Contents

P9-DDB-526

PAGE 14

PAGE 76

PAGE 160

PAGE 186

PAGE 214

PAGE 258

PAGE 269

PAGE 292

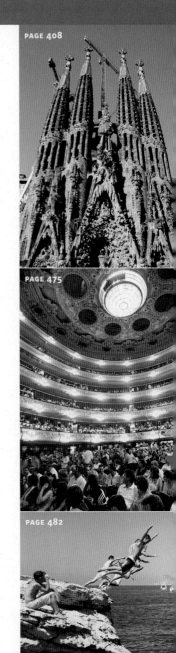

PAGE 408

PAGE 475

PAGE 482

PAGE 534

PAGE 549

PAGE 627

PUBLISHED BY

Wiley Publishing, Inc.

111 River St., Hoboken, NJ 07030-5774

ISBN 978-0-470-49769-2

Frommer's®

Editorial by Frommer's

EDITOR	PHOTO EDITOR
Emil J. Ross	Cherie Cincilla
CARTOGRAPHER	CAPTIONS
Elizabeth Puhl	Kathryn Williams
COVER PHOTO EDITOR	COVER DESIGN
Richard Fox	Paul Dinovo

Produced by Sideshow Media

PUBLISHER	MANAGING EDITOR
Dan Tucker	Megan McFarland
PROJECT EDITOR	PHOTO RESEARCHER
Kathryn Williams	John Martin
DESIGN	SPOTLIGHT FEATURE DESIGN
Kevin Smith, And Smith LLC	Em Dash Design LLC

For information on our other products and services or to obtain technical support, please contact our Customer Care Department within the U.S. at 800/762-2974, outside the U.S. at 317/572-3993 or fax 317/572-4002.

Wiley also publishes its books in a variety of electronic formats. Some content that appears in print may not be available in electronic formats.

MANUFACTURED IN CHINA

5   4   3   2   1

How to Use This Guide

The Day by Day guides present a series of itineraries that take you from place to place. The itineraries are organized by time (The Best of Madrid in 1 Day), by region (The Costa del Sol), by town (Girona), and by special interest (Gastronomic Valencia). You can follow these itineraries to the letter, or customize your own based on the information we provide. Within the tours, we suggest cafes, bars, or restaurants where you can take a break. Each of these stops is marked with a coffee-cup icon ☕. In each chapter, we provide detailed hotel and restaurant reviews so you can select the places that are right for you.

The hotels, restaurants, and attractions listed in this guide have been ranked for quality, value, service, amenities, and special features using a **star-rating system.** Hotels, restaurants, attractions, shopping, and nightlife are rated on a scale of zero stars (recommended) to three stars (exceptional). In addition to the star-rating system, we also use a kids icon kids to point out the best bets for families.

The following **abbreviations** are used for credit cards:

AE American Express **MC** MasterCard
DC Diners Club **V** Visa
DISC Discover

A Note on Prices

Frommer's lists exact prices in local currency. Currency conversions fluctuate, so before departing consult a currency exchange website such as **www.oanda.com/currency/converter** to check up-to-the-minute conversion rates.

In the "Take a Break" and "Best Bets" sections of this book, we have used a system of dollar signs to show a range of costs for 1 night in a hotel (the price of a double-occupancy room) or the cost of an entree at a restaurant. Use the following table to decipher the dollar signs:

COST	HOTELS	RESTAURANTS
$	under $150	under $15
$$	$150–$250	$15–$25
$$$	$250–$350	$25–$40
$$$$	$350–$450	$40–$50
$$$$$	over $450	over $50

How to Contact Us

In researching this book, we discovered many wonderful places—hotels, restaurants, shops, and more. We're sure you'll find others. Please tell us about them, so we can share the information with your fellow travelers in upcoming editions. If you were disappointed with a recommendation, we'd love to know that, too. Please email us at frommersfeedback@wiley.com or write to:

Frommer's Spain Day by Day, 1st Edition
Wiley Publishing, Inc.
111 River Street
Hoboken, NJ 07030-5774

Travel Resources at Frommers.com

Frommer's travel resources don't end with this guide. **Frommers.com** has travel information on more than 4,000 destinations. We update features regularly, giving you access to the most current trip-planning information and the best airfare, lodging, and car-rental bargains. You can also listen to podcasts, connect with other Frommers.com members through our active reader forums, share your travel photos, read blogs from guidebook editors and fellow travelers, and much more.

An Additional Note

Please be advised that travel information is subject to change at any time—and this is especially true of prices. We suggest that you write or call ahead for confirmation when making your travel plans. The authors, editors, and publisher cannot be held responsible for the experiences of readers while traveling. Your safety is important to us, so we encourage you to stay alert and be aware of your surroundings.

About the Authors

Patricia Harris and **David Lyon** (chapters 1–13 and 16–20) have journeyed the world for American, British, Swiss, and Asian publishers to write about food, culture, art, and design. They have covered subjects as diverse as elk migrations in western Canada, the street markets of Shanghai, winter hiking on the Jungfrau, and the origins of Mesoamerican civilization in the Mexican tropics. In the name of research, they have eaten hot-pepper-toasted grasshoppers, English beef, and roasted armadillo in banana sauce. When good wine or craft beer is unavailable, they drink Diet Coke. Wherever they go, they are continually drawn back to Spain for the flamenco nightlife, the Moorish architecture of Andalucía, the world-weary and lust-ridden saints of Zurbarán, and the phantasmagoric visions of El Greco—and the sheer joy of conversing with the regulars in a thousand little bars while drinking the house wine and eating tapas of Manchego and chorizo.

Neil Edward Schlecht (chapters 1, 3, 14, 15, and 19) is a freelance writer based in northwestern Connecticut. His first exposure to Spain was teaching English for a summer at a Col·legi Sant Ignasi in Barcelona. He returned to the Catalan capital just before the 1992 Olympics and spent most of the decade there, working on social and economic development projects for the European Union and later as a contributing writer for a Spanish art and antiques magazine. Neil is the author or co-author of a dozen travel guides, including *Frommer's Peru, Frommer's Cuba, Frommer's South America, Frommer's New York, Frommer's Texas,* and *Spain For Dummies.* But little motivates him like the chance to discover new restaurants and wines in Spain.

Acknowledgments

Patricia Harris and David Lyon would especially like to thank Pilar Vico of the Tourist Office of Spain and Estefanía Gómez of the Community of Madrid for their sage advice and friendship. They are also grateful to the regional tourism authorities in all of the autonomous regions of Spain for their support, enthusiasm, and invaluable information.

About the Photographers

Sergi Camara works as an independent photographer, combining his love of photography with audiovisual and documentary work. His series on Melilla, a town bordering Spain and Morocco, entitled *Assault on the Wall of Europe: Morocco,* was published as an exclusive in *La Vanguardia* magazine. Ireland-born **Denis Doyle** grew up in Dublin, later moving to Spain as an Associated Press (AP) staff shooter. He freelances as a photojournalist for clients such as Getty Images, *The New York Times,* and the *Guardian.* **Niccolò Guasti** is an Italian photojournalist living in Sevilla, where he shoots freelance editorial photography, in addition to personal projects. Native Spaniard **Jorge Guerrero** has studied photography in Barcelona, Madrid, and Sevilla. He currently works for Agence France-Presse (AFP). South African–born **Sean Mitchell-Henry** is currently based in Barcelona, where he shoots for a wide range of editorial and commercial clients. **Xaume Olleros** (www.xaumeolleros.com), a press and documentary photographer based in Valencia, works for newspapers and press agencies, as well as other Spanish and international clients. Based in northwest Spain, photographer **Oscar Pinal** (www.lightstalkers.org/oscar-pinal-rodriguez) has been contributing to regional publications, specializing in sports, documentary, and social photography. After spending 2 years freelancing in China, **Markel Redondo** (www.markelredondo.com) is a freelance photographer based in Bilbao. Some of his clients include *Le Monde, The New York Times,* and UNESCO. **Rafa Rivas** was born in the Basque Country and is based in Bilbao. He has worked for Agence France-Presse since 2000, as well as for several Spanish journals and news agencies. **Kirsten Scully** (www.scullyfoto.com), tireless adventure-seeker, photographer, and filmmaker, uses her love of travel and extreme sports as an excuse to make a living; her work has been published in major international travel and sailing magazines. Spain-based freelance photographer **Diego Vivanco** (www.diegovivanco.es) regularly contributes to major institutions, newspapers, and magazines in Spain and abroad.

The Best of Spain

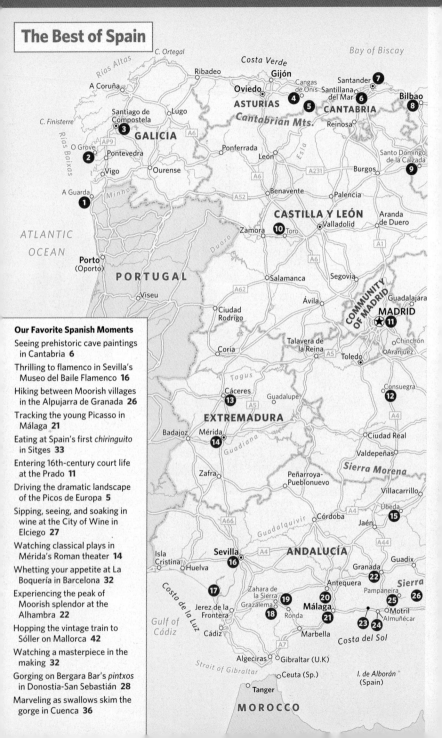

The Best of Spain

Our Favorite Spanish Moments

Seeing prehistoric cave paintings in Cantabria **6**

Thrilling to flamenco in Sevilla's Museo del Baile Flamenco **16**

Hiking between Moorish villages in the Alpujarra de Granada **26**

Tracking the young Picasso in Málaga **21**

Eating at Spain's first *chiringuito* in Sitges **33**

Entering 16th-century court life at the Prado **11**

Driving the dramatic landscape of the Picos de Europa **5**

Sipping, seeing, and soaking in wine at the City of Wine in Elciego **27**

Watching classical plays in Mérida's Roman theater **14**

Whetting your appetite at La Boquería in Barcelona **32**

Experiencing the peak of Moorish splendor at the Alhambra **22**

Hopping the vintage train to Sóller on Mallorca **42**

Watching a masterpiece in the making **32**

Gorging on Bergara Bar's *pintxos* in Donostia-San Sebastián **28**

Marveling as swallows skim the gorge in Cuenca **36**

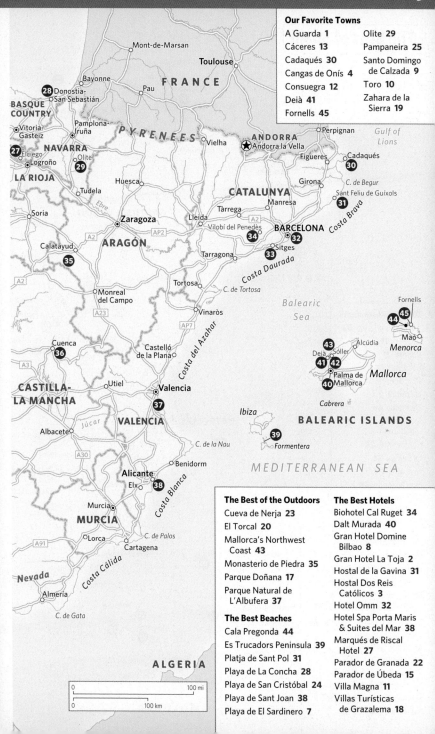

Our Favorite Towns

A Guarda **1**	Olite **29**
Cáceres **13**	Pampaneira **25**
Cadaqués **30**	Santo Domingo
Cangas de Onís **4**	de Calzada **9**
Consuegra **12**	Toro **10**
Deià **41**	Zahara de la
Fornells **45**	Sierra **19**

The Best of the Outdoors

Cueva de Nerja **23**
El Torcal **20**
Mallorca's Northwest
  Coast **43**
Monasterio de Piedra **35**
Parque Doñana **17**
Parque Natural de
  L'Albufera **37**

The Best Beaches

Cala Pregonda **44**
Es Trucadors Peninsula **39**
Platja de Sant Pol **31**
Playa de La Concha **28**
Playa de San Cristóbal **24**
Playa de Sant Joan **38**
Playa de El Sardinero **7**

The Best Hotels

Biohotel Cal Ruget **34**
Dalt Murada **40**
Gran Hotel Domine
  Bilbao **8**
Gran Hotel La Toja **2**
Hostal de la Gavina **31**
Hostal Dos Reis
  Católicos **3**
Hotel Omm **32**
Hotel Spa Porta Maris
  & Suites del Mar **38**
Marqués de Riscal
  Hotel **27**
Parador de Granada **22**
Parador de Úbeda **15**
Villa Magna **11**
Villas Turísticas
  de Grazalema **18**

The Best of Spain

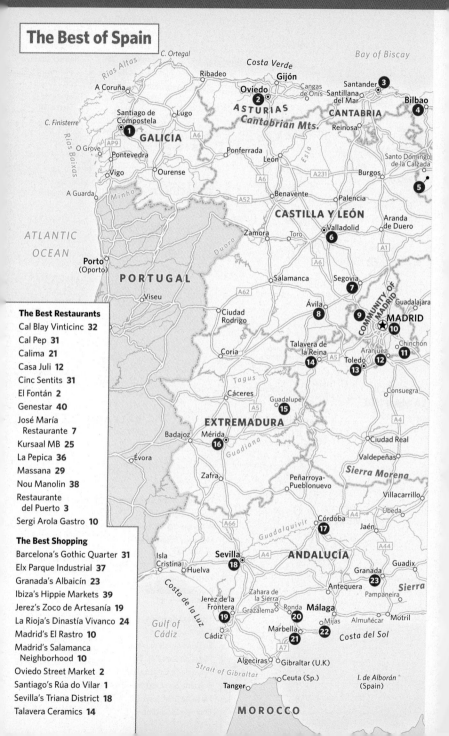

The Best Restaurants

Cal Blay Vinticinc **32**
Cal Pep **31**
Calima **21**
Casa Juli **12**
Cinc Sentits **31**
El Fontán **2**
Genestar **40**
José María Restaurante **7**
Kursaal MB **25**
La Pepica **36**
Massana **29**
Nou Manolin **38**
Restaurante del Puerto **3**
Sergi Arola Gastro **10**

The Best Shopping

Barcelona's Gothic Quarter **31**
Elx Parque Industrial **37**
Granada's Albaicín **23**
Ibiza's Hippie Markets **39**
Jerez's Zoco de Artesanía **19**
La Rioja's Dinastía Vivanco **24**
Madrid's El Rastro **10**
Madrid's Salamanca Neighborhood **10**
Oviedo Street Market **2**
Santiago's Rúa do Vilar **1**
Sevilla's Triana District **18**
Talavera Ceramics **14**

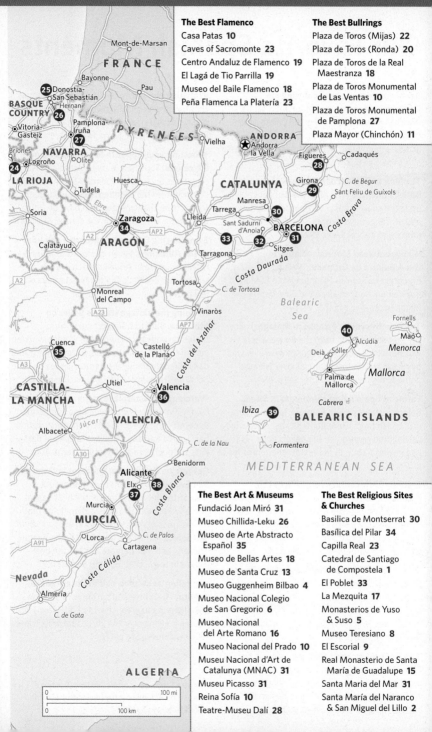

The Best Flamenco
Casa Patas **10**
Caves of Sacromonte **23**
Centro Andaluz de Flamenco **19**
El Lagá de Tio Parrilla **19**
Museo del Baile Flamenco **18**
Peña Flamenca La Platería **23**

The Best Bullrings
Plaza de Toros (Mijas) **22**
Plaza de Toros (Ronda) **20**
Plaza de Toros de la Real
Maestranza **18**
Plaza de Toros Monumental
de Las Ventas **10**
Plaza de Toros Monumental
de Pamplona **27**
Plaza Mayor (Chinchón) **11**

The Best Art & Museums
Fundació Joan Miró **31**
Museo Chillida-Leku **26**
Museo de Arte Abstracto
 Español **35**
Museo de Bellas Artes **18**
Museo de Santa Cruz **13**
Museo Guggenheim Bilbao **4**
Museo Nacional Colegio
 de San Gregorio **6**
Museo Nacional
 del Arte Romano **16**
Museo Nacional del Prado **10**
Museu Nacional d'Art de
 Catalunya (MNAC) **31**
Museu Picasso **31**
Reina Sofía **10**
Teatre-Museu Dalí **28**

**The Best Religious Sites
& Churches**
Basilica de Montserrat **30**
Basílica del Pilar **34**
Capilla Real **23**
Catedral de Santiago
 de Compostela **1**
El Poblet **33**
La Mezquita **17**
Monasterios de Yuso
 & Suso **5**
Museo Teresiano **8**
El Escorial **9**
Real Monasterio de Santa
 María de Guadalupe **15**
Santa Maria del Mar **31**
Santa María del Naranco
 & San Miguel del Lillo **2**

Our Favorite Spanish Moments

Seeing prehistoric cave paintings in Cantabria. Someone put that handprint up 15,000 years ago—and then he painted the bison he hoped his tribe could kill. It's an artistic straight line through the ages to Picasso and Miró. See p. 272.

Thrilling to flamenco in Sevilla's Museo del Baile Flamenco. You can't help but get caught up in the soaring passions, intricate rhythms, and swirling movement of Spain's signature music and dance. See p. 592.

Hiking between Moorish villages in the Alpujarra de Granada. Walking the mountain trails from Pampaneira to Bubión is a trek unchanged since the days before the Reconquista. See p. 577.

Tracking the young Picasso in Málaga. Follow the precocious child from the house where he was born to the baroque church where he was baptized. His footprints are all over Málaga, home to his legacy museum. See p. 654.

Eating at Spain's first *chiringuito* in Sitges. Before Ferran Adrià or Juan Marì Arzak, there was beach food. Chiringuito has been serving casual fried seafood on the beach since 1913 and gave its name to the restaurant genre. See p. 376.

Entering 16th-century court life at the Prado. The longer you look at *Las Meninas* by Diego Velázquez (see p. 672), the more you understand the private life, triumphs, and sorrows of Felipe IV and his family—and of the painter who witnessed it all. See p. 20.

Driving the dramatic landscape of the Picos de Europa. Soaring cliffs and rushing rivers are only half of it. The mountain villages of Asturias and Cantabria are the real gems in these mountains; Spain was born in revolt against the Moors here. See p. 268.

Sipping, seeing, and soaking in wine at the City of Wine in Elciego. The great La Rioja producer Marqués de Riscal hit a home run when it engaged Frank Gehry to design its bodega, hotel, and spa. See p. 333.

Watching classical plays in Mérida's Roman theater. Peel back 2,000 years as the ancient mysteries again take the stage on Mérida's Roman proscenium. See p. 187.

Whetting your appetite at La Boquería in Barcelona. Top chefs and regular folks alike haunt this legendary food market for fresh seafood from the Mediterranean, wild mushrooms from the Pyrenees, and olive oil from L'Empordà. It's a feast for the senses. See p. 410.

Experiencing the peak of Moorish splendor at the Alhambra. Seven centuries of refined Muslim culture in Andalucía achieve sumptuous perfection in the Nasrid palaces. See p. 610.

Hopping the vintage train to Sóller on Mallorca. Built to transport citrus from mountain valleys to Palma, the vintage wooden cars of this 1912 narrow-gauge train still shuttle daily through orange and lemon groves and the Serra de Tramuntana mountains. See p. 486.

Watching a masterpiece in the making. Day by day, Barcelona workmen come ever closer to completing Antoni Gaudí's phantasmagoric basilica, La Sagrada Família, the apex of Barcelona's Modernista architecture. See p. 406.

Gorging on Bergara Bar's *pintxos* in Donostia-San Sebastián. Brilliant invention meets Basque tradition for some of the best casual bar food in Spain. Popular opinion holds that the Basques make the best food in Spain, that San Sebastián has the best food in the Basque Country, and that Bergara Bar has the best *pintxos* in town. Diet begone! See p. 311.

Marveling as swallows skim the gorges in Cuenca. At sunrise and sunset, cliff swallows take flight in the great chasm of open air. The houses hanging over the gorge resemble those swallows' nests. See p. 172.

> PAGE 1 *Segovia's fairytale Alcázar.* OPPOSITE PAGE *The Alhambra is the pinnacle of Muslim architecture in Spain.*

Our Favorite Towns

> *Just south of the French border on the Costa Brava, Cadaqués, with its narrow and winding slate streets, was a retreat for a number of 20th-century artists.*

A Guarda. Like the toy blocks of an infant Neptune, the granite cubes of A Guarda's breakwater shelter one of the most productive fishing harbors on the harsh coast of Galicia. Tall, slender fishermen's houses ring the harborfront in an array of pastels. Along the docks, fishermen mend their nets, and heaps of wire lobster and crab traps sit beneath protective tarps. See p. 239.

Cáceres. The old houses in this Extremaduran city are fortified palaces built by warrior knights of the Reconquista. The "new" ones date from the 16th century, when their great-great-grandsons made their fortunes in the New World. The pedestrian Old City is a virtual museum of old Spain—made all the more picturesque during the nesting season when dozens of storks raise their young in big twiggy nests on almost every tower and parapet. See p. 184.

Cadaqués. This Catalan village clings like a seabird's nest to its stony cliffside beach. Of all the surrealist painters who summered here before the Civil War, only Salvador Dalí (born in nearby Figueres) remained a presence into the 1960s. A small museum preserves his workshop-home, and his sketches dot the walls of many restaurants. See p. 370.

Cangas de Onís. This pretty little village stretched out along a river has been around since Neolithic times, judging by the dolmen-dotted burial ground a few steps off the main street. Fishermen come to catch salmon, hikers to visit the Picos de Europa, and history buffs to see the tomb of the first Christian king Pelayo, hidden by a waterfall. See p. 265.

Consuegra. A line of 11 windmills and a crusader castle top the high ridge above this Manchegan village, giving it the look of a set for *Man of La Mancha.* Consuegra is also ground zero for the labor-intensive saffron industry and celebrates the world's most expensive spice with a colorful festival at the end of every October. See p. 159.

Deià. Perhaps the most picturesque village in Mallorca, this tiny green gem perched on a hillside, with the Mediterranean to one side and steep mountains on the other, is a sun-dappled portrait of honey-colored stone houses, tiled roofs, and green shuttered windows. No wonder artists, writers, and expats have long been so enamored of the place. See p. 486.

Fornells. Facing a pretty marina on a sheltered inlet, this whitewashed Menorcan fishing village is a destination for windsurfers, sailors, and above all gourmands; it's renowned for its seafood restaurants and *caldereta de llagosta,* a rich lobster stew. See p. 502.

Olite. Few castles in castle-intense Spain are as harmonious and picturesque as the one Carlos III of Navarra had constructed here in 1406. In fact, once you've entered the gates, it's often hard to tell where the castle ends and the town begins. Tour the royal palace, but don't miss the wine museum, champion of the little-known but splendid Navarra reds. See p. 321.

Pampaneira. Hikers step off to the peaks and valleys of the Parque Natural de Sierra Nevada from this gateway village of the High Alpujarra, south of Granada in Andalucía. More than a staging point, Pampaneira is a colorful mountain village in its own right, where weavers sell their colorful shaggy rugs and ham producers offer their wares on the small town square. See p. 578.

Santo Domingo de la Calzada. Pilgrims on the road to Santiago de Compostela have been stopping at this atmospheric medieval town ever since Santo Domingo founded it for them in 1044. The first place they head is the cathedral, where Domingo (James) is laid out in an elaborate tomb and live chickens cackle in a cage high on one wall. See p. 326.

> Santa María la Real Church, next to Olite's Palacio Real in Navarra.

Toro. Hometown of one of the hottest new red wine regions of Spain, Toro is not just a great place to eat and drink: Its 13th-century Colegiata church features one of the most beautifully carved Gothic portals in Spain. See p. 200.

Zahara de la Sierra. Whitewashed buildings huddle around a mountain peak capped by the ruins of an Arabic castle. Hike up to the fortress for views of every mountain pass in the eastern Sierra de Grazalema. Zahara is the staging ground for expeditions to see the *pinzapo* trees, living fossils from the Ice Age that survive in the high mountains. See p. 552.

The Best of the Outdoors

> A lush park, complete with 60m (197-ft.) waterfall, gives the Monasterio de Piedra its reputation as the "garden district" of Aragón.

Cueva de Nerja. Discovered in 1959, the Nerja caves opened a year later to reveal the spectacular result of 225 million years of geological activity. Only about one-third of the caverns can be visited, but names such as Hall of the Cascades or Hall of Hercules' Columns hint at the fantastic stalagmites and stalactites within. See p. 547.

El Torcal. What water did to the underground limestone in Nerja, wind and water did to the limestone hoodoos of El Torcal. A road undulates through the surreal landscape of scrubby growth and tortured rocks. Even better, follow the hiking paths to explore this otherworldly land where lizards skitter from rock to rock and 30 species of orchids bloom largely unseen. See p. 556.

Mallorca's Northwest Coast. The jagged northwest coast of Mallorca, from Port de Andratx to the lunarlike Formentor peninsula, is a landscape of sheared-off cliffs dropping to cool blue surf, camera-ready *miradors* (viewpoints), ancient hilltop villages, and secluded cove beaches. See p. 494.

Monasterio de Piedra. Spain's largest private natural park was established during the 19th-century aesthetic movement that celebrated Nature as a mystical force. The lakes, grottoes, and long, arcing waterfalls on the grounds of this Cistercian monastery, built in 1195, could make a believer out of any environmental agnostic. See p. 353.

Parque Doñana. Of the three rivers that have shaped Spain's history, the Guadalquivir might be the most important, since it was the gateway between Sevilla and the Atlantic. The vast wetlands where the Guadalquivir empties into the Bay of Cádiz are a magical world. About half the songbirds of Europe touch down here on their migrations, and the famous shellfish of Sanlúcar thrive in the estuaries. See p. 557.

Parque Natural de L'Albufera. The short-grained rice essential to paella was introduced around A.D. 712 by Berber farmers. Most of the heritage strains are still grown in these freshwater wetlands south of Valencia, where barrier beaches long ago blocked out the sea. The range of ecosystems—from forest to marsh to tidal beach—is almost unparalleled in Spain. See p. 516.

The Best Beaches

> *With almost 5,000km (3,107 miles) of coastline, Spain is home to many white-sand beaches, like Platja de Sant Pol.*

Cala Pregonda (Menorca). The secluded north coast is unequalled for dramatic scenery, with earthy red sands and sea stacks that glow golden in the late-afternoon sun. Because it's a 20-minute hike to get here, Pregonda—many Menorcans' favorite beach—is never crowded. See p. 502.

Es Trucadors Peninsula (Formentera). The tiny island of Formentera consists of gorgeous beaches and little more. The slender peninsula jutting north into the Mediterranean has Ses Illetes and Platja de Llevant, with fine white sand, translucent waters, and nude sunbathers. See p. 506.

Platja de Sant Pol (Sant Feliu de Guíxols). Bracketed on one side by a handsome port town and on the other by the circa-1900 gated resort of S'Agaró, Sant Pol offers a long stretch of white sand with some pretty good beach breaks and one major reef break for surfing. Unlike most Costa Brava beaches, it has few shops or restaurants. See p. 373.

Playa de La Concha (Donostia-San Sebastián). Possibly the most beautiful and cleanest urban beach in Europe, La Concha fans out around the bay of San Sebastián. Its golden sands are popular with families—the gradual slant of the beach means the water doesn't get deep too quickly and the waves are gentle. See p. 309.

Playa de San Cristóbal (Almuñécar). The rocky sand is a little rough underfoot, but the beach is full of character and popular with surfers. Once you watch the fishermen push their open boats off from the sand early in the morning, you can take your pick of beachfront *churrerías* (*churro* stands) for a good, greasy breakfast. See p. 546.

Playa de Sant Joan (Alicante). Downtown Alicante has only a tiny beach, but you can hop the tram to the barrier-beach community of Playa de Sant Joan, where the sand just won't quit and the surf is both big enough to ride and sedate enough to swim. See p. 526.

Playa de El Sardinero (Santander). It's hard to imagine how the Belle Epoque ladies and gentlemen who made this northern Spain's fanciest beach resort in the 1850s would regard the state of dress (or undress) on the beach today. Perhaps the nicest and largest beach on the Bay of Santander, Sardinero is an egalitarian strand fronted by symbols of privilege. See p. 284.

The Best Hotels

> *Spain's state-run* parador *system transformed historic buildings into luxury hotels, like the Parador de Úbeda.*

Biohotel Cal Ruget (Vilobí del Penedès). For anyone who has ever harbored fantasies of owning a charming little vineyard in Europe, this 19th-century wine estate turned gracious small hotel is just the ticket. From the outdoor pool, guests gaze across rows of vineyards to the jagged profile of Montserrat in the distance. See p. 385.

Dalt Murada (Palma de Mallorca). Ensconced in the old quarter, this old-school hotel overflows with old-world charm. Huge rooms in the 17th-century mansion are built around a de-

lightful patio and are filled with antiques. See p. 493.

Gran Hotel Domine Bilbao. Frank Gehry's design for the Guggenheim Museum raised the bar for architecture in Bilbao, and guests are the beneficiaries at this sleek new hotel that neatly blends high style and comfort. Aptly named Buenas Vistas ("good views"), a terrace allows for unparalleled views of the Guggenheim and the revitalized riverfront. See p. 316.

Gran Hotel La Toja (O Grove). If a stay in a historic spa hotel on a parklike island doesn't work its healing magic, a relaxing soak in the thermal waters will surely cure what ails you. Modernized in 2005, this Belle Epoque grande dame has lost none of its charm. See p. 249.

Hostal de la Gavina (Sant Feliu de Guíxols). Set on a cliff and surrounded by lush gardens, the gracious white hotel with red roof and green shutters is a Costa Brava landmark, offering a refined and relaxing retreat from the seaside bustle. The rooms exude traditional good taste, and a gorgeous saltwater pool overlooks the ocean. See p. 375.

Hostal Dos Reis Católicos (Santiago de Compostela). It's hard to imagine another hotel with the historic resonance of this hostelry founded by Fernando and Isabel in 1492 to lodge Santiago pilgrims. Now part of Spain's *parador* system, the building echoes with the footsteps of history, from the grand front lobby to the quiet hidden courtyards. See p. 260.

Hotel Omm (Barcelona). The city's design craze is evident in every other new hotel in the city, but this temple of sleek modern design in the heart of L'Eixample takes it to a new level. Architecture buffs will love the privileged rooftop views of Gaudí's La Pedrera. See p. 472.

Hotel Spa Porta Maris & Suites del Mar (Alicante). All rooms have a water view at this modern hotel on a pier next to the cruise port walkway. Guests can choose to gaze at the lively marina or at waves breaking on the beach below the ancient castle ruins. Some suites even have an ocean view from the shower. See p. 528.

Marqués de Riscal Hotel (Elciego). Book a room at this Frank Gehry–designed hotel in the heart of a historic vineyard for immersion in wine culture—from bodega tours and wine tastings to wine therapy spa treatments. The two fine restaurants have excellent food and wine pairings. See p. 332.

Parador de Granada. Fernando and Isabel may have driven the Moors from Granada in 1492, but you can still imagine how the Nasrid nobles must have felt when they woke up each morn-

> Hotel Omm is known for its ultra-chic decor as well as its stunning view of La Pedrera.

ing to the sight of their lush gardens. This unforgettable experience is available to those who plan ahead and book one of the 40 rooms in a former 15th-century convent on the Alhambra grounds. See p. 620.

Parador de Úbeda. This 16th-century palace was designed by Andrés Vandelvira, perhaps Spain's most accomplished Renaissance architect. His poetic sense of proportion and order created an exceptionally harmonious and comfortable hostelry arrayed around an elegant central courtyard. Some rooms look out on the other architectural gems on Úbeda's Plaza Monumental. See p. 587.

Villa Magna (Madrid). Feel like a rock star, matador, or media celebrity—or at least run into one in the elevator. The hotel's 2009 50€-million renovation proved that top-of-the-line luxury doesn't have to be stuffy or showy. Of course, you can opt for the suite that comes with its own butler, driver, and Maserati. . . . See p. 141.

Villas Turísticas de Grazalema. This simple hostelry exudes rustic charm with its turned-wood furniture and cool tile floors. With an outdoor pool and dining room serving hearty local specialties, it's the perfect base for exploring the Sierra de Grazalema Natural Park. Apartments with fireplaces are popular with families. See p. 563.

The Best Restaurants

> Gone are the days of "Don Ernesto" Hemingway, but La Pepica is still the place to come for traditional Valencian paella.

Cal Blay Vinticinc (Sant Sadurní d'Anoia). This "enogastronomic" offshoot of the popular Cal Blay deli operation transformed a 1905 Modernista wine cellar into a showcase of the cuisine of the Alt Penedès—with a wine list of nearly all the Cava producers of Sant Sadurní and still wine producers of nearby towns. See p. 385.

Cal Pep (Barcelona). Once a connoisseur's secret, this overwhelmingly popular joint at the edge of La Ribera now requires standing and waiting for a seat at the long counter—but for some of the best, freshest seafood in Barcelona, the wait is worth it. There's no menu, so you'll just have to let gravelly voiced Pep deliver whatever's freshest. See p. 460.

Calima (Marbella). Chef Dani García creates dishes from classical Andalucían flavors (mountain ham, grilled fish, grassy Córdoban olive oil) the way jazz saxophonist Dexter Gordon used to spin delicious riffs from old ballads. The food that results is hauntingly familiar yet always surprising. See p. 569.

Casa Juli (Aranjuez). No one has bothered to read the menu here in years. The waiter simply announces what goodies the chef has scored that morning, and you order accordingly— white asparagus in spring, wild mushrooms in fall, and milk-fed lamb or kid whenever it's available. See p. 134.

Cinc Sentits (Barcelona). This is strictly haute cuisine, in keeping with Barcelona's famed gourmet scene, but it's family run and a bit less pricey and intimidating than some hot spots. In that way, it's a good place to see what the city's creative culinary boom is all about. See p. 460.

El Fontán (Oviedo). With the central food market downstairs, Fontán defines market cuisine. Asturian cooking is popular all over Spain—and often oddly expensive for what is essentially peasant and fisherman fare. Here it's brilliant and inexpensive to boot. See p. 281.

Genestar (Mallorca). Just outside Alcúdia's thick walls, this surprising little restaurant, a one-man show, is foodies' best-kept secret; the five-course tasting menu isn't just creative and delicious, it's an outstanding bargain. See p. 489.

José María Restaurante (Segovia). Not even religion or politics can ignite such heated arguments among Castilians as the proper way to roast a suckling pig. Chef-proprietor José María Ruiz's version, with its succulent meat and

> *Michelin-starred chef Sergi Arola opened his latest eponymous culinary venture in 2008.*

crispy skin, is the benchmark against which all others are measured. See p. 223.

Kursaal MB (Donostia-San Sebastián). Basque superchef Martín Berasategui knows that not every diner can get into (or afford) his flagship namesake restaurant, so he endowed this classy, casual spot with some of his greatest-hits recipes and talented staff. Dine on greatness for a relative pittance. There's even a bargain small-plates tasting menu in the bar. See p. 311.

La Pepica (Valencia). You've seen paella all over Spain. You've never actually eaten it until you come to this temple of Valencian rice dishes. Ernest Hemingway loved the place, and it hasn't changed much since his time. If you can't find what you want among nearly 100 rice choices, go for the fresh fish. See p. 523.

Massana (Girona). Pere Massana's sparely modern dishes reinvent simple Catalan food with explosive flavors and winning textures. The affordable haute cuisine restaurant is known for its warm welcome and perfect service. The exquisite wine cellar is full of great finds from small Catalan wineries. See p. 397.

Nou Manolín (Alicante). Where do the top Michelin-starred chefs of Catalunya and Paris go when they want to eat perfect, authentic tapas? Nou Manolin. Grilled shrimp are always a hit, and the gazpacho is the best north of Andalucía. See p. 529.

Restaurante del Puerto (Santander). The waiters might all wear white tuxedos, the clientele often sport tailored suits, and it's hard to beat the elegant preparation and presentation of Cantabrian seafood at this upscale restaurant, but it was founded by fishermen as a bar featuring their aunties' cooking. See p. 285.

Sergi Arola Gastro (Madrid). The flagship of Madrid's most famous resident chef offers a showcase of an insane number of tiny, perfect plates that delight with their artistry, amuse with their wit, and satisfy with their flavors. There are no big plates here, just tasting menus of nonstop delicious bites. See p. 135.

The Best Shopping

> *Setting up their wares at dawn and pulling up stakes for siesta, vendors at Madrid's El Rastro flea market hawk everything from bric-a-brac to cool jewelry.*

Barcelona's Gothic Quarter. Against a backdrop of centuries-old shops, churches, and Gothic and Renaissance palaces, the tangle of dark alleyways of the Born and Barri Gòtic districts is suddenly chic, home to dozens of edgy fashion, food, home design, and antiques shops. See p. 402.

Elx Parque Industrial. Since Elx (Elche in Castilian) is one of Europe's major shoe manufacturing towns, shoe brands figure heavily among the 24 outlet shops grouped on the east side of town. With beautiful sewn details and fine leather, Pikolinos is perhaps the most popular, but other outlets offer good deals on soccer and other sport shoes, as well as clothing and housewares. See p. 519.

Granada's Albaicín. Braving the crowds along the narrow streets of Calderería Nueva and Calderería Vieja is the next best thing to visiting a Moroccan souk. Practice your bargaining skills and you'll get a deal on glittery embroidered bedcovers or a hand-stitched leather

bag. Truthfully, the merchandise changes little from shop to shop, but it's still fun to browse. See p. 614.

Ibiza's Hippie Markets. Before the club kids descended on Ibiza to party all night, a generation of hippies landed on the island in the 1960s, transforming it into an alternative international hangout. On the northeast coast, bohemian traditions and fashions continue at weekly markets, favorites of international fashion designers. See p. 506.

Jerez's Zoco de Artesanía. Perfect for one-stop shopping, the Zoco gathers more than 20 shops under one roof. Artisans often work in their small but bright spaces, and you might meet the person who sculpted the clay figurine or stitched bright floral designs on the recycled denim jacket that catches your eye. See p. 649.

La Rioja's Dinastía Vivanco. As one of the region's largest wine producers, Dinastía Vivanco has taken a lead in welcoming visitors with a lovely restaurant and state-of-the-art wine

> *Talavera de la Reina's style of colorful glazed pottery was brought to the New World by the Spanish in the 16th century.*

museum. As in most good museums, there's an excellent gift shop, with the company's wines as well as shelf upon shelf of wine- and food-related items, including beautiful stemware and every conceivable style of corkscrew. See p. 334.

Madrid's El Rastro. As many as 1,000 vendors might set up tables and spread blankets to display their goods at Spain's most famous flea market. Impossible numbers of buyers and browsers survey the goods, then stop in bars for a tapa and a beer before continuing their search for an out-of-print CD or a vintage shawl. See p. 111.

Madrid's Salamanca Neighborhood. At the other end of the economic spectrum, the wide sidewalks in Madrid's most decorous and fashionable neighborhood are made for window-shoppers who want to check out the latest offerings from Spain's top names in fashion. See p. 85.

Oviedo Street Market. The charming streets and plazas radiating from Plaza del Fontán in Oviedo's Old City make one of the most pleasant quarters to hunt for bargains at the Sunday flea market or at the Thursday and Saturday markets of newer goods, clothing, and fresh flowers. Expect lots of knockoff designer handbags. See p. 280.

Santiago's Rúa do Vilar. Along the city's gracious, arcaded shopping drag, you'll certainly rub elbows with pilgrims picking out enamel crosses or scallop-shell necklaces to celebrate the completion of their journey (or new pairs of soft, cushy shoes to reward their feet). Even if you arrived by car, not by foot, there's no reason not to browse and buy. See p. 258.

Sevilla's Triana District. The city's former fishing port and traditional Gypsy quarter is also home to a flourishing ceramics industry. Founded in 1870, Cerámica Santa Ana is the largest of several *alfarerías* (pottery shops) carrying on a tradition that began with the Romans and flourished when the Moors introduced the colorful geometric patterns that seduce buyers to this day. See p. 596.

Talavera Ceramics. You've probably seen Talavera tiles covering the facades of buildings throughout Spain without realizing that they came from Castilla-La Mancha's famous ceramics center. Fortunately, the artisans here also make beautiful platters, bowls, and pitchers more suitable for use at home. Many shops will pack and ship your purchases. See p. 157.

The Best Art & Museums

> *Frank Gehry's Guggenheim Bilbao was the centerpiece of a massive revitalization plan for the Basque city.*

Fundació Joan Miró (Barcelona). Great Catalan architect Josep Lluís Sert reinvented traditional Mediterranean architecture to create a bright and airy space to display the most complete collection of works by great Catalan artist Joan Miró. The rooftop sculpture garden is a delight. See p. 418.

Museo Chillida-Leku (Hernani). The powerful steel sculptures by Basque artist Eduardo Chillida are displayed in museums and public spaces throughout his home territory. At this beautiful estate near San Sebastián, you can view the works as Chillida arranged them. See p. 298.

Museo de Arte Abstracto Español (Cuenca). With a collection that focuses on artists who worked in Cuenca, this museum provides an unusual opportunity to reflect on the nature of artistic inspiration. Study the works hanging on the walls and then gaze out the windows at the astonishing landscape that drew the artists to this precarious village on a hill. See p. 173.

Museo de Bellas Artes (Sevilla). It would be treat enough to enter this former monastery where the tile work in the courtyard rises to the level of art. But the museum holds the country's second-largest collection of Spanish painting, with a strong concentration on works by local artists Bartolomé Estebán Murillo and Francisco de Zurbarán. See p. 593.

Museo de Santa Cruz (Toledo). The largest collection of El Greco paintings in Toledo are shown to great effect in the galleries of this 16th-century former convent. Artists often set up their own easels in front of *La Asunción de la Virgen (The Assumption of the Virgin)* to try to absorb El Greco's masterful handling of paint and space. See p. 168.

Museo Guggenheim Bilbao. More than 10 years after it opened, Frank Gehry's radical design for a museum has not lost its power to surprise. Temporary exhibitions are often equally unexpected, but Jeff Koons's gigantic flower-covered *Puppy* on the plaza out front remains the local favorite. See p. 312.

Museo Nacional Colegio de San Gregorio (Valladolid). Spanish sculpture from the 15th to the 18th century gets due recognition in the galleries ringing a courtyard of an elegant former mansion. Pride of place goes to the 16th-century local masters who imbued their polychrome wooden figures with unsurpassed levels of emotion and expression. See p. 201.

Museo Nacional del Arte Romano (Mérida). The superb quality of the sculptures, mosaics, and other artifacts underscores the fact that Augusta Emerita—now Mérida—was one of Rome's most important cities on the Iberian Peninsula. The pieces receive the artistic attention they deserve in this stunning museum designed by Rafael Moneo. See p. 186.

Museo Nacional del Prado (Madrid). The monarchs created this museum to prove that Spanish art was equal to that of other European nations. They needn't have worried. The works of Diego Velázquez and Francisco de Goya alone chart the course of Spanish history and reveal the depth of Spanish genius. See p. 72.

Museu Nacional d'Art de Catalunya (MNAC; Barcelona). This extraordinary collection of medieval and Renaissance religious art, ranging from Romanesque altarpieces and frescoes found in small churches across Catalunya to paintings by Spanish Old Masters, is a treat. See p. 416.

Museu Picasso (Barcelona). The largest collection of Picasso's works in Spain, this ever-popular museum concentrates on his "Blue Period." Nearly as noteworthy is the museum itself, which occupies several 15th-century palaces and courtyards on one of La Ribera's most atmospheric streets. See p. 410.

Reina Sofía (Madrid). The opportunity to contemplate Picasso's masterpiece of anguish, *Guernica* (see p. 294), is reason enough to visit. But this dynamic museum in a former hospital also draws attention to such other 20th-century masters as Joan Miró, Juan Gris, and Salvador Dalí, while offering a fresh interpretation of 20th-century art. See p. 74.

Teatre-Museu Dalí (Figueres). Mix an old theater building and the unbridled imagination of Salvador Dalí and the result is this extravaganza of art, showmanship, and wit. You'll have to look hard to catch even a fraction of the visual puns. See p. 373.

> A painted wood masterpiece at the Museo Nacional Colegio de San Gregorio.

DECODING *LAS MENINAS*

The Sly Masterpiece That Injected Psychology into Painting

BY PATRICIA HARRIS & DAVID LYON

DIEGO VELÁZQUEZ (1599–1660) served as court painter and curator of the art collection of King Felipe IV during the 1640s and 1650s. *Las Meninas* is both his most psychologically complex and artistically inventive work. Ostensibly a portrait of the royal family, it captures an intimate glimpse of court life as if in a snapshot. *Las Meninas* hangs in the Prado amid works by other masters that Velázquez assembled for the king. The enigmatic composition of this 1656 painting poses questions about reality and illusion and creates an uncertain relationship between the viewer and the figures depicted. Just who was Velázquez painting?

The Players

FELIPE IV AND MARIANA
A mirror in the background reflects the royal couple. Many critics assume that the king and queen are posing for a portrait. But the king may have been sensitive about his age—and the trick of composition was Velázquez's diplomatic attempt to preserve Felipe's ego.

INFANTA MARGARITA
The young *infanta* was summoned to relieve boredom while her parents posed for their portrait. But Velázquez actually may have painted Margarita while her parents looked on.

VELÁZQUEZ
The painting is set in Velázquez's studio and also serves as a self-portrait of the artist. He wears the red cross of the Order of Santiago, which he did not receive until after *Meninas* was completed. Felipe IV probably had this award added to the painting after Velázquez's death.

MARÍA BARBOLA
Velázquez painted ten portraits of dwarves, always depicting them with dignity and appreciation of their individual personalities. Here, sturdy and independent-looking María Barbola stands in sharp contrast to the delicate, pampered *infanta*.

DON JOSÉ NIETO VELÁZQUEZ
The queen's chamberlain may have also been a relative of the painter. He pauses on the steps with his knee bent. Is he coming or going? The backlight behind the open doorway draws viewers even further into the painting.

The Painter's Painter

In *Las Meninas*, Velázquez created a royal portrait with surprisingly visionary modernism. Francisco de Goya acknowledged his debt to Velázquez 150 years later (he was among the first painters to see Velázquez's works, which hung in private quarters), and the public unveiling of Velázquez's paintings at the Prado in the early 19th century influenced the bold brushwork of Edouard Manet, in particular. Picasso recreated *Las Meninas* in 58 Cubist versions in 1957, and Irish painter Francis Bacon repeatedly drew on Velázquez compositions for his own work in the mid-1950's.

The Best Religious Sites & Churches

Basilica de Montserrat. This church located halfway up one of the most surreal massifs in Spain is also one of the holiest sites in the country. The large complex with a monastery and hotel is constructed around a 12th-century image of the Black Virgin, making it a virtual city of prayer. The train from Barcelona connects to the cable car station. See p. 386.

Basilica del Pilar (Zaragoza). Pilgrims from all over Spain flood into this shrine to the manifestation of the Virgin Mary known as El Pilar. According to church tradition, the Virgin Mary appeared to St. James here in A.D. 40 and gave him a statue of herself mounted on a column, or *pilar,* of jasper. The tiny statue and column are revered on the altar of the Holy Chapel of this massive baroque church. See p. 350.

Capilla Real (Granada). Small is beautiful. It can also be grand if it happens to be the burial site of Spain's famous co-monarchs, Fernando and Isabel, who rest beneath somber and serene sarcophagi. The grill around the main altar is a masterpiece of ironwork. An adjacent museum holds Fernando's sword and Isabel's favorite paintings. See p. 612.

Catedral de Santiago de Compostela. It's impossible not to be moved by the joy, relief, and devotion of the faithful who complete their pilgrimage by embracing a statue of Santiago behind the altar. The sheer artistry of the Romanesque interior is a just reward for the arduous journey to one of Europe's most famous pilgrimage sites, once declared the equal of Rome and Jerusalem by the Pope. See p. 256.

El Poblet. Deep beneath the powerful stone buildings of this 12th-century Cistercian monastery lie the mortal remains of the kings of Aragón, once rulers of all of northeastern Spain. The tour includes a visit to the monks' cellar dormitory, which was emptied each fall so it could serve as a fermentation vat for new wine. See p. 389.

La Mezquita (Córdoba). No church in Spain can compete with Córdoba's mosque for simple grandeur and unadorned spirit. Even the

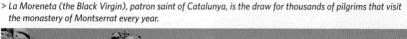

> *La Moreneta (the Black Virgin), patron saint of Catalunya, is the draw for thousands of pilgrims that visit the monastery of Montserrat every year.*

> *A festival in October celebrates the Virgen del Pilar, seen at bottom right here, with parades and bullfights.*

baroque Christian cathedral built inside could not still the echoes of 500 years of Islamic prayer. See p. 630.

Monasterios de Yuso y Suso. These two remote monasteries trace the history of religious life and architecture from the Visigothic foundations of Suso through the striking 16th-century church at Yuso. Not only can you see the first written examples of the Castilian and Basque languages, you can also purchase a bottle of Rioja wine made by Yuso's small monastic community. See p. 325.

Museo Teresiano (Ávila). After visiting the convent where Santa Teresa took her vows in 1535 and another that she founded in her later years, this small museum on the site of her childhood home is the best place to learn about her life and enduring legacy. The museum's hagiography only serves to make the flesh-and-blood woman all the more tangible. See p. 226.

El Escorial (Madrid). Religious fervor and secular power share the stage in this lavish palace outside Madrid. Felipe II spared no expense in honoring his royal lineage and expressing his religious devotion, and his architects managed to reflect the chastening, ascetic spirit of the Counter-Reformation in the unadorned facades and severely rectangular layout. The interior decorations are another matter, as Felipe's successors went for baroque. See p. 90.

Real Monasterio de Santa María de Guadalupe. The discovery of another Dark Virgin statue with the power to create miracles made this tiny village of Extremadura into one of Spain's chief pilgrimage sites in the 14th century. Today the ancient statue is rivaled by the basilica's paintings by local boy Francisco de Zurbarán. See p. 181.

Santa Maria del Mar (Barcelona). This stunningly beautiful Catalan Gothic church has such graceful dimensions and architectural perfection that you don't even have to be one of the faithful to be moved to tears. See p. 402.

Santa María del Naranco & San Miguel del Lillo (Oviedo). The primitive, almost tribal Catholic faith that drove the Reconquista originated in powerful, sturdy pre-Romanesque churches along the northern rim of the Iberian Peninsula. This pair built in 848 still embody that passionate, unquestioning faith. See p. 280.

The Best Flamenco

> *At night, the Museo del Baile Flamenco is filled with the sounds of clapping and flamenco guitar.*

Casa Patas (Madrid). Founded in 1985, this restaurant and *tablao* (flamenco club) played a big role in the current flamenco revival. Every up-and-coming artist dreams of playing to an enthusiastic audience in the performance space behind the restaurant. Shows start late, but plan to arrive early for a drink and a few tapas at the bar. See p. 75.

Caves of Sacromonte (Granada). The sounds of voices, guitars, and hands clapping reverberate against the low ceilings and rounded walls of the limestone caves in Granada's "Gypsy" district of Sacromonte. Attending one of these *tablaos,* such as Venta El Gallo, offers a peek at the lifestyle of this tight-knit community, as well as an unforgettable evening of music and dance. See p. 623.

Centro Andaluz de Flamenco (Jerez). Scholars prize this archive of books, music, and videos located in the city where many believe flamenco originated. But even those with more casual interests can enjoy the daily screenings of performance videos and try to keep time to the flamenco background music as they study the paintings and posters on the walls. See p. 648.

El Lagá de Tio Parrilla (Jerez). Family members of one of the Jerez flamenco dynasties operate this bar-nightclub flamenco show. You can buy some of the guitarists' albums anywhere, but only here can you see their sisters dance. See p. 649.

Museo del Baile Flamenco (Sevilla). If you weren't a flamenco fan when you entered this engaging museum, you'll become one before you leave. Founder Cristina Hoyos put all her performer's instincts to work creating a space alive with movement and sound. Study the videos of the seven flamenco performance styles and then return for an evening concert. By the end, you might be able to tell the *bulería* from the *soleá.* See p. 592.

Peña Flamenca La Platería (Granada). Performance dates are limited and the stage is short on ambiance, but it's worth seeking out this enthusiast's club where you might see the next big flamenco star on his or her way up. *Peña* members are dedicated to nurturing artists and know talent when they see it. See p. 623.

The Best Bullrings

> The Festival of San Fermín in Pamplona sees the running of the bulls from the Old Town to the Plaza de Toros.

Plaza de Toros (Mijas). This oval bullring from 1900 has blossomed into a major tourist attraction. Buses bring fans from across the Costa del Sol. Views are astounding—not just of the *corrida* (fight), but also of the pretty village spread out below. See p. 549.

Plaza de Toros (Ronda). Visitors to one of the most historic bullrings in Spain are not accompanied by a guide, so they may stand in the ring for as long as it takes to ponder what has been called the "oscillation between luck and death" that each matador faces as he steps onto the sands. A small museum is full of photographs and matadors' "suits of light." See p. 639.

Plaza de Toros de la Real Maestranza (Sevilla). This 18th-century bullring is one of Spain's most beautiful and most intimate. The museum does a good job of tracing the evolution of the contests from the 17th century forward. The tour puts a human face on the sport, with stops in the chapel where matadors stop to pray before entering the ring and to the infirmary that they are probably praying never to visit. See p. 597.

Plaza de Toros Monumental de Las Ventas (Madrid). Opened in 1931, this Mudéjar-style building lacks the long history of other stadiums. But in a country where matadors can rise to the status of rock stars, this is the ring where the best of the bunch come to show their stuff. For visitors troubled by the sport, the guided tour gives insight into its place in Spanish culture. See p. 103.

Plaza de Toros Monumental de Pamplona. The July "running of the bulls" has garnered such international attention that it almost completely upstages this 1922 ring—which is the bulls' final destination. The fourth-largest bullring in the world is made of reinforced concrete in a form that suggests a triumphal arch. See p. 340.

Plaza Mayor (Chinchón). For most of the year, people shop and dine on Chinchón's atmospheric main square. But during summer and fall feast days, the plaza is converted into a *corrida* and fans pack the wooden balconies for the best views. It's a step back to the old days, when many main squares did double duty as bullrings. See p. 88.

2
Strategies for Seeing Spain

Strategies for Seeing Spain

No matter where you go in Spain or how much time you budget, it will never be enough. There's always another painting to see, dish to eat, mountain to climb, or wave to ride. But if you're smart about your time, you won't come home feeling that you missed opportunities—just that you want to go back and do more. Here are some strategies that will help. Above all, remember that the point of your journey is to experience Spain, so dance to its rhythms and enjoy.

> PREVIOUS PAGE *Street signs in Spain are likely to be in the regional language.* THIS PAGE *Madrid's Atocha train station.*

Tip #1: Let Spain change you.

Don't fight it—Spain will make you a different person. You won't think twice about dinner at 10pm, flamenco at midnight, and a nightcap afterward. That's how the Spanish do it. You'll learn to eat a 2-hour lunch and catch a nap in the afternoon. You'll talk to strangers in a bar and make instant new friends you'll never see again.

Tip #2: Tailor your transportation to your itinerary.

If you need to go long distances, say between Barcelona and Bilbao, don't shy away from flying. Travelers who fly on Iberia to Spain can pre-purchase "Abono Transportes" coupons for domestic flights that can cost as little as 55€ per segment. A 90-minute flight definitely beats 9 hours on the train at about the same price. But you'll probably find that more often, the high-speed trains will better suit your needs, as you can watch the scenery whiz past outside the window and wander down to the cafe car for a snack. (Alas, the national train network, RENFE, has the gall to serve instant coffee in its food service.) Now that so many high-speed lines are open—and more are coming—it can be faster to get from Madrid to a distant city than it is to fly, if you factor in airport hassles. Don't overlook local trains and buses for side trips once you reach your hub (see Tip #4, below). But don't rule out car rental if you want to have the freedom and flexibility to explore more off-the-beaten-path destinations or experience the thrill of driving the coastal rim or the mountain switchbacks. Besides, you'll dine out on driving stories for years.

> *Spaniards eat late; Cafetería El Molino in Pamplona doesn't heat up until almost midnight.*

Tip #3: Leave your food preconceptions at home.

The Spaniards may find more plants, sea life, animals, and animal parts edible than any other culture, with the possible exception of the Chinese. They also know how to make everything taste good. Going to Spain should be a mind-opening and palate-educating experience. Try everything once before you ask what it is. You probably have a mental list of things you will *never* eat. Never. If you're like a lot of English speakers, this includes most organ meats, snails, unfamiliar sea creatures such as giant barnacles, fish whose mouths are bigger than their bodies, bull's tail, and the various extremities of the pig (trotters, snout, and ears). But go ahead and try them. You can ease your way into the tastes of Spain by eating tapas. The portions are small and relatively inexpensive, and you might discover that you absolutely love something you never thought would pass your lips. If you're not certain how to attack a given food, the person sitting next to you at the bar will undoubtedly assist with amusement. You get points for trying.

Tip #4: Pick your hotels using an airline model.

Many of the most successful airlines operate on a hub-and-spoke system. Sometimes it's useful to stay in a single hotel and make day trips to multiple destinations, if they are close enough and you have either a car or good public transport. Other airlines operate a point-to-point network, and that model can also work for choosing hotels if you plan to cover a larger territory and move quickly. Plot your itinerary, carry your bags, and check into new digs every few days.

Tip #5: Pack light and dress well.

Light packing is especially critical if you're traveling by train and staying in several hotels. You do not need more than two pairs of shoes—one comfortable pair for walking and another comfortable but nicer pair for going to dinner or a show. Leave the hoodies and sweatpants at home. The biggest mistake most English-speakers make in Spain is dressing like they came to mow the lawn. Show some respect by dressing smart casual most of the time, and you'll get respect in return. This is especially important when visiting Spain's many religious

> *The midday meal is the largest in Spain, and dinner is late, but Spaniards tide themselves over with tapas.*

sites. If in doubt about whether, say, to cover your head, take your lead from the faithful. The good Lord may have made your body, but his worshipers are not all that keen on seeing it in church. Packing light has another advantage when you're coming home, as you'll have more space in your luggage for all the purchases you've made.

Tip #6: Don't overload your itinerary.

Trying to see three major museums in a day is like speed-reading the classics—it will all be a blur. Pace yourself so you can linger over a glass of wine at a cafe, see the temporary exhibition as well as the permanent collection at a museum, or have time to walk to your next stop instead of trying frantically to find a taxi. Keep in mind that summer heat in Spain is likely to slow you down. Don't beat yourself up for not finishing the checklist. Tomorrow is

another day. Getting lost is okay. Serendipity is the grace that happens to people who are open to the unexpected.

Tip #7: Pick the day's key activity and plan around it.

You surely have some "must sees" on your Spanish wish list. Focus on one or perhaps two per day and research other sites, shops, and restaurants in the same vicinity. Sometimes it's the small, unexpected stuff that makes your day. Be prepared to wing it now and then. It's called an adventure.

Tip #8: Go online.

The world has gone digital, and that includes Spain. Hotels and museums generally have a Web presence and often their own websites where you can book in advance. Moreover, most websites have an English version, although you may have to go to the Spanish pages for the

> *RENFE, Spain's national rail service, has worked in recent years to improve its fleet's speed and comfort.*

most complete or up-to-date information. You can also get tickets to many of Spain's cultural events, from individual concerts to admissions to the Alhambra, through ServiCaixa (www.servi caixa.com). The national rail network, RENFE, has an especially good and quick website (www. renfe.es) that lets you check timetables in a snap and make reservations on high-speed and long-distance trains. Even if your Blackberry or iPhone doesn't function on the Spanish networks, you can stay connected without lugging a netbook or laptop around. Most hotels have computers for guest use, and Internet cafes are common. It can be a great relief to be lost, buy 15 minutes in an Internet cafe to consult Google Maps, and come out knowing where you are, where you're going, and how to get there.

Tip #9: Learn a little Spanish.

Thanks to the Internet and pop culture, English has emerged as Spain's most commonly spoken foreign language. Nonetheless, knowing some Spanish is immensely helpful if you need to, say, look things up in a phone book. It's for precisely that reason that this guide uses local Spanish, Catalan, Basque, or Gallego names for towns, streets, buildings, and establishments. That's how the maps and signs will read! Most Spaniards appreciate it if you make an effort to speak with them in their own language; if they sense that your Spanish is even worse than their English, they might switch to your tongue. Learning Spanish—especially menu Spanish (see p. 701 for a glossary)—might also avert unwelcome surprises on your plate (see Tip #3). It definitely helps for striking up conversations in crowded tapas bars.

Tip #10: Manage your money wisely.

Use plastic judiciously. Check to see if your credit card imposes a foreign currency charge (most do), and get a card that waives that fee. Even with bank fees for foreign currency transactions, it will be far cheaper for you to withdraw cash from your home bank account at an ATM than it will be to exchange cash or traveler's checks, which typically get poor exchange rates and incur a transaction fee to boot. Usually you're better off withdrawing 300€ once than 50€ six times, as most banks also charge a per-transaction fee. When you do go to charge, the credit card system may ask if you want the charge in your home currency or in euros. Choose euros every time—you'll get the wholesale bank exchange rate on your credit card bill, which is usually better than the retail rate charged at the point of purchase.

3
The Best All-Spain Itineraries

Highlights of Spain

Spain in a week or two? Think of it like a first date. Everything is fresh, you might fall in love, and you can look forward to learning more another time. On your first (full) seven days, you'll have time to see the elegant capital, followed by two of the most iconic cities of ancient castles and grand cathedrals. After that, you'll head south to the medieval streets of Córdoba and flamenco-filled nights in Sevilla. If you have more than a week to spend in Spain, your second week can include other iconic Spanish highlights, notably the sophisticated Catalan capital of Barcelona. Then fly north to Bilbao, a city literally transformed by art. Explore surfing beaches and fishing villages along the Basque coast, ending in the Belle Epoque resort of San Sebastián, where a great beach meets an even greater dining scene.

START Fly into Madrid's Barajas airport.

❶ Madrid. Start at the **Prado** (see p. 72, ❶), one of the world's greatest art museums. Don't be waylaid by Fra Angelico and Titian—you're in Spain, not Italy. Concentrate on galleries devoted to Diego Velázquez and Francisco de Goya, whose greatest works are here.

The **Reina Sofía** (see p. 74, ❺) picks up where the Prado leaves off. The museum's radical rethinking of recent art emphasizes creative vision over aesthetic polemics—although the most striking work is still Pablo Picasso's highly political *Guernica* (see p. 294). Spend the rest of the day shopping in beehivelike **Puerta del Sol** (see p. 74, ❻). At

> PREVIOUS PAGE *Spain's social life revolves around its public plazas.* THIS PAGE *Some of the 2,000 rooms of Madrid's Palacio Real are still open to the public.*

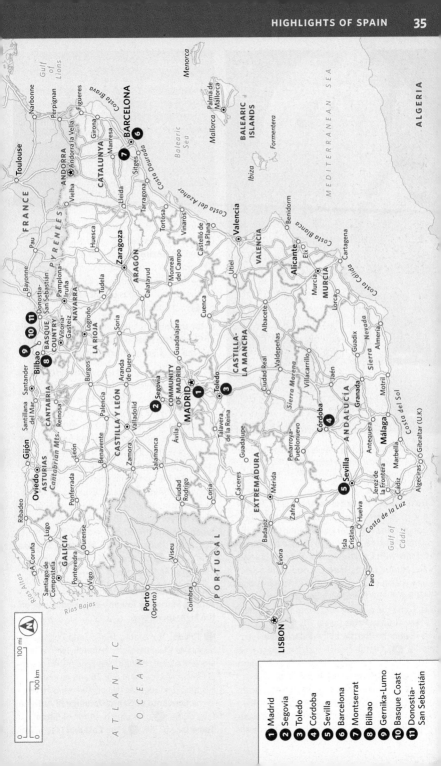

1. Madrid
2. Segovia
3. Toledo
4. Córdoba
5. Sevilla
6. Barcelona
7. Montserrat
8. Bilbao
9. Gernika-Lumo
10. Basque Coast
11. Donostia-San Sebastián

> La Mezquita, built on the site of a Visigoth basilica that replaced a Roman temple, is a UNESCO World Heritage Site.

Travel Tip

Although it can be more expensive to make advance reservations (a must on most high-speed trains) from home rather than after arriving, your time is at a premium, and you don't want to be left without a seat. If you're going during the summer or around the holidays, make train reservations before you leave. See p. 692 for more on train travel in Spain.

trod by blue-blooded nuns in the **Monasterio de las Descalzas Reales** (see p. 81, ❽). Circle around the **Teatro Real,** or Ópera (see p. 80, ❻), and stop for a drink and to people-watch on **Plaza del Oriente** (see p. 80, ❹) before exploring the elegant arcades of **Plaza Mayor** (see p. 81, ❾). ⏱ 2 days.

In the morning, take a train from either Atocha or Chamartín stations to Segovia (about 2 hr.) and the no. 3 bus to Plaza Mayor.

❷ **Segovia.** It's hard to tell which end of the Old City is more iconic: the 166 arches of the **Aqueducto** (see p. 218, ❶), which supplied water to Segovia for 1,900 years, or the **Alcázar de Segovia** (see p. 220, ❹), a fairy tale castle at the other end of the boat-shaped bluff where the city stands. The aqueduct conjures the might and skill of the Romans, the castle the pomp and clout of the Castilian monarchy. Segovia rewards exploration, from its Renaissance-noble barrio on one side of **Plaza Mayor** (see p. 218, ❷) to the ancient Judería neighborhood on the other. Don't miss the Gothic sculptures in the **Museo de Segovia** (see p. 221, ❺) or a meal of roast suckling pig. Return to Madrid to sleep. ⏱ 1 day.

On day 4, take an early-morning train from Atocha Station to Toledo—only a half-hour on the high-speed line.

❸ **Toledo.** The Arabic, Jewish, and Christian history of the citadel city is literally written in stone. Its spirit, though, was rendered in oils by El Greco, who came at age 26 and never left. His best paintings remain as well. Study them in the **Convento de Santo Domingo El Antiguo** (see p. 166, ❷), his parish church of **Santo Tomé** (see p. 169, ❾), the **Catedral** (see p. 168,

6pm, walk to **Plaza Santa Ana** (see p. 74, ❽) and make new friends as you belly up to the bar in a succession of tapas joints. (You're just getting started, so it's okay to ease into Spanish cuisine with *tortilla española,* a potato omelet, and *patatas bravas,* fried potatoes with a spicy paprika sauce.) By 10pm, the restaurants open. Jet lag is your friend—it's hours earlier in the U.S. End the evening with a late-night flamenco show at **Casa Patas** (see p. 75, ❾).

Begin the 2nd day at the **Palacio Real** (see p. 76, ❶). Let the crowds rush the palace while you explore the armory. Think of the plate armor as Hapsburg formalwear. It was all custom-made, so you see the real size of those kings whose portraits you saw yesterday. Enjoy the splendors of Bourbon taste in the palace rooms. Spend an hour in the hushed but art-filled halls

7), and the **Museo de Santa Cruz** (see p. 168, **5**). Then enjoy wandering the tangle of narrow streets, where deep blue shadows offer respite from the sun.

Toledo had one of Spain's most dynamic Jewish communities until Fernando and Isabel expelled them in 1492. The **Museo Sefardí** (see p. 170, **10**), housed in Toledo's last surviving synagogue, the 1355 Sinagoga del Tránsito, tells the city's Jewish history and, by extension, the broader lot of Jewish life in Spain. ⏱ 1 day.

On day 5, take an early-morning train back to Atocha, where the high-speed AVE will whisk you to Córdoba in 2 hr.

4 **Córdoba.** Winding streets summon the Córdoba of 1,000 years ago, when Christians, Jews, and Muslims made the capital of the Caliphate the most cultured city in Europe. Start at **La Mezquita** (see p. 630, **4**), the largest mosque built in western Europe. The forest of red and white arches vanishing into the distance evokes the ascetic spirituality of a desert people, and it is easy to imagine the majesty of 40,000 worshipers bowing as one.

The best parts of the **Alcázar de los Reyes Cristianos** (see p. 630, **5**), a palace for the caliphs that Fernando and Isabel gut-renovated, are the Arabic baths (which they left alone) and the formal gardens (constructed centuries

later). Several sites in the atmospheric Judería evoke the era when philosophers like Moses Maimonides and Averroës walked these streets. Visits to the **Casa de Sefarad** (see p. 631, **9**) and its counterpart, the **Casa Andalusí** (see p. 631, **10**), will illuminate daily life in the 12th century for Córdoban Jews and Muslims, respectively. ⏱ 1 day.

On day 6, hop the AVE for a half-hour ride to Sevilla, where you'll stay for 2 days.

5 **Sevilla. La Giralda** (see p. 590, **3**) was the minaret of the main mosque before it became the cathedral's bell tower. Now it is the iconic image of Sevilla. The **Catedral** (see p. 590, **2**) itself—the third-largest Gothic cathedral in Europe—obliterated the mosque to leave no doubt who won the Christian-Muslim struggle. The beautiful Patio de Naranjas, the mosque's ablution courtyard where the faithful washed before prayer, remains an integral and evocative part of the complex.

The **Real Alcázar** (see p. 591, **4**) was the last word about Castilian power and might. Europe's oldest royal residence still in use consists of two palaces, several connecting structures, and beautiful gardens. Focus on the Palacio Mudéjar, constructed at the end of the 14th century in much the same style—and, tradition says, by many of the same artisans—

> *Toledo, surrounded on three sides by the Tajo River, overlooks the plains of Castilla from its hilltop perch.*

> *A ramp will lead you to the top of La Giralda, the most recognizable monument of Sevilla.*

as Granada's Alhambra. Take an hour to explore the colorful medieval streets of **Barrio Santa Cruz** (see p. 592, ❻).

Sevilla grew fat and sassy from the 16th to 18th century by monopolizing trade with the New World colonies. Great wealth meant a building boom, with cash left over to patronize the arts. Do not miss master paintings, especially those by Francisco Zurbarán in the **Museo de Bellas Artes** (see p. 593, ❾), and absorb the exuberance of Spanish baroque architecture at the **Basílica de Nuestra Señora de la Macarena** (see p. 593, ❿). Squeeze in time to peruse the ceramics factories (see p. 601), sample tapas, and catch flamenco in the **Barrio Triana** (see p. 596, ⓰). ☺ 2 days.

On day 8, fly on to Barcelona to continue the 2-week itinerary. If you're only spending a week in Spain, fly home from Sevilla's Aeropuerto San Pablo.

❻ **Barcelona.** Waste no time getting to **La Sagrada Família** (see p. 406, ❶), the soaring legacy of the Modernista visionary Antoni Gaudí. A century after his death, this landmark basilica is finally nearing completion. Gaudí's apartment building, **La Pedrera** (see p. 408, ❷), another symbol of the city, stands in the heart of L'Eixample. Just down **Passeig de Gràcia** (see p. 426, ❺) is **Manzana de la Discordia** (the "Block of Discord"), where other seminal Modernista works huddle together. Grab lunch in L'Eixample and then head to Plaça de Catalunya and the great strolling boulevard **La Rambla** (see p. 410, ❼), which remains the centerpiece of life in the capital. **Mercat de la Boquería** (see p. 410, ❽), the legendary food market, is set back from La Rambla, about halfway down.

Getting your second wind? Head to Montjuïc and the **Museu Nacional d'Art de Catalunya** (MNAC; see p. 416, ❶), a top museum of medieval religious art. **Fundació Joan Miró** (see p. 418, ❺) features the Catalan surrealist's unique artistic language in both painting and sculpture. Back down in the center, **El Palau de la Música Catalana** (see p. 418, ❻) is a wonderfully ornate music hall open for daily tours and concerts. Finally, get a great late-afternoon view of Barcelona and relax in Gaudí's whimsical **Parc Güell** (see p. 419, ❼).

On your second day, set out for **Museu Picasso** (see p. 410, ❿), the largest collection of Picasso's art in Spain. Peruse the Born district's hip fashion boutiques and art galleries en route to **Santa Maria del Mar** (see p. 411, ⓫), an exquisite Catalan Gothic church. Cross Vía Laeitana to see the **Catedral de Barcelona** (see p. 410, ❾) and wander the **Barri Gòtic,** stopping for a drink in **Plaça del Pi.** On the far side of the Barri Gòtic, continue down La Rambla to **Port Vell** (see p. 414, ❻), the old port, fronted by a pleasant boardwalk. Saunter east to the colorful beachfront barrio of **Barceloneta.** Keep going to reach the city's revamped beaches and **Port Olímpic** (see p. 414, ❼), the neighborhood created for the '92 Olympics. ☺ 2 days.

> *The sinuous lines of the Guggenheim Bilbao, with Jeff Koons's* Puppy *topiary in front.*

On day 10, hop the R-5 train for the 1-hr. trip to Montserrat, where you can transfer to the cable car up the mountain.

7 Montserrat. The jagged outline of Montserrat *looks* like a magical mountain, and monks established a facility on its flanks to house *La Moreneta,* a 12th-century carving of Virgin and Child with reputed miraculous properties. A monkish city has grown up around the pilgrimage site. The 1m-high (3¼-ft.) statue is ensconced in a chapel above the main altar of the basilica, where pilgrims file past to kiss her extended hand. Quickly tour the **Museu de Montserrat** to see art donated by the faithful before catching the cable car and train back to Barcelona. ⏰ 6–8 hr. See p. 364, **1**.

On day 11, fly from El Prat in Barcelona to Bilbao (about 1 hr. 10 min.).

8 Bilbao. The architectural distinction of this city begins even before you land. The main terminal of the airport, designed by Santiago Calatrava in 2000, is called **La Paloma** ("The Dove") because its two wings sweep back from

> *La Rambla, a bustling, tree-lined boulevard, stretches from the Barri Gòtic to Barcelona's revitalized harbor.*

> *Northern Spain's Basque coast is dotted with traditional fishing villages and seductive seaside resorts.*

a beaklike tip. Frank Gehry's innovative architecture for the **Museo Guggenheim Bilbao** (see p. 312, ❷) creates a harmonious package but oddly shaped interiors. Get a free audio guide when entering to understand how to tour the space. The contemporary art is cutting edge, and so is the museum experience. By contrast, the **Museo de Bellas Artes** (see p. 314, ❹) is strikingly comprehensive, with strengths in Gothic art and Basque regional painting.

Gehry's titanium dinosaur jump-started the transformation of Bilbao from decayed industrial city to architectural showcase, and nowhere are the changes more evident than in the **Abandoibarra** (see p. 314, ❸), with new riverfront sculptures, buildings, and cafes. Follow the riverside path to the Casco Viejo (Old Town) for tapas or dinner under the arches of the neoclassical **Plaza Nueva** (see p. 315, ❽). ⏲ 2 days.

In Bilbao, rent a car one-way to San Sebastián. Follow the A-8 east about 17km (10 miles) to exit 100 for the BI-635 to Gernika-Lumo, about 15km (9 miles).

❾ **Gernika-Lumo.** Since the village was founded in the mid–13th century, Basque leaders have traveled to Gernika to meet beneath a special oak tree. That symbol of Basque independence drew the wrath of Generalissimo Francisco Franco, who had the German Luftwaffe bomb the village on April 26, 1937. Although the barrage killed hundreds, perhaps thousands, the Nazis missed their main target. The petrified trunk of the ancient oak still stands atop a hill on the grounds of the former Basque parliament, the **Casa de Juntas.** To understand more of the complex culture and even more complicated politics of the Basques, visit the **Museoa Euskal Herria,** or Basque Heritage Museum. The Gernika Peace

> *Perhaps the best nightlife in Donostia-San Sebastián is a traditional tapas-crawl through the seaside town's abundant dining establishments.*

Museum, **Fundación Museo de la Paz de Gernika,** emphasizes the prevention of future wars. A disturbing audiovisual re-creation of the bombing and gripping exhibits about the attack and its aftermath may be the best arguments ever for peace. ⊕ 3 hr. See p. 292, ❹.

Drive the BI-2238 northeast 23km (14 miles) for about 25 min. to Lekeitio. In Lekeitio, pick up the coastal road, BI-3438, for the 15km (9-mile) eastward drive to Ondarroa.

❿ **Basque Coast.** The prosperous tuna-fishing town of **Lekeitio** (see p. 302, ❸) has a pair of splendid swimming beaches.

After driving along sea cliffs, you'll enter **Ondarroa** (see p. 303, ❹), the leading Basque fishing port. Attractions break down into three categories: lively bars and restaurants of the port district, medieval landmarks of the old quarter, and the secluded nudist beach of Playa Saturrarán on the east end of town. ⊕ 6 hr. with stops, 2 hr. without.

Continue east from Ondarroa on GI-638 for 8km (5 miles) to the A-8, which will whisk you into San Sebastián in 30km (18 miles), where you can get rid of the car.

⓫ **Donostia-San Sebastián.** Spain's answer to Cannes and Biarritz, San Sebastián is the most glamorous resort in Spain. Explore the narrow streets of **Parte Vieja** (see p. 306, ❶), walk the **Paseo Nuevo** (see p. 308, ❷), and ascend Monte Urgull for views of the harbor. Save time to check out sharks and turtles in the **Aquarium Donostia-San Sebastián** (see p. 308, ❹). After lunch, indulge by sunbathing and swimming in the brisk waters. If you go to the gym a lot, you'll feel at home on the surfer's beach, **Playa de Zurriola** (see p. 308, ❻). If a family scene is more comfortable, then the broad **Playa de la Concha** (see p. 309, ❾) is perfect. The westerly **Playa de Ondarreta** (see p. 309, ⓫) has an ambience somewhere between the two. If the beach isn't for you, hop a G2 bus to visit the **Museo Chillida-Leku** (see p. 298, ❸), an inspiring rustic studio dedicated to celebrated Basque abstract sculptor Eduardo Chillida (1924–2002). You'll want to be back in time to enjoy the tapas scene in the **Gros** barrio ("neighborhood"; see p. 308, ❼). ⊕ 1 day.

Take the 5-hr. train from San Sebastián to Madrid to fly home from Barajas.

Undiscovered Northwest Spain

Despite the enduring draw of the pilgrimage site of Santiago de Compostela, surprisingly few travelers venture to the north, especially to the northwest mountains and sea. These towns are less "undiscovered" than they are the road less traveled. Among them are the lyrical Asturian city of Oviedo, the elegant seaside resort of Santander, and the historic capitals of Burgos and León. History, pageantry, faith, and seaside frolics all await. You'll start this weeklong trip by flying in, but you'll switch to train travel the rest of the way.

> *According to tradition, all roads in Spain once led to the tomb of St. James (Santiago) below the Cathedral of Santiago de Compostela.*

START Fly into Santiago's Aeropuerto de Lavacolla and catch the Freire bus to downtown Santiago de Compostela.

1 Santiago de Compostela. According to Christian tradition, Santiago (better known as St. James the Apostle), who preached the faith to Roman Hispania after the death of Christ, was beheaded in Jerusalem in A.D. 44. His disciples carried his body by sea to the Galician coast for burial. Pilgrimages to the area began when Santiago's tomb was discovered

in A.D. 814 and continue to this day. More than a millennium of pilgrims have transformed Santiago into a fascinating town. Begin at the **Catedral** (see p. 256, **1**), where the faithful make it their first business to climb the stairs and embrace a Gothic statue of Santiago, whose remains lie in the crypt beneath the altar.

The **Praza do Obradoiro** (see p. 258, **2**) is the Old Town's central square, graced on one side by the cathedral, on another by the lodging for pilgrims established in 1492 by Fernando

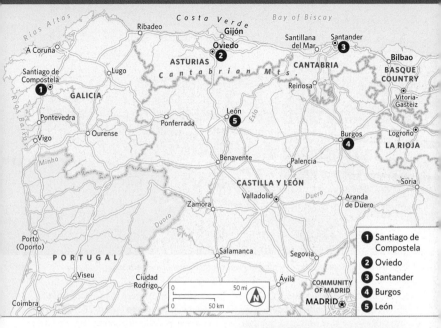

1	Santiago de Compostela
2	Oviedo
3	Santander
4	Burgos
5	León

and Isabel (now the Hostal Dos Reis Católicos; see p. 260). Look for the brass scallop shell, symbol of Santiago, in the center of the plaza. Behind the cathedral, the new **Museo das Peregrinacións** (see p. 259, **5**), or Museum of Pilgrimages, details everything you would ever want to know about Santiago the saint, Santiago the city, and the Camino de Santiago (pilgrimage route). As you might expect, the city has no shortage of eating and drinking establishments, found mostly on **Rúa da Raína** and **Rúa do Franco** (see p. 258, **3**), and shops, found on **Rúa do Vilar** (see p. 258, **4**). As you wander about, you'll hear street musicians playing flutes, guitars, and Galician bagpipes. ☉ 2 days.

Catch the afternoon train to Oviedo, about a 3-hr. trip.

2 Oviedo. The compact medieval quarter of the capital city of the Principality of Asturias flows seamlessly into gridlike modern shopping streets. Despite its hilly layout, Oviedo is a walking city of broad streets that follow the contours of the land, offering new vistas at every corner. Start at the **Catedral** (see p. 278, **1**) in the heart of the Old City. The 15th-century church was constructed around a

> *The 9th-century Cross of the Angels is one of the first and finest examples of Asturian religious art.*

beautiful pre-Romanesque chapel, the **Cámara Santa,** which holds the 9th- and 10th-century jeweled crosses that are the symbols of Oviedo and Asturias.

> *The fishing port of Santander's bay waters are warmer than most of northern Spain.*

One of the striking things about Oviedo is that its ancient quarters often predate other Spanish cities by several centuries. Some of that age is revealed in the early paintings in the splendid **Museo de Bellas Artes** (see p. 278, ❸). A rather fantastic altarpiece of the life, martyrdom, and resurrection of 2nd-century-A.D. Galician martyr Santa Marina captures the mix of Christian belief and Celtic legend that persisted here through the Middle Ages.

Oviedo's real charm shines in its street life, whether around the **Plaza del Fontán** (see p. 280, ❼), which swirls with a street market and folk dancing from Thursday to Sunday, or along the urbane, contemporary **C/ Uría** (see p. 280, ❾), with its boutiques and bronze likeness of Woody Allen, who set part of his 2008 film *Vicky Cristina Barcelona* here. ⏲ 1–1½ days.

Catch the early-morning train to Santander, a trip of about 3½ hr.

❸ **Santander.** You'll arrive in time for a leisurely lunch. Wander from the waterfront through the downtown **Jardines de Pereda** (see p. 282, ❶) and into the heart of the city. There's very little ancient about Santander, since a 1941 fire gutted the Casco Viejo (Old Town). But follow the narrow streets uphill and watch for eateries where people are congregating outside with drinks. Santander is a great fishing port, and even the humblest fish restaurants are often very good.

After lunch, return to the waterfront to **Muelle de Albaredo** (see p. 282, ❷) to hop either an inexpensive harbor ferry or a sightseeing boat to see the great bowl of the Bay of Santander. This city is all about the sea—or the beach, where land meets ocean. The **Museo Marítimo del Cantábrico** (see p. 284, ❻), part aquarium and part maritime history museum, relates the long tale of Santander and the water.

Take time to stroll the **Peninsula de la Magdalena** (see p. 284, ❽). Santander lured the royal family here from 1913 to 1930 by building them a summer palace at the tip of this peninsula, now turned into a public park with a minizoo of penguins and sea lions. Finally, no visit to Santander is complete without either enjoying the long strand of **El Sardinero** (see p. 284, ❾) or at least admiring the Belle Epoque mansions, casino, and hotels that rise on the hill above the beach. ⏲ 1½ days.

Book ahead for 1 of the 2 evening Regional Express trains to Burgos and cut your travel time by two-thirds, to 47 min. Hop the no. 11 bus from the new Rosa de Lima station to the Plaza de España.

❹ **Burgos.** Burgos could be called the first medieval strip mall, since the city coalesced in the early 11th century along the pilgrimage route to Santiago. It was a crossroads of scholarship and power throughout the medieval era and is considered by many the cradle of the Castilian language. Even today its residents speak textbook Spanish. Start exploring at **Plaza del Cid,** where a heroic statue depicts local hero Rodrigo Díaz de Vivar, aka El Cid, as a knight-warrior on horseback. (Half the monarchies of Europe can claim the legendary 11th-c. warrior as an ancestor; see p. 210.)

Follow the leafy **Paseo del Espolón** along the river to Puente de Santa María to enter the Old City via the triumphal **Arco de Santa María.** Perhaps the first thing you'll spot in the broad Plaza de San Fernando is a bronze statue of a weary Santiago pilgrim sitting on a bench. The real pilgrims will be making their way to the adjacent **Catedral de Burgos** (see p. 209, **❽**), an airy, soaring example of French Gothic architecture. El Cid and his wife lie in beautifully carved sepulchres in front of the altar. ⊕ 1 day.

Reserve ahead for the midafternoon AVE train to León. Travel time is about 1 hr. 40 min.

❺ León. A great medieval power with vassal territories reaching all the way to the Rhône in the 11th century, León made the transition to holy city with an upsurge of Santiago pilgrims in the 13th century.

The stonemasons, carvers, painters, and iron sculptors who built the soaring French Gothic **Catedral de León** (see p. 208, **❼**) formed one of the greatest workforces of medieval times. In the end, the glass artists outshone them all with stained-glass windows that dazzle everyone who walks in. Nearby, the 11th-century **Colegiata de San Isidoro** (see p. 202, **❹**) is less showy, but its adjoining convent holds the graves of 11 kings of León, laid out beneath extraordinary 12th-century ceiling frescoes that have never been conserved yet remain vivid and largely intact. ⊕ 1 day.

Reserve ahead for the early-morning high-speed ALVIA train to Madrid (2 hr. 50 min.), where you can take the Metro to Barajas airport to fly home.

> *As well as the tombs of the kings of León, La Colegiata houses the remains of San Isidoro and his wife.*

The Two Castillas

When the kings of Castilla began to dominate central Spain in the 11th century, they planted churches to assert the primacy of Christianity and castles to retain their new dominions. Take 10 days to 2 weeks to discover the sun-drenched plains of La Mancha and fortified hilltop cities like Cuenca, Toledo, Segovia, and Ávila. Walk with scholars and dreamers in Salamanca, and never forget that the wine press won more land than the sword as you taste through Zamora and Toro. Use this tour to extend a visit to Madrid, or as a jumping-off point for "Undiscovered Northwest Spain" (see p. 42).

> *Physics be damned! Cuenca is known for its seemingly gravity-defying* casas colgadas *(hanging houses).*

START Rent a car in Madrid and follow signs to the A-3, going 86km (53 miles) to the A-40, then continuing 80km (50 miles) to Cuenca. **TRIP LENGTH** 888km (552 miles).

❶ Cuenca. Like a castle in the air, this steep little village consists of Arabic streets, Renaissance and Gothic palaces, and an improbably Anglo-Norman 12th-century **Catedral** (see p. 172, **❷**). It rises on an abrupt limestone spur with vertigo-inducing drop-offs to the Huécar and Júcar rivers. Famed for a few death-defying buildings cantilevered over the gorges, Cuenca has *three* excellent small **museums of contemporary abstract art** (see p. 173, **❹**; p. 174, **❾**, **❿**). ⏲ 1½ days.

Head west on the A-40 for 125km (78 miles) to merge onto the A-4 north. In 14km (8⅔ miles), take exit 52 and follow signs to Aranjuez.

❷ Aranjuez. While he plotted his burial at El Escorial (see p. 90, **❹**), Felipe II also had a splendid **Palacio Real** and beautiful parks built in the hilly farm country south of Madrid.

1. Cuenca
2. Aranjuez
3. Toledo
4. Segovia
5. Ávila
6. Salamanca
7. Zamora
8. Toro
9. Valladolid

A gracious town with great restaurants has flourished there ever since. To preview the serene mood of this regal retreat, listen to the Miles Davis interpretation of *Concierto de Aranjuez* on the legendary *Sketches of Spain* album. ⊙ 1 day. See p. 89, **3**.

Head north on the A-4 for 8km (5 miles) to exit 44. Pick up AP-41 for 18km (11 miles) to Toledo.

3 Toledo. The medieval city of Toledo rises like a mirage from the plains of La Mancha. A bridge enters the walls from a hillside across the river, but most approaches are from the valley. Take an outdoor escalator up to the Old City walls and walk the rest of the way. The winding, narrow streets link important buildings and their adjoining plazas. In the middle of the maze is the soaring **Catedral** (see p. 168, **7**) with extensive Mudéjar decoration. The sacristy holds several works by El Greco.

As you explore the atmospheric city, don't miss the **Museo de Santa Cruz** (see p. 168, **5**), where you can get nose to nose with some of El Greco's saints, and the **Museo Sefardí** (see p. 170, **10**), which relates the proud—and sad—history of Jews in Toledo and the rest of Spain. ⊙ 1–2 days.

> *Medieval suits of armor greet visitors to Segovia's once impregnable Alcázar.*

Follow the AP-41 north 60km (37 miles) to the exit for R-5/A-5. In 30km (19 miles), merge onto the A-6 and continue 39km (24 miles). Take the AP-61 for 28km (17 miles) to Segovia.

4 Segovia. Many observers liken Segovia's Old City to a steamship, with the fairy tale **Alcázar** (see p. 220, **4**) as the prow, the **Catedral** (see p. 220, **3**) with its glorious Churriguera altar as the mast, and the Roman **Aqueducto** (see p. 218, **1**) as the rudder.

Board her from the stern, enjoying the street life of the plaza around the aqueduct's great arches, and wind your way to the **Plaza Mayor** (see p. 218, ). Then shop from the cathedral to the palace fortress, where the Hall of Monarchs traces the Castilian royal line from Pelayo (d. 737) to Isabel and Fernando's haunted daughter, Juana la Loca (1479–1555). End your day with roast suckling pig at **José María Restaurante** (see p. 223). ⏲ 1 day.

Head southwest on the AP-61 for 28km (17 miles) and pick up the A-6/AP-6 northwest for 21km (13 miles). At exit 81, take the AP-51 30km (19 miles) to Ávila.

❺ Ávila. The appearance of yet another fortified city on a hilltop is a good reminder of how Castilla got its name. You can walk atop the **12th-century walls** (see p. 224, ❷) that earned Ávila UNESCO World Heritage status. But the enduring influence of mystic and reformer Santa Teresa (1515–82) put the city on the pilgrimage map. Although psychologists may have a field day with Teresa's ecstatic visions, she and her friend and confessor San Juan de la Cruz (1542–91) founded the order of Carmelitas Descalzos, or Barefoot Carmelites, which steered Spanish Catholicism to a more ascetic path. The **Museo Teresiano** (see p. 226,

❹) provides a good overview of the saint's life and legacy. ⏲ 1 day.

From Ávila, follow the A-50 west for 98km (61 miles) to the N-501 for 5km (3 miles) to Salamanca.

❻ Salamanca. The 1218 founding of the **University of Salamanca** (see p. 228, ❶, ❷; p. 230, ❸) set this city on a cerebral path. The life of the mind is even evident in the local style of carving the soft, golden Villamayor limestone of the University's buildings. Some of the earliest examples are the capitals in the cloister of **Convento de las Dueñas** (see p. 232, ❾), where for centuries, only the Dominican nuns enjoyed the fantastic flying goat heads, wicked devils, and winged horses. Some of the finest carvings, including a frog that has become a good-luck talisman, adorn the doorway to the **Escuelas Mayores** (see p. 230, ❸). Panhandlers love to point out the 1992 updates (including an astronaut) to the carvings around the Puerta Ramos of the **Catedral Nueva** (see p. 230, ❻), which shares a wall with its elder sister, the **Catedral Vieja** (see p. 231, ❼). Together they trace architectural styles from Gothic to baroque. ⏲ 1–2 days.

From Salamanca, follow the A-66 north for 53km (33 miles) to Zamora.

> *The fortified walls of Ávila are a reminder of Spain's violent history, a country divided and reunited time and again.*

> *In its heyday, the University of Salamanca was one of the leading intellectual institutions of Europe.*

7 Zamora. This lovely city on the banks of the Río Duero changed hands between Moors and Christians constantly between the 9th and 11th centuries. When Castilla's King Alfonso VII (self-dubbed "Alfonso the Emperor") seized it for good, he and his successors built one of Spain's greatest Romanesque cathedrals, the **Catedral de Zamora,** and 23 other churches in the 12th and 13th centuries that remain active today. One of the best restored is the humble **Magdalena,** where the portals are carved with flowers and vines. ◷ 1 day. See p. 198, **1**.

Follow the A-11 40km (25 miles) to Toro.

8 Toro. You have to give the stone carvers who created the main entry to the 13th-century **Santa María la Mayor (Colegiata)** credit for audacity. Their depiction of the Last Judgment shows God saving the musicians first, while the virgins and martyrs wait their turns. Today Toro is the namesake center of a rising-star wine district, built on the *tinta de Toro* grape, a vigorous version of Spain's signature *tempranillo* grape. Enjoy the luscious reds at every bar, and save time to visit the *bodegas* (wine cellars). ◷ 1 day. See p. 200, **2**.

Follow A-11 east 30km (19 miles) to pick up the A-62 for 28km (17 miles) to Valladolid.

9 Valladolid. In this last capital of the Kingdom of Castile, you'll find the only house still standing where Miguel de Cervantes lived. The **Museo Casa de Cervantes** shows the author's modest lifestyle, even as a court hanger-on. You'll be introduced to the artistry of sculptor Juan de Juni when you visit the **Catedral,** and you can examine more of his polychrome wooden masterpieces at the **Museo Nacional Colegio de San Gregorio** (formerly the Museo Nacional de Escultura). ◷ 4 hr. See p. 201, **3**.

Follow the A-62 southwest to exit 151. Follow the A-6 to Madrid, watching for signs to Aeropuerto de Barajas. The complete drive of 233km (145 miles) takes a little under 3 hr. Fly home from Barajas.

Moorish Spain by Train

On this 5-day tour, you'll have an advantage the Christian kings of northern Spain who laid siege to the Moorish dominions of the south would have killed for: You don't have to march (or ride a horse). You can hop the train to see the glories of Muslim Spain from the original power center of Córdoba to the final blossoming of Nasrid artistry in Granada's Alhambra. Motorcoach tours often follow this route because it hits the jackpot of Moorish art and architecture.

> Toledo's Mudéjar legacy can be seen in the city's architecture, like the Puerta del Sol's horseshoe arch.

START From Madrid, take an early-morning train from Atocha station to Toledo (35 min.).

❶ Toledo. Christian and Muslim forces traded Toledo back and forth for 2 centuries, but citizenry of both faiths flourished during that time (as did Jewish settlement). Around A.D. 1000, Toledo emerged as an intellectual crossroads of great scholarly traditions, where ancient Greek learning would be translated into Arabic, from Arabic into Castilian for dissemination in Spain, and from Castilian to Latin for dissemination in Europe. Catholic conquerors prized their Muslim subjects, whether scholars or artisans. The legacy of the Toledo School (as the translators were known) is that the Western world now has the works of Aristotle, Plato, and Pythagoras.

The legacy of the Muslim artisans remains in the brickwork all over Toledo—the decorative Mudéjar style. It is most pronounced in the bell tower of **Santo Tomé** (see p. 169, **❾**), which became El Greco's parish church, and the 12th-century **San Román,** which was closed for renovations when this book went to press. Located in the heart of the Muslim quarter, San Román not only has a proud Mudéjar tower, but its interior looks precisely like a mosque, right down to the *mihrab* (the niche indicating the direction of Mecca)—except that the walls are covered with Romanesque Christian murals. ⊕ 1 day.

Take an early-morning train back to Atocha, where the high-speed AVE will whisk you to Córdoba in 2 hr.

1	Toledo
2	Córdoba
3	Sevilla
4	Granada

2 Córdoba. Headquarters of the Caliphate that ruled al-Andaluz—the Moorish lands that once included the entire Iberian Peninsula south of the Cantabrian mountains—Córdoba represented the high-water mark of Muslim power and culture in western Europe. Its winding, narrow streets are so ancient that centuries of whitewash have rounded the corners of the buildings. The old section of the city is called the **Judería,** but that name came later—after the Christian conquerors kicked out the Muslims and allowed the Jews to remain. The most powerful Muslim symbol in Spain is **La Mezquita** (see p. 630, **4**), the largest mosque ever built in western Europe.

To understand the complex, intertwined history of the cultures of Córdoba, visit the **Torre de la Calahorra** (see p. 628, **1**), where a beguiling audio tour introduces you to the likes of the Torah scholar Moses Maimonides (1135–1204) and Muslim philosopher and mathematician Averroes (1126–98).

Two modern cultural sites, the Jewish **Casa de Sefarad** (see p. 631, **9**) and its Muslim counterpart, the **Casa Andalusí** (see p. 631, **10**), vividly conjure life in 12th-century Córdoba, just as fundamentalist politics began to tear the city apart. After the day-trippers have left, you'll hear canaries sing in the back streets and watch the stars blink on overhead, one by one. ⊙ 1 day.

Hop the AVE for a half-hour ride to Sevilla.

3 **Sevilla. La Giralda** (see p. 590, **3**), the mosque's minaret repurposed as the bell tower of the **Catedral** (see p. 590, **2**), is the most obvious reminder of Moorish Sevilla. Traces of the Almohad dynasty's palace also remain in some of the rooms of the **Real Alcázar** (see p. 591, **4**), and a distinctly Nasrid decorative style is found throughout the complex's Palacio Mudéjar—built about the same time as the Alhambra, and possibly by some of the same artisans. As you explore the city, you'll also find crumbling Arabic walls near the exuberantly Spanish baroque **Basilica de Nuestra Señora de la Macarena** (see p. 593, **10**). Take some time to wander the surrounding **Barrio Santa Cruz** (see p. 592, **6**), whose basic street layout dates from the Córdoban Caliphate. Wherever you walk, you'll be overwhelmed by the profusion of colorful tiles of geometric patterns that cover major buildings and humble homes alike. The artistry of Andalucían painted tiles reached its apogee here and was revived in the 19th century in the workshops of the **Barrio Triana** (see p. 596, **16**). Another form of artistry also flourishes here: You'll see women stitching flamenco garb in small storefronts and hear the rhythmic strumming of guitars and lonesome wail of flamenco drifting from the bars at night. ☺ 2 days.

Take the regional (R-598) train to Granada, a 3-hr. trip.

4 **Granada.** The last Andalucían city to fall to the Reconquista, Granada retains the strongest Moorish ambience of any city in western Europe. The labyrinthine streets of the **Albaicín** (see p. 614, **12**) seem little changed from the 15th century, when it was the main residential barrio of Nasrid Granada. Indeed, Granada's new mosque is here.

The narrow alleys of **Calderería Vieja** and **Calderería Nueva** (see p. 613, **5**) rise up behind the royal chancellery like a North African souk, bustling with merchants selling rugs and trinkets. Their teahouses serve delightful traditional

> *The Generalife, with its extravagant gardens and courtyards overlooking the Alhambra, was the sultans' summer retreat.*

> *Our photographer happened upon this lively scene in the narrow streets of Cordoba's Judería, or Jewish Quarter.*

Muslim pastries of honey and nuts. But the (literally) crowning glories of Granada are the **Alhambra and Generalife** (see p. 610, ❶), a hilltop complex behind fortified walls. So popular are these sites that you will need to plan in advance, since tickets are timed to limit the number of visitors (see "Getting into the Alhambra & Generalife," p. 627). It's worth every bit of the trouble. The palaces, built from 1318 to 1391, are elegantly shaped constructions, playing on the Nasrid dynasty's—the last Moorish kings of Spain—love of sinuous lines, graceful arches, and the ever-present sound of moving water. The patterns of the sumptuous decoration in carved plaster and wood evoke a heaven of the Koran without ever becoming representational. The gardens surrounding the buildings are equally serene—a discordant note, considering the **Alcazaba** (see p. 627, ❿), your last stop in the Alhambra, was a fortified citadel. Finish by climbing the 8th-century Torre Vela in the Alcazaba for splendid views of the city below. ☺1–2 days.

From Granada, take the Altaria train back to Madrid (just under 5 hr.) for your flight home.

> *The Albaicín quarter of Granada has retained the labyrinthine, whitewashed charm of its medieval Moorish past.*

Gastronomic Northeast Spain

Is there something in the Catalan language that gives its cooks special talents in the kitchen? The traditional dishes of Catalunya and Valencia run the gamut from seafood-rice casseroles to delicate timbales of vegetables and wild mushrooms. The wines of the regions, if not yet quite famous, are nonetheless perfectly matched to the cuisine. This 10-day tour explores gastronomic wonders from the fish-obsessed Costa Brava to simply food-obsessed Barcelona, passes through the best of the wine country, and winds down to heritage rice plantations around Valencia, birthplace of true paella. There are only three meals a day, so the trip could take some time. See the chapters on Catalunya, Barcelona, and Valencia and the Costa Blanca for ideas on what to do between meals. *Buen apetito!*

> *The proprietors at Quimet i Quimet are as serious about their libations as they are about their* montaditos.

START Roses. TRIP LENGTH 559km (347 miles).

❶ Roses. This Costa Brava town has such a splendid beach that in the height of summer you can hardly see the sand for all the pink northern European skin. Tucked back in the hills above town is **elBulli** (see p. 56), where chef Ferran Adrià serves his madly inventive 30-course meals to the lucky few who manage to get reservations.

Roses is more than just a beach resort—it is a great fishing village. Even Adrià is a champion of honest traditional food, and you won't find a better *suquet* (Catalan fish stew) in town than at **La Cala** (see p. 375). If you're still hungry, drive out on the peninsula to **Cadaqués** (see p. 370, ❶) to feast on the *Zarzuela de Salvador y Gala*—a medley of fish and shellfish served at **Restaurant Sa Gambina** (see p. 375) and

1. Roses
2. Girona
3. Barcelona
4. Sant Sadurní de Anoia
5. Cambrils
6. Parque Natural del Delta de l'Ebre
7. Valencia
8. L'Albufera

named for frequent patrons Mr. and Mrs. Salvador Dalí. ⏱1 day. See p. 371, ❷.

From Roses, follow the C-6 west for 15km (9⅓ miles). Take the N-II south for 6km (3¾ miles). Follow the AP-7 south 27km (17 miles) to Girona.

❷ **Girona.** There are at least a dozen good excuses to visit Girona—the creation tapestry in the **Catedral** (see p. 396, ❼) or the atmospheric Roman walls, for example. But for a more delicious reason to stay the night in this handsome inland city, look to **Massana** (see p. 397). Two decades ago, Pere Massana opened up a simple *asador*—a restaurant that roasted meat over a wood fire. But he has created nothing less than a modern, spare, and intense rethinking of traditional Catalan cooking in which flavors seem to explode off the plate. The price is right, especially for one of Catalunya's best fine-dining spots. ⏱1 day.

Follow the AP-7 south 85km (53 miles). Follow signs to C-33/Barcelona and continue 12km (7½ miles) to Barcelona.

❸ **Barcelona.** In the elBulli off season (Nov–Mar), Ferran Adrià makes his base in Barcelona, and his experimental kitchen has helped

> *Devilishly decadent hot dark chocolate with fresh whipped cream at Barcelona's Granja Viader "milk bar."*

> Codorníu was the first vineyard to produce Spain's sparkling wine, Cava.

Bully for Bulli

Catalan-speaking chefs haven't been satisfied to sit on the laurels of tradition. Ferran Adrià joined the staff at **elBulli** in 1983, and Spanish cuisine hasn't been the same since. Although his foam days are largely past, Adrià put modern gourmet cooking on a scientific footing. Yet like so many of his peers, Adrià has returned to an emphasis on ingredients over technique and a belief in engaging all the senses. Radical Catalan cuisine, in short, has come home to its roots. To get a taste of Adrià's magic, you can try booking a reservation at elBulli online in late December at **www.elbulli.com**, but don't hold your breath—requests outnumber seats 250 to 1. That said, Adrià announced that elBulli would be closing in 2012 and reopening as a foundation dedicated to food arts in 2014, so you might want to try for a table now. C/ Montjoi, 30. Roses, Girona. ☎ 972-15-04-57. Tasting menu cost varies by season and year, but expect to pay upwards of 200€. AE, DC, MC, V. Dinner Tues–Sat most months.

galvanize local chefs into making the city one of the world's hottest dining scenes. Beyond the avant-garde and *cuina de autor* (haute cuisine) found in chic restaurants, foodies will be in heaven at food markets, shops, and tapas bars. Start your gastronomic pilgrimage at the **Mercat de la Boquería** (see p. 410, ❽), the incredible food market overflowing with fresh seafood, wild mushrooms, vegetables, and little kiosk bars, including **Bar Pintxo** and **El Quim.** Tucked away on a small alley in the Raval neighborhood, **Granja Viader** (see p. 432, ⑤) is literally a taste of old-school Barcelona, the oldest "milkbar" in the city (since 1870), known for its thick chocolate drinks. **Colmado Quílez** (see p. 432, ❻), a famous 1908 *colmado* (grocery store and wine shop), has floor-to-ceiling shelves stocked with gourmet packaged goods. A great spot for lunch in L'Eixample is **Restaurant Embat** (see p. 463), part of a trend of smart, low-key restaurants labeled "bistronomic"—creative Catalan cuisine at neighborhood prices. Early evening snacks are unequaled at **Quimet i Quimet** (see p. 433, ⑭), a standing-room-only tapas joint in Poble Sec that serves dozens of creative *montaditos*, little gourmet sandwiches. Another tapas bar that has gotten a lot of attention right from its inception—it is the brainchild of Adrià's brother—is **Inopia** (see p. 461). Off the beaten track, and trafficking not in experimental stuff but in straightforward and largely traditional tapas, Inopia has quickly become a classic. **Cinc Sentits** (see p. 460) is one of the most accessible of Barcelona's haute cuisine restaurants, a great introduction to gourmet Catalan dining. Since 1851, **E & A Gispert** (see p. 433, ⑪), near Passeig del Born, has dispensed coffee and teas, dried fruits and nuts, and honey and jams from an atmospheric shop with a unique old wood-burning nut roaster. To taste some Catalan wines, pop into **La Vinya del Senyor** (see p. 479), a stylish wine bar with a great roster of Spanish wines and a popular terrace overlooking Santa Maria del Mar. ⏱ 2–3 days.

From Barcelona, take the Ronda Litoral B-10 for 9km (5⅔ miles) to merge onto the A-2. Continue (it becomes the AP-2) for 15km (9⅓ miles). Take the AP-7 west 20km (12 miles) to Sant Sadurní de Anoia.

> *Excellent fish restaurants and markets are found in Cambrils on Spain's Costa Daurada (Golden Coast).*

4 Sant Sadurní d'Anoia. You have to love a town where most of the buildings are thick-walled storage for sparkling wines. About 40 cellars are open for **visits and tastes** (see p. 383, **5**), though most ask that you call ahead if you want to see the facilities. As a general rule, you can drop in to buy wine anytime they're working (generally Mon–Fri 10am–2pm and Mon–Thurs 4–6pm). Most of these producers of Cava, the Catalan answer to champagne, are very small. Two of the biggest, however, can be visited by calling or emailing only a few hours ahead: **Freixenet,** which pioneered overseas sales of Cava as an inexpensive champagne substitute, does much of its tour by video. The

other giant, **Codorníu,** occupies an extraordinary Modernista winery designed by Josep Puig i Cadafalch and built from 1895 to 1915. The tasting includes some eye-opening select wines that are a world apart from the producer's entry-level Cava. You don't have to visit any winery to taste the wines, of course. **Cal Blay Vinticinc** (see p. 385), a self-appointed "eno-gastronomic" restaurant in a 1905 Modernista wine cellar, carries nearly all Cavas made in Sant Sandurní and pairs dishes to match them. For a crash course in Alt Penedès gastronomy, opt for the *cupatges* menu of four courses and dessert, accompanied by four Cavas. ⊕ 1 day.

> *Mussels, anchovies, and cod fish croquettes are on the menu at Valencia's Casa Montaña.*

Head southwest on the AP-7/A-7 for 90km (56 miles) to Cambrils.

5 Cambrils. This Costa Daurada town has long, sandy beaches with gentle waves and a busy fishing port where one of the great attractions is watching the boats unload their catches every afternoon. Count on some being set aside for Joan Gatell, chef of the eponymous **Joan Gatell Restaurant** (see p. 379). Gatell's gastronomic menu (65€ and up) is a four-course feast of great fish with a Catalan accent and cutting-edge technique. From absurdly expensive baby eels in spring to tuna roe in fall, Gatell gets the best seasonal fish and has the elegant presentation to match. ⏱ 4 hr. See p. 378, **3**.

From Cambrils, follow the coastal road to AP-7 (toward Valencia) and continue 50km (31 miles) to exit 39A. Follow signs for 15km (9⅓ miles) to TV-3402 and the village of Deltebre.

6 Parque Natural del Delta de l'Ebre. The Riu Ebre (Río Ebro to the rest of Spain) sweeps from mountain streams in Cantabria down across Iberia until it reaches the Mediterranean here on the border between Catalunya and Valencia. Full of breeding colonies of the greater flamingo and other wading birds, this amazing muddy delta is ruled off in agricultural squares, each with its own rice paddy. A large portion of Spain's rice is grown here. ⏱ 4 hr. See p. 367, **6**.

From Deltebre, follow AP-7/A-7 south for 193km (120 miles) to Valencia.

7 Valencia. Even larger than La Boquería in Barcelona, the **Mercado Central** (see p. 520, **1**) in Valencia is a celebration of all things culinary—in a Modernista building to boot. Nearby **Mercado Colón** (see p. 522, **3**), another Modernista masterpiece of iron and

> *L'Albufera, a large freshwater lagoon separated from the Mediterranean by only a thin sandbank, is known for fishing and rice growing.*

glass, has been mostly converted into a classy food mall of good cafes, but Mangliano, on the lower level, was named best gastronomic boutique in Spain in 2009. While you're near the markets, it's worth a visit to **Cervecería Maipi** (see p. 522, ❺), where the owner is the master of the tapa of *manitas,* or stewed pig's feet. **Horchatería El Siglo** (see p. 522, ❼) has been concocting *horchata,* a milky beverage made from tiger nuts and beloved by Valencianos, since 1836.

Valencia, of course, is known for its seafood and its paella. Head to the El Cabanyal district to visit the **Museo del Arroz** (see p. 523, ❾) and get a grasp on traditional rice growing and processing. Stop at **Casa Guillermo** (see p. 523, ❿) for the house-cured anchovy fillets, and then pop across the street to **Casa Montaña** (see p. 523, ⓫) for steamed mussels and one of a choice of up to 1,000 different wines. Keep heading toward the sea, and you'll soon arrive at the kitchen entrance to **La Pepica** (see p. 523, ⓬), the palace of paella where you can get authentic paella Valenciana—with chicken, rabbit, snails, and garden vegetables instead of seafood. ⏲ **2 days.**

From Valencia, follow harbor road CV-500 toward El Salou for 10km (6¼ miles) to L'Albufera.

❽ **L'Albufera.** Arabic for "Little Sea," L'Albufera is the largest lake in Spain. It appears to be one of the first places on the Spanish coast where rice cultivation was introduced by the North Africans in the early 8th century, and the lagoons and wetlands around the lake are still the chief growing region for heritage strains of rice, like the Bomba, so prized for paella. The **Racó de l'Olla Centre d'Interpretación** gives a good overview of the complex ecosystems in the natural park that surrounds the lake, including the sandy barrier beach that protects it from the salty Mediterranean. ⏲ **1 day. See p. 516, ❶.**

Return to Valencia to fly home.

Spain for the Whole Family

Traveling with children is a great way to meet Spaniards.
Every town has a park where youngsters kick around soccer balls, and your kids can join in while you chat with other parents. Young children may not be ready for Spain's glorious art museums and churches, but they will probably be intrigued by the castles (even if they liken each one to Hogwarts Academy). This tour can be done in about 10 days and highlights kid-friendly spots in some of Spain's major destinations. Don't forget that one parent can spend the afternoon shopping while the other takes the kids to the museum. And count on eating well: All but the fanciest restaurants welcome children, and there is nothing more Spanish than a big family meal at an outdoor cafe on Sunday afternoon. This tour is easily accomplished by train.

> Weekends are a popular time to rent rowboats on the pond in Madrid's Parque de Buen Retiro.

START Fly into Madrid.

❶ **Madrid.** The armory at the **Palacio Real** (see p. 76, ❶) enthralls children raised on Harry Potter books. In addition to swords and daggers, you'll see the suits of armor worn by kings and nobles—and their horses. Give mom a breather to poke around the boutiques of **Salamanca** (see p. 85, ❼) while Dad accompanies the kids to the **Museo Arqueológico Nacional** (see p. 84, ❹) to see the replica of the Altamira cave, and to the nearby **Museo Naval** (see p. 102, ❺) to look

at models of the ships that sailed in the Spanish Armada.

On weekends, everyone descends on **Parque de Buen Retiro** (see p. 82, ❶), where free puppet shows grab the youngest and the teenagers head for the rowboats on the pond. Keep close watch on the kids at the grand Sunday street market of **El Rastro** (see p. 111, ⓬); they'll be dazzled by the hustle and bustle. Go ahead—let them chase the pigeons in **Plaza Mayor** (see p. 81, ❾) while you sip wine at a cafe table. 🕐 2 days.

1 Madrid
2 Barcelona
3 Valencia
4 Granada
5 Málaga
6 Costa del Sol

Take the high-speed AVE train from Atocha Station to Barcelona. Travel time is around 3 hr.

2 Barcelona. Children will love **La Rambla**'s (see p. 410, **7**) bird sellers and theatrical assortment of human statues. Walk (with an eye on your kids and your valuables) down La Rambla to **Mirador de Colom** (see p. 414, **4**), where you can take an elevator up for panoramic waterfront views. The **Rambla del Mar,** a drawbridge across the old port, leads to **L'Aquàrium de Barcelona** (see p. 414, **5**), Europe's second-largest aquarium. Just east, Barcelona's boardwalk-lined urban beaches are full of families, volleyball players, surfers—and topless sunbathers.

Children will love soaring high above the city aboard the **Transbordador Aeri** (see p. 444, **1**) cable car from the beach to Montjuïc. On summer evenings at the base of Montjuïc below the Palau Nacional, the colorful **Font Màgica** (see p. 445, **7**) fountains make for a fun light and pop-music show.

Gaudí's two best-known buildings, **Casa Milà** (also known as La Pedrera; p. 408, **2**)—where the rooftop chimneys look like Star Wars figures—and **La Sagrada Família** (see p. 406, **1**) are well worth visiting, but the top

> Four sun discs decorate the vaulted mosaic ceiling of Parc Güell's would-be market.

> *Barcelona's aquarium has 35 tanks, featuring 11,000 marine animals and 450 different Mediterranean species.*

Modernista sight for children is **Parc Güell** (see p. 419, **7**), a fantasyland with plenty of green space for them to let off steam. ⏲ 2 days.

Whisk down to Valencia on the Alaris high-speed train in 2½ hr.

3 Valencia. First get the lay of the land in the Old City from the bell tower of the cathedral, **El Miguelete** (see p. 514, **5**). With its heaps of spices and wide-eyed whole fish, the **Mercado Central** (see p. 512, **1**) is nothing like grocery stores at home. After they've seen the produce stalls, your kids might consider eating their vegetables.

Even skeptics of zoos are won over by the **Bioparc** (see p. 532, **9**), with replicated habitats of equatorial Africa, the African savannas, and the island of Madagascar. Barriers keep the big beasts at bay, but the lemurs scamper everywhere.

There's something for all ages at the futuristic **City of Arts & Sciences** (see p. 533, **13**). If you hit a rainy day, make a beeline to the IMAX cinema in **L'Hemisfèric** (see p. 534, **B**). Interactive exhibits at the **Museu de les Ciències Príncipe Felipe** (see p. 534, **C**) let the young ones play with insects and marvel at a model of Leonardo da Vinci's flying machine. With performances by bottlenose dolphins, the underground **L'Oceanogràfic** (see p. 535, **D**) is more than just an aquarium.

Even the pickiest eater can find some variety of paella to appeal at **La Pepica** (see p. 523, **12**). Someone in the crowd is bound to want one with snails. . . . ⏲ 2 days.

Sightsee out the windows on the 8-hr. ride aboard the García Lorca train to Granada.

4 Granada. Even if they get tired visiting the **Alhambra and Generalife** (see p. 610, **1**), your kids will thank you later for showing them this wonder of the world. Some stories of palace intrigue (like the king who piled up the heads of his wife's lover's family in a fountain) resemble gruesome fairy tales. But kids usually prefer the fortress of the **Alcazaba** (see p. 627, **10**), where they can climb the 8th-century Torre de la Vela and imagine raining down arrows on invaders below.

Children and adults alike are fascinated by the **Museo Cuevas del Sacromonte** (see p. 615, **15**), which shows how Gypsies have dwelt in the caves above town for centuries. The architectural fragments in the **Museo Arqueológico** (see p. 614, **10**) might evoke a yawn, but wait until the kids encounter the massive stone bull from 500 B.C.

Hop a city bus rather than making a steep climb by foot through the **Albaicín** (see p. 614, **12**) to **Mirador San Nicolás** (see p. 615, **13**). This lively plaza is like a giant balcony on the city, full of playing children, flamenco street musicians, and casual cafes. ☉ 1 day.

Take whichever train suits your schedule to Málaga. Slow trains take 2 hr., fast trains about 20 min. less.

5 Málaga. This ancient coastal city is an easy hike for kids, as most of it lies on a relatively flat plain at the base of a hill. Do the hill first (by bus) to visit the ruins of the **Castillo de Gibralfaro** (see p. 655, **8**), with its sweeping views. Walk back down on Paseo de Don Juan Tamboury for a bird's-eye view of the bullring.

The kids will love scampering through the patios and along the walls of the old fortress, the **Alcazaba** (see p. 654, **7**). And street performers and elaborately garbed living statues provide free entertainment on the broad pedestrian shopping artery of **C/ Marqués de Larios** (see p. 656, **10**). If it's cool enough for hot chocolate, order steaming cups and a plate of *churros* at **Casa Aranda** (see p. 656, **11**). If it's hot, cool off at the in-city beach. ☉ 1 day.

Local trains run every half-hour to Torremolinos (25 min.) and Fuengirola (45 min.) on the Costa del Sol.

6 Costa del Sol. Frequent buses connect the beach towns of Costa del Sol—just when you think the beach is ending, you'll round a point and another begins. High-priced amusement parks abound, but for simple fun head to the **Parque de la Batería** in Torremolinos (see p. 570, **1**), where you can rent a rowboat for a pittance. **Sea Life Benalmádena** (see p. 570, **3**) is a nifty little aquarium and minigolf

> *Old-school but effective—and fun—burro taxis are one form of transportation on the Costa del Sol.*

complex right at Malapesquera beach. The biggest and best family attraction on the coast, though, is the **Fuengirola Zoo** (see p. 571, **7**), a model cage-free zoo with more than 1,300 animals. You can also hop a bus every half-hour to **Mijas Pueblo** (see p. 571, **8**), where children can ride around the village in a cart pulled by a ribbon-bedecked donkey. For more ideas, see p. 570, "The Costa del Sol with Kids." ☉ 2 days.

Fly home from Málaga.

Wine Country Rambles

Spanish vineyards make some of Europe's most exciting new wines. This 6-day tour focuses on the heartland of fine Spanish table wines in La Rioja, Ribera del Duero, and the ascendant districts of Rueda and Toro. "Enotourism" is just developing, but most wineries have an office where you can buy the products, and bodegas included here encourage tours and tastings. It's wise to call or e-mail ahead for a reservation.

> *The robust* tinto de Toro *grape (a synonym for* tempranillo*) saw a boom in popularity in the 1980s.*

START Fly into Bilbao Airport and rent a car. Take the AP-68 for 107km (66 miles) to Haro, about a 1-hour drive. **TRIP LENGTH** 633km (393 miles).

1 Haro. This handsome town is the capital of La Rioja Alta, and you can learn the history, science, and aesthetics of Rioja wines at the **Centro de Interpretación del Vino de la Rioja.** Most bodegas are close to the rail station. A good bet for a tour and tasting is **CVNE,** which

has been making wines since 1879—when the *Phylloxera* louse decimated French vineyards and La Rioja stepped up to supply Europe with elegant reds. You'll start to understand why La Rioja is a DOCa (*Denominación de Origen Calificada),* Spain's highest wine classification. ⏲ 1 day. See p. 335, **5**.

Drive southeast on N-232 for 19km (12 miles) to Cenicero. Turn left and follow LR-211 for 6km (3¾ miles) to Elciego.

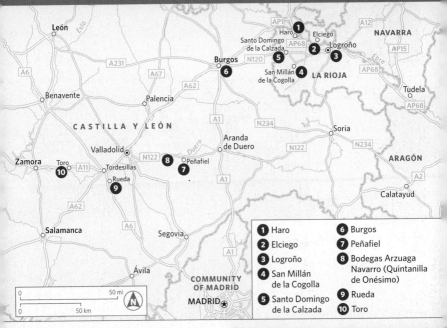

Haro 1
Elciego 2
Logroño 3
San Millán de la Cogolla 4
Santo Domingo de la Calzada 5
Burgos 6
Peñafiel 7
Bodegas Arzuaga Navarro (Quintanilla de Onésimo) 8
Rueda 9
Toro 10

2 Elciego. The Rioja classification includes properties outside the Autonomous Region of Rioja, including this Basque village where the Marqués de Riscal pioneered Bordeaux-style winemaking in 1862. In 2006, the company engaged Frank Gehry to build the **City of Wine,** a complex that includes the historic winery and a Gehry hotel that seems to be wearing a multi-tinted beribboned titanium toupee. Relax with wine therapies in the spa or take a bodega tour. There's a cafe and sales room for visitors in a hurry. ⊕ Half-day. See p. 333, 3.

Backtrack 6km (3¾ miles) on the LR-211 to Cenicero and turn left to follow N-232 for 23km (14 miles) to Logroño, about a half-hour drive.

3 Logroño. Like Haro, Logroño is a "capital" of the Rioja wine district, but it's also a stopover for pilgrims on the Camino de Santiago. For in-town sipping, head to the tapas bars along C/ Laurel or C/ San Juan. One of the easiest wineries to visit on the outskirts of town is **Bodegas Ontañón** (see p. 331). The barrel-aging warehouse and tasting room has an impressive display of wine-themed sculpture, fine art, and stained glass. ⊕ Half-day. See p. 330, 1.

> A guided tour of the CVNE winery in Haro gives visitors a glimpse into the making of legendary Riojas.

> *Frank Gehry's surreal luxury hotel overlooks the historic Marqués de Riscal winery.*

From Logroño, go west 15km (9⅓ miles) on the A-12 to exit 21. Follow signs for LR-205/San Millán to drive 25km (16 miles) through rural vineyards to San Millán de la Cogolla.

④ San Millán de la Cogolla. This small village has been making poetry (Gonzalo de Berceo was born here) and wine since at least the 13th century. The **Monasterio de Yuso** (see p. 325, ③) is a beautiful monastic compound that ranges from 11th-century walls to a 16th-century church. Its treasures include the earliest manuscripts written in Castilian and Basque. The monks support themselves by agriculture, which means grapes. Yuso makes wonderful, reasonably priced Riojas, available for sale in the store or at the monastery's hotel. ⏱ 3 hr.

Follow the LR-205/LR-206 northwest for 12km (7½ miles) to pick up the LR-240 for the last 9km (5⅔ miles) into Santo Domingo de la Calzada.

⑤ Santo Domingo de la Calzada. The town is named for the 12th-century saint who built a church for pilgrims on the way to Santiago de Compostela. He also built them a lodging, a handsome Romanesque structure that now operates as the classy state-run **Parador de Santo Domingo de la Calzada** (see p. 327). Plenty of great Rioja wine is made around Santo Domingo, but bodegas aren't a big part of city life. The *parador*'s dining room, however, has a deep cellar to complement the hearty meat and game dishes. ⏱ Half-day. See p. 326, ④.

Follow the N-120—which parallels the Camino de Santiago footpath—for 68km (42 miles) to Burgos.

⑥ Burgos. This big city with a gorgeous cathedral and associations with El Cid was the initial capital of the Kingdom of Castilla. It is surrounded by vineyards and marks the beginning of the Ribera del Duero wine district, which earned DOCa status in 2008.

The area grew wine grapes in antiquity, but they were wiped out by Muslim domination and reintroduced in the 12th century by Benedictines from Cluny in Burgundy. ⊕ Half-day. See p. 203, **5**.

Follow the A-1 south for 52km (32 miles) to exit 185. Take BU-110 to BU-111 to BU-130 for a total of 42km (26 miles). Turn right on N-122 and continue 10km (6¼ miles) to Peñafiel.

7 Peñafiel. Peñafiel is the de facto capital of the Ribera del Duero wine region. Even the town's mountaintop turreted fortress was built to protect the vineyards. The citadel now serves as the **Castillo-Museo Provincial del Vino,** an exhaustive wine museum that also offers an interesting tour of the castle. The high-tech exhibits are all in Spanish, but CD players with commentary in other languages are available. A good bet for a bodega visit is **Bodega Convento San Francisco,** which occupies a 12th-century convent in the heart of the village. ⊕ Half-day. See p. 212, **1**.

From Peñafiel, drive west on the N-122 for 10km (6¼ miles).

8 Bodegas Arzuaga Navarro (Quintanilla de Onésimo). The N-122 parallels the Río Duero across the center of Spain, a river nearly on par with the Rhine and Rhône for its vineyards. (The Duero becomes the Douro in Portugal's port country.) Arzuaga Navarro isn't the oldest winery in the region, but it's well set up for tours and tastings, which can range from a few sips to a minicourse in Ribera del Duero wines. ⊕ 3 hr.

Continue west on N-122 for 30km (19 miles) until it becomes VA-11. Continue 15km (9⅓ miles) to the Ronda Sur around Valladolid. Take exit 151 to get on A-6 south. Continue to km 172 to reach Rueda.

9 Rueda. Beneath the parched soil of this village lie cool cellars where wine has been aged since the 12th century. Rueda is the heart of the Ruedo DO (*Denominación de Origen;* wine region) that stretches along both sides of the A-6 highway south to **Medina del Campo** (see p. 206, **4**) and north to Tordesillas. This is white wine country, with the best made from the native *verdejo* grape and aged in French and American oak. Make an appointment to tour **Bodegas Antaño** to see some of the 4km (2½

> *The fermented fruits of the Marqués de Riscal's labor.*

miles) of 400- to 500-year-old cellars and the modern tasting room. ⊕ Half-day. See p. 214, **3**.

From Rueda, drive north for 11km (6¾ miles) on the A-6 to Tordesillas to pick up the N-122 west. Follow the N-122 for 40km (25 miles) through vineyards to Toro.

10 Toro. The Fariña bodega applied scientific winemaking to the venerable *tinta de Toro* grape in the 1980s, and suddenly every big-name Spanish winemaker had to have a bodega in Toro. The town's utter charm is aided by wine shops offering free tastings every few paces. Visit the **Santa María la Mayor Colegiata** church to see the 13th-century carved portal that exalts music above chastity and martyrdom. Then see the place that launched a thousand crates, **Bodegas Fariña.** The company's oak-aged flagship red is named Colegiata in honor of the church. ⊕ Half-day. See p. 216, **4**.

From Toro, drive east on N-122 for 40km (25 miles). Pick up the A-6 toward Madrid, watching for signs to Barajas Airport as you approach Madrid. The complete drive (240km/149 miles) takes a little under 3 hr. Fly home from Barajas.

Our Favorite Moments

Madrid knows how to have a good time—the city doesn't waste any part of the 24-hour day. You can spend all day touring the incomparable museums, seeing royal monuments, and patronizing the shops. And when day is done, the night of drinking, dining, dancing, and socializing is just about to begin.

> PREVIOUS PAGE *The Cibeles Fountain.* THIS PAGE *Background music in the Plaza Mayor.*

❶ Sitting at a cafe table in Plaza Mayor. Surveying the length and breadth of the city's most decorous square, for just a moment you are no longer a visitor—you belong here. See p. 81, ❾.

❷ Spending Sunday in Parque de Buen Retiro. You can row a boat, catch a charming puppet show, and still have time to stop and smell the roses. See p. 82, ❶.

❸ Reliving Spanish history with Goya's paintings. No history book can match the anguish of Francisco de Goya's painting *Dos de Mayo,* which shows French troops crushing the Spanish spirit. See p. 72, ❶.

❹ Shopping for a picnic at Mercado de la Paz. Every tasty delight in Spain eventually comes to Madrid. But for a picnic, all you'll need is cheese, some sausage, a loaf of bread, a bowl of olives, a bottle of wine. . . . See p. 85 ❼.

❺ Seeing how the royalty lived. Whatever you think of the powdered wigs and knee breeches, the quarters at the Palacio Real show that Carlos III enjoyed a sumptuous house. See p. 76 ❶.

❻ Tapas hopping around Plaza Santa Ana. In a single evening, you can make six new friends and try five things you never thought you'd eat. See p. 74, ❽.

❼ Being electrified by flamenco at Casa Patas. You don't need to understand the words to be caught up in the soaring passions, intricate rhythms, and swirling movement. See p. 75, ❾.

❽ Dipping *churros* in hot chocolate at Chocolatería San Ginés. While this combination makes a great breakfast, it makes an even better bedtime snack around 3am. See p. 132.

❾ Encountering *Guernica* in the Reina Sofía. One of the iconic images of the 20th century is even more powerful in person. See p. 74, ❺.

❿ Getting a shoeshine with tapas at José Luis. Just because you're standing at a bar eating little sandwiches with your fingers doesn't mean you can't look natty. See p. 85, ❻.

⓫ Bargaining at El Rastro. You didn't even know that you needed a baroque-style mantle clock, but the price is too good to pass up. See p. 111, ⓬.

⓬ Getting lost in Hapsburg Madrid. The layout of the tangled streets of La Latina have barely changed since Felipe II moved the court here in 1561. See p. 108.

⓭ Watching the Cibeles and Neptuno fountains at night. Emblematic of Madrid's regal side at any time of day, illuminated statues take on a thrilling grandeur at night. See p. 92, ❶.

⓮ Greeting the *madrugada* after dancing all night at Sala Flamingo. You know you're becoming a Spaniard when you don't call it a night until early morning, or *madrugada.* See p. 148.

⓯ Watching a Real Madrid match with fans in a bar. Soccer is in the DNA of Madrileños. If Real Madrid is playing, all other life comes to a halt. See p. 147.

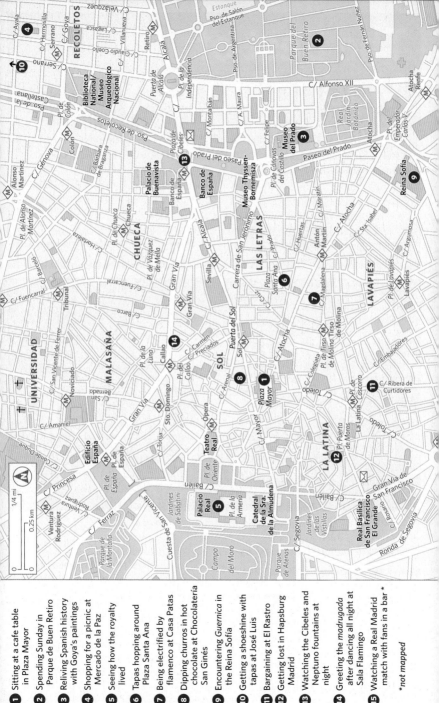

1 Sitting at a cafe table in Plaza Mayor

2 Spending Sunday in Parque de Buen Retiro

3 Reliving Spanish history with Goya's paintings

4 Shopping for a picnic at Mercado de la Paz

5 Seeing how the royalty lived

6 Tapas hopping around Plaza Santa Ana

7 Being electrified by flamenco at Casa Patas

8 Dipping churros in hot chocolate at Chocolatería San Ginés

9 Encountering Guernica in the Reina Sofía

10 Getting a shoeshine with tapas at José Luis

11 Bargaining at El Rastro

12 Getting lost in Hapsburg Madrid

13 Watching the Cibeles and Neptuno fountains at night

14 Greeting the madrugada after dancing all night at Sala Flamingo

15 Watching a Real Madrid match with fans in a bar *

*not mapped

The Best of Madrid in 1 Day

Madrid is a monumental city, full of the trappings of empire, with its royal palace, burbling mythological fountains, and splendid art museums. Its public spaces encompass broad plazas, leafy *paseos,* and sweeping green parks. But unlike some capitals, Madrid doesn't close at the end of the workday. In fact, the street and cafe life are just beginning. However many days you can spend in the city, don't let one side of Madrid distract you from the others. See the art museums, but don't miss a walk in the park and an evening literally rubbing elbows at a tapas bar. If you have only one day to spend, enjoy the genius of Spanish painting, stop to smell the flowers, and wade into the vibrant street life of two of the city's public squares.

> *Madrileños will tell you a good evening in the capital city begins in Plaza Santa Ana.*

START Metro to Atocha or Banco de España.

❶ ★★★ Museo Nacional del Prado. If this is your first visit to the Prado, one of the world's greatest art museums, avoid the temptation to skim through the collection. Focus instead on the rooms devoted to two of the three pillars of Spanish art: Diego Velázquez (1599–1660) and Francisco de Goya (1746–1828). (The other pillar is Picasso, but more about him below.) You'll find Velázquez's *Las Meninas* (1656) in Sala 12 on the first floor of the Villanueva

building. Ostensibly a portrait of the 4-year-old Infanta Margarita and her entourage, it's a complex work of extraordinary artistic and psychological innovation and one of the touchstones of Spanish art (see p. 20).

Most of the Goya works are on the second floor and run the gamut from cheery rural scenes and royal portraits to his late paintings of war and suffering found in Salas 66 and 67. His *Saturn Devouring His Son* (1819–23) remains one of the most frightening images ever rendered in oil. ⏱ 2–3 hr. See p. 96.

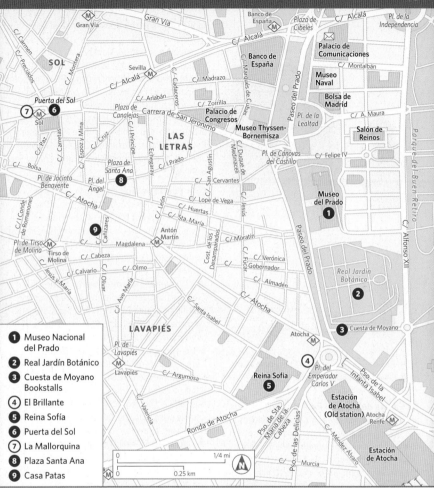

1 Museo Nacional del Prado
2 Real Jardín Botánico
3 Cuesta de Moyano Bookstalls
4 El Brillante
5 Reina Sofía
6 Puerta del Sol
7 La Mallorquina
8 Plaza Santa Ana
9 Casa Patas

2 **Real Jardín Botánico.** The adjacent Parque de Buen Retiro (see p. 93, 3) is a vast swath of landscaped greenery. But this gated enclosure planted with more than 3,000 plants and 100-plus species of trees is a living reminder of the best of the 18th century, when the garden was founded. More than merely beautiful, it combines a love of order (reflected in formal plantings) with scientific curiosity (most specimens are labeled). The grounds are rarely crowded, so it's a great place to catch your mental breath. ⊙ 30 min. Plaza de Murillo, 2. ☎ 91-420-30-17. www.rjb. csic.es. 2€, 1€ students, free for seniors and kids 10 & under. May–Aug 10am–9pm, Apr and Sept 10am–8pm, Mar and Oct 10am–7pm, Nov–Feb 10am–6pm. Metro: Atocha or Banco de España.

> The size of the Prado's collection can be overwhelming; the museum will help you choose wisely.

> *The Reina Sofía picks up where the Prado leaves off, though not in a linear fashion.*

❸ Cuesta de Moyano Bookstalls. Dealers in secondhand books line this street adjacent to the botanical garden, from Atocha Station up to the gates of Parque de Buen Retiro. Most volumes are in Spanish, but it's still fun to browse among the art books. ⏱ 20 min. Cuesta de Moyano. No phone. Daily 10am–7pm, liveliest Sun morning.

④ ☕ **El Brillante.** Before going into the Reina Sofía, pop into one of Madrid's pop-culture icons, El Brillante. The cavernous sandwich shop (it stretches a full block between streets) has every kind of sandwich you could imagine but specializes in *bocadillos* filled with fried calamari. C/ Atocha, 122. ☎ 91-468-05-48. $$.

❺ Reina Sofía. The Prado ends with the 19th century, and the Museo Nacional Centro de Arte Reina Sofía picks up with the 20th. In 2009, the museum opened new floors and rearranged the collection in a curatorial coup d'état. Rejecting both the "linear narratives of modernity" and the "banal oblivion of post-modernist history," the galleries now display a logic of association. Gallery 206 centers on Picasso's *Guernica,* arguably the 20th century's greatest work of political art and a turning point in Spanish art history equal to *Las Meninas* by Velázquez. Surrounding galleries include many of the preliminary drawings and works by other artists who also exhibited at the 1937 Spanish Pavilion in Paris: Alexander Calder, Joan Miró, and war photographer Robert Capa. ⏱ 2 hr. See p. 94, ❹.

❻ ★ Puerta del Sol. If all Spain comes to Madrid, all Madrid comes to Sol. It is the figurative heart of the city: When citizens were moved to protest—or even to outright rebellion, as they were in 1808, against Napoleon's soldiers—they generally chose Sol as their battleground. And Madrileños gather in Sol on New Year's Eve armed with a bottle of Cava and a dozen grapes, one for each chime counting down to midnight. But Sol is also the literal heart of Madrid: It's the crossroads of the city's metro and bus systems, and the official bull's-eye center of the country. Kilómetro Cero, the zero-mile indicator for all roads in Spain, is marked on a plaque in front of the ocher-colored Casa de Correos, the former post office. Directly across the square, tourists usually pose in front of the landmark statue of a bear and strawberry tree, the central image of the city's official seal. The shopping streets of C/ Preciados, C/ Mayor, and C/ Arenal radiate from Sol, or walk up the small streets behind the post office to find the city's quirkier stores. ⏱ 30 min. Metro: Sol.

⑦ ☕ **La Mallorquina.** The best vantage on Sol is from one of the second-floor window tables at this pastry shop that first opened in 1894—ideally while you enjoy a *café con leche* and a soft meringue. Puerta del Sol, 8. ☎ 91-521-12-01. $$.

❽ ★ Plaza Santa Ana. In the best of all possible worlds, you'll get to this popular noshing and socializing square for tapas time. The square itself and the surrounding streets contain some of Madrid's most venerable tapas bars, including Villa Rosa, where filmmaker Pedro Almodóvar filmed a bar scene in *High Heels,* and Las Bravas (see p. 133), which

> *The statue of the bear and strawberry tree in the Puerta del Sol is called "El Oso y el Madroño" by locals.*

invented (and patented) the spicy sauce for fried potatoes that is a staple of Spanish bar food. The square is also a gateway to the Barrio de las Letras (see p. 116), so called because Miguel de Cervantes and Lope de Vega lived in the neighborhood. ⏱ 1 hr. Metro: Sol, Antón Martín. See p. 117, ⑤.

❾ ★★ **Casa Patas.** Flamenco may have been born in Andalucía, but it finally grew up in Madrid, when the leading practitioners began to converge on the capital in the late 1980s. This bar-restaurant with a performance room in back is run by people passionate about the art—it's co-owned by a founding member of the flamenco-jazz fusion group Pata Negra. Programs vary from virtual unknowns to scions of the Amaya, Montoya, and Habichuela family dynasties. ⏱ 2 hr. See p. 148.

> *Some say Casa Patas is the best, and most authentic, flamenco in Madrid.*

The Best of Madrid in 2 Days

With two of the three big art museums under your belt, you're ready to spend your second day enjoying the royal splendor of Madrid by experiencing the pomp and circumstance of the Palacio Real and its gardens, the rich interior life lived by blue-blooded nuns, and the 19th-century decorum of Isabelline Madrid. In the end, though, you'll rejoin the common folk in the people's square.

> Isabel II's 1850 Teatro Real has been updated with state-of-the art equipment that affords elaborate opera and ballet productions.

START C/ Bailén.

SITE GUIDE PAGE 78

❶ ★★★ **Palacio Real.** Felipe II may have moved the national capital from Toledo to Madrid in 1561, but the obsessive builder of royal castles never got around to making a proper one here. The first fortress on this hillside overlooking the Río Manzanares was constructed in 863 by Muhammad I, the emir of Córdoba, to guard against invasion of Toledo by the Christian kings of the north. When Alfonso VI swept through in 1083 en route to conquering Toledo, the alcázar simply changed hands. Once Madrid was the capital, Felipe II and his successors gussied up the gloomy medieval fort enough to spend a few days a year living there while spending most of the time in country palaces. But fire ravaged the alcázar in 1734, and Felipe V saw his chance to emulate the grandeur of the Versailles digs of his French Bourbon cousins. Fortunately for the crown, vast wealth from the American colonies was pouring in to support construction of the stone-vaulted fireproof palace. The original plans were modeled on Bernini's work in Italy, but the palace took a more neoclassical turn before it was completed in 1764 in time for Felipe's son, Carlos III, to move in. See p. 78.

❷ **Mural Árabe.** Just down C/ Bailén from the palace, you can see the A.D. 863 remains of one wall that supported the base of the original Muslim fortifications of Madrid. It serves as the backdrop for a small park, where the gates are usually locked unless there's a concert scheduled. **Parque del Emir Muhammad I.**

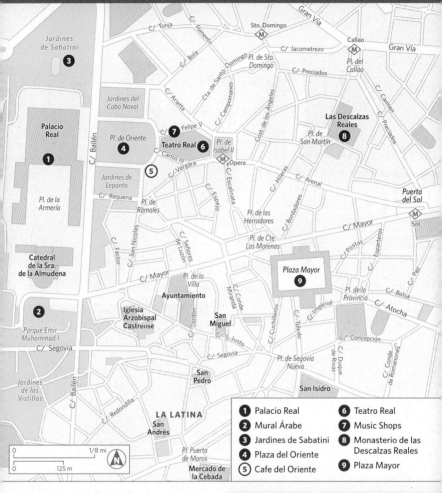

Map labels:

Gran Vía
C/ Torija
C/ Fomento
Sto. Domingo M
C/ Jacometrezo
Callao
Gran Vía
Jardines de Sabatini ❸
C/ Bola
Cta. de Santo Domingo
Pl. de Sto. Domingo
Pl. del Callao
C/ Preciados
C/ Arrieta
C/ Campomanes
Cost. de los Ángeles
C/ Carmen
Jardines del Cabo Noval
Felipe V ❼
Las Descalzas Reales
Palacio Real
C/ Bailén
Pl. de Oriente ❹
Teatro Real ❻
Pl. de Isabel II
Pl. de San Martín ❽
❶
Carlos III
C/ Vergara
M Opera
C/ Hileras
C/ Arenal
Puerta del Sol
Pl. de la Armería
Jardines de Lepanto
❺
C/ Espejo
C/ Escalinata
Pl. de las Herradores
C/ Bordadores
C/ Mayor
M Sol
C/ Requena
Pl. de Ramales
Pl. de Cte. Las Morenas
C/ Postas
C/ Esparteros
Catedral de la Sra. de la Almudena
C/ San Nicolás
C/ Factor
C/ Señores de Luzón
Pl. de la Villa
Plaza Mayor ❾
Pl. de la Provincia
C/ Paz
C/ Bolsa
❷
C/ Mayor
C/ Conde Miranda
C/ Cuchilleros
C/ Toledo
C/ Imperial
C/ Atocha
Parque Emir Muhammad I
Ayuntamiento
C/ Concepción
C/ Segovia
Iglesia Arzobispal Castrense
San Miguel
C/ Lepanto
C/ S. Justo
C/ Duque de Rivas
C/ Conde de Romanones
Jardines de las Vistillas
C/ Bailén
C/ Segovia
Pl. de Segovia Nueva
San Pedro
San Isidro
C/ Redondilla
LA LATINA
San Andrés
Pl. Puerta de Moros
Mercado de la Cebada

0 — 1/8 mi
0 — 125 m

❶	Palacio Real	❻	Teatro Real
❷	Mural Árabe	❼	Music Shops
❸	Jardines de Sabatini	❽	Monasterio de las Descalzas Reales
❹	Plaza del Oriente		
❺	Cafe del Oriente	❾	Plaza Mayor

❸ **Jardines de Sabatini.** The north side of the royal palace is anchored by formal 18th-century-style gardens with symmetrically trimmed hedges, a pool, fountains, and statues of Spanish monarchs originally sculpted for the palace, not the gardens. A cool and tranquil spot, especially during the summer, the gardens honor Francesco Sabatini (1722–97), the final architect who worked on the Palacio Real. He

Travel Tip

Palacio Real and Monasterio de las Descalzas Reales are free to citizens of the European Union on Wednesdays. If you're not from the EU, visit on another day to avoid crowds.

> The Palacio Real's neoclassical Sabatini Gardens, named after the Italian architect who designed the royal stables the gardens replaced.

SITE GUIDE

❶ Palacio Real

Just as El Escorial (see p. 90, ❹) is a monument to the Hapsburgs, the Palacio Real embodies the opulence and love of decorative excess of the first generations of Bourbon kings. The current royal family chooses to live in the more modest Palacio de la Zarzuela on the Madrid outskirts.

Set apart from the palace, start at the ❹ **kids Armory.** The royal suits of armor thrill kids—and most adults. Separate admission is available.

Make your way into the Palacio Real up the ❺ **Main Staircase** (right). The stairs of slabs of Toledo marble create a grand entry. Head to the ❻ **Hall of Columns,** filled with busts of Roman emperors and hung with 17th-century tapestries saved from the 1734 fire. This hall is used for formal events.

Note the supreme flattery of Tiepolo's ceiling fresco, *The Apotheosis of the Spanish Monarchy,* in the ❼ **Throne Room,** before heading to the ❽ **Gasparini Room.** In Carlos III's dressing room, embroidered silver silk covers the walls, stucco fruit and flowers adorn the ceiling, and swirling marble makes the floor dance.

The ceiling of ❾ **Carlos III's Bedroom** depicts the creation of the Order of Carlos III, an homage to the man by grandson Fernando VII.

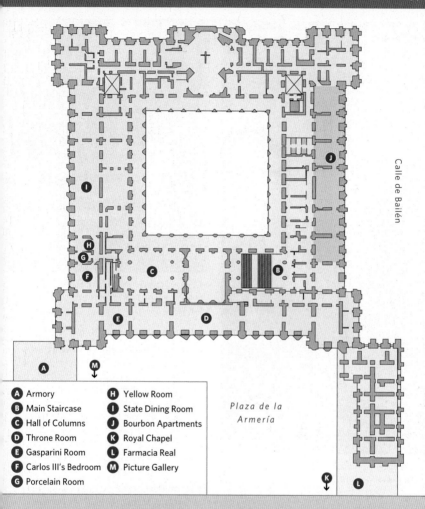

Calle de Bailén

Plaza de la
Armería

A Armory
B Main Staircase
C Hall of Columns
D Throne Room
E Gasparini Room
F Carlos III's Bedroom
G Porcelain Room
H Yellow Room
I State Dining Room
J Bourbon Apartments
K Royal Chapel
L Farmacia Real
M Picture Gallery

Moving on, fine 18th-century porcelain from the Real Fábrica de Porcelana de Buen Retiro, founded by Carlos III, fills the cases of the G **Porcelain Room.** Rich tapestries of birds and flowers, woven at the Real Fábrica de Tapices (see p. 95, 6), envelop the study of Carlos III, called the H **Yellow Room.**

The I **State Dining Room** was created in 1879 to celebrate Alfonso XII's marriage. The grand hall seats 145 diners. It's a short walk to the J **Bourbon Apartments,** smaller rooms that show the domestic life of the monarchs from 1880 to 1931. Swirling frescoes of heaven fill the dome of the K **Royal Chapel,** a jewel

box church. But equally enchanting is the L **Farmacia Real;** old stills and apothecary jars dominate the 16th-century potion-making facility.

Finally, end your visit at the M **Picture Gallery.** Art that once hung in the palace is shown in changing exhibitions. C/ Bailén, s/n. ☎ 91-454-88-00. www.patrimonionacional.es. Guided visit 10€, unguided 8€, students and ages 5–16 3.50€; Picture Gallery 1€ additional; separate admission for Armory 3.40€ adults, 1.70€ students and ages 5–16. Apr–Sept Mon–Sat 9am–6pm, Sun 9am–3pm; Oct–Mar Mon–Sat 9:30am–5pm, Sun 9am–2pm. Metro: Ópera.

> *Flamenco fans can find guitars, books, costumes, and sheet music at El Flamenco Vive, adjacent to the Ópera.*

> *The opulence of the Palacio Real rivals even Versailles.*

had designed the royal stables that stood on this spot until 1933. King Juan Carlos opened the gardens to the public in 1978. ⏱ 30 min. C/ Bailén. Free. Daily 9am–dusk.

④ Plaza del Oriente. Facing the Palacio Real, this graceful semicircular plaza of gardens and even more royal statuary (including a truly imposing equestrian figure of Felipe IV) has a marvelous, decadent elegance befitting its early-19th-century origins. Joseph Bonaparte launched construction when his younger brother, Napoleon, installed him as king of Spain (1808–13). The project languished, but was finally completed in the 1840s under Isabel II.

⑤ 🍴 **Cafe del Oriente.** This elegant Belle Epoque restaurant has both French and Spanish haute cuisine dining indoors, but the outdoor cafe tables remain one of Madrid's best places to see and be seen—you'll note that the clientele is among the city's best dressed. Drinks come at a premium, but pretend that your embassy is picking up the tab. Plaza de Oriente, 2. ☎ 91-541-39-74. $$.

❻ Teatro Real. Isabel II was a busy queen in this corner of Madrid. In 1850 she decreed the destruction of the Old City opera house and the creation of this gingerbread theater that opened just 5 months later. The building, often simply called Ópera, served many functions over the years but reopened in 1997 as an opera house. It is also the home of the Orquesta Sinfónica de Madrid. The opera season usually includes 16 or 17 productions, along with a few ballets and many musical recitals. See p. 149.

❼ Music Shops. Some of Madrid's best shopping for musical instruments and sheet music is found in the streets adjacent to the Ópera, including C/ Felipe V and C/ Carlos III. ⏱ 20 min. See p. 122.

> *The Monasterio de las Descalzas Reales is where Spain's well-heeled daughters once came to devote their lives to prayer.*

⑧ ★★ Monasterio de las Descalzas Reales.
Founded in 1559 by Juana de Austria, sister of Felipe II, this Franciscan convent historically received women from noble families who wished, for one reason or another, to retire from the world. They often brought artistic riches from their families with them. The former dormitory, for example, is hung with tapestries woven from cartoons by Peter Paul Rubens. The main staircase, covered with murals of saints, angels, and Spanish monarchs, explains in a glance the aristocracy's obsession with religion, power, and art. ⏱ 1 hr. Plaza de las Descalzas, 3. ☎ 91-454-88-00. www.patrimonionacional.es. 5€ adults, 2.50€ students. Entrance limited to 20 people at a time Tues–Thurs and Sat 10:30am–12:45pm and 4–5:45pm, Fri 10:30am–12:45pm, Sun 11am–1:45pm. Metro: Ópera.

⑨ ★★★ Plaza Mayor. There's hardly a public activity in Madrid that hasn't taken place in Plaza Mayor, first constructed as an open-air market at the edge of town in 1619. It has been revised every century since, as the city soon engulfed the square. Over the years it has seen everything from bullfights to executions to the public confessions of the Inquisition. (The royal family had an apartment facing the square with a catbird seat on the proceedings.)

Nowadays the main spectacles are the Sunday coin and stamp market and the December Christmas market. But the plaza is at its best as a grand stage set where tourists and locals shop beneath the arcades and sit at sunny cafe tables eating, drinking, and talking. The Casa de Panadería (built for the once all-powerful Bakers' Guild) on the north side is adorned with murals of the zodiac in a vaguely medieval style, but don't be fooled by the seeming antiquity of the paintings—they were added when the plaza was last reformed in 1992. The powerful arches that serve as the nine gates to the plaza were added in 1854, including the **Arco de Cuchilleros** (Arch of the Knife-Sharpeners) on the southwest corner. Musicians often set up here to take advantage of the echoing acoustics. The arch also leads to the barrio of La Latina (see p. 108). ⏱ 1 hr. Metro: Sol, Ópera.

The Best of Madrid in 3 Days

Another magnificent art museum (and an artist's home and studio) await you on your third day of touring Madrid. You'll walk the length of the city's grandest park and explore some of the most elegant boulevards and neighborhoods.

START Plaza de Independencia.

1 ★★ **Parque de Buen Retiro.** On a weekend in warm weather, almost everyone in Madrid heads to this magnificent public park to stroll the walkways, row boats on the pond, and enjoy puppet shows with their kids. The private grounds of the royal retreat called Buen Retiro began their transformation into gardens and parkland in the 1630s. Carlos III opened the grounds to the aristocracy in 1767, and after Napoleon's armies effectively destroyed the royal residence, subsequent kings focused on enhancing the park for public rather than private use. ⏱ 1½ hr. For details on park attractions, see p. 93, **3**.

> The wide, picturesque boulevards, called paseos, that run through the capital city are destinations as much as thoroughfares.

2 **Paseo del Prado.** In the late 18th century, Carlos III earned his sobriquet as the "mayor king" by remaking the face of the city. One major improvement was the creation of a north–south boulevard on the western flank of his Buen Retiro property. Now known as the Paseo del Prado, it has been remodeled many times, notably to accommodate motor vehicle traffic. You'll have plenty of company as you stroll along the leafy park that runs up the middle. Extensions of the boulevard created the Paseo de Recoletos and Paseo de Castellana, which now form the axis of Madrid.

3 ★★ **Museo Thyssen-Bornemisza.** You have to give Baron Hans Heinrich Thyssen-Bornemisza points for self-confidence. He chose to establish a museum for his private art

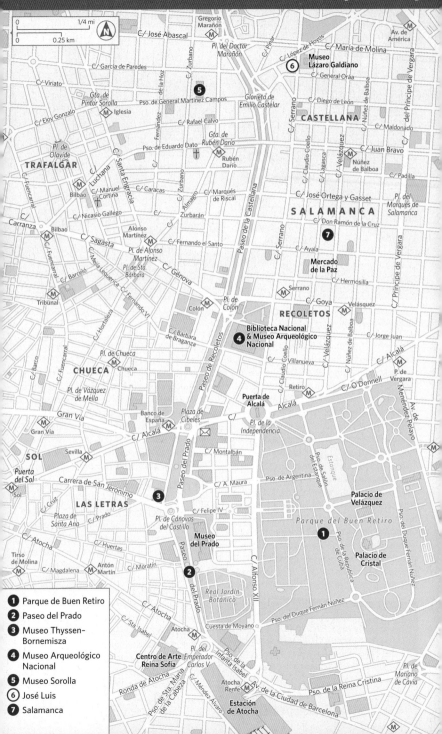

> *The widow of painter Joaquín Sorolla turned over the couple's elegant townhouse and garden to become a museum and memorial to the artist.*

collection in Madrid, a city already blessed with the Prado and the Reina Sofía. But then his private collection, sold to the Spanish government for a nominal fee in 1993, is one of the greatest amassed in the 20th century and neatly supplements the other two institutions. The museum itself consists of the neoclassical 18th-century Palacio de Villahermosa, redesigned by Rafael Moneo, and a 2004 addition created to house the collections of the baron's Spanish-born fifth wife, Carmen Cervera.

The collections, which span the 13th through 20th centuries, remain separate but equal. The baron made some major finds in Italian and German Gothic art and was in the right auction houses when the gavel came down on some stunning works by Impressionist and Post-Impressionist painters. The baroness, on the other hand, snapped up some seminal works by

Picasso (*Man with a Clarinet*, 1911–12) and Miró (*Catalan Peasant with a Guitar*, 1924) and sagely purchased a number of works by American abstract expressionists. The couple seemed to have a joint passion for German expressionism between the world wars, with her favoring Max Pechstein and him Ernst Ludwig Kirchner. ⏲ 2 hr. Paseo del Prado, 8. ☎ 91-369-01-51. www.museo thyssen.org. 6€ adults, 4€ seniors and students. Tues–Sun 10am–7pm. Metro: Banco de España.

❹ ★ **Museo Arqueológico Nacional.** You'd think that a museum established in 1867 and filled with pottery shards and old bones would be a pretty stable place, but this extraordinarily dynamic museum is always recasting its exhibits. In recent decades, many artifacts have been repatriated to regional museums, and scientists have reached a more nuanced understanding of the past. As a result, galleries relating to the earliest human habitations on the Iberian Peninsula are closed for overhaul. New discoveries about the Celtiberian culture that preceded Phoenician, Greek, and Roman incursions have resulted in fascinating new galleries. Be sure to see the 5th-century-B.C. statue of the Dama de Baza, a seated figure discovered in 1971 near Granada. ⏲ 1½ hr. See p. 102, ❹.

Travel Tip

On a hot summer night, you can enjoy great views of the Paseo at dinner from **La Mirador del Museo** (☎ 91-420-39-44), the terrace restaurant serving contemporary Mediterranean cuisine on the roof of the Museo Thyssen-Bornemisza. Menus start at 60€.

⑤ ★★ Museo Sorolla. Valencia-born Joaquín Sorolla (1863–1923) was one of Spain's sunniest painters, known for rendering landscapes, seascapes, and even portraits with saturated colors. This museum is located in the Andalucían-style house and studio he built from 1911 to 1917, just as the nearby neighborhood of Salamanca was taking shape. Unfinished paintings on easels in his studio create the illusion that the painter will be back in a few minutes to add more brushstrokes. The downstairs rooms—filled with slightly faded family photographs—reflect the domestic life of a painter serene in his good fortune, his talent, and his fame.

The upstairs galleries are a more conventional museum, in this case organized by theme rather than date, since Sorolla came early to his technique of modeling light rather than form. You might notice that his society portraits rely extensively on compositions from Velázquez. Don't miss the folkloric paintings that served as studies for the mural Sorolla painted at the Hispanic Society of New York in 1912 to 1919. But the painter from the Levante was at his best on the seashore, charging his canvases of waves, rocks, and sandy beaches with a vibrant, often erotic, passion. English signage is good, though Spanish plaques add more detail. ⏱ 1½ hr. Paseo General Martínez Campos, 37. ☎ 91-310-15-84. http://museosorolla.mcu.es. 3€ adults, free for kids 18 & under, free to all Sun. Tues–Sat 9:30am–8pm, Sun 10am–3pm. Metro: Gregorio Marañon.

⑥ 🍳 **José Luis.** Before you head out to explore the shopping avenues of Salamanca, fortify yourself with a slice of *tortilla española* at the bar of this legendary restaurant, where a shoeshine man is always available. C/ Serrano, 89–91. ☎ 91-484-43-00. $$.

⑦ ★ Salamanca. The Marquis de Salamanca, a legendary financier and bon vivant, turned real estate developer in the 1870s by financing a new upscale neighborhood north of the Parque de Buen Retiro. It took 50 years to finish, but still remains the most elegant Madrid barrio, with broad, tree-lined streets and Belle Epoque buildings with wrought-iron balconies. Not only do C/ Serrano, C/ Goya, and C/ Velázquez boast the boutiques of Spain's top fashion designers, but the neighborhood has Madrid's fanciest fresh food market, **Mercado de la Paz** (C/ Ayala, 28).

> *Two birds, one stone: Customers can get a shoe shine and a snack at Salamanca's famous José Luis restaurant.*

The Best Side Trips from Madrid

When Felipe II moved the Spanish capital to Madrid in 1561, the city wasn't the only spot that boomed. The monarch began building palaces and churches in the adjacent countryside. Those royal digs account for most of the attractions in the Community of Madrid, the autonomous region around the capital. The exceptions are cute little Chinchón and Alcalá de Henares, a city that predates Madrid by more than a millennium. All are popular getaways for Madrileños. As few travelers visit more than one of these destinations, directions are given from Madrid; the whole tour could be done in 4 days using Madrid as a base of operations.

> Playwright and poet Lope de Vega once studied behind the Plateresque facade of the Colegio Mayor de San Ildefonso.

START From Madrid, take the A-2 east 25km (16 miles) to Alcalá de Henares.

❶ **Alcalá de Henares.** The country's progenitor of the modern Spanish language, Miguel de Cervantes, was born in Alcalá in 1547. Although the Cervantes family left Alcalá when Miguel was a boy, the central square of the old town is called Plaza de Cervantes and boasts a heroic bronze statue of the author. The ★ **Museo Casa Natal de Cervantes** re-creates family life among the 16th-century middle class in the structure where Cervantes was probably born. A room of *Don Quixote* editions (including

CASTILLA Y LEÓN

COMMUNITY OF MADRID

Manzanares el Real

Embalse de Santillana

CASTILLA-LA MANCHA

Guadarrama

Colmenar Viejo

San Lorenzo de El Escorial ④

Collado Villalba

Galapagar

COMMUNITY OF MADRID

Alcobendas   San Sebastián de los Reyes

Las Rozas de Madrid ⑤

Barajas Int'l Airport

Alcalá de Henares ①

Villanueva de la Cañada   Majadahonda

Pozuelo de Alarcón

MADRID ★

Torrejón de Ardoz

Coslada

Alcorcón

Móstoles   Leganés

Getafe

Fuenlabrada

Arganda del Rey

El Álamo

Parla   Pinto

Griñón

Valmojado

Valdemoro

Ciempozuelos

Chinchón ②

Colmenar de Oreja

Yuncos

Aranjuez ③

Añover de Tajo

Villarubia de Santiago

Noblejas

Ocaña

CASTILLA-LA MANCHA

0 ___ 10 mi
0 ___ 10 km

① Alcalá de Henares
② Chinchón
③ Aranjuez
④ El Escorial
⑤ El Pardo

many in other languages) hints at how inspiring many artists found the ungainly knight, displaying illustrations by Goya, Doré, and even Salvador Dalí.

The buildings in Alcalá are old and the population is young—as befits the city where the Spanish Renaissance was born, when Cardinal Francisco Jiménez de Cisneros founded its university in 1499. When the Inquisition was closing minds, Alcalá was opening them. The first classes at the university met in 1508, but the college moved to Madrid in 1836. The Universidad de Alcalá de Henares, founded in 1977, now occupies many of the old buildings, including the **Colegio Mayor de San Ildefonso,** the original 16th-century heart of the university.

> *A scene of 16th-century middle class domesticity at the Museo Casa Natal de Cervantes.*

> *The picturesque arcaded Plaza Mayor of Chinchón captivated Goya, whose portrait of the Countess of Chinchón now hangs in the Prado.*

Student-guided tours of the Colegio begin with the 1543 Plateresque facade, which students compare to a graphic novel for its wealth of historical, mythical, and religious figures. You'll also see the beautiful Capilla San Ildefonso, built from 1500 to 1512 in a mix of Mudéjar and Gothic styles, and the stunning Gothic-Mudéjar examination room where the Miguel de Cervantes Prize is awarded every year to honor the life's work of an author writing in Spanish.

Tours begin at the university's shop, which sells T-shirts and backpacks emblazoned with the logo of two swans, or *cisnes,* facing each other—a pun on founder Cisneros. But the town is better known for another bird: Approximately **90 pairs of white storks** nest here on the ancient buildings around the university.

Wildlife in these parts was significantly more ferocious some 780,000 years ago, judging by the bones of saber-toothed tigers, ur-wolves, and rhinoceroses exhibited at the ★ **Museo Arqueológico Regional.** Clear signage and vivid exhibits make this 1999 institution one of the most rewarding archaeological museums in the country. Don't miss the wonderful murals

recovered from Complutum, the city founded by the Romans in 1 B.C. upon which Alcalá is built. Museo Cervantes: ◷ 30 min. C/ Mayor at C/ Imagen. ☎ 91-889-96-54. Free. Tues–Sat 11am–7pm, Sun 11am–3pm. Colegio: ◷ 1 hr. Plaza San Diego. ☎ 91-885-64-87. 4€ adults, 2€ students and seniors. Guided visits Mon–Fri every hour 10am–1pm and 4–7pm, Sat–Sun every half-hour 11am–2:30pm. Museo Arqueológico: ◷ 1½ hr. Plaza Bernardas. ☎ 91-879-66-66. www.madrid. org. Free. Tues–Sat 11am–7pm, Sun 11am–3pm.

From Madrid, follow the A-3 45km (28 miles) south to Chinchón.

❷ **Chinchón.** This authentic village of the central *meseta* (high plains) might be best known for its powerful (150-proof and higher) anise liqueur, *anís de Chinchón,* but Madrileños often come here to get in touch with their rural roots. Cars parked in a ring in the middle of Plaza Mayor almost obscure the anachronistic qualities of the square, which lies in a hollow where the Old City's cobbled streets converge. The three-story wooden houses, some hundreds of years old, that surround the plaza are united by running balconies connecting one to another. During feast days in July to September, they are front-row seats as Chinchón holds *corridas* (bullfights) on the hard-packed sands of Plaza Mayor.

From Madrid, follow the N-4 47km (29 miles) south to Aranjuez.

❸ **Aranjuez.** Spanish monarchs built so many palaces and hunting lodges around Madrid that it's easy to conclude that they preferred the countryside to the city. For more than 400 years, they've been coming to Aranjuez in the spring, when the region's white asparagus and tangy strawberries are in season. Beyond the superb produce, Aranjuez's main attractions are the striking gardens and royal residences.

The ★★ **Palacio Real** is often called the Spanish Versailles, perhaps because the main expansion of Felipe II's country palace was orchestrated by Carlos III, the Bourbon king who had more than a passing familiarity with the court of his French cousins. When the Spanish monarchs go to the countryside, they don't exactly rough it. Several centuries of accreted ornamentation have created a labyrinth of rooms that resemble Fabergé eggs.

The monarchs didn't just look after their own comforts. They constructed immense

Travel Tip

The royal compound at El Escorial is so large that you might want to take the **Chiquitrén**, a narrated tourist train that makes stops along the way from the palace to the far end of the Jardín del Príncipe. It departs from Palacio Real (☎ 902-088-089) and costs 5€.

gardens to offer local residents shady respite from the heat and dust of summer. **Jardín de la Isla** is adjacent to the palace on a man-made island surrounded by a canal and the Río Tajo. Full of mature trees, its elaborate decorative fountains function only a few minutes daily to conserve water.

The more immense **Jardín del Príncipe** stretches 2.5km (1½ miles) from the riverbank eastward to form the northern border of the city. It too consists of a network of walkways shaded by mature leafy trees and punctuated by flower beds. The garden contains the **Museo de las Falúas,** which preserves the ornate 17th- to 19th-century royal pleasure barges, where musicians entertained monarchs and their entourages. But the height of ornamental excess might be the ★★ **Casa del Labrador,** a minipalace built for Carlos IV at a time when

> *The gardens of the royal palace in Aranjuez offered Spain's Bourbon monarchs more than just a stroll in the countryside.*

> *A funicular runs to the Valle de los Caidos.*

03-05. www.patrimonionacional.es. 5€. Apr-Sept Tues-Sun 10am-6:15pm; Oct-Mar Tues-Sun closes 5:15pm. Reserve ahead; limited to 10 people per hour.

From Madrid, take the A-6 45km (28 miles) northwest to San Lorenzo de El Escorial.

❹ ★★★ **El Escorial.** With their extensive home renovations, Bourbon monarchs put their own—often frilly—stamp on Madrid's Palacio Real. If you want to see Hapsburg vanity and fervor at its purest, do not miss the Real Monasterio de San Lorenzo de El Escorial, which Felipe II commissioned after the death of his father, Carlos V. He intended the monastery palace and its mausoleum to be an eternal memorial to the Hapsburg line, and with the aid of original architect Juan Bautista de Toledo and his successor, the great Juan de Herrera, Felipe's wildest aspirations were realized.

The basilica is the most impressive part of the immense complex. Crowned by a dome inspired by St. Peter's, it has 43 sumptuously decorated altars. Beneath the basilica, the royal vaults contain 26 black-marble graves of the Hapsburg and Bourbon monarchs from Carlos V to Alfonso XII. The Palacio de los Asturias, by comparison, is rather spare, though one room is festooned with frescoes of Hapsburg battle victories. Felipe II's private quarters are nearly monastic—except that the bedroom overlooks the basilica main altar. The Museo de Arquitectura recounts the relatively swift construction of El Escorial (27 years); its art gallery contains paintings by El Greco, Zurbarán, Ribera, Titian, and Rubens.

When the founder of the Falange Española (Franco's fascist party) died, the Generalissimo had him interred at El Escorial—and surviving monarchists cried foul. So Franco built the **Valle de los Caidos,** a humongous memorial to the Civil War dead, and buried his hero there. (Franco's own remains are behind the high altar.) Originally intended to honor only

the monarchy's days looked numbered. **Palacio:** ⏲ 2 hr. ☎ 91-891-07-40. www.patrimonionacional.es. 4.50€ adults unguided, 5€ guided, 2.50€ students and seniors. Apr-Sept Tues-Sun 10am-6:15pm; Oct-Mar closes 5:15pm. Jardín de la Isla: ⏲ 30 min. Daily 8am-8:30pm. Free. Jardín del Principe: ⏲ 2 hr. Daily 8am-8:30pm. Free. Museo: ⏲ 30 min. Jardín del Principe, s/n. ☎ 91-891-07-40. www.patrimonionacional.es. 3€. Apr-Sept Tues-Sun 10am-6:15pm; Oct-Mar closes 5:15pm. Casa: ⏲ 45 min. Jardín del Principe, s/n. ☎ 91-891-

Travel Tip

Every year on November 20, admirers of Franco congregate at the Valle de los Caidos to celebrate the memory of El Caudillo. It's a good day to skip, as violence sometimes breaks out.

> *If the Palacio Real belongs to the Bourbons stylistically, El Escorial belongs to the Hapsburgs.*

Nationalist casualties, the gigantic cross and underground basilica were eventually dedicated to all the fallen, or *caidos*. Whatever your politics or taste in memorial art, there's no denying the impressiveness of the cross, which towers 150m (492 ft.) on a peak of the Sierra Guadarrama. There's a funicular from the basilica to the base of the cross for outstanding scenic views. El Escorial: ⏱ Half-day. C/ Juan de Borbón, San Lorenzo de El Escorial. ☎ 91-890-59-02. www.patrimonionacional.es. 8€ adults, 10€ guided tours, 4€ students and ages 5–16, free Wed. Apr–Sept Tues–Sun 10am–6pm; Oct–Mar closes 5pm. Valle de los Caidos: ⏱ 30 min. ☎ 91-890-56-11. 5€ adults, 3€ seniors and students. Funicular 2.50€. Apr–Sept Tues–Sun 9:30am–6pm; Oct–Mar Tues–Sun 10am–7pm. Bus: 660 from San Lorenzo de El Escorial.

From Madrid, follow the M-30 6km (4 miles) north to the M-607. El Pardo is another 5km (3 miles) north along M-607.

❺ **El Pardo.** Far less monumental than El Escorial, the Palacio Real de El Pardo was also built by Felipe II, though its moat and defensive towers were the work of his father.

Gutted by fire in the 18th century, El Pardo was rebuilt with Enlightenment pomp under Carlos III. Today the palace is a study in contrasts. Until his death in 1975, Francisco Franco made El Pardo his private residence, and his presence lingers like an uninvited guest. Franco's personal suite displays a functional simplicity of modern plumbing and austere bedrooms. Only the dressing room devoted to ceremonial uniforms reveals his extravagant side. The rest of the palace is a tour de force of decorative arts, as carved and gilded furniture fills voluminous rooms where formal portraits of the Bourbon kings from the 18th to the 20th century peer down. Goya and his brother-in-law created the designs for tapestries—mostly sweet country landscapes or stylized hunt scenes—that were woven to cover the walls like wallpaper. El Pardo also serves as the residence of foreign heads of state during official visits to Madrid. ⏱ 1½ hr. C/ Manuel Alonso, Monte de El Pardo. 91-376-15-00. www.patrimonionacional.es. 4€, 2.30€ seniors and students. Mon–Sat 10:30am–5:45pm (Oct–Mar closes 4:45pm); Sun 10am–1:30pm.

Bourbon Madrid

The Bourbon monarchs considered their capital city an extended living room and made it a better place to live—in contrast to their French cousins, who lost their heads over estrangement from their subjects. Bourbon improvements begun in the 18th century remade Madrid into a monumental city of pleasant amenities—a trend the monarchs continued until the Civil War.

> *Go at the right time to the Cibeles fountain, and you might hear footballers chanting "Hala Madrid!"*

START Plaza de Cortes.

1 Fuente de Neptuno & Fuente de Cibeles.
Son of a bricklayer, Ventura Rodriguez went to work at age 10 helping his father build the Palacio Real de Aranjuez (see p. 89, **3**). A fast learner, he became head of architectural studies at the Real Academia de Bellas Artes (see p. 95, **7**) at age 35. He was also the go-to guy for Carlos III when it came to civil engineering. Passed over for more glamorous jobs at the Palacio Real, Rodriguez went beyond road work to design the decorative fountains that now define the *paseos,* or avenues, of Madrid.

The **Fuente de Neptuno,** executed in 1780, shows the sea god wielding his trident from atop a chariot. Fans of the Atlético football team head here to celebrate victories. The fountain marks the Plaza de Cortes, where Carrera de San Jerónimo meets the *paseos.* Facing off on opposite sides of the circle are the **Ritz** and **Palace** hotels (see p. 141), two properties built after guests at Alfonso XIII's 1906 wedding couldn't find luxury rooms.

The **Fuente de Cibeles,** designed from 1777 to 1782, shows the Anatolian goddess of fertility sitting on a chariot pulled by two lions. The preferred celebration spot for fans of the Real Madrid football team, the fountain marks the end of the Paseo del Prado and the beginning of the Paseo de Recoletos.

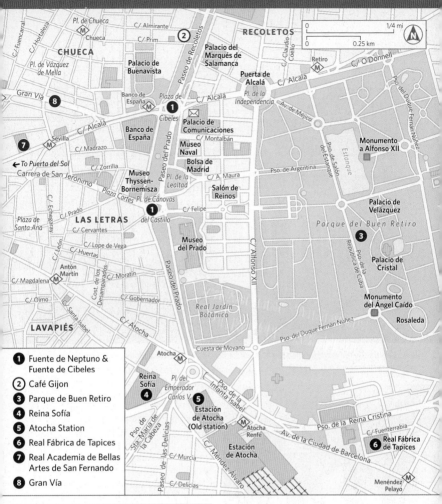

0   1/4 mi
0   0.25 km

- **1** Fuente de Neptuno & Fuente de Cibeles
- **2** Café Gijon
- **3** Parque de Buen Retiro
- **4** Reina Sofía
- **5** Atocha Station
- **6** Real Fábrica de Tapices
- **7** Real Academia de Bellas Artes de San Fernando
- **8** Gran Vía

② ☕ **Café Gijon.** For the most elegant cup of coffee on the *paseos,* stop at this site of many *tertulias,* or literary discussion groups, founded in 1888. Paseo de Recoletos, 21. ☎ 91-522-37-37. $–$$.

❸ Parque de Buen Retiro. Since it opened to the public in 1868, Buen Retiro has been one of Madrid's most popular parks. Enter at Plaza de Independencia by the triumphal arch and walk up the steps to the Avenida de Méjico. Small children will be captivated by the **puppet theater** on the right. On the left, just beyond the fountain covered in stone dolphins and bronze turtles, is the **Estanque.** Felipe IV had it dug in 1631 to stage mock naval battles, but

nowadays families can take a tranquil glide in rented rowboats. The grandiose **Monumento a Alfonso XII** dominates the lake. Conceived as a morale booster after Spain lost its colonies in 1898, it wasn't finished until 1922. Beyond the lake, the **Palacio de Velázquez,** an 1883 exhibition pavilion with decorative tiles by Daniel Zuloaga, now houses temporary art exhibitions. Just beyond it is the 1887 **Palacio de Cristal,** created to exhibit tropical plants and inspired by London's Crystal Palace. It's a favorite spot for wedding photos. In a completely different vein, the **Monumento del Ángel Caído** sculpture depicts Lucifer's descent to Hell. On the left is the aromatic **Rosaleda,** a

> *Buen Retiro's Crystal Palace, called the "Chocolate Box" by locals, was built as a hothouse but today hosts exhibitions of modern art.*

> *Over 120 years old, Café Gijon is as much intellectual salon as restaurant.*

specimen garden of hundreds of rose varieties. ⏱ 1½ hr. Free. Summer 7am–midnight; winter 7am–10pm. Metro: Retiro.

❹ **Reina Sofía.** Two free-standing glass elevators on the main facade of the old General Hospital announce that the Museo Nacional Centro de Arte Reina Sofía isn't just another huge hall of art. This museum is about upsetting order to forge new ideas. Just take a look at Jean Nouvel's 2007 ultramodern addition on the back, which alters the paradigm of rectilinear space.

While Richard Serra's minimalist sculptural homage to Picasso (*Equal-Parallel: Guernica-Bergasi,* referring to the 1986 U.S. bombings of Libya) on Floor 1 sets a distinctly polemical tone, the heart of the exhibits are above. Floor 2 galleries deconstruct the *ism*s of 20th-century art to show what was happening in Spain: hyperrealism in reaction to cubism, Miró's experiments to blend constructivism with surrealism, and the underappreciated Juan Gris and his reordering of modernism. Set your preconceptions aside. One of the best is Salvador Dalí's nearly realistic rendering of a young Luis Buñuel. ⏱ 2 hr. C/ Santa Isabel, 52. ☎ 91-774-10-00. www.museoreinasofia.es. 6€ adults, 3€ students, kids and seniors free, free to all Sat 2:30–9pm. Mon and Wed–Sat 10am–9pm; Sun 10am–2:30pm. Metro: Atocha.

> *The Royal Tapestry Factory's most famous cartoonist (that is, preliminary sketch artist) was Francisco Goya himself.*

5 Atocha Station. Fire destroyed the 1851 wooden Mediodía train station. It was rebuilt in 1892 in a grand wrought-iron style in consultation with Gustave Eiffel. The current version was designed in 1985 by Rafael Moneo, who divided tracks for conventional and high-speed trains and converted the old terminal into a glass-roofed concourse with a tropical garden, shops, and cafes. ⏱ 20 min. Metro: Atocha.

6 Real Fábrica de Tapices. The first Bourbon king, Felipe V, founded the Royal Tapestry Factory in 1721 to emulate Louis XIV's Gobelins Manufactury in Paris. Goya worked here in the mid–18th century designing cartoons for tapestries in El Pardo (see p. 91, **5**), and a few of his drawings are on display. Weavers work at the original wooden hand looms, making rugs and wall tapestries and restoring historic pieces. ⏱ 1 hr. C/ Fuenterrabia, 2. ☎ 91-434-05-50. www.realfabricadetapices.com. 4€ adults, 3€ kids. Guided tours Mon–Fri 10am–2pm. Closed Aug. Metro: Atocha.

7 Real Academia de Bellas Artes de San Fernando. Founded in 1752, the art academy has been in this palace off Puerta del Sol since 1773. Although Goya was twice rejected as a student, he ultimately became director. The lower galleries—culminating in 13 of Goya's paintings and his final palette under glass—still reflect his theory of Spanish painting: that all roads lead to Goya. Galleries of 19th- and 20th-century art close if staff are not available. ⏱ 1 hr. C/ Alcalá, 13. ☎ 91-524-08-64. http://rabasf.insde.es. 3€ adults, 1.50€ students, free for seniors and kids 17 & under. Tues–Sat 9am–5pm; Sun 9am–2:30pm. Metro: Sevilla or Sol.

8 Gran Vía. A grand diagonal linking the new neighborhoods of Salamanca and Argüelles was bandied about in the late 19th century, but Alfonso XIII repackaged the idea as a thoroughfare for automobiles. Alfonso dug the ceremonial first shovel in 1910, and several Art Nouveau buildings (such as Metropolis at the corner of C/ Alcalá) recall the high hopes for the street—later dashed by economic collapse. Cinemas and theaters near the Callao Metro station are the bright heart of Gran Vía nightlife.

The Best of the Prado

The Spanish monarchs gathered the core collections of the Prado, and Carlos III commissioned the museum from Juan de Villanueva in 1785. Delayed by warfare, the Prado finally opened in 1819—the first time anyone but members of the court saw many of its works. The holdings of Spanish art are unrivaled, but as one of the world's greatest museums, the Prado has other treasures as well. This tour hits many of the highlights.

> *Much of architect Rafael Moneo's extension of the Prado, completed in 2007, is underground.*

START **Goya gate, Paseo del Prado.**

❶ **Jerónimos Building: Cloister.** Rafael Moneo's clever and graceful extension of the Prado sets this 16th-century cloister built for the once-adjacent Jerónimos monastery into a glass display cube. Statues excavated from Hadrian's Villa at Tivoli are displayed in the courtyard.

❷ **Gallery 51C: Romanesque Murals.** A recreation of the 12th-century hermitage chapel of Santa Cruz de Maderuelo in León features 19 painstakingly preserved murals that mix Old and New Testament stories with depictions of the Apostles and Evangelists.

Travel Tip

The main entrance is through Rafael Moneo's 2007 extension in back, but purchase tickets first at the Goya gate on the north side of the building.

❸ **Gallery 49: Fra Angelico & Raphael.** Fra Angelico's moving *Annunciation* (1426–27) is perhaps the Prado's earliest masterpiece. The gallery of Italian painting from 1300 to 1800 also contains several works by Raphael, including his *Holy Family with Little St. John* (ca. 1520), in which an infant John the Baptist hands a ribbon inscribed AGNUS DEI ("Lamb of God") to the infant Jesus.

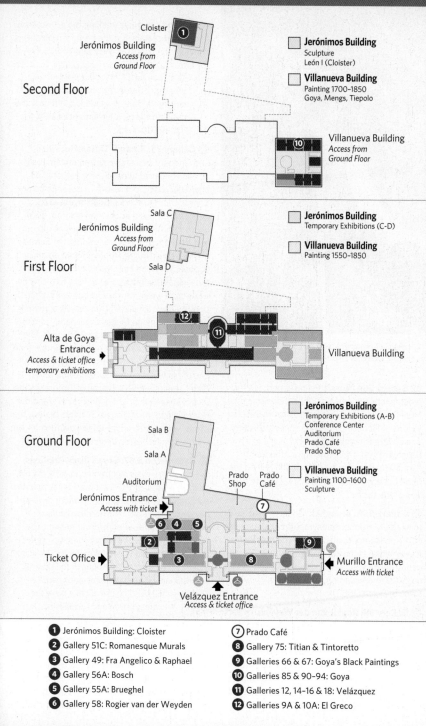

Second Floor

Cloister

Jerónimos Building
*Access from
Ground Floor*

Jerónimos Building
Sculpture
León I (Cloister)

Villanueva Building
Painting 1700–1850
Goya, Mengs, Tiepolo

Villanueva Building
*Access from
Ground Floor*

First Floor

Sala C

Jerónimos Building
*Access from
Ground Floor*

Sala D

Jerónimos Building
Temporary Exhibitions (C–D)

Villanueva Building
Painting 1550–1850

Alta de Goya
Entrance
*Access & ticket office
temporary exhibitions*

Villanueva Building

Ground Floor

Sala B

Sala A

Auditorium

Jerónimos Entrance
Access with ticket

Prado
Shop

Prado
Café

Jerónimos Building
Temporary Exhibitions (A–B)
Conference Center
Auditorium
Prado Café
Prado Shop

Villanueva Building
Painting 1100–1600
Sculpture

Ticket Office

Murillo Entrance
Access with ticket

Velázquez Entrance
Access & ticket office

1 Jerónimos Building: Cloister
2 Gallery 51C: Romanesque Murals
3 Gallery 49: Fra Angelico & Raphael
4 Gallery 56A: Bosch
5 Gallery 55A: Brueghel
6 Gallery 58: Rogier van der Weyden

7 Prado Café
8 Gallery 75: Titian & Tintoretto
9 Galleries 66 & 67: Goya's Black Paintings
10 Galleries 85 & 90–94: Goya
11 Galleries 12, 14–16 & 18: Velázquez
12 Galleries 9A & 10A: El Greco

> A detail of Hieronymus Bosch's The Garden of Earthly Delights *(1500–05).*

④ Gallery 56A: Bosch. Felipe II, perhaps the most fanatically religious of the Spanish kings, had a special affinity for the surreal moralistic visions of Flemish painter Hieronymus Bosch. The bizarre triptych of *The Garden of Earthly Delights* (1500–05) is the star of the room. Paradise is depicted on the left and hell on the right. In between, Bosch deliciously details the sins of the flesh.

⑤ Gallery 55A: Brueghel. Modern taste tends to exalt the somber but sympathetic depictions of the peasantry by the Flemish painter Pieter Brueghel the Elder. But Brueghel shared Bosch's darkly apocalyptic sensibility, evidenced by the dogs scavenging among the bones in *The Triumph of Death* (1562).

⑥ Gallery 58: Rogier van der Weyden. In part because they also ruled the Low Countries for many years, Spanish monarchs had a soft spot for Flemish painting. Isabel I was particularly fond of 15th-century master of grief and suffering Rogier van der Weyden. One of his largest surviving works, *The Descent from the Cross* (ca. 1435), dominates this gallery. The artist did

not sign his paintings, making the provenance of many uncertain. But the composition of this canvas is pure van der Weyden.

⑦ 🍵 Prado Café. Rest your eyes while you sip coffee in the sleek silvery monochrome of this new cafe located near the main entrance. Main entrance hall. ☎ 91-330-28-00. $–$$.

⑧ Gallery 75: Titian & Tintoretto. Titian and Carlos V must have gotten on famously, as each believed himself the greatest of his age. The Venetian master's massive *Emperor Carlos V on Horseback* (1548) invented the genre of the grand equestrian portrait, drawing from both medieval depictions of knights and the Roman sculptural tradition of heroes on horseback. But it's more than an act of sycophancy—Titian penetrated the bravado of the king at the Battle of Mühlberg to reveal an aging man weary of war. His unusual composition of *Adam and Eve* (1550) depicts a seated Adam reaching up to stay Eve's hand from the apple offered by a boy-snake in the tree. The same room contains several works by the great Venetian colorist Tintoretto. Among them is one of his finest portraits, *Gentleman with a Gold Chain* (ca. 1555). Typical of Tintoretto, the face is shaped in bright highlights to stand out from the dark background. Scholars believe that Diego Velázquez purchased the painting for the court when he visited Venice.

⑨ Galleries 66 & 67: Goya's Black Paintings. Welcome to Goya's nightmares. In 1819, the old, deaf, and war-weary Goya moved to the Quinta del Sordo, a small house outside Madrid where he covered the walls with horrific visions of death, decay, and suffering never meant to be exhibited. The so-called Black Paintings were ineptly transferred to canvas in the 1870s, losing much of their pigment but none of their power. His visionary distortion of time and space (as in *The Fates*) and slashing use of color were precursors of expressionism and surrealism.

⑩ Galleries 85 & 90–94: Goya. A sunnier, younger Goya holds forth in the second-floor galleries filled with bright cartoons painted for the tapestries that would eventually line the walls of El Pardo (see p. 91, **⑤**). Children frolic in the countryside, noble men and ladies picnic in the fields, and nary a cloud crosses the path

> *El Greco's* The Coronation of the Virgin *(ca. 1591–92).*

of the benevolent sun. The resolute cheeriness almost seems cloying, but it helped Goya land a paying job as court painter.

⑪ Galleries 12, 14–16 & 18: Velázquez. For most of his adult life, Diego Velázquez served the kings of Spain, and most of his paintings remained for royal eyes only until the Prado opened. The enduring power of art comes to the fore when schoolchildren visit Gallery 12 and sit enraptured before *Las Meninas* (see p. 20), their small bodies echoing the entourage around the Infanta Margarita. Although more than 50 Velázquez paintings perished in the 1734 fire at the Alcázar, many more survived, including portraits of the royal family. Maybe the most telling is his *Felipe IV in Hunting Clothes* (ca. 1653). The pose is nearly identical to one the painter used 20 years earlier, but Felipe's face is filled with the deep melancholy of his eventual decline.

⑫ Galleries 9A & 10A: El Greco. Never a favorite of the Spanish crown, El Greco wasn't even categorized as a Spanish painter by the Prado until the early 20th century. Born in Crete and trained in Venice and Rome, he painted like no one else. While most of his religious canvases feature a sky with whirlpool clouds and sudden shafts of light illuminating saints, take a close look at *Fable* (ca. 1600), which shows

> *The Prado houses several Raphaels, including* The Holy Family of the Oak Tree *(ca. 1518).*

a young man blowing on burning embers in the company of a trickster boy and a monkey. Some scholars consider it an allegory of sexual desire. Paseo del Prado. ☎ 91-330-28-00. www.museodelprado.es. 8€ adults, 4€ students, free for kids 17 & under, free to all Tues–Sat 6–8pm and Sun 5–8pm. Tues–Sun 9am–8pm. Metro: Atocha or Banco de España.

The Best Historical Museums

Madrid is a young city by Spanish standards, but it has packed a lot of history into 4½ centuries as the national capital. These history museums will give you a good overview of it all. Some of the museums complement each other (Naval and América, in particular), while others, like the clothing museum, see the past in a single narrow vision.

> The Museo de San Isidro chronicles the history of Madrid from the Paleolithic era to the present day.

START Metro to Moncloa or Ciudad Universitaria, to Avenida Juan de Herrera

❶ ★ **Museo del Traje.** A quick stroll past the shop windows in Salamanca (see p. 228) will give you a sense of the confidence and accomplishment of Spain's contemporary fashion designers. But if you'd like to explore the links between fashion and history, visit this "costume" museum. It traces the evolution of Spanish style from the 18th century through the present day, with special attention to such style-setters as Balenciaga. Because fabrics are so perishable, few examples of Spanish clothing before the 18th century survive. ⏲ 1 hr. Avenida Juan de Herrera, 2. ☎ 91-550-47-00. http://museodeltraje.mcu.es. 3€ adults, free for seniors and kids 17 & under, free to all Sat after 2:30pm and Sun. Tues–Sat 9:30am–7pm; Sun 10am–3pm. Metro: Moncloa or Ciudad Universitaria.

❷ ★★ **Museo de América.** Although Carlos III was usually preoccupied with building projects in Madrid, he was the quintessential Enlightenment monarch and made time to assemble a "cabinet" of curiosities from Spain's colonies in the Americas. The museum's collection of 25,000 objects gathered during archaeological and scientific expeditions is an outgrowth of that fascination with the New World. The collection has a number of amazing pieces, including Mayan stone carvings, Incan textiles, Mexican pottery, and the Códice Tudela, a 16th-century manuscript with Mayan drawings and text by a Spanish missionary. But the museum has moved well beyond the mere display of curiosities. Exhibits balance the excitement and adventure of discovery with

1 Museo del Traje
2 Museo de América
3 Museo de San Isidro
4 Museo Arqueológico Nacional
5 Museo Naval
6 Plaza de Toros Monumental de Las Ventas

> *Balenciaga appears alongside bullfighting costumes at the Museo del Traje.*

sensitive portrayals of New World cultures that would be forever changed by the encounters. The building itself is reminiscent of New World Spanish structures, with an arched entry, baroque tower, and central courtyard. ⏱ 1½ hr. Avenida Reyes Católicos, 6. ☎ 91-549-26-51. http://museodeamerica.mcu.es. 3€ adults, 1.50€ kids, free to all Sun. Tues–Sat 9:30am–3pm; Sun 10am–3pm. Metro: Moncloa.

❸ Museo de San Isidro. The old palace holding this city history museum sits on the site believed to have been the 12th-century home of San Isidro Labrador (patron saint of Madrid) and his wife, Santa María de la Cabeza. Indeed, a centerpiece of one exhibit is the couple's well.

According to legend, when their infant son fell into the well, the couple's prayers caused the water to rise and deliver him to safety. Part of the museum deals with the saints, the legends surrounding them, and the political machinations around their canonizations. But the museum's main exhibits chronicle the growth of Madrid since the first appearance of human hunters on the banks of the Río Manzanares some 300,000 years ago. ⏱ 45 min. For details on the exhibits, see p. 110, ❽.

❹ ★ Museo Arqueológico Nacional. Still undergoing major renovations to galleries dealing with Paleolithic and Neolithic Spain, this sweeping museum often tiptoes between archaeology and history. Shortly after the Prado opened, most of the crown's holdings in ancient Greek, Phoenician, Egyptian, and Roman art were deaccessioned from the art museum and deposited here—accounting for the rather unsystematic antiquity collections. But once the museum

> *A statue outside Las Ventas reminds visitors what can happen to unlucky matadors.*

begins to deal with the Visigoths, things really pick up. The Treasure of Guarrazar—crowns and other gold jewelry fashioned from 621 to 672—should banish any image of the Germanic invaders as barbarian hordes. The goldsmithing is on a technical and aesthetic par with any age. The museum's collection of Mudéjar works in ceramics, wood, and glass speaks to the vibrancy of a hybrid culture of Muslim traditions that survived after the Spanish Reconquista. Note that while the museum is free during renovations, there will be an admission charge when the work is done. Outside, a re-creation of the Cueva de Altamira (see p. 272) and its 15,000-year-old painted walls is entered from the front lawn. ⏱ 1½ hr. C/ Serrano, 13. ☎ 91-577-79-12. http://man.mcu.es. Free. Tues–Sat 9:30am–8pm; Sun 9:30am–3pm. Metro: Serrano.

❺ ★★ Museo Naval. Security is so tight that you'll have to show your passport to enter this museum housed on the first floor of the Spanish navy headquarters. The navy began

> *The Museo Naval extensively covers Spain's formidable naval exploits from the time of Columbus.*

collecting historical materials in the late 18th century, and the maps, paintings, nautical instruments, and ship models offer a fascinating overview of Spain's maritime pursuits. Exhibits begin with the discovery and exploration of the Americas, including a scale model of Columbus's surprisingly small flagship, the *Santa Maria*. The museum's most treasured artifact dates from those heady days of exploration: Juan de la Cosa's 1500 handwritten map of the New World. The central patio is devoted to shipbuilding during the 18th century, when Spain and England struggled with each other for maritime hegemony. Proud even in defeat, the museum displays heroic paintings of the 1805 Battle of Trafalgar. For a glimpse of shipboard life, don't miss the re-creations of the wardroom of a 16th-century frigate and the 19th-century cabin of a ship commander. ⏱1 hr. Paseo del Prado, 5. ☎ 91-523-87-89. www.museo navalmadrid.com. Free. Tues–Sun 10am–2pm. Metro: Atocha or Banco de España.

⑥ ★ Plaza de Toros Monumental de Las Ventas. It is not a museum, per se, but a guided tour here takes you into the stands and onto the sands of what many consider Spain's most important bullring. Opened in 1931, Las Ventas is a Mudéjar tour de force of red brick, carved plaster, and decorative tile and ironwork. During the March to October season, the ring's 24,000 seats are usually packed with passionate fans who come to analyze the skills of Spain's most accomplished matadors. Don't miss the Grand Portal: Only matadors who are awarded the highest honor at the conclusion of a match can exit through this ceremonial gate—usually swept up by a sea of admirers. Whatever your feelings about bullfighting, this is a good place to get some insight into its place in Spanish history and culture. ⏱1 hr. C/ Alcalá, 237. ☎ 91-556-92-37. www.las-ventas.com. 7€ adults, 5€ ages 4–12. Tues–Sun 10am–2pm. Metro: Ventas.

DEATH IN THE AFTERNOON

The Moment of Truth in Spain's Most Controversial Spectacle BY PATRICIA HARRIS & DAVID LYON

THE MODERN SPANISH *CORRIDA*, or bullfight, dates from the early 18th century, when Francisco Romero of Ronda ritualized the spectacle by donning a small cape and dispatching the wounded beast with a sword through the shoulder blades. The quintessentially Spanish sport remains a popular but controversial part of national life in Spain today: Though Catalunya, for one, periodically threatens to ban the *corrida*, top matadors are often more famous in Spain than rock, football, or movie stars.

Bullfighting Fashion

The *traje de luces,* or "suit of lights," is modeled on 18th-century Andalucían formal dress: The matador wears a suit with many golden threads, while his assistants wear suits in silver (*traje de plata*). The pants are usually skin-tight and the shoulders of the jacket heavily padded.

Stages of the Fight

A typical *corrida* features three matadors, each of whom faces two bulls. Each matchup is divided into thirds, or *tercios,* announced by a trumpet. Following the ceremonial introduction of the matador and his *cuadrilla* (entourage), the bullfighter performs a series of passes with a dress cape and assesses the bull's behavior in the first *tercio de varas;* a *picadero,* or man on horse, follows this by lancing the bull in the neck hump. In the *tercio de banderillas,* three *banderilleros* each plant two sharp barbed sticks, or *banderillas,* into the bull's shoulders. In the final stage, the *tercio de muerte,* the matador returns to the ring with a red cape and sword to exhaust the bull before finally thrusting his sword between the shoulders and into the bull's heart.

The Best Bullrings

LAS VENTAS, MADRID: During the 3-week Fiesta de San Isidro in late May and early June, the 25,000-seat Las Ventas stages daily bullfights. The season continues on weekends into October. See p. 103.

PLAZA DE TOROS DE LA REAL MAESTRANZA, SEVILLA: One of the most famous venues, Sevilla's bullring was constructed in 1758. The season begins during the April Feria festival and continues intermittently into October. As the ring seats only 12,000 to 14,000, spectators are often close to the action. See p. 597.

PLAZA DE TOROS, RONDA: Built in 1785, Ronda's bullring hosts infrequent *corridas* between April and October. The *Corrida Goyesca,* in which matadors dress in the style depicted by Goya, is held in early September and honors Pedro Romero. See p. 639.

Who's Who

PEDRO ROMERO (1754–1839) Grandson of Francisco Romero of Ronda, Pedro Romero established the matador as artist. He is said to have slain more than 5,000 bulls before retiring (unharmed) in 1799. Legend holds that he made a single comeback appearance at the age of 80, killing several bulls before a large crowd in Madrid.

JUAN BELMONTE (1892–1962) Frequently gored because he fought close to the bull's horns, Belmonte ruled Spanish bullfighting between the World Wars and was a confidante of Ernest Hemingway. When his doctor told him that he could no longer smoke, drink, or carouse with women, Belmonte committed suicide after drinking two bottles of wine, smoking several cigars, and romping with two prostitutes.

MANOLETE (1917–47) Manuel Laureano Rodríguez Sánchez is considered by some aficionados the greatest matador of all time. He often stood unwaveringly still, maneuvering the bull around him with cape and gestures. When he died after being gored by a bull called Islero in Linares, Spain observed an official 3 days of mourning.

EL CORDOBÉS (b. 1936) Born Manuel Benítez Pérez, El Cordobés introduced an acrobatic, risk-taking style to bullfighting in the 1960s. The first "rock star" matador, he embodied celebrity excess, both inside and outside the ring. He retired in 1971, only to return to the ring in 1979. His last fight was in 2000.

ENRIQUE PONCE (b. 1971) Perhaps the greatest of Spain's active matadors, the Valencia-born Alfonso Enrique Ponce Martínez is considered the first matador superstar of the 21st century.

The Best Small Art Museums

Madrid's large art institutions are only the beginning of the city's aesthetic glories. Escape the crowds at these more tightly focused smaller institutions.

> Dance on the Banks of the River Manzanares *by Francisco Goya (1777).*

START Metro to Príncipe Pío to Glorieta de San Antonio de la Florida.

① **La Ermita de San Antonio de la Florida.** To accommodate the city's growing pains, this church on the banks of the Río Manzanares was twice demolished and rebuilt. Fortunately, the third version proved to be a keeper—it was declared a national monument in 1905. The crowning glories of this petite masterpiece, originally constructed from 1792 to 1798, are the Francisco de Goya frescoes on the walls and ceiling. In addition to scenes from the life of San Antonio de Padua, Goya created images of angels to rival any of the Italian Renaissance masters. Goya's remains were interred in the

Now Showing

A host of cultural centers that mount temporary art exhibitions—often of contemporary art and photography—supplement Madrid's superb traditional art museums. Check their websites (below) for schedules, or consult *Guia del Ocio*, the weekly guide to Madrid art, culture, and entertainment available at all newsstands.

CaixaForum: Paseo del Prado, 36. ☎ 91-330-73-00. http://obrasocial.lacaixa.es. Free. Daily 10am–8pm. Metro: Atocha.

Centro Cultural Conde Duque: C/ Conde Duque, 11. ☎ 91-588-58-34. www.munimadrid.es/condeduque. Free. Tues–Sat 10am–2pm and 6–9pm; Sun 10:30am–2pm. Metro: Plaza de España.

Circulo de Bellas Artes: C/ Marqués de Casa Riera, 2. ☎ 91-360-54-00. www.circulobellasartes.com. 2€. Tues–Sat 11am–2pm and 5–9pm; Sun 11am–2pm. Metro: Banco de España.

Fundación Juan March: C/ Castelló, 77. ☎ 91-435-42-40. www.march.es. Free. Mon–Sat 11am–8pm; Sun 10am–2pm. Metro: Núñez de Balboa.

Matadero Madrid: Paseo de la Chopera, 14. ☎ 91-480-49-69. www.mataderomadrid.com. Free. Tues–Fri 4–10pm; Sat–Sun 11am–10pm. Metro: Legazpi.

mausoleum in 1919. ⏱ 30 min. Glorieta de San Antonio de la Florida, 5. ☎ 91-542-07-22. www.munimadrid.es/ermita. Free. Tues–Fri 9:30am–8pm; Sat–Sun 10am–2pm. Metro: Príncipe Pío.

1 La Ermita de San Antonio de la Florida
2 Museo Lázaro Galdiano
3 Museo Nacional de Artes Decorativas
4 Museo Sorolla

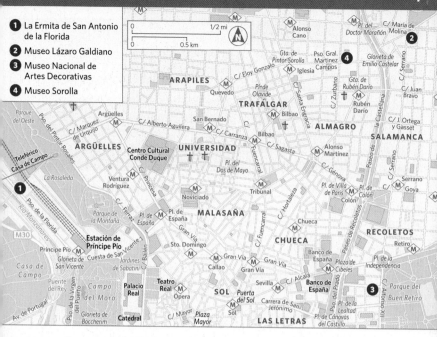

2 Museo Lázaro Galdiano. When Lázaro Galdiano died in 1947, he willed his 1909 Renaissance-style mansion and his personal collections to the Spanish government. The museum, which opened in 1951 and was recently renovated, occupies some of the lavish spaces of the 35-room mansion but does not attempt to re-create family life. Nonetheless, you'll get a sense of the taste and lifestyle of the wealthy financier as you study his collections of arms and armor, bronze miniatures, antique coins, clocks and watches, porcelain, crystal, and more. Galdiano also collected drawings, prints, and more than 750 paintings, including works by the Spanish masters Goya, El Greco, and Velázquez. The Fundación Lázaro Galdiano also sponsors concerts and lectures. ⏱ 1½ hr. C/ Serrano, 122. ☎ 91-561-60-84. www.flg.es. 4€, free on Wed. Wed–Mon 10am–4:30pm. Metro: Rubén Darío or Gregorio Marañón.

3 Museo Nacional de Artes Decorativas.
This seemingly encyclopedic museum has its roots in the early-20th-century movement to further the teaching and study of the industrial arts. Less than a third of the 40,000-object collection is displayed on five floors of a late-19th-century palace. Most work is Spanish, though the museum's Ming- and Qing-dynasty pieces reflect the enduring Spanish interest in Chinese design. The collections of furniture, rugs, textiles, glass, and ceramics are arranged chronologically, so it is possible to trace the evolution and influences of design over the centuries. Don't miss the 18th-century Valencian kitchen on the fourth floor. The blue and white tiles, depicting a lady of the time surrounded by her servants and animals, are an artistic tour de force, providing a snapshot of domestic life. Save the lower-level contemporary design galleries—repudiating all that's gone before—for last. ⏱ 1½ hr. C/ Montalban, 12. ☎ 91-532-64-99. http://mnartesdecorativas.mcu.es. 3€. Tues–Sat 9:30am–3pm; Sun 10am–3pm. Metro: Banco de España.

4 ★★ Museo Sorolla. Perhaps Spain's most successful artist in the late–19th and early–20th centuries, Joaquín Sorolla clearly enjoyed his talent, his family, and his commercial success. All three are amply covered at this museum in his former home/studio. See p. 85, 5.

La Latina

La Latina, the neighborhood from Plaza Mayor to the Puerta de Toledo, is part of the Old City of Madrid. In fact, it is older than Old Madrid, and predates the arrival of the Hapsburgs. Long impoverished and dilapidated, La Latina has been in the throes of gentrification for some time and boasts one of the city's best tapas districts.

START Plaza de San Miguel.

1 Mercado de San Miguel. You used to see butchers carrying sides of meat on their shoulders and fishmongers with cod strung by their gills going in and out of this venerable fresh market. Following several years of renovation, the gritty market reopened as a "Centro de Cultura Culinaria" of upscale wine bars, pastry shops, and casual restaurants. You can still buy great fish and meat, but most customers come to drink, snack, and socialize. ⊙ 30 min. Plaza de San Miguel, s/n. www.mercadodesanmiguel.es. Free. Mon–Wed and Sun 10am–10pm; Thurs–Sat 10am–2am. Metro: Ópera.

2 Plaza Mayor. Cut through the grand plaza past the equestrian statue of Hapsburg king Felipe III to the Toledo gate on the south side. See p. 81, **9**.

3 Colegiata de San Isidro. This rather dour hulk of a church was built by the Jesuits in the 16th century on a patch of land purchased through the will of Empress María de Austria. When Carlos III booted the Jesuits out of Spain in 1767 for meddling in politics, he had the Colegiata rededicated to San Isidro and Santa María de la Cabeza. Their remains are displayed on the main altar. ⊙ 20 min. C/ Toledo, 37. ☎ 91-364-40-50. Open for Mass only. Metro: La Latina.

4 Plaza Tirso de Molina. A short walk east brings you into this square of flower sellers named for the Golden Age dramatist Tirso de Molina (1583–1648). A central playground amuses children while their parents look on from cafe terraces. Just outside the plaza, you'll find **Yelmo Cines Ideal** (see p. 147), which shows movies in their original languages,

> Plaza Mayor grew in importance—and infamy—under the Hapsburgs, who used it as the site of autos-da-fé during the Inquisition.

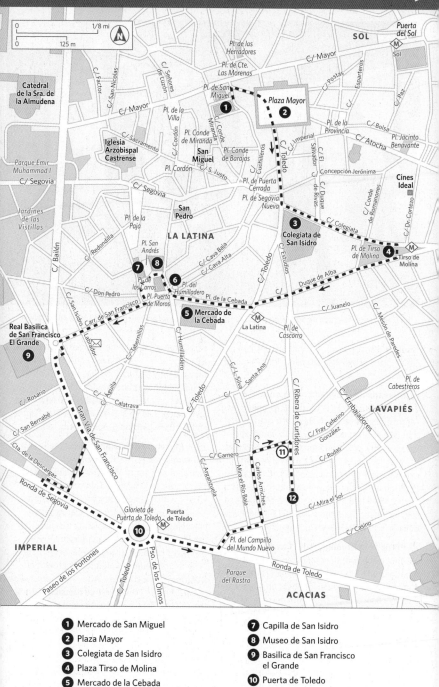

1 Mercado de San Miguel

2 Plaza Mayor

3 Colegiata de San Isidro

4 Plaza Tirso de Molina

5 Mercado de la Cebada

6 Plaza de la Humilladero & Cava Baja

7 Capilla de San Isidro

8 Museo de San Isidro

9 Basilica de San Francisco el Grande

10 Puerta de Toledo

11 Toma que Toma

12 El Rastro

> *In recent years, Mercado de San Miguel has transformed from a gritty food market to a gourmand haven.*

whether it's Mandarin, Japanese, French, or (most often) English. ⏱ **20 min. Metro: Tirso de Molina.**

⑤ Mercado de la Cebada. Walk down C/ Conde del Duque del Alba, past La Latina Metro entrance to reach this fresh market that is everything Mercado San Miguel used to be: earthy, gritty, and for some, even a little too real. It's a great place to marvel over the extraordinary fish sold in landlocked Madrid, or to purchase fresh fruit, bread, and cheese for a picnic. You'll find good buys on staples like sea salt, spices, and canned goods. ⏱ **30 min. Plaza Cebada, s/n. ☎ 91-365-91-76. Metro: La Latina.**

⑥ Plaza de la Humilladero & Cava Baja. Keep walking west from the market and the street broadens into Plaza de la Humilladero, always a good bet for cheap eats. The bars on adjoining C/ Cava Baja and C/ Cava Alta make up one of Madrid's most popular tapas zones. ⏱ **10 min. Metro: La Latina.**

⑦ Capilla de San Isidro. This small chapel dedicated to Madrid's patron saint is all that remains of San Andrés, the adjoining church burned during street fighting in the Civil War. The brick chapel, which was built to hold the

saint's relics (now in the Colegiata, see p. 108, **③**), was severely damaged and has been only recently restored. Niches in the support structure for the cupola hold statues of the 12 Apostles and four Evangelists. ⏱ **30 min. Plaza San Andrés, 1. ☎ 91-365-48-71. Free. Mon–Thurs and Sat 8am–1pm and 6–8pm. Metro: La Latina.**

⑧ ★ Museo de San Isidro. This is really two museums in one: the house of San Isidro Labrador and Santa María de la Cabeza, and the Museo de Orígenes. The former deals largely with legends associated with the two 12th-century Madrileños and features some charming religious art depicting various miracles. (San Isidro was no dummy—while he prayed, an angel ploughed his fields.) The "origins" museum devoted to the growth of Madrid is more complex. After a cursory sweep through the first few hundred thousand years, the exhibits become more focused after Madrid becomes the national capital in 1561. Much of the story is related with portraits of the artists, kings, poets, playwrights, and soldiers for whom city streets are named. Signage is all in Spanish, but if you can read it, you'll get a history reminder with every street sign. ⏱ **1 hr. Plaza de San Andrés, 2. ☎ 91-366-74-15. www.**

> *Dedicated bargain hunters can find just about anything at El Rastro (literally "thieves' market").*

munimadrid.es/museosanisidro. Free. Tues–Fri 9:30am–8pm; Sat–Sun 10am–2pm. Metro: La Latina.

⑨ Basilica de San Francisco el Grande. Erected at the end of the 18th century and heavily remodeled at the end of the 19th, San Francisco was the main church in Madrid until the Catedral de la Almudena near the Palacio Real was finally completed in 1993. San Francisco's main claim to fame is that it's *really* big (it boasts the largest cupola in Spain) and that many famous people attended services here a century ago. The museum holds conventional religious art and jewels—mainly of interest to silversmiths studying chalice construction—but the recently restored ceiling murals of Mary Queen of Heaven are quite striking. If you skip the museum, you can visit the church during morning Mass, every hour on the hour from 8:30am. ⏲ 30 min. Plaza San Francisco, 11. ☎ 91-365-38-00. 3€ adults. Tues–Sat 11:15am–12:45pm and 5:15–7pm. Metro: La Latina.

⑩ Puerta de Toledo. Joseph Napoleon commissioned this impressive granite monument to his own imperial presence in 1812. By the time it was finished a year later, French troops had withdrawn from Spain and the arch became the ceremonial gate through which Fernando VII entered the city to restore the Bourbon monarchy. A frieze on the monument commemorates the event. ⏲ 10 min. Metro: Puerta de Toledo.

⑪ 🍺 **Toma que Toma.** You should have worked up a thirst by now, so pop into this handsomely tiled bar for a *caña* (a small draft beer) and a cheap *tosta,* or toast, with sliced sausage. C/ del Carnero and C/ Ribera de los Curtidores. No phone. Metro: Puerta de Toledo. Cash only. $.

⑫ ★ **El Rastro.** Every Sunday morning, C/ Ribera de Curtidores becomes a sea of bargain hunters at Madrid's celebrated flea market. From the Ronda de Toledo all the way up the steep hill to Plaza de Cascorro, vendors at stalls hawk African crafts, Chinese jewelry, knockoff purses, pashminas, underwear and socks, miscellaneous hardware, old lamp parts, and zillions of music CDs. Pickpockets have a field day, so watch your belongings. The market begins to unravel around 2pm, when even the vendors hit the tapas bars. ⏲ 1 hr. C/ Ribera de Curtidores and nearby streets. Sunday 8am–2pm. Metro: Puerta de Toledo or La Latina.

Chueca & Malasaña

North of Gran Vía, the chic neighborhoods of Chueca and Malasaña have come a long way since Pedro Almodóvar's 1990 film *¡Átame! (Tie Me Up! Tie Me Down!)* showed Antonio Banderas being beaten by drug dealers in Plaza Chueca. These days, the wildest Chueca gets is during Gay Pride Week (end of June), with its flamboyant parade. Young designers have gravitated here (making for some great shopping) and the bohemian vibe attracts a youthful, alternative crowd. Shop in the afternoons and stick around for the nightlife.

> *A colorful tiled mural adorns a Chueca pharmacy.*

START Metro to Gran Vía.

❶ C/ Hortaleza & C/ Fuencarral. It's a toss-up which of these parallel streets is Chueca's main shopping drag. Both have many small boutiques—some mainstream, some not—catering to a young crowd. Look for surf fashion at **Quicksilver** (C/ Fuencarral, 22) or nifty hats at **Cocoa** (C/ Hortaleza, 28). **Corleone's Company** (C/ Hortaleza, 37) is a veritable temple of contemporary ready-to-wear. ⊕ 45 min. Metro: Gran Vía.

❷ C/ Augusto Figueroa. You can always tell Americans from Europeans by their shoes. To blend in (stylishly), head here for designer shoe outlets. Prices are cut drastically for classics at legendary Mallorcan manufacturer **Barrats,** C/ Augusto Figueroa, 20, and for the latest styles at **Farrutx,** C/ Augusto Figueroa, 18. ⊕ 45 min. Metro: Chueca.

❸ Plaza de Chueca. Find a seat at one of the cafe tables on the plaza to enjoy the street scene. There are some good boutiques as well, like **L'Habilleur,** Plaza de Chueca, 8, with designer clothing bargains. ⊕ 30 min. Metro: Chueca.

④ 🍴 ★ Antigua Casa Ángel Sierra. This is both an attraction in itself (just wait until you see the Andalucían tiles inside) and a good spot to sip the house vermouth with a dish of tuna in vinaigrette. C/ Gravina, 11. ☎ 91-531-01-26. $$.

❺ Santa Bárbara. Chueca isn't all boutiques and bars. The church of Santa Bárbara, in a monastery complex off Plaza de Santa Bárbara, anchors a refined residential neighborhood. Queen Bárbara de Bragança (1711–58) established the monastery expecting to retire there as a widow. She died before her husband, Fernando VII (1713–59), and they're buried together in extravagant marble tombs in the baroque church. Spain's Supreme Court occupies the monastery buildings. ⊕ 30 min. C/ Bárbara de Braganza, 1–3. ☎ 91-319-48-11. Church open for Mass only. Metro: Chueca, Colón.

❻ Palacio Longoria. Return to C/ Hortaleza along C/ Fernando VI, where you'll encounter the cream-colored, swirl-decorated home of the **Sociedad General de Autores y Editores,** central clearinghouse for royalties for Spanish authors. It is one of Madrid's most striking Modernista buildings. ⊕ 15 min. C/ Fernando VI, 4. ☎ 91-349-95-50. Metro: Alonso Martínez.

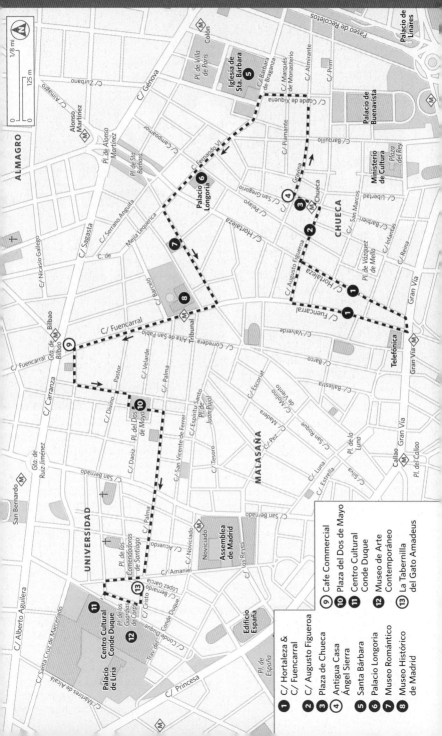

ALMAGRO

CHUECA

MALASAÑA

UNIVERSIDAD

1. C/ Hortaleza &
   C/ Fuencarral
2. C/ Augusto Figueroa
3. Plaza de Chueca
4. Antigua Casa
   Ángel Sierra
5. Santa Bárbara
6. Palacio Longoria
7. Museo Romántico
8. Museo Histórico
   de Madrid
9. Cafe Commercial
10. Plaza del Dos de Mayo
11. Centro Cultural
    Conde Duque
12. Museo de Arte
    Contemporáneo
13. La Tabernilla
    del Gato Amadeus

> *A zinc bar, Andalucían tiles, and house vermouth attract a mixed crowd at Antigua Casa Ángel Sierra.*

⑦ Museo Romántico. The Marqués de Vega-Inclán lived in the 20th century but belonged to another era. The dedicated aesthete made it his life's work to rescue everything picturesque about Spain, serving Alfonso XIII as Royal Commissioner of Tourism and Popular Artistic Culture. The Marqués had a special affinity for the Romantic period, and his collections of early-19th-century paintings, books, furniture, and curiosities are gathered into this idiosyncratic museum. Alas, he was better at acquiring than conserving. The museum is closed indefinitely for restoration, so just enjoy the handsome exterior of the 18th-century palace. ⏱ 15 min. C/ San Mateo, 13. ☎ 91-448-01-63. http://museo romantico.mcu.es. Metro: Tribunal.

⑧ Museo Histórico de Madrid. Baroque architect Pedro Ribera installed a terrific Churrigueresque doorway on the Hospital de San Fernando that he built from 1721 to 1726. For the time being, you'll have to be satisfied with studying its extravagant swirls: The wonderful city history museum, with its exquisite scale model of circa-1600 Madrid, is undergoing restoration. ⏱ 15 min. C/ Fuencarral, 78. ☎ 91-701-18-63. www.munimadrid.es/museodehistoria. Metro: Tribunal.

⑨ 🍷 Cafe Commercial. Stroll up C/ Fuencarral (or hop the Tribunal Metro one stop) to the Glorieta de Bilbao to enjoy a coffee at this meeting place. Artists and intellectuals have been admiring themselves in the mirrored walls since 1870. Glorieta de Bilbao, 7. ☎ 91-521-56-55. $.

⑩ Plaza del Dos de Mayo. Filled by day with teens skateboarding the plaza and children laughing in the playground, and by night with young adults socializing in cafes, this Malasaña plaza was twice the scene of revolt. On May 2, 1808, army commanders Daoíz and Velarde (whose barracks were here) led an uprising against the French occupiers after 15-year-old seamstress Manuela Malasaña was shot for defending herself with scissors. A double statue commemorates the heroes. And on May 2, 1976, a couple disrobed atop the statues as an expression of the rebirth of Spanish spirit after the death of Franco—an event some critics pinpoint as the birth of the Movida Madrileña, the hedonistic counterculture and newfound sense of freedom. ⏱ 10 min. Metro: Bilbao, Tribunal.

⓫ Centro Cultural Conde Duque. This immense red-brick compound with an extravagant baroque entrance was constructed in 1717 to house the Royal Guards. In another Madrileño example of beating swords into plowshares, now it's one of the city's most significant cultural institutions, housing the music library, city archives, a concert hall, and exhibition spaces. ⏱ 30 min. C/ Conde Duque, 11. ☎ 91-588-58-34. www.munimadrid.es/condeduque. Free. Tues–Sat 10am–2pm and 6–9pm; Sun 10:30am–2pm. Metro: Plaza de España, Ventura Rodriguez.

⓬ ★ Museo de Arte Contemporáneo. The Conde Duque (see previous) is home to this contemporary art museum, which mounts lively temporary exhibitions that complement rather than compete with the grander shows at the Reina Sofía. There's always some kind of Spanish connection, but many of the artists come from other European countries. Media range from graphic arts and painting on canvas to film and video. ⏱ 1 hr. C/ Conde Duque, 9. ☎ 91-588-59-28. www.munimadrid.es/condeduque. Free. Tues–Sat 10am–2pm and 5:30–9pm; Sun 10:30am–2:30pm. Metro: Plaza de España, Ventura Rodriguez.

⓭ 🍽 La Tabernilla del Gato Amadeus. Conde Duque patrons often gravitate to this literal hole in the wall where actor Javier Bardem's sister Monica makes acclaimed croquettes and serves good wine at bargain prices. See p. 133. C/ Cristo, 2. ☎ 91-541-41-12. $$.

> *Jose Grases Riera's Modernista confection houses the Sociedad General de Autores y Editores.*

Barrio de Las Letras

Writers, artists, and professional bohemians have hung out in the "District of Literature" since the first open-air theater was erected in this neighborhood in 1583. Miguel de Cervantes and Lope de Vega both lived here during the 16th-century Golden Age of Spanish letters, and poets, painters, and intellectuals argued in the cafes here in the 19th and early–20th centuries. Hemingway, of course, drank here. Cleaned up and tastefully gentrified, it remains a fashionable nightlife neighborhood still haunted by its literary giants.

> By nightfall, Plaza Santa Ana is the capital city's premier tapas spot.

START Metro to Sol.

❶ Puerta del Sol. This ancient square, which used to be the eastern gate to the city (aka the "Gate of the Sun"), has been fixed in art and literature. Goya memorialized the May 1808 massacre of civilians by French soldiers here in chilling detail. And both Hemingway and Orwell wrote of the horror of the street fighting here during the Civil War. ⊕ 30 min. See p. 74, ❻.

❷ Carrera de San Jerónimo. Walk up San Jerónimo, where a youthful Hemingway stayed at the Hostal Aguilar in 1923 because "that's where the bullfighters live." A plaque at the corner of C/ Victoria marks the spot of a legendary cafe, **Fontana del Oro.** If you want to meet the real bohemians, continue up Victoria to **Taberna Alhambra** (see p. 135), where Federico García Lorca (1898–1936) is said to have drunk when he had a play in town. Farther down San Jerónimo is **L'Hardy,** at Carretera San Jerónimo, 8, a tony cafe and restaurant that has been patronized by authors since it opened in 1839. According to 150-year-old gossip, Isabel II entertained her lovers in the upstairs dining room. ⊕ 30 min.

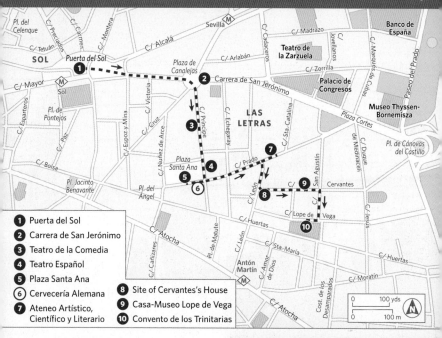

① Puerta del Sol
② Carrera de San Jerónimo
③ Teatro de la Comedia
④ Teatro Español
⑤ Plaza Santa Ana
⑥ Cervecería Alemana
⑦ Ateneo Artístico, Científico y Literario
⑧ Site of Cervantes's House
⑨ Casa-Museo Lope de Vega
⑩ Convento de los Trinitarias

③ **Teatro de la Comedia.** Currently closed for refurbishment, this theater with its curlicue wrought-iron decorations was deemed radically modern when it opened in 1875. It is the home of the Compañía Nacional de Clásico, which presents Spanish classical drama. During renovations, the company is performing at the Teatro Pavón (C/ Embajadores, 9; http://teatroclasico.mcu.es), near the La Latina Metro station.

④ **Teatro Español.** This lovely neoclassical theater from 1807 stands on the site of Madrid's first outdoor theater, the Corral des Comedias de Principe, which opened in 1583 and entertained the masses through the Golden Age of Spanish drama. Medallions along the theater's facade represent a who's who of Spanish playwrights, from 16th-century dramatist Pedro Calderón de la Barca (1600–81), on the far right, to Federico García Lorca, appropriately enough on the far left. Lorca's *Blood Wedding* debuted here in 1933 to resounding popular and critical success. A year later, *Yerma* was resoundingly panned. That's the stage for you. The theater remains an active venue for both plays and concerts. ⏱ 5 min. See p. 149.

⑤ ★★ **Plaza Santa Ana.** Showing his customary antipathy to religious orders, Joseph

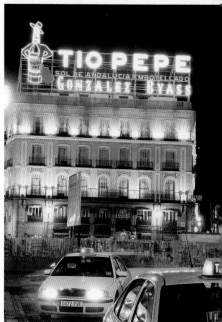

> *Public outcry at the removal of the hallmark Tío Pepe sign at Puerta del Sol brought the neon advertisement back.*

> *The Teatro Español runs a program of crowd-pleasing Spanish plays, dance, and music.*

> *Break for a café or cerveza in Plaza Santa Ana.*

Bonaparte had the Convento de Santa Ana torn down in 1810, replacing it with this square that is now bracketed by the coolly classic Teatro Español and the self-consciously stylish ME by Meliá hotel. Situated where the streets leading from the neighborhoods of Sol, Lavapiés, and La Latina all converge, Plaza Santa Ana is a busy spot. A thousand little dramas unfold at the cafe tables, on the benches, or on the children's playground. By evening, it's Madrid's premier tapas locale.

Filmmaker Pedro Almodóvar trained his cameras on the tiled walls of Villa Rosa, Plaza de Santa Ana, 15, when he needed a bar scene for *High Heels* (1991). Even newcomer bars on the square affect a sepia-toned antiquity to suggest that, yes, they served Orson Welles and Ernest Hemingway. Heck, they probably even served Lope de Vega. ⏱ 30 min. Metro: Sol or Antón Martín.

⑥ 🍺 **Cervecería Alemana.** When Hemingway drank beer (instead of rum or brandy), he often did so at this bar, which retains a Teutonic *bierkeller* pub atmosphere to this day. Swagger in for a pint and tapa of dynamite potato salad. Plaza Santa Ana, 6. ☎ 91-429-70-33. $$.

❼ **Ateneo Artístico, Científico y Literario.** Walk down C/ Prado from Plaza Santa Ana to have a gander at this marvelously old-fashioned institution. The private library for the study of

> *Houses-turned-museums dedicated to local writers, poets, and artists are big in Spain, and Lope de Vega's is worth a visit.*

arts and science was established in 1820 and has been at this location since the Civil War. If the doorman is indulgent, he might let you peek inside to see the glossy wooden stacks. ⏱ 5 min. C/ Prado 21. Metro: Antón Martín.

❽ Site of Cervantes's House. Poor Cervantes! The author who gave the Spanish people their language left few artifacts behind. Follow C/ León to the corner with C/ Cervantes, where a small plaque marks the spot where his very modest house stood until 1833. ⏱ 5 min.

❾ ★★ Casa-Museo Lope de Vega. Félix Lope de Vega y Carpio (1562–1635), who popularized the Madrid vernacular by putting it in the mouths of his characters, has fared somewhat better. He was astonishingly prolific—his 425 surviving plays are estimated to be only a third of his output. But this "lover, writer, husband, and priest," as the guides at his house-museum call him, did everything to excess. He married three times, fathered innumerable children (some legitimate, some not), and was embroiled in multiple lawsuits over his amorous pursuits. In a Renaissance version of rehab, he

became a priest at age 50 and had a window installed in his bedroom overlooking the altar of his chapel. The house was badly damaged in the Civil War, and the subsequent restoration takes some liberties with strictly historical interpretation. Lope de Vega wouldn't have minded—as long as the audience applauded. ⏱ 1 hr. C/ Cervantes, 11. ☎ 91-429-92-16. Free. Tues-Fri 9:30am–2pm; Sat 10am–2pm. Metro: Antón Martín.

❿ Convento de los Trinitarias. From the decadent old playwright-priest's house, turn right on C/ de Augustin and quickly right again on C/ Lope de Vega to reach this venerable convent. Daughters of both Cervantes and Lope de Vega became nuns here, and when Cervantes died in poverty in 1616, he was buried in the convent church. (His wife was also buried here.) Over the years, the exact location of the bones has been lost, but a large marble plaque on the exterior wall commemorates the author of *Don Quixote*. The convent is a closed order but the church is open for Mass. ⏱ 15 min. C/ Lope de Vega, s/n. Free. Masses Mon-Fri 9:30am; Sat 7:30am; Sun 10am and noon. Metro: Antón Martín.

Madrid Shopping Best Bets

Best Luxury Leather Goods
Loewe, C/ Serrano, 26 (see p. 121)

Best Traditional Garment Shop
Capas Seseña, C/ Cruz, 23 (see p. 125)

Best Flea Market
El Rastro, C/ Ribera de Curtidores (see p. 111)

Best One-Stop Shopping
Príncipe Pío, Paseo de la Florida, s/n (see p. 122)

Best Shoe Splurge
Gaytan, C/ Jorge Juan, 15 (see p. 125)

Best Shoe Bargain
Casa Hernanz, C/ Toledo, 18 (see p. 125)

Best All-Around Flamenco
El Flamenco Vive, C/ Conde de Lemos, 7 (see p. 125)

Best Gifts
Perfumería Alvarez Gómez, C/ Serrano, 14 (see p. 125)

Best Bargain Style
Zara, C/ Preciados, 18 (see p. 122)

Most Theatrical Boutique
Agatha Ruiz de la Prada, C/ Serrano, 27 (see p. 121)

> *Fans of El Rastro flea market.*

Madrid Shopping A to Z

Antiques & Art

Galerías Piquer LAVAPIÉS

Antiques dealers have set up shop on the lower end of Ribera de Curtidores, and this grouping of about 70 small dealers offers a little something for everyone. The courtyard setting makes for tranquil browsing. C/ Ribera de Curtidores, 29. No central phone. www.dai.es/piquer. Metro: La Latina.

Artisanal Crafts

El Arco Artesanía LA LATINA

The selections of leather work, ceramics, and silver jewelry are particularly strong in this shop displaying the work of contemporary Spanish artisans. Plaza Mayor, 9. ☎ 91-365-26-80. AE, MC, V. Metro: Ópera.

Ceramics

★ Antigua "Casa Talavera" GRAN VÍA

The helpful proprietor will watch your bulky bags as you browse carefully in this small shop filled to the brim with hand-painted ceramics in traditional and more modern styles. It's the perfect place to find a showpiece pitcher or a fun olive serving dish. C/ Isabel La Catolica, 2. ☎ 91-547-34-17. AE, MC, V. Metro: Santo Domingo.

Contemporary Fashion

Agatha Ruiz de la Prada SALAMANCA

The bright colors and playful designs of this popular Spanish designer adapt beautifully to clothing (for men, women, and children), housewares, and stylish accessories. Don't miss the sunglasses. C/ Serrano, 27. ☎ 933-19-05-51. www.agatharuizdelaprada.com. AE, MC, V. Metro: Serrano.

★★ Loewe SALAMANCA

Gorgeous leather goods and high-fashion clothing have the classic good taste that befits investment-level prices. C/ Serrano, 26. ☎ 91-577-60-56. www.loewe.es. AE, MC, V. Metro: Serrano.

> *Traditional ceramics at Antigua "Casa Talavera."*

> *Department store El Corte Inglés has a little bit of everything.*

Zara SOL

This hugely popular Spanish fashion chain specializes in interpreting the latest runway styles for fashionistas on a budget—and in a hurry. One of several branches in the city. C/ Preciados, 18. ☎ 91-521-09-58. www.zara.com. AE, DC, MC, V. Metro: Sol or Callao.

Department Stores & Shopping Centers
ABC Serrano SALAMANCA

A neoclassical former newspaper building has been converted to a shopping center to meet the needs of the discerning residents of the Salamanca neighborhood. Entrances at C/ Serrano, 61, or C/ Castellana, 34. ☎ 91-577-50-31. www.abcserrano.com. AE, DC, MC, V. Metro: Serrano or Núñez de Balboa.

★★ El Corte Inglés SOL

Smaller branches of this all-purpose department store are scattered around the city, but the main installation at Preciados has the most thorough selections of almost anything you'd want to buy. The grocery store is strong on Spanish wines and olive oils, while cosmetics has all the Spanish powders and scents. C/ Preciados, 3. ☎ 91-379-80-00. www.elcorteingles.es. AE, DC, MC, V. Metro: Sol.

★ Príncipe Pío PRÍNCIPE PÍO

The soaring height and glass roof of a landmark 19th-century train station make for an especially light and bright shopping center, with a good mix of shops, restaurants, and even a movie theater. Paseo de la Florida, s/n. ☎ 91-758-00-40. www.ccprincipepio.com. Metro: Príncipe Pío.

Guitars & Music
Conde Hermanos ÓPERA

One of the legendary custom makers of

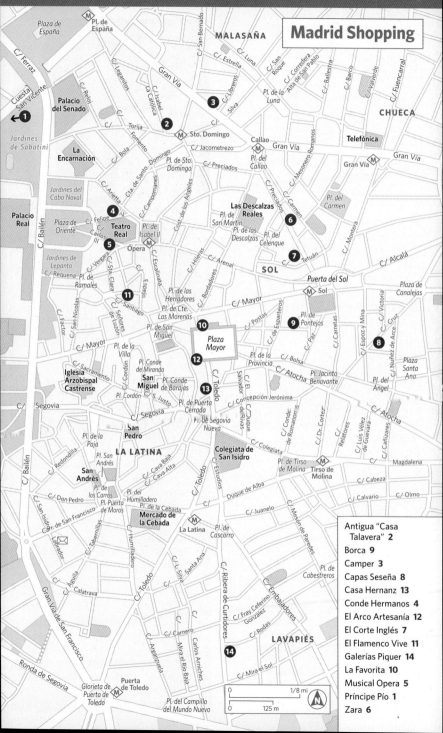

Madrid Shopping

Antigua "Casa Talavera" **2**

Borca **9**

Camper **3**

Capas Seseña **8**

Casa Hernanz **13**

Conde Hermanos **4**

El Arco Artesanía **12**

El Corte Inglés **7**

El Flamenco Vive **11**

Galerías Piquer **14**

La Favorita **10**

Musical Opera **5**

Príncipe Pío **1**

Zara **6**

Salamanca Shopping

ABC Serrano **1**
Agatha Ruiz
   de la Prada **2**
Gaytan **4**
Loewe **3**
Perfumería Alvarez
   Gómez **5**

Destination Shopping

Dedicated shoppers know that no one store (not even El Corte Ingles) satisfies all cravings. Here's where the browsing is best:

C/ Preciados

This street stretching between Puerta del Sol and Gran Vía not only has the city's largest branch of El Corte Ingles, but it also boasts the electronics (and music) giant FNAC and a host of small *perfumerías* and boutiques.

Chueca

The most gay-friendly neighborhood in Madrid also happens to have the city's best shoe shopping, especially in factory outlet stores of brands such as Barrats and Figueroa. Find the best concentration of footwear and other leather goods on C/ Augusto Figueroa.

Salamanca

Even if you're just peering in the windows, this upscale neighborhood epitomizes Madrileño fashion—less self-conscious than Barcelona, hipper than Paris.

★ El Rastro

At the other end of the economic spectrum, this venerable Sunday street market streams down C/ Ribera de Curtidores with inexpensive clothes, household goods, pop-culture collectibles, and even a few antiques (see p. 111, **12**).

classical and flamenco guitars, Conde Hermanos maintains a salesroom here at Ópera, while the factory is in Las Letras. Prebuilt models are also available. C/ Felipe V, 2. ☎ 91-429-93-33. www. condehermanos.com. AE, MC, V. Metro: Ópera.

★★ El Flamenco Vive ÓPERA
This shop is the nerve center of Madrid's flamenco scene. If there's a performance in town, the staff will know. Guitars, dance shoes and dresses, sheet music, books, and CDs are jammed into the tiny space. If it's flamenco, it's here. C/ Conde de Lemos, 7. ☎ 91-547-39-17. AE, MC, V. Metro: Ópera.

Musical Opera ÓPERA
Spanish music isn't all about guitars, though Musical Opera does carry a wide range of student guitars. But the classical instruments—from tubas and trumpets to timpani and xylophones—are this music shop's forte. It also carries an excellent selection of sheet music in every genre from classical études to modern jazz. C/ Carlos III, 1. ☎ 91-540-16-72. www.musical opera.com. MC, V. Metro: Ópera.

Shoes
Camper GRAN VÍA
Comfort and quirky style are the hallmarks of this wildly popular Spanish shoe manufacturer. This is one of several outlets in the city. Gran Vía, 54. ☎ 91-547-52-23. www.camper.es. AE, DC, MC, V. Metro: Gran Vía.

★★ Casa Hernanz LA LATINA
Don't be put off by the line of women snaking out the door. Helpful counter clerks keep things moving quickly in this tiny shop that specializes in hand-sewn espadrilles. C/ Toledo, 18. ☎ 91-366-54-50. MC, V. Metro: Ópera.

★★ Gaytan SALAMANCA
If you're ready to splurge on a pair of hand-crafted leather shoes, this is the place to do it. A custom pair of shoes takes 2 to 3 weeks and can be shipped to the United States. C/ Jorge Juan, 15. ☎ 91-435-28-24. AE, MC, V. Metro: Serrano or Velázquez.

Toiletries
★ Perfumería Alvarez Gómez SALAMANCA
This charmingly old-fashioned perfume manufacturer is best known for the citrus-based Agua de Colonia, but it offers a wide variety of soaps and concentrated bath gels

> *El Flamenco Vive, for the enthusiast.*

and shampoos. C/ Serrano, 14. ☎ 91-431-16-56. AE, DC, MC, V. Metro: Serrano.

Traditional Fashion
Borca SOL
Whatever your price range, this is a good place to look for a classic embroidered fringed shawl, or *mantilla*. C/ Marqués Viudo de Pontejos, 2. ☎ 91-532-61-53. AE, MC, V. Metro: Sol.

★★ Capas Seseña SOL
This shop has been supplying Madrileños with capes for more than a century. They offer a variety of styles and fabrics to suit every taste, with prices you'd expect for a fine, hand-sewn garment. C/ Cruz, 23. ☎ 91-531-68-40. www. sesena.com. AE, MC, V. Metro: Sol.

La Favorita LA LATINA
The slightly more constructed Basque cap is the Spanish answer to the French beret. You'll find a variety of styles and colors for both men and women. Plaza Mayor, 25. ☎ 91-366-58-77. www.lafavoritacb.com. AE, DC, MC, V. Metro: Ópera.

IBERIAN COMFORT FOOD

Tapas on the Menu

BY PATRICIA HARRIS & DAVID LYON

TAPAS (known in the Basque country as *pintxos*) are how Spaniards avoid drinking on an empty stomach. These little plates (the most common of which are listed below) make up the unofficial fourth meal of the day, best enjoyed in boisterous bars before the 10pm dinner hour. The morsels are a Spanish way of life—the purest distillations of iconic Iberian flavors.

PIMIENTOS
Baked stuffed *piquillo* peppers grace bars all over Spain, but they become especially artful plates in the Basque country, where the peppers are grown. Depending on the season, they may be red or green, but the stuffing is almost always a blend of salt cod and mashed potato.

vinegar, or olive oil. *Boquerónes* are usually pickled.

TORTILLA ESPAÑOLA
Spaniards have the recipe for this thick potato omelet imprinted in their genes, yet every cook has a personal twist, sometimes adding diced red peppers, onion, sausage, ham, or flakes of tuna.

ALBÓNDIGAS
These pork mini-meatballs in gravy are usually served in small casserole dishes, often with a few slices of bread to sop up the gravy. *Albóndigas* are popular winter tapas, eaten with strong spirits to ward off the chill.

BOQUERÓNES
Nobody can rival the Spaniards for their love of anchovies, which are eaten grilled or deep-fried when fresh, or as fillets on a plate when preserved in salt,

JAMÓN SERRANO
This air-dried mountain ham is among the country's greatest delicacies. Accompanied by breadsticks, it is usually sliced so thin that you could see through it—if there were more light in the bar.

PATATAS BRAVAS
Invented by the Bravas bar in Madrid (which holds the patent), these fried potatoes smothered in piquant, bright-orange paprika-garlic sauce have become a national standard. Spear the potatoes with toothpicks.

What's on Tap

The *tapa* (Spanish for "cover") originated in 19th-century Andalucía as a lid for sherry glasses to keep flies out of the drink, and sherry is still the beverage of choice in many tapas bars of southern Spain. Nationwide, the most common beverage consumed with tapas is probably *cerveza*, or beer, usually ordered by the small glass, or *caña*. Very traditional bars often encourage patrons to drink what the house has in barrels—either a local wine or the rough but bracing native *vermut* (vermouth). In Asturias, Cantabria, and some parts of the Basque country, *sidra* (hard apple cider) is the preferred libation. But you can also order tapas with nonalcoholic beverages.

Madrid Restaurant Best Bets

Best for Gourmets
Sergi Arola Gastro $$$$ C/ Zurbano, 31
(see p. 135)

Best *Tortilla Española*
Cervecería José Luis $$ C/ Serrano, 89–91
(see p. 132)

Best Traditional Tapas
Taberna del Alabardero $$ C/ Felipe V, 6
(see p. 135)

Best Bargain Creative Food
Bazaar Restaurant $ C/ Libertad, 21
(see p. 129)

Best Fresh Market Cuisine
Casa Juli $$ C/ Gobernación, 12, Aranjuez
(see p. 129)

Best Bullfight Atmosphere
Taberna de Antonio Sanchez $ C/ Méson de
Paredes, 13 (see p. 135)

Best Tourist Magnet
Restaurante Botín $$$ C/ Cuchilleros, 17
(see p. 134)

Best Healthy Fast Food
Fast Good $ C/ Tetuan, 3 (see p. 133)

Best *Asador*
Casa Julián de Tolosa $$$ Cava Baja, 18
(see p. 129)

Best Traditional Tiles
Taberna Alhambra $ C/ Victoria, 9 (see p. 135)

Best *Bocadillos*
El Brillante $ C/ Atocha, 122 (see p. 132)

Best Creative Tapas
Estado Puro $ Plaza Cánovas del Castillo, 4
(see p. 133)

Best *Chocolate con Churros*
Chocolatería San Ginés $ C/ Pasadizo de San
Ginés, 5 (see p. 132)

> *Suckling pig goes into the oven at Restaurante Botín.*

Madrid Restaurants A to Z

★ **Bazaar Restaurant** CHUECA *CONTEMPORARY*
This chic spot with all-white decor opens unusually early at 8:30pm, but you won't be seated only with fellow tourists unaccustomed to dining at 10pm—the reasonably priced small plates are popular with young Spaniards. C/ Libertad, 21. ☎ 91-523-39-05. Entrees 7€–13€. AE, DC, MC, V. Lunch & dinner daily. Metro: Chueca.

Bocaito CHUECA *SPANISH*
Families pack the tables, but many diners order full meals (fried pork sweetbreads, for example, or a pork chop with salad and fries) to eat standing at one of the two bars. It's loud, smoky—and delicious. C/ Libertad, 4–6. ☎ 91-532-12-19. Entrees 8€–20€. AE, DC, MC, V. Lunch & dinner Mon–Sat. Metro: Chueca.

Casa Juli ARANJUEZ *CASTILIAN*
You won't need a menu—the waiter will tell you what the cook purchased at the market. April to June, that means white asparagus; May to July, fresh strawberries. Local lamb (spring to early summer) is some of the best in the world. C/ Gobernación, 12. ☎ 91-892-58-43. Entrees 12€–17€. AE, DC, MC, V. Lunch Tues–Sun, dinner Tues–Sat.

★ **Casa Julián de Tolosa** LA LATINA *BASQUE*
This spectacular Basque *asador* (grill shop) in the midst of casual tapas bars upholds its Tolosa roots with perfect steak and red peppers. Cava Baja, 18. ☎ 91-365-82-10. Entrees 14€–24€. AE, MC, V. Lunch daily, dinner Mon–Sat. Metro: La Latina.

Casa Marta ÓPERA *SPANISH*
In some restaurants, the bar crowd can overwhelm the diners. But in this family-run spot, the bar is for a quick drink while waiting for a table. The menu is strong on comfort fare such as tuna croquettes, veal-and-almond meatballs, and garlic soup. C/ Santa Clara, 10. ☎ 91-548-28-25. Entrees 6€–12€. MC, V. Lunch & dinner daily. Metro: Ópera.

> *A small plate at Bazaar.*

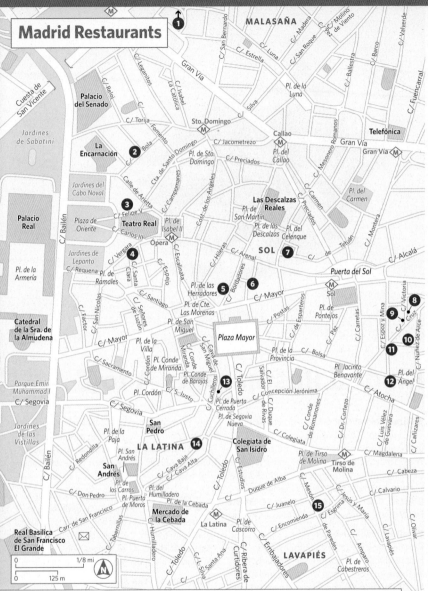

Madrid Restaurants

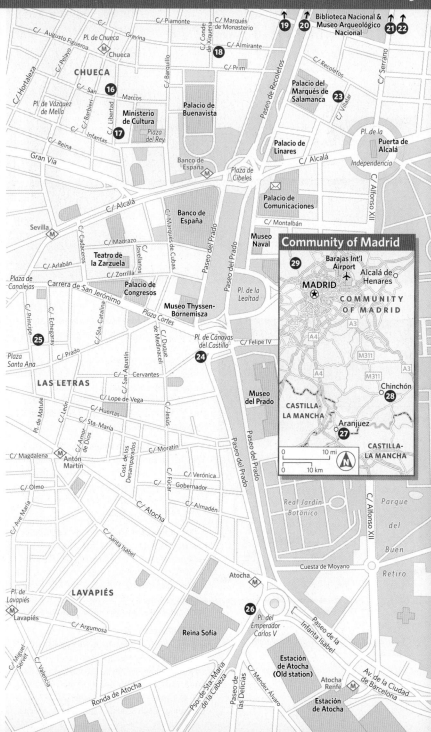

> Montaditos *coming up (or down) at José Luis.*

> Churros *and hot chocolate at Chocolatería San Ginés.*

★★ **Cervecería José Luis** SALAMANCA *SPANISH*
An outdoor relief sculpture of a dining room identifies this Serrano stalwart, but the scene inside is even more interesting. Diners stand at the marble-paneled bar to nibble *montaditos* (small sandwiches) while having their shoes shined. C/ Serrano, 89–91. ☎ 91-563-09-58. Entrees 12€–20€. AE, MC, V. Lunch & dinner daily. Metro: Gregorio Marañon.

★★ **Chocolatería San Ginés** SOL *CAFE*
This institution, with a classy marble bar, knows that hot chocolate and *churros* are perfect any time of day—or night. C/ Pasadizo de San Ginés, 5. ☎ 91-365-65-46. Daily 9am–6am. No credit cards. Metro: Sol or Ópera.

★ **Dassa Bassa** RECOLETOS *CONTEMPORARY SPANISH* Popular TV chef Dario Barrio produces adventurous cuisine based on seasonal produce. Dishes combine sensational tastes with wit and panache. C/ Villalar, 7. ☎ 91-576-73-97. Entrees 24€–42€. AE, DC, MC, V. Lunch & dinner Tues–Sat, closed 3 weeks in Aug. Metro: Atocha.

★ **El Brillante** PASEOS *SPANISH*
Overstuffed sandwiches on fresh rolls lure diners all day. A fried calamari sandwich will stave off hunger while you're visiting the Reina Sofía museum on the same plaza. C/ Atocha, 122. ☎ 91-468-05-48. Sandwiches 2.50€–7€. Cash only. Lunch & dinner daily. Metro: Atocha.

> *A dining room at Restaurante Botín.*

El Ñeru SOL *ASTURIAN*
A lively tapas scene signals the popularity of this Asturian restaurant. Head to the dining room downstairs to try hake braised in cider or hearty *fabada Asturiana,* a stew of white beans, ham, and sausage. C/ Bordadores, 5. ☎ 91-541-11-40. Entrees 10€–20€. AE, MC, V. Lunch & dinner Tues–Sun. Metro: Sol or Ópera.

★ Estado Puro PASEOS *CONTEMPORARY SPANISH* Celebrity chef Paco Roncero turns classic tapas inside out at this whimsical bar where a *tortilla española* is deconstructed into a soup. Plaza Cánovas del Castillo, 4. ☎ 91-573-95-54. Plates 4€–15€. AE, DC, MC, V. Lunch daily, dinner Tues–Sat. Metro: Atocha.

Fast Good SOL *CONTEMPORARY SPANISH* Spanish superchef Ferran Adrià is the mastermind behind this casual eatery with fast service and healthy food. It's not high cuisine, but you'll be happy with a mushroom panino or roast chicken and couscous. C/ Tetuan, 3. ☎ 91-523-04-56. www.fast-good.com. Salads and sandwiches 5€–7€. MC, V. Lunch & dinner daily. Metro: Sol.

Ginger LAS LETRAS *CONTEMPORARY SPANISH* The small and artfully plated dishes are not much larger than some of the tapas served in Plaza Santa Ana bars. But they are reasonably priced, and you'll be able to sit at a table in the pretty dining room. Plaza del Ángel, 12. ☎ 91-369-10-59. www.restauranteginger.com. Entrees 7€–10€. AE, MC, V. Lunch & dinner daily. Metro: Tirso de Mólina.

La Bola Taberna ÓPERA *CASTILIAN*
This is the place to try Madrid's classic *cocido,* a stew of mixed meats and sausages that includes tripe and other offal. Not feeling adventurous? Select a few tapas and still enjoy the atmosphere of this 1870s Madrid institution. C/ Bola, 5. ☎ 91-547-69-30. Entrees 6.50€–20€. Cash only. Lunch daily, dinner Mon–Sat. Metro: Ópera.

★★ La Casa del Abuelo LAS LETRAS *SEAFOOD* This family-run restaurant opened in 1906 to serve shrimp, langostinos, and sweet wine. It proved to be a winning formula. Share a small plate of simply grilled shrimp and another of breaded shrimp fried in olive oil. C/ Victoria, 12. ☎ 91-521-23-19. www.lacasadelabuelo.es. Entrees 8€–14€. DC, MC, V. Lunch & dinner daily. Metro: Sevilla.

★ Las Bravas LAS LETRAS *SPANISH* Potatoes doused with *bravas* sauce are a bar staple. Try them at the spot that claims to have invented the spicy red paprika sauce. It's equally good on *tortilla española.* C/ Espoz y Mina, 13. ☎ 91-521-35-07. Entrees 4€–10€. Cash only. Lunch & dinner daily. Metro: Sevilla.

> *Taberna de Antonio Sanchez.*

> *Sergi Arola's ubermodern Gastro.*

La Tabernilla del Gato Amadeus MALASAÑA

SPANISH You probably won't see actor Javier Bardem here in his sister Monica's tiny bar. But her ham or *bacalao* (salted cod) croquettes are so good that you'll forget to be disappointed. C/ Cristo, 2. ☎ 91-541-41-12. Entrees 6€–13€. Cash only. Lunch Tues–Sun, dinner daily. Metro: Plaza de España.

La Trucha LAS LETRAS *SPANISH*

La Trucha's smoked trout on toast rates high on most lists of top Santa Ana tapas. But you can also enjoy a full meal of roast cod or home-style stewed oxtail in the small dining room or outdoor terrace. C/ Manuel Fernández y González, 3. ☎ 91-429-58-33. Entrees 12€–26€. AE, MC, V. Lunch & dinner daily. Metro: Antón Martín.

★ Maitetxu Asador CHUECA *BASQUE*

Madrid has more famous Basque restaurants, but this small spot with a big wood-burning grill

is a neighborhood favorite. A whole grilled sea bream for two is the house specialty. C/ Almirante, 2. ☎ 91-531-01-09. Entrees 11€–31€. MC, V. Lunch Mon–Sat, dinner Thurs–Sat. Metro: Chueca.

★★ Pedro Larumbe Restaurante SALAMANCA

CONTEMPORARY SPANISH This award-winning chef prepares dishes that are as elegant as his richly furnished late-19th-century dining rooms. His genius is to reimagine the familiar, like a napoleon of foie gras and caramelized mango. C/ Serrano, 61. ☎ 91-575-51-11. Entrees 16€–26€. AE, DC, MC, V. Lunch Mon–Fri, dinner Mon–Sat. Metro: Serrano.

Restaurante Botín LA LATINA *SPANISH*

Admittedly a tourist trap, Botín has been in business since 1725, and its atmospheric warren of tiny dining rooms will enhance your enjoyment of the house-specialty roast suckling pig or other roasted or grilled meats. C/ Cuchilleros, 17. ☎ 91-366-42-17. Entrees 9€–27€. AE, DC, MC, V. Lunch & dinner daily. Metro: Ópera.

Restaurante El Torreon EL PARDO *SPANISH*

Opt to dine outdoors on the lawn at this lovely restaurant popular for first communions and other big family events. You can eat lighter and more casually from the large tapas selection at the bar. Carretera Cristo de El Pardo, s/n. ☎ 91-376-09-46. Entrees 12€–24€. AE, DC, MC, V. Lunch & dinner daily.

Restaurante Plaza Mayor CHINCHON *SPANISH*

Wood-beamed dining rooms exude rustic charm, but the prize tables are on the balcony

> Montaditos *at Taberna del Alabardero.*

overlooking the plaza. It's hard to go wrong with either roast lamb or veal chops. Plaza Mayor, 10. ☎ 91-894-09-29. Entrees 13€–21€. AE, DC, MC, V. Lunch Tues–Sun, dinner Tues–Sat.

★★★ **Sergi Arola Gastro** CHAMBERI
CONTEMPORARY SPANISH This flagship of superchef Sergi Arola has been called formal, sexy, and surprising—and it's all three. Arola believes in plating a few intense flavors per dish, cooking the way Miró painted. It's all or nothing here—no ordering a la carte. C/ Zurbano, 31. ☎ 91-310-21-69. Tasting menus 85€–130€. AE, DC, MC, V. Lunch Mon–Fri, dinner Mon–Sat. Metro: Rubén Darío.

Taberna Alhambra LAS LETRAS *ANDALUCIAN*
The walls of this 1929 tavern are covered with tiles designed by Alfonso Romero, the tile master of Las Ventas bullring. The best food choices are easy to eat while standing in a crowd: sausages, croquettes, or smoked and dried tuna. C/ Victoria, 9. ☎ 91-521-07-08. Tapas and *raciones* 3€–14€. Cash only. Lunch & dinner daily. Metro: Sevilla.

Taberna de Antonio Sanchez LAS LETRAS
SPANISH You'll probably dine in the company of bullfight fans in this 1830s bar with photos of matadors on the wall. Don't expect culinary innovation, just solid versions of classic tapas and small casseroles, such as white beans, sausage, or meatballs in wine. C/ Méson de Paredes, 13.

☎ 91-539-78-36. Entrees 9€–14€. Cash only. Lunch & dinner daily. Metro: Tirso de Mólina.

★★ **Taberna del Alabardero** OPERA *BASQUE*
This Basque-style restaurant is part of a group that trains youth for restaurant careers. Good deeds aside, they take the food seriously. Try the hake and clams in parsley sauce or oxtail stewed with honey and cinnamon. C/ Felipe V, 6. ☎ 91-547-25-77. Entrees 18€–25€. MC, V. Lunch & dinner daily. Metro: Ópera.

Taberna La Fragua de Vulcano LAS LETRAS
SPANISH It may be new, but with its old-style Andalucían tiles and classic choices of Spanish tapas, the "forge of Vulcan" feels like it's been around since the mythological blacksmith was a pup. It even serves some saffron rice dishes sold as either seafood or chicken paella. C/ Alvarez Gato, 9. ☎ 91-522-36-05. Entrees 5€–12€. Cash only. Lunch & dinner daily (closed Mon Jan–Sept). Metro: Sol.

★★★ **Villa Magna by Eneko Atxa** RECOLETOS
CONTEMPORARY BASQUE Madrid's new power dining room features innovative cuisine bound to make you smile. You have to love a chef who cooks an egg yolk from the inside out by injecting it with superheated truffle juice. Paseo Castellana, 22. ☎ 91-587-12-34. Entrees 36€–48€. AE, DC, MC, V. Lunch & dinner daily. Metro: Rubén Darío.

Madrid Hotel Best Bets

Best Contemporary Luxury
Villa Magna $$$$ Paseo Castellana, 22
(see p. 141)

Best for Backpackers
IYH Posada de Huertas $ C/ Huertas, 21
(see p. 140)

Best for Museumgoers
HUSA Hotel Paseo del Arte $$ C/ Atocha, 123
(see p. 140)

Best for Families
Room Mate Laura $$$ Travesía de Trujillos, 3
(see p. 141)

Best Old City Location
Hotel Moderno $$ C/ Arenal, 2 (see p. 140)

Best Affordable Charm
Hotel Plaza Mayor $$ C/ Atocha, 2 (see p. 140)

Best Boutique Hotel
Vincci SoMa $$$ C/ Goya, 79 (see p. 141)

Best for Would-Be Aristocrats
The Ritz $$$$ Plaza de la Lealtad, 5 (see p. 141)

Best Traditional Elegance
Westin Palace $$$$ Plaza de las Cortes, 7
(see p. 141)

Best for the Young & Hip
Room Mate Óscar $$$ Plaza Vásquez de Mella,
12 (see p. 141)

Best for Romance
Hotel Ópera $$ Cuesta de Santo Domingo,
2 (see p. 140)

> *Hotel Plaza Mayor on Plaza Santa Cruz.*

Madrid Hotels A to Z

AC Recoletos RECOLETOS
This gracious hotel in a stately 19th-century neoclassical building makes a good base for museum hopping and Salamanca shopping. The updated interior features clean-lined furniture and a soothing neutral color palette. C/ Recoletos, 18. ☎ 91-436-13-82. www.ac-hotels. com. 63 rooms. Doubles 120€–170€. AE, DC, MC, V. Metro: Colón.

Best Western Premier Santo Domingo ÓPERA
The owner's vast collection of mostly baroque art and antiques lends this hotel an air of decorum. Rooms are spacious and comfortable. Plaza de Santo Domingo, 13. ☎ 91-547-98-00. www.hotelsantodomingo.com. 119 rooms. Doubles 75€–178€. AE, MC, V. Metro: Santo Domingo.

Catalonia Las Cortes LAS LETRAS
Opened in 2006, this updated traditional hotel adds some formality to the busy streets near Plaza Santa Ana. In a superior room, you might sleep beneath a ceiling mural from the original 18th-century palace. C/ del Prado, 6. ☎ 91-389-60-51. www.hoteles-catalonia.com. 65 rooms. Doubles 89€–160€. AE, MC, V. Metro: Sevilla.

High Tech-Petit Palace Posada del Peine SOL
The hotel has rental bicycles, but you won't need one to explore the Old City from this central spot between Plaza Mayor and Puerta del Sol. Every room in this contemporary hotel in a historic shell sports a computer. C/ Postas, 17. ☎ 91-523-81-51. www.hthoteles.com. 71 rooms. Doubles 80€–114€. AE, MC, V. Metro: SOL.

★ Hostal Macarena LA LATINA
Cheery plantings of geraniums on the balconies hint at the care that goes into maintaining the simple but stylish rooms in this second-floor *hostal*. Rooms are large for budget lodging near Plaza Mayor. Cava de San Miguel, 8. ☎ 91-365-92-21. www.silserranos.com. 18 rooms. Doubles 59€–79€. MC, V. Metro: Ópera.

> *The stained-glass rotunda of the Westin Palace.*

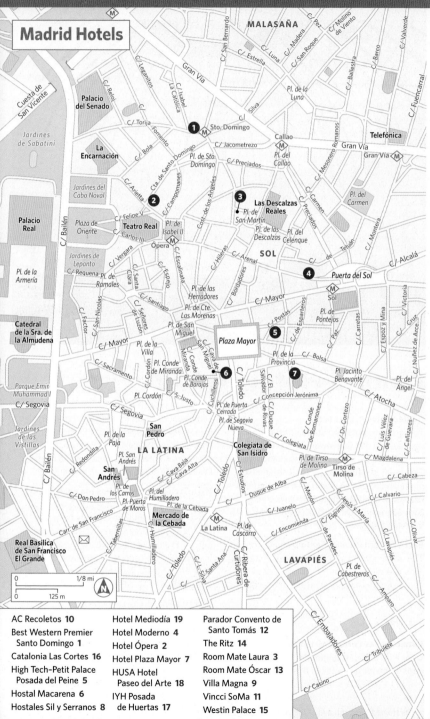

Madrid Hotels

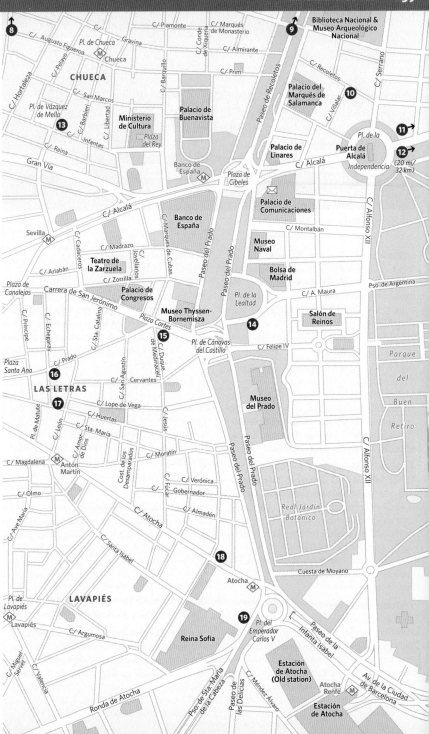

> *HUSA Hotel Paseo del Arte offers real deals.*

★ Hostales Sil y Serranos CHUECA
Triple or quadruple rooms are a good option for families in this recently renovated *hostal*. Most rooms have new marble and tile bathrooms and unfussy traditional decor. C/ Fuencarral, 95, 2nd floor. ☎ 91-448-89-72. www.silserranos.com. 29 rooms. Doubles 59€–79€. MC, V. Metro: Gran Vía.

Hotel Mediodía PASEOS
Built in 1914 in the neoclassical French style, Mediodía has generous public spaces for relaxation. Many of the bright, basic guest rooms look out on the Reina Sofía museum or Atocha train station. Plaza del Emperador Carlos V, 8. ☎ 91-530-70-08. www.mediodiahotel.com. 173 rooms. Doubles 65€–90€. AE, MC, V. Metro: Atocha.

★★ Hotel Moderno SOL
The same family has run this hotel since it opened in 1939, and their dedication is obvious in the ongoing updates and careful choice of colors and furnishings. If you splurge on 1 of 17 rooms with an outdoor terrace, ask for one facing C/ Arenal for the best view. C/ Arenal, 2. ☎ 91-531-09-00. www.hotel-moderno.com. 97 rooms. Doubles 75€–162€. AE, DC, MC, V. Metro: Sol.

★★ Hotel Ópera ÓPERA
The hotel's boxy exterior won't win any awards, but the rooms are full of contemporary style and character. Some have sloping ceilings with skylights, while five have outdoor terraces with sweeping city views. Cuesta de Santo Domingo, 2. ☎ 91-541-28-00. www.hotelopera.com. 79 rooms. Doubles 99€–149€ w/breakfast. AE, DC, MC, V. Metro: Ópera.

★★ Hotel Plaza Mayor LA LATINA
Fitting a modern hotel into a 200-year-old church building made for some oddly shaped rooms, but that only adds to the charm. The hotel sits on Plaza Santa Cruz; book a superior room for a view of the lovely old square. C/ Atocha, 2. ☎ 91-360-06-06. www.h-plazamayor.com. 34 rooms. Doubles 69€–95€. AE, DC, MC, V. Metro: Tirso de Mólina.

★★ HUSA Hotel Paseo del Arte ATOCHA
This 2006 hotel with contemporary international style often hosts small conferences. But the level of service and comfort can't be beat, and the location near the art museums is terrific. You could land a real deal on a slow night. C/ Atocha, 123. ☎ 91-298-48-00. www.husa.es. 260 rooms. Doubles 90€–160€. AE, DC, MC, V. Metro: Atocha.

★ IYH Posada de Huertas LAS LETRAS
Rooms around a central patio encourage camaraderie in this well-run hostel. Eight-bed dorms are furnished to maximize privacy. Some double rooms are available. Guests share bathrooms, laundry, computers, and a kitchen. C/ Huertas, 21. ☎ 91-429-55-26. www.posadadehuertas.com. 152 beds in rooms for 2–8. 18€–24€ per person. MC, V. Metro: Antón Martín.

★★ Parador Convento de Santo Tomás
ALCALÁ DE HENARES Built inside the walls of a Renaissance convent, this 2009 hotel shakes up the usual *parador* paradigm in favor of luxurious high style. It has an attached conference center and futuristic spa. C/ Colegios, 8. ☎ 91-888-03-30. 128 rooms. Doubles 180€–225€. AE, DC, MC, V.

> A suite at Room Mate Laura.

> Putting on the Ritz in Madrid.

★★ The Ritz PASEOS

Whether you're seeking a rich sense of history or modern comforts and pampering, you'll find both at this landmark hotel that opened in 1910 to emulate its namesakes in Paris and London. Plaza de la Lealtad, 5. ☎ 91-701-67-67. www.ritzmadrid.com. 167 rooms. Doubles 572€–690€. AE, DC, MC, V. Metro: Banco de España.

★ Room Mate Laura ÓPERA

Families needn't sacrifice style for space (and a kitchen) in this friendly hotel that combines self-consciously cutting-edge design with homey comfort. Many rooms feature loft sleeping areas. Travesía de Trujillos, 3. ☎ 91-701-16-70. www.room-matehotels.com. 36 rooms. Doubles 105€–211€ w/breakfast. AE, DC, MC, V. Metro: Ópera.

★ Room Mate Óscar CHUECA

With a relaxed vibe and playful design (brightly stenciled walls and see-through shower stalls, for example), Óscar epitomizes the youthful style of the neighborhood. Breakfast is served until noon so night owls can sleep in. Plaza Vásquez de Mella, 12. ☎ 91-701-11-73. www.room-matehotels.com. 75 rooms. Doubles 105€–200€ w/breakfast. AE, DC, MC, V. Metro: Gran Vía.

★★★ Villa Magna PASEOS

Feel like a rock star when you stay at this 1972 luxury hotel that reopened in 2009, after a 2-year, 50€-million renovation. Rooms are huge, suites are even bigger—and run up to 15,000€ a night (with butler and chauffeur). Paseo Castellana, 22. ☎ 91-587-12-34. www.villa-magna.com. 150 rooms. Doubles 340€–380€. AE, DC, MC, V. Metro: Rubén Darío.

★ Vincci SoMa SALAMANCA

Jaunty red awnings on the exterior signal the contemporary flair of this boutique hotel in the heart of Salamanca. Romantics should book a room with outdoor terrace; families can opt for an apartment. C/ Goya, 79. ☎ 91-435-75-45. www.vinccihoteles.com. 170 rooms. Doubles 95€–195€. AE, MC, V. Metro: Goya.

★★ Westin Palace PASEOS

All of Madrid society has passed beneath the grand stained-glass dome of the central rotunda of this luxury hotel, opened in 1912. Recent renovations to the guest rooms have added Westin trademark amenities without diminishing the Belle Epoque style. Plaza de las Cortes, 7. ☎ 91-360-80-00. www.westinpalacemadrid.com. 468 rooms. Doubles 198€–339€. Metro: Banco de España.

Madrid Nightlife & Entertainment Best Bets

Best Flamenco
Casa Patas, C/ Cañizares, 10 (see p. 148)

Best Classic Cocktails
Museo Chicote, Gran Vía, 12 (see p. 146)

Best Relic of the *Movida Madrileña*
La Vía Lactea, C/ Velarde, 18 (see p. 143)

Best Sports Bar
Zahara Restaurante Cervecería, Gran Vía, 31 (see p. 147)

Best Celebrity Spotting
The Penthouse, ME by Meliá Hotel, Plaza Santa Ana, 14 (see p. 146)

Best Modernista Movie House
Cine Doré, C/ Santa Isabel, 3 (see p. 147)

Best Kitsch Nightlife
Tupperware, Corredera Alta de San Pablo, 26 (see p. 148)

Best Outdoor Dance Club
Ananda, Estación de Atocha, Avenida Ciudad de Barcelona, s/n (see p. 147)

Best Hemingway-esque Haunt
Cervecería Alemana, Plaza Santa Ana, 6 (see p. 143)

Best Summer Performing Arts Festival
Los Veranos de la Villa (see p. 146)

Best Historic Stage
Teatro Español, C/ Principe, 25 (see p. 149)

Best Place to Meet the Next Almodóvar
Angelika Cinema Lounge, C/ Cava Baja, 24 (see p. 143)

Best Romantic Jazz Club
Central Cafe, Plaza del Angel, 10 (see p. 149)

> *Cervecería Alemana, an old Hemingway haunt.*

Madrid Nightlife & Entertainment A to Z

Bars & Pubs

Angelika Cinema Lounge LA LATINA
Join the intelligentsia in this relaxed, nonsmoking tapas bar (a rarity), where there's always a film screening in its original language on the plasma TVs and you can enjoy intense discussions about cinematography while sipping a gin and tonic. C/ Cava Baja, 24. ☎ 91-366-04-94. Metro: La Latina.

Café Antic CHUECA
This romantic gay-neighborhood classic with dark corners and flickering candlelight is a favorite for hand-holding trysts. The martini menu has almost every variation on gin and vodka drinks you could imagine. C/ Hortaleza, 4. No phone. Metro: Gran Vía.

★ Cervecería Alemana LAS LETRAS
Hemingway often drank brandy here with a beer chaser, and many a member of the American press corps (back when there were still overseas bureaus) followed suit. If you can keep from muttering through your short white beard about bullfights and boxing, it's still a great place for malt and conversation. Plaza Santa Ana, 6. ☎ 91-429-70-33. Metro: Sol.

Fulanito de Tal CHUECA
The two-level disco bar shakes as often with live music as recorded. Popular with Chueca's lesbian community, it's also a hit with gender-bending fashionistas. C/ Conde de Xiquena, 2. ☎ 91-522-02-06. Metro: Chueca.

La Vía Lactea CHUECA
When all the pent-up passion burst into La Movida Madrileña in the late 1970s and early 1980s, the "Milky Way" was the hippest bar in town. A new generation strikes its own alternative poses, surrounded by posters of Movida movies and bands. C/ Velarde, 18. ☎ 91-446-75-81. Metro: Bilbao or Tribunal.

> Zarzuela *at Joy Eslava.*

Madrid Nightlife & Entertainment

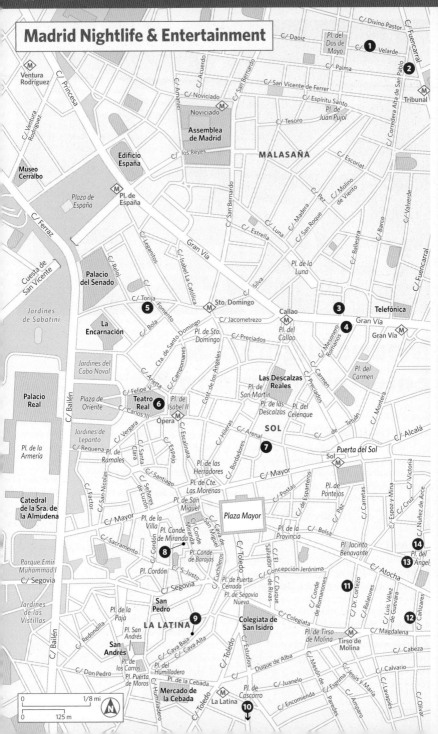

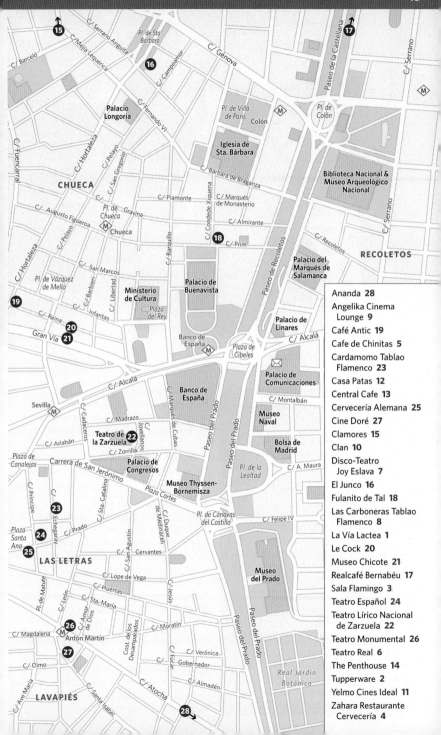

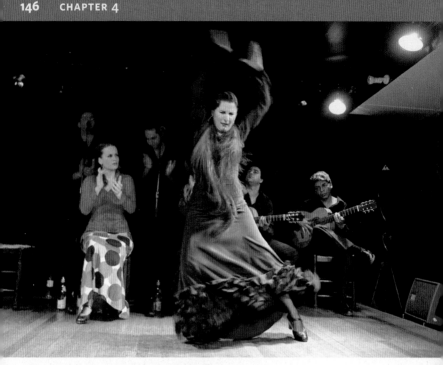

> *Dinner and dancing at Las Carboneras Tablao Flamenco.*

Arts Extravaganzas

Suma Flamenco

Replacing a shorter winter flamenco festival of years past, this 6-week blow-out of performances almost every night starting in early May is organized by the Community of Madrid. Prices and venues vary. See www.madrid.org for details.

Los Veranos de la Villa

Two solid months of concerts, dance, theater, *zarzuela*, and even poetry take place around the city from the end of June to the end of August. The festival includes a series of free street concerts. See www.esmadrid.com/veranosdelavilla for details.

Festival de Otoño

Internationally famous performers and companies fill the theaters and concert halls from mid-October to mid-November. There's even a program of contemporary circus acts. See www.madrid.org for details.

★ Le Cock CHUECA

Name and location suggest a raunchy bar, but Le Cock is actually suave and upscale—more like the lounge of a classy hotel, where you can sprawl on the sofas, sip tall drinks through a straw, flirt, and converse. Decibel levels rise as the evening progresses. C/ Reina, 16. ☎ 91-532-28-29. Metro: Gran Vía.

★ Museo Chicote GRAN VÍA

This classy joint with Art Deco decor was Madrid's first real American cocktail bar—the kind of place where Frank Sinatra drank when he was in town. The "museo" part of the name is just a joke about the bar's longevity. Come early for a martini, or late for mixed drinks as DJs spin throbbing house music. Gran Vía, 12. ☎ 91-532-67-37. Metro: Gran Vía.

★ The Penthouse LAS LETRAS

The rooftop bar at the ME by Meliá Hotel aims to attract the beautiful people to sip cocktails as they preen for each other. They're amusing to watch, if you can tear yourself from the great views of Madrid's old quarter. Plaza Santa Ana, 14. ☎ 91-701-60-00. Metro: Sol.

> *A show at Teatro Lírico Naciónal de Zarzuela.*

Cinema

★ Cine Doré LAS LETRAS

This classic repertory house in a 1922 Modernista theater screens films in their original languages with Spanish subtitles, when needed. It's a great way to build your Spanish vocabulary. C/ Santa Isabel, 3. ☎ 91-369-11-25. Tickets 2.50€. Metro: Antón Martín.

Yelmo Cines Ideal LA LATINA

With nine screens running simultaneously, Ideal can show the best of current film from around the world, always in the original language. C/ Doctor Cortezo, 6. ☎ 902-22-09-22. http://yelmocines.es. Tickets 6€–8€. Metro: Tirso de Mólina.

Dance Clubs

★ Ananda PASEOS

This warm-weather outdoor scene near the Atocha parking garage reserves Wednesday and Sunday nights for gay dance parties. Estación de Atocha, Avenida Ciudad de Barcelona, s/n. ☎ 91-524-11-44. Cover 15€. Metro: Atocha.

Disco-Teatro Joy Eslava SOL

Every cheap hotel in Madrid has handouts touting Joy Eslava—and for good reason. The cavernous space was built in the 19th century for the uniquely Madrileño style of light opera called *zarzuela,* and you need to get a crowd for disco to work. Doors open around 11pm, but the dancing doesn't get serious until 1am or later. C/ Arenal, 11. ☎ 91-366-37-33. www.joy-eslava.com. Cover 12€. Metro: Sol.

Bouncing with the Balls

Madrileños don't choose their soccer loyalties. You're born into either an Atlético family or a Real Madrid family. Marriages over those lines are as star-crossed as a liaison between a Capulet and a Montague. Chances that you will be able to buy tickets to a match between the two Madrid teams are slimmer than the odds of winning Once, the state-run lottery. You might be able to find tickets to other matches, though (see "Listings & Tickets," p. 149). But you don't have to go to either stadium to join in the fun. Whenever either Madrid team plays, the TV in every bar and restaurant around town is tuned to the match. Two places stand out for simultaneous sipping and cheering:

★ **Realcafé Bernabéu.** The away matches of Real Madrid are always broadcast at this cafe-bar at the stadium. Arrive early if you want to get a seat with decent sightlines to the screen. Gate no. 30 of Estadio Santiago Bernabéu, Paseo de la Castellana, 144. ☎ 91-458-36-67. www.realcafebernabeu.es. Metro: Bernabéu.

★ **Zahara Restaurante Cervecería.** This pop-culture icon of hamburgers, pizza, and beer also has big-screen televisions hanging from the ceiling so that no one need miss a kick. As long as you keep ordering food or drink, you can keep watching. Gran Vía, 31. ☎ 91-521-84-24. Metro: Callao.

> *Isabel II's Belle Epoque Teatro Real.*

★ Sala Flamingo CHUECA
The crowd (and cover charge) in this hip end of Chueca varies by night, with bouncy reggae on Thursdays, retro hip thrash music on Fridays, and a mix of heavy metal and trance for the goths on Saturdays. C/ Mesoneros Romanos, 13. ☎ 91-541-35-00. Cover 7€–12€. Metro: Gran Vía.

Tupperware CHUECA
Although this two-level kitsch-o-rama extravaganza is technically a bar rather than a club, you'll find plenty of people dancing in front of the Barbie dolls. The music's too loud for conversation anyway. Aim for a table upstairs, where the cool kids are. Corredera Alta de San Pablo, 26. ☎ 91-446-42-04. No cover. Metro: Tribunal.

Flamenco
★ Cafe de Chinitas ÓPERA
In flamenco's dark days, when tourist shows featured castanets, frilly dresses, and dubious guitar licks, Chinitas kept the wolf from the door of many dedicated musicians and dancers.

Despite the air of a flamenco "nightclub," this is a great place to see journeymen performers who've been at the game since long before some of the ponytailed hotshots were born. C/ Torija, 7. ☎ 91-559-51-35. www.chinitas.com. Cover 35€–37€. Metro: Santo Domingo.

Cardamomo Tablao Flamenco LAS LETRAS
The flamenco revival has nurtured a new generation of singers, musicians, and dancers, and this is one of the clubs where the up-and-coming come to get up. Performances don't begin until the air has turned a sufficiently deep shade of nicotine blue. C/ Echegaray, 15. ☎ 91-369-07-57. www.cardamomo.es. Cover 10€ with 1 drink. Metro: Sevilla or Sol.

★★★ Casa Patas LAS LETRAS
Even guys drinking beer at the bar wear ponytails and black shirts open halfway to the waist, and the wisecracks tend to be exchanged in an almost incomprehensible Andaluz dialect. But the music and dance in the back room are the real thing. Casa Patas is run for flamenco

aficionados by people who live the flamenco life. C/ Cañizares, 10. ☎ 91-369-04-96. www.casapatas.com. Cover 28€–31€. Metro: Tirso de Mólina or Antón Martín.

Clan LAVAPIÉS

Rock bands and jazz combos often fill the windowfront stage of this restaurant-nightclub in the evenings, but the flamencos take over a little after midnight on Fridays and Saturdays. C/ Ribera de Curtidores, across from no. 30. ☎ 91-528-84-01. www.osclan.com. No cover. Metro: Puerta de Toledo or Embajadores.

★ Las Carboneras Tablao Flamenco LA LATINA

Many visitors to Spain over the last half century have been initiated into flamenco at one supper club or another near Plaza Mayor. Carboneras is the current champion, and perhaps the best yet. Expect a good mix of veteran performers and bright new stars. Plaza del Conde Miranda, 1. ☎ 91-542-86-77. www.tablaolascarboneras.com. Cover 29€ with 1 drink. Metro: Ópera or La Latina.

Jazz

★ Central Cafe LAS LETRAS

This classy bar-restaurant has championed the cause of modern and postmodern jazz for more than a quarter century, programming live concerts every night around 10pm with touring musicians from around the globe. Plaza del Angel, 10. ☎ 91-369-41-43. www.cafecentral madrid.com. Cover 8€–11€. Metro: Antón Martín.

Clamores MALASAÑA

This spacious club may program Spanish singer-songwriters more than any other genre of musician, but it's actually best known for live blues and jazz acts that play the basement stage. C/ Alburquerque, 14. ☎ 91-445-79-38. www.clamores.es. Cover 6€–12€. Metro: Bilbao.

El Junco CHUECA

Jam sessions on Sundays and Tuesdays have made this retro dive one of the don't-miss spots for jazz fans in Madrid. It's dark, it's smoky, and the music doesn't start until midnight. Plaza de Santa Bárbara, 10. ☎ 91-319-20-81. www.eljunco.com. Cover 10€–14€. Metro: Alonso Martínez.

Theater, Dance & Classical Music

★★ Teatro Español LAS LETRAS

This beautifully restored early-19th-century theater presents plays, concerts, and dance. If a Madrileño speaks of a "night at the theater,"

chances are he means the Teatro Español. C/ Principe, 25. ☎ 91-429-62-97. www.esmadrid.com/teatroespanol. Ticket prices vary. Metro: Tirso de Mólina or Antón Martín.

Teatro Lírico Naciónal de Zarzuela PASEOS

The decorated candy-box architecture of this theater is a perfect fit for the musical comedy confection of the *zarzuela*. C/ Jovellanos, 4. ☎ 91-524-54-00. http://teatrodelazarzuela.mcu.es. Ticket prices vary. Metro: Sevilla.

Teatro Monumental LAS LETRAS

Now that Madrid's symphony orchestra has moved to the Teatro Real (see below), this grand theater with superb acoustics is home to the Orquesta y el Coro de RTVE (the orchestra and choir of state radio and television). C/ Atocha, 65. ☎ 91-429-12-81. www.osm.es. Ticket prices vary. Metro: Antón Martín.

Teatro Real ÓPERA

Restored to its Belle Epoque glory, the opera house is the base for the Orquestra Sinfónica de Madrid, which presents several operas and ballets in addition to a full schedule of symphonic concerts. Plaza Isabel II, s/n. Tickets: ☎ 902-24-48-48. Information: ☎ 91-516-06-06. www.teatro-real.es. Ticket prices vary. Metro: Ópera.

Listings & Tickets

Every Thursday, the weekly *Guía del Ocio* hits the newsstands with up-to-date listings of concerts, movies, performances, and all manner of Madrid entertainment. Editorial is strictly Spanish but pretty straightforward. The giveaway English-language monthly *In Madrid* also carries fairly extensive entertainment listings geared largely to college-age students from abroad. It's also available online at www.in-madrid.com.

Advance tickets to most Madrid events are available at the various branches of **El Corté Inglés,** including C/ Preciados, 3 (☎ 902-40-02-22; www.elcorteingles.es). Other ticket services with less of a Madrid focus include **Tel-Entrada** (☎ 902-10-12-12; www.telentrada.com); **ServiCaixa** (☎ 902-33-22-11; www.servicaixa.com); and Ticketmaster's Spanish branch, **Tick Tack Ticket** (☎ 902-15-00-25; www.ticktackticket.com).

Madrid Fast Facts

> The new terminal at Barajas International Airport.

Arriving & Getting Around

BY PLANE **Madrid Barajas International Airport** (MAD) is the world's 10th-busiest airport, served by more than 100 airlines that handle more than 52 million passengers a year. Terminals 1 through 3 are home to SkyTeam and Star Alliance airlines (including SpanAir), while Iberia and its OneWorld Alliance partners (including American Airlines and British Airways) use Terminal 4, inaugurated in 2006. The quickest way into town is on **Metro Line 8** (pink), which runs from 6am to 1:30am between central Madrid and Terminals 4 and 2 (you can walk from 2 to Terminals 1 and 3). Metro service to and from the airport carries a 1€ surcharge. You have to change trains at Nuevas Ministerios, as the airport segment of the line uses different platforms. There is also **bus service** on lines 200 and 204 between the airport and the Avenida de America bus terminal. On a good day, either mode of transport takes 20 minutes; on a bad day, it can take 45 minutes. A taxi from the airport to downtown costs 30€ to 35€. **BY TRAIN** Most RENFE (Spanish national trains; ☎ 902-24-02-02; www.renfe.es) and international trains arrive at **Estación Atocha,** Glorieta del Emperador Carlos V (☎ 91-506-61-95; metro: Atocha), or **Estación Chamartín,** C/ Augustín de Foxa, s/n (☎ 91-323-15-15; metro: Chamartín). Atocha is Spain's largest rail station and the terminus for high-speed rail links with Barcelona, Valencia, Sevilla, and (soon) Bilbao. BY BUS It's a slow way to come, but buses service Madrid from most major capitals of western Europe. Most buses arrive at **Estación Sur de Autobuses de Madrid,** C/ Mendez Alvaro, 83 (☎ 91-468-42-00; www.estaciondeautobuses.com). Local buses 8, 37, 58, 102, 113, 148, and 152 service the city from Estación Sur. BY CAR This being the hub of Spain, there's a road from everywhere leading to the capital. From the Basque Country, the **A-1** is 507km (315 miles) from Irún at the French border to Madrid. From Barcelona, follow the **A-2** for 626km (389 miles). From Valencia, use the **A-3** for 349km (217 miles). From Cádiz, the **A-4** stretches 625km (388 miles) to Madrid. From Badajoz on the Portuguese border in Extremadura, the **A-5** runs 409km (254 miles). From A Coruña in Galicia, the **A-6** goes 602km (374 miles) to Madrid. Note that these highways sometimes change numbers. The limited access highway with an "A" designation becomes an "N" highway with a Roman numeral (N-I, N-II, N-III, and so on) when it has multiple access points, or an "AP" when it is a toll highway. BY METRO The **Metro** (☎ 902-44-44-03; www.metromadrid.es) is the most efficient way to get around town. It has 12 color-coded lines, and you can change lines without limit until you exit at a station. Single fares (*sencillo*) are 1€, or you can buy a Metrobús pass (10 trips on the Metro or a city bus) for 7€. The Metro runs daily from 6am to 2am, with fewer trains on Sundays and holidays. Most stations have a sign indicating how many minutes until the next train (usually less than 5).

ATMs

You'll find 24-hour ATMs in all Madrid neighborhoods. Most accept Maestro/MasterCard, Cirrus, and Visa.

Doctors & Hospitals

For emergency medical or dental attention, go to the *centro de urgencia* (emergency room) at **Hospital General Universitario Gregorio Marañón,** Dr. Esquerdo, 46 (☎ 91-568-80-00), or **Hospital Universitario La Paz,** Paseo de la

Castellana, 261 (☎ 91-727-70-00). Non-E.U. residents can consult national health service doctors for a relatively small fee; ask at your hotel for a list of doctors.

Pharmacies

To find an open pharmacy outside normal business hours, check the list of stores posted on the door of any drugstore or call ☎ **012.** By law, there's always a drugstore open around the clock in every neighborhood. Drugstores are called *farmacías.* When open, they display a neon green cross. A couple of central pharmacies open daily around the clock include **Farmacía de la Paloma,** C/ Toledo, 46 (☎ 91-365-34-58; www.farmaciadelapaloma.com), and **Farmacía del Globo,** C/ Atocha, 46 (☎ 91-359-20-00).

Post Office

Madrid's central post office is located at **Plaza de Cibeles, s/n** (☎ 91-523-0695), near the Prado. Post office hours are usually Monday to Friday 9am to 8pm and Saturday 9am to 7pm. Stamps are also sold at tobacco shops.

Safety

You should exercise the same caution in Madrid as in any large city, using common sense and avoiding deserted streets at night and during the afternoon closing hours. Never leave anything visible in a parked car, especially overnight. Be vigilant about your belongings in crowds, such as at El Rastro flea market, a favorite haunt of pickpockets, and in subway cars. Pickpockets often frequent the airport Metro line because passengers are so busy keeping their suitcases from falling over that they are lax about protecting their pockets or purses.

Visitor Information

Madrid Oficina de Turismo, Plaza Mayor, 27 (☎ 91-588-16-36; www.esmadrid.com), is open daily 9:30am to 8:30pm (metro: Sol or Ópera). **Colón Tourism Center,** Plaza de Colón in the walkway between C/ Génova and C/ Goya (www.turismomadrid.es), is open daily 9:30am to 8:30pm (metro: Colón). The Colón office does not accept phone calls and offers consultations only on a walk-in basis.

5
Castilla-
La Mancha

The Best of Castilla-La Mancha in 4 Days

Located in the heart of Spain, the sprawling province of Castilla-La Mancha stretches across Iberia's vast tableland from mountain range to mountain range. This 4-day tour starts in the eastern highlands, where Cuenca perches above two converging gorges. On a second day, you'll see the remains of the ancient Roman city of Segóbriga en route to majestic Toledo, the hilltop capital.

> PREVIOUS PAGE *The famed windmills of La Mancha.* THIS PAGE *El Puente de San Pablo spans the Huécar gorge, connecting Cuenca's Old Town with St. Paul's medieval convent.*

START Cuenca. TRIP LENGTH 269km (167 miles).

❶ **Cuenca.** Only warriors or monks would build a city suspended so high above a pair of river gorges. In Cuenca's case, warriors: Muslim invaders from North Africa shrewdly positioned this aerie to oversee all the strategic passes between the mountains and the flatlands. That was 714, and a Christian king didn't take the town until Alfonso VIII came marching up the hill in 1177. Only a crumbling wall and the Arco de Bezudo remain from the Muslim fortress— as well as the medieval street plan onto which the Christian conquerors shoehorned their Gothic and Renaissance palaces.

Travel Tip

For hotels and restaurants in Cuenca, see p. 175; for Toledo, see p. 171.

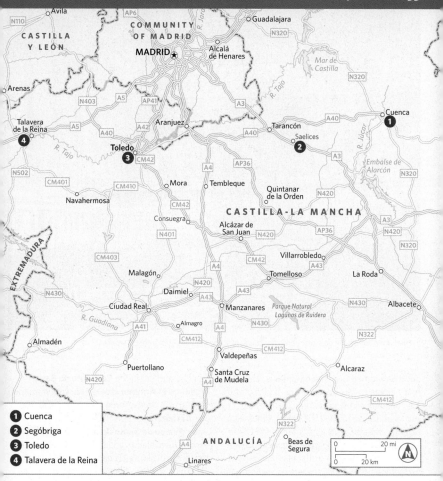

1 Cuenca
2 Segóbriga
3 Toledo
4 Talavera de la Reina

The **Museo de Cuenca** is a good place to get an overview of city history, as well as the broader history and prehistory of the surrounding area. It is particularly strong on two periods: the Roman occupation, and the 14th to the 16th century, when the wool and wine trades enriched the area.

Cuenca's improbable location and even more improbable architecture (a few houses actually dangle off the edge of their lots over the Huécar gorge) sometimes make the city seem more fantastic than real. Over the years, that unreality has proved very appealing to artists. One of Spain's main 20th-century movements, El Grupo Paso, was centered here. Its legacy includes three superb art museums (see p. 173, **4**; p. 174, **9** and

10). Museo de Cuenca: ⏱ 1 hr. C/ Obispo Valero, 12. ☎ 969-213-069. 1.20€ adults, .60€ students, free Sat and Sun. June 15–Sept 15 Tues–Sat 10am–2pm and 5–7pm, Sun 11am–2pm; Sept 16–June 14 Tues–Sat 10am–2pm and 4–7pm.

Follow A-40 west for 51km (32 miles) to exit 254. Follow CM-310 southwest 21km (13 miles) to Segóbriga.

2 Segóbriga. The best Roman statuary unearthed here has been moved to the Museo de Cuenca (see above), but otherwise this site is one of the better preserved Roman cities in Spain. Colonized in the 1st century B.C., Segóbriga was a shipping center for wheat grown on the surrounding plains and for lead

> *The high altar of Toledo's cathedral, the home of some of El Greco's greatest works.*

and silver mined from the mountains. The city really began to flex its muscle in the 1st century A.D., building all the structures that are hallmarks of Roman urban civilization: a theater, an amphitheater, a basilica, a temple to Diana, and a public bath complex. A **museum** on-site contains many smaller artifacts found during excavations. ⊙ 2–3 hr. Carretera de Saelices a Villamayor de Santiago. ☎ 629-752-257. www.patrimoniohistoricoclm.es. 4€ adults, 2€ students, free for seniors and kids 10 & under. Apr–Sept Tues–Sun 10am–9pm; Oct–Mar closes 6pm.

Go northeast on CM-310 for 2.5km (1½ miles) and follow A-3 for 19km (12 miles) to exit 84, watching signs to A-40. Continue 42km (26 miles) west on A-40, then 10km (6¼ miles) on A-4 to exit 52. Follow N-400 for 38km (24 miles) to Toledo.

❸ Toledo. You could easily prolong your stay in Toledo well past 2 days—El Greco came to paint some pictures in 1577 and never left. His artistic legacy is one of the many layers of Toledo attractions. Unlike most other Spanish painters, his best pictures are *not* in the Prado, but at home where they were painted in Toledo.

Check them out in the **Convento de Santo Domingo el Antiguo** (see p. 166, ❷); his parish church of ★ **Santo Tomé** (see p. 169, ❾); the ★★ **Catedral** (see p. 168, ❼); and the ★★★ **Museo de Santa Cruz** (see p. 168, ❺).

Much of Toledo's appeal is simply wandering the tangle of extremely narrow streets, where the deep blue shadows offer cool respite from the sun. (The impossibility of squeezing most autos down these streets leaves them largely open for pedestrians.) A less claustrophobic stroll follows the Old City walls, and gives you a chance to look out over the surrounding countryside and see some of the massive institutions built into the walls, such as the **Monasterio de San Juan de los Reyes** (see p. 170, ⓫).

Toledo also had one of Spain's most dynamic Jewish communities, until Fernando and Isabel crippled their just-reunited country with expulsion orders in 1492 for all Jews and Muslims who would not convert to Christianity. The ★★ **Museo Sefardí** (see p. 170, ❿), housed in Toledo's last surviving synagogue, the 1355 Sinagoga del Tránsito, tells the city's Jewish history and, by extension, the broader lot of Jewish life in Spain. See p. 166.

> *Visitors to Artesanía Talaverana can watch artisans throw and glaze authentic Talavera pottery.*

From Toledo, go west on the A-40 for 40km (25 miles). Continue west on the A-5 for 45km (28 miles) to Talavera de la Reina.

❹ **Talavera de la Reina.** During your stay in Toledo, you might want to consider a day trip to this handsome town known for its ceramics. The ★ **Museo Ruiz de Luna** traces a millennium of pottery making on the site of a former convent. The galleries chronicle the design evolution of Talavera pottery from cobalt-blue 16th-century pieces to 17th-century stylized hares, deer, and partridges. Over time, the tile designs became more complex, reaching their stylistic apex with the 1914 facade of the Ruiz de Luna ceramics factory (for which the museum is named).

If you're interested in buying ceramics, visit **Artesanía Talaverana,** Avenida de Portugal, 36 (☎ 925-802-909). It's the only shop where you can watch the artisans at work and see the whole process.

It figures that Talavera's main church, the ★★ **Basilica de Nuestra Señora del Prado,** would be so covered in painted tiles that the locals call it the "ceramic Sistine Chapel." Note the frieze of the Adoration on the main entry, with a line of women approaching Jesus on one side and a line of Spanish soldiers approaching on the other. Inside, Old Testament stories line the left side, New Testament the right. Museo: ⏱ 1 hr. Plaza de San Agustin, 13. ☎ 925-800-149. 1€. Tues-Sat 10am-2pm and 4-6:30pm; Sun 10am-2pm. Basilica: ⏱ 1 hr. Los Jardines del

> *Cuenca's hanging houses have unparalleled views of the gorges below.*

Prado, 6. No phone. Free. Mon-Fri 7am-2pm and 5-9:50pm; Sat 8am-2pm and 5-9:50pm.

The Best of Castilla-La Mancha in 1 Week

South and southeast of Toledo, the high plain is relieved only by hiccups of hills and the occasional limestone ridge that pokes from the soil like half-buried driftwood. For centuries, La Mancha was a battleground of Muslim and Christian armies, and it seems as if every high spot in the landscape is crowned by castle ruins. Today the region has reverted to farming. The Romans grew wheat and grapes. The Muslims introduced the saffron crocus and replaced the vineyards with olives. When the Christians returned, so did the vineyards. Follow "The Best of Castilla-La Mancha in 4 Days," and then divide your remaining 3 days between the picturesque village of Consuegra and the handsome urban capital of Castilla-La Mancha wine, Valdepeñas.

> Grapes, olives, wheat, saffron, and sheep have all made La Mancha an important agricultural region.

START Toledo. **TRIP LENGTH** 417km (259 miles), including "The Best of Castilla-La Mancha in 4 Days."

❶ Autovía de los Viñedos. The drive south on the "Vineyards Highway" of CM-42/CM-400 offers a study in edible landscape. Unlike the high trellising practiced in much of France and California, La Mancha's vines are cropped close to the ground, sometimes trained to a single low wire, and allowed to sprawl. For every vineyard, there is also a grove of *cornicabra* olives, a native varietal with fruit shaped like a ram's horn. Where water is scarce, shepherds tend herds of Manchegan sheep, the heritage breed that produces the milk for Manchego cheese.

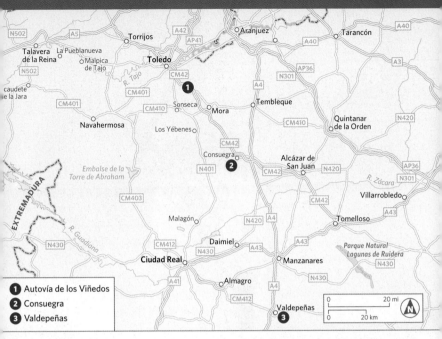

1 Autovía de los Viñedos
2 Consuegra
3 Valdepeñas

Follow CM-42 for 65km (40 miles) to Consuegra.

2 **Consuegra.** Few tourists visit this town, which is too bad, because Consuegra is magical and evocative. Drive into town in the brown heat of summer, and you'll see wandering herds of sheep—and a few adventurous goats—grazing on the outskirts. Their shepherd will be wearing a snap-brim cap pulled down to his eyebrows and will be standing in whatever shade is available while his dogs manage the livestock. Drive into town in October, when fall rains turn dry fields into mud, and you'll see dozens of villagers stooped over small garden patches, plucking the purple flowers of the saffron crocus.

The high limestone ridge that rises behind Consuegra is capped by the ★ **Castillo de la Muela,** a 12th-century castle being restored by students from Consuegra's technical school. (Communities all over Spain have trade schools to train youth in building restoration.) Three towers are now safe to climb for amazing views, and the cisterns and chapel have been restored. The castle was the Castilla

Wild About Saffron

Central La Mancha grows one of the priciest crops in the world: *Crocus sativus*, the purple flower prized for three bright red stigmas hidden among the petals. Properly cleaned and toasted, the tiny threads become saffron, worth more than its weight in gold. This corner of Spain supplies two-thirds of the world's culinary-grade saffron, so it's not surprising that Consuegra hosts a festival to celebrate the harvest. The **Fiesta de la Rosa del Azafrán,** or "Saffron Rose Festival," takes place on the last full weekend of October.

There is, of course, singing, dancing, eating, and the crowning of a beauty queen. But the festival's key events are the intense competitions between "strippers" to clean the most blossoms in a few minutes' time. Crowds gather to cheer these adepts, the best of whom pluck the stigmas with blinding speed. As day turns to evening, the heady aroma of saffron fills the night air as farmers toast the carefully cleaned threads. It is their red gold.

> *Miguel de Cervantes's well-meaning if bumbling hero, Don Quixote, jousted with windmills like those in Consuegra.*

headquarters for the Order of St. John of Jerusalem, a Crusader order now known as the Knights of Malta.

★★ **Eleven vintage windmills** follow the crest of the ridgeline. The one called "Bolero" contains the city's tourist office, and its grind works are in fine working order, so you can climb the stairs to see how the locals used to grind wheat into flour. Castillo: ◷ 1 hr. Monte Calderico. No phone. 3€. Mon–Fri 9:20am–1:45pm and 4:40–6:45pm; Sat–Sun 10:40am–1:45pm and 4:40–6:45pm. Windmills: ◷ 1 hr. Molino El Bolero, Monte Calderico. ☎ 925-475-731. www.consuegra.es. Free. Thurs–Mon 11:30am–2pm and 4:30–8pm.

Follow CM-400 for 3km (1⅔ miles). Drive the A-4 for 80km (50 miles) south to Valdepeñas.

❸ Valdepeñas. Gigantic amphorae, long used for winemaking, set along the road into town leave no doubt about the main industry here. (The street is even called Avenida del Viño, or Avenue of Wine.) The Romans shipped a veritable flood of wine from Valdepeñas, and when winemaking began again in the 12th century after 400 years of Islamic prohibition, makers revived the big terra-cotta vessels. Today the industry has shifted either to cement tanks or to stainless steel fermentation and judicious aging in small oak barrels. The focus here is no longer on mass production (the town

Spending the Night in Consuegra

Gracious ★ **La Vida de Antes** is a new hotel that feels like a 19th-century noble's guest house. Owners will loan you a bike for the steep pedal up to the windmills. C/ Colón 2. ☎ 925-480-609. www.lavidadeantes.com. 9 rooms. Doubles 65€–88€. MC, V.

A tiled mural of Don Quixote and Sancho Panza confronting windmills lifts the formality of the dining room at **Las Provincias.** Ambitious cuisine usually includes some saffron dishes and often highlights local small game, such as quail and partridge. Carretera Toledo-Alcázar, km 58.5. ☎ 925-482-000. Entrees 12€–18€. Lunch & dinner daily. MC, V.

> *The amphorae lining the road into Valdepeñas are for looks only but speak to the town's hundreds of years of winemaking history.*

was once known as the bulk wine capital of Spain); Valdepeñas has joined the drive toward lower production of better wines.

There are several approaches to boosting quality. ★★★ **Bodegas Real** (see p. 165, ❸) takes the scientific route. This sharp, contemporary winery is located in the middle of the vineyards to minimize time from picking to crush. Chardonnay grapes are even harvested and crushed at night to keep them cool. The approach at ★★ **Bodegas Dionisos** is more mystical, involving astrological signs and

> *Bodegas Real, a second generation family winery, seeks to bring the "concept of the chateau to the lands of La Mancha."*

Spending the Night in Valdepeñas

The 1960 kids **Hotel El Hidalgo** was an early project of Antonio Lamela, the style genius behind Terminal 4 of Madrid's Barajas airport. Most rooms have terraces around the pool. A-4, km 194. ☎ 926-313-088. www.hotelelhidalgo.es. 54 rooms. Doubles 60€. MC, V.

For a farm-fresh meal, **Bodegas Real**'s gourmet restaurant serves vegetables from the garden. See p. 165, ❸.

phases of the moon. The bodega is in the owner's 200-year-old home at the edge of the city, and the tour is colorful. More to the point, the wines are terrific. Dionisos: ⏱ 90 min. C/ Union, 82. ☎ 926-313-248. www.labodegadelasestrellas.com. Visit with tasting 5€. Mon-Fri 9am-2pm and 4-7pm with reservation.

Tracking Don Quixote

Miguel de Cervantes's self-deluded "knight" Don Quixote is perhaps the most famous character in Spanish literature. Cervantes never divulged where the man of La Mancha was born, but he mentioned several real Manchegan locales in the novel. Here's a tight cluster to visit in 2 days.

> *Most towns of La Mancha claim some connection to Cervantes's delusional knight on horseback.*

START El Toboso. **TRIP LENGTH** 151km (94 miles).

❶ El Toboso. The birthplace of Quixote's lady love, Dulcinea, has the uproarious **Museo de Humor Gráfico Dulcinea,** devoted to humorous images of her, mostly engravings, in a quixotically decorated house. The **Museo Cervantino** displays hundreds of editions of *Don Quixote* in a world of languages. Museo de Humor: ⏱ 30 min. C/ Doña Tolosa, 2. ☎ 925-568-226. 2€ adults, 1€ seniors and students. Tues–Sat 10am–2pm and 5–7pm; Sun 10am–2pm. Museo Cervantino: ⏱ 15 min. C/ Daoíz y Velarde, 3. ☎ 925-197-456. Same prices and hours as Dulcinea museum.

Follow TO-1101 southwest for 18km (11 miles).

❷ Campo de Criptana. Some scholars think the demented knight tilted against the windmills here. Ten of the original 32 remain on a hilltop outside of town, and one is the local tourist office. Windmills: ⏱ 30 min. C/ Barbero, 1. ☎ 926-562-231. Tues–Fri 10am–2pm and 4–6pm; Sat 10am–2pm.

Go west on N-420 for 13km (8 miles). Follow CM-42 north 30km (19 miles) to Consuegra.

❸ Consuegra. With 11 medieval windmills and an imposing 12th-century castle on the Monte Calderico ridge above town, Consuegra also could have been the nearsighted Quixote's battleground with "giants." See p. 159, ❷.

Follow CM-42 south 4km (2½ miles). Take A-4 south 14km (8⅔ miles) to Puerto Lápice.

❹ Puerto Lápice. Speaking of castles, Quixote was knighted at a Puerto Lápice country inn, or *venta,* that he mistook for a castle. **La Casa Rural La Blanquilla** is a modern renovation of a tiny 200-year-old *venta.* Casa Rural: CM-4120

Legend on map:

1. El Toboso
2. Campo de Criptana
3. Consuegra
4. Puerto Lápice
5. Argamasilla de Alba
6. Parque Natural Lagunas de Ruidera

km 21.7 (11km/6⅔ miles southwest of Puerto Lápice). ☎ 926-695-063. veroblanqui@hotmail.com. 6 rooms. Inquire for availability and rates. MC, V.

Head south on A-4 for 11km (6¾ miles). Take CM-3113 for 30km (19 miles).

5 Argamasilla de Alba. Around 1600, Cervantes began his novel while imprisoned here in a cellar that is now the **Museo Casa de Madrano**. It may also be here that Cervantes thought to write his novel in plain, everyday language—which accounts for much of the book's early success. Museo: ⊙ 30 min. C/ Cervantes, 7. ☎ 926-522-393. Free. Tues–Sat 10am–2pm and 5–8pm; Sun 10am–2pm.

Head southeast on CM-3115 for 31km (19 miles) and watch for signs to park.

6 Parque Natural Lagunas de Ruidera. The lakes of this lovely park are named for a story in *Don Quixote* in which a magician transforms some bothersome ladies into lakes. Visit the deep Montesinos cave, a setting for a Quixote episode. ⊙ 2–3 hr. Ossa de Montiel. ☎ 926-528-116. www.lagunasruidera.com. Free. Information center: Sept–June Wed–Sun 8am–6:30pm; Jul–Aug daily 8am–6:30pm.

> First published in 1605 and 1615, Don Quixote *still tops lists of the most influential works of fiction ever written.*

Tastes of La Mancha

The sun-baked *meseta* (plateau) of La Mancha yields some of Spain's most distinctive tastes. The landscape should tip you off: low-growing grapevines, olive groves, and flocks of sheep grazing on scrub brush. That translates into wine, olive oil, and the incomparable DO Manchego cheese. Gastro-tourism is just beginning here, so appointments are essential, but you can do this tour in 1 day.

> *Bodegas Real's celebrated Restaurante El Umbráculo, serving farm-fresh fare and wine from the cellar.*

START From Toledo, follow CM-4000 to Malpica and follow signs toward La Pueblanueva. **TRIP LENGTH** 154km (96 miles).

❶ ★★★ Finca Cotanillo. The Valderrama brand produces some of the world's top olive oils and runs this farm southwest of Toledo, which focuses on the piquant *cornicabra* varietal. During the January to February harvest season, Valderrama transforms olives to oil in 45 minutes to preserve the subtle flavors. A factory tour and olive oil tastings are available all year. Valderrama's superb contemporary restaurant onsite, **Instinto Básico,** emphasizes market cuisine. Finca: ⏲ 3 hr. with lunch. Carretera de Malpica a La Pueblanueva,

km 9.6. ☎ 925-860-069 or 676-462-730. www. valderrama.es. Free. Daily 9am–7pm. Instinto: ☎ 619-306-727. Entrees 12€–18€, midday menus 15€–22€. Lunch daily, dinner Wed–Sat. AE, MC, V.

From Toledo, follow CM-400 south 18km (11 miles) to CM-401 east 24km (15 miles).

❷ ★★★ Finca La Prudenciana. Best known under the internationally acclaimed Artequeso marque, this farmstead cheese maker produces only about 40,000 wheels a year. The cheese-making barn and its thick-walled aging "caves" stand adjacent to the family farmhouse. Fewer than a dozen workers operate the "factory" where raw milk is transformed into curds, then

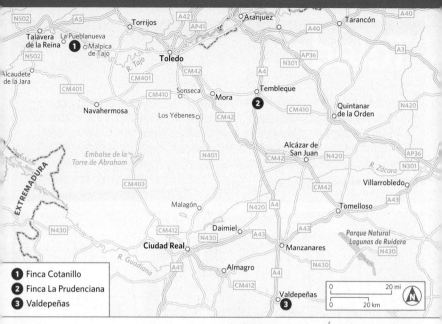

1 Finca Cotanillo
2 Finca La Prudenciana
3 Valdepeñas

pressed into wheel-shaped molds. The deeply refrigerated aging rooms are redolent with the sweet tang of Manchego. The *semicurado* is aged at least 4 months, the prestigious *curado* at least a year. ⏱ 2 hr. A-4 northbound, km 100, Tembleque. ☎ 925-145-192. www.artequeso.com. Free. Mon–Fri 9am–2pm.

From Tembleque follow A-4 south 112km (70 miles) to Valdepeñas.

3 **Valdepeñas.** Castilla-La Mancha produces more wine than the rest of Spain combined, and much of it comes from the town of Valdepeñas. You'll learn why at the **Museo del Viño,** housed in a 1901 bodega. Of the many bodega tours, the most impressive is ★★★ **Bodegas Real,** with its stunning new winery, reception center, and gourmet restaurant serving vegetables from the farm garden. Outstanding *tempranillo* reds might even be upstaged by Burgundy-style chardonnay. Museo: ⏱ 45 min. C/ Princesa, 39. ☎ 926-321-111. Free. Tues-Sat 10:30am–2pm and 6–8:30pm; Sun noon–2pm. Bodegas Real: ⏱ 3 hr. with lunch. Finca Marisánchez, Carretera a Cózar, km 12.8. ☎ 914-577-588. www.bodegas-real.com. Tours: Tues-Sun 11:30am and 1:30pm. Tour and tasting 6€, free for restaurant patrons. Bodegas Real restaurant: ☎ 926-360-323. Entrees 14€–22€. Lunch & dinner Tues-Sun. MC, V.

> *Manchego is a semifirm cheese made from the milk of the ancestral line of manchega sheep.*

Toledo

From high on a rock above the Río Tajo, this ancient citadel city surveys the sweeping La Mancha plains. It is the literal high point of Iberia's central tablelands and served as the regional or national capital from Roman times until 1560, when Felipe II moved the court to Madrid. Toledo remains the most medieval of Spain's large cities, a warren of narrow streets, where ancient buildings guarantee cool shadows even in the fierce heat of summer. Its Arabic, Jewish, and Christian history is written in stone—barely touched by the modern world.

> *Toledo's French Gothic cathedral is the final resting place of several Castilian kings.*

START Park in the car park at Paseo de Recaredo and take the La Granja outdoor escalator through the city gates. The Old City is best explored on foot.

1 Old City Walls & Gates. Only the south side of the city retains its fortified medieval walls, but some ceremonial gates remain. If you come to Toledo by the labor-saving outdoor escalator, you'll pass through **Puerta de Alfonso VI** at the base of the hill. At the top, turn left to walk toward **Puerta del Sol,** an original gate to the Muslim hilltop city that was rebuilt in Mudéjar style in the 14th century. **Mirador Barrio Nuevo,** across the street from the Museo Sefardí (see p. 170, **10**), has sweeping panoramic views.

2 Convento de Santo Domingo El Antiguo. Born in Crete and trained in Venice and Rome, Doménikos Theotokópoulos (1541–1614) came to Toledo in 1577 with a lucrative contract to paint nine canvases for this Dominican convent. His early version of the *Asunción* that hangs above the altar helped make his reputation. Known as El Greco ("The Greek"), he spent the rest of his life in Toledo. His tomb is deep in a crypt below the convent church. A tour of the church's museum includes the chance to look through a peephole into the burial vault. ☉ 30 min. Plaza Santo Domingo El Antiguo, s/n. ☎ 925-222-930. 2€. Mon–Sat 11am–1:30pm and 4–7pm; Sun 4–7pm.

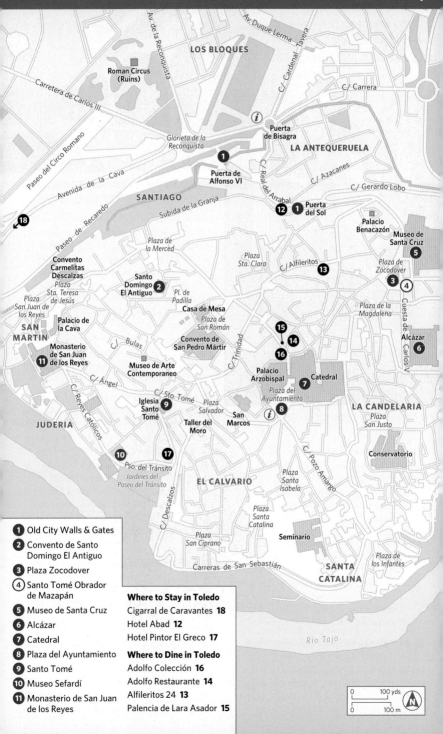

LOS BLOQUES

Roman Circus (Ruins)

Carretera de Carlos III

Av. Duque Lerma

C/ Carrera

Glorieta de la Reconquista

Puerta de Bisagra

LA ANTEQUERUELA

Paseo del Circo Romano

Avenida de la Cava

1 Puerta de Alfonso VI

C/ Azacanes

C/ Gerardo Lobo

SANTIAGO

Subida de la Granja

Paseo de Recaredo

12 **1** Puerta del Sol

Palacio Benacazón

Museo de Santa Cruz **5**

Plaza de la Merced

Plaza Sta. Clara

C/ Alfileritos **13**

Plaza de Zocodover

3 **4**

Convento Carmelitas Descalzas

Plaza Sta. Teresa de Jesús

18

Santo Domingo El Antiguo **2**

Pl. de Padilla

Casa de Mesa

Plaza de San Román

Pîaza de la Magdalena

Plaza San Juan de los Reyes

SAN MARTÍN

Palacio de la Cava

Monasterio de San Juan de los Reyes **11**

C/ Bulas

C/ Ángel

Museo de Arte Contemporaneo

Convento de San Pedro Mártir

15 **14**

16

Alcázar **6**

Cuesta de Carlos V

JUDERÍA

C/ Reyes Católicos

C/ Sto. Tomé

Iglesia Santo Tomé **9**

Plaza Salvador

Taller del Moro

San Marcos

Palacio Arzobispal **7** Catedral

Plaza del Ayuntamiento

8

LA CANDELARIA

Plaza San Justo

10

17

Pso. del Tránsito

Jardines del Paseo del Tránsito

C/ Descalzos

EL CALVARIO

Conservatorio

C/ Pozo Amargo

Plaza Santa Isabela

Plaza Santa Catalina

Plaza San Ciprano

Seminario

Carreras de San Sebastián

SANTA CATALINA

Plaza de los Infantes

Río Tajo

1 Old City Walls & Gates

2 Convento de Santo Domingo El Antiguo

3 Plaza Zocodover

4 Santo Tomé Obrador de Mazapán

5 Museo de Santa Cruz

6 Alcázar

7 Catedral

8 Plaza del Ayuntamiento

9 Santo Tomé

10 Museo Sefardí

11 Monasterio de San Juan de los Reyes

Where to Stay in Toledo

Cigarral de Caravantes **18**

Hotel Abad **12**

Hotel Pintor El Greco **17**

Where to Dine in Toledo

Adolfo Colección **16**

Adolfo Restaurante **14**

Alfileritos 24 **13**

Palencia de Lara Asador **15**

0   100 yds

0   100 m

> *El Greco's* Assumption of the Virgin *(1607–13).*

> *The Museo de Santa Cruz was originally a Renaissance hospice founded by Cardinal Mendoza.*

③ **Plaza Zocodover.** There's little logic to Toledo's streets, but corners are often signposted with arrows pointing either to the Catedral or to this cafe-lined former market square. City buses serving the lower barrios make this their only old-city stop.

④ 🔊 kids ★ **Santo Tomé Obrador de Mazapán.** Marzipan pastries (called *mazapán* here) have been a tradition in Toledo since the 12th century. Pop into this confectioner to pick a treat that looks too good to eat. Plaza Zocodover, 7. ☎ 925-221-168. $.

⑤ ★★★ **Museo de Santa Cruz.** Only steps off the plaza, this marvelous museum lets you get unusually close to its dozen or so El Greco paintings, including his masterpiece *La Asunción de la Virgen (Assumption of the Virgin)*, painted from 1607 to 1613. The painter's singular

genius prefigures later art movements with his handling of light, his proto-cubist treatment of space, and his action-painting impasto of rivulets of pigment. Most of the permanent collection here was removed from Toledo churches and convents, and its strengths are naturally in 16th-and 17th-century religious art. Scoot past the archaeological fragments in the courtyard to reach the upper galleries, where you can also admire the Mudéjar and Renaissance coffered ceilings. ⏱ 1 hr. C/ Cervantes, 3. ☎ 925-221-036. Free. Mon–Sat 10am–6pm; Sun 10am–2pm.

⑥ **Alcázar.** Across a small plaza from Santa Cruz, the Alcázar has been a fort since Roman times, although the great Renaissance sculptor-architect Alonso de Covarrubias constructed the present building in 1535. Besieged and heavily damaged by Republican forces in the Spanish Civil War, the resistance of the Nationalist troops inside became a symbol of the iron will of Franco's men. For many years, the Alcázar has been designated to become a museum of the army, a project yet to come to fruition.

⑦ ★★ **Catedral.** All streets in the center of the Old City eventually funnel down to the cathedral. Begun in 1227 and finally finished in 1497, it's one of only three French-style Gothic cathedrals in Spain. You'll be awed by the soaring interiors—once you find the door. (It's off C/ Hombre del Palo beneath the clock tower.) The archbishop of Toledo is the primate of Spain, and this house of worship is his home church. True to form, it stands on the site of the city's old mosque, which in turn displaced an earlier Visigothic basilica. Only fragments of

> *Plaza Zocodover, the heart of Toledo's Old City.*

the mosque remain, mostly as reused columns and capitals in some of the side chapels. The simple body of Gothic architecture is almost obscured by the vestments of baroque adornment—that is, you can hardly see the arches for the gilt. The cathedral also holds the ornate tombs of several Castilian kings and the all-powerful Cardinal Mendoza (1428–95). Its artistic masterpiece, however, may be the 1495 carved choir stalls by Rodrigo Alemán, showing the conquest of Granada only 3 years earlier. Several major El Grecos can be found in the sacristy: his portrait series of the Apostles and his famous 1577–79 *El Espolio* (*The Disrobing of Christ*). ⏱ 1½ hr. C/ Cisneros, s/n. ☎ 925-222-241. 7€, free Sun. Mon–Sat 10am–6:30pm; Sun 2–6:30pm.

❽ Plaza del Ayuntamiento. Since the cathedral's surrounding plazas were built up long ago, this small plaza in front of city hall and adjacent to the immense church functions as the city center. Kids kick soccer balls around under parents' watchful eyes, and tourists sit on benches to study their tourist office maps.

❾ ★ Santo Tomé. One rational thread in Toledo's street plan is the east-west corridor lined with shops and restaurants. At the head of city hall plaza, the street is called C/ de la Trinidad, but it soon becomes C/ Santo Tomé

Toledo Blades

Toledo's blacksmiths were the first artisans in Europe to rediscover how to make hardened Damascus steel, and any Crusader worth his salt wanted a sword of Toledo steel to take into battle in the Holy Land. Trinket shops sell a lot of junky souvenir swords, but there are a few authentic sword makers still practicing the ancient trade—mainly producing ceremonial swords and keeping fencing clubs in rapiers. On winter weekdays you can visit the shop of ★★ **Mariano Zamoraño Fábrica de Espadas y Armas Blancas,** C/ Ciudad, 19 (☎ 925-222-634), and see craftsmen heating, pounding, and stretching steel to make blades. During warmer weather, they assemble swords and do other less heat-intensive work. Even the supersharp kitchen cutlery made here carries the sword maker's MZ signature.

on the west. Walking west brings you to the church of Santo Tomé. Since it was his parish, El Greco gave a discount for the commission of *El Entierro del Conde Orgaz (The Burial of the Count of Orgaz)*, which many scholars consider his best work. Funerals of 16th-century nobles were generally carried out by other nobles, so the painting is really a multiple portrait of Toledo gentry. It is displayed in a foyer outside the church, and while the admission seems steep for a single painting, it *is* a great one. ⏱ 20 min. C/ Santo Tomé, s/n. ☎ 925-256-098. www.santotome.org. 2.30€. Summer daily 10am–6:45pm; winter closes 5:45pm.

🔟 ★★ **Museo Sefardí.** Former Royal Treasurer Samuel Leví extracted a special dispensation from Pedro I to construct the Sinagoga del Tránsito in 1355. New synagogues were banned, but Leví had clout, having served Pedro in several capacities. When the Jews were expelled in 1492, the building was Christianized as a church, and most of the carved scrollwork on the walls was unfortunately destroyed.

Partial restoration in 1910 under the culture ministry stalled, but in 1992, the old synagogue finally opened as a museum about Judaism from the time of the Romans (who settled many Jewish troublemakers in Spain) to 1492. Rather droll displays show how attitudes changed until Spain finally withdrew the expulsion order in 1869. ⏱ 1 hr. C/ Samuel Leví, s/n. ☎ 925-223-665. www.museosefardi.net. 2.40€ adults, 1.20€ seniors and students, free Sat afternoon and Sun morning. Feb 15–Nov Tues–Sat 10am–9pm, Sun 10am–2pm; Dec–Feb 14 closes 6pm Tues–Sat.

⓫ **Monasterio de San Juan de los Reyes.** Fernando and Isabel built this Franciscan monastery as their burial site, though they later opted for the greater symbolism of Granada. The central courtyard of the cloister is a junglelike garden, full of sunshine and birdsong. It's not hard to imagine being happy here for eternity. ⏱ 30 min. C/ San Juan de los Reyes, 2. ☎ 925-223-802. www.sanjuandelosreyes.org. 2.30€. Summer daily 10am–7pm; winter closes 6pm.

> In 1954, the Monasterio de San Juan de los Reyes and its cloistered gardens were turned over again to the Franciscans.

Where to Stay & Dine

> The stone-walled dining room of Alfileritos 24.

Adolfo Colección OLD CITY MANCHEGAN
Sample the cuisine of Toledo's top chef (see below) at this casual gourmet shop and bar with reasonably priced small plates. C/ Nuncio Viejo, 1. ☎ 925-224-244. Plates 6€–10€. Lunch & dinner daily. AE, DC, MC, V.

★★ Adolfo Restaurante OLD CITY MANCHEGAN
Toledanos favor this flagship room of local restaurateur Adolfo Muñoz for a big night out. The acclaimed wine list complements updated Manchegan cuisine, such as loin of lamb with white truffle, garlic, and thyme. C/ Granada, 6. ☎ 925-252-472. www.adolforestaurante.com. Entrees 25€–32€. Lunch daily, dinner Mon–Sat. AE, DC, MC, V.

★ Alfileritos 24 OLD CITY CONTEMPORARY SPANISH Ancient stone walls make a dramatic setting for munching on tapas and small plates, such as mushroom and langostino croquettes, in the tavern, or full meals in the dining room, like the duck breast with plums and caramelized onions. C/ Alfileritos, 24. ☎ 925-239-625. www.alfileritos24.com. Entrees 16€–20€, tavern 5€–11€. Lunch & dinner daily. AE, DC, MC, V.

★★ Cigarral de Caravantes SAN MARTIN
This hill-country estate across the Río Tajo has the Toledo views that inspired El Greco—and an outdoor pool. All rooms feature beamed ceilings and spacious terraces. It's on the no. 71 bus line, which runs to Plaza de Zocodover. Carretera Circunvalación, 2. ☎ 925-283-680. www.cigarralde caravantes.com. 22 rooms. Doubles 90€–120€. AE, DC, MC, V.

★ Hotel Abad OLD CITY
Abad brings a modern edge to a 19th-century blacksmith's shop with rich, saturated colors and shiny surfaces. But they couldn't improve on the aged wooden beams, exposed brick, and big windows that flood the building with light. C/ Real del Arrabal, 1. ☎ 925-283-500. www.hotelabad. com. 22 rooms. Doubles 74€–122€. DC, MC, V.

★ Hotel Pintor El Greco OLD CITY
About half the rooms here occupy a typical 17th-century brick and stucco building and are furnished accordingly with carved wooden furniture and wrought-iron accents. A 2008 modern addition features marble floors and leather furniture. Neither wing disappoints. C/ Alamillos del Tránsito, 13. ☎ 925-285-191. www.hotelpintorelgreco.com. 60 rooms. Doubles 60€–155€. AE, MC, V.

Palencia de Lara Asador OLD CITY MANCHEGAN
This elegant white-linen *asador* (grill) shows great respect for traditional dishes such as venison with red-wine sauce or pickled wild partridge. C/ Nuncio Viejo, 6. ☎ 925-256-746. Entrees 15€–24€. Lunch Tues–Sun, dinner Tues–Sat. MC, V.

Cuenca

When Tariq's Muslim armies fortified this high limestone spur in 714, they were literally building a castle in the air. Cuenca's old quarter looks down from a dizzying height to the gorges of the Río Huécar and Río Júcar. Space was tight on this steep hilltop, so when the city blossomed from the 12th to the 16th century, Cuencans erected angular, vertical buildings that push to the edge of the gorges—and beyond. The Spanish abstract artists known as El Grupo Paso discovered this vertical fantasy of a town in the 1950s—and well-to-do Madrileños soon followed on weekend getaways. *Note:* It's best to forego public transportation or a car for your feet.

> *Crossing Cuenca's Puente de San Pablo over the Huécar gorge is not for those with a fear of heights.*

START CU-914 to Plaza Mayor.

❶ Plaza Mayor. This wide triangle is anchored on the south (downhill) side by the 1733 Ayuntamiento, or town hall, which has three arches beneath it to let traffic pass through. The plaza is small but busy with cafes and shops along its edges. Matadors and bulls go at it here during the Fiesta de San Mateo (Sept 18–21). During Semana Santa, the brotherhoods gather here for Cuenca's processions, which are famous all over Spain. ⏲ 20 min.

❷ ★ Catedral de Cuenca. Six years after Alfonso VIII conquered Cuenca in 1177, he engaged Anglo-Norman masons to build this Gothic masterpiece with alabaster columns. (His wife was Anglo-Norman princess Eleanor Plantagenet.) Now anchoring the north end of Plaza Mayor, the cathedral's steps are a hangout for street musicians and a common meeting point for lost tourists. The church's multilingual audio guide (included in the admission) supplies a lively and detailed art-historical narrative. ⏲ 1 hr. Plaza Mayor, s/n. ☎ 969-224-626. 2.80€ adults, 2€ seniors and students. July–Sept Mon–Fri 10am–2pm and 4–7pm, Sat–Sun 10am–6:30pm; Oct–June daily 10:30am–1:30pm and 4–6:30pm.

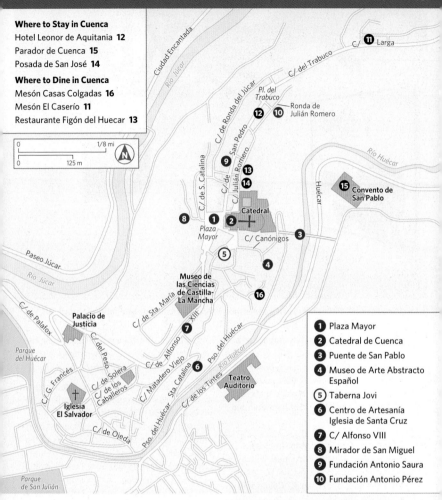

Where to Stay in Cuenca
Hotel Leonor de Aquitania **12**
Parador de Cuenca **15**
Posada de San José **14**

Where to Dine in Cuenca
Mesón Casas Colgadas **16**
Mesón El Caserío **11**
Restaurante Figón del Huecar **13**

1 Plaza Mayor
2 Catedral de Cuenca
3 Puente de San Pablo
4 Museo de Arte Abstracto Español
5 Taberna Jovi
6 Centro de Artesanía Iglesia de Santa Cruz
7 C/ Alfonso VIII
8 Mirador de San Miguel
9 Fundación Antonio Saura
10 Fundación Antonio Pérez

3 Puente de San Pablo. This wood and iron footbridge between the San Pablo convent (now a *parador*) and the Old City spans the Huécar gorge. Built in 1902, it replaced the original stone bridge constructed from 1533 to 1589. It's also a great place to photograph the *casas colgadas*, or "hanging houses," cantilevered over the gorge.

4 ★★ Museo de Arte Abstracto Español. This museum, founded by artist Fernando Zóbel (1924–84), occupies one of the *casas colgadas*. As a member of El Grupo Paso, Zóbel amassed a comprehensive collection of midcentury Spanish abstract art, and later works were acquired by the museum after the gift of his collection in

> *Plaza Mayor is a gathering spot for Cuenca's locals.*

> *The Museo de Arte Abstracto Español features some of Spain's most outstanding abstract artists.*

1980. In recent years, the museum has added a gallery for temporary exhibitions. Seeing a hanging house from the inside is an added bonus. ⏱1 hr. C/ Canónigos, s/n. ☎ 969-212-983. www.march. es/cuenca. 3€ adults, 1.50€ seniors and students. Tues–Fri 11am–2pm and 4–6pm; Sat 11am–2pm and 4–8pm; Sun 11am–2:30pm.

⑤ 🍴 **Taberna Jovi.** Reflect on Cuenca's man-made and natural wonders with a drink and a tapa at this artists' hangout since the days of El Paso. C/ Colmillo, 10. ☎ 969-214-284. $$.

❻ **Centro de Artesanía Iglesia de Santa Cruz.** In addition to its painters and sculptors, Cuenca has a strong history in fine crafts. This converted medieval church makes a splendid display space—half gallery, half sales room. ⏱30 min. C/ Santa Catalina, s/n. ☎ 969-233-184. Free. Tues–Sat 11am–2pm and 5–9pm; Sun 11am–2pm.

❼ **C/ Alfonso VIII.** Photographers and painters love this main avenue on the downhill side of Plaza Mayor for its colorful houses in faded pastels, many with medieval crests above their doors.

❽ **Mirador de San Miguel.** Most visitors gravitate—no pun intended—to the Huécar gorge. They never realize that the overlook by the San Miguel church, northwest of Plaza Mayor, has even more striking views down the green hillside to the Júcar river. ⏱30 min.

❾ ★ **Fundación Antonio Saura.** Another great abstract modernist and El Paso founder, Antonio Saura (1930–98) worked largely with a monochromatic palette. He developed a highly individual gestural vocabulary of forms to represent male and female bodies, crucifixes, and such Spanish mythic figures as Don Quixote and Goya's *Yellow Dog*. This museum displays both Saura's own work and his private collection of fellow artists. ⏱1 hr. Plaza de San Nicolas, 4. ☎ 969-236-054. www.fundacionantoniosaura. es. Free. Summer Mon and Wed–Sat 11am–2pm and 4–8pm, Sun 11am–2pm; winter closes 7pm Mon and Wed–Sat.

❿ ★ **Fundación Antonio Pérez.** More collector than artist, Antonio Pérez bequeathed this witty collection that's the perfect complement to the Saura foundation and the abstract art museum. Pérez exuberantly embraced Pop Art and his own artistic niche, Found Art. (His *Castrati* is a group of three bells minus their clappers.) Pérez found a lot, and therefore left a lot. ⏱1 hr. C/ Ronda de Julian Romero, 20. ☎ 969-230-619. www.fundacion antonioperez.es. Free. Summer Wed–Mon 11am–2pm and 5–9pm; winter closes 8pm.

Where to Stay & Dine

> *Cuenca's convent-cum-parador.*

Hotel Leonor de Aquitania OLD CITY
Eighteen rooms in this 18th-century palace
turned hotel have views of the Huécar gorge. All
feature a relaxed traditional style of pale walls,
tile floors, and colorful floral fabrics. C/ San Pedro,
60. ☎ 969-231-000. www.hotelleonordeaquitania.
com. 49 rooms. Doubles 103€–120€. AE, MC, V.

★ **Mesón Casas Colgadas** OLD CITY *MANCHEGAN*
You won't have to sacrifice food quality for a great
view in this fine dining establishment in one of
Cuenca's *casas colgadas*. Views of Huécar gorge
are outstanding, as are house specialties of fried
trout in ham and onion sauce, or roast lamb.
C/ Canónigos, s/n. ☎ 969-223-509. Entrees 14€–
24€. Lunch Wed–Mon, dinner Wed–Sat. AE, MC, V.

Mesón El Caserío CASTILLO *MANCHEGAN*
Locals favor this casual spot just outside the
Old City walls for wood-grilled meats and vegetables. The short walk uphill will build your
appetite for roast sirloin or lamb with grilled
asparagus. C/ Larga, 17. ☎ 969-230-021. Entrees
6€–15€. Lunch & dinner Wed–Mon. MC, V.

★★ **Parador de Cuenca** HUECAR GORGE
Designers mixed historic style and modern
comfort to transform this 16th-century former
convent into Cuenca's top lodging. Relatively

large rooms have high ceilings and traditional
decor; some look across the Huécar gorge
to the Old City. A long footbridge spans the
gorge—an exhilarating or frightening walk
depending on your tolerance for heights. Subida
San Pablo, s/n. ☎ 969-232-320. www.parador.es.
63 rooms. Doubles 133€–160€. AE, DC, MC, V.

★★ **Posada de San José** OLD CITY
There's an option for every style and budget—
from large rooms with terraces to cozy retreats
with shared bath. Meticulous owners emphasize
the building's venerable history with simple
wooden furniture, whitewashed walls, and a
fascinating collection of art and artifacts. There's
no air-conditioning, but night breezes cool the
rooms quickly. C/ Julián Romero, 4. ☎ 969-211-
300. www.posadasanjose.com. 31 rooms. Doubles
74€–100€. AE, DC, MC, V.

★ **Restaurante Figón del Huecar** OLD CITY
MANCHEGAN You might feel like a dinner-party
guest in this former home of singer José Luis
Perales. Start with *ajoarriero* (a traditional pâté
of potato, codfish, and garlic) before moving on
to such contemporary fare as cannelloni filled
with oxtail and braised apple. C/ Ronda Julián
Romero, 6. ☎ 969-240-062. Entrees 16€–20€.
Lunch Tues–Sun, dinner Tues–Sat. AE, MC, V.

Castilla-La Mancha Fast Facts

> *Castilla-La Mancha's transport system is connected to Madrid by air, rail, or road.*

Arriving & Getting Around

BY PLANE Most visitors to Castilla-La Mancha fly into Madrid's Barajas International Airport (see p. 150). **BY TRAIN** Toledo and Cuenca have excellent rail connections to Madrid via the national train system **RENFE** (☎ 902-240-202; www.renfe.es). Toledo's **Estación de RENFE** is in the new city at Paseo de la Rosa, s/n. On the high-speed train, Toledo is only 30 minutes from Madrid. Cuenca's **Estación de RENFE** is also in the new city, at the base of the hill, at C/ Mariano Catalina, 10. High-speed service on the Madrid–Valencia line is scheduled to begin in 2012. **BY BUS** A variety of bus lines service the cities and towns of Castilla-La Mancha, almost all with connections to Madrid. **Consuegra**'s bus stop is at Avenida de Castilla-La Mancha, s/n (☎ 925-480-553). **Cuenca**'s bus station is at C/ Fermín Caballero, 20 (☎ 969-227-087). **Talavera de la Reina**'s station is at Ronda Cañillo, 7 (☎ 925-800-400). The main **Toledo** bus station is at C/ de la Estación, s/n (☎ 925-215-850). The

Valdepeñas station is at C/ Feria del Vino, 1 (☎ 926-322-866). BY CAR From Madrid, the main access route to Toledo is via the **AP-41,** to Talavera via the **A-5,** and to Cuenca via the **A-3** to the **A-40.** The **A-4** shoots due south from Madrid, passing through Valdepeñas en route to Andalucía.

ATMs
You'll find 24-hour ATMs throughout the region, even in the smallest villages. Most accept Maestro, Cirrus, and Visa.

Doctors & Hospitals
For emergency medical or dental attention, go to the *centro de urgencia* (emergency room) of the nearest hospital. TOLEDO **Hospital Virgen de la Salud,** Avenida de Barber, 30 (☎ 925-269-200). CUENCA **Hospital Virgen de la Luz,** C/ Hermandad de Donantes De Sangre, s/n (☎ 969-179-900; www.hvluz.es). Non-E.U. residents can consult national health service doctors for a relatively small fee; ask at your hotel for a list of doctors.

Emergencies
The all-around emergency number in Spain is ☎ **112.** For an ambulance, call ☎ **061.** For national police, call ☎ **091.**

Internet Access
Wi-Fi has become common in hotels and is usually free except in business hotels.

Pharmacies
To find an open pharmacy outside normal business hours, check the list of stores posted on the door of any drugstore. By law, there's always a drugstore open somewhere. Drugstores are called *farmacías.* When open, they display a neon green cross.

Police
Call ☎ **091** for the national police or ☎ **092** for the local police.

Post Office
CONSUEGRA The office is at C/ Florinda, 5 Bajo (☎ 925-475-507). CUENCA The main office is at C/ Princesa Zaida, 5 (☎ 969-221-042). TOLEDO The main office is at C/ de la Plata, 1 (☎ 925-284-437). VALDEPEÑAS The main office is at C/ Bernardo Balbuena, 25 (☎ 926-322-596). Offices are generally open Monday to Friday 8am to 8pm and Saturday 9am to 2pm.

Safety
Cities and towns in Castilla-La Mancha are generally safe. Use common sense and avoid deserted streets at night. Take care not to leave anything visible in a parked car, especially overnight. Vandalism of cars parked on the street in Toledo's Old City is not uncommon, but you are more likely to be towed than vandalized.

Visitor Information
Toledo Oficina Provincial de Turismo, Puerta de Bisagra, s/n (☎ 925-220-843; www.visitclm.com), is open Monday to Saturday 9am to 7pm, Sunday 9am to 3pm, and provides information on Toledo, Consuegra, Talavera de la Reína, and villages in the Don Quixote tour. ARGAMASILLA DE ALBA **Oficina de Turismo,** C/ Cervantes, 7 (☎ 926-523-234), is open Tuesday to Saturday 10am to 2pm and 5 to 8pm, Sunday 10am to 2pm. CAMPO DE CRIPTANA **Oficina de Turismo,** C/ Barbero, 1 (☎ 926-562-231; www.campode criptana.info), is open Tuesday to Friday 10am to 2pm and 4 to 6pm, Saturday 10am to 2pm. CONSUEGRA **Oficina de Turismo,** Molino de Viento "Bolero" (☎ 925-475-731; www.consuegra.es), is open Thursday to Monday 11:30am to 2pm and 4:30 to 8pm. CUENCA **Oficina Municipal de Turismo,** C/ Alfonso VIII, 2 (☎ 969-241-051; www.turismocuenca.com), is open daily 9am to 9pm. EL TOBOSO **Oficina de Turismo,** C/ Daoíz y Velarde, 3 (☎ 925-568-226), is open Tuesday to Saturday 10am to 2pm and 5 to 7pm, Sunday 10am to 2pm. TALAVERA **Oficina de Turismo,** C/ Palenque, 2 (☎ 925-826-322; www.talavera.org/turismo), is open Monday to Friday 9:30am to 2pm and 5 to 7pm, Saturday to Sunday 10am to 2pm. TOLEDO **Patronato Municipal de Turismo,** Plaza del Ayuntamiento, s/n (☎ 925-254-030; www.toledo-turismo.com), is open Monday to Friday 10:30am to 2:30pm and 4:30 to 7pm, Saturday to Sunday 10:30am to 2:30pm. VALDEPEÑAS **Oficina de Turismo,** Plaza de España, s/n (☎ 926-312-552; www.valdepenas.es), is open Monday to Friday 10am to 2pm and 5 to 7pm, Saturday 10am to 2pm.

The Best of Extremadura in 5 Days

Mountainous Extremadura is a region of comings and goings. The Romans settled here to stake a claim to westernmost Europe. Pilgrims stream to Guadalupe to see the image of the Virgin, often continuing to Santiago de Compostela in Galicia. Hernán Cortés and Francisco Pizarro—conquerors of the Aztecs and Incas, respectively—were Extremadurans, as were many New World soldiers and administrators. And from late February into August, thousands of storks settle in to lay their eggs and raise their chicks. To cover the region at a leisurely pace, plan to spend 2 nights in Mérida and 1 each in Guadalupe, Trujillo, and Cáceres.

> PREVIOUS PAGE *Alfonso XI's mountain Monasterio de Santa María de Guadalupe.* THIS PAGE *The engineering feat of the Roman Acueducto los Milagros was a miracle for 2nd-century Augusta Merita.*

START Mérida. TRIP LENGTH 249km (155 miles).

❶ **Mérida.** The Roman mark is strong on Augusta Emerita, as this city was called when founded in 25 B.C. Approach from the north, and you cannot help but marvel at the **Acueducto los Milagros.** The remaining 38 arches tower 25m (82 ft.) high and stretch for 830m (2,723 ft.). They were constructed early in the 2nd century A.D. to bring water 4.8km (3 miles) to the city from the dammed Proserpina reservoir. The city's east gateway also has three remaining granite-and-brick arches of **Acueducto San Lázaro.**

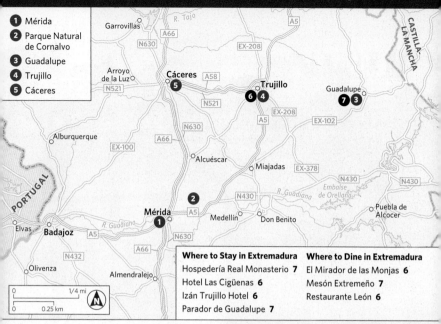

① Mérida
② Parque Natural de Cornalvo
③ Guadalupe
④ Trujillo
⑤ Cáceres

Where to Stay in Extremadura	Where to Dine in Extremadura
Hospedería Real Monasterio 7	El Mirador de las Monjas 6
Hotel Las Cigüeñas 6	Mesón Extremeño 7
Izán Trujillo Hotel 6	Restaurante León 6
Parador de Guadalupe 7	

These engineering marvels hint at the Roman traces left in Mérida. As you stroll the city, you'll discover fragments of walls or arches or the ruins of a temple in the middle of a residential neighborhood. Don't miss the truly impressive **amphitheater and theater,** or the **Museo Nacional del Arte Romano,** where Roman art, architecture, and daily life come together in the superb interpretive exhibitions. See p. 186.

Follow N-V east for 14km (8⅔ miles) until it merges with the E-90. Continue 2km (1¼ miles) to Carretera Trujillanos-Embalse de Cornalvo.

② **Parque Natural de Cornalvo.** Two mountain ranges frame this park of deep woods and rolling plains covered with wheat and olives. While Extremadura is often considered a dry land, this section is crisscrossed with small rivers dammed 2,000 years ago by the Romans to create *embalses* (reservoirs) still in use. Six different trail heads give you access to walks as short as an hour or as long as a day. Get a good overview of the terrain and bird life by hiking 8km (5 miles) around the Embalse de Cornalvo. **Centro de Interpretación: Carretera Trujillanos–Embalse, s/n. ☎ 630-12-51-72. Free. Daily 9am–2pm and 4–7pm.**

> *An excavated Augusta Emerita street at the Museo Nacional del Arte Romano.*

Retrace your route to E-90 east and continue 43km (27 miles). At exit 287, follow EX-102 east 75km (47 miles) to Guadalupe.

③ **Guadalupe.** This mountain village of narrow cobbled streets and wooden houses with hanging balconies is among the main pilgrimage sites of Spain. The modest village nestles around the skirts of the ★★ **Real Monasterio de Santa María de Guadalupe.** The early-14th-century monastery-church complex was commissioned by Alfonso XI of Castilla y León to house an

> *Celts, Romans, Moors, and Christians have inhabited Trujillo, but the Moors erected its imposing castle.*

ancient image of the Virgin Mary discovered near the Río Guadalupe a few years earlier. Pilgrims are drawn to the image of Nuestra Señora de Guadalupe (Our Lady of Guadalupe), the patroness of Extremadura, but the complex has other treasures as well, including 11 major paintings by Francisco Zurbarán (born in nearby Fuente de Cantos). Among them is one of his most important works, *La Apoteosis de San Jerónimo (The Apotheosis of St. Jerome).* The monastery

Pimentón de la Vera

Few spices are so characteristic of Spanish cuisine as the paprika known as *pimentón de la vera,* widely available in local shops. Cultivated in a handful of towns in the de la Vera region outside Cáceres since the 16th century, the three varieties of pepper (sweet, hot, and bittersweet) are harvested in October and hand-turned for 10 to 15 days in drying rooms heated by a smoky oak-log fire. Only a dozen producers qualify to use the DO Pimentón de la Vera label, the guarantee of authenticity and quality.

was an important scriptorium from the 14th to 19th century, and more than 90 hand-lettered miniature books are displayed in the monastery museum, along with several paintings by Goya and El Greco and a marble sculpture of the Crucifixion attributed to Michelangelo.

Plaza Santa María in front of the church remains the lively heart of town. The shops surrounding it sell souvenirs of Guadalupe, while the central fountain is where three American Indians brought back by Columbus on his second voyage were baptized. If you need a break, just off the plaza is **Pastelería-Cafe Atrium,** where you can try a slice of *técula mécula,* the local specialty almond tart. Monasterio: Plaza Juan Carlos 1, s/n. ☎ 927-36-70-00. Church free; tours of museum, sacristy, cloister 4€ adults, 3€ seniors, 1.50€ kids. Church open daily 8am–9pm, tours 9:30am–1pm and 3:30–6:30pm. Pastelería: C/ Alfonso el Onceño, 6. ☎ 927-36-70-40. Snacks 3€–8€. AE, MC, V. Lunch & dinner daily.

From Guadalupe, follow EX-102 west 43km (27 miles). At the fork, bear right on EX-208 for 26km (16 miles) to Trujillo.

> *A church fit for kings (and queens)—Fernando and Isabel once attended Mass at Santa María la Mayor.*

④ Trujillo. He's been dead since 1541, but the big man in town remains Francisco Pizarro, conqueror of the Incan empire and founder of Lima, Peru. A heroic-scale bronze of Pizarro on horseback dominates the 16th-century Plaza Mayor, but you'll need to hike uphill to the old quarter to get more personal with the conquistador at his grandfather's house, the ★ **Casa-Museo de Pizarro.** The conqueror-to-be spent much of his childhood here, and the lower level shows how the family lived. Upstairs, exhibits detail his career and explain a little about Inca culture.

Pizarro was actually only one of several local men who made his bones in the Americas. (New World riches funded many handsome Renaissance palaces in the lower town.) Another Trujillano, Francisco Orellana, is famed for exploring the length of the Amazon River in the 1540s. His bust stands in the plaza outside the town's fortresslike Romanesque church, ★ **Santa María la Mayor.** Built on the site of a mosque and consecrated in 1232, Santa María was part of the Christian effort to consolidate the Reconquista. Its extraordinary altarpiece consists of 25 paintings by Salamanca-born Francisco Gallego (1440–1507), one of the great Castillian painters of his day. Climb the bell tower for sweeping overviews of the countryside and the new city below the original town.

The bell tower is grand, but the Muslim governors under the Córdoban Caliphate had already nailed down the best views in town by building the **kids Castillo** atop the Cabeza de Zorro ("Head of the Fox") hill in the late–10th and early–11th centuries. Substantially modified from the 16th century forward, the castle's turrets provide views of Trujillo and neighboring towns.

Each year on the weekend closest to May 1, Trujillo hosts the Feria Nacional de Queso, or national cheese fair. If you miss it, you can still get a pretty good overview of local cheese making at the **Museo del Queso y el Vino de Trujillo,** located in an old convent. The museum also offers tastings of local cheese and wine. Casa-Museo: C/ Martibés, s/n. No phone. 1.40€ adults, free for kids. Daily 10am–2pm and 4:30–7:30pm. Santa María: Plaza Santa María.

> *Francisco Pizarro was a local boy done good when he conquered the Incan Empire and founded modern-day Lima.*

No phone. 1.40€, free for kids. Daily 10am–2pm and 4:30–7:30pm. Castillo: Cabeza de Zorro. No phone. 1.40€ adults, free for kids. Daily 10am–2pm and 4:30–7:30pm. Museo del Queso: C/ Francisco Pizarro, s/n. ☎ 927-32-30-31. www.quesovino.com. 2.30€ with tasting of wine and cheese, 1.30€ without; free for kids. Summer daily 11am–3pm and 6–8pm; winter daily 11am–3pm and 5:30–7:30pm.

From Trujillo, follow the N-521/A-8 west 46km (29 miles) to Cáceres.

5 Cáceres. The New World wealth that graced remote Trujillo also built many a trophy home in the old quarter of this provincial capital—often complete with defensive towers for warring with the neighbors. In some ways, the city of fortified mansions is a study in the warrior mentality, since about half of it was built by knights of the Reconquista, while the remainder was constructed for those who had vanquished the native peoples of the Americas. For details on the Cáceres architectural sites, see p. 190.

The machismo apparently abated over the centuries. The 1837 facade of the **Palacio Episcopal** on Plaza Santa María prominently features medallions of an Aztec woman on one side and the head of a Moor (complete with bristling, swept-back moustache and beard) on the other. They appear to have been placed there, *menos* irony, as nostalgic, decorative motifs in the height of the Romantic era.

Rather more clear-headed artistry is the province of the nearby **Centro Provincial de Artesanía.** Set in a 15th-century palace, this center showcases the work of Extremaduran artists working in stone, wood, leather, and ceramics. Plaza de Santa María, s/n. ☎ 927-22-74-53. Free. Tues-Sat 10am–2pm and 5:30–8:30pm; Sun 10am–2pm.

Travel Tip

For lodging and dining in Mérida, see p. 189.
For lodging and dining in Cáceres, see p. 192.

Where to Stay & Dine

> A room at the 15th-century Parador de Guadalupe.

El Mirador de las Monjas TRUJILLO *EXTREMA-DURAN* Specializing in meats roasted on a wood fire, the stylish dining room is empty when the weather is good enough to sit outside in the gardens below the castle. Plaza de Santiago, 2. ☎ 927-65-92-23. Menus 19€–20€. MC, V. Lunch & dinner Wed–Mon.

★ **Hospedería Real Monasterio** GUADALUPE Rooms in this former monastery are far too comfortable and updated to feel monastic. A quiet haven with a pretty courtyard, the hotel is at the back of the church complex. Plaza Juan Carlos 1, s/n. ☎ 927-36-70-00. 47 rooms. Doubles 65€. MC, V.

kids Hotel Las Cigüenas TRUJILLO This well-maintained circa-1970 hotel is popular with families, as some rooms accommodate extra beds. At the edge of town overlooking a pasture, the hotel is a 15-minute stroll to Plaza Mayor. Avenida de Madrid, 52. ☎ 927-32-13-00. www.hotelasciguenas.com. 77 rooms. Doubles 75€–94€. MC, V.

★ **Izán Trujillo Hotel** TRUJILLO A stunning courtyard salon and rich upholstery set the tone for this new hotel in a 16th-century convent. For a touch of local color, the hotel sells beautiful linens made at a nearby convent. Plaza del Campillo, 1. ☎ 927-45-89-00. www.

izanhoteles.es. 77 rooms. Doubles 70€–120€. AE, DC, MC, V.

Mesón Extremeño GUADALUPE *EXTREMA-DURAN* To eat light (so to speak), order charcuterie from the bar menu, especially the house *morcilla* (sausage). Steaks are grilled on a wood fire, while lamb, kid, and suckling pig are roasted in a wood-burning oven. Plaza Santa María, 3. ☎ 927-15-43-27. Entrees 8€–23€. MC, V. Lunch & dinner Wed–Mon.

★ **Parador de Guadalupe** GUADALUPE A central courtyard filled with orange trees signals that this 15th-century former hospital is as peaceful as the Hospedería (see above)—but with more luxury and services. Its restaurant focuses on updated versions of Extremaduran recipes handed down through the religious orders. C/ Marqués de la Romana, 12. ☎ 927-36-70-75. www.parador.es. 42 rooms. Doubles 70€–185€. Entrees 15€–28€. AE, DC, MC, V.

kids Restaurante León TRUJILLO *EXTREMADURAN* Families flock to this bullfight-themed *taberna* (tavern), with its brick and stone arches and flatscreen TV always showing a *corrida*. Quieter dining rooms are available in the rear. C/ General Mola, 23. ☎ 927-32-17-92. Entrees 8€–16€. MC, V. Lunch & dinner daily.

Mérida

Founded as Augusta Emerita in 25 B.C., Mérida still wears a Roman face. In most of Spain, the Roman era survives only in foundation stones beneath a cathedral built on a mosque built on a Visigothic church built on a Roman temple. But Mérida's streets are lined with Roman ruins, ghosts of this former capital of the westernmost Iberian province of Lusitania. The remains are rivaled only by those of Tarragona (see p. 390), the bookend capital of eastern Iberia.

> The architect of the Prado's addition designed the statuary hall at the Museo Nacional del Arte Romano.

START Corner of C/ Santa Eulalia and C/ Moreno Vargas.

❶ C/ Santa Eulalia. Today's chief commercial drag was one of two main Roman streets in ancient Mérida. A section of the 6m-wide (20-ft.) Roman pavement is exposed next to the tourist office.

Travel Tip

Single admissions to Mérida's many Roman sites add up, but the **Conjunto Monumental** pass gets you into all but the Museo for 10€ adults, 6€ kids. The sites also have a **gift shop,** C/ Reyes Huertas, 5 (☎ 924-30-15-13), with nice reproduction jewelry, ceramics, mosaics, and Roman-themed souvenirs.

❷ ★★★ Museo Nacional del Arte Romano. Rafael Moneo made this museum as monumental as the art it displays. "Art" is the right word—the museum treats the statues, carved columns and capitals, and gigantic floor mosaics as reverently as the Prado treats its Goya paintings. Superb signage sets every object in the context of life in Augusta Emerita, as if the emperor will be back after lunch. When construction began, a Roman neighborhood was uncovered—now it's the basement exhibit. ⏱ 1 hr. C/ José Ramón Mélida, s/n. ☎ 924-31-16-90. http://museoarte romano.mcu.es. 3€ adults, free for kids, free Sat afternoon and Sun. Dec–Feb Tues–Sat 10am–2pm and 4–6pm, Sun 10am–2pm; Mar–Nov Tues–Sat 10am–2pm and 4–9pm, Sun 10am–2pm.

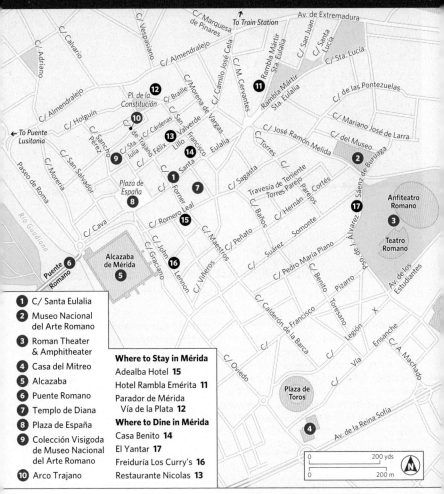

1. C/ Santa Eulalia
2. Museo Nacional del Arte Romano
3. Roman Theater & Amphitheater
4. Casa del Mitreo
5. Alcazaba
6. Puente Romano
7. Templo de Diana
8. Plaza de España
9. Colección Visigoda de Museo Nacional del Arte Romano
10. Arco Trajano

Where to Stay in Mérida
Adealba Hotel 15
Hotel Rambla Emérita 11
Parador de Mérida Vía de la Plata 12

Where to Dine in Mérida
Casa Benito 14
El Yantar 17
Freiduría Los Curry's 16
Restaurante Nicolas 13

③ ★★★ Roman Theater & Amphitheater.

Excavations of these arenas of high art and blood sport, respectively, began in 1910, which might be why they are the best preserved of their kind. Walk the floor of the 1st-century-A.D. amphitheater, peering into caves where wild beasts were caged before they were unleashed on gladiators as 14,000 spectators screamed. The theater, built around 15 B.C., has a decorous grace and more limited seating, as befits a hall where actors would recount the ageless mysteries. Performances of classical theater are still held July to August. ⏱ 1 hr. C/ José Ramón Mélida, s/n. ☎ 924-00-49-08. 7€ adults, 6€ kids and seniors. Winter daily 9:30am–1:45pm and 4–6:15pm; summer daily 9:30am–1:45pm and 5–7:15pm.

> Mérida's Roman theater, built by General Agrippa around 15 B.C., can seat up to 3,000 people.

> *Excavations have uncovered Roman mosaics like this one at Casa del Mitreo, just outside Mérida.*

❹ **Casa del Mitreo.** Just outside the old walls, this "suburban" estate (ca. A.D. 100), with exquisite mosaic floors and some painted walls, evokes a rich complex arranged around three patios. A Roman and Visigoth burial ground is in the same enclosure. ⏱ 45 min. Vía Ensanche, s/n. ☎ 924-00-49-08. 4€. Winter daily 9:30am–1:45pm and 4–6:15pm; summer daily 9:30am–1:45pm and 5–7:15pm.

Instead of following city streets, walk along the green strip of the riverbank to the Alcazaba.

❺ **Alcazaba.** The Romans built the bridge (see below), but the Moors defended it with this A.D. 835 stone fort on the riverbank—one of the first Arabic *alcazabas* (forts) in Spain. ⏱ 30 min. C/ Graciano, s/n. ☎ 924-00-49-08. 4€. Winter daily 9:30am–1:45pm and 4–6:15pm; summer daily 9:30am–1:45pm and 5–7:15pm.

❻ ★ **Puente Romano.** Built in 25 B.C., this 60-arch, 792m (2,600-ft.) span over the Río Guadiana has been restored every 600 to 700 years and is now limited to pedestrians. The end closest to the city is the best preserved. A ramp provides access to the walking paths on the island in the middle of the river.

❼ ★ **Templo de Diana.** Mérida's only religious Roman building survived, in part, because a powerful duke annexed the temple for part of his 16th-century palace. The soaring structure with Corinthian columns was built around A.D. 100 for the cult of the emperor.

❽ **Plaza de España.** Méridanos gather here at the cafes in front of the 1883 town hall, where storks nest on top. Santa María Church on the west side has a spare Romanesque beauty later encrusted with baroque ornamentation. Its tiny stained-glass windows have the intensity of manuscript illuminations.

❾ **Colección Visigoda de Museo Nacional del Arte Romano.** Often dismissed as barbarians, the Visigoths had rich artistic traditions that married Roman form to simple lines drawn from nature. This collection is one of the richest troves of Visigothic design in Spain. ⏱ 30 min. C/ Santa Julia, s/n. ☎ 924-31-16-90. Free. June–Sept Tues–Sat 10am–2pm and 5–7pm, Sun 10am–2pm; Oct–May Tues–Sat 10am–2pm and 4–6pm, Sun 10am–2pm.

❿ **Arco Trajano.** The marble facings and other lavish decorations are long gone, but this 15m-high (49-ft.) arch that once spanned a major Roman street maintains an air of great ceremony. Archaeologists hypothesize that it was the approach to a temple dedicated to worship of the emperor.

Where to Stay & Dine

> A meal at Casa Benito.

★★ Adealba Hotel

This tranquil hotel opened in 2009 in a 15th-century house steps from the Templo de Diana. Sleek, minimalist decor doesn't stint on space or comfort. A small spa features a Turkish bath. C/ Romero Leal, 18. ☎ 924-38-82-71. www.hoteladealba.com. 18 rooms. Doubles 112€–189€, with breakfast. AE, MC, V.

★ Casa Benito EXTREMADURAN

The cozy dining rooms here must have a poster or photo of every bullfight since Benito opened in 1870. The wood-burning ovens and grill produce smoky suckling pig and saddle of lamb. A shaded outdoor patio is popular, and there's a weekday 10€ menu. C/ San Francisco, 3. ☎ 924-33-07-69. Entrees 14€–24€. MC, V. Lunch & dinner daily.

El Yantar EXTREMADURAN

This corner of Spain produces distinctive cheeses and some of the top acorn-fed Iberian hams. Taste the best here as tapas or *raciones* (large versions of tapas). Paseo De José Álvarez Sáenz de Buruaga, s/n. ☎ 924-31-63-54. www.jamoneselyantar.com. Tapas 1.50€–1.80€, raciones 4€–13€. AE, DC, MC, V. Lunch & dinner Wed–Mon.

Freiduría Los Curry's SEAFOOD

This casual fish fry restaurant serves magnificent shrimp from Sanlúcar and North Atlantic lobster and steamed mussels from Galicia—all at bargain prices. C/ John Lennon, 17. ☎ 656-79-35-84. Entrees 6€–8€. Cash only. Lunch & dinner Tues–Sun.

Hotel Rambla Emérita

Intense colors brighten these basic rooms with tiled bathrooms. Some rooms overlook the Rambla's strip of green park. The helpful staff make Emérita a good budget choice. C/ Rambla Mártir Santa Eulalia, 17. ☎ 924-38-72-31. www.hotelemerita.com. 28 rooms. Doubles 54€–72€. MC, V.

★★ Parador de Mérida Vía de la Plata

This stately 18th-century convent is a quiet retreat, yet handy to bustling Plaza de España. Vaulted ceilings, tiled floors, and cream-white masonry walls emphasize the spaciousness of even a typical double room. The restaurant is a showcase of Extremaduran cuisine. Plaza Constitución, 3. ☎ 924-31-38-00. www.parador.es. 82 rooms. Doubles 143€–155€. Entrees 14€–29€. AE, DC, MC, V.

★ Restaurante Nicolas EXTREMADURAN

Eat local in the lovely upstairs dining room, which features veal and lamb as well as fresh vegetables and foraged wild mushrooms. Veal steak in a sauce of local peppers is a sure bet. There's also an excellent and extensive Extremaduran wine list. C/ Felix Valverde Lillo, 13. ☎ 924-31-96-10. Entrees 7€–22€. MC, V. Lunch & dinner daily.

Cáceres

The 12th-century Almohad-dynasty ramparts surrounding the old quarter of this UNESCO World Heritage city have succeeded in keeping the modern world at bay. The streets are lined with great stone private palaces with family crests above the doors—some built in the 13th and 14th centuries by warrior knights of the Reconquista, others financed with plunder from the New World. Storks favor these ancient structures as nesting sites, and in early May the city celebrates the birds with a weeklong festival.

> Even family homes, like this 15th-century mansion with machicolation, were fortified in medieval Spain.

START Plaza Mayor.

❶ **Plaza Mayor.** Just outside the Old City walls, this lively plaza laid out in the 13th century remains the city's gathering place. Restaurants and shops operate beneath its 16th-century arcades. Streets at the south end lead to the modern shopping district; those on the north are filled with bars, taverns, and discos.

❷ **Arco de la Estrella.** From Plaza Mayor, this 18th-century gate leads uphill into the Old City.

❸ **Casa de los Toledo-Moctezuma.** Built in the late 16th century by the Spanish son-in-law of the last Aztec emperor, the building (now a public archive) is covered with stork nests. Peek in to see the lovely Renaissance patio.

❹ **Palacio y Torre de Carvajal.** This handsome Gothic/Renaissance palace was restored in the late 20th century for the regional tourist office. A display area highlights historical and natural attractions of the city and countryside. ⏱ 20 min. C/ Amaguro, 1. ☎ 927-25-55-97. Free. Mon-Fri 8am-9pm; Sat 10am-2pm and 5-8pm; Sun 10am-2pm.

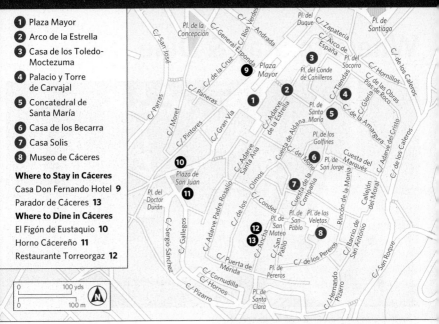

1 Plaza Mayor
2 Arco de la Estrella
3 Casa de los Toledo-Moctezuma
4 Palacio y Torre de Carvajal
5 Concatedral de Santa María
6 Casa de los Becarra
7 Casa Solis
8 Museo de Cáceres

Where to Stay in Cáceres
Casa Don Fernando Hotel **9**
Parador de Cáceres **13**

Where to Dine in Cáceres
El Figón de Eustaquio **10**
Horno Cácereño **11**
Restaurante Torreorgaz **12**

5 **Concatedral de Santa María.** The bulk of the cathedral attests to its 13th-century Romanesque beginnings, but the nave's soaring Gothic arches create an airy house of worship further brightened by stone carvings with plant motifs. Many of the gold and silver chalices and tabernacles in the treasure room were made in Mexico. ⏱ 30 min. Plaza de Santa María. ☎ 927-22-36-11. 1€. Summer daily 9:30am–2pm and 5:30–9pm (winter afternoons 4:30–8pm).

6 **Casa de los Becarra.** Temporary art exhibits are often mounted in this 15th-century fortified mansion so typical of Cáceres. Art students sketch in the pocket plaza in front, with its statue of civic patron San Jorge. ⏱ 20 min. Plaza de San Jorge, 2. ☎ 927-22-36-11. Free. Tues–Sat 11am–2pm and 5–8pm; Sun 11am–2pm.

7 **Casa Solis.** A striking family seal depicting the sun makes this 15th-century fortified mansion a city landmark.

8 ★ **Museo de Cáceres.** Most notable among the archaeological exhibits is the largest Moorish cistern in Spain, but the museum's art wing surprises with holdings in contemporary art. ⏱ 45 min. Plaza de las Veletas, 1. ☎ 927-01-08-77. 1.20€. Tues–Sat 9am–2:30pm and 5–8:15pm (Oct to mid-Apr afternoons 4–7:15pm); Sun 10:15am–2:30pm.

> A stork makes itself at home on a spire of the Casa de los Toledo-Moctezuma.

Where to Stay & Dine

> A sitting area at the medieval Parador de Cáceres.

★★ Casa Don Fernando Hotel

Just across from the Arco de la Estrella and the town hall, this former grand private home opened in summer 2008 as a contemporary boutique hotel with spacious rooms, chic decor, and a strict no-smoking policy. It's worth the 20€ to 30€ premium for the "superior" rooms on the front of the building, with even more space and sweeping views of Plaza Mayor and the walls of the Old City. Plaza Mayor, 30. ☎ 927-21-42-79. www.casadonfernando.com. 36 rooms. Doubles 75€–120€. AE, MC, V.

★★ El Figón de Eustaquio *EXTREMADURAN*

An outstanding local chef presents exquisite versions of traditional Extremaduran cuisine in this rustic room brightened by white linens and a formally dressed wait staff. Unusual country dishes, including some with frog or organ meats, are balanced by a wide choice of roast meats and Galician seafood. The wine list is almost all Spanish, with an emphasis on the wines of the Cáceres region. Ask about the after-dinner cigar list. Plaza de San Juan, 12–14. ☎ 927-24-81-94. Entrees 12€–22€. AE, MC, V. Lunch & dinner daily.

Horno Cácereño *EXTREMADURAN*

The kitchen at Cácereño knows how to play with fire. House specialties include roast suckling pig, lamb, and kid, and grilled wild boar and venison. Don't miss the vegetable dishes with seasonal mushrooms or truffles. Plaza San Juan, 15. ☎ 927-22-22-37. Entrees 12€–30€. MC, V. Lunch & dinner daily.

★★ Parador de Cáceres

Staying in this 14th-century palace gives you an immediate sense of what it was like to live in Cáceres in its medieval heyday between the Reconquista and the conquest of the New World. Rooms vary widely in size and shape but are comfortably appointed in the traditional Old Castillian style of tile floors and natural woods. In contrast to the preponderance of tan stone, the extremely comfortable public areas and courtyards make striking use of rich color. C/ Ancha, 6. ☎ 927-21-17-59. www.parador.es. 33 rooms. Doubles 143€–155€. AE, DC, MC, V.

Restaurante Torreorgaz *EXTREMADURAN*

Parador de Cáceres's restaurant emphasizes such local delicacies as venison with *Torta del Casar* (a soft sheep's-milk cheese) and *zarangollo* salad of roasted red peppers and onions. Weather permitting, the best seats are tables in the lovely garden. C/ Ancha, 6. ☎ 927-21-17-59. Entrees 15€–22€. AE, DC, MC, V. Lunch & dinner daily.

Extremadura Fast Facts

Arriving & Getting Around

BY PLANE Extremadura has no direct air service. Your best bet is to fly into Madrid (see p. 150). **BY TRAIN** Both Mérida and Cáceres have excellent connections to Madrid by rail as well as frequent trains between the two cities. **Estación del RENFE Mérida** is on C/ Cardero, about a 5-minute walk north of Plaza de España, while **Estación del RENFE Cáceres** is on Avenida Alemania south of town. Both stations use the national RENFE number: ☎ 902-24-02-02. An hourly Cáceres bus shuttles passengers to downtown Plaza de América. **BY BUS** The **Mérida bus station** is on Avenida de la Libertad (☎ 924-37-14-04), with frequent service to Madrid, Sevilla, and Cáceres. The **Cáceres bus station** is on Carretera de Sevilla (☎ 927-23-25-50). Frequent service is available to Madrid, Sevilla, Mérida, and Trujillo, along with less frequent service to Guadalupe, Córdoba, Lisbon, and Valladolid. **BY CAR** The **N-V** highway between Madrid and Lisbon cuts east–west through Extremadura. The north–south **A-66** connects to Salamanca in the north and Sevilla in the south.

ATMs

Even the smallest villages have 24-hour ATMs that accept Maestro/MasterCard, Cirrus, and Visa.

Doctors & Hospitals

For emergency medical or dental attention, go to the *centro de urgencia* (emergency room) of the nearest hospital. **MÉRIDA Hospital de Mérida, C/Miguel Servet,** s/n (☎ 924-38-10-00). **CÁCERES Complejo Hospitalario de Cáceres,** Avenida Pablo Naranjo, s/n (☎ 927-25-62-00).

Emergencies

The all-around emergency number in Spain is ☎ 112.

Pharmacies

To find an open pharmacy outside normal business hours, check the list posted on the door of any drugstore. When open, they display a neon green cross.

Police

For national police, call ☎ **091;** for local police, call ☎ **092.**

Post Office

Most post offices in Extremadura are open Monday to Friday 8am to 9pm, Saturday 9am to 2pm. Main offices are identified on city maps.

Safety

Extremadura's towns and cities are extremely safe. Avoid deserted streets and take care not to leave anything visible in a parked car.

Visitor Information

CÁCERES Información Turística de Cáceres, at Plaza Mayor, 3 (☎ 927-01-08-34; www.turismoextremadura.com), is open Monday to Friday 8:30am to 2:30pm and 4 to 6pm, Saturday and Sunday 10am to 2pm. **GUADALUPE Oficina de Turisme Guadalupe,** at Plaza de Santa María de Guadalupe (☎ 927-15-41-28; www.puebladeguadalupe.net), is open Monday to Friday 10am to 2pm and 4 to 6pm, Saturday 10am to 2pm. **MÉRIDA Oficina de Turismo Mérida,** at C/ Santa Eulalia, 64 (☎ 924-33-07-22; www.turismoextremadura.com), is open daily 9:30am to 2pm and 4:30 to 7pm. **TRUJILLO Oficina de Turismo Trujillo,** at Plaza Mayor (☎ 927-32-26-77; www.trujillo.es), is open Tuesday to Friday 9:30am to 2pm and 4 to 7:30pm, Saturday to Monday 10am to 2pm and 4 to 7pm.

The Best of Castilla y León in 3 Days

The story of Castilla y León, Spain's largest autonomous region, is a tale of the consolidation of power. For the first 3 days in the high *meseta* and long river valleys, you'll visit three cities that embody the power of the sword, the power of faith, and the power of knowledge.

> PREVIOUS PAGE *The medieval walls surrounding the city of Ávila.* THIS PAGE *Fernando and Isabel first met in Segovia's 12th-century Alcázar.*

START Bologna. **TRIP LENGTH** 265km (165 miles).

1 Segovia. The Old City on a wedge of rock stretches from the Roman feet of its signature aqueduct to the imperial head of its royal palace. With 166 iconic arches, the ★★★ **Aqueducto** (see p. 218, **1**) was so efficiently engineered that it supplied water to the city for 1,900 years. At the other end of the rocky outcrop, the ★★ **Alcázar de Segovia** (see p. 220, **4**) commands the countryside from a high bluff. Perhaps the most evocative castle in Spain, it conjures the pomp and might of the Castilian monarchy. Segovia is a city that rewards exploration, from its Renaissance noble barrio on one side of **Plaza Mayor** (see p. 218, **2**) to the ancient Judería on the other. Don't miss the Gothic sculptures in the ★ **Museo de Segovia** (see p. 221, **5**).

Drive south 26km (16 miles) on the AP-61 to the AP-6. In 24km (15 miles), take exit 81 to the AP-51 for 30km (19 miles) to Ávila.

Travel Tip

For detailed coverage of hotels and restaurants in Segovia, see p. 223; for Ávila, see p. 227; and for Salamanca, see p. 233.

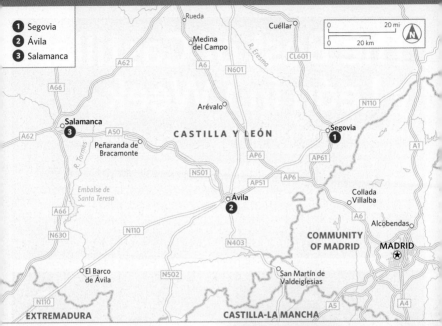

1 Segovia
2 Ávila
3 Salamanca

2 Ávila. Wrapping the city like a nun's voluminous habit, ★★ **Las Murallas,** the medieval walls of Ávila (see p. 224, **2**), give the city an air of cloistered mystery. Santa Teresa—the influential mystic and church reformer—was born here in 1515, and her spirit still has Ávila in thrall. The ★ **Museo Teresiano** (see p. 226, **4**), on the site of her childhood home, provides an excellent overview of the saint and her impact. Visit the **Monasterio de la Encarnación** (p. 226, **6**) to see where she took the veil, and the austere **Convento de San José** (see p. 226, **5**) to see how seriously she took the vows of poverty.

Follow A-50 100km (62 miles) to Salamanca.

3 Salamanca. A scholar's city since the ★★ **University of Salamanca** (see p. 228, **1**, **2**; p. 230, **3**) was founded here in 1218, Salamanca has a rare open plan, free of castles and defensive walls. The city loves a joke—the humor of the carved facades of its churches and university buildings is a subtle knock on pomp—and it readily embraces the new. Students hang out in shaded Renaissance doorways with their laptops, tapping the wireless networks inside. Its **two cathedrals** (see p. 230, **6**; p. 231, **7**) are harmonious,

> *St. Teresa, a 16th-century Catholic mystic and reformer, founded the Convento de San José.*

light-filled churches appealing to the better angels of the intellect. The student population guarantees a lively tapas and nightlife scene.

The Best of Castilla y León in 1 Week

The more northerly tier of Castilla y León is less monumental than the south, yet equally intriguing. It is the countryside that gave Spain such figures as El Cid and most of the kings named Alfonso—the Battler, the Avenger, and the Wise, among others. It is also the land where the Río Duero has watered the parched soil to produce two major crops introduced by the Romans: wheat and wine grapes. After following the previous 3-day itinerary (see p. 196), spend your fourth day in Zamora and Toro, and the remainder in the erstwhile royal capitals of Valladolid, León, and Burgos.

> The Catedral de León's 125 stained-glass windows are so heavy they have strained its walls.

START From Salamanca, follow the A-66 67km (42 miles) north to Zamora. **TRIP LENGTH** 646km (401 miles), including "The Best of Castilla y León in 3 Days."

1 Zamora. Sometimes called a museum of Romanesque architecture, tiny Zamora is graced with two dozen churches from the 12th and 13th centuries, including the voluminous ★ **Catedral de Zamora** and the much tinier parish church the ★ **Magdalena,** with its beautiful carved proto-Gothic sepulchers

and doorway carvings of fruits, vines, and vegetables. This ostentatious holiness was calculated by the kings of León, who were creating spiritual fortifications on the borderland between their dominions and the Muslim realm.

The **Portillo de la Traición** ("Treason Gate") on the northwest corner of the city commemorates the duplicitous assassination of the Castilian king Sancho II in 1072. (He and El Cid were laying siege to the city in a battle

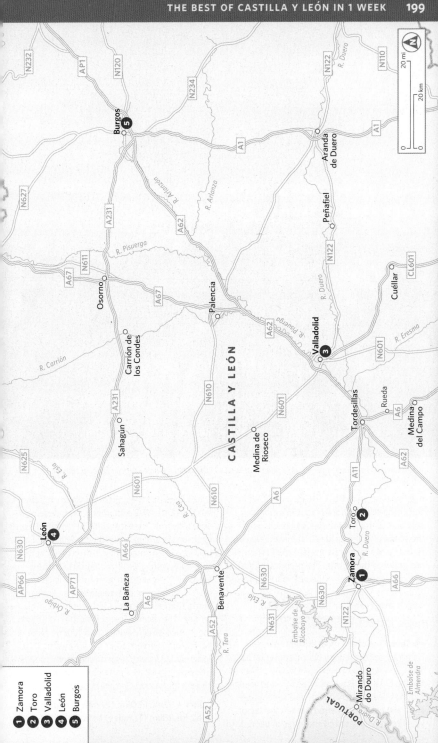

> *The town of Toro looks over a fertile plain that is a DO (Denominación de Origen) for bold red wines.*

over succession to the Castilian crown.) It is surprising that Zamora's monuments have survived so many centuries, as the city was also the scene of fierce battles in the war between Isabel I and Juana la Beltraneja, the Portuguese pretender to the throne. The memory of that struggle is preserved in the old Spanish proverb *"No se ganó Zamora en una hora,"* or "Zamora wasn't won in an hour." See p. 206, ❸.

Follow A-11 40km (25 miles) to Toro.

❷ **Toro.** One of the most ancient towns in Castilla y León, the agricultural center of Toro was conquered by Hannibal in 220 B.C. Set on the Río Duero, it is surrounded by a fertile plain that has been largely devoted to wine grapes since the early 10th century, when the region was first repopulated by the kings of León. Toro wines filled half the hold of the *Pinta* on Columbus's historic 1492 exploration, and these powerful reds from the local clone of *tempranillo* are again on the ascendancy. Built in the shape of a fan, Toro is surrounded by 10th-century defensive walls with wide 17th- and 18th-century gates. At the geographic center of the community stands ★★ **La Colegiata,** also known as **Santa María la Mayor,** a 13th-century Gothic temple. The recently conserved main entrance, the Pórtico de la Majestad, is a tour de force of polychrome carved stone. It portrays the Last Judgment, concentrating on the happy groups (musicians, virgins, martyrs) who have been chosen for heaven. See p. 216, ❹.

Follow A-11 east 30km (19 miles) to pick up A-62 for 28km (17 miles) to Valladolid.

3 Valladolid. The de facto capital of Castilla y León is both the gateway to the northern tier of the autonomous region and the main railhead for the Duero valley wine region. An important center in solidifying the Reconquista, Valladolid flowered in the 12th century and became important under Fernando and Isabel, who were married here. It even served briefly as the national capital under Carlos V and his son Felipe II, who was born here in 1527.

Felipe left his mark on his native city by engaging El Escorial architect Juan de Herrera to design a monumental house of worship on the ruins of a 13th-century church. In typical fashion, construction of the **Catedral de Valladolid** stretched over several centuries. In the 18th century, the solid, blocky structure was embellished by architect Alberto Churriguera in his family's distinctive baroque style (see p. 231). The interior of the church features lifelike figures from carved and painted wood by Juan de Juni. A 1€ coin illuminates the main altar so that you can study de Juni's masterful 1551 altarpiece.

Altarpieces by de Juni and other artists similarly skilled in woodworking are displayed at the **Museo Nacional Colegio de San Gregorio.** In a separate small building, you can examine the *"pasos,"* or enormous processional scenes borne through the streets during Holy Week—without having to brave the crowds.

Opened in June 2002 in a 16th-century monastery, **Patio Herreriano Museo de Arte Contemporáneo Español** offers a more up-to-date survey of Spanish art, focusing on works from 1918 forward, displayed in airy galleries surrounding a contemplative courtyard.

Before window-shopping along pedestrian C/ Santiago, take an outdoor table at **Cafe del Norte** to enjoy a *blanco y negro* (coffee with a scoop of ice cream) and survey the scene in Plaza Mayor.

A short detour from the shops of C/ Santiago brings you to ★ **Museo Casa de Cervantes,** the early-17th-century dwelling where Miguel de Cervantes lived from 1601 to 1606, when the court of Felipe III was based in Valladolid. The simple but comfortable home is furnished with period pieces similar to those described by Cervantes in letters to friends and family, with a small bedchamber, several desks and tables, and a salon with low Arab-style seating. Catedral: ⊙ 30 min. C/ Arribas, 1. ☎ 983-30-43-

> Whitewashed walls, terra cotta floors, and exposed wood beams warm the Museo Casa de Cervantes.

62. Free. Tues–Fri 10am–1:30pm and 4:30–7pm; Sat–Sun 10am–2pm. Museo de San Gregorio: ⊙ 30 min. C/ Cadenas de San Gregorio, 1 and 2. ☎ 983-25-03-75. http://museosangregorio.mcu. es. 2.40€ adults, 1.20€ seniors and students. Mid-Mar to Oct Tues–Sat 10am–2pm and 4–9pm, Sun 10am–2pm; Nov to mid-Mar Tues–Sat closes 6pm, Sun 10am–2pm. Museo de Arte: ⊙ 30 min. C/ Jorge Guillén, 6. ☎ 983-36-29-08. 3€ adults, 2€ seniors and students, 1€ for all on Wed. Tues–Fri 11am–8pm; Sat 10am–8pm; Sun 10am–3pm. Cafe del Norte: Plaza Mayor, 11. ☎ 983-35-66-02. Snacks from 2€. AE, MC, V. Lunch & dinner daily. Museo de Cervantes: ⊙ 45 min. C/ del Rastro, s/n. ☎ 983-30-88-10. 3€. Tues–Sat 9:30am–3pm; Sun 10am–3pm.

Follow A-62 west 25km (16 miles) to A-62 north. In 25km (16 miles), take A-6 north for 87km (54 miles). Follow A-66 for 57km (35 miles) to León.

> *The royal burial vaults of the Colegiata, dedicated to San Isidoro de Sevilla in 1063, are painted with magnificent Romanesque frescoes.*

4 León. Unification of Castilla and León into one autonomous region may have stilled rivalries between the two, but the Leónese still like to boast of their ancient lineage, saying, "León had 24 kings before Castilla even had laws." There's some truth to the claim, and the final resting place of many of those royals is both beautiful and spooky enough to make the hair stand up on the back of your neck.

Built at the end of the 11th century, the ★★ **Colegiata de San Isidoro** is a Romanesque gem, as squat—and as graceful—as a Greco-

Roman wrestler. The León royal burial vault in the adjoining convent contains the remains of 11 kings, 14 queens, and other nobles—many in tiny stone coffins. Their unadorned sepulchers are watched over by fanciful 12th-century ceiling frescoes depicting biblical scenes and medieval court life.

The artistry of the royal pantheon, however, is trumped by the extraordinary stained-glass windows of the nearby ★★★ **Catedral de León** (see p. 208, **7**). You can be forgiven for thinking you have stepped into the tube of a kaleidoscope. From Bible scenes as detailed as any painting to floral motifs to coats of arms, the windows embrace every style of liturgical stained glass over the past 8 centuries. You can buy modern illuminated pages replicating the cathedral windows at **El Escribiano,** a shop dedicated to the artistry of the medieval scribe.

A similar strain of medieval revivalism inspired the late-19th-century **Casa de Botines.** It was designed by famed Catalan Modernista architect Antoni Gaudí (see p. 428) to evoke a medieval fortress—right down to the facade's sculpture of St. George sticking it to the dragon. A modern bronze of the architect with a sketch pad sits on a bench facing the building.

León's artistry didn't end with the churches. **MUSAC** (Museo de Arte Contemporáneo de Castilla y León), which opened in 2005, won the E.U.'s Mies van der Rohe architecture prize for its innovative design. The white concrete

El Cid

Rodrigo Díaz de Vivar (1040–99), otherwise known as El Cid, was Spain's quintessential medieval knight and is celebrated as a national hero. A brilliant military tactician, he served the kings of Castilla until he was exiled in 1080. As a mercenary, he spent 7 years in service to the Muslim kings of Zaragoza before being recalled to Castilla. He mustered a combined Muslim and Christian army to carve out his own fiefdom in Valencia, defending it against Aragón, the counts of Barcelona, and the Muslim rulers of Córdoba. Several medieval epic poems, most notably *Cantar de Mio Cid,* turned the warrior and statesman into a legend. See p. 210 for more on El Cid.

building has 3,351 windows—it's designed as a digitized version of a 13th-century stained-glass image from the cathedral. Most exhibitions are temporary, but the museum has an ongoing series of workshops and lectures. Free guided tours are available in Spanish and English. **Colegiata:** ⏱ 30 min. Plaza de San Isidro. ☎ 987-87-61-62. 4€. Sept–June Mon–Sat 10am–1:30pm and 4–6:30pm, Sun 10am–1:30pm; July–Aug Mon–Sat 9am–8pm, Sun 9am–2pm. **Escribiano:** C/ Fernando Gonzalez Regueral, 6. ☎ 987-07-32-22. MC, V. **Casa de Botines:** ⏱ 10 min. C/ Ancha, across from Plaza San Marcelo. **MUSAC:** ⏱ 1 hr. Avenida de los Reyes Leoneses, 24. ☎ 987-09-00-00. www.musac.es. Free. Tues–Fri 10am–3pm and 5–8pm; Sat–Sun 11am–3pm and 5–9pm. Bus: 7, 11, 12.

Follow CL-630 9km (5⅔ miles) south to A-231 and drive east 156km (97 miles) to exit 157. Follow N-120 9km (5⅔ miles) to Burgos.

⑤ Burgos. Although it was repopulated in 884, Burgos began to flourish a century later when it became the capital of Castilla and a key stop on the Camino de Santiago. In fact, the historic city is virtually a medieval strip mall along the pilgrimage route. A good place to begin exploring is at **Plaza del Cid,** where a

heroic statue depicts El Cid as the prototypical knight-warrior on horseback. A few steps up C/ Santander is **Casa del Cordón,** a striking 15th-century palace with elaborate Gothic details at the roofline. Best known as the spot where Columbus met with Fernando and Isabel in 1497 after his second voyage, it is now a bank. Double back to El Cid and follow the leafy **Paseo del Espolón** along the river to Puente de Santa María so that you can enter the Old City via the triumphal **Arco de Santa María,** one of a dozen medieval gates to the city.

The gate opens into **Plaza de San Fernando,** where a sympathetic bronze statue of a weary pilgrim sits on one of the benches. Towering over the plaza is the spacious and bright **Catedral de Burgos,** the best example of French Gothic church architecture in Spain. The sepulchers of El Cid and his wife occupy the place of honor where the nave and transept cross. The cathedral's museum is the best signed and interpreted in Spain.

Behind the cathedral, the **Arco Fernán González** gate leads up to a scenic overlook of the hillside above the city, where Napoleon's troops destroyed the **Castillo de Burgos** in 1813. See p. 209, **⑧**.

> *A dozen medieval gates, including the Arco de Santa María, protect Burgos, the "cradle of Castilla."*

Castles & Cathedrals

The modern Spanish state was forged in the territories of Castilla and León, rival kingdoms united by marriage in 1230. Whenever the northern kings took back a city during the Reconquista, they built a defensive castle and a cathedral. Nearly a millennium later, these turf-claiming monuments in stone still define the region. The ones on this tour are the most dramatic, and can be seen in a (full) week.

> In the Middle Ages, La Mota ("mota" means defensive hill) was the center of Medina del Campo.

START Segovia. **TRIP LENGTH** 741km (460 miles).

❶ Segovia. Rebuilt along idealized lines after an 1862 fire, the ★★ kids **Alcázar de Segovia** (see p. 220, ❹) looks like a Victorian story-book castle. The enchanting structure is both majestic and almost too orderly to be real. Impressive rooms present a virtual museum of the Castilian monarchy.

Segovia's Reconquista-era church burned down in 1520 when burghers rose up against the crown. The ★ **Catedral** (see p. 220, ❸) that replaced it is the last Gothic structure of its kind built in Spain.

Drive south 26km (16 miles) on the AP-61 to pick up the AP-6 west. In 24km (15 miles), take exit 81 to the AP-51 for 30km (19 miles). At exit 111, follow A-50 100km (62 miles) to Salamanca.

❷ Salamanca. This sunny city of learning may lack a castle, but it compensates with *two* cathedrals. The ★★★ **Catedral Vieja** (see p. 231, ❼) is an atmospheric Romanesque temple from the 12th and 13th centuries. Nominally Gothic in form, the ★★★ **Catedral Nueva** (see p. 230, ❻) benefited from having the Churriguera brothers (see p. 231) oversee its

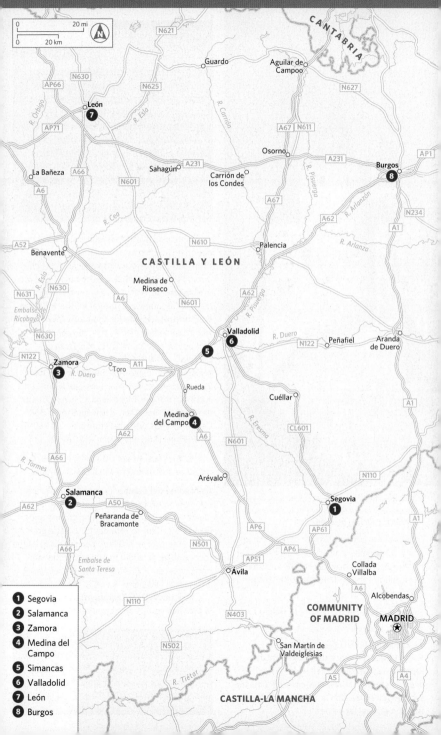

0   20 mi
0   20 km

CANTABRIA

N621

Guardo

Aguilar de
Campoo

N627

N630

AP66

León **7**

AP71

R. Orbigo

R. Esla

R. Carrión

Osorno

A67 N611

A231

Burgos **8**

AP1

La Bañeza

A66

Sahagún

A231

Carrión de
los Condes

A67

R. Pisuerga

R. Arlanzón

N234

A52

N601

A62

R. Arlanza

A1

Benavente

N610

Palencia

CASTILLA Y LEÓN

R. Esla

N631

N630

Medina de
Rioseco

A6

N601

A62

R. Pisuerga

Embalse de
Ricobaya

N630

Valladolid **6**

5

R. Duero

N122

Peñafiel

Aranda
de Duero

N122

Zamora **3**

R. Duero

Toro

A11

Rueda

A1

Cuéllar

Medina
del Campo **4**

A6

N601

R. Eresma

CL601

A62

A66

R. Tormes

Arévalo

N110

Salamanca **2**

A50

Segovia **1**

Peñaranda de
Bracamonte

A1

A66

Embalse de
Santa Teresa

N501

AP51

AP6

AP61

AP6

Collada
Villalba

A6

Alcobendas

N110

Ávila

COMMUNITY
OF MADRID

MADRID ✪

N403

1 Segovia

2 Salamanca

3 Zamora

4 Medina del
Campo

5 Simancas

6 Valladolid

7 León

8 Burgos

N502

San Martín de
Valdeiglesias

A5

A4

R. Tiétar

CASTILLA-LA MANCHA

> *Recent excavations of Segovia's Alcázar have uncovered granite blocks similar to those used in the nearby Roman aqueduct.*

construction. Look closely for carvings of an astronaut floating in space and a monkey eating an ice-cream cone, part of the witty 1992 "restoration" of the elaborate 16th-century Puerta Ramos.

Follow A-66 north for 67km (42 miles) to Zamora.

❸ **Zamora.** One of Spain's greatest Romanesque buildings, the ★ **Catedral de Zamora** was swiftly erected from 1151 to 1174, and its Byzantine scaled dome has become the symbol of the city. Don't miss the striking collection of medieval tapestries.

Spending the Night in Zamora

Tranquil decor and large modern rooms characterize the serene ★★ **NH Palacio del Duero,** which engulfed two medieval convents and a former winery. Plaza de la Horta, 1. ☎ 980-50-82-62. www.nh-hotels.com. 49 rooms. Doubles 70€–107€. AE, DC, MC, V.

The creative chef at ★★ **El Rincón de Antonio** champions local products in innovative dishes. Sample his style in miniature with a bar-only tasting menu of four tapas, wine, dessert, and coffee for 11€. Rúa de Los Francos, 6. Entrees 12€–26€. Lunch daily, dinner Mon–Sat. AE, MC, V.

The town's 67,000 residents also have the option of worshiping at any of the other 23 12th- and 13th-century Romanesque churches around the city, including the lovingly restored ★ **Magdalena.** With so many medieval monuments, Zamora was a natural for the ★ **Centro de Interpretación de las Ciudades Medievales,** which elucidates medieval culture, life, and architecture. Catedral: ⏱ 45 min. Plaza de Catedral, s/n. ☎ 980-53-06-44. 3€ adults, 1.50€ seniors and students. Apr–Sept Tues–Sun 10am–2pm and 5–8pm; Oct–Mar Tues–Sun 10am–2pm and 4:30–6:30pm. Magdalena: ⏱ 15 min. Campo de Marte, 17. Free. Daily 10am–1pm and 5–8pm. Centro: ⏱ 1 hr. Cuesta del Pizarro, s/n. ☎ 980-53-62-40. Free. Daily noon–2pm and 5–8pm.

Follow A-11 east 66km (41 miles) to A-6 south for 30km (19 miles) to Medina del Campo.

❹ **Medina del Campo.** One of Castilla's largest castles, ★★ **La Mota** sits above this historic market town. Used as a training ground under Franco, the 12th- to 15th-century castle previously served as an artillery magazine and as the royal archive. In addition to walking the ramparts, you can visit the great keep, the chapel, and a royal bedroom.

The **Palacio Real Testamentario de Isabel la Católica** stands on a corner of the arcaded

Travel Tip

Medina del Campo is a historic market town. As such, all the shops are closed on Thursdays and open on Sundays, when the national cattle market takes place.

Spending the Night in Medina del Campo

A spa hotel in cattle country, the **Palacio de las Salinas** dates from 1912 and combines old-fashioned grace with modern spa treatments. A paved path for walking or biking leads to town. Carretera de las Salinas, km 4. ☎ 983-80-44-50. www.palaciodelassalinas. es. 64 rooms. Doubles 174€ with breakfast, discounts for additional nights. MC, V.

main square with a statue of the queen out front. Isabel I executed her will and died here in 1504. The interpretation center recounts the life and death of the dynamic monarch. Mota: ⏰ 1 hr. Avenida del Castillo. ☎ 983-80-10-24. Free. Apr–Sept Mon–Sat 11am–2pm and 4–7pm (4–6pm Oct–Mar), Sun 11am–2pm. Palacio: ⏰ 1 hr. Plaza Mayor de la Hispanidad. 2€ adults, 1.50€ students and seniors. Apr–Sept Mon–Sat 10am–1:30pm and 5–8pm (4–6pm Oct–Mar), Sun 11am–2pm.

Go north on A-11 to exit 181. Follow A-62 east 17km (11 miles) to exit 135 at Simancas.

> TOP The Hall of Monarchs was once the most important room of Segovia's Alcázar. BOTTOM Salamanca's Catedral Nueva.

> *Philip II moved Spain's national archives to Simancas's castle in 1563.*

⑤ Simancas. Though the striking 15th-century **Castillo**—transformed from a fort to a castle by royal architects—is now a royal archive open only to researchers, it's worth stopping to explore the compact, prosperous town of Simancas. The twisting, narrow streets are lined with distinctive houses built largely of mortared stone blocks, many with coats of arms over the doors.

Staff at the tourist office will unlock the heavy door to **El Salvador,** a late-Gothic 16th-century church edifice with an original 12th-century bell tower. Soaring vaults make the interior truly monumental, while the high windows pour light down on the heavily gilded Plateresque *retablo* (devotional painting) of the Resurrection, by Inocencio Berruguete. At the far edge of town, **Plaza del Mirador** provides views of the green countryside and the Río Pisuerga, crossed by a 13th-century bridge built on Roman footings.

After you've worked up an appetite, do your own taste test at **Patio Martín,** which has twice won national competitions for its *tortilla española* (a Spanish omelet with potatoes). Salvador: Plaza Mayor. ☎ 983-59-04-09. Free. Tues–Sat 10am–1:30pm and 5–7:30pm; Sun 10am–2pm. Patio Martín: C/ Las Tercias, 3. ☎ 983-59-11-33. Main courses 30€. AE, MC, V. Lunch daily, dinner Thurs–Sat.

Travel Tip

Valladolid has no castle, but Peñafiel, less than an hour's drive east, has one of Castilla's most unusual and best restored. See p. 212, ❶.

Spending the Night in Valladolid

A block off Plaza Mayor, the Renaissance palace that now holds the **Hotel Imperial** has taken in lodgers since the 1840s. Compact, simply decorated rooms contrast with heavily marbled and gilded public areas. C/ Peso, 4. ☎ 983-33-03-00. www.himperial.com. 63 rooms. Doubles 55€–90€. MC, V.

Heavy wooden furniture set within the stone walls of a former monastery lend old-time atmosphere to ★ **La Parrilla de San Lorenzo,** a local favorite for lamb roasted in a wood oven. Cloistered nuns make the dessert pastries. C/ Pedro Niño, 1. ☎ 983-33-55-88. Entrees 15€–21€. Lunch daily, dinner Mon–Sat. DC, MC, V.

Follow A-62 east 13km (8 miles) to Valladolid.

⑥ Valladolid. Rugged and powerful, the **Catedral de Valladolid** exemplifies the spare, unadorned style of Juan de Herrera with its massive, squared-off columns of rough-cut stone. One of the few Renaissance cathedrals in northern Spain, it is renowned for its collection of liturgical music. Free organ concerts on the new 19,000-digital-tube organ are offered all year.

The cathedral's main altarpiece by Juan de Juni is a masterwork in the polychrome wooden style characteristic of Valladolid. To truly appreciate the mid-16th-century artists' ability to convey emotion, examine works by masters such as de Juni and Alonso Berruguete in the well-lit galleries of the **Museo Nacional Colegio de San Gregorio.** See p. 201, ❸.

Follow A-62 west 25km (16 miles) to A-62 north. In 25km (16 miles), take A-6 north for 87km (54 miles). Follow A-66 for 57km (35 miles) to León.

⑦ León. It's hard not to feel for the stonemasons, carvers, iron sculptors, and painters who adorned the soaring ★★★ **Catedral de León:** The saturated color of the stained-glass windows outshines everything, making it feel as if you had stepped into a religious jewel box. Created between the 13th and 20th centuries, the windows cover about 1,800 sq. m (19,375 sq. ft.) with Bible stories, coats of arms, and a joyous celebration of the wonders of the Creation. Catedral: ⏱ 45 min. Plaza de la Regla. ☎ 987-87-57-70. Free. Oct–June Mon–Sat 8:30am–1:30pm

> *El Cid Campeador, Spain's greatest national hero, was born near Burgos and now rests in its Catedral.*

and 4–7pm (4–8pm July–Sept), Sun 8:30am–
2:30pm and 5–7pm (5–8pm July–Sept).

Follow CL-630 9km (5⅔ miles) south to A-231
and drive east 156km (97 miles) to exit 157.
Follow N-120 9km (5⅔ miles) to Burgos.

8 Burgos. With soaring, light-filled spaces,
the **Catedral de Burgos,** begun in 1221, may be
the stateliest in Spain. Even side chapels built
as family tombs in the 16th century display a
Renaissance proportion and balance that
oversized recumbent sculptures of the
deceased cannot spoil. El Cid and his wife
Doña Jimena rest beneath a modest slab at the
center of the Latin cross, where shafts of light
shoot down from the dome above.

The **Castillo de Burgos,** where the city
was refounded in 884, has lain in ruins since
Napoleon's troops destroyed it in 1813. You
can see it from a *mirador* (viewpoint) reached
by climbing steps from Arco Fernán González.
Catedral: ⏱ 1 hr. Plaza de San Fernando. ☎ 947-
20-47-12. 5€ adults, 4€ students and seniors, 1€
kids 7–14. Daily 9:30am–7:30pm (closed Tues
3–3:30pm), no admission after 6:30pm.

Spending the Night in León

A plain, narrow facade on a busy street near
the cathedral hides the modern and comfortable **Hotel Paris** with freshly renovated
(if often cozy) rooms. Some larger rooms
and a spa were added in 2008. C/ Ancha, 18.
☎ 987-23-86-00. www.hotelparisleon.com. 61
rooms. Doubles 73€–95€. AE, DC, MC, V.

Plaza San Martín is one of the liveliest
spots in the bar- and cafe-filled Barrio Húm-
edo. The downstairs dining room of **Mesón
San Martín** is a good bet for a quiet meal of
roasted pork, lamb, or veal chops. Plaza San
Martín, 8. ☎ 987-25-60-55. Entrees 7€–19€.
MC, V. Lunch & dinner Tues–Sun.

For a quick bite or a break, sit at the
bar at **Taberna Bar Cuervo** to taste León's
famous *embutidos* (sausages) and charcuterie. C/ Sal, 6. ☎ 987-25-40-03. Raciones
7.50€–15€. AE, MC, V. Lunch & dinner daily.

Spending the Night in Burgos

Hotel Velada Burgos sits on the Santiago pilgrimage route, and pilgrims are hard-pressed
to resist this soothing modern boutique hotel
in a 17th-century mansion. All rooms are
junior suites. C/ Fernán González, 6–10. ☎ 947-
25-76-80. www.veladahoteles.com. 64 rooms.
Doubles 65€–90€. AE, DC, MC, V.

For a quick meal, order *huevos al estilo
Tomares* (fried eggs that you stir into a cas-
serole of tomato sauce and fried potatoes)
at the bar of **La Favorita Taberna Urbana.**
Or opt for the pretty dining room and a
T-bone steak from the wood-fired grill. C/
Avellanos, 8. ☎ 942-20-59-49. Entrees 10€–
18€. MC, V. Lunch & dinner daily.

SIX DEGREES OF EL CID

Spain's Medieval Man in the Middle

BY PATRICIA HARRIS & DAVID LYON

RODRIGO DÍAZ DE VIVAR (1040–99) was celebrated in epic poetry as the warrior knight El Cid, and today, his life could be a soap opera: He fought for both sides as brothers Sancho II of Castilla and Alfonso VI of León struggled with each other and the Moors. Relieved of his Christian command and sent into exile, he turned mercenary and led victorious Moorish armies in Aragón and Catalunya. Recalled by Alfonso VI, he rose to his greatest fame by reconquering Valencia from the Almoravid Moorish invaders. Considered Spain's national hero, El Cid could also be the father of his country—or maybe his continent. The book of his descendants (all through two daughters, Cristina and María) runs more than 10,000 pages long. This is just a small sampling of how El Cid's blood has run through many of the royal families of Europe.

The Descendants of El Cid

Cristina

María

1100

GARCIA RAMÍREZ (ca. 1100–50), "THE RESTORER": A winemaking noble from La Rioja, he re-established Navarra's autonomy. His descendants became the kings of Castilla, León, Navarra, Portugal, and Aragón.

WILLIAM I (1131–66), "THE WICKED," AND WILLIAM II (1155–89), "THE GOOD": Norman kings of Sicily, they both lived in semi-seclusion at the royal palace in Palermo.

1200

JAUME I OF ARAGÓN (1208–76), "THE CONQUEROR": Raised by the Knights Templar, he reconquered Valencia (again) and the Balearic Islands; wrote the *Book of Wisdom*, containing proverbs from various authors; and codified marine law in the Mediterranean.

1300

1400

ROGER-BERNARD III OF FOIX (1243–1302): Ruler of the independent county of Foix in France, he was renowned as a poet and troubadour.

FERNANDO II OF ARAGÓN (1452–1516), "THE CATHOLIC": One half of the power couple of Fernando and Isabel, he led the final unification of Spain when he maneuvered Navarra into the fold in 1511.

*Intermarriages in the 14th century among the houses of Aragón (Cristina), Mallorca (María), and Naples (María) united the bloodlines of El Cid's daughters into one central European lineage, the House of Bourbon.

1500

ANNE OF BRITTANY (1477–1514): Queen consort of France twice, as wife of Charles VIII and Louis XII, she was the richest woman in Europe in her day.

1600

1700

MARY I OF ENGLAND (1516–58), "BLOODY MARY": The daughter of Catherine of Aragón and Henry VIII, she tried to reconvert England to Catholicism.

HENRI IV (1553–1610), "THE GREAT": Perhaps the last king of France popular with his subjects, he was the progenitor of the main Bourbon family line.

1800

JUAN CARLOS I OF SPAIN (b. 1938): The current constitutional monarch of Spain, he oversaw the transition from dictatorial Franco to democracy.

1900

GRAND DUKE HENRI (b. 1955): The current ceremonial head of state of Luxembourg, his family line—and that of El Cid—encompasses the House of Bourbon-Parma, the House of Spain, the House of France, the House of Capet, and the Robertians.

2000

Castilla y León for Wine Lovers

Like the Rhone and Rhine, the Duero is one of Europe's great wine rivers. Small and sluggish in the high country of Burgos, it picks up major tributaries as it flows through the Ribera del Duero district, becoming broad and deep as it continues west through Toro and on to the Portuguese border. The Romans made bulk wines here, and by the late Middle Ages, the Spanish court favored the region for powerful reds and cask-aged whites. Modern winemaking techniques and the rediscovery of local strains of *tempranillo* and *verdejo* grapes have transformed the Castilian stretch of the Duero into Spain's most exciting wine region. **Note:** Wine tourism is in its infancy. In most cases, you'll have to call ahead to visit bodegas, but you'll be lavished with personal attention. This tour can be done in 3 or 4 days.

> Castilla y León has nine high quality wine-growing regions designated Denominaciones de Origen.

START Peñafiel. **TRIP LENGTH** 107km (66 miles).

① Peñafiel. The de facto capital of the red-wine district of Ribera del Duero, Peñafiel lies on the N-122, the main road that parallels the Duero. Small outlets for major producers abound, and the tourist office has a list of bodegas open for visits and tastings in the surrounding towns. Ask the office to call.

Located in the middle of town in a 12th-century convent, **Bodega Convento San Francisco,** a small producer, is the most convenient for visits. If you haven't booked an English-language tour in advance and can handle a visit in Spanish, ask the tourist office to call.

The ★★ kids **Castillo-Museo Provincial del Vino** recounts wine history, growing and

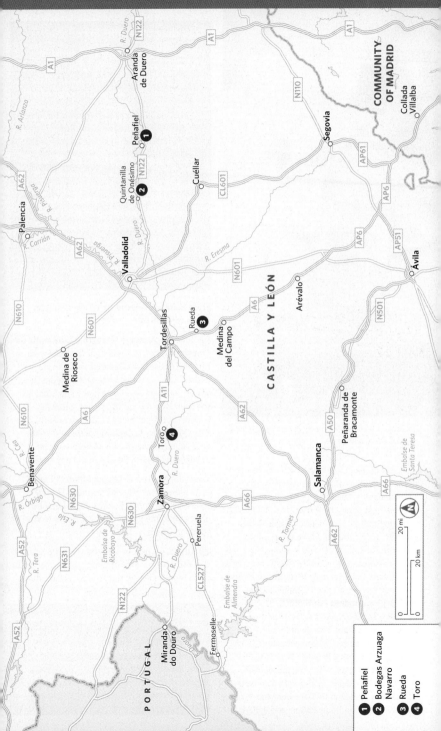

PORTUGAL

Miranda
do Douro

Fermoselle

CL527

Embalse de
Almendra

Pereruela

R. Duero

Zamora

Toro

R. Duero

Benavente

Medina de
Rioseco

Palencia

Tordesillas

Valladolid

Rueda 3

Medina
del Campo

Arévalo

Peñaranda de
Bracamonte

Salamanca

Embalse de
Santa Teresa

Ávila

CASTILLA Y LEÓN

Cuéllar

Quintanilla
de Onésimo 2

Peñafiel 1

Aranda
de Duero

Segovia

COMMUNITY
OF MADRID

Collada
Villalba

R. Duero

R. Arlanza

R. Carrión

R. Pisuerga

R. Eresma

R. Tormes

R. Órbigo

R. Esla

R. Tera

R. Cea

Embalse de
Ricobayo

A1

N122

A1

N110

AP61

AP6

AP51

A6

AP6

N601

N601

A6

N501

A62

A50

A66

A62

A11

N630

N630

N631

A52

N610

N610

A52

N122

CL601

N122

A62

A62

Bodegas Arzuaga
Navarro

1 Peñafiel
2 Bodegas Arzuaga
   Navarro
3 Rueda
4 Toro

20 mi

20 km

N

> *Rueda, once known for sherry, is now known for its crisp verdejo whites.*

From Peñafiel, drive west on the N-122 for 10km (6¼ miles).

❷ **Bodegas Arzuaga Navarro (Quintanilla de Onésimo).** Stop to taste, tour the winery, or tour the entire farm. Tastings range from short and simple to a minicourse in Ribera del Duero wines. Arzuaga also has a fancy spa hotel on the premises, for multiday wine getaways (200€-300€ per person). Carretera N-122, km 325, Quintanilla de Onésimo. ☎ 983-68-11-46. www.arzuaganavarro.com. Bodega visits in Spanish and English 5€-25€. Call 1 day ahead.

Continue west on N-122 for 30km (19 miles) until it becomes VA-11. Continue 15km (9⅓ miles) to the Ronda Sur around Valladolid. Take exit 151 to get on A-6. Continue to km 172 to reach Rueda.

❸ **Rueda.** Rediscovery of the *verdejo* grape and the introduction of controlled cold fermentation rocketed Rueda's whites to world-class status

winemaking techniques, and the finer points of appreciating local wines. Signage is in Spanish, but a headset CD player provides English commentary. Best of all, the museum is inside one of the region's most romantic castles, which looks like a ship stranded on a mountaintop. Oficina de Turismo: Museo de la Radio, Plaza San Miguel de Reoyo, 2. ☎ 983-88-17-15. www.turismo penafiel.com. Oct-Mar daily 10:30am-2pm and 4:30-7pm; Apr-Sept daily 10:30am-2:30pm and 5-8:30pm. Bodega Convento: C/ Calvario, 22. ☎ 983-87-80-52. 5€-10€. Oct-Apr Mon-Fri 9am-2pm and 4-7pm; May-Sept Mon-Fri 7am-3pm. Castillo-Museo: ⏱ 40 min. (castle), ⏱ 1 hr. (museum). Castillo de Peñafiel. ☎ 983-88-11-99. Castle guided tour 3€, with wine museum 6€, free for kids 11 & under. Tasting with commentary 9€. Oct-Mar Tues-Sun 11:30am-2pm and 4-7pm; Apr-Sept Tues-Sun 11am-2:30pm and 4:30-8pm.

> *Bodegas Arzuaga Navarro, on Ribera del Duero's* ruta del vino (wine route), *has a hotel and state-of-the-art spa as well as vineyards.*

in the late 1970s, but some cellars date from the 12th century. The village is the capital of the DO Rueda district, stretching south to Medina del Campo (see p. 206, ❹) and north to Tordesillas.

At ★★ **Bodegas Antaño,** make an appointment to tour the historic cellars (stretching 4km/2½ miles), the beautiful wine library, and the art collection of owner José Luis Ruiz Solaguren, founder of the José Luis restaurants in Madrid and Salamanca. The underground galleries are 400 to 500 years old, but the winery is computerized and ultracontemporary. Carefully crafted wines range from fresh young whites to elegant verdejos aged in French and American oak.

★ **Tienda Bodegas Félix Sanz,** on Rueda's main street, sells the wines of this sixth-generation family operation. A pioneer in rehabilitating the *verdejo* grape, Sanz focuses on tangy, fruit-forward whites with a lingering finish.

★★ **Bodegas Prado Rey** is a top producer in both Rueda and Ribera del Duero, and it's doing its part for wine tourism with a new store and restaurant at the bodega on the edge of town. Call ahead a few days to get an English-speaking guide.

Rueda is also a controlled denomination for superb aged sheep's-milk cheeses. **La Quesera de Rueda,** an artisanal producer, makes cheeses that mate perfectly with Rueda wines. Bodegas Antaño: ⏲ 1–2 hr. C/ Arribas, 7–9. ☎ 983-86-85-33. www.bodegasantano.com. Tour 10€. Store Mon–Fri 9:30am–7:30pm, tours by arrangement Mon–Fri 11am–7pm. Tienda: C/ Santissimi Cristo, 26. ☎ 983-86-80-44. www.bodegasfelixsanz.es. Shop Mon–Fri 9am–2pm and 3:30–6:30pm. Bodega visits with 2–3 days' notice 5€. Bodegas Prado Rey: ⏲ 1–2 hr. Carretera A-6, km 172.5. ☎ 983-44-40-48. www.pradorey.com. Store daily 10am–9pm. 45-min. tour 6.50€, 75-min. tour with tasting 12€. Restaurant serves lunch & dinner daily. Entrees 14€–19€. AE, MC, V. Quesera: Carretera A-6, km 172.1. ☎ 983-86-82-98. www.laqueseraderueda.com. Mon–Fri 8am–2:45pm and 3:30–8pm, Sat 8am–2:45pm.

From Rueda, drive north on A-6 to Tordesillas, taking exit 179 and merging onto VA-515

> *The Pórtico de la Majestad on Toro's Colegiata still retains its original polychrome paint job.*

for total distance of 12km (7½ miles). From Tordesillas, follow the N-122 40km (25 miles) west through wine country to Toro.

④ Toro. It took scientific winemaking to harness the potential of the *tinta de Toro* grape, a local strain of *tempranillo,* but ever since Manuel Fariña led the way in the early 1980s, the biggest names in Spanish wine have crowded into this medieval provincial capital. Some believe that Toro is the Holy Grail of red wines: powerful enough for long aging, supple and velvety enough to drink young. Bodegas are scattered in the countryside, but most have exclusive agents in the charming Old City.

The small shop of **Bodegas Bajoz-Liberalia** distributes (and pours) the wines of Liberalia, Bajoz, and the esteemed Sobreña, which is experimenting with organically produced red wine. Quiz the shop owner about the city—he's the author of a guidebook to Toro's artistic and historic highlights.

Don't miss the fabulous wines of ★ **Bodegas Fariña,** the bodega that put Toro on the map

with earlier harvests, controlled fermentation, and judicious aging. The wines are named for the most beautiful church in town, the Colegiata. To simply taste and buy, visit exclusive distributor **Isabel Caballero Calvo.**

While you'll only find sacrificial wine at the 13th-century church of ★★ **Santa María la Mayor (Colegiata),** it's a can't-miss stop, even on a wine tour. The Pórtico de la Majestad, or main entry, is one of the finest concentrations of Gothic painted stone carving in Spain. Perhaps expressing the biases of the designer, the depiction of the Last Judgment shows musicians as the first to be saved—ahead of the virgins and martyrs. Bajoz: C/ Corredera, 25. ☎ 980-69-03-59. Mon–Sat 10am–2pm and 5–8pm. Fariña: Camino del Palo, s/n. ☎ 980-57-76-73. www.bodegasfarina.com. Visits by appointment Mon–Fri 10:30am–1pm and 4–5:30pm; Sat 10:30am–1:30pm. Calvo: Avenida Carlos Pinilla, 2. ☎ 980-69-31-85. Mon–Fri 10am–2pm and 5–8pm; Sat 10am–2pm. Colegiata: ⏱ 30 min. Plaza Santa María, s/n. 1€. Mon–Sat 10am–2pm and 5–7:30pm; Sun 10am–2pm.

Spending the Night Around Toro

Business folk in the wine trade favor the **Hotel María de Molina,** a clean and comfortable hotel with traditional Spanish decor. Plaza de San Julián de los Caballeros, 1. ☎ 980-69-14-14. 33 rooms. Doubles 59€–70€. AE, MC, V.

Now that Toro wines have made their splash in the international gastronomic scene, Toro has discovered the culinary ferment shaking Madrid, Barcelona, and San Sebastian. The stylish bar of **La Viuda Rica** is the perfect place to sample *tapas creativas:* innovative plates prepared like little works of art. C/ Rejadorada, 7. ☎ 980-69-15-81. Entrees 9.50€–22€. MC, V. Lunch Tues–Sun, dinner Tues–Sat.

For an afternoon snack, watch *todo* Toro walk past from the shady arcade of **Restaurante-Bar Alegría** when you stop for a sandwich and glass of red wine. Plaza Mayor, 10. ☎ 980-69-00-85. Entrees from 8€. MC, V. Lunch & dinner daily.

For an interesting option outside of Toro, head west to Zamora (see p. 206, ❸) and pick up CL-527 west toward the Portuguese border. About 15km (9 miles) west of Zamora, you'll pass through the pottery town of Pereruela. Continue another 41km (25 miles) west to the outskirts of Fermoselle. There you'll find **Hacienda Unamuno.** The long driveway into the Unamuno estate says it all. Olive trees grow leaf by leaf with vines, and the Duero is visible in the distance. Since the Arribes del Duero region is not a full-fledged DO, more varietals are grown here, with Syrah and sauvignon blanc giving the native *tempranillo* and *verdejo* a run for their money. This tiny and beautiful hotel with a large complement of wine-related activities is the perfect spot to glimpse the wine culture of an area still 20 years from being discovered. The estate's restaurant, open to all, shows the influence of nearby Portugal with an emphasis on pork and salt cod dishes, as well as squid in their own ink. The dining room looks through glass to the barrels of the estate's aging cellar. CL-527, km 56. ☎ 980-61-41-40. www.haciendas-espana.com. Tours 6€, Thurs–Sat noon and 6pm, Sun noon. Store 9am–8pm. Hotel 10 rooms. Doubles 120€. Restaurant entrees 17€–20€. AE, MC, V. Lunch & dinner Thurs–Sun.

Segovia

Geography dictated Segovia's destiny. Like a thick slice of cake laid on its side, the Old City tapers uphill from its signature Roman aqueduct to the high bluff of a fanciful castle fortress—the frosting on the cake. The physical arrangement made Segovia highly defensible, but it also constrained growth in the Old City. A medieval economic, military, and religious powerhouse, Segovia's star declined after the Castilian revolt against the crown failed in 1520. The aqueduct and Alcázar are the leading attractions, but many Spaniards also make the pilgrimage here to dine on roast suckling pig.

> *The Romans used some 24,000 Guadarrama granite blocks to construct Segovia's remarkable aqueduct.*

START Plaza del Avendaño.

❶ ★★★ **Aqueducto.** This extraordinary example of Roman plumbing and civil engineering remains as impressive as it was 2,100 years ago, when the 15km (9½-mile) water channel was constructed to slake Segovia's thirst with water from the Sierra Guadarrama. The channel of granite blocks fitted together without mortar remained the city's main water supply into the 19th century. The waterway is a ground-level channel for most of its distance, but its 166 arches (28m/92 ft. at the highest) cross a

valley before continuing all the way to the Alcázar. The aqueduct is one of those rare sights that photographs well from every angle, but the most striking vantage is at eye level at the Avendaño *mirador,* where the aqueduct enters the Old City.

❷ **Plaza Mayor.** Most streets in Segovia converge on Plaza Mayor, making it the sunburst center of the city. Surrounded by the cathedral, arcades of shops and offices, and a handsome theater, it is the city's social and mercantile heart. On Thursdays it's filled with a lively market.

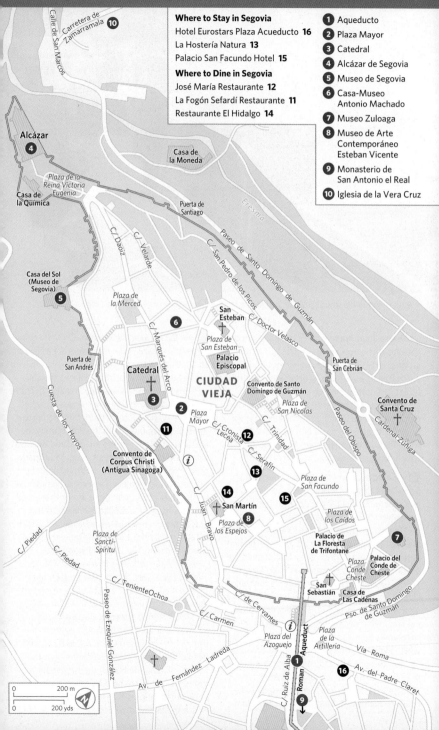

Where to Stay in Segovia

Hotel Eurostars Plaza Acueducto **16**

La Hostería Natura **13**

Palacio San Facundo Hotel **15**

Where to Dine in Segovia

José María Restaurante **12**

La Fogón Sefardí Restaurante **11**

Restaurante El Hidalgo **14**

1 Aqueducto

2 Plaza Mayor

3 Catedral

4 Alcázar de Segovia

5 Museo de Segovia

6 Casa-Museo Antonio Machado

7 Museo Zuloaga

8 Museo de Arte Contemporáneo Esteban Vicente

9 Monasterio de San Antonio el Real

10 Iglesia de la Vera Cruz

> At the heart of the city, Segovia's Plaza Mayor typifies Old Castilla (now Castilla y León).

Teatro Juan Bravo frames the east side of the plaza. The neoclassical building, first inaugurated in 1918, was thoroughly restored and renovated as a performing arts center in 1989. It features dance, theater, concerts, and variety shows from September to June, including the extravaganza festival of marionettes, Festival Titirimundi de Segovia, in late April or early May. **Teatro: Plaza Mayor, s/n. ☎ 921-46-00-39. www.teatrojuanbravo.org.**

❸ ★ Catedral. Something of an anachronism, Segovia's cathedral was the last Gothic cathedral erected in Spain—per order of Carlos V. He wanted to imitate the old cathedral that had been destroyed in the 1520 armed revolt of the Castilian cities against the crown. The first stones were laid in 1525, but impoverished Segovia was unable to complete the building until 1768. The cathedral's art represents the dark side of Spanish Catholicism, with an emphasis on the Crucifixion and other scenes of suffering and martyrdom. One uplifting exception is the Capilla Santisimo Sacramento (ca. 1700), which gleams with a gold-encrusted ornamental altar designed by José de Churriguera (see p. 231). ⊕ 30 min. **C/ Marqués del Arco, s/n. ☎ 921-46-22-05. 3€, free Sun 10am-1pm. Tues-Fri 10am-2pm and 4-8pm, Sat-Sun 10am-8pm.**

❹ ★★ kids Alcázar de Segovia. On first seeing Segovia's Alcázar, many travelers are relieved to finally encounter a storybook castle (instead of the more clunky fortress-palaces typically constructed by Spanish warrior kings). In truth, it never looked like this when it was an active fort. The original 13th-century fortress burned in 1862, giving the crown the opportunity to "restore" it to conform to an idealized 19th-century concept of a medieval castle. Many parts of the older castle remain, but the Romantic notions of the medieval period are highlighted by the suits of German plate armor that greet you as you enter. Castilian monarchs often stayed here in the late medieval period, which is reflected by the sumptuous tapestries and Mudéjar decorative tiles and woodwork.

Isabel I raced to this fortress in 1474 when she received word that her brother, Enrique IV, had died. A Galley Chamber mural shows her marching from the Alcázar to Plaza Mayor to be proclaimed queen of Castilla, launching a 5-year war with Portugal over rights to the throne. Her great-grandson Felipe II papered over all the inconvenient historical blips by commissioning the Hall of the Monarchs; a ceiling-height frieze here represents every king or queen in the Castilian line from Pelayo, credited with starting the Reconquista in 722 (see

> *The majestic Catedral de Segovia stands on the site where Isabel I was crowned queen of Castilla.*

p. 663), to Juana la Loca, Isabel's daughter and Felipe's grandmother. ⏱ **2 hr. Plaza de la Reina Victoria Eugenia, s/n.** ☎ **921-46-07-59. 4€, 3€ seniors and students. Apr–Sept daily 10am–7pm; Oct–Mar closes 6pm.**

❺ ★ Museo de Segovia. This provincial museum, founded as a repository for art and artifacts seized from closed churches, was installed a few years ago in Casa del Sol, a medieval Jewish slaughterhouse at the edge of the Old City. Now a thoroughly modern museum, it blends archaeological artifacts and liturgical art with striking historical exhibits to tell the story of the region. It covers a timeline from the geological forces that shaped the landscape up through some of the crown's efforts to encourage industrialization in the 19th century. Exhibits on the history of the wool industry, in particular, elucidate the 1520 revolt that spelled Segovia's economic downturn. While the museum contains a handful of superb paintings, its greatest artistic strength lies in the mix of Roman, Gothic, and Renaissance sculpture, including an especially moving alabaster Pieta. ⏱ **1 hr. C/ Socorro, 11.** ☎ **921-46-06-13. 1.20€, .60€ students, free Sat–Sun. Oct–June Tues–Sat 10am–2pm and 4–7pm; July–Sept Tues–Sat 10am–2pm and 5–8pm, Sun 10am–2pm.**

> *Suited "knights" on horseback help lend a fairy-tale feel to the Alcázar.*

> *Inside the Iglesia de la Vera Cruz is a temple where the Knights Templar held initiation rites.*

⑥ Casa-Museo Antonio Machado. A key figure in the Generation of '98, a group of Spanish writers active in Spain after the Spanish-American War, Machado has emerged as Spain's best-loved poet. From 1919 to 1932, he taught French in Segovia, having moved here to be close to his brother and playwright collaborator, Manuel. The sparse furnishings suggest Machado lived a monkish existence at this boardinghouse. His poetry says otherwise, recounting a long affair with a married Segoviana who had three children. ⏱ 30 min. C/ Desamparados, 5. ☎ 921-46-03-77. 1.50€, free Wed. Guided tours Wed–Sun 11am–6:30pm.

⑦ Museo Zuloaga. In 1908, ceramic artist Daniel Zuloaga established his pottery studio in the ruins of the medieval San Juan church. One of the most influential decorative artists of 20th-century Spain, Zuloaga and his firm created many of the painted tiles found on public facades all over the country. This small museum at the studio site highlights the painterly achievements of the Zuloaga clan. ⏱ 30 min. Plaza de Colmenares, s/n. ☎ 921-46-33-48. 1.20€, .60€ students, free Sat–Sun. Oct-June Tues–Sat 10am–2pm and 4–7pm; July–Sept Tues–Sat 10am–2pm and 5–8pm, Sun 10am–2pm.

⑧ Museo de Arte Contemporáneo Esteban Vicente. Segovia-born Vicente was the Forrest Gump of modern art, popping up wherever the action was. A member of the Madrid avant-garde of the 1920s, he joined the Picasso-Dufy circle in Paris and spent the end of his career in the whirlwind of abstract expressionism in New York in the 1950s. The core collection consists of 150 works donated by Vicente. ⏱ 30 min. Plazuela de las Bellas Artes, s/n. ☎ 921-46-20-10. www.museoestebanvicente.es. 2.40€ adults, 1.20€ seniors and students, free Thurs. Tues–Fri 11am–2pm and 4–7pm; Sat 11am–7pm; Sun 11am–2pm.

⑨ Monasterio de San Antonio el Real. Fewer than a dozen Clarisa nuns remain at this lovely 15th-century monastery established by Enrique IV, so they have turned over the greater part of the complex to a museum. Flemish and Spanish religious paintings hang side by side with naive religious art painted by the sisters. The guided tour pauses in the salon so you can admire Segovia's only original Mudéjar carved wooden ceiling. ⏱ 45 min. C/ San Antonio El Real, 6. ☎ 921-42-02-28. Donation. Tues–Sat 10am–2pm and 4–7pm; Sun 10am–2pm.

⑩ ★ Iglesia de la Vera Cruz. Consecrated more than 800 years ago, this house of worship was built to a complex mystical plan for the Knights Templar. The plan is modeled on Jerusalem's 12-sided Church of the Holy Sepulchre, and every niche and fragmentary wall mural has a mystical association. Long abandoned, the church has been partially restored by the last surviving crusader order, the Knights of Malta. Carretera de Zamarramala, s/n. ☎ 921-43-14-75. 1.75€. Tues 4–7pm; Wed–Sun 10:30am–1:30pm and 4–7pm.

Where to Stay & Dine

> *Diners come to chef José María Ruiz's namesake restaurant for the* cochinillo.

★★ Hotel Eurostars Plaza Acueducto NEW CITY This contemporary deluxe business hotel offers bargain rates on stylish large rooms. Near the aqueduct and Plaza del Azoguejo, it's convenient for strolling into the Old City. Avenida Padre Claret, 2–4. ☎ 921-41-34-03. www.eurostarshotels.com. 72 rooms. Doubles 60€–110€. AE, MC, V.

★★★ José María Restaurante OLD CITY *CASTILIAN* Segovianos take roast suckling pig *very* seriously. There's even an organization to certify chefs. In pig-roasting circles, chef-proprietor José María Ruiz is legendary for producing succulent meat with crackling skin. A meal of *cochinillo* is pricey, but ranks among the best in the world. C/ Cronista Lecea, 11. ☎ 921-46-11-11. Entrees 14€–31€. MC, V. Lunch & dinner daily.

★ La Fogón Sefardí Restaurante OLD CITY *CASTILIAN* The kitchen isn't kosher by a long shot, but the emphasis on grains and vegetables is a welcome respite from heavy Castilian cookery. Segovia's strong Jewish tradition is reflected in such dishes as curried lamb with eggplant and garden vegetables. C/ Judería Vieja, 17 and 19. ☎ 921-46-62-50. Entrees 7€–14€. AE, MC, V. Lunch & dinner daily.

kids La Hostería Natura OLD CITY Each room in this 17th-century noble mansion surprises with bright colors and stylish decor. For a romantic getaway, ask for room no. 103, with its high canopy bed and small balcony, or no. 114, with a four-poster wrought-iron bed and hydromassage tub. Room no. 111, a two-bathroom suite with a master bedroom and a second room with three twin beds, is great for families. C/ Colón, 5 and 7. ☎ 921-46-67-10. www.naturadesegovia.com. 17 rooms. Doubles 70€–90€. MC, V.

★★ Palacio San Facundo Hotel OLD CITY This lodging was built as a convent, was converted into a private palace in the 1500s, and became a hotel in 2006. Arrayed around the glass-covered courtyard, rooms are decorated in a clean contemporary style with either wrought-iron or padded-leather headboards and glass-slab bathroom sinks. Plaza San Facundo, 4. ☎ 921-46-30-61. www.hotelpalaciosanfacundo.com. 33 rooms. 99€–140€ with breakfast. AE, MC, V.

Restaurante El Hidalgo OLD CITY *CASTILIAN* An atmospheric restaurant in the Renaissance-era patio of a restored 13th-century house, Hidalgo serves simple local food, including the famous green beans of La Granja and roast lamb and pig. C/ José Canalejas, 4. ☎ 921-46-35-29. Entrees 6€–12€. MC, V. Lunch Tues–Sun; dinner Tues–Sat.

Ávila

Standing high on a hill, Ávila is one of the most striking walled cities in Spain. Mystic reformer Santa Teresa, one of the most influential women in Spanish Catholicism, was born here in 1515. You can trace her life as you explore the still largely medieval city. Part of her childhood home remains, as do the convent where she took her vows and another that she founded—all pilgrimage sites for believers.

> The city of Ávila, and its well-preserved medieval walls, is a UNESCO World Heritage Site.

START Los Cuatro Postes.

① Los Cuatro Postes. About 1.5km (1 mile) outside the city, a four-posted canopy marks the spot where Teresa's uncle captured her when she ran away seeking martyrdom. The site is a small shrine, so it has a roadside pullout for parking. It is also the best vantage for photographing the entire walled city, especially in the late afternoon.

② ★★ kids Las Murallas de Ávila. Largely an 11th-century defensive system built shortly after the Reconquista, the city walls stretch 2.5km (1½ miles). You can walk the ramparts about 40% of the distance, climbing into guard posts and imagining invading armies trying to storm the unassailable heights. Not only can you see the entire surrounding countryside, but you also get a stork's-eye view of twiggy nests on the city towers. ⏱ 1 hr. Entrances at C/ Carnicerías, Alcázar and Ronda Vieja. ☎ 920-25-50-88. 4€. Apr-Oct 15 daily 10am-8pm; Oct 16-Mar daily 11am-6pm.

③ Catedral de Ávila. Built into the city walls, Ávila's cathedral is a prime example of a fortress-church. Its multiple columns create significant visual clutter, but every personage of note in Ávila is entombed here, filling every nook. The Capilla del Cardenal holds some true artistic treasures: Gothic polychrome wooden statues of the saints. Unsurprisingly, a side altar is dedicated to Santa Teresa. ⏱ 30 min. Plaza de la Catedral. ☎ 920-21-16-41. 4€. Apr-Oct Mon-Fri 10am-6pm, Sat 10am-7pm, Sun noon-5pm; Nov-Mar Mon-Fri 10am-5pm, Sat 10am-6pm, Sun noon-5pm.

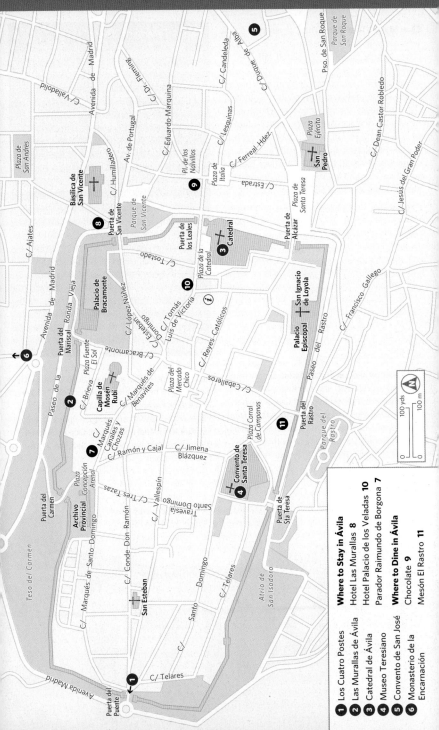

Where to Stay in Ávila

Hotel Las Murallas **8**
Hotel Palacio de los Veladas **10**
Parador Raimundo de Borgona **7**

Where to Dine in Ávila

Chocolate **9**
Mesón El Rastro **11**

1 Los Cuatro Postes
2 Las Murallas de Ávila
3 Catedral de Ávila
4 Museo Teresiano
5 Convento de San José
6 Monasterio de la Encarnación

❹ ★ **Museo Teresiano.** The Convento de Santa Teresa now stands on the site of her childhood home, but the museum associated with the convent has preserved her garden. Not merely an exercise in hagiography, the museum places Teresa in the context of 16th-century Catholicism and traces her influence through the ages. Among the artifacts are letters between Juan de la Cruz and Teresa, who displayed a vigorous, no-nonsense penmanship. ⏱ 1 hr. C/ La Dama, s/n. ☎ 920-21-10-30. 2€. Apr–Oct Tues–Sun 10am–2pm and 4–7pm; Nov–Mar Tues–Sun 10am–1:30pm and 3:30–5:30pm.

❺ **Convento de San José.** Founded by Teresa in 1562 a few blocks east of the city walls, this was the first Barefoot Carmelite convent. Its small museum presents unexpected artifacts, including Teresa's clavicle and the saddle on which she rode around Spain on convent business. There's also a re-creation of her original cell, including a narrow bed with log pillow and a window seat where she sat to write. ⏱ 20 min. C/ Las Madres, 4. ☎ 920-22-21-27. 1.20€. Apr–Oct daily 10am–1:30pm and 4–7pm; Nov–Mar daily 10am–1:30pm and 3–6pm.

❻ **Monasterio de la Encarnación.** Teresa took the habit here in 1535 and eventually served as prioress, yet Encarnación did not embrace her reforms until the 20th century. The sisters lived in comparative luxury—each spacious room had a small kitchen. Visitors familiar with Teresa's writings will thrill at seeing the small receiving

Santa Teresa de Jesús

Born into an exceedingly pious family, Teresa Sánchez de Cepeda y Ahumada was devoted even as a child to stories of the lives of the saints—running away at age 7 in hopes of being martyred by Moors. (She didn't get far before her uncle brought her home.) At age 20, she entered the Carmelite convent outside town, taking the name Teresa de Jesús. As a novice, she fell sick and experienced religious ecstasies that provided the foundation for her later mystical writings. At 45, she set about reforming her order on principles of absolute poverty, ceremonial flagellation, and the removal of shoes. With her friend and confessor San Juan de la Cruz, she founded the order of Carmelitas Descalzos, or Barefoot Carmelites, and emerged as one of the leading writers and organizers of the Spanish Counter Reformation. Although persecuted in her later years, she was exonerated before the Inquisition and canonized in 1622, 40 years after her death. In 1970, Pope Paul VI named her a Doctor of the Church.

rooms where Teresa and Juan de la Cruz jointly experienced being "lifted up in ecstasy." ⏱ 1 hr. Paseo de la Encarnación, s/n. ☎ 920-21-12-12. 1.70€. May–Sept Mon–Fri 9:30am–1pm and 4–7pm, Sat–Sun 10am–1pm and 4–6pm; Oct–Apr Mon–Fri 9:30am–1:30pm and 3:30–6pm, Sat–Sun 10am–1pm and 4–6pm.

> Eighty-two semicircular guard towers stand sentinel over the "City of Saints and Stones."

Where to Stay & Dine

> *The Renaissance Hotel Palacio de los Veladas.*

Chocolate NEW CITY *CASTILIAN*
This stylish bar-restaurant may look like a candy box with its postmodern red and brown decor, but the kitchen is serious about its beef. It's hard to beat the massive T-bone steak, or *chuletón de Ávila*—as tasty a steak as you'll find in Spain. Plaza de Nalvillos, 1. ☎ 920-21-16-79. Entrees 9€–13€. Cash only. Lunch & dinner daily.

Hotel Las Murallas NEW CITY
Just a 5-minute walk from the cathedral gate, this simple, modern hotel is a bargain in a pricey city. A few rooms have striking views of the old walls; others have small terraces. Ample free on-street parking is available, though the hotel also has an underground garage. Ronda Vieja, s/n. ☎ 920-35-31-65. www.hotellas murallas.com. 16 rooms. Doubles 55€–90€. MC, V.

Hotel Palacio de los Veladas OLD CITY
With a prime location next to the cathedral, this lovely Renaissance palace has been thoroughly modernized as one of Ávila's best hotels. Deluxe furnishings layer subdued pattern on subdued pattern for a contemporary, opulent look. On weekends, you're likely to see wedding parties convene for cocktail receptions in the glamorous central courtyard. Plaza de la Catedral, 10. ☎ 920-25-51-00. www.veladahoteles.com. 145 rooms. Doubles 80€–210€. AE, MC, V.

Mesón El Rastro OLD CITY *CASTILIAN*
The motto of this hyper-traditional fine-dining restaurant built into Ávila's city walls seems to be that if it's meat, they serve it. Roast lamb and pig are popular choices, especially for large family groups, but the kitchen also specializes in organ meats and many unusual local casseroles, including beans with chorizo and pig's ears. Not everything on the menu is so heavy and exotic: Non-Spaniards often opt for the whole roast chicken. Plaza del Rastro, 1. ☎ 920-21-12-18. Entrees 10€–19€. AE, DC, MC, V. Lunch & dinner daily.

Parador Raimundo de Borgona OLD CITY
Set into the city walls in a 16th-century palace—complete with a defensive tower—this *parador* embodies the style and spirit of old Ávila. Warmly lit and decorated in traditional Castilian style, it retains ancient granite floors in many rooms. Most of its public lounges open onto a central courtyard with an inner gallery of columns. The restaurant emphasizes local dishes, including the pork and vegetable stew *pucheretes teresianos*. C/ Marqués Canales de Chozas, 2. ☎ 920-21-13-40. www.parador.es. 55 rooms. Doubles 103€–165€. AE, DC, MC, V. Entrees 15€–32€. Lunch & dinner daily.

Salamanca

Salamanca glows golden in the early-morning and late-evening sun, befitting a city that has been a beacon of learning since the university was founded here in 1218. The glow emanates from the sandstone of its major buildings, quarried at nearby Villamayor. Wit and wisdom have always powered Salamanca, and they are vividly evident in the sculptures and carvings that adorn the city facades. Do not look for defensive walls or cannon emplacements in Salamanca—look instead for the good-luck frog on the university portal, narrative reliefs of Bible stories on the churches, and sudden surprises of angels or gargoyles overhead.

> You could spend a full day studying the Plateresque carvings that adorn Salamanca's Escuelas Mayores.

START Patio de Escuelas Menores.

① Patio de Escuelas Menores. Most of the buildings of the University of Salamanca, which occupy about a quarter of the Old City, date from the school's 15th-and 16th-century heyday as one of Europe's leading universities. Tour groups often gather in this patio outside the undergraduate school, dominated by a heroic statue of 16th-century poet and scholar Fray Luis de León, who was imprisoned for 4 years during the Inquisition for translating the Biblical "Song of Solomon" into Castilian. When he returned to the classroom, the opening line of his lecture was "*Decíamos ayer...*" or "As we were saying yesterday...."

② ★★ **kids Cielo de Salamanca.** Pop into the darkened gallery off the plaza to see this mesmerizing art treasure. The remains of a mural painted in 1473 by Francisco Gallego on the vault of the university library set astronomical science in a mythic astrological framework. ⏱ 15 min. Patio de Escuelas Menores, s/n. No phone. Free. Tues–Sat 10am–2pm and 4–8pm; Sun 10am–2pm.

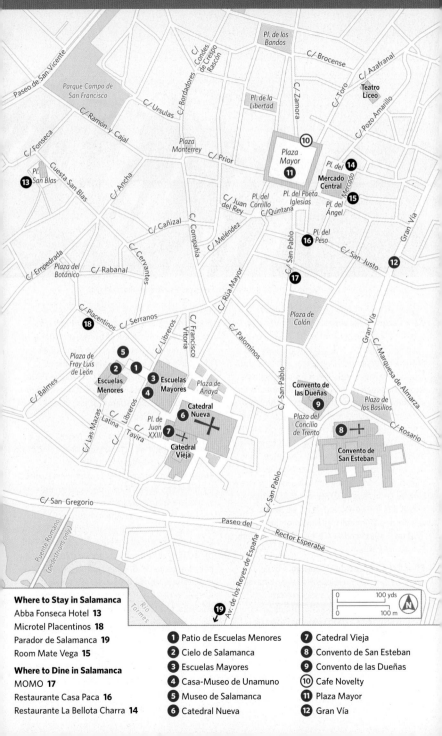

Where to Stay in Salamanca
Abba Fonseca Hotel **13**
Microtel Placentinos **18**
Parador de Salamanca **19**
Room Mate Vega **15**

Where to Dine in Salamanca
MOMO **17**
Restaurante Casa Paca **16**
Restaurante La Bellota Charra **14**

1 Patio de Escuelas Menores
2 Cielo de Salamanca
3 Escuelas Mayores
4 Casa-Museo de Unamuno
5 Museo de Salamanca
6 Catedral Nueva
7 Catedral Vieja
8 Convento de San Esteban
9 Convento de las Dueñas
10 Cafe Novelty
11 Plaza Mayor
12 Gran Vía

> *A costumed student singing group, called a* tuna, *serenades pedestrians on Plaza Mayor.*

3 ★ **Escuelas Mayores.** On any given day, dozens of people scrutinize the facade of the Escuelas Mayores, the original graduate school of the University of Salamanca. The carvings around the main entry are a tour de force of expressive high relief sculpture. On the right side, about a third of the way from the top, a frog perches on a human skull. School lore holds that spotting the frog brings good luck on exams. You can make a self-guided tour of the building, peeking into the old chapel redolent of incense, looking through the windows at the library, and visiting the classroom where Luis de León taught. ⏱ 30 min. C/ Libreros, s/n. ☎ 923-29-44-00, ext. 1150. 4€ adults, 2€ seniors and students, free Mon morning. Mon–Fri 9:30am–1:30pm and 4–7:30pm; Sat closes 7pm; Sun 10am–1:30pm.

4 ★ **Casa-Museo de Unamuno.** Poet, philosopher, and novelist Miguel de Unamuno served as the university's rector from 1900 to 1924 before he was forced into exile by the government. When General Primo de Rivera's dictatorship fell in 1930, he returned as rector until the outbreak of the Civil War in 1936. He called for "the resurrection of the man of thought who cries out against brute force and the failure of reason" and ended up under house arrest, where he died. The rooms of the museum—his quarters during his first stint as rector—are full of books, photographs, and mementos that hint at the mind of one of Spain's great intellectuals. ⏱ 45 min. C/ Libreros, 25. ☎ 923-29-44-00. 3€ adults, 1.50€ seniors and students. Tues–Fri 9:30am–1:30pm and 4–6pm; Sat–Sun 10am–1:30pm; closed afternoons July–Sept.

5 **Museo de Salamanca.** This recently renovated regional art museum originated in 1848 as a repository for paintings and statues from monasteries and convents seized by the state. Some of the most charming works are Gothic sculptures taken from country churches, but the masterpieces are Renaissance and baroque, including an intricate Churrigueresque altarpiece crafted at the end of the 17th century. Temporary exhibits display contemporary art on loan from the Reina Sofía in Madrid. ⏱ 30 min. Patio de las Escuelas, 2. ☎ 923-21-22-35. 1.20€ adults, free for seniors and students, free to all Sat–Sun.

6 ★★★ **Catedral Nueva.** Begun in 1513 and finally consecrated in 1733, the "new" cathedral represents a last gasp of Gothic architecture in Spain. Its anachronistic form was intended to harmonize with the old cathedral, with which it shares a wall. Only the baroque cupola and upper bell tower break with the Gothic

> *The relative simplicity of the Romanesque Catedral Vieja (Old Cathedral) contrasts with the ornamentation of its successor.*

style. All three Churriguera brothers served as supervising architects. Carvings around the Puerta Ramos are famous for their 1992 update of age-old imagery (see p. 204, ②). ☉ 30 min. Plaza de Anaya, s/n. ☎ 923-21-74-76. Free. Apr–Sept daily 9am–8pm; Oct–Mar daily 9am–1pm and 4–6pm.

7 ★★★ **Catedral Vieja.** Built in the 12th and 13th centuries as a Romanesque temple with Gothic vaults, the old cathedral is rarely used as a house of worship, functioning instead as a museum of the church, holding its early art and artifacts. Beautiful tombs of nobles and bishops fill the building, making it seem as if the new cathedral was built to make room for more burials of the illustrious dead. ☉ 1 hr. Entered through Catedral Nueva. ☎ 923-21-74-76. 4.25€ adults, 3.50€ seniors and students. Apr–Sept daily 10am–7:30pm; Oct–Mar daily 10am–12:30pm and 4–5:30pm.

8 ★ **Convento de San Esteban.** Dominicans from this convent accompanied Columbus to the New World and preached Christianity to the natives. History finally vindicated the

Going for Baroque

Some scholars think that sculptor-painter-architect Alonso Cano invented Spanish baroque with his 1667 facade for the Granada cathedral, but it took the Churriguera brothers of Salamanca to give it a name: Churrigue-resque. **José Benito Churriguera** (1665–1725) and his brothers **Joaquin** (1674–1724) and **Alberto** (1676–1750) were stone sculptors who became architects, and they were well-versed in the tradition of elaborately carved stone facades so characteristic of Salamanca buildings. (The soft sandstone used in most major constructions certainly encouraged intricate decoration.) Their sinuous, twisted columns and detailed, often gilded ornamentation are prefigured by Mudéjar surface decoration, but the brothers integrated the geometric fantasies into structural elements. The Churrigueresque style was popular from about 1690 to 1750. The most extreme examples are found not in Spain, but in Mexico.

Dominicans for their insistence on the rights and dignity of indigenous peoples, but the order suffered for its inconvenient and impolitic position in the go-go exploitation years of the 16th century. Members of the order still work as missionaries around the globe—and they still fight for social and economic justice, as many of the exhibits in their convent make clear. Don't miss the church's José Benito Churriguera altar and the baroque choir with an illustrated hymnal large enough that all 118 monks could read the music from their seats. ⏱ 1 hr. Plaza del Concilio de Trento, s/n. ☎ 923-21-50-00. 3€ adults, 2€ seniors and students. Daily 10am–2pm and 4–8pm.

⑨ kids ★ Convento de las Dueñas. The cloistered nuns of San Estéban's sibling institution open the arcaded cloister and rose garden of their lovely 15th-century convent to visitors. Carvings on the arcade pillars are some of the most accomplished in Salamanca. In addition to Bible stories, they feature enough angels, griffins, flying goat heads, winged horses, and deliciously malevolent devils to satisfy even the most extreme fan of modern graphic novels. ⏱ 45 min. Plaza del Concilio de Trento, s/n. ☎ 923-21-54-42. 1.50€. Mon–

Fri 10:30am–12:45pm and 4:30–6:45pm; Sat 10:30am–12:45pm.

⑩ 🍴 Cafe Novelty. If you need a break, look for a table outside this Art Nouveau landmark, and enjoy one of their ice-cream specialties. Plaza Mayor, 2. ☎ 923-21-49-56. $.

⑪ ★★★ Plaza Mayor. Constructed in the 18th century from designs by Alberto Churriguera (see p. 231), this center of city life is a harmonious marriage of neoclassical proportions and baroque decoration. Lined with three-story buildings with arched arcades, the square has a rhythmic grace. The *ayuntamiento,* or city hall, on the north side features a steeple decorated with allegorical figures. All around the plaza are medallions depicting rulers, heroes, and figures from Salamanca history—including Carlos V, Cervantes, and Santa Teresa. In the evenings, university singing groups called *tunas* often dress in 17th-century minstrel costumes to perform for tips.

⑫ Gran Vía. Nearly empty by day except for a few bars and cafes, this street starts to wake around 8pm. By midnight, the bars and clubs are hopping.

> *The arched arcade of Salamanca's Plaza Mayor welcomes students to take a study break.*

Where to Stay & Dine

> *Snacks on parade at Restaurante Casa Paca.*

Abba Fonseca Hotel
A 5-minute walk from the cathedrals, this modern hotel inside a golden sandstone building offers the comforts of great beds and thick towels, room to spread out, and all the network and power plugs to work on the road. Plaza San Blas, 2. ☎ 923-01-10-10. www.abbahotels.com. 86 rooms. Doubles 65€–110€. AE, MC, V.

Microtel Placentinos
Romantic rooms with soft contemporary furnishings and rich colors are set in a 16th-century sandstone building surrounded by the university. Some double rooms feature whirlpool tubs, and all share a terrace with a Jacuzzi. C/ Placentinos, 9. ☎ 923-28-15-31. www.microtel placentinos.com. 9 rooms. Doubles 67€–92€ with breakfast. MC, V.

MOMO *CONTEMPORARY SPANISH*
A little self-consciously stylish (the owners describe it as "Berlin club industrial"), MOMO makes terrific contemporary food modeled on the classics. The kitchen consistently wins regional contests for creative tapas, and the dining room expands on those plates with dishes like smoked tongue smothered in roasted red peppers. C/ San Pablo, 13–15. ☎ 923-28-07-98. Entrees 14€–22€. MC, V. Lunch & dinner Mon–Sat.

Parador de Salamanca
Though it's a bit of a walk to the Old City, this modern building across the river has striking views of historic Salamanca and the usual *parador* system comforts. C/ Teso de la Feria, 2. ☎ 923-19-20-82. www.parador.es. 110 rooms. Doubles 103€–176€. AE, DC, MC, V.

Restaurante Casa Paca *CASTILIAN*
While it's tempting to simply graze on the generous tapas served free with each 3€ drink, Casa Paca also has one of the best traditional dining rooms in town, with a specialty in roast kid and suckling pig. Plaza del Peso, 10. ☎ 923-21-89-93. Entrees 12€–22€. AE, DC, MC, V. Lunch & dinner daily.

Restaurante La Bellota Charra *CASTILIAN*
Locals favor this casual room by the public market for generous plates of sausage or a combination meal of meat pâtés and vegetable terrines. Plaza del Mercado, 8–10. ☎ 923-21-96-57. Entrees 7€–14€. AE, DC, MC, V. Lunch & dinner daily.

Room Mate Vega
Close to Plaza Mayor and the public market, this ultracontemporary hotel is both comfortable and stylish—and breakfast is served until noon to accommodate night owls. Plaza del Mercado, 16. ☎ 923-27-22-50. www.room-matehotels.com. 38 rooms. Doubles 65€–120€ with breakfast. AE, MC, V.

Castilla y Léon Fast Facts

> *An intimidating post office letter box in Ávila.*

Arriving & Getting Around

BY PLANE Of the cities in this chapter, only Valladolid has direct commercial air service, with daily flights from Barcelona landing at **Aeropuerto Vallanubla** (☎ 983-41-55-00; www.aena.com). **BY TRAIN** All cities in this chapter have good train connections to Madrid, if not always to each other. Valladolid is a hub for north–south trains between Madrid and Burgos and east–west trains linking Segovia, Ávila, and Salamanca. Rail information for all stations is available at ☎ 902-24-02-02 and www.renfe.es. The stations, all called **Estación del RENFE**, are located as follows: in **Ávila,** at Avenida José Antonio, s/n; in **Burgos,** at Avenida de Conde Guadalhorce; in **León,** at Avenida de Astorga, 2; in **Salamanca,** at Plaza de la Estación de Ferrocarril; in **Segovia,** at Paseo Obispo Quesada, s/n; in **Valladolid,** at C/ Recondo, s/n; and in **Zamora,** at C/ Alfonso Peña. **BY BUS** Bus service among the cities of Castilla y León is excellent. Station locations are as follows. **Ávila:** Avenida Madrid & Portugal (☎ 920-25-65-65); **Burgos:** C/ Miranda, 4 (☎ 947-26-20-17); **León:** Paseo Ingeniero Saenz de Miera (☎ 902-42-22-42); **Salamanca:** Avenida Filiberto Villalobos, 71 (☎ 923-23-67-17); **Segovia:** Paseo de Ezequiel González, 10 (☎ 921-42-77-07); **Valladolid:** Puente Colgante (☎ 983-23-63-08); **Zamora:** C/ Alfonso Peña, 3 (☎ 980-52-09-52). **BY CAR** Salamanca, Valladolid, and Burgos are linked by the **A-62.** Segovia, Ávila, and Salamanca are usually reached from Madrid by connecting roads branching from the **A-6,** which continues north to León. Zamora, Toro, Valladolid, and the Ribera del Duero wine country are linked by the **N-122.**

ATMs

You'll find 24-hour ATMs throughout the region, even in the smallest villages. Most accept Maestro, Cirrus, and Visa.

Doctors & Hospitals

For emergency medical or dental attention, go to the *centro de urgencia* (emergency room) of the nearest hospital. **ÁVILA Hospital Provincial,** C/ Jésus del Gran Poder, 42 (☎ 920-22-22-22). **SALAMANCA Hospital Clínico Universitario,** Paseo San Vincente, 182 (☎ 923-291-100).

SEGOVIA **Hóspital General de Segovia,** C/ de Ávila, s/n (☎ 921-41-91-00). Non-E.U. residents can consult national health service doctors for a relatively small fee; ask at your hotel for a list of doctors.

Emergencies

The all-around emergency number in Spain is ☎ **112.** For an ambulance, call ☎ **061.** For national police, call ☎ **088.**

Internet Access

Wi-Fi has become common in most hotels and is increasingly offered as a free amenity except in business hotels. Hotels without in-room Internet connections may provide access through a public computer. Internet cafes are common.

Pharmacies

To find an open pharmacy outside normal business hours, check the list of stores posted on the door of any drugstore. By law, there's always a drugstore open somewhere. Drugstores are called *farmacías.* When open, they display a neon green cross.

Police

Call ☎ **088** for the national police or ☎ **092** for the local police.

Post Office

ÁVILA Plaza de la Catedral, 2 (☎ 920-35-31-06). BURGOS Plaza Conde de Castro, s/n (☎ 947-26-27-50). LEÓN Jardin De San Francisco, s/n (☎ 987-87-60-81). SALAMANCA Gran Vía, 25–29 (☎ 923-28-11-17). SEGOVIA Plaza del Doctor Laguna, 5 (☎ 921-46-16-16). VALLADO-LID Plaza de Rinconada, s/n (☎ 983-36-22-70). ZAMORA C/ Santa Clara, 15 (☎ 980-50-90-59). Offices are generally open Monday to Friday 8am to 8pm and Saturday 9am to 2pm.

Safety

Cities through Castilla y León are generally quite safe. Use common sense and avoid deserted streets at night and during the afternoon closing hours. Take care not to leave anything visible in a parked car, especially overnight.

Visitor Information

Tourist offices are as follows. ÁVILA **Centro de Recepción de Visitantes,** Avenida de Madrid, 39 (☎ 902-10-21-21; www.avilaturismo.com), is open daily 9am to 8pm. BURGOS **Oficina de Turismo,** Plaza de San Fernando, s/n (☎ 947-28-88-74; www.aytoburgos.es), is open Monday to Thursday 10am to 2pm and 4:30 to 7:30pm, Friday to Sunday 10am to 8pm. LEÓN **Oficina de Turismo,** Plaza de la Regla, 3 (☎ 987-23-70-82; www.turismocastillayleon.com), is open Monday to Friday 9am to 2pm and 5 to 8pm, Saturday to Sunday 10am to 2pm and 5 to 8pm. MEDINA DEL CAMPO **Oficina del Turismo,** Plaza Mayor de la Hispanidad (☎ 983-81-13-57; www.medinadelcampo.es), is open Monday to Friday 8am to 3pm and 4 to 7pm, Saturday 10am to 2pm and 4 to 7pm, Sunday 10am to 2pm. RUEDA **Oficina de Turismo,** C/ Santissimo Cristo, s/n (in the Casa Consistorial; ☎ 983-86-80-02), is open mid-October to June Monday–Wednesday and Friday 8am–3pm, Thursday 4–7pm; July to mid-October also open Saturday 9am–noon. SALAMANCA **Oficina de Turismo,** Plaza Mayor, 32 (☎ 923-21-83-42; www.salamanca.es), is open Monday to Friday 9am to 2pm and 4:30 to 8pm, Saturday 10am to 8pm, Sunday 10am to 2pm. SEGOVIA **Centro de Recepción de Visitantes,** Plaza del Azoguejo, 1 (☎ 921-46-67-20; www.turismodesegovia.com), is open daily 10am to 8pm. SIMANCAS **Oficina de Turismo,** C/ Miravete, 11 (☎ 983-59-01-23; www.aytosimancas.es), is open Tuesday to Saturday 10am to 1:30pm and 5 to 7:30pm, Sunday 10am to 2pm. TORO **Oficina de Turismo,** Plaza Mayor, 6 (☎ 980-69-47-47; www.toroayto.es), is open Tuesday to Saturday 10am to 2pm and 4 to 8pm (7pm in winter), Sunday 10am to 2pm. VALLA-DOLID **Oficina de Turismo,** Plaza Zorrilla, s/n (☎ 902-20-30-30; www.turismocastillayleon.com), is open Monday to Saturday 9:30am to 2pm and 4 to 7pm, Sunday 9:30am to 5pm. ZAMORA **Oficina de Turismo,** Plaza de Arias Gonzalo, 6 (☎ 980-53-36-94; www.zamoradipu.es), is open April to September daily 10am to 2pm and 5 to 8pm, October to March daily 10am to 2pm and 4 to 7pm.

8

Galicia

The Best of Galicia in 5 Days

With its bagpipes, green hills, and sea-wracked cliffs, Galicia can seem more Irish than Spanish. Even the local dialect is a melodic blend of Latin and Gaelic tongues. Though small, the region is diverse and hypnotically fascinating. In 5 days, you can explore the rugged coast and two leading fishing ports, spend a day treading the pedestrian streets of a city that's practically a museum of Renaissance architecture, and experience one of Christendom's top pilgrimage cities.

> PREVIOUS PAGE *The storied cathedral of Santiago de Compostela.* THIS PAGE *Pontevedra was once a bustling port town at the mouth of the River Lérez.*

START Tui. **TRIP LENGTH** 195km (121 miles).

1 Tui. This handsome city on the north bank of the Río Miño (Riu Miño in Gallego) that divides Spain from Portugal wears a medieval crown: the massive **Catedral de Tui.** It is no coincidence that the fortress-cathedral commands a major bend in the river: Emperor Alfonso VII—ruler of Galicia, Castilla, León, and the formerly Muslim kingdom of Toledo—had just put down Muslim incursions on his turf and wanted to protect his southwest border. When he built the church, he made sure it could do military double duty. ⏱ 1 day. See p. 244, **1**.

From Tui, follow PO-552 toward A Guarda for 27km (17 miles).

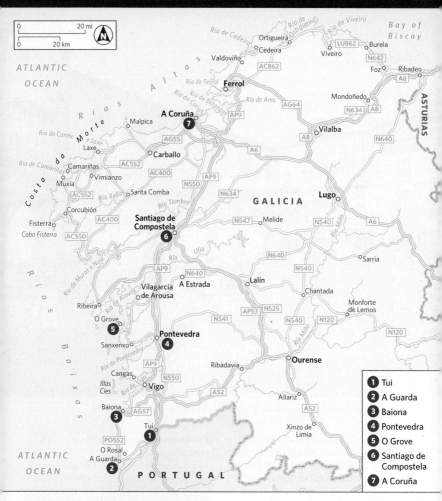

Travel Tip

For information on lodging and dining in Tui, A Guarda, Baiona, Pontevedra, and O Grove, see p. 249. For information on lodging and dining in Santiago, see p. 260.

2 A Guarda. The banks of the Río Miño are lined with vineyards from Tui to A Guarda. "A Guarda" is an ancient Celtic place name denoting a watchtower fortress, but there's nothing pugnacious these days about this affluent fishing port. Modern fishing vessels and plastic nets may lack the romance of dories and hand-knit webbing, but this is an authentic fishing community and a great place to eat—all of Spain craves its swordfish, crabs, and lobster. Work up an appetite by walking out to the breakwater that protects the harbor and touring the **Museo do Mar.** ◷ Half-day. See p. 245, **3**.

Continue on PO-552 for 30km (19 miles) to Baiona.

3 kids Baiona. Half a dozen sandy beaches have ensured Baiona's role as a vacation town, but it also boasts a picturesque stone castle complex, the **Fortaleza de Monterreal.** Bobbing among the yachts in the harbor is a replica of the **Carabela *Pinta,*** one of Christopher Columbus's vessels on his historic 1492 voyage. ◷ Half-day. See p. 246, **4**.

> *Mansions built with maritime fortunes line the cobbled alleys of Pontevedra's Old Town.*

Continue on PO-552 about 3km (1¾ miles) to the AG-57. Head north toward Pontevedra and continue 22km (14 miles) to AP-9. Follow signs north 31km (19 miles) to Pontevedra.

④ Pontevedra. If you arrive in the evening after exploring the scenic coast en route from Baiona, you'll be amazed at the near silence of the streets in the historic quarter. In fact, Pontevedra has forgotten more history than many towns in Spain can remember. A Roman administrative center, it flourished in the late medieval period as a ship-building town and shipping center.

The **Museo de Pontevedra** is one of Galicia's most comprehensive history museums. It occupies five separate buildings, including the ruins of the 14th-century Santo Domingo convent. ⊙ Half-day. See p. 248, **⑥**.

Leave Pontevedra on the PO-308 coastal road toward Sanxenxo, continuing 28km (17 miles) before turning onto PO-316 into O Grove.

⑤ O Grove. Well ahead of the curve, this fishing village began to transform itself into a summer resort in the mid-19th century. Remarkably beautiful long tidal flats (which produce prodigious quantities of shellfish) make O Grove worth a detour. Cross the bridge to the island of **A Toxa** (La Toja), center of the resort trade. ⊙ Half-day. See p. 248, **⑦**.

Leave O Grove on the PO-316 for 6km (3¾ miles) to the VRG-4.1 to connect to AP-9. Santiago is about 48km (30 miles) away.

⑥ Santiago de Compostela. One of Europe's first tourist destinations, Santiago became a magnet for the faithful when the tomb of St. James the Apostle was discovered and certified by the pope around A.D. 814. Christian kings of northern Spain needed a rallying point for their efforts to regain the Iberian Peninsula from the North African Muslim armies that had conquered it a century earlier—and a major

Christian shrine was just the ticket. Pilgrims to Santiago included popes, bishops, and kings, as well as scholars, poets, and untold numbers of regular folk. The pilgrimage route reunited Spain with the rest of Europe and spurred the economic recovery of the northern rim of the peninsula after centuries of warfare. ⏱ 1 day. See p. 256.

7 A Coruña. The smell of the sea permeates this financial and industrial capital of Galicia set on a knob of land jutting into the Atlantic. On one side of the isthmus are its sandy bathing beaches; on the other, protected by headlands, is Spain's second-largest port. The port is split between container vessels and the *lonja,* or fish market, that ships seafood all over Spain. Along the edge of the port, the glassed-in balconies of the high buildings gave A Coruña the nickname "City of Crystal." Below, the blooming green strip of **Jardines Mendez Núñez** is heady with roses in May and June. The gardens lend an air of grace to the big-shouldered working port.

Gardens line the seaside path to the ★ kids **Castelo de San Antón,** now home to the **Museo Arqueolóxico e Histórico.** This small museum collapses A Coruña's long history in a series of exhibit rooms, starting with a stunning display of Celtic gold jewelry dating from 2500 to 500 B.C. The city became a prominent Roman port after Julius Caesar arrived in 61 B.C. Extensive displays of Roman pottery, burial remains, and metalwork show how the settlement flourished until it was nearly destroyed by the Normans in the 5th century. A Coruña was reestablished as a seaport in the 13th century. The ill-fated Spanish Armada sailed from here in 1588, and a year later Sir Francis Drake returned the favor of an invasion by laying waste to the harbor—an action that led Felipe II to commission this fort.

The headland near the fort neatly encapsulates A Coruña's surviving Romanesque religious structures. **Convento das Bárbaras,** a 14th-century monastery now home to Las Clarisas nuns, occupies a plaza by the same name. You might hear the cloistered sisters in prayer around midday at the church, or you can purchase pastries from their *torno,* a small revolving door built into the vestibule.

Walk along the ancient monastery walls and you'll reach **Santa María do Campo,** where a 12th-century church constructed by the

> *A climb to the top of Torre de Hércules provides fantastic views over A Coruña, Spain's second-largest port.*

mariners' guild forms the heart of a collegiate complex. The first chapel inside the door on the left is dedicated to Mary Magdalene, a favorite of sailors.

The final stop in the Old Town is **Praza María Pita,** which honors the young woman who fired a cannon in 1589 to warn the city of the approach of Drake's fleet. Once the site of

> *The beaches of A Coruña get crowded in July and August; Ríazor, in town, is a good, fairly wide one.*

the workshops of stonemasons who built A Coruña's solid docks, the plaza served to divide the port from the city. Today it's a gathering place for social and political events (the town hall anchors one side). Cafes, bars, and restaurants are tucked beneath its protective arcades. Several shopping and dining streets lead off the plaza, including Rúa Real, where 13-year-old Pablo Picasso had his first exhibition in a furniture store in 1894. (His family lived here from 1891 to 1895.)

From the Paseo Marítimo, you can ride bus no. 3 or 3A to reach the city's other attractions. The **kids** **Torre de Hércules** is Europe's oldest working lighthouse. It was built by the Romans in the 2nd century A.D., though continued modernization has obscured its origins. A climb to the top provides great views of A Coruña's bay and port.

On the next headland, the ultramodern **kids** **Acuarium Finisterra** handles a subject dear to the heart of every A Coruñan: the creatures of the ocean. The tanks replicate marine environments around the world.

More than a dozen sandy beaches make A Coruña a summer resort playground. Two

Spending the Night in A Coruña

Have the best of both worlds—the bustling city and the soft sand and high surf of Orzán and Riazor beaches—at the **Meliã María Pita.** Set at the edge of the beaches at the narrows of A Coruña's isthmus, the hotel is about a 10-minute stroll from Praza María Pita. Avenida Pedro Barrié de la Maza, 1. ☎ 981-20-50-00. www.solmelia.com. 133 rooms. Doubles 70€–140€. AE, DC, MC, V.

★ **Pablo Gallego Restaurante,** a favorite of local fishmongers, is one of the Praza María Pita's best dining options. Chomp down on octopus either in balsamic vinegar (cold) or stewed with potatoes and spicy paprika (*pulpo Galego*), or opt for the elegance of mixed brochettes of monkfish and langostinos. Praza Maria Pita, 11 bajo. ☎ 981-20-88-88. Entrees 15€–28€. MC, V. Lunch & dinner Mon–Sat.

The Camino de Santiago

Pilgrims have been walking across Europe to the tomb of St. James the Apostle for nearly 12 centuries, and from spring to fall, they're ubiquitous in northern Spain. The **Camino de Santiago** (Way of St. James) pilgrimage takes several routes, though the main one is the French Route, stretching 780km (485 miles) from St. Jean-Pied-du-Port in France to Santiago de Compostela. Like a mighty river, it is joined by many tributaries, including the Camino del Norte through Bilbao, the Camino Primitivo through Oviedo, and the Camino Aragónese that crosses Aragón to Pamplona. In the countryside, pilgrimage routes often parallel main roads. In cities, they are marked with brass scallop shells (the symbol of Santiago) in the pavement. Other popular routes include the Camino Portugués from Lisbon through southern Galicia, and the Via Plata from Sevilla through Extremadura.

> *Praza María Pita, named after a local heroine.*

adjoining in-town strands are kids **Praia do Orzán** and **Praia de Ríazor,** both on the 3/3A bus route.

Finally, the kids **Ascensor Panorámico Monte San Pedro** elevator climbs 100m (328 ft.) to the top of a mountain at the western edge of town—a great spot for sunsets or for looking down on the Torre de Hércules. ⏱1 day. Castelo: ⏱45 min. Paseo del Parrote, s/n. ☎ 981-18-98-50. www.ctv.es/USERS/sananton. 2€ adults, 1€ seniors and students. Tues–Sat 10am–7:30pm; Sun 10am–2:30pm. Bárbaras *torno:* Mon–Fri 10:30am–12:30pm and 4:30–5:45pm; Sat 10:30am–noon. Santa María: ⏱15 min. Rúa da Santa María. Torre: ⏱30 min. Avenida de Navarra, s/n. ☎ 981-22-37-30. 2.50€, 1.50€ seniors and students. Apr–Sept daily 10am–6:45pm; Oct–Mar daily 10am–5:45pm. Acuarium: ⏱1 hr. Paseo Alcalde Francisco Vázquez, 34. ☎ 981-18-98-42. www.casaciencias.org. 10€ adults, 4€ seniors and students. Sept–June Mon–Fri 10am–7pm, Sat–Sun 10am–8pm; July–Aug daily 10am–9pm. Ascensor: ⏱1 hr. Sea Promenade at Millennium Obelisk at San Pedro Park. No phone. 2€ one-way. Every 30 min. Oct–May Sun–Fri 11:30am–7:30pm and Sat 11:30am–9:30pm; June–Sept Tues–Sun 11:30am–9pm.

Galicia's South Coast

No wonder Galicians identify with the sea. Geological fault lines and ancient river valleys make maps of Galicia's southern coastline look as if land and sea were playing ping-pong. Long estuaries—called *rias* in Galego—characterize the coast, which juts in and out for a total of 1,400km (870 miles). The sea comes to the doorstep of communities that look as if they should be far inland. This 2-day tour samples some of the Rias Baixas (or "lower *rias*") from the Portuguese border north toward Santiago de Compostela.

> *For visitors coming from Valença do Minho in Portugal, the city of Tui is the first taste of Galicia.*

START Tui. TRIP LENGTH 147km (91 miles).

❶ Tui. Near the tidal limit of the Río Miño that divides Portugal and Spain, the city of Tui (Tuy in Castilian) assumed its current form in the 12th century, when the kings of Castilla (who had recently inherited Galicia) followed their usual public works policy by erecting a cathedral to claim the town for God, and a defensive wall to claim it for the crown. Although Tui saw action in the 17th-century war with Portugal, it's largely been a prosperous, learned city on a hill surrounded by rich farmland and vineyards. The old landing at the canoe club begins the Spanish leg of the Portuguese pilgrimage route of Santiago.

The whole town is pleasant to wander, but the main sight is **Catedral de Tui,** the fortresslike Romanesque church at the highest point. Building began in 1120, and the church was consecrated in 1225. It received Gothic embellishments over the next few centuries and sturdy exterior buttresses after the Lisbon earthquake of 1755.

At the edge of town, a marked but unnamed road leads inland to ★ kids **Parque Natural Monte Aloia.** Crisscrossed with hiking paths, the highest sector of this mountainous park is an interesting complex of ancient religious sites and overlooks with long views of the countryside and Miño valley. Stop at the top of the mountain for an empanada and a drink at the outdoor picnic tables of **Bar Monte Aloia.** Catedral: ⏱ 1 hr. Plaza de San Fernando, s/n. ☎ 986-60-05-11. Church free; museum, cloister, tower, and gardens 2€. Daily 9am–2pm and 4–9pm. Parque: ⏱ 1 hr. Centro de Información off N-550.

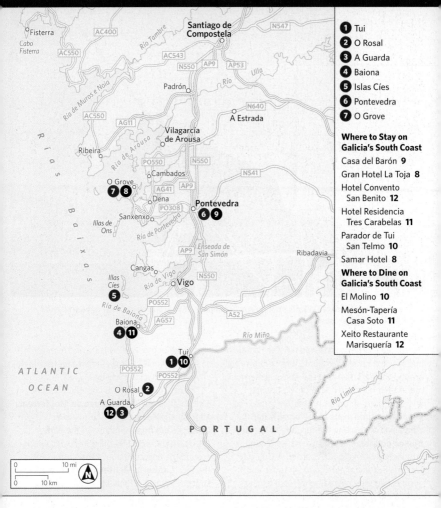

① Tui

② O Rosal

③ A Guarda

④ Baiona

⑤ Islas Cíes

⑥ Pontevedra

⑦ O Grove

Where to Stay on Galicia's South Coast

Casa del Barón **9**

Gran Hotel La Toja **8**

Hotel Convento San Benito **12**

Hotel Residencia Tres Carabelas **11**

Parador de Tui San Telmo **10**

Samar Hotel **8**

Where to Dine on Galicia's South Coast

El Molino **10**

Mesón-Tapería Casa Soto **11**

Xeito Restaurante Marisquería **12**

☎ 986-68-50-95. Free. Tues–Fri 10am–2pm and 4–7pm; Sat–Sun 11am–2pm and 4–7pm. Bar: Rúa Monte Aloia. ☎ 986-68-51-60. Entrees 5€–15€. MC, V. Lunch & dinner daily.

From Tui, follow PO-552 toward A Guarda. This road is also the Ruta do Viños in the southernmost section of the Rías Baixas DO (wine region).

② **O Rosal.** About 16km (10 miles) into the drive, the PO-552 (which parallels the Río Miño) suddenly sprouts side roads leading to vineyards around the town of O Rosal. Grapes line the roadside in tracts as small as backyard gardens and as big as fields reaching over the hillside. The dominant grape is *albariño,* which makes a fruit-forward, slightly acidic wine with a long finish. Several winemakers offer tastings, including **Bodegas Terras Gauda.** Terras Gauda: ⏱ 1 hr. PO-552, km 55. ☎ 986-62-10-01. www.terrasgauda.com. Tasting room Mon–Sat 11am–2pm and 4–8pm, Sun 11am–2pm; winery tours (free) Mon–Sat 5:30pm, Sun 12:30pm.

The road continues another 11km (6¾ miles) to A Guarda. Head to the port.

③ ★★ **A Guarda.** The Río Miño meets the Atlantic at A Guarda, an ancient Celtic port that now boasts Europe's most important swordfish fleet as well as many in-shore

> THIS PAGE *The replica of Columbus's surprisingly compact* Pinta *in Baiona's harbor.* OPPOSITE PAGE *Pontevedra's craggy coast.*

fishermen trapping crabs and lobster. Pastel houses, restaurants, and bars form a cubist wall around the harbor. Along the docks, fishermen mend their nets and heaps of wire lobster and crab traps sit under protective tarps. The **Paseo Marítimo** leads to the breakwater, with a walkway along the top, and to the tiny **Museo do Mar,** in a replica of the cannon emplacement that once guarded A Guarda. Exhibits include a few aquarium tanks and good explication of traditional local fishing equipment and vessels. Museo: ⊙ 30 min. Paseo Marítimo, s/n. ☎ 986-61-00-00. Free. Mid-Sept to early June Sat-Sun 11am-2pm and 4-7pm; early June to mid-Sept 11am-2pm and 6-9pm.

Continue on PO-552 for 30km (19 miles) to Baiona, passing Santa María de Oia. Roadside *miradores* offer dramatic views of waves crashing on the rocky coast.

❹ ★ kids **Baiona.** This deep harbor on the lip of the southernmost *ría* was a major cargo port in the late Middle Ages, but is best known in maritime circles as the first place in Europe to learn of Columbus's discoveries. Navigated by a local sailor, the *Pinta* made landfall here on March 1, 1493. A replica of the ship constructed for the quincentennial bobs in the harbor among power cruisers and recreational sailboats. The kids **Carabela *Pinta*** is shockingly small for such a long voyage.

There's no missing the crenellated stone walls of Baiona's kids **Fortaleza de Monterreal,** a fortification constructed fitfully over centuries but finally finished in the early 1600s. About 3km (1¾ miles) of walls wrap around the headland above the harbor. After the fort, **Cafetería Monterrey** makes a good spot to snack on a local favorite, *empanada de zamburiñas,* filled with a mix of chopped shellfish, onion, and roasted red peppers.

Six long kids **sandy beaches,** mostly on the east end of town, mean that today Baiona is more resort than port or fort. Pinta: ⊙ 20 min. Porto do Baiona. ☎ 986-68-70-67. 1€. Daily 11am-2pm and 4:30-7:30pm. Fortaleza: ⊙ 45 min. ☎ 986-68-70-67. 1€. Daily 10am-9pm. Cafetería: Rúa Ramon y Cajal, 5. ☎ 986-35-54-90. 2€-5€. Cash only. Daily breakfast & lunch.

❺ ★ kids **Islas Cíes.** This archipelago of three islands at the mouth of the Ría de Vigo is a national **maritime park.** The largest island of Cíes can be reached by ferry from Baiona and Vigo. A good 90-minute hike following the dramatic coastline begins at the long sand

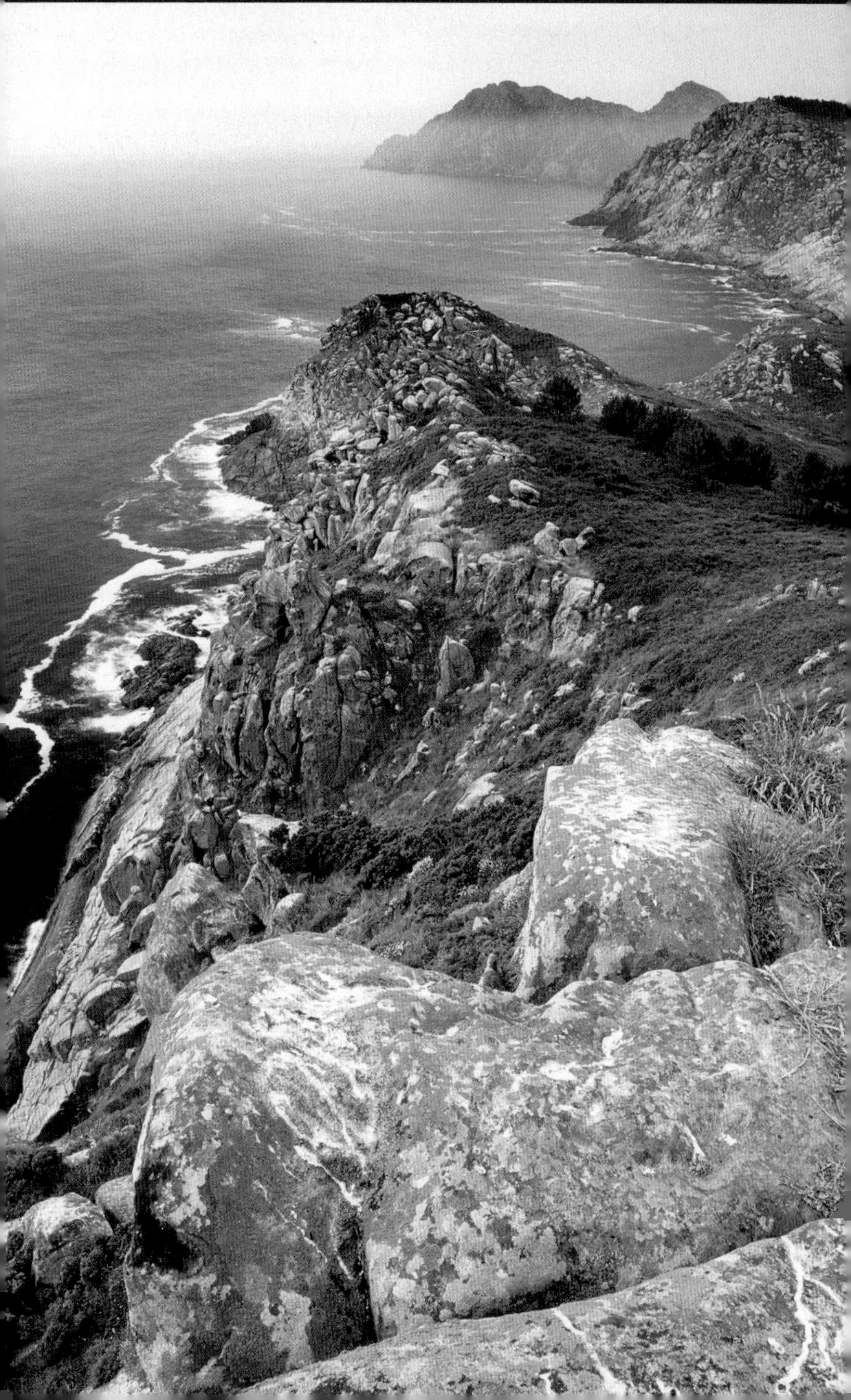

On your way out of town toward O Grove (see below), the north coast of the **Ría Pontevedra** offers spectacular vistas of the bay's deep cut into the rocky land. The road is lined with picturesque stone houses. What look like stone dollhouses on stilts are actually household grain storage buildings. Museo: ⏱ 1 hr. Rúa Pasantería, 10. ☎ 986-85-14-55. www.museo.depo.es. Free. Tues–Sat 10am–2pm and 4–7pm; Sun 11am–2pm.

Leave Pontevedra on PO-308 coastal road toward Sanxenxo. Follow PO-308 for 28km (17 miles); then take PO-316 into O Grove.

⑦ ★ O Grove. This small town at the end of a peninsula surrounded by shellfish flats and 8km (5 miles) of beaches is as much fishing village as summer getaway. (A shellfish auction is held at the docks weekdays at 5pm.) Drive to well-marked **Mirador Monte A Siradella** for panoramic views of a landscape where land and sea merge. Or tour the shoals aboard a  kids **glass-bottomed catamaran,** complete with a tasting of mussels.

Southwest of the village next to mussel farms, the kids **Acuarium Galicia** focuses on the majestic Galician coastal environment, exhibiting sea otters, turtles, and local fish.

Locals gather shellfish in the shallows near the bridge between the village and the island of A Toxa (La Toja in Castilian). Despite overblown condo development, A Toxa remains Galicia's most famed resort. Photographers can't resist tiny Capilla de San Caralampio, covered with scallop shells. Catamaran: ⏱ 75 min. Estación Autobuses and Catamaranes, C/ Beiramar, s/n. ☎ 986-73-12-46. 13€ adults, 6€ kids. Apr–Sept; call for times. Acuarium: ⏱ 1 hr. Punta Moreiras, Peninsula de O Grove. ☎ 986-73-15-15. www.acquariumgalicia.com. 10€ adults, 7.50€ seniors, 6.50€ kids 6–12. Sept–June Fri–Sun 10am–8pm; July–Aug daily 10am–9pm.

Leave O Grove on PO-550 for 6km (3¾ miles) toward Dena, a village covered in *albariño* grapevines and rose bushes. Continue into Cambados to see locals gather clams and periwinkles. The VRG-4.1 connects to northbound AP-9, passing through Padrón (where Santiago's body was brought from Jerusalem) en route to Santiago de Compostela.

> Take a glass-bottomed catamaran cruise and then sample nécora, O Grove's local species of crab.

beach of Praia das Rodas and ends at the Faro de Porta lighthouse. ⏱ Half-day. Ferry: ☎ 986-22-52-72. 18€ round-trip, free for kids 11 & under. www.mardeons.com. Park: Ile da Cíes. ☎ 986-68-75-02. http://reddeparquesnacionales.mma.es.

Continue on PO-552 for about 3km (1¾ miles) to the AG-57. Head north toward Pontevedra and continue 22km (14 miles) to AP-9. Follow signs north 18km (11 miles) toward Pontevedra. Cross the Autopista del Atlántico (AP-9) suspension bridge—the best vantage to appreciate Ría de Vigo. Continue 13km (8 miles) to Pontevedra.

⑥ Pontevedra. The pedestrian Old City is a virtual museum of architectural styles, from Gothic to baroque. Pontevedra flourished in the Renaissance, and its standout buildings feature graceful arcades and formal coats of arms. Look for small ancient statues in almost every square. The five buildings of the **Museo de Pontevedra** encompass the design history of this city of stone, and its collections summarize the evolution of Galician society.

Where to Stay & Dine

> *Wine and dine at Xeito Restaurante Mariquería.*

★★ Casa del Barón PONTEVEDRA
This 16th-century palace *parador* (government-run hotel) occupies a choice spot in the pedestrian Old City. The marvelous garden is an ideal place to enjoy lunch. Rúa Barón, 19. ☎ 986-85-58-00. www.parador.es. 45 rooms. Doubles 103€–160€. Entrees 18€–28€. AE, DC, V. Lunch & dinner daily.

El Molino TUI *GALICIAN*
Grilled river and ocean fish are specialties of this local favorite in Tui's new city. C/ A.G. Besada, 19. ☎ 986-60-30-12. Entrees 9€–22€. AE, MC, V. Lunch & dinner daily.

Gran Hotel La Toja O GROVE
This famed Belle Epoque resort hotel with thermal baths and a spa has been crisply modernized. Isla de La Toja, s/n. ☎ 986-73-00-25. www.granhotellatoja.com. 197 rooms. Doubles 130€–270€ with breakfast. AE, DC, MC, V.

★★★ Hotel Convento San Benito A GUARDA
This stunning 1561 convent just above the fishing harbor became a quietly luxurious hotel with furniture in 18th- and 19th-century styles—and bathrooms with all modern conveniences. Plaza de San Benito, s/n. ☎ 986-61-11-66. www.hotelsanbenito.es. 24 rooms. Doubles 57€–108€. MC, V.

Hotel Residencia Tres Carabelas BAIONA
These modest digs are right in town, steps from the attractions and a small beach below the castle. C/ Ventura Misa, 61. ☎ 986-35-51-33. www.hoteltrescarabelas.com. 12 rooms. Doubles 43€–62€. MC, V.

Mesón-Tapería Casa Soto BAIONA *GALICIAN*
A charming tiled dining room with a glass roof is the perfect spot for platters of wood-roasted meats and fish. Rúa Laxe, 7. ☎ 986-35-57-08. Entrees 9€–18€. MC, V. Lunch & dinner Thurs–Tues.

★★ Parador de Tui San Telmo TUI
This modern hotel feels like a country estate, but it's a pleasant 15-minute stroll to town along the banks of the Río Miño. Avenida Portugal, s/n. ☎ 986-60-03-00. www.parador.es. 32 rooms. Doubles 124€–160€. AE, DC, V.

★★ Samar Hotel O GROVE
All but one room at this spacious and pretty 2005 hotel have terraces to enjoy sea breezes on Playa La Lanzada—far from downtown but next to the sand and surf. Rúa La Lanzada, 9. ☎ 986-73-83-78. www.samarhotel.com. 14 rooms. Doubles 70€–100€ with breakfast. MC, V.

★★ Xeito Restaurante Mariquería A GUARDA
SEAFOOD Sit on the rocky point overlooking crashing waves to enjoy grilled swordfish or rice and shellfish casseroles. Rúa Fernández Albor, 19. ☎ 986-61-04-74. Entrees 15€–30€. MC, V. Lunch & dinner daily.

Costa da Morte

Myth, legend, and hyperbole are intertwined along this dramatic coast between Santiago and A Coruña—a region called the "Coast of Death" because so many ships have foundered on its rocky shores. This route begins at the "End of the Earth," or *"Fisterra"* in Galego—a name bestowed by the Roman legions who came here to behold the nightly departure of the sun from Europe. Roads cannot hug the cliffs of the convoluted shore, so this 1-day-long scenic drive passes through rolling, lushly green countryside before plunging down to sheltered, sandy harbors on the windy, sea-blasted coast.

> *The lighthouse at Cabo Fisterra, about 90km (56 miles) from Santiago de Compostela, is a welcome sight for many weary pilgrims.*

START From Santiago de Compostela, go west on the AC-543 toward Negreira and stay on the same road (which changes numbers) to Dumbría. Pass through Corcubión and Cee, which share a beautiful harbor, and follow signs to Fisterra. **TRIP LENGTH** 90km (56 miles).

1 Fisterra. The road rises on coastal headlands even before it reaches the fishing village of Fisterra. Just before town, a scenic turnoff

affords a dramatic view of the tight crease of the harbor where the village huddles. There is almost no arable land around Fisterra, so the people of this remote village wrest their living from the sea. Their brave fishing traditions are well-recounted at the small **Museo da Pesca** at the handsome harbor.

The high cliffs of the nearby lighthouse promontory, ★★ **Cabo Fisterra,** are surrounded by a wild and swirling sea that ensures a mystical mistiness on the sunniest days—befitting

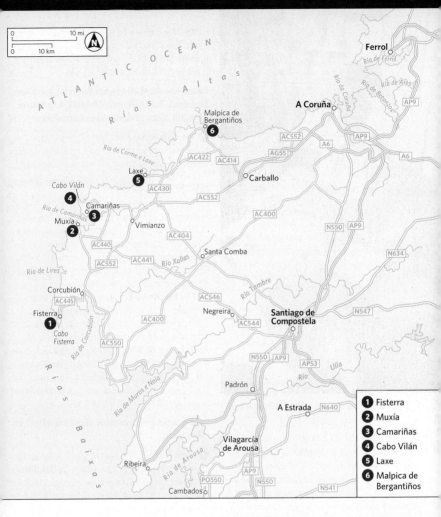

1	Fisterra
2	Muxía
3	Camariñas
4	Cabo Vilán
5	Laxe
6	Malpica de Bergantiños

a site where legend says ancient Celts made sacrifices to their sun god and where the most die-hard pilgrims to Santiago conclude their long walk. (There's a bronze hiking boot honoring them.) **Museo:** ☉ 20 min. C/ Paseo da Riviera, s/n. ☎ 981-74-07-07. www.cofradiafisterra.org. 1€. May–Aug daily 10:30am–2:30pm and 5–7pm; Sept–Apr Tues–Sat 10:30am–1:30pm and 3:30–6:30pm, Sun 10:30am–1:30pm.

From Fisterra, backtrack 16km (10 miles) and turn left onto CP-2303 for a 16km (10-mile) drive to Muxía.

Spending the Night in Fisterra

Standing 143m (469 ft.) above the sea, the inn at the lighthouse, ★ **O Semáforo,** has to be one of the most scenic lodgings in Spain. Reserve ahead, especially during the May to September main pilgrimage season. The dining room serves simple Gallegan fare, usually fish and potatoes. Faro de Fisterra, s/n. ☎ 981-72-58-69. www.osemaforo.com. 5 rooms. Doubles 90€–110€. Entrees 11€–30€. MC, V. Lunch & dinner Wed–Mon, Tues hotel guests only. Closed Nov.

> *The art of handmade bobbin lace is alive and well in Camariñas.*

❷ ★ **Muxía.** A vigorous fishing port with a deep, sheltered harbor, Muxía has had a rough history: It was destroyed by 12th-century Norman and Saxon pirates and again by Napoleon in the early 1800s. Sharing a prominent point with a lighthouse is the striking, mostly 16th-century church known locally as the **Santuario da Virxe da Barca,** or Virgin of the Boat—a reference to the tradition that a dispirited St. James (Santiago) was reinvigorated in his efforts to spread the Gospel in Spain when the

Virgin Mary appeared to him in a boat on this point. The church, formerly a Celtic pagan worship site, is another final destination for Santiago pilgrims. Santuario: ⏱ 30 min.

Follow the AC-440 toward Berdoias for 10km (6 miles). Turn left onto CP-1603, and follow signs for 15km (9⅓ miles) to Camariñas.

❸ ★★ **Camariñas.** Two institutions at the broad, scenic harbor sum up Camariñas: On the water side of the street stands the fishermen's brotherhood building. Directly across is the lace-maker's association.

The town has been famous for its lace for a millennium, and every girl starts learning the craft at about age 5. (Peek in windows in town, and you'll often see women sitting near the light, working away with their bobbins.) Since 1991, Camariñas has also sponsored an annual international exhibition of the art.

The **Museo do Encaixe** displays historic examples of lace, mostly from the 19th and 20th centuries, as well as works in progress. A good spot to purchase exquisite lace is **M. Julia Encaje de Bolillos.** Museo: ⏱ 30 min. Praza Insuela, s/n. ☎ 981-73-63-40. www.camarinas. net. 2€. Tues–Sat 11am–2pm and 4–7pm; Sun 11am–2pm and 4–6pm. Bolillos: C/ Cantón Miguel Feijon, s/n. ☎ 981-73-71-71. MC, V.

Follow signs from town for 6km (3¾ miles) to Cabo Vilán.

❹ **Cabo Vilán.** The Coast of Death lives up to its name here at this cape, where the **English cemetery** contains the graves of more than 170 English sailors of the HMS *Serpent* who perished in the 1890 wreck.

The road approaching the Cabo Vilán **lighthouse** passes through a large, almost intimidating wind farm of giant turbines, but the payoff is spectacular. This headland is one of the most primeval stretches of this coast—it looks as if the rocks were snapped off at the sea. The landscape changes as you put the cape behind you and pass through green inland farmland that resembles the west of Ireland. At the village of Traba, long cultivated furrows stretch down to a shore of sandy beaches.

Follow route AC-432 toward Vimianzo for 17km (11 miles). Turn left and follow AC-433 for 14km (8⅔ miles) to Laxe.

Spending the Night in Camariñas

If you simply want a good fish meal before continuing or have been seduced into a romantic overnight stopover, you can find both at **Hotel Rústico Puerto Arnela.** Rúa do Carmen, 20. ☎ 981-70-54-77. www.puerto arnela.es. Doubles 45€ with breakfast. Entrees 9€–23€. MC, V. Lunch daily, dinner Mon–Sat.

Travel Tip

It's best to explore this area by car, though it can be managed by public transport: Buses run five to seven times daily from A Coruña to Malpica, with intermittent service down to Fisterra.

5 Laxe. This prosperous fishing port sits on the north side of a striking estuary, where the sea intrudes far inland with sheer rock walls on either side. It marks the northern end of the geological majesty of the coast. As you drive north from Laxe, you will see long sandy beaches stretching into the distance. Behind the dunes are fertile marshlands that extend, in some cases, a kilometer (⅔ mile) or more inland.

Follow AC-431 east toward Ponteceso. In 9km (5⅔ miles), turn left onto DP-4307 and follow signs 12km (7½ miles) to Malpica.

6 kids Malpica de Bergantiños. The headlands above the shipping and fishing port of Malpica provide an exceptional overview of the **Illas Sisargas,** a set of small rocky islands about 1km (⅔ mile) offshore that are a sanctuary and protected breeding area for seabirds. The town's long white-sand beach is fully exposed to the Atlantic, making it a premier destination for wet-suit surfing. (The water is *cold.*)

Leave Malpica on AC-418. In 15km (9⅓ miles), connect with AG-55 for 32km (20 miles) to A Coruña.

> *ABOVE* The lighthouse at Cabo Vilán was Spain's first to run on electricity. *BELOW* The sandy white beaches of Laxe.

SET IN STONE

Revelations (and the Rest of the Bible, Too)

BY PATRICIA HARRIS & DAVID LYON

SINCE THE 13TH CENTURY, the cathedral at Santiago de Compostela has been one of the most important pilgrimage sites in Christendom. Although the cathedral has been embellished over the years, the original church remains the core of the complex and embodies its most striking artistry. Most striking of all is the Pórtico da Gloria, a colonnade behind the western facade created between 1168 and 1188 by Maestro Mateo. It is the premier masterpiece of Romanesque sculpture in Spain—a veritable New Testament in stone.

APOSTLES COLUMN
The column on the right side of the central arch depicts the apostles Peter (holding keys), Paul (holding an epistle), James the Lesser

(with a carpenter's saw), and John (with an eagle at his feet).

CENTRAL ARCH TYMPANUM
Christ is flanked by the four evangelists, who are depicted

with their symbols: the eagle of John, the writing desk of Matthew, the bull of Luke, and the lion of Mark.

MAIN COLUMN SUPPORTING THE CENTRAL TYMPANUM The dominant figure at the top of the mullion is the seated image of Santiago, declared the patron saint of Spain in the early 9th century. Christian forces fighting the Moors went into battle under his banner.

RIGHT ARCH TYMPANUM
The Book of Revelation was a profound influence on Mateo. This section features the heads of God the Father and God the

Son flanked by two groups of figures: Heaven is represented by angels carrying

the blessed in the folds of their robes, while Hell is depicted by demons torturing the damned.

Santiago de Compostela

In the western Iberian Peninsula, all roads lead to Santiago; in the city, all streets lead to the cathedral. Pilgrims have been coming here since the discovery of the body of St. James the Apostle (*"Santiago"* in Galego and Castellano) in the 9th century. By the 12th century, they were so numerous that the pope named Santiago as equal to Rome and Jerusalem for Christian pilgrims. Their presence made Santiago one of the first tourist cities in Europe. The religious aspect of visiting Santiago, however, saves the city from being a tourist trap. It is a truly monumental place, steeped in history and lore, and beautiful both rain and shine.

> *The triple portal of the Portico de Gloria was the magnum opus of Romanesque sculptor Master Mateo.*

START C/ Praza do Obradoiro.

❶ ★★★ **Catedral.** One of Christendom's holiest sites, this masterpiece Romanesque church masked by a series of baroque facades offers just the sort of welcome you'd hope for after walking all the way across northern Spain from France (the most popular pilgrimage trail,

called the French route). On arrival, pilgrims traditionally climb the stairs behind the altar to embrace a polychrome statue of Santiago. Starting in 1168, Maestro Mateo spent 20 years directing the construction of the cathedral and its masterful stone carvings. His artistry is best displayed in the **Pórtico da Gloria** (see p. 254). Restoration work obscures the carvings,

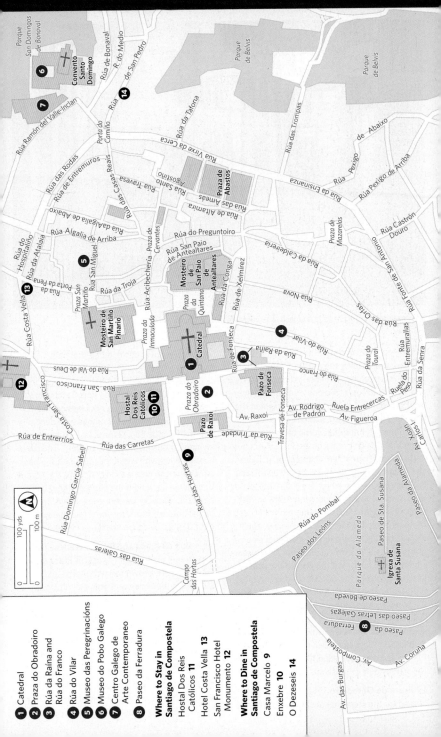

1 Catedral
2 Praza do Obradoiro
3 Rúa da Raina and
   Rúa do Franco
4 Rúa do Vilar
5 Museo das Peregrinacións
6 Museo do Pobo Galego
7 Centro Galego de
   Arte Contemporaneo
8 Paseo da Ferradura

Where to Stay in
Santiago de Compostela
Hostal Dos Reis
Católicos 11
Hotel Costa Vella 13
San Francisco Hotel
Monumento 12

Where to Dine in
Santiago de Compostela
Casa Marcelo 9
Enxebre 10
O Dezeseis 14

> *Sometimes pilgrims need to let loose too—nightlife on Rúa da Raína.*

but you can get up close and personal with the statuary by climbing the scaffolding on a free guided tour; prior reservation is required (www.reservasportico.es). You can also see the floor-level self-portrait of Mateo, against which the people of Santiago gently knock the heads of their babies in hope that some of his genius will rub off. The saint's remains are in a silver chest in the crypt. The cathedral **museum** includes some special chapels, the Gothic cloister, and the treasure rooms, which are more interesting than most because they contain 12th- to 18th-century statuary, including the ruins of Maestro Mateo's carved stone choir (ca. 1200). You'll also see ancient coins left by medieval pilgrims from as far away as Istanbul and Russia. Architecture buffs find the visit to the **roof** an intriguing look at the construction techniques. ⏱ 1½ hr. C/ Praza do Obradoiro, s/n. ☎ 981-56-93-27. www.catedraldesantiago.es. Catedral: Free. Daily 9am–9pm, Mass only noon–1pm. Museo: 5€ adults, 1€ kids. June–Sept Mon–Sat 10am–1pm and 4–8pm, Sun 10am–2pm; Oct–May Mon–Sat 10am–1:30pm and 4–6:30pm, Sun 10am–1:30pm. Roof: 10€, same hours as museum.

❷ Praza do Obradoiro. The central plaza is named for the stonemasons' workshops once located here. It is enclosed by the main entrance to the cathedral, the hospital for pilgrims established in 1492 by Fernando and Isabel (now the Hostal Dos Reis Católicos; see p. 260), the imposing neoclassical Pazo de Raxoi (now the seat of city government), and the Pazo de San Xerome (a 15th-century structure housing university offices). The plaza is often filled with weary pilgrims bearing backpacks and carrying walking sticks as they crane their necks to behold the cathedral that has been their goal for days or even weeks. In the very center of the plaza, you'll find the symbol of St. James, a scallop shell.

❸ ★ Rúa da Raína and Rúa do Franco. These two streets leading southwest off Praza do Obradoiro are known for restaurants and nightlife—roles they have probably played since they were constructed in the 12th century. Raína is named for the queen of Portugal, who established a hospital here during her 1324 pilgrimage. "Franco" is what pilgrims who came from beyond the Pyrenees were once called, whether they were French or not.

❹ ★ Rúa do Vilar. Now lined with arcades (handy when it rains), this 10th-century street features Santiago's best shopping for pastry

> A display on the trades of the sea at the Museo do Pobo Galego (Museum of the Galician People).

treats and for souvenirs that range from crosses carved from *azabache* (jet) to plastic cigarette lighters emblazoned with the silhouette of a pilgrim in full stride. **Lar Das Meigas** specializes in local arts and crafts, including weaving, lace, *Gaita de Barquin* (bagpipes), ceramics, and jewelry. Check the shop for its schedule of walking tours and concerts of traditional music. **Meigas:** Vilar, 47. ☎ 981-56-51-22. www.lardasmeigas.com. Hours for activities vary.

❺ ★ **Museo das Peregrinacións.** Almost any question you'd have about Santiago the city or the saint is answered in this superb Museum of Pilgrimages. Dioramas, artifacts, and wall texts examine the phenomenon of pilgrimages around the world, the legend and facts regarding the transfer of the body of St. James the Apostle here after his death in A.D. 44, and the growth of Santiago as a pilgrimage site from the 11th century onward. One set of displays deals with the major pilgrimage roads to Santiago. ⏱ 1 hr. C/ San Miguel, 4. ☎ 981-58-15-58. www.mdperegrinacions.com. 2.40€. Tues–Fri 10am–8pm; Sat–Sun 10:30am–1:30pm.

❻ **Museo do Pobo Galego.** A Gothic church from the 13th and 14th centuries forms the heart of the monastery complex housing the Museum of the Galician People. Remarkable sepulchers in the church include a depiction of a knight in armor, but the museum is more interested in exploring Galician folkways and culture than simply honoring the dead. Alas, there is no English signage, but excellent displays give insight into fishing practices and such arts as weaving and lace making. One photo display depicts the construction of a *Gaita de Barquin*, the Galician version of the bagpipe. ⏱ 45 min. Rúa San Domingos de Bonaval. ☎ 981-58-36-20. www.museodopobo.com. Free. Tues–Sat 10am–2pm and 4–8pm; Sun 11am–2pm.

❼ **Centro Galego de Arte Contemporaneo.** Right across from the Museo do Pobo Galego, this unadorned modern building with white walls and gleaming marble and wood floors makes a serene backdrop for changing exhibitions of often challenging contemporary art. ⏱ 45 min. Rúa Ramón del Valle Inclan, s/n. ☎ 981-54-66-29. www.cgac.org. Free. Tues–Sun 11am–8pm.

❽ **Paseo da Ferradura.** The pilgrim-filled narrow medieval streets of Santiago can begin to seem a little claustrophobic, especially during the busy summer months. Follow the lead of the locals and take a stroll on the tree-lined paths of the Alameda park. Along the Paseo de Ferradura, you can still enjoy picturesque views of the cathedral—at a comfortable remove from the crowds.

Where to Stay & Dine

> *The Hostal Dos Reis Católicos, next to the cathedral.*

★★ **Casa Marcelo** *CONTEMPORARY SPANISH*
Beloved by the national Spanish gourmet society as well as a certain French tire company, Marcelo's contemporary cuisine is a breeze of fresh air after the sturdy peasant fare of Galicia. All nine courses are small, and each focuses on a single, often subtle flavor experience. The market-driven menu (as in all of Galicia) features a lot of seafood. Wines are extra. Rúa Hortas, 1. ☎ 981-55-85-80. 60€ tasting menu. AE, MC, V. Lunch Tues–Sat, dinner Thurs–Sat.

Enxebre *GALICIAN*
You've probably never been in such a rollicking *parador* dining room as this traditional Galician tavern. Locals flock here to share big plates of small bites like croquettes, chicken and clams, or potato and sausage omelets while downing 2€ glasses of Galician wine. Hostal Dos Reis Católicos, Praza do Obradoiro, 1. ☎ 981-58-22-00. Entrees 7€–17€. AE, DC, MC, V. Lunch & dinner daily.

★★★ **Hostal Dos Reis Católicos**
The monumental landmark palace on the cathedral's main plaza was established in 1492 by Fernando and Isabel as lodging for pilgrims. Today it's one of Spain's most luxurious and history-steeped *paradores.* Praza do Obradoiro, 1. ☎ 981-58-22-00. www.parador.es. 138 rooms. Doubles 150–265€ with breakfast. AE, DC, MC, V.

★ **Hotel Costa Vella**
Set at the edge of the medieval city, this fully modern hotel features low-key traditional decor with such rustic touches as exposed stone walls. On nice days, breakfast (5.50€ extra) is served in beautiful rear gardens. The best four rooms overlook the gardens. C/ Porta da Pena, 17. ☎ 981-56-95-30. www.costavella.com. 14 rooms. Doubles 70€–87€. AE, DC, MC, V.

O Dezeseis *GALICIAN*
This local favorite just outside the old walls offers bargain prices on Galician fish and beef dishes. The selection of wines from Galicia and León is outstanding. Rúa de San Pedro, 16. ☎ 981-57-76-33. Entrees 11€–13€, menu 12€. MC, V. Lunch & dinner Mon–Sat.

★★ **San Francisco Hotel Monumento**
This former convent was founded by St. Francis of Assisi when he and his companions made a pilgrimage to Santiago in 1214. Contemporary design meets monastic tradition in superbly comfortable rooms in the 16th-century cloister. The location is literally steps from the cathedral, and an ideal choice for drivers, as it has extensive parking. Campillo San Francisco, 3. ☎ 981-58-16-34. www.sanfranciscohm.com. 82 rooms. Doubles 90€–150€. AE, MC, V.

Galicia Fast Facts

Arriving & Getting Around

BY PLANE Overseas travelers typically fly to Galicia after changing planes in Barcelona or Madrid. Iberia flies daily from Madrid to A Coruña's **Aeropuerto de Alvedro** (☎ 981-18-72-00), which is 10km (6 miles) outside town. Iberia also flies three times a week from Barcelona and six times per week from Madrid to Santiago's **Aeropuerto de Lavacolla** (☎ 981-54-75-01), which is 11km (6¾ miles) outside town. **BY TRAIN** A Coruña has the best long-distance train connections in Galicia. Trains arrive at **Estación San Cristóbal** at Praza San Cristóbal (☎ 902-24-02-02). Both Santiago and Pontevedra are well-served by trains from A Coruña. The Santiago train station is at C/ Hórreo, 75A. Pontevedra's station is at Praza de Calvo Sotelo, s/n. Two trains daily also service Santiago from Madrid. **BY BUS** Bus service to A Coruña and Santiago takes 8 to 10 hours from Madrid, but both cities have six to eight arrivals per day. For information, call **Alsa** (☎ 981-58-61-33; www.alsa.es). Regional service is frequent and thrifty, with hourly buses between A Coruña and Santiago. For information, call **Monbus** (☎ 981-55-57-60; www.monbus.es). Pontevedra is linked by hourly bus service to Santiago. For information, call ☎ 902-29-29-00. **BY CAR** The **AP-9 toll road** links Tui, Pontevedra, Santiago, and A Coruña, with side roads leading to other coastal communities. The main east-west access is via the A-6 in the north and the A-52 in the south.

Booking Services

Compostur (☎ 902-19-01-60; www.santiagoreservas.com), in the Santiago de Compostela tourist office (see below), assists with determining hotel room availability from May to October.

Doctors & Hospitals

For emergency medical or dental attention, go to the *centro de urgencia* (emergency room) of the nearest hospital. Non-E.U. residents can consult national health service doctors for a relatively small fee; ask at your hotel for a list of doctors.

Emergencies

The all-around emergency number in Spain is ☎ **112**. For an ambulance, call ☎ **061**. To report a forest fire, call ☎ **085**.

Language

Most Galicians speak Galego, sometimes classified as a dialect of Spanish and sometimes considered a separate language. It is very similar to Portuguese, with some additional vocabulary inherited from Gaelic. Signage is generally in Galego, with secondary signage in Castilian Spanish. English is almost always the default common non-Spanish language.

Pharmacies

To find an open pharmacy outside normal business hours, check the list of stores posted on the door of any drugstore. By law, there's always a drugstore open somewhere. Drugstores are called *farmacías*. When open, they display a neon green cross.

Police

For national police, call ☎ **091;** for local police, call ☎ **092;** for traffic police, call ☎ **062.**

Post Office

Urban post offices in Galicia are generally open Monday to Friday 8am to 9pm, Saturday 9am to 2pm. **A CORUÑA** The main post office is at C/ Manuel Casas, 1 (☎ 981-22-51-75). **PONTEVEDRA** The main post office is at C/ García Borbón, 53 (☎ 981-85-16-77). **SANTIAGO** The main post office is at Travesía Fonseca, s/n (☎ 981-58-12-52).

Safety

Galicia's towns and cities are extremely safe. Use common sense. If hiking the Camino de Santiago, stay with groups of other pilgrims.

Visitor Information

For information on the autonomous region of Galicia including the Rías Baixas, or South Coast, and the Costa da Muerte, check with the following offices: **A CORUÑA** **Oficina de Turismo de Galicia,** Dársena da la Marina, s/n (☎ 981-22-18-22; www.turgalicia.es), open Monday to Friday 10am to 2pm and 4 to 7pm, Saturday 11am to 2pm and 5 to 7pm, Sunday 11am to 2pm. **SANTIAGO DE COMPOSTELA** **Oficina de Turismo de Galicia,** Rúa do Villar, 30–32 (☎ 981-58-40-81; www.turgalicia.es), open Monday to Friday 10am to 8pm, Saturday 11am to 2pm and 5 to 7pm, Sunday 11am to 2pm.

9
Asturias &
Cantabria

The Best of Asturias & Cantabria in 4 Days

Asturias and Cantabria join Galicia and the Basque Country as España Verde, or "Green Spain," where the climate often seems more northern European than Mediterranean. Walled off from Castilla y León by the towering peaks and ridges of the Cordillera Cantábrica, which trap moisture coming in from the Atlantic, both regions are verdant and wet. The earliest evidence of human habitation in Spain (up to 140,000 years ago) is found in the limestone mountains—along with the stunning scenery and superb hiking—in the Parque Natural Picos de Europa. The coastal communities, famous for their fishing and shipping since Roman days, are among the country's best beach resorts.

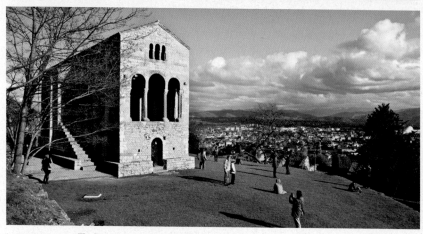

> PREVIOUS PAGE *The limestone massifs of the Picos de Europa.* THIS PAGE *Before it was a church, Santa María del Naranco was the hunting lodge of Ramiro I.*

START Oviedo. TRIP LENGTH 169km (105 miles).

❶ Oviedo. The compact medieval quarter—almost entirely pedestrian—of this capital city of the Principality of Asturias flows seamlessly into the gridlike modern shopping streets. Despite its hilly layout, Oviedo is a walking city of surprisingly broad streets that twist and turn with the contours of the land, offering new vistas at every corner. Oviedo was repopulated in the 8th century as the capital of the Asturian kingdom, the only Christian realm in Spain at the time. Hints of that heritage remain in the 9th-century ★★★ **Cámara Santa** in the cathedral (see p. 278, ❶) and the churches of ★ **Santa María del Naranco** and **San Miguel del Lillo** (see p. 280, ❿) on the hill above town.

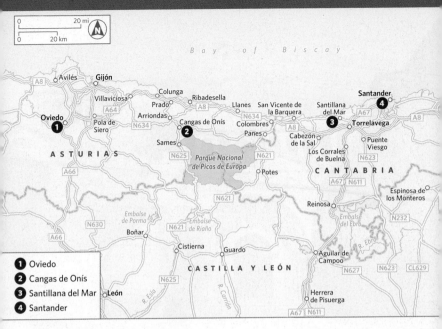

1 Oviedo
2 Cangas de Onís
3 Santillana del Mar
4 Santander

From Oviedo, follow A-66 and A-64 to N-634 east for 38km (24 miles) to Cangas de Onís.

2 Cangas de Onís. Following a successful revolt against Muslim rulers in 722, this mountain village became the first capital of Asturias before the crown was moved to Oviedo. Cangas is an inordinately attractive and prosperous mountain town, featuring a number of handsome homes built by 19th-century Asturians who retired here after making their fortunes in the Americas. Today it serves as a laid-back base town for excursions into the mountains of the Parque Natural Picos de Europa, Spain's first national park (established in 1918). Cangas itself offers excellent scenic hiking (and salmon fishing, for that matter) along the Río Sella. The town also makes a good base for visits to the Paleolithic cave art at ★ **Cueva El Buxu** (see p. 272, **2**). ★★ **Covadonga** (see p. 269, **2**), a scenic mountain site where Pelayo, the warrior who led the revolt against the Muslims, is buried in a shrine, is a village of the Cangas

municipality. It also offers beautiful river-gorge hiking.

Follow N-634 for 19km (12 miles) to A-8. Continue 85km (53 miles) to exit 234. Follow signs 5km (3 miles) to Santillana del Mar.

3 Santillana del Mar. Contrary to its name, Santillana is far from the ocean—it's an inland village surrounded by dairy pastures. The medieval walled town is extraordinarily well preserved, right down to the quaint 12th- to 15th-century cobble-paved streets, despite the fact that it is also a 21st-century working community.

The town is named for Santa Juliana, the martyr whose relics were thought to be held at the monastery church (ca. 870) that later grew into the Romanesque **Colegiata de Santillana del Mar.** Most of the church as it now stands dates from the 11th and 12th centuries. The 17th-century altarpiece is a baroque masterpiece fashioned from Mexican silver. The rhythmic arches of the cloister, with their exquisitely carved capitals, give the complex a sturdy grace.

Stone carving seems to be a theme in Santillana. The **Museo Jesús Otero Oreña** is located near the Colegiata in the house where its namesake sculptor was born in 1908 and

Travel Tip

For hotels and restaurants in Oviedo, see p. 281; for Cangas de Onís, see p. 271; and for Santander, see p. 285.

> ABOVE *Santillana del Mar's Romanesque Colegiata church.* BELOW *Archaeology exhibits at the Museo de Altamira try to recreate the magic of the cave.*

died in 1994. The permanent collection encompasses both his low- and high-relief works, which often represent rural figures or heroic workers in a style that owes a great deal to the expressionism of the 1930s.

Santillana often serves as a base for visiting the nearby ★★ **Museo de Altamira** (see p. 272, **❶**), dedicated to the Paleolithic cave-art legacy of Cantabria. If you want to see some of the great cave art *in situ,* the ★★★ **Cueva de El Castillo** (see p. 273, **❸**) is also nearby.

Just outside of town, ★ **Zoo Santillana del Mar** offers the spectacle of more than 450 species of animals from around the world—though the hundreds of storks and herons settling into the trees around the zoo at dusk might rival any exhibit inside the facility. Part of the zoo is devoted to the flora and fauna contemporaneous with the inhabitants of the Altamira cave—European bison, Przewalski horses, deer, wild boar, lynx, and gray wolves. Colegiata: ⏱ 45 min. Plaza del Abad Francisco Navarro, s/n. ☎ 942-84-03-17. 3€. Tues–Sun 10am–1:30pm and 4–7:30pm. Museo Jesús Otero:

> *Make sure to walk Santander's seaside promenade, restored with large parts of the Old Town after a 1941 fire.*

Spending the Night in Santillana

Modern construction in the ★ **Parador de Santillana** retains the historic style of old-fashioned Santillana—at a significant discount over nearby Parador Gil Blas. (The two share parking and dining.) Plaza Ramón Pelayo, s/n. ☎ 942-81-80-00. www.parador.es. 28 rooms. Doubles 103€–155€. AE, MC, V.

There's no shortage of tourist eateries in Santillana, but you'll eat better if you join the locals at **Casa Cossio** for a real meal of grilled meat, bread, and a bottle of red wine to enjoy at outdoor tables. Plaza del Abad Francisco Navarro, 12. ☎ 942-81-83-55. Entrees 9€–24€. AE, MC, V. Lunch & dinner Wed–Mon.

🕐 30 min. Plaza del Abad Francisco Navarro, s/n. ☎ 942- 81-88-06. Free. Daily 10am–1pm and 4–7:30pm. Zoo: 🕐 2 hr. N-133, km 2. ☎ 942-81-81-25. www.zoosantillanadelmar.com. 16€ adults, 9€ kids 4–12. Daily 9:30am–nightfall.

❹ **Santander.** The great bowl of the Bay of Santander creates an unusual climate in this resort community. The air is always so laden with moisture that it seems to glow softly in the sunlight. Bay waters are also warmer than most on the north coast of Spain, adding to the appeal of Santander's beaches. Since the middle of the 19th century, the city has competed with San Sebastian for recognition as the most elegant resort of northern Spain. The king and queen even spent their summers here, from 1913 to 1930, in an English-style palace built for them on the **Peninsula de la Magdalena** (see p. 284, ❽). Most of the Belle Epoque resort structures can be found along ★★ **Playa de El Sardinero** (see p. 284, ❾), the longest and widest of Santander's many fine beaches.

Picos de Europa

Sculpted by glaciers and etched by rivers, the limestone massifs of the Picos de Europa tower 2,400m (7,874 ft.) and higher. Much of the area is a protected park, and its more remote reaches harbor such endangered species as the brown bear, lynx, and gray wolf. Unless you go mountain trekking, you're unlikely to see these big predators, but the entire region is rich with birds and its streams are practically clogged with salmon in spring and summer. Hitting all the stops on this tour would take at least 2 days.

> The Puente Romano, adorned with a cross, arches over the Río Sella in Cangas de Onís.

START Cangas de Onís. **TRIP LENGTH** 117km (73 miles).

1 Cangas de Onís. This delightful mountain town is a traditional base for excursions into the natural park. People have lived here a long time, as attested by archaeological finds in nearby caves and the **Dolmen de Santa Cruz,** a Neolithic burial chamber formed by five massive stones. The tiny Capilla de Santa Cruz was erected atop the stones in 737; the tour, alas, consists solely of a video.

Another hint of the antiquity of Cangas is the **Puente Romano** that arches over the Río Sella at the edge of town. Frequently rebuilt, its current form is a medieval arch on Roman footings. The Paleolithic ★ **Cueva El Buxu** (see p. 272, **2**) is located about 2km (1¼ miles) outside town.

If you don't have a car, you can take a bus from Oviedo and use local transport to reach nearby trail heads. The tourist office supplies maps. **Jaire Adventure** is one of several

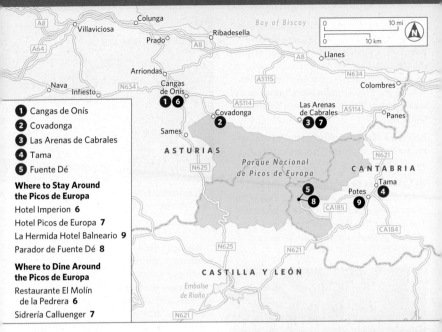

outfitters offering more strenuous adventures such as canoeing, canyon trekking, or caving. Dolmen: ⏱ 20 min. Avenida Constantino González, s/n. ☎ 985-84-80-05. 1€. Mon–Sat 10am–noon and 4–5:15pm. Jaire: Avenida Covadonga, 14. ☎ 985-84-14-64. www.jairecanoas.com. Excursions 25€–40€.

Take AS-114, following signs to AS-262, for 10km (6¼ miles) total to Covadonga.

❷ **Covadonga.** Many units of the Spanish Army have been called "Covadonga," one of the most resonant names in Spanish history. The Battle of Covadonga in 722 is regarded as the beginning of the Reconquista. Details of the battle have metamorphosed into myth, but certain points are clear: A small Christian army led by the elected Visigoth king Pelayo successfully routed a small Muslim army here and ended Moorish governance of Asturias. Pelayo was crowned king—the beginning of the line that would eventually become the rulers of Spain.

Pelayo's sarcophagus at ★★ **Sanctuario de Santa Cueva** rests in a niche high on a rock wall. A dramatic waterfall marks the spot, and visitors can climb stairs to the niche and an adjacent chapel to the Virgin Mary. Parking is tight in the summer; park along AS-262 and walk the rest of the way along the river.

> The Picos de Europa, nearly impassable in the Middle Ages, today challenge Europe's most intrepid climbers.

During the summer, Picos de Europa natio-nal park limits access to the **Lagos de Cova-donga**—two sparkling lakes surrounded by monumental shaftlike mountains of limestone karst—to public buses only. Sanctuario: ⏱ 45 min. AS-262. Free. Daylight hours. Lagos: Bus 7€ adults, 3€ kids. Check at park office in Cangas de Onís (see p. 287).

Backtrack 7km (4⅓ miles) to the AS-114, and follow it east for 27km (17 miles) to Las Are-nas de Cabrales.

❸ **Las Arenas de Cabrales.** Set in the Río Cares valley, tiny Las Arenas (pop. 797) is the market village for the surrounding mountains. The tourist office (see p. 287) provides maps of an extensive system of trails for hikes of 45 minutes to 5 hours.

> Sheep contribute to the region's distinctive Queso de Cabrales.

Although most Cabrales cheese is made by shepherds in the hills, it comes to Las Arenas to be shipped worldwide. The exhibition center at the ★ **Cueva del Queso** shows how the cheese is made—and what makes it distinctive. Cueva: Barrio Pares. ☎ 985-84-51-23. 4.50€ adults, 2€ kids. Spring and summer daily 10am–2pm and 4–8pm; rest of year Sat–Sun only. Tours begin 15 min. after the hour.

Continue east on AS-114 for 21km (13 miles). Turn right on N-621 toward Potes. Continue 24km (15 miles) south toward Tama.

❹ **Tama.** The drive from Las Arenas is fantasti-cally scenic, as it winds along the bottom of river valleys squeezed between high mountains. At the state-of-the-art ★★ kids **Centro de Visi-tantes de Sotama,** life-size photos and striking sound effects make you feel as if you're actually hiking the trails of the Picos. Centro: ⏱ 1 hr. Ave-nida Luis Cuevas, 2. ☎ 942-73-81-09. www.mma. es. Free. Daily 9am–6pm; July–Aug closes 8pm.

Continue on N-621 for 4km (2½ miles) to Potes. Turn right on CA-185 for 24km (15 miles) to Fuente Dé.

❺ **Fuente Dé.** Four hiking trails ranked easy to moderate ascend surrounding slopes. They range from 5km (3 miles) to 11km (6¾ miles). For great views without the effort, the kids **Tele-férico,** built in 1966, starts at 1,070m (3,510 ft.) and zooms up to 1,823m (5,981 ft.) in just 3 minutes. The gondola holds 20 passengers. Teleférico: ⏱ 1½ hr. ☎ 942-73-66-10. 14€ adults, 4€ kids. Mar to mid-Nov or first heavy snowfall daily 10am–6pm.

Cabrales with a Side of Sidra

Pungent blue Cabrales cheese, or **Queso de Cabrales,** is made in small batches with a blend of raw milk from cows, goats, and sheep (in winter, cows only). It's aged in natural limestone caves, where cool temperatures and good ventilation aid the growth of the penicillin mold characteristic of blue cheeses.

Asturian natural cider, or **sidra,** is the perfect companion to Cabrales. Fermented very dry from tart apples, the cider should be poured from a bottle raised about a me-ter (3 ft.) above the glass, to allow oxygen to enter the brew and release the flavor.

Where to Stay & Dine

> *Vertiginous views at the Parador de Fuente Dé.*

Hotel Imperion CANGAS DE ONIS
Near the "Roman" bridge, this hotel with spacious rooms makes a good base for mountain explorations—or just enjoying the elegant small town. Five rooms have terraces. C/ Puente Romano, s/n. ☎ 985-84-94-59. www.hotelimperion.com. 18 rooms. Doubles 55€–100€. AE, MC, V.

★ **Hotel Picos de Europa** ARENAS DE CABRALES
Antique maps add rustic charm to this fine country hotel with quietly contemporary decor. C/ Mayor, s/n. ☎ 985-84-64-41. www.hotelpicosdeeuropa.com. 36 rooms. Doubles 45€–99€ with breakfast. AE, MC, V.

★ **La Hermida Hotel Balneario** POTES
Opened in 2006, this luxurious hotel incorporates thermal baths that have been acclaimed since the 17th century. Carretera La Hermida a Potes, s/n. ☎ 942-73-36-25. www.balneariolahermida.com. 57 rooms. Doubles 170€ with breakfast. AE, MC, V.

★★ **Parador de Fuente Dé** FUENTE DÉ
Built the same year as the cable car, this hotel achieves the brawny feel of a mountain lodge, with ample rooms furnished with dark wood and rich fabrics. After a day of hiking, enjoy a hearty meal in the elegant, white-linen restaurant. Fuente Dé. ☎ 942-73-66-51. www.parador.es. 77 rooms. Doubles 60€–127€. Entrees 18€–32€. AE, DC, MC, V. Lunch & dinner daily.

Restaurante El Molín de la Pedrera CANGAS DE ONIS CANTABRIAN Chorizo and cider dominate the tapas scene at this hip riverfront complex. For a full meal, try the stewed beef on corncakes. C/ Río Güeña, 2. ☎ 985-84-91-09. Entrees 12€–24€. MC, V. Lunch Thurs–Tues, dinner Thurs–Mon.

★★ **Sidrería Calluenger** ARENAS DE CABRALES CANTABRIAN This casual *sidrería* (cider house) features local Cabrales cheese in such dishes as stuffed piquillo peppers with cheese sauce, or fried apples with honey, cheese, and walnuts. They also pour a properly aerated cider. Plaza Castaneu, s/n. ☎ 985-84-64-41. Entrees 6€–14€. Cash only. Lunch & dinner Thurs–Tues.

Prehistoric Caves

The limestone caves of the Cantabrian mountain range are a treasure-trove of Paleolithic art. Since the late 19th century, more than 50 caves have been discovered with haunting images of human hands, bison, deer, horses, mammoths, and other creatures. Some of the caves open to the public are listed below. It's worth going out of your way—and planning ahead—to experience the human creativity of 10,000 to 35,000 years ago. The number of visitors is often limited, and age restrictions may apply.

> Life-size replicas of the world-famous Altamira Paleolithic cave drawings, deemed the "Sistine Chapel of prehistoric art."

START Santillana del Mar. **TRIP LENGTH** 333km (207 miles).

❶ ★★ **Museo de Altamira.** Sophisticated bison drawings on the ceiling made Altamira so famous that it had to be closed in the 1990s to protect it. This museum's life-size re-creation lacks the original magic but compensates with superb archaeology exhibits. Stop for an overview before visiting another cave. 2km (1¼ miles) outside Santillana del Mar. ☎ 942-81-80-05. www.museodealtamira.es. 3€ adults, 1.50€ seniors and students, free Sat afternoon and Sun.

May–Oct Tues–Sat 9:30am–8pm, Sun 9:30am–3pm; Nov–Apr Tues–Sat closes 6pm.

Follow A-8 for 85km (53 miles) to N-634. Take N-634 19km (12 miles) to Cangas de Onís.

❷ ★ **Cueva El Buxu.** Only 25 people per day are allowed to enter this small cave to see charcoal drawings and rock engravings, including striking Ice Age elk. Cardes, s/n (2km/1¼ miles from Cangas de Onís). ☎ 608-17-54-67. 3€ adults, 1.50€ seniors and students, free Wed. Phone for reservations 3–5pm Wed–Sun; tours Mon–Wed.

1 Museo de Altamira
2 Cueva El Buxu
3 Cueva de El Castillo
4 Cueva de Covalanas
5 Cueva El Soplao

Follow A-8 88km (55 miles) to N-623. Continue on N-623 another 5km (3 miles) to Puente Viesgo.

3 ★★★ **Cueva de El Castillo.** Touring this beautiful cave is a journey to the dawn of art, going back to handprints that may have been clan signs. Later paintings include graceful horses, deer, and bison that would have seemed alive in flickering firelight. Follow signs from Puente Viesgo. ☎ 942-59-84-25. http://cuevas.culturadecantabria.com. 3€ adults, 1.50€ kids. May–Sept daily 10am–2pm and 4–6:30pm; Oct–Apr Wed–Sun 9:30am–4:55pm.

Take N-623 north to N-634. After 20km (12 miles), merge onto A-8, continuing west for another 26km (16 miles).

4 ★★ **Cueva de Covalanas.** This small cave is known as the "Cave of the Red Hind" for its iron oxide drawings of a flock of deer, seemingly poised to flee from hunters. Monte Panda, Ramales de la Victoria. ☎ 942-64-65-04 or 629-13-54-44. http://cuevas.culturadecantabria.com. Oct–Apr Wed–Sun 10am–1pm; May–Sept Wed–Sun 10am–noon and 4–6pm.

Take N-629 19km (12 miles) north to the A-8. Follow A-8 71km (44 miles).

> Consider yourself lucky to get into Cueva El Buxu, only 25 people a day allowed.

5 ★ **Cueva El Soplao.** Discovered in the early 20th century, Soplao features amazing mineral formations—the work of nature, not man. For those with an Indiana Jones spirit, the "adventure tourism" visit plumbs 3km (1¾ miles) deep into the earth. Exit 269, A-8, La Florida. ☎ 902-82-02-82. www.elsoplao.es. General visit 10€ adults; 7.50€ seniors, students, and kids 4–16. Adventure tourism 30€ kids 12 and up, kids 11 & under not permitted. Mon–Fri 8am–10pm; Sat 10am–10pm; Sun 9am–3pm.

The Cantabrian Coast

The Picos de Europa extend east from Asturias all the way into Cantabria. But the autonomous region of Cantabria is best known for its dramatic 200km (124-mile) coastline, not for mountains. The more than 70 sandy beaches along this route are punctuated by high headlands and sheer cliffs. This driving tour cruises through fishing ports and resort towns both east and west of the largest resort of all, Santander. Depending on how much beach time you'd like, plan for at least 4 days.

> Santander is popular with locals as well as Brits coming from Portsmouth and Plymouth on the ferry.

START Unquera. **TRIP LENGTH** 118km (73 miles).

❶ Unquera. Where the Río Deva flows from the mountains to the sea, the estuarine system blooms with marshes, shellfish-filled mud flats, and long sandy beaches. Follow signs for **Mirador Tina Menor,** on an 8km (5-mile) loop off C-380, for outstanding vistas of rocky bluffs to the east and green mountains sloping to the sea on the west. Access roads lead to three public beaches.

Follow N-634 east 9km (5⅔ miles) to San Vicente.

❷ San Vicente de la Barquera. As you begin the descent into town, you'll be treated to the quintessential image of the Cantabrian coast: a 13th-century castle and church high above a harbor filled with fishing boats. The **Castillo del Rey,** a sturdy defensive fort, was begun in 1210, when San Vicente was engaged in the Reconquista of Andalucía. Fernando and Isabel converted the castle to a prison, but it has been restored to its medieval appearance.

A stop on the coastal pilgrimage route to Santiago, San Vicente remains a significant

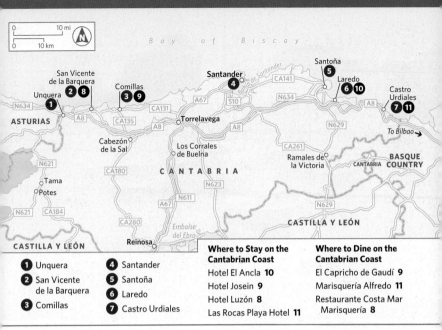

Bay of Biscay

1 Unquera
2 San Vicente de la Barquera
3 Comillas
4 Santander
5 Santoña
6 Laredo
7 Castro Urdiales

fishing port known for *sorropotún,* a tuna and potato stew. But fishermen share the coast with beachgoers and surfers. The 3km-long (1¾-mile) **Playa de Gerra,** for example, has superb surfing waves. To try them out, hit **Surfnsoul. com** for rentals on boards and individual and group lessons. Castillo: ☉ 1 hr. ☎ 942-71-07-97. 1.40€. Tues–Sun 11am–2pm and 5–8pm. Surfnsoul: Playa de Gerra, Parque Natural de Oyambre. ☎ 699-92-40-09. www.surfnsoul.com. Board and wetsuit 10€/hr. Group courses start at 119€.

Follow CA-131 for 11km (6¾ miles) to Comillas.

3 **Comillas.** The quaint resort town of Comillas, whose main beach is framed by a rocky headland and the fishing port, has a handful of Modernista buildings. The **Palacio de Sobrellano,** designed by Catalan architect Joan Martorell, and the **Capilla Panteón** beside it, designed by Josep Llimona and Agapit Vallmitjana, were built in the late 1870s. Both exteriors are updated Gothic buildings—the modern details are all inside.

A young Antoni Gaudí (see p. 428) designed the more fanciful ★ **El Capricho de Gaudí,** a summer home built from 1883 to 1885. The architect's Mudéjar Revival roots are evident in the brick facade with rows of ceramic

> *The familiarly fantastic architecture of Gaudí's summer palace, El Capricho.*

tile. The ground floor is now a restaurant (see p. 277), and a gift shop sells Gaudíana.

The **town cemetery gates** on the hill above the beach are the most Modernista of all— created in 1893 by Luis Doménech y Montaner. Palacio: ☉ 30 min. Palacio Sobrellano, s/n. ☎ 942-72-03-39. 3€ palace, 3€ chapel. Guided tours only

> *Boats in the harbor of Castro Urdiales, once a whaling port and still a fishing center for bonito and hake.*

Tues–Sun 9:30am–2:30pm and 3:30–6pm. El Capricho: ⏱ 30 min. Bajo Sobrellano, s/n. ☎ 942-72-03-65. Shop Tues–Sun 10:30am–7:30pm.

Leave Comillas on CA-135 to A-8. In 18km (11 miles), take exit 230 to A-67. In 22km (14 miles), merge onto S-10 for Santander.

4 Santander. This elegant city is the major resort of Cantabria. Be sure to walk the seaside promenade and visit Playa El Sardinero and the Magdalena peninsula. See p. 282.

Follow S-10/A-67 for 9km (5⅔ miles) toward Bilbao. Continue 28km (17 miles) on A-8 to exit 177. Follow N-634 for 2km (1¼ miles) to CA-241. Santoña is 5km (3 miles).

5 Santoña. This beach town offers the easiest access to the **Reserva Natural Marismas de Santoña y Noja.** This large area of coastal marshes and tidal mud flats is northern Spain's most important stopover for migrating birds

Travel Tip

For lodging and dining in Santander, see p. 285.

and the only breeding site in northern Spain of the purple heron and red-crested pochard. Guided birding tours are sometimes offered; inquire at the tourist office (see p. 287).

Follow CA-241 south to N-634 east. Continue 12km (7½ miles) to Laredo.

6 Laredo. Three rivers feed through the Santoña marshes. Where they reach the sea, a long beach of fine sand, Playa Salvé, lines the shore of Laredo. Though the town has limited amenities, it's a great getaway spot to enjoy sand, surf, and sun.

Head east on N-634 2km (1¼ miles) to A-8. Take exit 151 and follow signs into Castro Urdiales.

7 Castro Urdiales. The medieval fort converted to a lighthouse and the 13th-century Gothic **Santa María** church (with gorgeously carved portals) lend a medieval air to this one-time whaling port that remains a major fishing center for hake and bonito. The bars and restaurants around the port serve fish to rival any on the north coast of Spain. The town's three extensive sandy beaches also make it a major summer resort.

Where to Stay & Dine

> *Wrought iron details at San Vicente's Hotel Luzón.*

El Capricho de Gaudí COMILLAS *INTERNATIONAL*
The dining room in this design landmark is a crystal jewel box, with formal white linens and porcelain—and a dining experience to match. Bajo Sobrellano, s/n. ☎ 942-72-03-65. Entrees 16€–22€. MC, V. Lunch Tues-Sun, dinner Tues-Sat.

Hotel El Ancla LAREDO
The smartly modern rooms here are a surprise against the naively old-fashioned nautical theme of the public areas. The hotel circles a tranquil, pretty garden in a fine residential neighborhood, yet it's just a block from astonishing Playa Salvé strand. Half board (breakfast and dinner included) can be a very good deal here, especially in the low season. C/ González Gallego, 10. ☎ 942-60-55-00. www.hotelelancla. com. 42 rooms. Doubles 73€–132€. MC, V.

kids Hotel Josein COMILLAS
Every room faces the ocean at this older motel-like lodging high on a bluff. Sleep to the sound of surf. It also has its own staircase down to the beach. C/ Manuel Noriega, 27. ☎ 942-72-02-25. www.hoteljosein.com. 28 rooms. Doubles 75€–100€ with breakfast. MC, V. Open Mar–Oct.

Hotel Luzón SAN VICENTE
This graceful, old-fashioned small hotel with lacy wrought-iron details holds down a key location at the turn of the harbor. Some rooms have views of the pleasure boats. Avenida Miramar, s/n. ☎ 942-71-00-50. www.hotelluzon.net. 36 rooms. Doubles 50€–70€. MC, V.

★ Las Rocas Playa Hotel CASTRO URDIALES
Steps off Playa Brazomar and a short walk to town along Paseo Marítimo, Las Rocas is bright, cheerful, and a steal anytime but August. Rooms are flooded with shore light, especially the corner rooms, nos. 216, 316, and 416. Avenida de la Plaza, s/n. ☎ 942-86-04-00. www. lasrocashotel.com. 67 rooms. Doubles 66€–140€ (usually 78€). AE, MC, V.

★★ Marisquería Alfredo CASTRO URDIALES
SEAFOOD There's a menu of sorts, but knowledgeable diners simply go to the bar and point at an array of seafood tapas. The bar selection may be the greatest work of consumable art on the coast. C/ Santa María, 2. ☎ 942-86-36-43. Most shellfish market price by kilogram. Entrees 5€–30€. MC, V. Lunch & dinner Wed-Mon.

Restaurante Costa Mar Marisquería SAN VICENTE *SEAFOOD* Fin fish or shellfish? This handsome tiled harbor restaurant offers great deals on platters for two. The only other decision you need to make is red, white, or rosé. C/ Generalísimo, s/n. ☎ 942-71-01-01. Entrees 11€–23€. MC, V. Lunch & dinner Fri-Wed.

Oviedo

One of Spain's most graceful, lyrical cities, Oviedo was rebuilt after it became the court of the northern kings leading the Reconquista in 808. The capital moved to León in 910, but Oviedo still flourished as a key stopover on a Santiago pilgrimage route. (Those pilgrims continue to earn their stripes scaling the high mountains.) Every bit as romantic as depicted in Woody Allen's 2008 film, *Vicky Cristina Barcelona*, Oviedo's tan sandstone medieval city flows seamlessly into a modern commercial center.

> *The capital of Asturias is still pleasant in summer, when most of the rest of Spain is unbearably hot.*

START Plaza de la Catedral.

① ★ **Catedral.** Mostly constructed in flamboyant Gothic style during the 15th century, the airy cathedral has an extraordinary altarpiece of 20 panels that seem to drip gold. The cathedral is the heart of the medieval city, and the heart of the cathedral is the 9th-century ★★★ **Cámara Santa,** built for Alfonso II (759–842). This pre-Romanesque chapel holds the gold and gem-encrusted 9th-century Cross of Angels (the symbol of Oviedo) and the 10th-century Cross of Victory (the symbol of Asturias). But the architectural columns carved with expressive portraits of the apostles are equally beautiful. ⏱ 1 hr. Plaza de la Catedral, s/n. ☎ 985-20-31-17. Church free. Cámara Santa 2€, with museum and cloister 3.50€. Oct–June Mon–Fri 10am–1pm and 4–8pm, Sat 10am–1pm and 4–6pm; July–Sept Mon–Fri 10am–8pm, Sat 10am–6pm.

② **Plaza Porlier.** Adjacent to the plaza of the cathedral, Plaza Porlier is surrounded by monumental 18th-century palaces. At one corner sits the original 1608 University building, now filled with administrative offices. Inside the colonnaded cloister stands a statue of archbishop Fernando de Valdés Salas (1483–1568), who left funds in his will to establish the school.

③ ★★ **Museo de Bellas Artes.** The major art museum of the Principality of Asturias displays one of only three sets of portraits of the Apostles by El Greco (painted 1585–90). Head upstairs, past the multipanel life and martyrdom of Santa Marina (who, in one resurrection, pops from the belly of a dragon), to the 19th- and 20th-century work by Asturian artists. Some depicted self-consciously folkloric scenes, while others captured the gritty realism

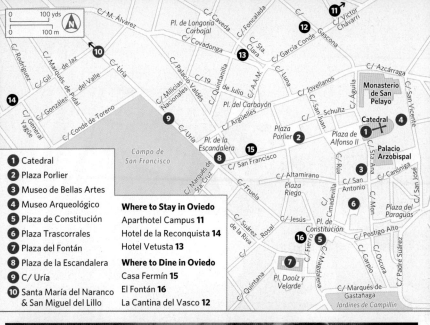

Where to Stay in Oviedo
Aparthotel Campus **11**
Hotel de la Reconquista **14**
Hotel Vetusta **13**

Where to Dine in Oviedo
Casa Fermín **15**
El Fontán **16**
La Cantina del Vasco **12**

1. Catedral
2. Plaza Porlier
3. Museo de Bellas Artes
4. Museo Arqueológico
5. Plaza de Constitución
6. Plaza Trascorrales
7. Plaza del Fontán
8. Plaza de la Escandalera
9. C/ Uría
10. Santa María del Naranco & San Miguel del Lillo

> *The Cámara Santa (Holy Chamber) of Oviedo's Catedral de San Salvador looks like the inside of a treasure chest.*

of the lives of Asturian coal miners—making the region's Republican leanings in the Civil War utterly understandable. ⏱ 1 hr. C/ Santa Ana, 1. ☎ 985-21-30-61. www.museobbaa.com. Free. Sept–June Tues–Fri 10:30am–2pm and 4:30–8:30pm, Sat 11:30am–2pm and 5–8pm, Sun 11:30am–2:30pm; July–Aug Tues–Sat 10:30am–2pm and 4:30–8:30pm, Sun 10:30–2:30pm.

④ **Museo Arqueológico.** Known for its collection of pre-Romanesque sculptures salvaged from churches throughout Asturias, this museum behind the cathedral is closed for a multiyear renovation until 2012. That said, the building itself, an old monastery, may be worth a look. C/ San Vicente, 3. ☎ 985-21-54-05.

> *On weekends, pipers carrying the Asturian* gaita *(a Spanish bagpipe) take to the streets with music.*

⑤ Plaza de Constitución. Essentially the secular answer to the cathedral's plaza, this bustling civic center is dominated by the old Jesuit church of San Isidro el Real and by the town hall. The arch beneath the town hall—representing the Old City gate by which pilgrims entered Oviedo to visit the cathedral—opens into C/ Cimadevilla, full of shops and restaurants.

⑥ Plaza Trascorrales. The weathered old fish market, now a cultural center, dominates this plaza; bronze statues have replaced fishmongers. The ground levels of the surrounding houses are filled with restaurants. Adjacent C/ Mon is a center of late-night revelry.

⑦ Plaza del Fontán. Cafes and a few shops surround the city's most colorful and most diminutive plaza, where bagpipe and folk dance troupes often perform. On Thursdays and weekends, the surrounding streets (and adjacent Plaza Daoíz y Velarde) bustle with street vendors selling everything from clothing to fresh-cut lilies. Sunday brings the flea market, mostly on Plaza Daoíz y Velarde, where you might find everything from vintage costume jewelry to World War II–era cameras. Thurs, Sat, Sun outdoor markets 10am–2:30pm.

⑧ Plaza de la Escandalera. Medieval and modern Oviedo converge at this open plaza at the corner of Parque San Francisco. The clock on the Chastur savings bank marks the hour to the strains of the Asturian regional anthem.

⑨ C/ Uría. This boutique shopping street leads from Escandalera into the largely pedestrian mercantile heart of the new city. At the corner of C/ Milicias Nacionales, a 2003 bronze of Woody Allen slumps along in full stride.

⑩ ★ Santa María del Naranco & San Miguel del Lillo. Architecture buffs might want to make the 3km (1¾-mile) trip up Monte Naranco to visit these splendid examples of 9th-century design. The two churches were centuries ahead of their time in both sculpture and construction techniques. **Monte Naranco.** ☎ 638-26-01-63. 3€ adults, 2€ kids, free Mon mornings. Oct–Apr Sun–Mon 9:30am–1pm, Tues–Sat 9:30am–1pm and 3:30–7pm; May–Sept daily 10am–12:30pm and Tues–Sat 3–4:30pm. Bus: 10.

Where to Stay & Dine

> *The silver screen–ready Hotel de la Reconquista.*

kids Aparthotel Campus

Less than a 10-minute stroll from the cathedral, these spacious, modern apartments include small kitchens in both studio and one-bedroom configurations. One child 11 or under stays free. The surrounding neighborhood, just a few streets out of the old quarter, is a vibrant residential area with markets, shops, and Oviedo's only self-service laundromat. C/ Fernando Vela, 13. ☎ 985-11-16-19. www.aparthotelcampus.es. 65 units. Studio and 1-bedroom apts 55€–129€. MC, V.

★ Casa Fermín *ASTURIAN*

Founded in 1924, Fermín pioneered the transformation of Asturian home cooking into haute cuisine. Fine linens and formally dressed waiters are no hindrance to enjoying *fabada* (beans stewed with pork) or pig's trotters with a large grilled shrimp. C/ San Francisco, 8. ☎ 985-21-64-52. Entrees 15€–26€. AE, DC, MC, V. Lunch & dinner Mon–Sat.

★★ El Fontán *ASTURIAN*

Simple food is always best close to the source, in this case upstairs from the city's fresh food market. Daily menus are a bargain, especially since they include a half bottle of wine. Try the *merluza* (hake) or the rib-sticking *pote Asturiano,* a stew of white beans, kale, potatoes, and assorted sausages (with a hambone for seasoning). C/ Fierro, 2. ☎ 985-22-23-60. Entrees 11€–23€, menu 10€. MC, V. Lunch & dinner until 8pm daily.

Hotel de la Reconquista

Oviedo's grandest historic hotel has been home to kings and princes, but it's best known now as the romantic hotel in *Vicky Cristina Barcelona.* Built as an 18th-century orphanage and hospital, it was transformed into a luxury property with historic ambience in the 1970s. C/ Gil de Jaz, 16. ☎ 985-24-11-00. www.hoteldelareconquista.com. 142 rooms. Doubles 140€–240€. AE, DC, MC, V.

Hotel Vetusta

This chipper, friendly, small hotel has renovated its compact rooms in a sleek contemporary style—all hard surfaces and minimal decoration. You can't miss the red facade with wood-and-glass enclosed balconies. C/ Covadonga, 2. ☎ 985-22-22-29. www.hotelvetusta.com. 16 rooms. Doubles 60€–107€ with breakfast. AE, MC, V.

La Cantina del Vasco *ASTURIAN*

C/ Gascona is celebrated as the "Boulevard of Cider," where tavern waiters delight in pouring cider into a glass from a great height. It's the perfect drink with hearty Asturian comfort food. C/ Gascona, 15. ☎ 985-22-01-98. Entrees 6€–18€. MC, V. Lunch & dinner daily.

Santander

A half-dozen spectacular beaches curled around a large, boat-filled bay make Santander one of northern Spain's most appealing resorts. An important port since Roman times, the city enjoys a steady flow of British tourists via overnight ferries from Portsmouth and Plymouth, but is also popular with Spaniards, for whom it is a lower-priced alternative to San Sebastián (see p. 306). A massive fire gutted much of the Casco Viejo ("Old City") in 1941, but lively shops and restaurants have long since filled the gaps, ensuring that there's plenty to do on a rainy day.

> Santander's main resort district lies along the three beaches of the town's northeast coast.

START Jardines de Pereda.

① ★ kids **Jardines de Pereda.** Every resort town should have such a lovely downtown park. The two-deck **carousel** decorated in Belle Epoque style twirls to '80s and disco tunes (1.70€ per ride). The gardens also have the central stand for ★★ **Tus Bic** (www.tusbic.es), rental bikes that are free with a 150€ credit card deposit.

② kids **Muelle de Albaredo.** Harbor ferries and sightseeing boats leave from this wharf across from the Jardines de Pereda. The schooner **Cantabria Infinita** makes trips around

the harbor with narrative about Cantabrian maritime history. Ticket price includes admission to the Museo Marítimo (see below). Or see the bay on the cheap with **Los Reginas, S.A. Excursiones Marítimas,** which services the beaches, including more secluded Pedreña and Somo. *Infinita:* ⏱ 1½ hr. ☎ 902-99-59-06. 10€, free for kids 4 & under. Sails Wed and Fri–Mon. Los Reginas: ⏱ 45 min. ☎ 942-21-67-53. www.losreginas.com. 2.20€ one-way to Pedreña or Somo beaches, 4.10€ round-trip. Sightseeing trip around bay 4.10€.

Where to Stay in Santander

Hotel Bahía **16**
Hotel Hoyuela **10**
Hotel Real **11**

Where to Dine in Santander

Casa Goria **12**
La Casa del Indiano **15**
Restaurante Cañadio **13**
Restaurante del Puerto **14**

1 Jardines de Pereda
2 Muelle de Albaredo
3 Catedral de Santa María de la Asunción
4 Museo de Bellas Artes
5 Biblioteca Menéndez y Pelayo
6 Museo Marítimo del Cantábrico
7 Southern Beaches
8 Peninsula de la Magdalena
9 Northeast Beaches

> *Scholar Marcelino Menéndez y Pelayo was generous with the city where he was born and buried.*

❸ Catedral de Santa María de la Asunción. The main cathedral was ravaged by the 1941 fire, but the Capilla del Cristo Baja escaped. Before leaving downtown, enter the south portico to see this squat but lovely Romanesque chapel. A glass floor reveals Roman thermal baths discovered in 1982 excavations. ⏱ 30 min. Plaza del Obispo José Eguino y Trecu, s/n. ☎ 942-22-60-24. Free. Mon–Fri 10am–1pm and 4–7:30pm; Sat 10am–1pm and 4:30–8pm; Sun 10am–1:30pm and 5–9pm. Free guided visits July–Aug.

❹ Museo de Bellas Artes. Near the cathedral, the city's modest art museum has interesting local landscapes among its collections. The museum also mounts excellent contemporary exhibitions. ⏱ 30 min. C/ Rubio, 6. ☎ 942-20-31-20. Free. June 15–Sept 15 Mon–Fri 11:15am–1pm and 5:30–9pm, Sat 10:30am–1pm; Sept 16–June 14 Mon–Fri 10:15–1pm and 5:30–9pm, Sat 10am–1pm.

❺ Biblioteca Menéndez y Pelayo. Walk up the steps adjacent to the museum to see the 50,000-volume library that critic and scholar Marcelino Menéndez y Pelayo bequeathed to his native city in 1912. ⏱ 10 min. C/ Rubio, 6. ☎ 942-23-45-34. Free. Mon–Fri 9–11:30am.

❻ ★★ kids Museo Marítimo del Cantábrico. Part aquarium, part history museum, part state-of-the-art maritime education center, this institution hunkers down along the shore between the downtown docks and the beaches. ⏱ 1½ hr. C/ San Martin de Bajamar, s/n. ☎ 942-27-49-62.

www.museosdecantabria.com. 6€ adults, 4€ kids 4-12. May–Sept daily 10am–7:30pm (last entry 6:30pm); Oct–Apr Tues–Sun 10am–6pm. Bus: 1–4, 7, 13.

❼ kids Southern Beaches. Stretching along the southern arm of the Magdalena peninsula, **Playas de Los Peligros, La Magdalena,** and **Los Bikinis** are among the most popular with Santanderos. Magdalena is often filled with young children attending watersports classes. Bus: 1–7, 9, 13, 15.

❽ ★ kids Peninsula de la Magdalena. The delightful rolling park of this headland peninsula leads to the Palacio de la Magdalena, where Alfonso XIII and Queen Eugenia summered from 1913 to 1930. Admission to the park is free but controlled by a single gate. A group of caravels on dry land hint at local seafaring traditions. Children generally prefer the penguins and sea lions of the minizoo. ⏱ 2–3 hr. Daily 8am–8:30pm. Bus: 1–4, 7, 9, 10, 13, 15.

❾ ★★ Northeast Beaches. Extending more than 2km (1¼ miles) north from the Magdalena peninsula, the golden strands of **Playas del Camello, de la Concha,** and **de El Sardinero** make up Santander's main summer resort district. Many late-19th-century hotels and mansions stand on the hills above the beaches. The soccer stadium is also at El Sardinero. Bus: 1–7, 9, 13, 15 (only buses 1 and 2 for north end).

Where to Stay & Dine

> *Contemporary Basque cuisine at Restaurante Cañadio.*

Casa Goria *CANTABRIAN*
The bar here anchors a lively tapas scene, and the rustic restaurant with an open kitchen serves full meals of local standards like grilled langostinos or roast leg of lamb. C/ Río de la Pila, 12. ☎ 942-22-22-86. Entrees 10€–18€. MC, V. Lunch & dinner daily.

★ Hotel Bahía
Adjacent to the ferry port and Jardines de Pereda, this modern business hotel is comfortably appointed and centrally located for exploring the Old Town and waterfront. Avenida de Alfonso XIII, 6. ☎ 942-20-50-00. www.grupo sardinero.com. 188 rooms. Doubles 150€–210€. AE, DC, MC, V.

Hotel Hoyuela
A new construction in classic style, Hoyuela sits between the casino and the beach in the heart of the classy El Sardinero summer resort district. Avenida de los Hoteles, 7. ☎ 942-28-26-28. www.gruposardinero.com. 55 rooms. Doubles 90€–235€. AE, DC, MC, V.

★★ Hotel Real
This early-20th-century society hotel recalls the days when Spanish royalty summered in Santander. Even the most modest rooms have outside-facing windows. The luxurious seawater spa in a separate building offers a full treatment menu. C/ Pérez Galdós, 28. ☎ 942- 27-25-50. www.hotelreal.es. 123 rooms. Doubles 120€–350€. Spa treatments begin at 28€. AE, DC, MC, V.

La Casa del Indiano *CANTABRIAN*
The "Indianos" were Cantabrians who made their fortunes overseas, then came home to live like lords. Their nostalgic style informs the decor of this otherwise conventional Cantabrian restaurant, located in a food market with several smaller eateries. Mercado del Este, 4 (at C/ Hernán Cortes). ☎ 942-07-46-60. Entrees 4€–16€. MC, V. Lunch & dinner daily.

★★ Restaurante Cañadio *CONTEMPORARY*
The chef here, a disciple of Juan Mari Arzak (grandfather of cutting-edge Basque cuisine), offers ambitious cuisine at good prices. On weekdays, try his style on the cheap with the 9€ "soup" of the day in the cafe. It could be a real soup—or a hearty rice with chicken. C/ Gómez Oreña, 15. ☎ 942-31-41-49. Entrees 13€–24€. MC, V. Lunch & dinner Mon–Sat.

★★★ Restaurante del Puerto *SEAFOOD*
Established by a fishing family in the 1930s, Puerto has evolved into Santander's power seafood restaurant: Waiters in white tuxedos attend diners in tailored suits. C/ Hernán Cortés, 63. ☎ 942-21-30-01. Entrees 16€–30€, shellfish market price. AE, MC, V. Lunch Tues–Sun, dinner Tues–Sat (lunch & dinner daily in Aug).

Asturias & Cantabria Fast Facts

> Brittany Ferries at port in Santander.

Arriving & Getting Around

BY PLANE Most overseas travelers wishing to fly into Asturias or Cantabria change planes in Madrid. The **Aeropuerto de Santander** (☎ 942-20-21-00; www.aena.com) has frequent daily connections to Madrid, Barcelona, and London. It is convenient to the city via an inexpensive cab ride. By contrast, the **Aeropuerto de Asturias** (☎ 985-12-75-00; www.aena.com) is located 47km (29 miles) from Oviedo in Santiago del Monte, Ranón. Several carriers use the airport, with direct service to many cities in Spain, Lisbon, London, Paris, and Brussels. **BY TRAIN** RENFE (☎ 902-24-02-02; www.renfe.es) offers daily service from Madrid to both Santander and Oviedo. The narrow-gauge Transcantábrico line operated by **FEVE** (☎ 985-28-44-12; www.feve.es) connects Oviedo and Santander with Bilbao and San Sebastián. **BY BUS** Buses servicing the communities in Asturias and Cantabria are generally operated by **ALSA** (902-42-22-22; www.

alsa.es). In most cases, you will have to depend on either Oviedo or Santander as a hub to go from town to town. ALSA also operates long-distance buses from Madrid. **BY CAR** The main high-speed highway along the north coast is the A-8. **BY FERRY** **Brittany Ferries** (☎ 0871-244-0871 in the U.K. or ☎ 942-36-06-11 in Spain; www.brittany-ferries.co.uk) runs overnight auto and passenger service from Portsmouth and Plymouth in the U.K. to Santander.

ATMs

You'll find 24-hour ATMs throughout the region, even in the smallest villages. Most accept Maestro, Cirrus, and Visa.

Booking Services

There are no booking services per se in Asturias and Cantabria. Local tourist offices, however, will advise on lodging availability.

Doctors & Hospitals

For emergency medical or dental attention, go

to the *centro de urgencia* (emergency room) of the nearest hospital. OVIEDO **Hospital Universitario Central de Asturias,** C/ Celestino Villamil, s/n (☎ 985-108-000). SANTANDER **Hospital Marqués de Valdecilla,** Avenida Valdecilla, s/n (☎ 942-20-25-20). Non-E.U. residents can consult national health service doctors for a relatively small fee; ask at your hotel for a list of doctors.

Emergencies
The all-around emergency number in Spain is ☎ 112. For an ambulance, call ☎ 061.

Internet Access
Wi-Fi has become common in most hotels and is increasingly offered as a free amenity except in business hotels. Hotels without in-room Internet connections may provide access through a public computer. Internet cafes are common.

Pharmacies
To find an open pharmacy outside normal business hours, check the list of stores posted on the door of any drugstore. By law, there's always a drugstore open somewhere. Drugstores are called *farmacías*. When open, they display a neon green cross.

Police
Call ☎ 091 for the national police or ☎ 092 for the local police. The Guardia Civil can be reached at ☎ 062.

Post Office
OVIEDO The main post office is at C/ Santa Susana, 18 (☎ 985-20-88-84). SANTANDER The main post office is at Plaza Alfonso XIII, s/n (☎ 942-36-55-19). Both are open Monday to Friday 8am to 6pm, Saturday 10am to 2pm.

Safety
Both the cities and the countryside are quite safe in Asturias and in Cantabria. Use common sense and avoid deserted streets at night and during the afternoon closing hours. Take care not to leave anything visible in a parked car, especially overnight or at the beach.

Visitor Information
Info Asturias, C/ Cimadevilla, 4, Oviedo (☎ 985-21-33-85; www.infoasturias.com), supplies information about the entire Principality of Asturias; the office is open daily 10am to 7pm. **Oficina de Turismo del Gobierno de Cantabria,** C/ Jesus Otero, 20, Santillana del Mar (☎ 942-81-82-51; www.turismodecantabria.com), is open daily 9am to 1pm and 4 to 7pm and offers information about the entire autonomous region. ARENAS DE CABRALES **Oficina de Turismo,** Carretera General, s/n (☎ 985-84-64-84), is open Monday to Thursday 10am to 2pm and 4 to 8pm, Friday to Sunday 9am to 9pm. CANGAS DE ONÍS **Oficina de Turismo,** Avenida de Covadonga, 1 (☎ 985-84-80-05; www.cangasdeonis.com), is open daily 10am to 2pm and 4 to 6pm. CASTRO URDIALES **Oficina de Turismo,** Avenida de la Constitución, s/n (☎ 942-87-15-12; www.turismodecantabria.com), is open daily 9:30am to 1pm and 4 to 7pm. COMILLAS **Oficina de Turismo,** C/ Joaquin del Pielago, 1 (☎ 942-72-25-91; www.comillas.es), is open September to June daily 9am to 2pm and 4 to 6pm, July to August daily 9am to 9pm. LAREDO **Oficina de Turismo,** Avendia Miramar, s/n (☎ 942-61-10-96; www.turismodecantabria.com), is open daily 9:30am to 1pm and 4 to 7pm. OVIEDO **Oficina de Turismo,** Plaza Constitución, 4 (☎ 984-08-60-60; www.oviedo.es), is open June daily 10am to 7pm, July to September 9:30am to 7:30pm, October to May 10am to 2pm and 4:30 to 7pm. PICOS DE EUROPA **Parque Nacional de los Picos de Europa,** Casa Dago, Avenida de Covadonga, 43, Cangas de Onís (☎ 985-84-86-14; www.picosdeeuropa.com), is open daily 8:30am to 2:30pm, also Friday to Sunday 3 to 5pm in summer. SANTANDER **Oficina de Turismo,** Jardines de Pereda, s/n (☎ 942-20-30-00; www.santander.es), is open Monday to Friday 9am to 7pm, Saturday 10am to 7pm, Sunday 10am to 2pm. SANTOÑA **Oficina de Turismo,** Palacio Duque de Manzanedo, C/ Manzanedo, s/n (☎ 942-66-00-66; www.turismodecantabria.com), is open daily 9:30am to 1pm and 4 to 7pm. SAN VICENTE DE LA BARQUERA **Oficina de Turismo,** Avenida Generalísimo, 6 (☎ 942-71-07-97), is open Monday to Saturday 10am to 1:30pm and 4:30 to 7pm, Saturday 10:30am to 1:30pm.

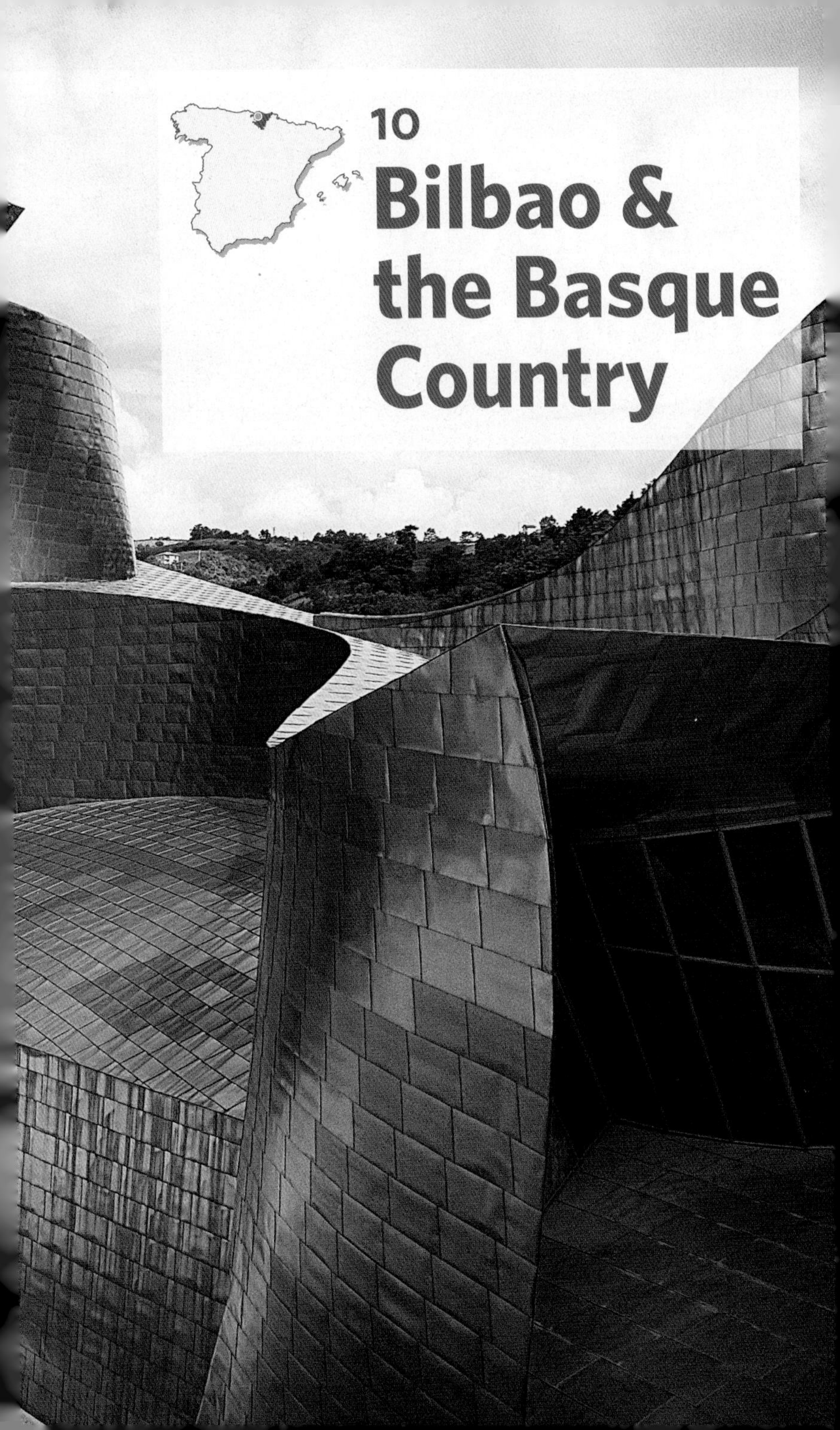

10 Bilbao & the Basque Country

The Best of the Basque Country in 3 Days

Many international travelers have been lured to northern Spain just to see the amazing Guggenheim Bilbao Museum, only to be seduced by the stirring mountains and dramatic coastline that make up the Basque Country. Begin your first of 3 days in Bilbao visiting the Guggenheim, among other treats. Then spend a day exploring some of the nearby Basque Coast, winding up in historic Gernika, the Basque capital from its founding in 1366 until the 19th century.

> *PREVIOUS PAGE The Guggenheim Bilbao has a 50m-high (165-ft.) atrium. THIS PAGE Bilbao's riverside Casco Viejo (Old City).*

START Bilbao. **TRIP LENGTH** 57km (35 miles).

❶ Bilbao. You (and 90% of visitors) came to Bilbao to see the ★★★ **Museo Guggenheim Bilbao,** so make it your first stop. Frank Gehry's innovative architecture creates a harmonious package, but some rather oddly shaped interiors. The more peculiar the space, the more likely it will hold video art. In keeping with the museum's postmodern sensibility, there is no linear way to tour. Don't miss works in hidden side galleries.

By contrast, the ★★ **Museo de Bellas Artes** is refreshingly conventional with its layout of square galleries and framed paintings on walls.

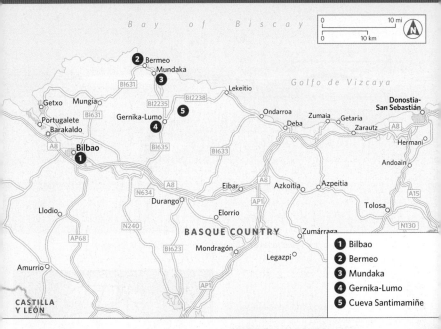

It's strikingly comprehensive, with special strengths in Gothic art and Basque regional painting.

The Guggenheim Bilbao jump-started the transformation of Bilbao from decayed industrial city to architectural showcase, and nowhere are the changes more evident than in the ★★ **Abandoibarra** neighborhood, with new riverfront sculptures, architecture, and cafes. You can even walk along the riverside path all the way to the Casco Viejo ("Old City") for tapas or dinner under the arches of the handsome neoclassical **Plaza Nueva.** Guggenheim: ⏱ 3 hr. See p. 312, ❷. Bellas Artes: ⏱ 1½ hr. See p. 314, ❹. Abandoibarra: ⏱ 45 min. See p. 314, ❸. Plaza Nueva: See p. 315, ❽.

From Bilbao, follow BI-631 for 37km (23 miles) to Bermeo.

❷ **Bermeo.** Begin sampling the Basque coast by wandering the medieval streets of this ancient fishing and whaling port. Its fishing heritage is detailed at the ★ kids **Museo del Pescador,** while you can understand some of the whaling history aboard the schooner ★ kids **Aita Guria Baleontzia.** You might want to have lunch here at **Restaurante Jokin** (see p. 305). ⏱ 3 hr. See p. 300, ❶.

> Bilbao's arcaded Plaza Nueva hosts bars, restaurants, and colorful markets.

Follow BI-2235 south 5km (3 miles) to Mundaka.

❸ **Mundaka.** A sandbar in the tidal waters of the long mouth of the Río Urdaibai creates one of the world's greatest pipelines—a 60m-long (200-ft.) tunnel of curving water. Where there's a wave like that, there are surfers. Even if you don't surf, this is a great village to swim, sunbathe, and watch the daredevils. See p. 302, ❷.

> *Surfers come from all over the world to take on Mundaka's 60m-long (200-ft.) pipeline.*

Continue another 11km (7 miles) south on BI-2235.

❹ **Gernika-Lumo.** Picasso (and hence the world) knew this historic Basque village by its Castilian name, **Guernica,** but the Spanish name isn't used here. After all, it was the eventual leader of Spain, Francisco Franco, who invited the German *Luftwaffe*'s air raid on Gernika on April 26, 1937, choosing a market day to maximize casualties. Between 200 and 2,000 people died in the 3½-hour hail of bombs, and much of Gernika was leveled. The symbolic target was the 1,000-year-old Foral Oak, where Basques had elected their leaders since the Middle Ages. The bombs missed, and the rebuilt city has prospered.

The petrified trunk of the oak stands atop a hill on the grounds of the former Basque parliament, the ★★ **Casa de Juntas.** An incongruous neoclassical pavilion covers the trunk, which is surrounded by living trees nurtured from its acorns. Feel the majesty of history in this former assembly hall—all the pomp and formality is the culmination of 700 years of Basques convening in this village to ensure self-government.

The Foral Oak always made Gernika special to Basques, but Franco's punishment of the town cemented Gernika as the emblem of Basque identity and nationalism. To begin to understand the complex culture (and its complicated politics), visit the ★★ **Museoa Euskal Herria,** or Basque Heritage Museum. Politics are soft-pedaled to emphasize history and

> *An elaborate stained-glass ceiling depicting the Foral Oak lights up Gernika-Lumo's Casa de Juntas.*

culture. Extensive exhibits illustrate traditional Basque dance, music, games, and sports (including jai alai, a game somewhat like handball in which the ball is whipped around a court by wicker baskets strapped to the wrist). Some visitors trance out just listening to the music

> *The Santimamiñe Cave takes its name from the chapel of San Mamés (St. Amandus) nearby.*

tracks on the audio guides, which are available in English, Spanish, and French—but not German.

The ★ **Fundación Museo de la Paz de Gernika** tries to put the emphasis on efforts to avoid future wars. A disturbing audiovisual recreation of the bombing and gripping exhibits about the attack and its aftermath may be the best arguments ever for peace. Casa de Juntas: ⏱ 30 min. Juntetxea. ☎ 946-25-11-38. Free. June–Sept daily 10am–2pm and 4–7pm; Oct–May daily

10am–2pm and 4–6pm. Museoa: ⏱ 1½ hr. C/ Allendesalazar, 5. ☎ 946-25-54-51. www.bizkaia. net/euskalherriamuseoa. 3€ adults, 1.50€ seniors and students. Tues–Sat 10am–2pm and 4–7pm; Sun 11am–4pm. Fundación: ⏱ 30 min. Plaza Foru, 1. ☎ 946-27-02-13. www.museodelapaz.org. 4€ adults, 2€ seniors and students, free for kids 11 & under. Sept–June Tues–Sat 10am–2pm and 4–7pm, Sun 10am–2pm; July–Aug Tues–Sat 10am–8pm, Sun 10am–3pm.

From Gernika, take the ring road toward Lekeitio, and then follow BI-638 to the Barrutia roundabout. Continue on BI-2238 through Idokiliz and turn right on BI-4244 for a total of 4km (2½ miles). Santimamiñe parking lot is at the end of the road.

5 ★ **Cueva Santimamiñe.** Only minutes out of Gernika, the Santimamiñe cave has the most Paleolithic cave paintings in Basque Country. The charcoal drawings made between 12,500 and 10,000 B.C. include bison, horses, goats, and even a bear and a deer. Long-halted archaeological exploration has resumed, limiting visits to the cave's initial chambers. Advance booking by phone or email is essential. ⏱ 1 hr. BI-4244, Kortezubi. ☎ 944-65-16-57 or 944-65-16-60. santimamiñe@bizkaia.net. 5€ adults, 2€ seniors and students, free for kids 6 & under. Tues–Sun 10am–12:30pm and 4:30–6pm.

Spending the Night in Gernika-Lumo

Many travelers treat Gernika as a day trip, but **Hotel Gernika** makes a convenient overnight stay before continuing up the Basque Coast. The simply furnished rooms are reasonably spacious and the bathrooms are fully modern. C/ Carlos Gangoiti, 17. ☎ 946-25-03-50. www.hotel-gernika.com. 40 rooms. Doubles 72€–82€. AE, DC, MC, V.

Asador Zollo Barri prizes the taste of both land and sea. Grilled scallops, for example, are served with pickled onions and creamed white asparagus, flounder with rice redolent of parsley and garlic. Wood-grilled meats are always a good bet. C/ Juan Kaltzada, 79. ☎ 946-25-52-39. Entrees 14€–20€. AE, MC, V. Lunch Tues–Sun, dinner Tues–Sat.

IN EARLY 1936, officials of Spain's elected government commissioned a mural from Pablo Picasso for the 1937 International Exposition of Arts and Techniques in Modern Life, to be held in Paris. Picasso procrastinated until after the Spanish Civil War broke out. On April 26, 1937, German Luftwaffe planes terror-bombed the Basque town of Gernika-Lumo (Guernica in Castilian) at the invitation of General Francisco Franco, and Picasso found his subject. He worked furiously to complete *Guernica* in time for the May 24 opening of the Spanish Pavilion and bring the cause of Spanish suffering before the world.

Picasso's Mysterious Images

THE BULL
Many critics believe the bull is Picasso's self-portrait—the imperial, steely mind observing the human brutality.

LIGHTBULB & LANTERN
The lightbulb is Picasso's representation of the sun. Traditionally a symbol of Spain, it has been reduced to a technological device in the darkness of the atrocity. A figure coming in the window holds a lantern to attempt to illuminate the scene.

WOMAN HOLDING DEAD CHILD
This figure echoes Picasso's images of rape victims from a 1935 to 1936 series, "Dreams and Lies of Franco."

THE HORSE
Traditionally an image of Spanish nobility, the horse is the enemy of the bull, intended to show Franco's imperial power to ride roughshod over the Spanish people. Echoing a Goya composition, Picasso shows the horse having kicked two men to death.

Seeing in Black and White

The bombing of Gernika didn't hit newspapers for a few days, but Picasso was immediately infuriated when he saw the black and white photos in Parisian papers. The stippled grayscale of the canvas evokes those first reports—and the dark cloud of war.

PICASSO'S GUERNICA

Bringing Spanish Suffering to the World's Attention

BY PATRICIA HARRIS & DAVID LYON

Why Gernika?

Since medieval times, regional leaders of the Basque people gathered beneath an ancient oak tree, the 1,000-year-old Foral Oak, in Gernika to govern themselves. The fierce independence of the Basques offended Francisco Franco, as they were nearly alone in northern Spain in opposing his bid to overthrow the elected government. The bombing by Franco's German allies was intended to destroy the ancient oak. The 3½-hour bombing, deliberately staged on a market day, killed between 200 and 2,000 citizens but missed the tree. It nonetheless demonstrated Franco's might—and his brutality.

Guernica in Exile and at Home

Picasso vowed that *Guernica* would never be exhibited in Spain as long as Franco lived. At the outbreak of the Spanish Civil War, the painting was in Paris. When the Exposition came down in November 1937, *Guernica* was displayed in London before traveling to the U.S. The painting was exhibited in San Francisco, Los Angeles, Chicago, and New York to raise funds for Spanish Loyalists. In 1939, Picasso loaned the painting to the Museum of Modern Art in New York, where it remained until repatriation to Spain in 1981. After several years in its own building adjacent to the Prado, it was moved into its own gallery at the Museo Nacional Centro de Arte Reina Sofía.

The Best of the Basque Country in 1 Week

This tour continues on from "The Best of the Basque Country in 3 Days." You'll spend another day exploring the coast before you settle into the seductive rhythms of Donostia-San Sebastián for 2 more. Finally, follow one of the historic Santiago pilgrimage routes to the high-country Basque capital, Vitoria-Gasteiz.

> The climate at Donostia-San Sebastián's Playa Ondaretta is more Atlantic than Mediterranean.

START From Gernika, take A-8 for 48km (30 miles) to exit 12, then N-634 into Zumaia.
TRIP LENGTH 164km (102 miles), including "The Best of the Basque Country in 3 Days."

1 Zumaia. As you walk the beaches, you'll spot ammonite fossils embedded in the rock cliffs. The light is magical—or so painter Ignacio Zuloaga (1870–1945) certainly thought. See his studio, art collection, and paintings in the **Museo Zuloaga.** ⏱ 3 hr. See p. 303, **5**.

Follow N-634 for 11km (6¾ miles) to Zarautz.

2 Zarautz. Which is more amazing—the 3km (1¾-mile) beach or the hip sculpture that lines the beach promenade? It's all in how you look, which is also the take-away lesson from the exhibits at **Photomuseum.** ⏱ 3 hr. See p. 304, **7**.

Follow A-8 east for 13km (8 miles) to exit 9 and follow signs into Donostia-San Sebastián.

Bay of Biscay

Golfo de Vizcaya

Bermeo
Mundaka
BI631
Lekeitio
Getxo Mungia
BI2238
Ondarroa
Zumaia Getaria
Donostia-San Sebastián ③
Portugalete
BI631 Gernika-Lumo
BI2235
Deba ① Zarautz ②
A8
Barakaldo
Hermani
Bilbao
BI635
BI633
Andoain
N634 A8
A8
Eibar Azkoitia Azpeitia
A15
Llodio
Durango
AP1
Tolosa
N240
Elorrio
N130
AP68
BI623
Zumárraga
Amurrio
Mondragón
Beasain
BASQUE COUNTRY
Legazpi
Idiazábal ④
AP1
Embalse de Ulibarri-Ganboa
N622
A1 A10
Altsasu
NAVARRA
Vitoria-Gasteiz ⑤
Salvatierra
E5 E80
Alegría-Dulantzi
NA120
AP68
A132
A1
CASTILLA Y LEÓN
AP1 Miranda de Ebro
CASTILLA Y LEÓN

① Zumaia
② Zarautz
③ Donostia-San Sebastián
④ Centro de Interpretación del Queso Idiazábal
⑤ Vitoria-Gasteiz

③ **Donostia-San Sebastián.** Indulge yourself with a day of sunbathing and swimming in the brisk waters. If you are young and buff, you might prefer the surfer's beach, **Playa de Zurriola** (see p. 308, ⑥). If a family scene is more comfortable, then the broad ★★★ **Playa de la Concha** (see p. 309, ⑨) is perfect. The westerly **Playa de Ondarreta** (see p. 309, ⑪) has an ambience somewhere between the other two.

Spend your second day exploring the narrow streets of ★ **Parte Vieja** (see p. 306, ①), walking the ★ **Paseo Nuevo** (see p. 308, ②), and ascending Monte Urgull for great views of the harbor. Save time to check out the sharks

> El Palco de las Presidentas *by Basque painter Ignacio Zuloaga.*

> *After almost 10 years of development and renovation projects, visitors to the Donostia-San Sebastián aquarium can literally immerse themselves in sea life.*

and turtles in the ★★ **Aquarium Donostia-San Sebastián** (see p. 308, ④).

Apart from the beach, the biggest attraction in town is the dining (see p. 311 for suggestions on where to eat).

From San Sebastián, it's a short bus ride to the inspiring ★★ **Museo Chillida-Leku,** which covers the life of celebrated Basque abstract sculptor Eduardo Chillida (1924–2002). Chillida bought the property in 1982 and restored and redesigned its 1543 farmhouse to display his powerful works in steel, as well as smaller pieces in such media as paper and alabaster. In addition, more than 40 Chillida sculptures dot the wooded grounds. Museo: ⏱ 45 min. Barrio Jáuregui, 66, Hernani. ☎ 943-33-60-06. www.museochillidaleku.com. 8.50€ adults, 6.50€ seniors and students. Sept–June Wed–Mon 10:30am–3pm; July–Aug Mon–Sat 10:30am–8pm and Sun 10:30am–3pm. Bus: G2 from San Sebastián.

From San Sebastián, follow the A-8 west. At exit 10, go south on the N-I/A-15 35km (22 miles) to exit 412 toward Idiazábal.

④ kids **Centro de Interpretación del Queso Idiazábal.** The nutty, pungent Idiazábal cheese made from raw sheep's milk is a star of Basque cuisine. This center in its hometown explains the heritage breed of sheep and the whole cheese-making process. You can also visit the adjacent factory for a tasting. A program aimed at children is clearly designed to make them into little cheese heads. ⏱ 45 min. C/ Nagusia, 37, Idiazábal. ☎ 943-18-82-03. www.idiazabal gaztarenmuseoa.com. 2€, 4€ with tasting. Sept 16–June 14 Mon–Fri 10:30am–12:30pm; June 15–Sept 15 daily 10:30am–1:30pm and 3:30–6:30pm.

⑤ **Vitoria-Gasteiz.** Basque Country government is the least centralized in Spain. Even though Vitoria-Gasteiz became the capital of

Spending the Night in Vitoria-Gasteiz

The **Barceló Gasteiz Hotel** is located near the convention center on a boulevard that circles the old city. With contemporary decor and well-appointed bathrooms, it is a good base for exploring the old town. Avenida Gasteiz, 45. ☎ 945-22-81-00. www.barcelo.com. 150 rooms. Doubles 51€–85€. AE, DC, MC, V.

In the shadow of the cathedral, **El Portalón** began as a 15th-century coach-house inn. Its menu is a virtual living museum of Basque cuisine: cod in *pil-pil* sauce, lamb's feet in red pepper sauce, partridge, and lentil salad. C/ Correría, 147. ☎ 945-14-27-55. Entrees 15€–26€. AE, DC, MC, V. Lunch & dinner daily.

> *Kids play soccer on Playa de la Concha.*

the autonomous region in 1987, the trappings of governance are virtually invisible. Start at **Plaza de España** right outside the medieval quarter. The neoclassical arcaded plaza is lined with cafe tables—a popular hangout for university students. Just west of Plaza de España is the long, rectangular **Plaza de la Virgen Blanca.** The three-tiered monument topped by a winged Victory commemorates the June 1813 battle here in which English, Portuguese, and Spanish troops under the Duke of Wellington drove the French out of Spain.

A clever fountain shoots water straight up from paving stones. The plaza climbs toward the 13th-century church of **San Miguel** (open Mon–Fri 11am–3pm). A niche in front of the church holds a late Gothic polychrome statue of the Virgen Blanca, the city's patroness, that is, alas, behind a nearly opaque acrylic panel. The church marks the south end of Gasteiz's medieval city, which is built in stepped levels on an elliptical hilltop. On the east side, outdoor escalators make it easy to get into the old city.

But you'll have to walk down Cantón de San Francisco Javier to visit ★★ **Artium,** a contemporary art museum that embraces all media, including video and installation art. The collections emphasize Spanish and Basque artists but also reach out internationally. The big names of Spanish 20th-century art—Picasso, Dalí, Miró—are here, but the museum also spotlights lesser-known artists. Two signature works are in the lobby: a 1972 ceramic wall mural by Miró, and a 2001 glass sculpture by Javier Pérez that appears to be floating in air. Actually, it's suspended from the ceiling.

> *Vitoria-Gasteiz's patron, the White Virgin.*

The **Catedral de Santa María** marks the north end of the medieval quarter. A wonderful Gothic hulk of a fortress-cathedral, Santa María was originally part of the city's defensive walls. The cathedral is undergoing restoration until 2014, and visitors have the rare chance to see the work in progress. A separate city-walls tour begins at the remains of an 11th-century wall found inside the cathedral, then branches out to other city sites. Artium: ⏱ 1½ hr. C/ Francia, 24. ☎ 945-20-90-20. www.artium.org. 4€ adults, 1€ kids. Tues–Sun 11am–8pm. Catedral: ⏱ 2 hr. C/ Fray Zacaras. ☎ 945-25-51-35 for tour reservations. www.catedralvitoria.com. Catedral tour 5€, city walls tour 2€. Both tours daily 11am–2pm and 5–8pm. Reservations required.

The Basque Coast

Basque poet Kirmen Uribe summed up the appeal of his native coastline between Bilbao and San Sebastián: "I cannot choose. I'm going to stay here—between the green waves and the blue mountains." When you arrive in one of these villages, where rugged cliffs suddenly drop down to long sands swept by waves of mythic proportions, you may well decide that you too aren't going anywhere.

> A scenic overlook offers a view of the hermitage atop San Juan de Gaztelugatxe, near Bermeo.

START From Bilbao, follow BI-631 for 37km (23 miles) to Bermeo. **TRIP LENGTH** 135km (84 miles).

1 Bermeo. Shield your eyes from the brawny fleet of steel-clad, diesel-powered trawlers in the harbor and you could think Bermeo was lost in a medieval time warp. Its 14th-century Gothic church, the ancient San Juan arch connecting the fishing port to the village, and the 15th-century Ercilla tower barely hint of modern times. But there's no escaping the boats, even if the original pocket harbor surrounded by fishermen's houses has been converted to a pleasure marina. The kids ★ **Aita Guria Baleontzia**, a replica whaling schooner built from 2002 to 2005 from 17th-century plans, lies berthed against the stone wharves. Bermeo's whalers hunted along the Cantabrian coast until the late 15th century, but soon began to venture to Greenland, Canada, and Maine, processing their catch on shore and returning home with holds full of oil.

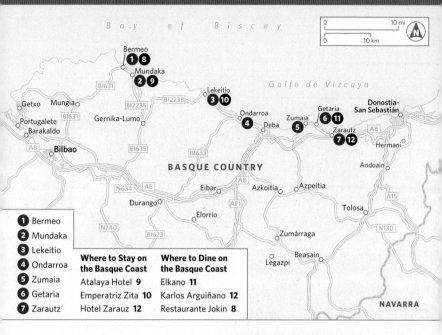

Bay of Biscay

0 ___ 10 mi
0 ___ 10 km

Bermeo **1** **8**
Mundaka **2** **9**
Lekeitio **3** **10**
Golfo de Vizcaya
Getxo
Mungia
BI631
BI2235
BI2238
Ondarroa **4**
Deba
Zumaia **5**
Getaria **6** **11**
Zarautz **7** **12**
Donostia-San Sebastián
Portugalete
Barakaldo
BI631
Gernika-Lumo
Hermani
Bilbao
A8
BI635
BI633
Andoain

BASQUE COUNTRY

N634   A8
Eibar
A8
Azkoitia
Azpeitia
A15
Durango
AP1
Elorrio
Tolosa
N240
BI623
Zumárraga
N130
Beasain
Legazpi

NAVARRA

1 Bermeo
2 Mundaka
3 Lekeitio
4 Ondarroa
5 Zumaia
6 Getaria
7 Zarautz

Where to Stay on the Basque Coast	**Where to Dine on the Basque Coast**
Atalaya Hotel **9**	Elkano **11**
Emperatriz Zita **10**	Karlos Arguiñano **12**
Hotel Zarauz **12**	Restaurante Jokin **8**

The ★ kids **Museo del Pescador** fills the Torre Ercilla, the last remaining fortified tower of more than 30 that once ringed the village. The museum is entirely devoted to Bermeo's long history with the sea. You'll learn that the town helped Magellan's armada prepare to circumnavigate the globe—but Bermeo's sailors usually stayed closer to home, as attested by photographs of fishermen's wives plucking fat anchovies from nets on the docks. One entire floor is dedicated to the techniques of preserving fish by drying and canning. Stirring displays explain how the fishermen created their brotherhood in the 19th century to manage the fishery, extract a fair price, and help families of men lost at sea. Bronze statues at the sea wall in front of the museum show a woman, two children, and grandparents pointing anxiously to the horizon and exclaiming, "Here he comes." *Aita Guria Baleontzia:* ⏱ 1 hr. C/ Lamera, s/n. ☎ 946-17-91-21. www.aitaguria. bermeo.org. 5€ adults, 3€ kids 4–14, free for kids 3 & under. Apr–Oct Tues–Sat 10am–2pm and 4–7pm; Sun 11am–2pm. (Times can vary with extreme tides.) Museo: ⏱ 1 hr. Torre Ercilla, C/ Torronteroko enparatza, 1. www.bizkaia.net/museodelpescador. 3€, free for kids 11 & under. Tues–Sat 10am–2pm and 4–7pm; Sun 10am–2:15pm.

> Bermeo's Museo del Pescador (Fisherman's Museum) has occupied the Tower of Ercilla, a national monument, since 1948.

> *The 15th-century Basilica de Santa María de la Asunción watches over the Bay of Biscay in Lekeitio.*

Follow BI-2235 south 5km (3 miles) to Mundaka.

❷ Mundaka. Bermeo revolves around what's under the sea; Mundaka is about what's on top. Long rollers and a huge left-curling pipeline speed up the narrowing mouth of the river here, creating some of Spain's top surfing conditions in what is otherwise a gentle little fishing town with great swimming beaches. In early October, the Billabong Pro Mundaka surfing competition fills every lodging within an hour's drive. To get into the spirit, visit the **Mundaka Surf Shop** to rent gear or even take lessons.

The surf-shop staff can tell you where to surf, and they can tell you where the surfers socialize. Chances are they'll send you to **Bar Los Txopos** for beer and burgers. Follow the advice. Surf Shop: Paseo Txorrokopunta, 10. ☎ 946-87-67-21. www.mundakasurfshop.com. Board rentals 10€–15€ half-day, 18€–25€ full day. Bar: C/ Kepa Duenaren, s/n. ☎ 946-87-64-82. 3€–10€. Lunch & dinner daily.

Continue south on BI-2235 for 11km (6¾ miles) toward Gernika, picking up BI-2238 east for 22km (14 miles) to Lekeitio.

❸ Lekeitio. Marking the east end of the Bay of Biscay, Lekeitio is a prosperous fishing town with a major tuna fleet, although historically it was a cod town. Two sheltered swimming beaches, one on each side of the mouth of the Río Lea, look out to the island of San Nicolás, which you can walk to at low tide. The Gothic **Basilica de Santa María de la Asunción,** with its dramatic flying buttresses, overlooks the harbor. Panels on the gold-plated Flemish altarpiece depict scenes from the life of the Virgin and the Passion of Christ. Basilica: ⏱ 20 min. C/ Abaroa, s/n. ☎ 946-84-09-54. www.basilicadelekeitio.com. Free. Mon–Sat 8am–noon and 5–7:30pm.

Follow the twisting sea road, BI-3438, east for 15km (9⅓ miles) to Ondarroa.

④ Ondarroa. The Basque Country's leading fishing port has a lively harbor lined with even livelier restaurants and bars. Take time to stroll the charming medieval quarter with its two main landmarks, the 15th-century watchtower called **Torre Likon** and the fortresslike Gothic church of **Santa María,** which seems to rise from the rock. On the east edge of town lies **Playa Saturrarán,** a 300m (984-ft.) white-sand beach hemmed in by mountains. It is the most famous of the Basque Country's nudist beaches.

Follow GI-638 east for 8km (5 miles) to Deba and pick up N-634 for 24km (15 miles) to Zumaia.

⑤ Zumaia. A fortified medieval town at the mouth of two rivers, Zumaia's two outstanding beaches bracket a geological rarity—sheer, fossil-laden cliffs where the rock strata go back 100 million years. Basque painter Ignacio Zuloaga (1870–1945) lived and worked here, and a visit to his museum shows immediately why he was so enamored of the shore light. The **Museo Zuloaga** occupies a former hermitage acquired by Zuloaga to house his art. Along with splendid examples of Zuloaga's own work, it also shows a few paintings by El Greco, Goya, and Zurbarán. Museo: ⏱ 1 hr. C/ Santiago Etxea, s/n. ☎ 943-86-22-41. www.ignaciozuloaga.com. 6€ adults, 3€ seniors and students, free for kids 4 & under. Easter–Sept Wed–Sat 4–8pm, Sun 11am–2pm; Oct–Easter Sat 4–7pm, Sun 11am–2pm.

Continue east on N-634 for 7km (4 miles) to Getaria.

⑥ Getaria. This fishing village squats on the lee side of a peninsula known as the "Getaria mouse," but there's nothing timid about Getarians: Their coat of arms shows a whale with a harpoon stuck in its back. Juan Sebastián Elcano, Magellan's navigator, hailed from Getaria, as did fashion king Cristóbal Balenciaga. A handsome port with two long beaches, the town is perhaps best known for its *txakolí,* a lightly sparkling white wine with bracing acidity that is a perfect match for seafood. Its Gothic main church, **San Salvador,** has an unusual trapezoidal plan, and the central vault of the nave is pierced with star windows. San Salvador: ⏱ 20 min. C/ Nagusia, s/n. ☎ 943-89-60-24. Free. Winter Mon–Sat 10am–7:30pm; summer also open Sun 10am–12:30pm.

Continue east on N-634 for 6km (3½ miles) to Zarautz.

> *Playa Saturrarán is known for its natural views as much as its naturist views.*

> *Weekend crowds stroll along a narrow lane in the handsome port of Getaria.*

Who Are the Basques?

Euskadi, as the Basques call their region, is a culture apart. Unrelated to any other tongue, Euskera (the Basque language) is spoken in the Basque lands of Spain and France and in much of Navarra. Many towns have different names in Castilian Spanish ("standard" Spanish) and Euskera. (San Sebastián is Donostia in Basque, Vitoria is Gasteiz, and so on.) Fortunately, most road signs use both names. Ironically, most Basques also speak textbook Castilian.

The origin of the Basques remains a puzzle, but mainstream archaeology classifies them as survivors of the migrants who first populated the area roughly 35,000 years ago. Fiercely independent, the Basques cut power-sharing deals with the Romans to respect Basque law and tradition—and extracted promises from a long succession of Visigoth, Castilian, and Navarrese monarchs to abide by these *fueros*. The *fueros* were abrogated by the Spanish crown in 1876, setting off the first stirrings of Basque separatism. Unfortunately, Basque separatism today is probably best known for the terrorist acts of the separatist group ETA. The ETA's last major attack was the Madrid Barajas airport bombing in 2006.

Basque nationalists have defined Basques as anyone of Basque descent living in the region *and* as anyone living in the region who speaks Euskera. Although the Basque Country is largely self-governing under modern Spanish and European Union law, a popular political movement for full separation from Spain (and, to a lesser extent, France) remains.

⑦ Zarautz. Another whale-hunting town, Zarautz (Zarauz in Castilian) turned to tourism in the 19th century and is now the biggest Basque resort after San Sebastián. Its surfing rivals Mundaka's (see p. 302, ❷), and its seaside promenade along the 3km (1¾-mile) beach is lined with avant-garde contemporary sculpture. The town also boasts an excellent museum of photography and cinema, **Photomuseum.** Extensive exhibits detail the development of the medium, and collections are especially strong in daguerreotypes and wet-plate scenic photography of the 19th century. Changing exhibitions often feature Basque photographers. Photomuseum: ⏱ 30 min. C/ San Inazio, 11. ☎ 943-13-09-06. www.photomuseum.name. 6€ adults, 3€ seniors and students. Tues-Sun 10am–1pm and 5–8pm.

Where to Stay & Dine

> *A room at Lekeitio's popular seaside Emperatriz Zita.*

★ **Atalaya Hotel** MUNDAKA
This charming family-run hotel is steps from the best surfing, yet adjacent to a quiet, tree-shaded waterfront park. Grass mats here and there create a tropical air—and catch the sand before it scratches the lovingly polished floors. C/ Itxaropen, 1. ☎ 946-17-70-00. www.atalaya hotel.es. 13 rooms. Doubles 98€–108€. AE, MC, V.

★★★ **Elkano** GETARIA *SEAFOOD*
This legendary seafood grill restaurant could change the whole way you approach eating fish. The waiter may even take away your silverware and insist that you eat with your hands for the full-immersion experience. Preparations are simple, but the products are carefully chosen and handled. C/ Herrerieta, 2. ☎ 943-14-00-24. Entrees 16€–40€. AE, DC, MC, V. Lunch Tues–Sun, dinner Tues–Sat.

★★ **Emperatriz Zita** LEKEITIO
Constructed on the ruins of the palace where Zita, the last empress of the Austro-Hungarian empire, lived out her exile, this modern spa-hotel sits right on the ocean. A big hit for weddings, it's also a straight-out bargain. C/ Santa Elena, s/n. ☎ 946-84-26-55. www.aisiahoteles. com. 42 rooms. Doubles 64€–98€, suites 125€. AE, MC, V.

kids **Hotel Zarauz** ZARAUTZ
Set just 2 blocks back from the beach, this pleasant resort/business hotel in a traditional villa has eight quadruple rooms in its mix, ideal for families. One child 7 or under can stay in his or her parent's room for free. C/ Nafarroa, 26. ☎ 943-83-02-00. www.hotelzarauz.com. 75 rooms. Doubles 90€–120€. MC, V.

★★ **Karlos Arguiñano** ZARAUTZ *CREATIVE BASQUE* This landmark restaurant showcases the New Basque cuisine of chef Mikel Mayán. One intimate room offers a set gourmet menu, while a larger room with sea views permits more economical dining. While the a la carte menu preserves some of Mayán's greatest hits, it focuses on more traditional Basque grilled meat and seafood. C/ Mendilauta, 13. ☎ 943-13-00-00. Entrees 18€–24€, tasting menu 60€. AE, DC, MC, V. Lunch Thurs–Tues, dinner Fri–Sat.

★★ **Restaurante Jokin** BERMEO *SEAFOOD*
With fantastic views of the fleet from this glass-box restaurant perched above the stone wharves, it's easy to connect what's on your plate with who caught it. Daily menus hit local highlights like cod "meatballs" or roasted bonito with fresh asparagus. C/ Eupeme Deuna, 13. ☎ 946-88-40-89. Entrees 12€–26€. AE, DC, MC, V. Lunch daily, dinner Mon–Sat.

Donostia-San Sebastián

There are three main reasons to come to San Sebastián: to admire the Belle Epoque resort, to frolic on the spectacular beaches, and to eat brilliantly. Napoleon sacked and burned the city in 1813, and the resort that rose from the ashes has been devoted to refined hedonism ever since. Set along 6km (3¾ miles) of white-sand beaches between the headlands of Monte Urgull and Monte Igeldo, San Sebastián (Donostia in Basque) gleams like an oyster in its pearly shell.

> Take an antique funicular up Monte Igeldo for sweeping views of Donostia-San Sebastián's beaches.

START Plaza de Constitución.

❶ ★ Parte Vieja. Simply called the "Old Part," the medieval streets of San Sebastián were rebuilt after the 1813 fire, starting with the main square, **Plaza de Constitución.** The numbered, white-painted balconies off the stately neoclassical square are the only remaining sign that it was constructed as the town's bullring. The streets of the narrow quarter bustle at all hours of the day and night, but none more than bar-lined C/ Fermín Calbetón, one of San Sebastián's principal *pintxos* routes. (*Pintxos* is Basque for tapas on steroids.)

On a square above the main grid of the old city, an old Dominican convent houses the **Museo San Telmo.** For many years the museum was the city's attic—full of artwork (including some Goyas and Zurbaráns), musical instruments, ceramics, archaeological finds, farm tools, and photographs donated by citizens. Closed for reorganization and renovation in 2008, the museum should reopen with all new exhibits in 2011. Museo: ⏱ 30 min. Plaza Zuloaga, 1. ☎ 943-48-15-80. www.santelmomuseoa.com.

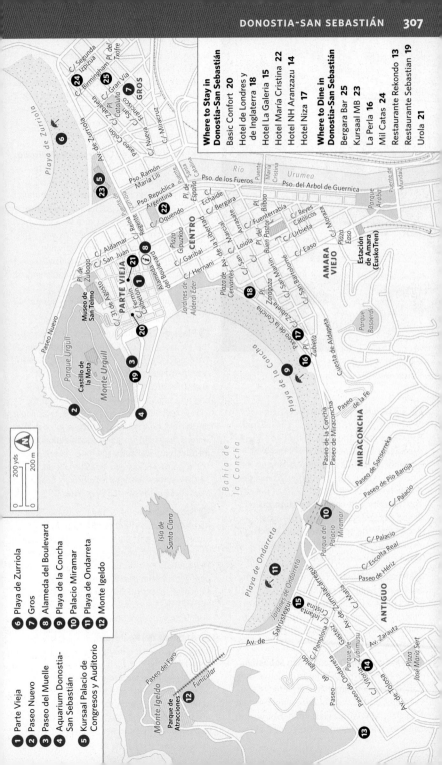

Where to Stay in Donostia-San Sebastián
Basic Confort 20
Hotel de Londres y de Inglaterra 18
Hotel La Galeria 15
Hotel María Cristina 22
Hotel NH Aranzazu 14
Hotel Niza 17

Where to Dine in Donostia-San Sebastián
Bergara Bar 25
Kursaal MB 23
La Perla 16
Mil Catas 24
Restaurante Rekondo 13
Restaurante Sebastián 19
Urola 21

1. Parte Vieja
2. Paseo Nuevo
3. Paseo del Muelle
4. Aquarium Donostia-San Sebastián
5. Kursaal Palacio de Congresos y Auditorio
6. Playa de Zurriola
7. Gros
8. Alameda del Boulevard
9. Playa de la Concha
10. Palacio Miramar
11. Playa de Ondarreta
12. Monte Igeldo

> *Spear the* pinxtos *on the bar with toothpicks; the bartender will tally them up at the end of the night.*

2 ★ **Paseo Nuevo.** This walking path circumnavigates Monte Urgull, the hill that rises abruptly at the edge of the Parte Vieja. A pleasant 20-minute stroll will take you along the peninsula's shore. Walking up the "mountain" takes about another 20 minutes. You're rewarded with great views of the city's bay from the 12th-century **La Mota** castle (open daylight hours). The castle is barely visible from the city below because a chapel with a huge statue of the Sacred Heart of Jesus was erected in front of it in 1950.

3 **Paseo del Muelle.** The fishing port lining the harbor beneath the shadow of the Urgull headland is a fascinating and busy place where small boats unload their catches for the seafood restaurants that occupy the old fishermen's stalls.

4 ★★ **Aquarium Donostia-San Sebastián.** Fully renovated in 2008 for its 100th birthday, San Sebastián's aquarium is devoted to the creatures and ecology of the Cantabrian Sea. The giant tank with a glass tunnel for visitors provides a full-immersion experience of the sharks and other large fish swimming about. ⏱ 1½ hr. Plaza Carlos Blasco de Imaz, 1. ☎ 943-44-00-99. www.aquariumss.com. 12€ adults, 8€ students and seniors, 6€ kids 4–12, free for kids 3 & under. Oct–Easter Tues–Sat 10am–7pm; Easter–June and Sept Mon–Fri 10am–8pm, Sat–Sun 10am–9pm; July–Aug daily 10am–9pm.

5 **Kursaal Palacio de Congresos y Auditorio.** Just across the Puente Zurriola from Parte Vieja, the sleek Rafael Moneo cubes of the Kursaal were conceived as two rocks grounded on the seashore. Since opening in 1999, the facility has become ground zero for San Sebastián's big festivals, notably the venerable (since 1953) international film festival in September and the nearly as established (since 1956) jazz festival in July. It also hosts many concerts and theatrical productions. ⏱ 10 min. Avenida Zurriola, 1. ☎ 943-00-30-00, tickets 943-00-12-00. www.kursaal.org.

6 **Playa de Zurriola.** Just east of the Kursaal, this long, unprotected stretch of beach stands exposed to the full force of the Atlantic Ocean. And the people who come here like it that way. They are mostly young, deeply tanned, and often minimally clothed—except for the folks in wet suits. Big rollers also make Zurriola the surfers' beach. (Didn't bring your board? Across the street from the beach, **Pukas Escola de Surf** rents wet suits and long-, short-, and bodyboards.) Pukas: Avenida Zurriola, 24. ☎ 943-32-00-68. www.pukassurfeskola.com. Boards start at 10€, wet suits at 5€ per hour.

7 **Gros.** The opening of the Kursaal in 1999 had a salubrious effect on the surrounding streets on the east side of the Río Urumea, and gentrification of the neighborhood continues. Few tourists ever venture here, which is too bad: Most of the best *pintxo* bars (which serve tapaslike snacks) in San Sebastián are located in the Gros. Take some time to look around—and bring your appetite.

8 **Alameda del Boulevard.** Back on the west side of the river, the Boulevard marks the spot where the city walls used to end. The busy street lined with tourist shops and cafes effectively divides Parte Vieja from the 19th-century resort community that blossomed after the royal family started coming to San Sebastián for the summer in 1845.

> *If the kids are scared of sharks, you can head upstairs to the aquarium's maritime museum.*

9 ★★★ **Playa de la Concha.** The beach closest to the city, La Concha, is also the most popular. A broad *paseo* (promenade) follows the water above the sand, and there are bath houses and changing rooms at the midpoint of the beach. If you want to walk the entire strand from Centro to the Igeldo headland, plan on spending 45 minutes. You can also hop buses nos. 5 and 25 from one end to the other.

10 **Palacio Miramar.** Only one small spit of land divides the beaches of San Sebastián's bay, and a graceful English-cottage-style estate stands on the high ground. This was the summer residence of the Spanish court under María Cristina, queen regnant from 1885 to 1902. The building remains private, but the gardens are open. ⏱ 30 min. Paseo de Miraconcha, 48. ☎ 943-48-11-66. Free. Daily 9am–8pm.

11 ★ **Playa de Ondarreta.** The bay's western beach is generally less crowded than Playa de la Concha, but there are fewer amenities. On the rocks at the point stands Eduardo Chillida's monumental 1977 sculpture, *Peine del Viento* (Comb of the Wind), a magical abstraction of three pieces of steel anchored in the rock.

> *Sculptor Eduardo Chillida's wave-battered* Comb of the Wind *(1977).*

12 **Monte Igeldo.** The panoramic view of the sweep of the beaches rushing toward the dense clot of Parte Vieja is best from the gazebo at the top of the western headland. It's a steep walk, but from April to October you can ride the funicular, which dates from 1912. ⏱ 1 hr. Funicular: Plaza del Funicular de Igeldo, 4. ☎ 943-21-02-11. Round-trip 2.50€ adults, 1.80€ kids 7 & under; one-way 1.40€ adults, 1€ kids 7 & under. Apr–June Mon–Fri 10am–8pm, Sat–Sun 10am–9pm; July–Oct Mon–Fri 10am–9pm, Sat–Sun 10am–10pm. Bus: 16.

Where to Stay

> *The palatial Hotel Maria Cristina.*

Basic Confort VIEJA
Well named, this small guest house divided between two old-quarter buildings sports smartly stylish rooms themed on great cities of Spain and the world. Everything is new, fresh, and scrupulously maintained. The only potential shortcoming is lack of air-conditioning, as nearby streets can be loud. C/ Puerto, 17, 2nd floor. ☎ 943-42-25-81. www.basicconfort.com. 10 rooms in 2 locations. Doubles 70€–90€. MC, V.

★ **Hotel de Londres y de Inglaterra** CENTRO
The Abba hotel group recently took over this Belle Epoque grande dame, a truly elegant resort that looks a bit like a beached ocean liner. Romantic Victorian furnishings with plush carpets and drapery are augmented by modern bathrooms. C/ Zubieta, 2. ☎ 943-44-07-70. www.hlondres.com. 148 rooms. Doubles 169€–254€. AE, MC, V.

Hotel La Galeria ONDARRETA
Set in a French Empire manse right at Playa Ondarreta, this modest hotel with antique-style furnishings and rooms themed to French and Spanish painters is steps from the Mount Igeldo funicular and the sandy beach. C/ Infante Cristina, 1–3. ☎ 943-31-75-59. www.hotellagaleria.com. 23 rooms. Doubles 110€–135€. AE, MC, V.

★★★ **Hotel María Cristina** CENTRO
This 1912 classic overlooking the Río Urumea (yet only a short walk from the beaches) is San Sebastián's most palatial hotel. Public areas are grand, even imperial, and even basic guest rooms are spacious and luxuriously appointed. It's probably the best spot in town for celebrity spotting during the film festival. Paseo Republica Argentina, 4. ☎ 943-43-76-41. www.luxurycollection.com/mariacristina. 136 rooms. Doubles 180€–710€. AE, MC, V.

★★ **Hotel NH Aranzazu** ONDARRETA
This outstanding modern business hotel with spacious rooms in sleek contemporary decor is located in a quiet residential neighborhood about a 7-minute walk from Playa Ondarreta. C/ Vitoria-Gasteiz, 1. ☎ 943-21-90-77. www.nh-hotels.com. 180 rooms. Doubles 95€–185€. AE, DC, MC, V.

★ **Hotel Niza** CENTRO
The rooms in this small family-run hotel are simple, airy, and full of light, and 18 of them have windows opening onto Playa de la Concha. Sea- and streetview rooms are the same price. The hotel will even loan you a laptop for the free wireless network, if you really must work. C/ Zubieta, 56. ☎ 943-42-66-63. www.hotelniza.com. 40 rooms. Doubles 123€–145€. AE, MC, V.

Where to Dine

> Pintxos *sampling in one of C/ Fermín Calbetón's many bars.*

★★★ Bergara Bar GROS *BASQUE*

Maybe the best *pintxo* bar in Spain, Bergara offers an immense spread of inventive dishes grounded in Basque tradition. The anchovy "false lasagna," for example, is brilliant. Squeeze to the bar and order by pointing. C/ General Artetze, 8. ☎ 943-27-50-26. Pintxos 2.50€. Cash only. Lunch & dinner Mon–Sat.

★★ Kursaal MB GROS *CONTEMPORARY BASQUE*

Sample superchef Martín Berasategui's clean, inventive, and intense cuisine in a casual atmosphere at a casual price. If you're more curious than hungry, try the bar's 10€ tasting menu of three tapas and a glass of wine. Avenida Zurriola, 1. ☎ 943-00-31-62. Menus 25€, 29€, 48€, and 73€. AE, DC, MC, V. Lunch Wed–Sun and dinner Thurs–Sat.

La Perla CENTRO *BASQUE*

Perched just above the sands of Playa de la Concha, Perla serves the Basque seafood classics. To save a bundle, eat at the bar-cafeteria on the east side. Paseo de la Concha, s/n. ☎ 943-46-24-84. Restaurant entrees 13€–20€. Bar-cafeteria 4€–10€. AE, MC, V. Lunch & dinner daily.

Mil Catas GROS *BASQUE*

Creative *pintxos* at this lively wine bar include the likes of goat cheese with apple jelly, escarole, pine nuts, and black-olive tapenade. They rightly call it "haute cuisine in miniature." C/ Zabaleta, 55. ☎ 943-31-16-56. Pintxos 2€–4€. MC, V. Lunch & dinner daily.

★★ Restaurante Rekondo IGELDO *BASQUE*

It's worth climbing the hill to this wood-burning Basque *asador,* celebrated as one of Spain's best meat and seafood grills. The cellars hold nearly 100,000 bottles, including many trophy bordeaux and Rioja wines. Paseo de Igeldo, 57. ☎ 943-21-29-07. Entrees 22€–27€. MC, V. Lunch Thurs–Tues, dinner Thurs–Mon.

★★ Restaurante Sebastian VIEJA *SEAFOOD*

The fishermen unload their catch in front, and the cooks hustle the fish inside. Feast on the *menú del día* (which always includes a fish soup) for 28€, or celebrate with a shellfish roast for two for around 150€. Muella, 14 bajo. ☎ 943-42-58-62. Entrees 12€–40€ (most under 25€). AE, MC, V. Lunch & dinner Wed–Mon.

Urola VIEJA *BASQUE*

Pintxos and draft cider at this atmospheric spot are great, but come back at dinner for wood-grilled whole monkfish for two or the huge, juicy prime rib. C/ Fermín Calbetón, 20. ☎ 943-42-34-24. Restaurant entrees 14€–24€, pintxos 2.50€. AE, MC, V. Lunch & dinner Thurs–Tues (closed Sun dinner).

Bilbao

More handsome than pretty, Bilbao (Bilbo in Basque) is a city of amplitude dominated by broad *paseos*, river vistas, and a veritable sculpture park of dynamic architecture. Yet as recently as the 1980s, it was a steel and ship-building city in dire decline. Bilbainos thought the government was crazy to court a major museum and a name architect to create a new landmark. But civic audacity paid off. The opening of the Guggenheim Bilbao in 1997 jump-started a transformation of the riverfront and turned a provincial city of 355,000 into what Guggenheim architect Frank Gehry has called a laboratory for contemporary architecture. In the world of architects, you're nobody unless you have a building in Bilbao.

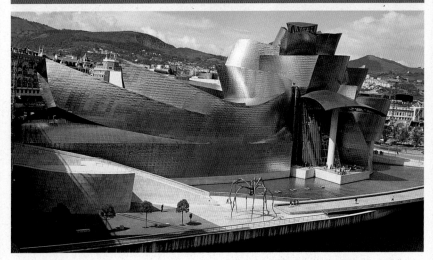

> *Louise Bourgeois's 9m (30-ft.) bronze spider sculpture,* Maman, *greets visitors to the Guggenheim Bilbao.*

START Plaza de Funicular.

❶ Funicular de Artxanda. Zip up the slope of Mount Artxanda in 3 minutes for an overview of the city, nestled in the valley of the Río de Bilbao. Along the sinuous river, the bronze and silver cluster of the Guggenheim seems to gleam in the sun. ⏱ 30 min. Plaza de Funicular, off C/ Castaños. ☎ 944-45-49-66. www.bilbao. net. .90€. Mon-Sat 7:15am-10pm, Sun 8:15am-10pm; June-Sept weekends closes 11pm.

❷ ★★★ Museo Guggenheim Bilbao. The armored beast shows its form best when viewed from across the river. Get a free audio guide when entering—the initial tracks explain how to journey through the space. The contemporary art is cutting edge, and so is the museum experience. Exploring the building from the inside is like walking through a grand sculpture. Signage in Basque, Spanish, and English does an excellent job of placing individual exhibitions in art-historical context and helping visitors appreciate them beyond the immediate "wow" factor. ⏱ 3 hr. Abandoibarra Etorbidea, 2. ☎ 944-35-90-00. www.guggenheim-bilbao.es. 13€ adults, 7.50€ students and seniors, free for kids 11 & under. Sept-June Tues-Sun 10am-8pm; July-Aug daily 10am-8pm. Metro: Moyúa. Tranvia: Guggenheim.

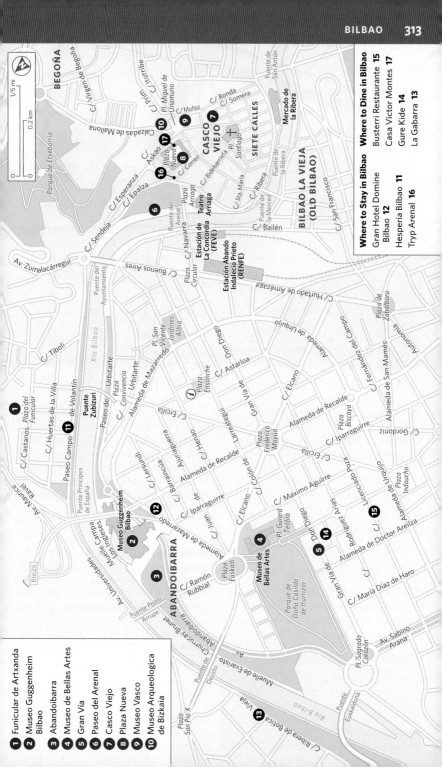

Where to Stay in Bilbao
Gran Hotel Domine Bilbao **12**
Hesperia Bilbao **11**
Tryp Arenal **16**

Where to Dine in Bilbao
Busterri Restaurante **15**
Casa Victor Montes **17**
Gure Kide **14**
La Gabarra **13**

1 Funicular de Artxanda
2 Museo Guggenheim Bilbao
3 Abandoibarra
4 Museo de Bellas Artes
5 Gran Vía
6 Paseo del Arenal
7 Casco Viejo
8 Plaza Nueva
9 Museo Vasco
10 Museo Arqueologica de Bizkaia

> *Chillida's suspended concrete sculpture* Meeting Place IV *(1999) at the Bilbao Museum of Fine Arts.*

❸ ★★ Abandoibarra. Until the 1980s, Bilbao's new signature waterfront district was home to dying steel mills, rail yards, and shipyards along a polluted river. Under the master plan of architect Cesar Pelli, it has assumed new walkways, intriguing contemporary sculpture, and an architectural zoo of innovative projects by world-famous architects—all since the Guggenheim opened. Santiago Calatrava's elegant (if controversial) footbridge, the **Pasarela Zubizuri,** summarizes the spirit of the new Abandoibarra: sinuous and monumental, yet built to a human scale. ⏱ 45 min.

❹ ★★ Museo de Bellas Artes. Don't overlook this gem of a conventional art museum—a place with rectangular galleries, paintings on the walls, and sculpture on the floor (unlike the

Guggenheim). The primarily Spanish collection ranges from powerful 12th- to 14th-century Gothic sculpture and painting, to early-20th-century regional painting. Among the modern works are abstract pieces in iron and stone by Basque sculptor Eduardo Chillida. ⏱ 1½ hr. Museo Plaza, 2. ☎ 944-39-60-60. www.museobilbao.com. 5.50€ adults, free for kids 11 & under, free Wed. Tues–Sun 10am–8pm. Metro: Moyúa.

❺ Gran Vía. The broad boulevard is the backbone of the Ensanche, Bilbao's 19th-century city-wide expansion plan. Stretching 1.5km (1 mile) from Puente Euskalduna (built above the old shipyards) east to the Plaza Circular, it is the most elegant shopping district of Bilbao and headquarters of many financial institutions.

❻ Paseo del Arenal. The promenade of the Casco Viejo follows what was originally a sandy bend in the river. On Sundays, a flower market blooms beneath covered pavilions and the city band plays in the wedding-cake-like bandstand. Upstaged by Abandoibarra's Paseo de Ribera, it retains a genteel Victorian charm.

Travel Tip

The **"Bono Artean"** voucher provides admission to the Guggenheim and Bellas Artes museums for the same price as an adult admission to the Guggenheim alone. Purchase at either museum.

> *The tourist office has listings of current productions at the Teatro Arriaga.*

7 Casco Viejo. For nearly 8 centuries, the Old Town, a compact triangle nestled under a hill on a bend in the river, *was* Bilbao. The atmospheric streets are wider than most medieval quarters and eventually converge on Plaza Unamuno, making it hard to get lost. Two riverfront institutions anchor the Old City. The first, the **Teatro Arriaga,** dates from 1919, although the style might be called 19th-century neoclassic with froufrou. Restored by the city, it is a popular venue for dance, theater, opera, and concerts. Farther upriver, the three-level 1929 **Mercado de la Ribera** could be called a cathedral of food. The main entry to the three-floor market is a wall of stunning stained glass. Teatro: ⊙ 1 hr. Plaza del Arriaga, 1. ☎ 944-79-20-36. www.teatroarriaga.com. Mercado: ⊙ 15 min. C/ Ribera, s/n. www.mercadodelaribera.com. Free. Sept 16–June 14 Wed–Thurs 8am–2pm and 4:30–7pm, Fri 8am–2:30pm and 4:30–7:30pm, Sat 8am–2:30pm; June 15–Sept 15 Mon–Sat 8am–2:30pm, also Fri 4:30–7:30pm.

8 ★ Plaza Nueva. Designed in 1789 and completed in 1851, this handsome square is one of the last neoclassical plazas built in Spain. The bars, cafes, and restaurants under its graceful arches offer the best tapas in the Casco Viejo.

9 Museo Vasco. Basque identity is the real subject of this museum that celebrates such traditional lifestyles as fishing and sheepherding. Get a sense of the Basque idea of fun in a display of the 100 to 212kg (220–467-lb.) stones hefted by men in public contests of strength. Another case details the

> *We dare you not to salivate on a Basque tasting tour.*

style of signature Basque caps—which you can still buy at Sombreros Gorostiago, C/ Victor 19 (☎ 94-416-12-76). ⊙ 30 min. Plaza Miguel Unamuno, 4. ☎ 944-15-54-23. www.euskal-museoa.org. 3€ adults, 1.50€ students, free for seniors and kids, free Wed. Tues–Sat 11am–5pm; Sun 11am–2pm. Metro: Casco Viejo. Tranvia: Unamuno.

10 Museo Arqueologica de Bizkaia. Tracing the human presence in the Bay of Biscay region from the arrival of Neanderthal man 100,000 years ago to the emergence of a coherent Basque region in the Middle Ages, this sleek museum opened in April 2009. Plaques in Spanish and Basque explain the significance of prehistoric stone tools, Celtiberian stone carvings and jewelry, and pottery from Neolithic to Roman times. ⊙ 45 min. Calzadas de Mallona, 2. ☎ 944-04-09-90. www.bizkaia.net. 3€ adults, 1.50€ students and seniors, free for kids 11 & under, free last Fri of month. Metro: Casco Viejo. Tranvia: Unamuno.

Where to Stay & Dine

> Tasty pintxos at Busterri.

Busterri Restaurante ENSANCHE *BASQUE*
Licenciado Pozo is one of Bilbao's liveliest streets for *pintxos* (Basque tapas). If you don't fill up in the bar on treats like roast cod with tomato coulis, head to the dining room for classic Basque seafood. C/ Licenciado Pozo, 43. ☎ 944-41-50-67. Entrees 11€–18€. MC, V. Lunch & dinner Tues–Sat.

★ **Casa Victor Montes** CASCO VIEJO *BASQUE*
The magnificent Belle Epoque–style bar, cafe, and dining room is an excellent choice in the jumping bar scene on Plaza Nueva. Nosh on seafood tapas or mountain charcuterie—or enjoy full dinner service of fresh fish or roast pigeon. Plaza Nueva, 8. ☎ 944-15-70-67. Entrees 14€–29€. MC, V. Lunch & dinner daily.

★★ **Gran Hotel Domine Bilbao** ABANDOIBARRA
The least expensive rooms at this minimalist marvel across the street from the Guggenheim overlook the caged-rock sculpture of the atrium, but everyone gets the sweeping view of Gehry's design from the rooftop terrace at breakfast. C/ Alameda Mazarredo, 61. ☎ 944-25-33-00. www.granhoteldominebilbao.com. 135 rooms. Doubles 117€–175€. AE, DC, MC, V.

★★ **Gure Kide** ENSANCHE *BASQUE*
Chef Aitor Elola's "slow food" platters (grilled scallops in sauce with local cheese, for example) amplify his crisply updated Basque fish and meat classics. **Particular de Estraunza, 4-6.** ☎ 944-41-50-04. Entrees 16€–32€. AE, DC, MC, V. Lunch & dinner Mon–Sat.

Hesperia Bilbao DEUSTU
The chic contemporary design here includes a playful patchwork of colored windows facing the Guggenheim across the river. The hotel's rental bikes are handy on the bike paths along the river. The best prices are on weekends. Campo Volantín, 28. ☎ 944-05-11-00. www.hesperia-bilbao.com. 151 rooms. Doubles 70€–98€. AE, DC, MC, V.

La Gabarra DEUSTU *BASQUE*
Steaks on the grill and cider from the barrel make this one a classic among *asadors*—a style of roast-meat restaurant perfected by the Basques and enjoyed all over Spain. Ribera de Botica Vieja, 18. ☎ 944-47-70-62. Entrees 11€–29€. MC, V. Lunch & dinner Mon–Sat.

★ **Tryp Arenal** CASCO VIEJO
It's worth springing 10€ more for a bigger superior room in this tranquil modern hotel with tasteful Spanish decor. Walk from the edge of the old quarter to Gran Vía to shop, or stroll to the Guggenheim in 20 minutes. C/ Los Fueros, 2. ☎ 944-15-31-00. www.solmelia.com. 40 rooms. Doubles 65€–85€. AE, MC, V.

Bilbao & the Basque Country Fast Facts

Arriving & Getting Around

BY PLANE Bilbao's **Aeropuerto de Sordika** (☎ 944-53-33-40; www.aena.com) is the main air gateway to the Basque Country. **BY TRAIN** Bilbao, San Sebastián, and Vitoria-Gasteiz have excellent rail connections to Madrid and Barcelona via **RENFE** (☎ 902-24-02-02; www.renfe.es). Bilbao's RENFE station is **Estación de Abando,** Plaza Circular, 2, which also services the **Euskotren** light-rail system that connects Bilbao with nearby towns. San Sebastián's RENFE station is **Estación del Norte,** Paseo de Francia, s/n. Vitoria-Gasteiz's rail arrives at **Estación de RENFE,** C/ Eduardo Dato, 46. The narrow-gauge line operated by **FEVE** (www.feve.es) also connects San Sebastián and Bilbao. **BY BUS** Long-distance and regional bus services are excellent. Bilbao's main station is at C/ Gurtubay, 1 (☎ 944-39-50-77; www.termibus.es). San Sebastián's station is located at Plaza Pío XII (www.termibus.es, www.pesa.es). Vitoria-Gasteiz's bus station is at C/ Los Herrán, 50 (☎ 945-25-84-00). **BY CAR** Bilbao and San Sebastián are linked by the **A-8;** San Sebastián and Vitoria-Gasteiz are linked to the rest of Spain via the **A-1. BY FERRY P&O Ferries** (☎ 0871-664-5645 in the U.K. or ☎ 902-02-04-61 in Spain; www.poferries.com) runs overnight auto and passenger service from Portsmouth in the U.K. to Bilbao.

Booking Services

Bilbao Reservas (☎ 902-87-72-98 or 946-61-32-79; www.bilbaoreservas.com) offers hotel booking at the Bilbao tourist office at Plaza Ensanche, 11 (Mon–Fri 9am–2pm and 4–7:30pm; check for Sat–Sun hours July–Aug). **Central de Reservas** (☎ 902-44-34-42; www.sansebastianreservas.com) in San Sebastián, located in the tourist information office (see below), offers assistance with online and in-person hotel booking.

Hospitals

BILBAO The main hospital with emergency services is **Hospital de Basurto,** C/ Montevideo Etorbidea 18 (☎ 944-006-000). **DONOSTIA-SAN SEBASTIÁN Hospital Nuestra Señora de Aranzazu,** C/ Alto de Zorroaga, s/n (☎ 943-007-000).

Post Office

BILBAO The main office is at Alameda Urquijo, 19 (☎ 944-70-93-38). **DONOSTIA-SAN SEBASTIÁN** The main office is at C/ Urdaneta, 7 (☎ 943-44-68-26). **VITORIA-GASTEIZ** The main office is at C/ Postas, 9 (☎ 945-15-46-89). They are all open Monday to Friday 8am to 8pm and Saturday 9am to 2pm.

Visitor Information

BILBAO Bilbao Turismo (www.bilbao.net/bilbao-turismo) has several offices. For the **Ensanche office,** see the booking services above. The **Guggenheim** office at C/ Abandoibarra Etorbidea, 2 (no phone), is open September to June Tuesday to Friday 11am to 6pm, Saturday 11am to 7pm, Sunday 11am to 3pm; July to August Monday to Saturday 10am to 7pm, Sunday 10am to 6pm. The **Casco Viejo** office is at Arriaga Teatro, Plaza Arriaga, s/n (no phone), and is open September to June Monday to Friday 11am to 2pm and 5 to 7:30pm, Saturday 9:30am to 2pm and 5 to 7:30pm, Sunday 9:30am to 2pm; July to August daily 9:30am to 2pm and 4 to 7:30pm. **BERMEO Tourist Office,** at C/ Lamera, s/n (☎ 946-17-91-54; www.bermeo.org), is open Tuesday to Saturday 10:30am to 1:30pm and 4 to 7pm, Sunday 11am to 2pm. **DONOSTIA-SAN SEBASTIÁN Oficina de Turismo,** Avenida de Boulevard, 8 (☎ 943-48-11-66; www.sansebastianturismo.com), is open Monday to Thursday 9am to 1:30pm and 3:30 to 7pm, Friday to Saturday 9:30am to 7pm, Sunday 10am to 2pm. **GERNIKA-LUMO Oficina de Turismo,** C/ Artekalea, 8 (☎ 946-25-58-92; www.gernika-lumo.net), is open Monday to Saturday 10am to 2pm and 4 to 7pm, Sunday 10am to 2pm. **LEKEITIO Oficina de Turismo,** Plaza Independencia, s/n (☎ 946-84-40-17; www.lekeitio.com), is open Monday to Saturday 10am to 2pm and 4 to 7pm, Sunday 10am to 2pm. **VITORIA-GASTEIZ Oficina de Turismo,** Plaza General Loma, 1 (☎ 945-16-15-98; www.vitoria-gasteiz.org/turismo), is open Monday to Saturday 10am to 7pm, Sunday 11am to 2pm. **ZARAUTZ Oficina de Turismo,** C/ Nafarroa Kalea, 3 (☎ 943-83-09-90; www.turismozarautz.com), is open Monday to Saturday 10am to 2pm and 4 to 7pm, Sunday 10am to 2pm.

Navarra
& La Rioja

The Best of Navarra & La Rioja in 3 Days

Navarra and La Rioja are united by the Santiago pilgrimage route and the *tempranillo* wine grape. Basque by origin, Navarra is the more mountainous of the two autonomous regions—dotted with hilltop villages, castles, and monasteries. La Rioja has been shaped by the grape, so its attractions are by nature more mellow. This tour hits some of the highlights of northern Spain's geography and culture. Start with a day and a half in Navarra's capital, Pamplona, followed by a half-day in Olite, and a day investigating some of the pilgrim towns en route to La Rioja.

> PREVIOUS PAGE *The famous running of the bulls at the San Fermín festival in Pamplona.* THIS PAGE *Olite's Palicio Real was restored in the early 20th century.*

START Pamplona. TRIP LENGTH 113km (70 miles).

1 Pamplona-Iruña. Outside of Sanfermines in July, any bull in Pamplona's streets will likely be the hyperbole of tour guides, but there's still plenty to see and do. You can get a feel for the running of the bulls by following the **route** (see p. 340, **1**) through town. Hemingway's 1926 novel *The Sun Also Rises* paints Pamplona as a good city for eating and drinking, and that's still

true today, whether on **Plaza del Castillo** (see p. 342, **3**) or surrounding streets.

Don't miss the death statues of Carlos III and his wife, Leonor de Trastámara, in the ★ **Catedral de Santa María and Museo Diocesano** (see p. 342, **5**). You'll also be surprised by the sweep of art in the spacious and beautifully lit galleries of the ★★ **Museo de Navarra** (see p. 342, **6**). It's a tossup which is more striking: the Roman mosaics or the frescoes rescued from ancient Gothic churches. ⏱ 1½ days.

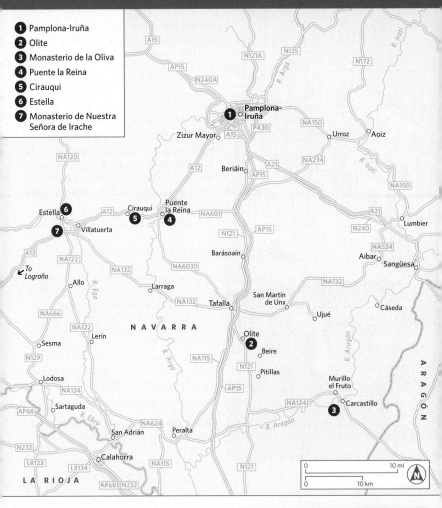

1 Pamplona-Iruña
2 Olite
3 Monasterio de la Oliva
4 Puente la Reina
5 Cirauqui
6 Estella
7 Monasterio de Nuestra
  Señora de Irache

Follow the AP-15/N-121 south 43km (27 miles) from Pamplona to Olite.

2 Olite. Until Navarra was finally absorbed into Spain in 1512, warfare with Castilla, Aragón, and France led to fortification of virtually every city and town. Few enjoyed such a harmonious and picturesque castle as Olite, which the strongest of all Navarra kings, Carlos III, ordered built in 1406. The fortifications of the **Palacio Real** embrace a large part of the old quarters. The town is also a center of the Navarra DO wine classification, and the new **Museo de la Viña y el Vino** makes a powerful case for the local industry. ⏲ Half-day. See p. 339, 5.

> Detail of a 14th-century fresco in Pamplona's cathedral.

and *garnacha* grapes. The monks keep a vow of silence except when they sing their prayers several times a day. The monastery is always open to tours, but visits to the Gothic bodega and its 1912 replacement, led by a guide who has not taken a vow of silence, are by prior arrangement. ⏲ 2 hr. Carretera de Lerida, s/n, Carcastillo. ☎ 948-72-50-06. 2€. Mon–Sat 9am–12:30pm and 3:30–6pm; Sun 9–11am and 4–6pm.

Backtrack to Olite and follow N-121 north for 6km (3¾ miles) to NA-132 west to connect to NA-6030. Continue 19km (12 miles) across broad fields of grain and vineyards to Puente la Reina.

❹ **Puente la Reina.** Alfonso the Battler established this town in the 12th century at the spot where pilgrimage roads from Toulouse and Paris converge. The old quarter evokes the medieval pilgrimages with its 12th- to 14th-century buildings along the narrow **Rúa Mayor.** The church of **Santiago,** largely rebuilt in the 16th century, retains two beautifully carved portals of the original Romanesque building. Stand on the 11th-century Romanesque bridge over the Río Arga and imagine the tens of thousands of pilgrims who walked over the six-arch span that gave the town its name. ⏲ 2 hr.

Follow A-12 west 7km (4⅓ miles) to Cirauqui.

❺ **Cirauqui.** This atmospheric and tiny village (pop. 480) with medieval wall and gates is built around a Gothic church. All streets radiate from the church and are lined with surprisingly large houses constructed from cut stone blocks inscribed with the owner's name and year of construction. The Camino de Santiago leaves the village on **Vía Romana,** which still has some Roman pavers, and crosses a Roman bridge. ⏲ 1 hr.

Follow A-12 west 5km (3 miles). Take exit 36 to NA-1110 and follow 5km (3 miles) to Estella.

❻ **Estella.** Also founded along the Santiago pilgrimage route, Estella flourished in the 13th and 14th centuries. In late July, townspeople recall the era by donning medieval garb for **Semana Medieval.** The **Palacio de los Reyes de Navarra,** built at the end of the 12th century, is the oldest nonreligious building in Navarra. It houses a museum primarily devoted to the paintings of Gustavo de Maeztu (1887–1947), but the real attraction is the building itself; one

> *The neoclassical Plaza de Castillo is the heart of modern Pamplona.*

From Olite, follow N-121 south for 6km (3¾ miles) and turn left onto NA-5330 for 10km (6¼ miles). Continue 10km (6¼ miles) to Carcastillo and follow signs for Monasterio de la Oliva.

❸ **Monasterio de la Oliva.** A bit out of the way, this early Cistercian monastery was founded in the 12th century to protect the southeast flank of Navarra from Aragónese incursions. The monks soon planted vineyards and created a bodega to support themselves. It proved a happy venture, as depicted in stone carvings on the 14th-century Gothic cloister showing monks tending vines and making wine. About two dozen Cistercian monks still live at the monastery, the only one in Spain making wine on-site from its own vineyards of *tempranillo*

> *Silent Cistercian monks still live and work, making wine, at the Monasterio de la Oliva in Carcastillo.*

> *Water or wine from the spigots at Monasterio de Nuestra Señora de Irache.*

of the narrative capitals relates the battle of Roland (Charlemagne's top warrior) with the Muslim giant Farragut. **Palacio:** ⊕ 30 min. C/ San Nicolás, 1. ☎ 948-54-60-37. www.museogustavodemaeztu.com. Free. Tues-Sat 11am-1pm and 5-7pm; Sun 11am-1:30pm.

Follow C/ Carlos VII (N-111A) south for 2km (1¼ mile).

❼ Monasterio de Nuestra Señora de Irache. Built in the 11th century and converted to a pilgrims' stopover in the 12th, this monastery will house a new ethnological museum due to open in 2010 or 2011. The working monastery makes wine, and you'll see pilgrims lining up to drink from the fountain on one side of the building—it spews red wine from one spout and water from the other. ⊕ 1 hr. N-111A, Ayegui. ☎ 948-55-44-64. Free. Nov-Mar Tues 10am-1:30pm, Wed-Sun 10am-1:30pm and 4:30-6pm; Apr-Oct Tues-Fri 9am-1:30pm and 5-7pm, Sat-Sun 9am-1:30pm and 4-7pm. Closed Christmas through New Year's.

Spending the Night in Puente de la Reina

Every pilgrim must dream of something like **Hotel El Peregrino,** a stone country house set in beautiful gardens outside of town. Sumptuously decorated rooms make a luxurious rural getaway for travelers with more secular agendas, too. C/ Irunbidea, s/n. ☎ 948-34-00-75. www.hotelelperegrino.com. 12 rooms. Doubles 100€-160€. AE, MC, V.

One of the nicest spots on Puente de la Reina's restaurant row, **La Conrada** emphasizes local vegetables in season, especially fresh artichokes, white asparagus, and green beans. Paseo de los Fueros, s/n. ☎ 948-34-00-52. Combination plates 8€-13€. MC, V. Lunch & dinner Thurs-Tues.

The Best of Navarra & La Rioja in 1 Week

If 3 days of art, history, mountain scenery, and religion in Navarra don't suffice (see "The Best of Navarra & La Rioja in 3 Days"), mix with heady Rioja wine to finish out the week. Start with 2 days in Logroño, a day to visit the historic winemaking and monastery towns, and a final day in gracious Santo Domingo de la Calzada, where you'll mix and mingle with the Santiago pilgrims.

> A statue of Santiago Matamoros (the politically incorrect St. James "the Moor slayer") above the south portal of Santiago El Real.

START Logroño. TRIP LENGTH 169km (105 miles), including "The Best of Navarra & La Rioja in 3 Days."

1 Logroño. The Codex Calixtinus, the 12th-century manuscript that was the first guidebook to the Camino de Santiago, singles out Logroño as a safe haven for travelers. The 11th-century **Puente de Piedra** (stone bridge), which still crosses the Río Ebro into town, was originally fortified with three guard towers. **Rúa Vieja** is the old pilgrim path, and it leads directly to the ancient **Pilgrim's Fountain** that predates the 16th-century **Santiago El Real** church, located at Barriocepo, 6. Use some of your time in Logroño to visit nearby bodegas or other towns outlined in "Wine Lovers' Rioja" (see p. 330). ⏱ 2 days.

Take the LO-20 west to merge onto A-12 for 25km (16 miles). Take exit 27 and follow N-120 into Nájera.

2 Nájera. The Río Najerilla, whose banks grow vast quantities of wine grapes, splits this historic town in half. Built in 1032, the **Monasterio de Santa María La Real** looks like a fortress on the outside and like a noble palace on the inside. The Claustro de los Caballeros—burial site of many knights—is renowned for the ornamental carvings of the capitals and walls. The church also holds a royal pantheon of 30 monarchs of Navarra.

Before leaving town to drive through a rolling countryside of almost unrelieved vineyards, fortify yourself with a glass of lightly aged Rioja and a deep-fried, cod-stuffed pepper at **La Taberna de Manu.** Monasterio: ⏱ 1½ hr. Plaza de Santa María, s/n. ☎ 941-36-10-83. www.santa marialareal.net. 3€. Tues–Sat 10am–1pm and

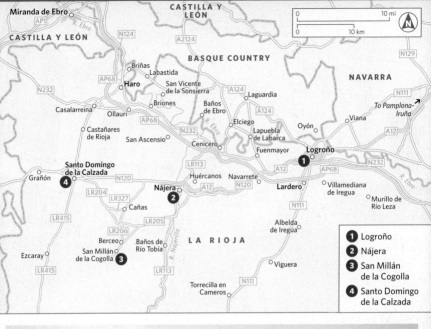

> *Pilgrims on the Camino de Santiago once crossed Logroño's Puente de Piedra under guard.*

4–7pm (winter 4–5:30pm), Sun 10am–12:30pm and 4–6pm (winter 4–5:30pm). Taberna: C/ Mayor, 3. ☎ 941-41-04-28. Entrees 10€–14€. AE, V. Lunch & dinner daily.

Head south on the LR-113 for 5km (3 miles). Turn right onto LR-205 to go 7km (4⅓ miles) to San Millan de la Cogolla.

❸ San Millán de la Cogolla. This small village was the home of 13th-century poet and author Gonzalo de Berceo, the first major literary figure to write in the Castilian dialect. He was

educated here by the monks of the **Monasterio de Yuso,** a magnificent compound that ranges from an 11th-century walled keep to a striking 16th-century church. The sacristy holds secular as well as religious treasures, including the first written examples of both the Basque and Castilian languages, which were removed from the nearby, vacant Suso monastery for safe-keeping.

Tickets are sold at the Yuso monastery for a strictly controlled visit via minibus to the more ancient **Monasterio de Suso** on the hill

> *The library at the Monasterio de Yuso houses over 300 documents dating from the 11th to the 15th centuries.*

> *The elaborately carved cloister of the Monasterio de Santa María La Real in Nájera.*

above town. Founded in 550, Suso consists of a Visigothic core with Mozarabic enlargements from the 11th century and a Romanesque section from the 13th. **Yuso and Suso:** ⏱ 1½ hr. ☎ 941-37-30-49. Each monastery 4€ adults, 3€ seniors, 1.50€ kids 8–14, free for kids 7 & under. Tues–Sun 10am–1:30pm and 4–6:30pm.

Go north on LR-206 for 8km (5 miles) to Cañas and turn left. Follow LR-327 3km (1¾ miles) to turn right onto LR-204/LR-240. Go 8km (5 miles) to Santo Domingo de la Calzada.

❹ **Santo Domingo de la Calzada.** La Rioja's quintessential pilgrimage town, Santo Domingo was founded specifically as a wayside for Santiago pilgrims. They still flock here, often staying a day to rest and do their laundry before continuing the remaining 550km (342 miles) to Santiago. You can spot them by the Crocs or flip-flops they wear to let their boots air out. In the old quarter, shops seem to be divided between those that sell shoes and foot remedies, and those that sell rain gear. Nonpilgrims will find the town an equally good base for exploring the Riojan countryside.

> *Santo Domingo de la Calzada's ornate Romanesque tomb of the city's namesake.*

To gain some insight into the history—and the day-to-day reality—of the pilgrimage, visit **kids** **El Camino Express Centro de Interpretación del Camino de Santiago.** At one point in the multimedia tour, you'll don pilgrim garb and imagine the trek.

The essential sight in Santo Domingo is the Gothic **kids** ★★ **Catedral,** begun in 1158. It must be the only cathedral with a hen and rooster in a cage high on a wall. Swapped out every few weeks for new fowl, they memorialize a medieval legend with many variants but one ending: a roasted hen and rooster sit up and crow to prove the innocence of a young pilgrim wrongfully accused of theft. Thus the Spanish saying, *"Santo Domingo de la Calzada, cantó la gallina después de asada"* ("Santo Domingo de la Calzada, where the chicken sang after being roasted"). An ornate tomb with a Romanesque carving of the town's founder and namesake stands near the entrance. Touch screens at each side altar or notable stop explain the history of the church and its treasures.

The church's **Torre Exenta** stands across the square. You can climb the 132 steps to the top for sweeping vistas of the countryside. You might even see pilgrims approaching on the horizon. El Camino: ⏱ 45 min. C/ Mayor, 33. ☎ 902-11-26-60. www.elcaminoexpress.com. 10€ adults, 8€ seniors, 6€ kids 4–12, free for kids 3 & under. Catedral: ⏱ 30 min. Plaza del Santo. ☎ 941-34-00-33. Free. Daily 10:30am–noon, 12:40–2pm, 5–5:30pm, and 6:15–7:15pm. Torre: ⏱ 30 min. Plaza del Santo. ☎ 941-34-05-31. 1.50€. Daily 10am–8pm.

Spending the Night in San Millán

One wing of the Yuso monastery was transformed into a comfortable and serene hotel, **Hospedería del Monasterio de San Millán,** in 1995. Monasterio de Yuso. ☎ 941-37-32-77. www.sanmillan.com. 25 rooms. Doubles 106€–135€. AE, DC, MC, V.

Popular with day-trippers and those who opt to stay the night, the **Asador de San Millán** is just a stone's throw from the monastery. House specialties are roast meats and the monastery's own superb red wine. C/ Prestiño, s/n. ☎ 941-37-32-43. Entrees 10€–18€. MC, V. Lunch & dinner Tues–Sun.

Spending the Night in Santo Domingo

Santo Domingo built a lodging for pilgrims next to the cathedral in the 12th century. Thoroughly modernized, the handsome Romanesque structure is now the ★★★ **Parador de Santo Domingo de la Calzada.** It's a safe bet that 12th-century pilgrims didn't have the fine linens, welcoming beds, or minibars that today's travelers enjoy. The restaurant offers hearty meat and game dishes well-suited to the local red wine. Plaza del Santo, 3. ☎ 941-34-03-00. www.parador.es. 61 rooms. Doubles 103€–160€. Entrees 14€–32€. AE, DC, V. Lunch & dinner daily.

A GRAPE GUIDE

Spain's Burgeoning Wine Regions   BY NEIL EDWARD SCHLECHT

WITH MORE LAND planted with wine grapes than any other nation, Spain is the third-largest producer of wine in the world (behind France and Italy). The global emergence of Spanish wine, in tandem with the flourishing of creative Spanish cuisine, has been one of the biggest gastronomy stories of the past decade: For years Spain was characterized by somnolent, old-school Rioja reds and fortified sherries, but a new wave of winemakers has infused Spanish wines with a sense of excitement and possibility. Yet much of the world is only waking up to the extraordinary diversity—and in many cases, extraordinary values—of wines from Spain.

The Lay of the Land

① LA RIOJA
The standard bearer of age-worthy dry reds (made with the native *tempranillo* grape) for more than 200 years. La Rioja today runs the gamut from old-world producers who age their wines in oak for a decade or more to modern stylists who've reinterpreted red.

② DUERO RIVER VALLEY
Land of powerful but elegant reds and two of Spain's legendary wineries (Pingus and Vega Sicilia), Ribera del Duero is the star of this region. The region also includes Toro, which produces big, rustic reds, and Rueda, known for its food-friendly, white *verdejos*.

③ NORTHWESTERN SPAIN "Green Spain" is celebrated for its lively *albariños* from Rías Baixas, ideally matched with seafood. But the region has emerged among connoisseurs for high-acid, richly mineral reds from steep mountains in Bierzo and Ribeira Sacra.

④ LEVANTE
A hot and dry emerging region of limestone-rich soil along the Mediterranean, where *monastrell* is the dominant grape. Highly extracted but excellent-value wines from Yecla, Murcia, Alicante, and especially Jumilla have suddenly gained a place at tables across the world.

⑤ ANDALUCÍA
The immense heat of southern Spain isn't ideal for many table wines, though it is perfect for fortified sherries and dessert wines, ranging from extremely dry to unctuous; prized are manzanilla, fino, *amontillado, oloroso,* and Pedro Ximénez.

⑥ CATALUNYA
Cava (sparkling wine made from *xarel·lo, macabeo,* and *parellada* grapes) comes from Penedés. Cult favorite Priorat, an ancient wine region resurrected in the last 2 decades, is coveted for its powerful (and expensive) reds with great slate-driven minerality.

Building a Better Winery

▲ **BODEGAS PROTOS (RIBERA DEL DUERO):** Sir Richard Rogers's series of curved parabolic roofs recall wine bottles resting in a cellar.

MARQUÉS DE RISCAL (LA RIOJA):
A mini-Bilbao Guggenheim and luxury spa hotel is incorporated into a 19th-century winery at Frank Gehry's "City of Wine."

BODEGAS YSIAS (LA RIOJA):
Santiago Calatrava fashioned an undulating structure that emulates the craggy outcroppings of surrounding mountains.

LOPEZ DE HEREDIA (LA RIOJA):
Zaha Hadid's startlingly modern addition to a starkly traditional 1877 winery resembles a sculptural decanter.

JULIÁN CHIVITE (NAVARRA):
This is a sleek and sensitive modern take by Rafael Moneo on traditional winery architecture for a winery with roots in the 17th century.

Spanish Wine Lingo

JOVEN Literally a "young" wine, sold 1 year after harvest.

CRIANZA Aged 2 years, with at least 1 year in *barricas* (oak barrels).

RESERVA Spent a minimum of 3 years aging, with 1 in the barrel.

GRAN RESERVA From outstanding vintage years; 2 years in the barrel and at minimum another 3 years aging in the bottle.

DENOMINACIÓN DE ORIGEN (DO) The law-designated wine-producing regions (similar to France's Appellation d'Origine Contrôlée); there are currently 62.

Wine Lovers' Rioja

Spain's first wine region to achieve international acclaim,

the Rioja blossomed when the 19th-century *Phylloxera* epidemic in France sent Bordeaux winemakers and landowners scrambling to reestablish themselves in Spain. The "French" style—fermentation in oak vats and extended aging in small oak barrels—came to characterize Rioja. To satisfy modern tastes for lighter wines, many vineyards have begun to age their wines in stainless steel rather than oak. Taste the difference for yourself with a journey along the Río Ebro, the central artery of the wine district. Most bodegas prefer that you reserve in advance for tours and tastings. Check the websites below.

> *Pilgrims and nonpilgrims alike partake of Rioja's finest on Logroño's Calle Laurel.*

START Logroño. **TRIP LENGTH** 40km (25 miles).

❶ **Logroño.** This handsome town poses a chicken-egg question: Which came first, the pilgrims or the wine? A major stopover on the Camino de Santiago since the 11th century, Logroño is also the capital of the Rioja wine district and the central shipping point for most producers. The Camino de Santiago enters town from the east and heads to **Santiago El Real,** located at Barriocepo, 6, open for evening services. The church has a striking statue of Santiago Matamoros over the main portal. The more elaborate cathedral is a few blocks away at **Plaza Mercado,** but the actual market—a 1929 Modernista structure full of fresh meat, fish, and produce (open Mon–Sat morning and afternoon)—is a few streets farther on Plaza de Abastos. The city's top tapas haunts can be found on C/ Laurel, which leads off the southwest corner of the market, and C/ San Juan, 2 blocks east.

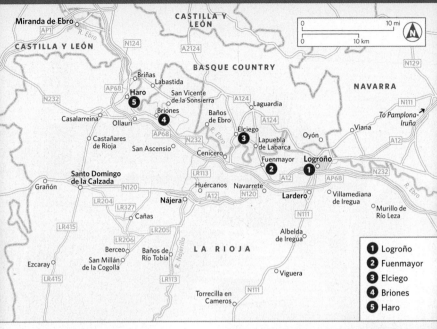

Miranda de Ebro
AP1
R. Ebro
CASTILLA Y LEÓN
N124
CASTILLA Y LEÓN
A2124
BASQUE COUNTRY
N129
Briñas
Labastida
AP68
Haro
San Vicente
de la Sonsierra
A124
Laguardia
N232
5
Briones
A124
NAVARRA
N111
Casalarreina
Ollauri
4
Baños
de Ebro
R. Ebro
To Pamplona-
Iruña
Castañares
de Rioja
AP68
N232
Elciego
3
Oyón
Viana
A12
San Ascensio
Cenicero
Lapuebla
de Labarca
Fuenmayor
Logroño
N232
R. Ebro
Santo Domingo
de la Calzada
LR113
2
1
AP68
Grañón
N120
Huércanos
Navarrete
A12
Villamediana
de Iregua
LR204
Nájera
A12
N120
Lardero
Murillo de
Río Leza
LR327
N111
Cañas
LR415
LR205
Albelda
de Iregua
LR206
Berceo
Baños de
Río Tobía
LA RIOJA
Ezcaray
San Millán
de la Cogolla
LR113
Viguera
Torrecilla en
Cameros
N111

0 ———— 10 mi
0 ———— 10 km

1 Logroño
2 Fuenmayor
3 Elciego
4 Briones
5 Haro

Wine shops are ubiquitous along C/ Portales and side streets in the old quarter. One boutique, **Nueva Antigua,** even makes vinotherapy skin-care products from wine and grape seeds.

Wineries are on the outskirts. **Bodegas Ontañón** receives visitors at its barrel-aging facility just east of town. You won't see grape-receiving bays or fermentation vessels, but the barrel rooms are highlighted by the Perez

Spending the Night in Logroño

Just outside the Casco Viejo, the **Hotel NH Herencia Rioja** is a convenient business hotel with a modern Spanish style based on glossy wood furniture and gold-veined marble floors. It's a good base to explore the old quarter on foot as well as to drive out to the bodegas. C/ Marqués de Murrieta, 14. ☎ 941-21-02-22. www.nh-hotels.com. 83 rooms. Doubles 70€–98€. AE, DC, MC, V.

Enjoy roasted lamb chops, beef steaks, or a broad variety of tapas at **Asador Mesón del Abuelo,** a great spot for a sit-down meal on one of Logroño's best tapas streets. C/ Laurel, 12. ☎ 941-22-46-63. Entrees 11€–17€. Cash only. Lunch & dinner daily.

> *A traditional stone hut, called a* guardaviña, *beside a Rioja vineyard.*

family's extensive collection of sculpture, art, and stained glass—almost all with a wine theme. Tours end at the tasting table. Nueva Antigua: C/ Portales, 28. ☎ 941-21-31-09. AE, MC, V. Ontañón: ⏱ 1½ hr. Avenida de Aragón, 3. ☎ 941-23-42-00. www.bodegasontanon.com. 4€ tour with tasting. Mon–Sat 11am, noon, 5pm, and 6pm; Sun 11am and noon by reservation.

> *Understatement is not Frank Gehry's style—his second whimsical masterpiece in Spain, the Marqués de Riscal vineyard's City of Wine.*

Spending the Night in Elciego

Frank Gehry's signature roof of anodized titanium strips makes the **Marqués de Riscal Hotel** look like a package with an elaborate ribbon. The 43 rooms (including 11 suites) draw their luxury from rich fabrics, marble bathrooms, and sweeping views of vineyards and Elciego. C/ Torrea, 1. ☎ 945-18-08-80. www.luxurycollection.com/marquesderiscal. 43 rooms. Doubles 325€–980€. AE, DC, MC, V.

The hotel's two restaurants (both open to nonguests) include the informal **Bistró 860,** known for impeccably prepared Riojan fare. Entrees 18€–41€, menus 29€–50€. AE, DC, MC, V. Lunch & dinner daily.

The **Restaurant Marqués de Riscal** is the gourmet dining option, serving cutting-edge contemporary Basque dishes. Consider the 11-course tasting menu to sample the chef's range. Entrees 18€–41€, tasting menu 91€. AE, DC, MC, V. Lunch & dinner Mon-Sat.

From Logroño, follow signs to the A-12 and continue 5km (3 miles) to N-232 to go 3km (1¾ miles) into Fuenmayor.

❷ Fuenmayor. Surrounded by vineyards and wineries, Fuenmayor is a small village with large wine warehouses. The two-lane N-232 highway paralleling the Río Ebro cuts through the heart of the Rioja Alta between Fuenmayor and Haro.

The huge modern facility of **Bodegas LAN** opened west of town in 1972 just as Rioja was regaining its international prestige. LAN makes only barrel-aged wines, using 100% *tempranillo* grapes for the *Crianzas* (aged 1 year) and 80% for the *Reservas* (aged 3 years) and *Gran Reservas* (aged at least 5 years). The tour passes along a catwalk above the barrel room with 25,000 barrels of wine in American, French, and Russian oak. When the tour guide opens the window, the heady aroma of the angels' share wafts out. Bodegas: ⏱ 1 hr. Paraje de Buicio (N-232 6km/3¾ miles west of town). ☎ 941-45-09-50. www.bodegaslan.com. Tours free by appointment. Tours and store: Mon-Fri 9:30am-noon and 3:30–5pm.

From Bodegas LAN, continue west on N-232 3km (1¾ miles) to turn right on LR-512 toward Cenicero. Make next right onto LR-211 and follow it, crossing the Ebro, to Elciego in the Basque Country. Total distance 9km (5⅔ miles).

❸ **Elciego.** The Rioja DOCa (*Denominación de Origen Calificada*, Spain's highest regional wine classification) isn't limited to the political region of La Rioja. It includes adjacent areas of Navarra and the Basque Country's Álava province. The Basque village of Elciego has a long history of producing fantastic Rioja Alta wines. Marqués de Riscal was a pioneer in Bordeaux-style winemaking, releasing its first vintage in 1862. In 2006, it expanded operations with a Frank Gehry–designed winery and hotel that complete what the company modestly calls the **Ciudad del Vino** ("City of Wine"). Built around the 19th-century winery, the Frank Gehry buildings are a grand gesture of fanciful style, giving the winery some of the aesthetic cachet that Bilbao enjoys from Gehry's Guggenheim museum. The winery also has a broad commitment to hospitality, with a top-flight spa (**Vino-thérapie Caudalíe,** treatments 60€–130€), a luxury hotel, and two fine-dining restaurants. The store and wine bar stand ready for casual visits—you can easily taste and buy. If there's room, you might be able to join a tour, although reservations are technically required. **Ciudad del Vino:** ◷ 2 hr. C/ Torrea, 1. ☎ 945-18-08-80. www. marquesderiscal.com. Tour and tasting 10€. Call for reservation and time. Store and wine bar daily 10am–7pm.

> Come summer, the vineyards of Rioja Baja, with a climate much like Arizona's, are lush and green.

Rioja: A Timeline

500 B.C.
Celtiberians make wine from local grapes.

100 B.C.–A.D. 300
Romans make wine for the legions.

715–1000
Riojans make wine in secret during Muslim occupation.

1000–1500
Monasteries dominate winemaking. Santiago pilgrims spread fame of Rioja.

1780
Oenologist Manuel Quintano introduces Bordeaux techniques of oak-vat fermentation and oak-barrel aging.

1850–80
Phylloxera hits French vineyards and many French winemakers relocate to Rioja.

1858
Marqués de Riscal establishes first Rioja winery operated on Bordeaux model. Marqués de Murrieta follows suit a few years later.

1914–65
Two world wars and Spanish Civil War cut market. Citing nationwide hunger, Spanish government limits vineyard acreage in favor of wheat and barley.

LATE 1960S
Rioja producers adopt American oak for aging barrels, creating a signature style with strong vanilla overtones.

1970
Century vintage vaults Rioja to international fame among connoisseurs.

> *Plan ahead for a tasting at the Museo de la Cultura del Vino at Dinastía Vivanco winery.*

> *Riojas ready to the drink at CVNE.*

Retrace route to N-232 and continue 16km (10 miles) west to km 442, just east of Briones.

❹ **Briones.** Like many Rioja Alta communities, Briones is a small village surrounded by vast vineyards. One of the town's largest producers, Dinastía Vivanco, operates the showcase **Museo de la Cultura del Vino.** Plan to take your time, as the museum alone will take a couple of hours and the tour of the winemaking facilities at least another hour. If time is limited, enjoy the Jardín del Baco—a display garden planted with 222 wine grape varieties, each with an explanatory plaque, and then peruse the wine, wine gadgets, glasses, and wine reference books and cookbooks in the shop. Plan ahead for the 2-hour wine-tasting class, offered Saturdays from noon to 2pm and 5 to 7pm for 21€. The facility also has a small restaurant, **Restaurante Dinastía Vivanco,** serving traditional Riojan dishes in an elegant setting. Museo: ◷ 3 hr. N-232, km 442. ☎ 902-32-00-01. www.dinastiavivanco.es. Museo 7.50€ adults, 6.50€ seniors, bodega tour/tasting 6.50€, museo and bodega combination 12€. Museo July–Sept Tues–Sun 10am–8pm; Oct–June Tues–Thurs and Sun

> *Wine at the award-winning (and huge) Bodegas LAN is aged in oak barrels for 1, 3, or 5 years.*

10am–6pm and Fri–Sat 10am–8pm. Guided visits Tues–Fri 10am and 4pm by reservation. Restaurante: ☎ 941-32-23-40. Entrees 16€–20€. AE, DC, MC, V. Lunch Tues–Sun, dinner Tues–Sat.

Continue west on N-232 for 4km (2½ miles). Turn right and follow N-124 for 3km (1¾ miles) to Haro.

❺ **Haro.** Wine has been very, very good to Haro, as you can tell by the 16th-century Plateresque and baroque architecture of the private palaces and churches. The center of the Old City is Plaza de la Paz, with a wedding-cake bandstand that echoes the tower of adjacent Santo Tomás church. The barrio known as **La Herradura** ("The Horseshoe") rises off the plaza as a tangle of medieval streets between C/ Santo Tomás and C/ Santo Martín. Every third storefront is a wine or gourmet shop, and most other doors open to tapas bars. A good bet for stuffed piquillo peppers and a glass of red wine is the tavern **Mesón Los Berones,** where most customers stand around wine barrels.

Many important Rioja producers have facilities near the Haro rail station, though most are closed to visitors in August and the first half of September. One good option for touring is **CVNE (La Compañía Vinícola del Norte de España),** a fixture here since 1879.

To delve deeper into the history, science, and aesthetics of Rioja wine, visit the new **Centro de Interpretación del Vino de la Rioja.** Three floors of exhibits, interactive computer displays, and video clips cover everything from planting the vine to shipping the bottles. Mesón: C/ Santo Tomás, 28. ☎ 941-31-07-07. Tapas 2€–3€, entrees 6€–12€. MC, V. Dinner Mon–Sat. CVNE: ⏱ 1½ hr. Barrio de la Estación, s/n. ☎ 941-30-48-09. www.cvne.com. Tour with tasting and tapa 8€. Tours Thurs–Mon 11am, 1pm, and 4pm by reservation. Shop Thurs–Mon 10am–6:30pm, Sun closes 2:30pm. Closed last 3 weeks in Aug. Centro: ⏱ 45 min. Estación de Enológica de Haro, C/ Bretón de los Herreros, 4. ☎ 941-30-57-19. www.vinodelarioja.org. 3€ adults, 2€ seniors and students. Tues–Fri 10am–2:30pm and 3:30–7pm; Sat 10am–7pm; Sun 10am–2pm.

Medieval Navarra

Turreted castles and atmospheric fortified monasteries high in the hills of Navarra attest to the turbulent Middle Ages in this corner of Spain. The kingdom of Pamplona (later renamed Navarra) was a stronghold where the Basques held off both the invading Muslims and the counterinvading French. But the price was endless war. Today those same mountain strongholds are peaceful sanctuaries where the hoofbeats of armies are only a passing dream.

> See the birthplace of one of the founders of the Jesuit Order at Castillo de Javier (Xavier).

START Yesa. **TRIP LENGTH** 79km (49 miles).

1 Monasterio de Leyre. Perched high enough on the slope of Mount Leyre to spot an invading army, this monastery was the spiritual center of medieval Navarra. The original church was constructed in the mid–9th century, in part to house relics of martyrs slain by Muslim conquerors. The monastery was established in the early 11th century and rebuilt by the Cistercians in the 13th century in the spare Cistercian Gothic style that became a monastic model throughout northern Spain. Fortunately, they retained the Romanesque portals with fanciful carvings mixing New Testament stories and mythological creatures. The facility was seized by the state in 1836, but was restored and came back to life as a Benedictine monastery in 1954. The monks make wine and offer tours of the church and the burial crypt of the kings of Navarra. You can hear the monks singing Gregorian chants during Monday to Saturday services.

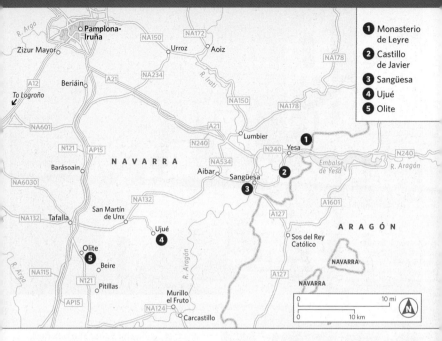

1. Monasterio de Leyre
2. Castillo de Javier
3. Sangüesa
4. Ujué
5. Olite

Spending the Night on Mount Leyre

Hotel Hospedería de Leyre occupies a portion of the monastery and offers simple but comfortable rooms. Its restaurant specializes in Navarra veal, a controlled regional designation under E.U. regulations. Monasterio de Leyre. ☎ 948-88-41-00. www.hotelhospederia deleyre.com. 32 rooms. Doubles 63€–76€. Entrees 16€–22€. MC, V. Lunch & dinner daily.

A hiking path to the summit of Mount Leyre departs from the monastery parking lot. An easier walk leads to a mountain spring and picnic area. ☺ 1 hr. Off N-240 outside Yesa. ☎ 948-88-41-50. 2.30€ adults, .60€ kids 6–12, free for kids 5 & under. Mon–Fri 10:15am–2pm and 3:30–7pm, Sat–Sun 10:15am–2pm and 4–7pm.

Follow signs toward Javier on N-240, taking turnoff on NA-5411 for total of 14km (8⅔ miles) to Javier.

❷ **Castillo de Javier.** The patron saint of Navarra, Francisco Javier (or Francis Xavier), was born in 1506 in this 11th-century castle. The Jesuit order, founded by Javier and Ignatius de Loyola in 1540, owns the property; visits to

Spending the Night near Castillo de Javier

There's a bigger hotel in the area around the castle, but the simple **Hotel El Mesón** has the edge on charm. Its restaurant focuses on Navarrese favorites like roast pork, beef, and salt cod. Plaza de Javier. ☎ 948-88-40-35. www.hotelmeson.com. 8 rooms. Doubles 65€. Entrees 9€–20€. AE, MC, V. Lunch & dinner daily.

the castle include Francisco's bedroom as well as the oratory and main keep. On weekends families picnic on the parklike castle grounds. ☺ 1 hr. NA-5411 between Yesa and Sangüesa. ☎ 948-88-40-24. 2€ adults, 1€ kids 6–12, free for kids 5 & under. Mar–Oct daily 10am–2pm and 3:30–7pm; Nov–Feb closes 6pm.

Follow signs toward Sangüesa on NA-5411 for 9km (5⅔ miles).

❸ **Sangüesa.** Sangüesa flourished in the Middle Ages as a stopover for Santiago pilgrims crossing northern Spain. The atmospheric Old Town is full of private palaces and small parish churches from the 12th to the 15th century.

> *The Gothic church next to Olite's fairy-tale Palacio Real is a popular place for wedding photos.*

> *Scenes from the Old and New Testaments adorn Santa María la Real in Sangüesa.*

At the main church of **Santa María la Real,** outstanding carved stone saints adorn the south portal. Santa María: ☉ 20 min. C/ Mayor, s/n. ☎ 948-87-10-84. Free. Daily 10am-1:30pm and 4:30-6:30pm.

Leave Sangüesa on the NA-132 toward Tafalla for a drive through rolling vineyards for 30km (19 miles) to San Martín de Unx. Turn left and follow NA-5310 8km (5 miles) to Ujué.

❹ **Ujué.** This medieval mountaintop village clutches the skirts of the hulking **Iglesia Fortaleza de Santa María de Ujué** castle, where villagers sought refuge during the ongoing warfare of the Middle Ages. Even though the Romanesque-Gothic structure is closed for restoration, it's worth walking up through town to see the main portal, where 12th-century stone carvings show laborers in the vineyards.

You can also enjoy chorizo and a glass of wine while shopping for local products at **Pastas Urrutia.** Iglesia: ☉ 1 hr. Off NA-5310 outside San Martín de Unx. ☎ 948-73-90-46. www.cfnavarra.es. Free. Closed at least through 2010 for restoration. Pastas: C/ San Isidro, 41. ☎ 948-73-92-57. Entrees 4€-10€. Cash only. Lunch & dinner daily.

> *Pilgrims climb the cobbled streets up to Ujúe's fortress-church—barefoot.*

Backtrack to San Martín and follow NA-5300 18km (11 miles) to Olite.

⑤ Olite. Carlos III of Navarra ordered the **Palacio Real** built in 1406. Even today its turreted high defensive walls give the town the air of a Gothic romance. Adjacent to the royal quarters is the beautiful Gothic church **Santa María la Real de Olite.** Wedding parties congregate for photos before the flower-carved main portal.

Navarra wines are little known outside Spain. The **Museo de la Viña y el Vino** chronicles winemaking since Roman days but concentrates on recent advances in viticulture and technology.

A tour of the **Bodega Marco Real** facility outside Olite will open your eyes—and taste buds—to Navarra wine. Palacio Real: ◷ 1 hr. Plaza Carlos III El Noble. ☎ 948-74-00-35. www. guiartenavarra.com. 3.10€, 6€ guided visit with Santa María. Mon–Fri 10am–7pm; Sat–Sun 10am–8pm. Guided tours Mon–Fri noon; Sat–Sun 12:30 and 5:30pm. Santa María: ◷ 10 min. Plaza Teobaldos, s/n. 948-74-17-03. www.turismo.navarra. es. Free. Mon–Sat 10am–7pm; Sun 11am–6:30pm.

Museo: ◷ 30 min. Plaza Teobaldos, 4. ☎ 948-74-12-73. www.museodelvinodenavarra.com. 3.50€ adults, 2€ seniors and students. Easter to mid-Oct Mon–Sat 10am–2pm and 4–7pm, Sun 10am–2pm; mid-Oct to Easter Mon–Sat closes 6pm, Sun closes 1pm. Bodega: ◷ 1 hr. N-121, km 38. ☎ 948-71-21-93. www.familiabelasco.com. 7€ guided tour and tasting. Fri–Sat 10:30am, 12:30pm, and 4:30pm; Sun 10:30am and 12:30pm.

Pamplona-Iruña

The capital of the Kingdom of Navarra since 824, Pamplona reached its apogee under Carlos III (1361–1425), who became king in 1387. An important stop on the French pilgrimage routes to Santiago, Pamplona (Iruña in Basque) has hosted popes, bishops, and kings. But its modern fame lies in Ernest Hemingway's 1926 depiction of the running of the bulls, or *encierro*, in *The Sun Also Rises.* With due respect to Papa, the sun also goes down, and when the air cools around sunset, everyone comes out into the blue shadows of the streets for drinks and tapas.

> Pamplona's encierro *terminates in the city's bullring; only the courageous, or foolish depending on which way you look at it, run in front of the bulls.*

START Coralillos de Santo Domingo.

❶ ★ Encierro Route. Unless you visit during the Sanfermines (San Fermín) festival, you won't see bulls running in the streets, but the route of the spectacle is a good introduction to the city. Begin at the **Coralillos** behind the Museo de Navarra, and follow **C/ Santo Domingo** past the **Mercado Publico** on Plaza Santiago. The bulls are just gaining speed when they turn onto **C/ Mercaderes** and make a tight 90-degree right onto **C/ Estafeta.** This is where camera crews film footage of bulls plunging into the crowds and where souvenir

hunters buy bull-emblazoned T-shirts at **La Curva de la Estafeta,** C/ Mercaderes, 23 (☎ 638-16-94-66; MC, V). Across the street, locals line up on Saturday mornings for fresh-baked cookies at **Confiteria Layana,** C/ Calceteros, 12 (☎ 948-22-11-24; cash only). The bulls race the length of Estafeta to the **Plaza de Toros** (where the leafy walkway next to the ring is—naturally—called Paseo Hemingway). Local clubs play Basque *pelota* (jai alai) at the Labrit Fronton, C/ Juan de Labrit, s/n (☎ 948-22-21-76), next to the **bullring.** Walk in and catch players practicing. ⊕ 1 hr.

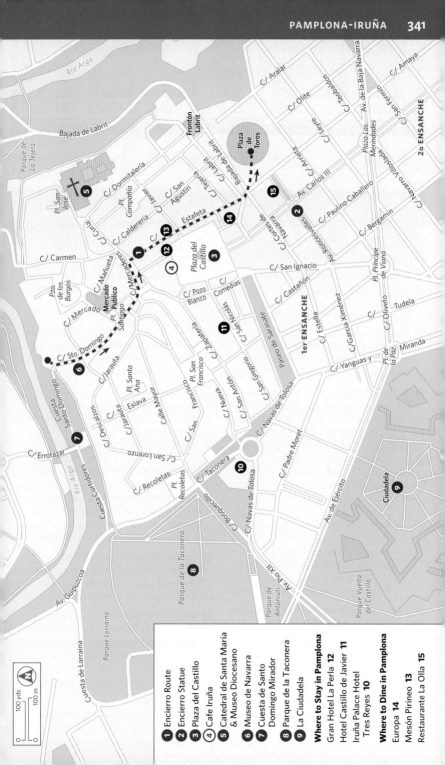

2o ENSANCHE

1er ENSANCHE

Río Arga

Parque de La Tejera

Bajada de Labrit

Frontón Labrit

Plaza de Toros

C/ Aralar
C/ Olite
C/ Teobaldos
Av. de la Baja Navarra
C/ San Fermín
C/ Amaya
C/ Leyre
Plaza Las Merindades
C/ Navarro Villoslada
C/ Dormitalería
Pl. San José
Pl. Compañía
C/ Javier
C/ San Agustín
C/ Tejería
C/ Labrit
Bajada de Labrit
Av. Carlos III
C/ Paulino Caballero
C/ Bergamín
C/ Curia
C/ Caldarería
Estafeta
C/ Roncesvalles
Av. de Cortes de Navarra
C/ Carmen
C/ Mañueta
C/ Mercaderes
Plaza del Castillo
C/ San Ignacio
C/ Príncipe de Viana
Pza. de los Burgos
Mercado Público
C/ Pozo Blanco
Comedias
C/ Castañón
Tudela
C/ Mercado
Pl. Santiago
C/ Estafeta
C/ San Nicolás
C/ García Ximénez
C/ Oliveto
Miranda
C/ Sto. Domingo
C/ Jarauta
Pl. Santa Ana
Pl. San Francisco
C/ Zapatería
Paseo de Sarasate
C/ Estella
Pl. de la Paz
C/ Yanguas y
Cuesta Santo Domingo
C/ Errotazar
Río Arga
Cuesta Curtidores
C/ Jarauta
C/ Descalzos
Eslava
Calle Mayor
C/ San Francisco
C/ Nueva
C/ San Antón
C/ San Gregorio
C/ Navas de Tolosa
C/ San Lorenzo
C/ Recoletas
Pl. Recoletas
C/ Bosquecillo
C/ Taconera
C/ Navas de Tolosa
C/ Padre Moret
Ciudadela
Av. de Ejército
Parque de la Taconera
Parque de Antoniutti
Av. Pío XII
Parque Vuelta del Castillo
Av. Guipúzcoa
Cuesta de Larraina
Parque Larraina

100 yds
100 m

Where to Stay in Pamplona

1. Encierro Route
2. Encierro Statue
3. Plaza del Castillo
4. Cafe Iruña
5. Catedral de Santa María & Museo Diocesano
6. Museo de Navarra
7. Cuesta de Santo Domingo Mirador
8. Parque de la Taconera
9. La Ciudadela

Where to Stay in Pamplona

Gran Hotel La Perla **12**
Hotel Castillo de Javier **11**
Iruña Palace Hotel Tres Reyes **10**

Where to Dine in Pamplona

Europa **14**
Mesón Pirineo **13**
Restaurante La Olla **15**

> *Hemingway saw his first bullfight in Pamplona in 1923; a good part of the rest of his time there was spent at Cafe Iruña.*

❷ Encierro Statue. This dynamic bronze captures the sheer animal exertion of the crowd running in the streets ahead of the bulls. Avenida de Roncesvalles.

❸ Plaza del Castillo. Cafe tables line this neoclassical grand square that is the heart of modern Pamplona. Less exciting than the Encierro statue, the soaring 1903 bronze of a female figure recalls the fight of the Navarrese and Basque people to hold onto their ancient charter of laws, or *fueros,* which the central government tried to abrogate in the late 19th century.

④ **🍸 Cafe Iruña.** You'll pay a premium to sip a dark rum outdoors at Cafe Iruña, but you'll be channeling Ernesto El Grande. The bar calls itself the *rincón de Hemingway* ("Hemingway's spot"). Plaza Castillo, 44. ☎ 948-22-20-64. $$

❺ ★ Catedral de Santa María & Museo Diocesano. The don't-miss sight here is the royal tomb with sculpted alabaster death statues of Carlos III and his wife, Leonor de Trastámara. The soaring Gothic vaults are also impressive, especially since Navarra was firmly stuck in Romanesque style when the church was begun in the late 14th century. The early sculptures in the museum have been so restored and stripped of their patina that they seem more reproduction than Gothic. ⏱ 1 hr. C/ Dormitalería,

3-5. ☎ 948-21-25-94. 4.40€ adults, 2.50€ kids. Mid-Sept to mid-July Mon–Fri 10am–2pm and 4–7pm, Sat 10am–2pm; mid-July to mid-Sept Mon–Fri 10am–7pm and Sat 10am–2pm.

❻ ★★ Museo de Navarra. The somber exterior of the former hospital conceals sweeping galleries inside. Start with the Roman mosaics (mostly 4th c. A.D.) before moving on to the Muslim stone carvings and the carved ivory chest (ca. A.D. 1000). The Gothic frescoes—admittedly faded glories—are some of the best of their kind in Spain. The museum's Goya is on the third floor. ⏱ 2 hr. C/ Santo Domingo, 47. ☎ 848-42-64-92. www.cfnavarra.es/cultura/museo. 2€ adults, 1€ seniors and kids, free Sat afternoon and Sun. Tues–Sat 9:30am–2pm and 5–7pm; Sun 11am–2pm.

❼ Cuesta de Santo Domingo Mirador. From the museum, the Cuesta de Santo Domingo and Cuesta de Curtidores follow the crest of the ancient city walls with striking westward views.

❽ Parque de la Taconera. You can enter the park by following Cuesta de Curtidores through an arch and over a highway bridge. A short walk into this green space leads to the old moat, where deer, goats, and peafowl intermingle in a strangely sweet Pamplonan peaceable kingdom.

❾ La Ciudadela. Now a park where youths play pickup soccer games, this pentagonal fortress was built from 1571 to 1645 and proved impregnable—until Napoleon came along.

Where to Stay & Dine

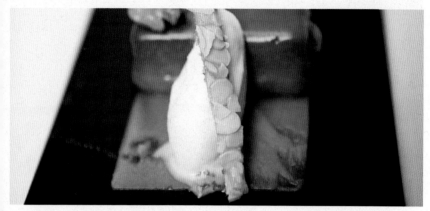

> *Cutting edge fare at Europa.*

★★ Europa CONTEMPORARY BASQUE
Just off Plaza de Castillo, this upstairs hideaway is the showcase of chef Pilar Idoate, a leader in the second generation of cutting-edge chefs who are reinterpreting Basque cuisine. The 62€ tasting menu will let you try a little of everything. The wine cellar is a brilliant cross-section of Rioja and the best of Navarra. C/ Espoz y Mina, 11. ☎ 948-22-18-00. Entrees 21€–25€. AE, MC, V. Lunch & dinner daily.

★ Gran Hotel La Perla
Some of Navarra's most famous visitors have slept in this stately 1881 grand hotel on the city's finest plaza. When the hotel reopened in 2007 after a 2-year restoration, each room was dedicated to one of these personages, including Hemingway, Charlie Chaplin, Orson Welles, and legendary matador Manolete. Plaza del Castillo, 1. ☎ 948-22-30-00. www.granhotellaperla.com. 44 rooms. Doubles 240€–325€. AE, DC, MC, V.

Hotel Castillo de Javier
This modern budget hotel occupies an old building in the heart of the nightlife district—a good location if you don't mind the party scene below your window. If you plan to turn in early, ask for an inside room. C/ San Nicolás, 50–52. ☎ 948-20-30-40. www.hotelcastillojavier.com. 19 rooms. Doubles 63€–69€. MC, V.

Iruña Palace Hotel Tres Reyes
Furnishings may be a little worn (though upgrades are ongoing), but you can't beat the location at the edge of the Taconera park, steps from the Old Town. Parkview rooms, with vistas of trees and distant mountains, make you feel like you're in the Navarra countryside. Jardínes de la Taconera, s/n. ☎ 948-22-66-00. www.hotel3reyes.com. 160 rooms. Doubles 112€–213€. AE, DC, MC, V.

Mesón Pirineo NAVARRESE
There's a quiet restaurant in back, but most patrons stop at the bar to fill up on generous tapas that offer new twists on traditional flavors. Try the ground meat and sausage in tomato sauce or shellfish in béchamel—both served in huge scallop shells. C/ Estafeta, 41. ☎ 948-20-77-02. Tapas 2.50€. V. Lunch & dinner daily.

Restaurante La Olla NAVARRESE
The name hints at only half the menu—casseroles featuring meat and vegetables from the nearby countryside. La Olla also puts its wood grill to work on veal chops and steaks. The Sunday special is roasted milk-fed lamb. Avenida Roncesvalles, 2. ☎ 948-22-95-58. Entrees 11€–21€. AE, DC, MC, V. Lunch & dinner daily.

Navarra & La Rioja Fast Facts

> *Safety first at* el encierro.

Arriving & Getting Around

BY PLANE Flying into Pamplona is an expensive proposition but sometimes there's no way around it. Flights from Madrid and Barcelona arrive daily at **Aeropuerto de Noaín** (☎ 902-40-47-04; www.aena.com), about 6.5km (4 miles) from town. A taxi (there's no bus) to town is about 13€. **BY TRAIN** **RENFE** (☎ 902-24-02-02; www.renfe.es) handles train service to Pamplona (Plaza Princípe de Viana), Logroño (Plaza de Europa, s/n), and Haro (Barrio de las Bodegas). **BY BUS** More than 20 bus lines service Pamplona's **Estacion de Autobuses,** C/ Conde Olivetto at corner of C/ Yanguas y Miranda (☎ 948-2-35-66). The **Logroño** station, Avenida de España, 1 (☎ 941-23-59-83), has bus connections with Madrid, Pamplona, and the **Haro** station at Plaza Castañares de Rioja, 4 (☎ 941-31-15-43). **BY CAR** The **A-68** highway parallels the Río Ebro, connecting the main towns of Rioja's wine districts and continuing to Zaragoza. The **AP-15** runs south from Pamplona through Olite, while the **A-12** runs west to Logroño. Access to Pamplona from Bilbao or Santander is via the **A-10.**

ATMs

You'll find 24-hour ATMs throughout the region, even in the smallest villages. Most accept Maestro/MasterCard, Cirrus, and Visa.

Booking Services

There are no booking services in Navarra and La Rioja. Local tourist offices, however, will advise on lodging availability.

Doctors & Hospitals

For emergency medical or dental attention, go to the *centro de urgencia* (emergency room) of the nearest hospital. **PAMPLONA-IRUÑA Hospital de Navarra,** C/ Irunlarrea, 3 (☎ 848-42-22-22). Non-E.U. residents can consult national health service doctors for a relatively small fee; ask at your hotel for a list of doctors.

Emergencies

The all-around emergency number in Spain is ☎ **112.** For an ambulance, call ☎ **061.**

Internet Access

Wi-Fi has become common in most hotels and is increasingly offered as a free amenity except in business hotels. Hotels without in-room Internet connections may provide access through a public computer. Internet cafes are common.

Pharmacies

To find an open pharmacy outside normal business hours, check the list of stores posted on the door of any drugstore. By law, there's always a drugstore open somewhere. Drugstores are called *farmacías*. When open, they display a neon green cross.

Police

Call ☎ **091** for the national police or ☎ **092** for the local police. The Guardia Civil can be reached at ☎ **062.**

Post Office

HARO The main post office is at Avenida de la Rioja, 10 (☎ 941-31-18-69). **LOGROÑO** The main post office is at C/ Perez Galdos, 40 (☎ 941-28-68-02). **PAMPLONA** The main post office is at C/ Pablo Sarasate, 9 (☎ 948-20-72-17). **SANTO DOMINGO DE LA CALZADA** The main post office is at Avenida Burgos, 10–12 (☎ 941-34-14-93).

Safety

Both cities and countryside are generally quite safe in Navarra and La Rioja, though it's prudent to hold your valuables close on the crowded drinking and tapas districts in Pamplona. The annual Sanfermines celebration also brings a rowdy crowd to town—steer clear of drunks. Use common sense and avoid deserted streets at night and during the afternoon closing hours. Take care not to leave anything visible in a parked car, especially overnight or at the beach.

Visitor Information

PAMPLONA Oficina de Turismo, C/ Eslava, 1 (☎ 848-42-04-20; www.turismo.navarra. es), also has information on the remainder of Navarra. It is open Monday to Saturday 10am to 2pm and 4 to 7pm, Sunday 10am to 2pm. **LA RIOJA Oficina de Turismo,** Paseo de El Espolón, Principe de Vergara, 1, Logroño (☎ 902-27-72-00; www.lariojaturismo.com), provides information on the entire autonomous region of La Rioja. It is open Monday to Friday 10am

to 2pm and 4 to 7pm, Saturday and Sunday 10am to 2pm and 5 to 7pm. **ESTELLA Oficina de Turismo,** C/ San Nicolás, 1 (☎ 948-55-63-01; www.turismo.navarra.es), is open Monday to Saturday 10am to 2pm and 4 to 7pm, Sunday 10am to 2pm. **HARO Oficina de Turismo,** Plaza Monseñor Florentino Rodríguez, s/n (☎ 941-30-33-66; www.beronia.org), is open July to September Tuesday to Saturday 10am to 2pm and 4:30 to 7:30pm, Sunday 10am to 2pm; from October to June it's open Monday to Friday 10am to 2pm, Saturday 10am to 2pm and 4 to 7pm. **JAVIER Oficina de Turismo,** C/ Zona Turística, s/n (☎ 948-88-43-87; www.turismo.navarra.es), is open Monday to Saturday 10am to 2pm and 4 to 7pm, Sunday 10am to 2pm. **LOGROÑO Oficina Municipal de Turismo,** C/ Portales, 50 (☎ 941-27-33-53; www.logroturismo.org), is open July to September daily 10am to 2:30pm and 5 to 8:30pm; October to June Monday to Saturday 10am to 2pm and 4:30 to 7:30pm, Sunday 10am to 2pm. **NÁJERA Oficina de Turismo,** Plaza San Miguel, s/n (☎ 941-36-00-41; www.najerasanmillan.com), is open Tuesday to Friday 10am to 1:30pm and 4 to 6pm, Saturday 10am to 2pm and 4 to 7pm, Sunday 10:30am to 2pm. **OLITE Oficina de Turismo,** Plaza de los Teobaldos (☎ 948-74-17-03; www.turismo.navarra.es), is open Monday to Saturday 10am to 2pm and 4 to 7pm, Sunday 10am to 2pm. **PUENTE DE LA REINA Oficina Municipal de Turismo,** C/ Mayor, 105, at Casa del Vínculo (☎ 948-34-08-45; www.puentelareina-gares.es), is open Monday to Saturday 10am to 2pm and 4 to 7pm, Sunday 10am to 2pm. **SANGÜESA Oficina de Turismo,** C/ Mayor, 2 (☎ 948-87-14-11; www.turismo.navarra.es), is open Monday to Saturday 10am to 2pm and 4 to 7pm, Sunday 10am to 2pm. **SAN MILLÁN DE LA COGOLLA Oficina de Turismo,** Monasterio de Yuso (☎ 941-37-32-59; www.lariojaturismo.com), is open Tuesday to Sunday 9:30am to 1:30pm and 3:30 to 6:30pm. **SANTO DOMINGO DE LA CALZADA Oficina de Turismo,** C/ Mayor, 33 (☎ 902-11-26-60; www.santodomingodelacalzada.org), is open Tuesday to Friday 11am to 7pm, Saturday and Sunday 10am to 8pm.

12
Aragón

The Best of Aragón in 4 Days

Best known as the home turf of King Fernando II, whose marriage to Isabel of Castilla y León in 1469 effectively united the Spanish crown, Aragón is often neglected by travelers. Yet this region of rich vineyards and orchards played a pivotal role in Spanish history. It was the northern locus of Islamic learning into the 11th century, and conquering Christian kings showed a wise tolerance that gave Aragón a vibrant medieval culture best evidenced in its splendid Mudéjar architecture.

> PREVIOUS PAGE *The belfry of Tarazona's Catedral.* THIS PAGE *A succession of churches have stood on the miraculous site of the Basilica del Pilar.*

START Tarazona. TRIP LENGTH 343km (213 miles).

1 Tarazona. Populated for most of the past 3,000 years, Tarazona reached its apex in the medieval period, when Jewish, Muslim, and Christian communities existed side by side. The atmospheric town is best appreciated on a walking tour to see the exteriors of the historic structures that tell its tale.

Tarazona's impressive **Catedral,** at Plaza La Seo, has been closed for restoration since the 1980s, though parts may reopen in 2010. Its exterior chronicles Aragonese architectural styles from Gothic to Renaissance. The heart of the building dates from the original 13th-century construction, but its towers are superb examples of Mudéjar design.

Hike through the Judería and adjacent Morería (the Jewish and Muslim barrios on the north hill in the center of town) to the hulking **Palacio Episcopal** at Plaza de Palacio. The Muslim palace was seized by the kings of Aragón as a royal residence and converted to the bishop's palace in the late 1300s. More Muslim than Mudéjar, the building sets the town's architectural tone.

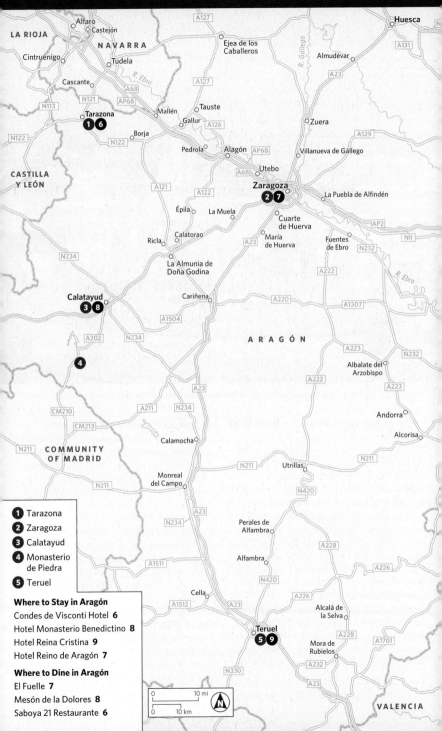

LA RIOJA
Alfaro
Castejón
NAVARRA
Huesca
Cintruénigo
Tudela
Ejea de los Caballeros
Almudévar
A127
A131
Cascante
R. Ebro
A68
A127
A23
N121
AP68
N113
Mallén
Tauste
Zuera
N122
Tarazona **1** **6**
Gallur
A126
Villanueva de Gállego
A129
Borja
Pedrola
Alagón
AP68
N122
A121
Utebo
Zaragoza **2** **7**
La Puebla de Alfindén
CASTILLA Y LEÓN
A122
Épila
La Muela
Cuarte de Huerva
AP2
NII
A23
María de Huerva
Fuentes de Ebro
N232
Ricla
Calatorao
R. Ebro
N234
La Almunia de Doña Godina
A222
Calatayud **3** **8**
Cariñena
A220
A1307
A1504
ARAGÓN
A202
N234
A223
N232
4
Albalate del Arzobispo
A222
A223
CM210
A23
A211
N234
Andorra
CM213
Calamocha
Alcorisa
N211
COMMUNITY OF MADRID
N211
N211
N211
Utrillas
Monreal del Campo
N420
N211
A23
N234
Perales de Alfambra
A228
A1511
Alfambra
A226
N420
Cella
A226
A1512
A23
Alcalá de la Selva
Teruel **5** **9**
A228
A1701
Mora de Rubielos
A232
N330
A23
VALENCIA

1 Tarazona
2 Zaragoza
3 Calatayud
4 Monasterio de Piedra
5 Teruel

Where to Stay in Aragón
Condes de Visconti Hotel **6**
Hotel Monasterio Benedictino **8**
Hotel Reina Cristina **9**
Hotel Reino de Aragón **7**

Where to Dine in Aragón
El Fuelle **7**
Mesón de la Dolores **8**
Saboya 21 Restaurante **6**

0   10 mi
0   10 km

> *Take the Ruta Turística for a panoramic view of Tarazona from Santa María Magdalena's Mudéjar tower.*

The adjacent late Romanesque **Santa María Magdalena,** Plaza de Palacio, dates from the early 15th century. The squat form of the church is lifted by a soaring Mudéjar tower.

Tarazona's Renaissance **Ayuntamiento** (town hall) at Plaza de España features a triumphal frieze of Carlos V entering Bologna in 1529 to be crowned Holy Roman Emperor. But Carlos is upstaged by much larger reliefs of Hercules performing heroic deeds—which tradition says took place on the slopes of Sierra del Moncayo, the 2,315m (7,595-ft.) mountain southeast of town. An abstract iron statue represents **El Cipotegato,** the local jester who races from the Ayuntamiento at noon on August 27 as townspeople pelt him with tomatoes. The messy event launches the 5-day festival of the town's patron, San Atilano. ⏱ 2 hr. Santa María Magdalena: Open for services only Sat 6pm, Sun 10am.

Follow the N-122 east for 35km (22 miles). Pick up the AP-68 for 45km (28 miles) to Zaragoza.

2 Zaragoza. Founded by Carthaginians, Zaragoza rose to prominence in the 1st century B.C. as the Roman colony of Caesaraugusta. It flourished from 1018 to 1118 as an independent Muslim *taifa* (principality) that joined forces with the Christians of Aragón to battle the Almoravids of Sevilla—an alliance that eased the inclusion of Muslims into Aragonese society. Modern Zaragoza is interwoven with the historic city that centers on **Plaza del Pilar.** Accented by a sculptural waterfall, the monumental plaza stretches from a segment of Roman wall at one end to the 12th-century cathedral at the other.

Between them stands the majestic ★★ **Basílica del Pilar,** built from 1681 to 1872 on the site where tradition holds that in A.D. 40, an apparition of the Virgin Mary presented St. James with a tiny statue of herself and a jasper column (the *pilar*). James built a chapel on the site a year later, and a succession of churches have followed to accommodate pilgrims. Even the

> *Zaragoza has seen uninterrupted human settlement for 2,000 years; here, the streets of its medieval quarter.*

exuberantly baroque basilica cannot diminish the simple appeal of the ancient small statue in the Capilla Sagrada.

St. James built his chapel just steps from the forum of the flourishing Roman town. A modern glass entrance leads to the **Museo del Foro de Caesaraugusta.** The subterranean facility integrates interpretive panels with portions of the forum buildings and related structures.

The east end of Plaza del Pilar is anchored by the ★★ **Catedral San Salvador.** A Romanesque church was constructed in the 12th century precisely where a Roman basilica, a Visigoth church, and the city's main mosque had once stood. When the church was heightened in the 14th century to incorporate Gothic ideas of light and volume, Mudéjar masters from Zaragoza and Sevilla created brick walls that are effectively polychrome geometric tapestries.

At this point, if you need a sightseeing break, stop for a tapa at **Las Palomas,** also on Plaza del Pilar. If you like what you try, come back in the evening for the tapas buffet.

One of Zaragoza's most spectacular examples of Mudéjar brick-and-tile architecture is the tower of ★ **Santa María Magdalena,** Plaza Magdalena, a few blocks behind the cathedral. The early-14th-century tower was modeled on an Almohad minaret.

> *A small statue with a large following—the Virgen del Pilar in Zaragoza's Holy Chapel.*

Not all central Zaragoza is Roman or Mudéjar. The ★ **Museo Ibercaja Camón Aznar,** in a Renaissance palace, has a Goya-centric vision of Spanish art—not surprising since the artist was raised in the city. One floor is filled with minor Goya paintings and a superb collection of his masterful, often surreal engravings. Other floors display earlier art leading up to Goya and later art proceeding from the master.

This city also harbors a masterpiece of Muslim architecture. ★★ **La Aljafería,** an 11th-century palace, captures the transition between the monumental architectural styles of Córdoba and Granada. Giuseppe Verdi was so taken with its defensive tower that he set his 1853 opera *Il Trovatore* here. Christian monarchs put their stamp on the complex by enlarging rather than destroying. Still, the core palace, with its delicate decoration of the *mihrab* (a niche in the wall that indicates the direction of Mecca), is the best part. Visits may be restricted when Aragón's regional government is in session. **Basílica:** ⏰ 30 min. Plaza del Pilar. ☎ 976-397-497. Free. Daily 6:45am–9:30pm. **Caesaraugusta:** ⏰ 45 min. Plaza de la Seo, 2. ☎ 976-399-752. www.zaragozacultural. com. 2.50€ adults, 1.80€ students, free for seniors. Tues–Sat 10am–1:30pm and 5–8:30pm; Sun 10am–1:30pm. Closed Sept 16–19. **Catedral:** ⏰ 30 min. Plaza de la Seo. ☎ 976-291-231. 3€ adults, 1.50€ seniors and students. Sept 16–June 15 Mon–Fri 10am–1:30pm and 4–6pm, Sat 10am–noon and 4–6pm, Sun 10–11:30am and 4–6pm; June 16–Sept

15 Mon–Fri 10am–6pm, Sat 10am–noon and 3–6pm, Sun 10am–noon and 2:30–6pm. **Las Palomas:** Plaza del Pilar, 16. ☎ 976-392-366. www.restaurantelas palomas.com. Buffet 9.75€. AE, MC, V. Lunch & dinner daily. **Ibercaja:** ⏰ 1 hr. C/ Espoz y Mina, 23. ☎ 976-397-328. Free. Tues–Sat 10am–2pm and 5–8:30pm; Sun 10am–2pm. **Aljafería:** ⏰ 2 hr. Parque de la Aljaferia. ☎ 976-289-685. www.cortesaragon. es. 3€ adults, 1€ seniors and students, free Sun. Daily 10am–1:30pm and 4:30–7:30pm.

Follow the A-2 toward Madrid for 91km (57 miles) to Calatayud.

❸ **Calatayud.** Above town, ruins of an 8th-century castle attest to how quickly the Moors took over the Iberian Peninsula. They founded Calatayud in 716, just 5 years after the North African invasion. Alfonso I of Aragón conquered Calatayud in 1120, but the Muslim artisans stayed and helped build many of the city's monumental structures in the Mudéjar style. Walk through the town to see the exteriors of some of the region's major examples of Mudéjar architecture.

From Plaza del Fuerte, head uphill to **Colegiata de Santa María,** C/ Baltasar Gracián (open only for services on Sat evenings and Sun mornings). The core of this church was built in the 13th century on the site of the main mosque. Most of the exterior is now baroque, but the lower portion of the tower preserves the original Mudéjar construction and the upper section imitates it. The extraordinary 16th-century carving in alabaster at the main entrance was originally conceived as an altarpiece.

Nearby **San Andrés,** Plaza San Andrés (open only for services on Sat evenings and Sun mornings), is another outstanding example of the medieval fortress-church of central Spain's Catholic/

> *Teruel's Mudéjar Iglesia de San Pedro.*

Muslim borderlands. Its three naves were originally a mosque, while its vaults date from the 14th and 15th centuries. Its Mudéjar decorative brickwork is the best preserved in Calatayud.

Turn downhill on C/ Rúa de Dato to **Plaza de España,** a charmingly old-fashioned plaza surrounded by 17th- and 18th-century houses that tilt at different angles. In the southeast corner, **Ciria Vinos y Licores,** Plaza de España, 32 (☎ 976-885-809; cash only), specializes in wines from DO Calatayud—a region celebrated for its *garnacha tinta* reds.

The short-lived Roman community of **Bilbilis,** off km 4.5 of the Carretera Soria, flourished in the 1st century A.D. The ruins outside of town, under excavation since 1971, are open for viewing. ☉ Half-day.

Follow the A-202 south for 31km (19 miles) to Monasterio de Piedra.

❹ ★★ **Monasterio de Piedra.** Founded at the height of the 19th-century Romantic movement's exaltation of Nature, this natural park around an 1195 Cistercian monastery boasts lakes, grottoes, and thunderous waterfalls. You might want to skip the fish farm, but the thrice-daily falconry demonstration (Mar–Oct) is fascinating. Guided visits include the monastery, a wine museum, a carriage museum, and an exhibition on history of chocolate. (The monastery claims to have been the first in Europe to make chocolate.) ☉ 1 day. A-2 exit 204 or 231, Carretera Nuévalos. ☎ 902-196-052. www.monasteriopiedra.com. 13€ adults, 9€ seniors and kids 4–12, free for kids 3 & under. Apr–Oct 9am–8pm; Nov–Mar 9am–6pm.

Follow A-2506 and A-1507 toward Calamocha for 75km (47 miles). Take A-23 66km (41 miles) to Teruel.

❺ **Teruel.** Virtually an open-air museum of Mudéjar architecture, Teruel is visually stunning. Most visitors approach from the north, walking up the 1920s neo-Mudéjar **L'Escalinata** stairs to enter town through the arch of the elaborately decorated 14th-century **Torre El Salvador.** The narrow street opens into the city's main square, **Plaza del Torico,** built around a fountain flowing from the mouth of a bull. The bull has been a civic symbol since Alfonso II captured the city in 1171. Teruel's Mudéjar style helped inspire 19th-century Modernista architecture, such as the striking **Caja Rural de Teruel,** Plaza Carlos Castel,

> *The woodland wonderland of the Monasterio de Piedra also includes a chocolate museum, monastery, and abbey-turned-hotel.*

a lilac-blue building with white floral designs. Jewelry at nearby **Tena,** C/ Tozal, 6 (☎ 978-612-314), reproduces the city's Mudéjar and Modernista motifs in miniature.

The 14th-century Mudéjar masterpiece ★★ **San Pedro** contains a chapel dedicated to Los Amantes, ill-fated medieval lovers whose legend looms larger than the church's towers. Visiting is a package deal—lots of high-tech Amantes displays eventually lead to the church.

The ★★★ **Catedral de Santa María de Mediavilla** is widely considered the most beautiful surviving example of Mudéjar architecture. Its towers, dome, and roof are all designated as part of UNESCO's World Heritage, but the coffered ceiling of the central nave is also a masterwork. San Pedro: ☉ 1 hr. Plaza de los Amantes. ☎ 978-618-398. www.amantesdeteruel.es. 8€ adults, 6€ seniors and kids 8–15, kids 7 & under free. Daily 10am–2pm and 4–8pm. Catedral: ☉ 30 min. Plaza de la Catedral. ☎ 978-618-016. 3€ adults, 2.40€ seniors and students. Summer Mon–Sat 11am–2pm and 4–8pm; winter closes 7pm.

MUDÉJAR ARCHITECTURE

Wedding Muslim Beauty to Christian Form

BY PATRICIA HARRIS & DAVID LYON

FROM ITS EMERGENCE in León in the 11th century to its apogee in Aragón in the 15th century, Mudéjar architecture represented the purest synthesis of architectural forms of Christian Europe with decorative motifs and construction techniques developed in the Muslim world. The term *Mudéjar* is a corruption of a medieval Arabic word for "domesticated," and refers to Muslim craftsmen who chose to remain in their home regions of Spain following the Christian Reconquista. Because Mudéjar style deals primarily with surfaces rather than structure, it is found on buildings that range from Romanesque to Renaissance. Mudéjar style lasted into the 16th century, when the expulsion of Muslims from Spain banished the craftsmen and architects to North Africa and the Middle East.

Pedro's Jewel

Begun in 1362 under orders of Pedro I ("the Cruel"), the **Palacio Mudéjar** in Sevilla's Real Alcázar (above) represents a convergence of at least three Islamic architectural traditions: formal construction techniques (including the horseshoe arch and patios surrounded by arcades), exquisite carved plaster friezes and doorway details (probably carved by artists from Granada who also worked in the Alhambra), and highly sophisticated tiling (probably by Sevilla's own Muslim ceramicists).

Mudéjar Mother Lodes

In 1986, UNESCO designated the cathedral and three other churches (including **San Pedro,** left) in Teruel as the Mudéjar Architecture World Heritage Site. In 2001, the designation was expanded to embrace six additional churches in Zaragoza, Calatayud, and the small town of Cervera de la Cañada. In addition to these sites in Aragón, other key locations to see Mudéjar style include León, Valladolid, Toro, Sahagún (near León), Toledo, and many of the early churches and convents throughout Sevilla.

The Hallmarks

BRICKS: Most Mudéjar buildings in Aragón are constructed of brick, a material that lends itself especially well to sophisticated geometric decoration. Walls of Romanesque and Gothic churches tended to be very thick, allowing craftsmen to configure the surface bricks with protruding corners that create complex patterns.

WOOD: Sophisticated combinations of carved panels and geometrically arrayed beams characterize Mudéjar wooden ceilings. They are usually found in rooms where the ceiling span does not exceed 6m (20 ft.), such as private chambers in palaces or small rooms in convents and monasteries. A major exception is the coffered ceiling of the main nave of the Teruel cathedral.

PLASTER: Plaster carving was a hallmark of the several Islamic architectural styles in Andalucía, and adaptations of those techniques decorate doorways, windows, and occasionally entire walls in Mudéjar build-

ings constructed in the Christian-dominated north.

TILES: Muslim craftsmen introduced tile artistry to Sevilla in the 8th century, and their abstract geometric tiles persist to this day as a popular decorative element in Spanish buildings. Mudéjar buildings often feature tiled floors, half-tiled walls, and tile decorations on their exteriors. The tower of San Salvador

in Teruel is often cited as one of the most harmonious combinations of Mudéjar tile and brickwork.

Where to Stay & Dine

> Locals favor grilled lamb and kid at El Fuelle.

Condes de Visconti Hotel TARAZONA

Occupying the minipalace of a Renaissance count, this charming small hotel is located only steps from Tarazona's main plazas. Some rooms are small, but all are imbued with character. C/ Visconti, 15. ☎ 976-644-908. www.condesdevisconti.com. 15 rooms. Doubles 68€–89€. AE, DC, MC, V.

El Fuelle ZARAGOZA ARAGONESE

Head for the Mudéjar tower of Santa María Magdalena to find this popular *asador* where locals favor wood-grilled Aragonese lamb or kid. C/ Mayor, 59. ☎ 976-398-033. Entrees 11€–16€. V. Lunch Tues–Sun, dinner Tues–Sat.

Hotel Monasterio Benedictino CALATAYUD

The monks in this 17th-century baroque structure would have been shocked by the bright color scheme and rich furnishings of the lush modern hotel, but guests are delighted. A market takes place on Tuesdays in the plaza in front. Plaza San Benito, 1. ☎ 976-891-500. www.hotelmonasteriobenedictino.com. 35 rooms. Doubles 77€–96€. AE, DC, MC, V.

Hotel Reina Cristina TERUEL

A convenient location with its own dedicated parking just outside the Torre El Salvador gate makes this ample, modern hotel an ideal location for exploring the Old City. Paseo del Óvalo, 1. ☎ 978-606-860. www.gargallohoteles.es. 81 rooms. Doubles 60–90€. MC, V.

Hotel Reino de Aragón ZARAGOZA

A short stroll from the historic district yet at the edge of a lively tapas scene, this superb business hotel has comfortable rooms and excellent service. Sixth-floor superior rooms have terraces with great views of the Mudéjar towers. C/ Coso, 8. ☎ 976-468-2000. www.hoteles-silken.com. 117 rooms. Doubles 65€–145€. AE, MC, V.

Mesón de la Dolores CALATAYUD ARAGONESE

Large portions and a creative approach to traditional cuisine make Dolores a town favorite. The menu features local vegetables from the Jalón valley and milk-fed lamb from the surrounding hills. Plaza de los Mesones, 4. ☎ 976-889-055. Entrees 13€–24€. AE, DC, MC, V. Lunch & dinner daily.

Saboya 21 Restaurante TARAZONA SPANISH

A classic Spanish menu emphasizes grilled beef and pork. Plus its proximity to La Rioja and Navarra guarantees a good selection of red and rosé wines. Plates tend to be generous, but light eaters can order half portions of many dishes. C/ Marrodán, 34. ☎ 976-643-515. Entrees 15€–20€. MC, V. Lunch Tues–Sun, dinner Tues–Sat.

Aragón Fast Facts

Arriving & Getting Around

BY PLANE Direct flights from Madrid and Barcelona arrive at the **Aeropuerto de Zaragoza** (☎ 976-712-300). **BY TRAIN** Train connections from Madrid and Barcelona are good for both Zaragoza and Calatayud. Trains arrive in Zaragoza at **Estación Delicias** just outside the city center (☎ 902-24-02-02). In Calatayud, trains arrive at **Estación Calatayud** on the south bank of the river dividing the town. **BY BUS** Service to Teruel from Barcelona is on **ABASA** (☎ 978-830-871), from Madrid and Barcelona on **Samar** (☎ 978-603-450), and from Zaragoza on **Terasa** (☎ 978-601-014). Tarazona, Zaragoza, and Calatayud are primarily serviced by **Alsa** (☎ 902-422-242; www.alsa.es). **BY CAR** The **A-2** links Zaragoza and Calatayud with the **AP-2** continuing to Barcelona. The **AP-68** links Zaragoza with Pamplona. Teruel is linked by the **A-23** to Valencia and, ultimately, to Zaragoza.

ATMs

Even the smallest villages have 24-hour ATMs. Most accept Maestro/MasterCard, Cirrus, and Visa.

Booking Services

Zaragoza Oficina de Turismo (see below) assists with walk-in hotel reservations but does not make bookings by phone or Internet.

Doctors & Hospitals

For emergency medical or dental attention, go to the *centro de urgencia* (emergency room) of the nearest hospital. **ZARAGOZA Hospital Miguel Servet,** Paseo Isabel la Católica, 1–3 (☎ 976-76-55-00).

Emergencies

The all-around emergency number in Spain is ☎ **112.**

Internet Access

Wi-Fi has become common in most hotels and is increasingly offered as a free amenity except in business hotels. Internet cafes are common.

Pharmacies

To find an open pharmacy outside normal business hours, check the list posted on the door of any drugstore. When open, they display a neon green cross.

Police

For national police, call ☎ **091;** for local police, call ☎ **092.**

Post Office

Most post offices in Aragón are open Monday to Friday 8am to 9pm, Saturday 9am to 2pm. Main offices are identified on city maps.

Safety

Aragón's towns and cities are extremely safe. Avoid deserted streets and take care not to leave anything visible in a parked car.

Visitor Information

CALATAYUD Oficina de Turismo, at Plaza Fuerte (☎ 976-886-322; www.calatayud.es), is open daily 9:30am to 1:30pm and 4 to 8pm. **TARAZONA Oficina de Turismo,** at Plaza de San Francisco, 1 (☎ 976-640-074; www.tarazona.es), is open daily 9am to 1:30pm and 4:30 to 7pm (opens 10am Sat–Sun). **TERUEL Oficina Municipal de Turismo,** at Plaza de los Amantes (☎ 978-624-105; www.dpteruel.es), is open Monday to Friday 10am to 2pm and 4 to 7pm, Saturday 10am to 2pm. **ZARAGOZA Oficina de Turismo,** at Plaza del Pilar (☎ 902-142-008; www.zaragozaturismo.es), is open daily from 9am to 9pm.

13
Catalunya

The Best of Catalunya in 3 Days

Soaring mountains, parched plains, and precipitous shoreline cliffs come together in a surrealist tableau in northeast Catalunya (Catalonia in English, Cataluña in Spanish), where one is tempted to say that native son Salvador Dalí simply painted what he saw. Three days is enough time to sample the medieval charms of Girona, spend a day visiting Dalí's own madcap museum and the dramatic landscapes of the north, and still explore the southern Costa Brava's sun-drenched beaches.

> PREVIOUS PAGE Girona's colorful medieval facades on the Riu Onyar. THIS PAGE Canyelles Petites beach in Roses.

START Girona, 115km (71 miles) northeast of Barcelona on the AP-7. TRIP LENGTH 117km (73 miles).

❶ **Girona.** The Romans who fortified Girona did such a fine job that it survived to be known as "the city of a thousand sieges"—most of them by French armies beginning with Charlemagne in A.D. 785 through Napoleon in 1809. The shape of the Old City remains Roman, even though the buildings are largely medieval. As a citadel city, Girona is blessedly compact and, while steep, walkable.

Crossing the Riu Onyar is much easier than in Roman times. Simply walk over the pedestrian footbridge to the 14th-century Romanesque hulk of **Sant Feliu** (see p. 394, ❸), one of the oldest churches outside the Roman walls. Roughly the same age, the handsome Benedictine monastery of Sant Pere de Galligants (St. Peter of the Cock Crows) houses the **Museu d'Arqueologia de Catalunya** (see p. 396, ❺), where Iberian and Roman artifacts chronicle the opening chapters of Girona's story.

Travel Tip

While Girona and Figueres have good train and bus service, bus connections to and between the coastal towns are infrequent and inconvenient. A car is best for following this itinerary. See p. 694 for car-rental information.

② **Northern Costa Brava.** Comfortably inland, **Figueres** (see p. 373, **④**) is the "big city" to the villages of the northern Costa Brava and a prosperous gateway for traffic and trade between Spain and France. Three showcase buildings of Modernista architecture can be found at nos. 16, 20, and 27 La Rambla, in the central shopping district. But it took native son Salvador Dalí to put Figueres on the international cultural

> Stairway to heaven: 89 steps (only some of which are pictured here) lead up to Girona's Catedral.

The medieval city revolves around the **Catedral de Girona** (see p. 396, **⑦**). Pass through the towering Roman gate into the plaza and crane your neck upward. The cathedral stands atop a stairway to heaven (actually, just 89 steps). Gironans are great storytellers; one legend says that the witch gargoyle on the facade was once a human witch, magically transformed into stone in the midst of curses and rants. Ever since, rainwater has washed blasphemy from her mouth.

Girona's medieval prosperity came in large part from its flourishing Jewish community, which was concentrated in the Call, the narrow streets near the cathedral. Carrer de la Força, where cyclist Lance Armstrong long kept an apartment, is the Call's main street, but photographers will want to explore the atmospheric side streets. The **Museu d'Història dels Jueus** (see p. 396, **⑨**) explains the basics of Jewish faith and culture and traces the role of Girona's Jewish community. See p. 394.

From Girona, follow AP-7 north 48km (30 miles) to Figueres. From Figueres, follow C-68 for 25km (16 miles) toward Roses, picking up GI-620 for another 9km (5⅔ miles) to Cadaqués.

> *The whitewashed charm of Costa Brava's Cadaqués.*

map. When the mayor invited Dalí to create a museum in 1961, the artist chose the ruins of the old municipal theater, destroyed in the Civil War. Asked why, he said, "Because I am a theatrical painter." It now receives more than a million visitors per year.

The road into **Cadaqués** (see p. 370, ❶) crosses the **Parc Natural del Cap de Creus,** a rugged peninsula where the narrow road clings to steep mountainside and daredevil competitive cyclists practice their mountain stages in the spring. Dalí spent more than 3 decades painting here, and his likeness in bronze strikes a rakish pose on the stony beach.

The better swimming beach is back in **Roses** (see p. 371, ❷), and during July and August the sands are nearly obscured with the mildly sunburned bodies of northern Europeans soaking in the sun. Hardly the most upscale resort, Roses has a busy working city that begins only a block from the shore. It is the leading fishing port of the northern coast and home of the revolutionary restaurant **elBulli** (see p. 56). Ferran Adrià, its chef, can be said to have done for Spanish cuisine what Picasso did for Spanish painting: He moved the goal posts.

Contrary to the tourist literature, the Costa Brava wasn't invented in the 1960s. Greeks made the Gulf of Roses a major trading center some 2,600 years ago, and the Romans treated the Greek town as their (literal) beachhead to conquer the Iberian Peninsula 300 years later. Discovered in 1908, the Greek and Roman ruins at **Empúries** (see p. 372, ❸) speak eloquently of archaic glories of both cultures. Much of the art removed from the site to other museums was returned in 2008 for the centenary of the excavations.

From L'Escala, follow GI-632 25km (16 miles) toward Torrent, picking up C-31 for another 10km (6¼ miles) to Palamós.

❸ **Southern Costa Brava.** The Bay of Palamós marks the beginning of the southern beaches of the Costa Brava. While **Palamós** (see p. 373, ❺) has some lovely beach resorts on its outer edges, the village itself is the leading fishing

> *The Greeks and Romans had trading posts in Empúries, which was excavated in the early 20th century.*

> *Tossa de Mar was once the picturesque haunt of artists like Marc Chagall.*

port of the southern coast. Its excellent **Museu de la Pesca** may answer every question you've ever posed to a Spanish waiter about the seafood menu.

The sea remains tantalizingly out of sight on the road south into **Sant Feliu de Guíxols** (see p. 373, ⑥). A shipbuilding center, Sant Feliu boasts an incredibly long and beautiful city beach. Local farmers bring their produce to **Plaça del Mercat** for an open-air food market Tuesdays to Sundays. On Sundays, vendors spill out into surrounding streets with clothing, "antiques," and other flea market goods.

One of the most scenic, twisting mountain roads on the Costa Brava, the GI-682, links Sant Feliu to the old Roman-Aragonese port of **Tossa de Mar** (see p. 374, ⑦). Just as the road traverses the final mountain pass and the smell of the sea reaches the heights, there is a great pullover for taking pictures of Tossa, with its hotel-lined beach cove backed by the turrets and walls of its fortified Vila Vella. Part of Tossa's charm lies in the character and distinctive architecture of its pre–Civil War buildings along the beach. Painter Marc Chagall settled in Tossa in 1933, calling it "blue paradise."

> *The wide, palm-lined Passeig dels Guíxols in Sant Feliu de Guíxols.*

The Best of Catalunya in 1 Week

If you have a week to spend in Catalunya, you can expand on the "Best of Catalunya in 3 Days" itinerary. Start by visiting the region's most revered religious shrine, more than halfway up one of Spain's most dramatic mountains. Then drive through the Penedès wine country before heading back to the shore. You'll even have time to explore the impressive Roman ruins in Tarragona and seek out graceful wading birds among the rice fields at the mouth of the Riu Ebre.

> The Basilica of Montserrat can be reached by road or train and aerial cable car; from there, take a funicular to the peak.

START Montserrat, 61km (38 miles) north-northwest of Barcelona off the A-2. TRIP LENGTH 332km (206 miles), including "The Best of Catalunya in 3 Days."

❶ Montserrat. You can see Montserrat's jagged peaks from all over eastern Catalunya. The sight is so striking—and so much a part of Catalan identity—that "Montserrat" is a commonly given name for women in the region (usually abbreviated to the nickname "Montse"). The single massif of pink conglomerate rises to 1,236m (4,055 ft.) at its highest peak, Sant Jeroni. It appears even higher because it rises abruptly from an inland river plain, and its 10km (6¼-mile) serrated ridgeline is otherworldly compared to Catalunya's more rounded peaks. Most of the mountain has been declared a natural park to protect its delicate alpine ecosystems, but hiking trails do cross its slopes, passing abandoned hermitages. The most important religious shrine, the **Basilica de Montserrat** (see p. 386, ❶), serves as the departure point for a number of high-altitude hikes, including one surprisingly easy path to the summit of Sant Jeroni. ⊕ 1 day.

From Montserrat, follow C-55 south 15km (9⅓ miles). Connect to the A-7/AP-7 west for 25km (16 miles) to Vilafranca del Penedès.

❷ Vilafranca del Penedès. The first cultivation of wine grapes in Catalunya took place in the Penedès about 2,700 years ago, and the region's winemakers haven't stopped yet. The

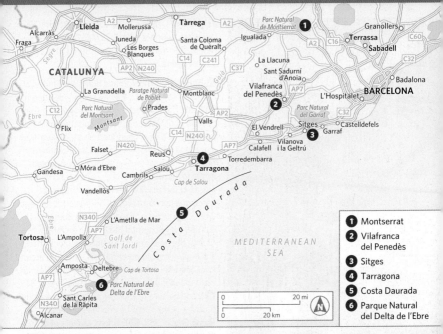

1 Montserrat

2 Vilafranca del Penedès

3 Sitges

4 Tarragona

5 Costa Daurada

6 Parque Natural del Delta de l'Ebre

Travel Tip

Each individual stop on this itinerary can be reached by train or bus from Barcelona, but if you want to string them together, rent a car.

> The Vinseum in Vilafranca del Penedès celebrates not just the region's wine, but wine culture.

rocky soils were celebrated in Roman times for their white wines, and white grapes still dominate the production of still wines and sparkling Cavas. In an afternoon in Vilafranca del Penedès, you can visit the **Vinseum** and tour the high-tech winemaking operations of the Torres company at the **Centre de Visites Torres** (see p. 382, **2**). ⏱ 3 hr. See p. 380, **1**.

From Vilafranca, follow C-15 south 10km (6¼ miles) and veer left onto C-15B, which wends through the scenic Garraf hills. Follow signs 12km (7½ miles) to Sitges.

3 Sitges. Long a beach escape for Barcelonans, Sitges became a resort town in the late 19th century, as artists, authors, and industrialists transformed the fishermen's houses into summer villas. Charismatic Modernista painter and longtime Sitges resident Santiago Rusiñol served as a magnet for avant-garde Catalan artists and thinkers from the late 1890s until nearly the eve of the

> The once staid days of Sitges are gone, replaced with a scene as swinging as Ibiza's.

Spanish Civil War. Striking displays at **Museu Cau Ferrat** exhibit both Rusiñol's own work and his private collection of mostly modern art. With its bohemian legacy, Sitges never really conformed to the social and political expectations of the Franco dictatorship, even becoming something of a hippie enclave in the late 1960s and 1970s. The secluded beach known as **Playa del Muerto** is famed for blending sunbathing and swimming with a gay social scene. The city is also famous for its raucous celebration of **Carnestoltes,** or Carnival, in the days leading up to the beginning of Lent. ⏱ 3 hr. See p. 376. ❶.

From Sitges, follow C-32 south for 30km (19 miles) to connect with E-15/AP-7 toward Valencia/Tarragona. Continue 33km (21 miles) to Tarragona.

❹ **Tarragona.** The Romans may have landed at Empúries (see p. 372, ❸) when they decided to drive the Carthaginians out of Iberia during the Second Punic War, but they made their military and administrative headquarters at Tarraco, now Tarragona. The most famous of the Roman roads on the peninsula, the Via Augusta, connected Rome to Tarraco, and pieces of it remain in the plazas of the city. Extensive Roman ruins in Tarragona constitute a UNESCO World Heritage Site. Just as the Catalans absorbed Roman culture, they absorbed the Roman architecture— mining the monuments for building blocks that show up in the old medieval city clustered around the **Catedral** (see p. 392, ❺). Follow the Roman walls along the **Passeig Arqueològic** (see p. 392, ❻), and be sure to walk through the long, arched passage of the Porta Triumphalis in the **Circ Romà** (see p. 392, ❾), where winners of chariot races would leave the circus. ⏱ 1 day. See p. 390.

From Tarragona, follow the E-15/AP-7 in the direction of Valencia for 25km (16 miles) to Cambrils.

❺ **Costa Daurada.** Since time is limited, base yourself in **Cambrils** (see p. 378, ❸) to enjoy the long beaches, eat at some of Spain's best seafood restaurants, and explore the coast by booking a catamaran cruise. Boats offer several options, including a regular shuttle back and forth to **Salou** (see p. 378, ❷) and trips to Tarragona's mighty harbor. More unusual options include a visit to one of the coast's remaining fishing villages, complete with a paella lunch cooked aboard ship. A variant of the fishing-village trip extends the day with a motorcoach tour of the delta lands at the mouth of the Ebro River (see below). ⏱ 1 day. See p. 376.

From Cambrils, follow the coastal road to AP-7 (in the direction of Valencia) and continue 50km (31 miles) to exit 39A. Follow signs for 15km (9⅓ miles) to TV-3402 and the village of Deltebre.

> *The wetlands of the Parque Natural del Delta de l'Ebre make it a favored breeding ground for birds.*

6 Parque Natural del Delta de l'Ebre. This park encompasses the verdant rice fields and wetlands at the mouth of the Riu Ebre (Río Ebro or Ebro River in the rest of Spain). One of the Iberian Peninsula's largest and most important rivers, it flows from headwaters in Cantabria to empty into the Mediterranean at the south end of the Costa Daurada. The delta is one of the largest in the western Mediterranean and contains lagoons, dunes, shallow bays, and beaches, as well as the river and its associated woodlands. The vast variety of watery terrain makes the delta prime habitat for breeding colonies of the greater flamingo and other wading birds, including the purple and night heron. Determined birders should contact **Audouin Birding Tours,** Partida Bochets, Freginals (☎ 649-286-086; www. audouinbirding.com), to arrange guided expeditions. ⏱ 3hr. See p. 378, **4**.

> *A slow day on the blue-flag Llevant Beach in Salou.*

THE "NATION" OF CATALUNYA

A Proud People with Curious Icons

BY NEIL EDWARD SCHLECHT

THE FIERCELY INDEPENDENT streak of Catalans is forged of a history, language, and culture unique from the rest of Spain—prompting Catalan nationalists to refer to their semiautonomous region as *un país* (literally "a nation"). The long, insular Franco dictatorship outlawed Catalan, but the ancient language has experienced a dramatic resurgence in modern, democratic Spain. It is now the principal language in public schools and on the streets of Catalunya (although in Barcelona, Spanish is spoken nearly as often). Franco also tried to systematically eradicate the unique symbols and touchstones of Catalan culture, but they have persevered. Consider this a guide to the most imaginative of these traditions.

A Catalan Cultural Primer

CORREFOCS
Part of city and regional festivals, these "fire runs"—like a parade—are the stuff of playful, dancing "devils" who run through the streets with hand-held fireworks and shower the crowds with sparks.

LA SARDANA
An ancient circle dance (frequently seen in Barcelona in front of the cathedral on Sunday mornings), this is the quintessential expression of Catalan culture,

invested with a sense of unity and pride. Strangers gather, join hands, drop their bags in the center, and perform precise, light-footed steps in unison as the circle grows to accommodate more dancers.

CASTELLERS
Performed during special regional and national celebrations, these thrilling "human towers" reach up to

nine levels. A base of strong-shouldered men—dressed in white pants, black sashes, and matching shirts—forms a conical pyramid, with progressively lighter boys and girls scrambling up their backs. When the smallest reaches the top, he or she waves four fingers, symbolizing the red stripes of the Catalan flag, and scrambles back down before the tower collapses.

GEGANTS & CAPGROSSOS
These distinctive folkloric costumes are the stars of parades and festivals, such as Barcelona's La Mercé. *Gegants* are giant hollow figures (usually

royal couples); the entire costume is supported by a single man or woman. *Capgrossos* (literally "big heads") are similar, usually caricatures featuring a large, papier-mâché head on a regular-sized body.

EL CAGANER
A nativity figure, originally a peasant with a traditional red stocking cap, in

the act of squatting and defecating, the character symbolizes Catalans' faith in the fecundity of the soil and the earth's cycle of regeneration. In a nod to pop culture, on sale at Christmas are now also figures of politicians, priests, Bart Simpson, and others, all assuming the position.

The Catalan Flag

The Senyera, the distinctive flag of Catalunya with four bold red stripes streaking across a yellow background, is steeped in legend. One apocryphal story involves the 9th-century Count of Barcelona, Wilfred the Hairy, who greatly expanded Catalunya's influence. Wounded in battle against the Moors during the siege of Barcelona, the Count was rewarded with a coat of arms by King Charles the Bald; prior to his death, Wilfred's bloodied fingers slid down the golden shield, giving birth to the symbol of the Catalan people.

Costa Brava

Along Catalunya's "wild coast" between the French border and Barcelona, mountain ranges spring from the ocean like Poseidon wading ashore. Dizzying heights overlook small coves where former fishing villages have turned from tuna to tourists as a means of employment. Although "Costa Brava" is synonymous with overbuilt package resorts of the 1960s, many of its communities retain a pre-exploitation charm.

> Trees cling to the still unspoiled rocky headland off Sant Feliu de Guíxols.

START Cadaqués, in the northeast corner of Catalunya. **TRIP LENGTH** 146km (91 miles).

❶ ★★ **Cadaqués.** Descending the winding, narrow road into town is a plunge into Picasso's cubist paintings of the summer of 1910. Magritte, Duchamps, Buñuel, and Man Ray also used to summer here, whiling away the days at bars and restaurants along the crescent-shaped

stony beach. Artists and their patrons still do the same. Salvador Dalí (from nearby Figueres) proved the most enduring presence, and his sketches dot the walls of many establishments. From 1930 to 1982, he worked at the fishing cove of Port Lligat in a labyrinth of fishermen's stalls. **Casa-Museu Salvador Dalí** preserves the artist's workshop, library, and lush gardens.

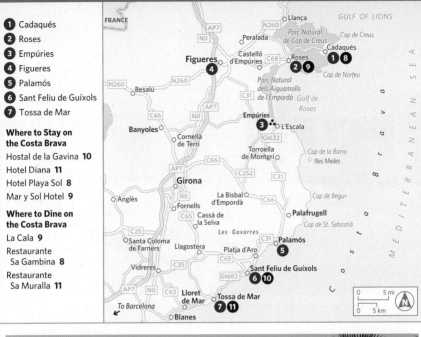

1. Cadaqués
2. Roses
3. Empúries
4. Figueres
5. Palamós
6. Sant Feliu de Guíxols
7. Tossa de Mar

Where to Stay on the Costa Brava

Hostal de la Gavina **10**
Hotel Diana **11**
Hotel Playa Sol **8**
Mar y Sol Hotel **9**

Where to Dine on the Costa Brava

La Cala **9**
Restaurante Sa Gambina **8**
Restaurante Sa Muralla **11**

> *The town of Roses offers some of the best, and most popular (read: crowded), beaches on the Costa Brava.*

Casa-Museu: ⏱ 1 hr. Port Lligat, s/n. ☎ 972-251-015. www.salvador-dali.org. 10€, 8€ seniors and students, free for kids 8 & under. Early Feb to mid-June and mid-Sept to early Jan Tues–Sun 10:30am–6pm; mid-June to mid-Sept daily 9:30am–9pm.

Follow GI-614 for 17km (11 miles) to Roses.

2 Roses. Tucked beneath the Cap de Creus at the head of a long bay, Roses has the longest and finest sand beaches of the northern Costa Brava. The geography guarantees nearly constant winds parallel to the beach, making Roses a capital for windsurfing and catamaran sailing. You can rent sailboards and catamarans or take lessons at the beach with **Windiscovery.**

> *Ruins of ancient villas with mosaic floors are the legacy of Empúries's Roman past.*

Although Roses becomes a brash tourist town in midsummer, it also retains a labyrinthine old quarter befitting a city founded 2,500 years ago by colonists from the Greek city of Rhodes. Get a handle on the rich past through exhibits at **L' Espai Cultural La Ciutadella,** where a history museum, archaeological site, and performing arts space occupy the forbidding walls of a 16th-century fortification. Windiscovery: Platja de Roses. ☎ 972-381-388. www.windiscovery.com. Gear rental starts at 12€ per hour. L' Espai: ⏲ 1 hr. Avinguda de Rhode, s/n. ☎ 972-151-466. www.laciutadella.cat. 3€. Oct–May Tues–Sun 10am–6pm (closes Oct–Jan Sun 2pm and all day Mon); June and Sept daily 10am–8pm; July–Aug daily 10am–9pm.

Follow C-68 west 6km (3¾ miles) to GIV-6216, which leads 8km (5 miles) south to Empúries at edge of L'Escala.

❸ ★★ **Empúries.** Greek commerce and Roman might are both writ large in the ruins of Empúries, which have been under excavation since 1908. Greeks founded the city in 600 B.C. as a trade port and then built a second city slightly inland in 550 B.C., naming it Emporion, or "trading place." (Today, the first settlement lies buried under an active fishing village.) Farther inland, Scipio

Africanus founded a military camp in 219 B.C. during his first invasion to oust the Carthaginians from the Iberian Peninsula. An amphitheater and villas with mosaics still attest to the flourishing Roman presence. A famous sculpture of Asclepius (god of medicine) was returned to the site from Barcelona in 2008. The **Museu d'Arqueologia de Catalunya** now interprets and chronicles the archaeological excavations.

You can walk along the seaside path from the ruins to the flourishing village of L'Escala. Salted anchovies from the town are famous all over Spain, and exhibits at the **Museu de l'Anxova i de la Sal** explain the local fishing industry from the 16th century to the present. Museu d'Arqueologia: ⏲ 2 hr. C/ Puig i Cadafalch, s/n. ☎ 972-770-208. www.mac.cat. 3€, free for kids 15 & under and seniors 65 & over. June–Sept daily 10am–8pm; Oct–May daily 10am–6pm. Museu de l'Anxova: ⏲ 30 min. Avinguda Francesc Macià, 1. ☎ 972-776-815. www.anxova-sal.cat. 2€. Mid-June to Sept Tues–Fri 10am–1:30pm and 5–8pm, Sat 11am–1pm and 6–8pm, Sun 11am–1pm; Oct to mid-June closed afternoons.

Follow GI-630 west 4km (2½ miles) from L'Escala to pick up C-31 for 19km (12 miles) northwest to Figueres.

4 Figueres. Native son Salvador Dalí established the flamboyant ★★★ **Teatre-Museu Dalí** here in 1974. On his death in 1989, thousands of artifacts and artworks from throughout his life passed to the Fundació Gala-Salvador Dalí, which maintains the museum. Dalí spent his last 4 years living here in the Torre Galatea (named for his wife), and was buried beneath the great dome depicting the eye of a fly as seen through a microscope. Don't miss the artist's first Cadillac in the courtyard, where it rains *inside* the car. Teatre-Museu: ⏱ 2–3 hr. Plaça Gala-Salvador Dalí, 5. ☎ 972-677-500. www.salvador-dali.org. 11€, 8€ students and seniors. Jan–Feb and Nov–Dec Tues–Sun 10:30am–5:45pm; Mar–May and Oct Tues–Sun 9:30am–5:45pm; June daily 9:30am–5:45pm; July–Sept daily 9am–7:45pm.

From Figueres, follow C-31 south for 24km (15 miles) and continue 9km (5⅔ miles) on C-252 to C-66. Go south 11km (6¾ miles) to C-31 for 7km (4⅓ miles) to Palamós.

5 Palamós. Now that so many Costa Brava fishing villages have been transformed into high-rise resorts, *someone* still has to catch all that fish served in the restaurants. One of the biggest fleets calls Palamós home, and the state-of-the-art **Museu de la Pesca** details both the fish and the fishing industry. Finally you can make the connection between the menu description and what will appear on your plate.

To get closer to the sea yourself, **Estació Nàutica** rents boats, kayaks, windsurfing boards, and jet skis and offers snorkeling, diving, and boating excursions. Museu: ⏱ 1 hr. Moll Pesquer, s/n. ☎ 972-600-424. www.museu delapesca.org. Free. Mid-June to mid-Sept daily 11am–9pm; mid-Sept to mid-June Tues–Sat 10am–1:30pm and 3–7pm, Sun 10am–2pm and 4–7pm. Estació Nàutica: C/ Arc, 6. ☎ 902-200-413. www. estacionauticabadia.com. Rentals start at 12€; extended expeditions start at 100€.

Follow C-31 southwest 15km (9⅓ miles) to C-65. Continue 4km (2½ miles) to Sant Feliu de Guíxols.

6 ★★ Sant Feliu de Guíxols. This beautiful harbor and fishing port is framed on one side by a rocky headland holding the luxury residential area of S'Agaro and on the other by a 10th-century Benedictine monastery and church. While the monastery is closed for restoration, **Mare de Déu dels Angels** remains an active parish church filled with a millennium of religious art, some of it quite powerful.

> *The Teatre-Museu Dalí, the self-proclaimed largest surrealist "object" in the world, lives up to the flamboyant extravagance of its namesake.*

> *The Arc de San Benet at the Benedictine monastery of Sant Feliu de Guíxols.*

> *Seven 14th-century round towers guard the walled Old Town of Tossa de Mar.*

Also a part of the monastery complex, the **Museu d'Història** explains the local cork industry that made Sant Feliu wealthy in the late 19th century—just in time for cork barons to build the marvelous Modernista houses along Platja de Sant Pol. Mare de Déu: ⏱ 30 min.

Plaça del Monestir. Free. Daily 9am–12:30pm and 7–8:30pm. Museu: ⏱ 30 min. Plaça del Monestir. ☎ 972-821-575. Free. Tues–Sat 10am–1pm and 5–8pm; Sun 10am–1pm.

Follow the coastal highlands road, GI-682, 22km (14 miles) south to Tossa de Mar.

7 ★ **Tossa de Mar.** High headlands surrounding the splendid sandy crescent of Tossa's beach saved it from rampant development—hotel developers ran out of space in the Vila Nova, or New Town. The **Vila Vella,** or Old Town, dates from the 12th to 14th centuries and rises on one of the headlands. Its seven round towers guard the ruins of a medieval church and governor's palace. A lighthouse at the top of the Old Town is sometimes open for tours, but the views are the main appeal. As you descend, follow signs to Plaça del Pintor J. Villalonga, where you'll find steps that let you walk along the medieval ramparts.

In 1914, archaeologists uncovered the ruins of one of the grandest Roman villas on the Costa Brava, **Els Ametllers Roman Villa.** Inhabited from the 1st century B.C. to the 6th century A.D., it was the headquarters of a vast tract of vineyards producing wine for export to Rome. During the summer, beautiful mosaic floors of the rooms are uncovered for viewing. Ametllers: ⏱ 1 hr. C/ del Pelegrí, 5–13. No phone. Free. Daylight hours.

Where to Stay & Dine

> *Mar y Sol's restaurant serves fresh Costa Brava seafood daily.*

★★★ Hostal de la Gavina SANT FELIU

This elegantly romantic hotel has grown from an 11-room inn established in 1932 on an estate above Platja de Sant Pol. Stunning grounds, a saltwater pool overlooking the sea, and easy access to coastline walking paths make La Gavina one of the great Costa Brava stays. The formal restaurant (entrees 15€–24€) is one of the best on the southern coast. Plaça Rosaleda, s/n, S'Agaró. ☎ 972-321-100. www.lagavina.com. 74 rooms. Doubles 150€–350€. AE, DC, MC, V.

Hotel Diana TOSSA DE MAR

This seafront hotel facing Tossa's stunning beach adapts the Modernista architecture of Gaudí's contemporaries to resort lodging. Rooms are small, but the price is right. Plaça d'Espanya, 6. ☎ 972-341-886. www.hotelesdante.com. 21 rooms. Doubles 80€–168€. AE, DC, MC, V.

★ Hotel Playa Sol CADAQUÉS

Set off from the beach hubbub on one point of Cadaqués harbor, this casually elegant beach hotel has been in the same family for more than 50 years. The gardenlike grounds offer a tranquil retreat. C/ Riba es Pianc, 3. ☎ 972-258-100. www.playasol.com. 50 rooms. Doubles 73€–191€. AE, DC, MC, V. Closed Dec–Jan.

La Cala ROSES MEDITERRANEAN/SEAFOOD

If you were to ask the local fishmonger for the best place in town for *suquet,* a Catalan seafood stew, she'd send you here. Fishnets on the tiled walls seem hokey, but the dishes are the real deal. C/ Sant Sebastià, 61. ☎ 972-256-171. Entrees 10€–21€. AE, DC, MC, V. Lunch & dinner daily.

kids Mar y Sol Hotel ROSES

Every light and airy room in this modern hotel overlooks the water and can sleep up to four people, making it great for families. Walk across the street to swim or sunbathe. The restaurant serves fresh seafood. Plaça Catalunya, 20. ☎ 972-252-111. www.prestigehotels.com. 37 rooms. Doubles 80€–115€ with breakfast. MC, V.

★ Restaurant Sa Gambina CADAQUÉS SEAFOOD

Salvador Dalí and his wife, Gala, had many a wild meal at this fun restaurant at the edge of the harbor. For a splurge, order the wacky couple's favorite dish, the copious *zarzuela* (stew) of fish and lobster named for them. C/ Riba Nemesio Llorens, s/n. ☎ 972-258-127. Entrees 17€–39€. MC, V. Lunch & dinner daily (Nov–Feb lunch only).

Restaurant Sa Muralla TOSSA DEL MAR

SEAFOOD Few places do quite such a good job with *cim-i-tomba,* the traditional Tossa dish of fish and potato layered with aioli. Pescaphobes can choose grilled meats. C/ Portal 16. ☎ 972-341-128. 13€–26€. MC, V. Mid-Mar to Sept lunch & dinner daily; Oct to mid-Mar lunch daily.

Costa Daurada

Golden sand beaches east and west of Tarragona earned this region the sobriquet of Costa Daurada (Dorada in Castilian), or "Gold Coast." Only the low Garraf hills separate the inland vineyard country from the coastal plain, creating a gentler landscape than along the Costa Brava. Pine trees reaching from the hills to the beaches signal a Mediterranean ecosystem, and the long beaches of wave-battered sand are the most impressive in Catalunya.

> The Església de Sant Bartomeu i Santa Tecla clings to the promontory along Sitges.

START Sitges. **TRIP LENGTH** 150km (93 miles).

① **Sitges.** Sometimes acclaimed as a gay resort, Sitges is a quick getaway for Barcelonans of every orientation. Breaking surf pounds its shores, and breakwaters segment the beach. Along the Passeig de la Ribera, two landmarks define seaside

Sitges: The first is **Chiringuito,** the restaurant founded in 1913 that's likely the source of the nickname given to every casual beachside bar/ cafe in Spain. Booming surf soaks the stone steps leading to Plaça del Baluart, where the second landmark, the 17th-century baroque **Església de**

Sant Bartomeu i Santa Tecla, overlooks the harbor. So does a single cannon, the last of six that drove off English warships in 1797.

Modernista artist Santiago Rusiñol (1861–1931) set Sitges on the art-colony path when he built a combined studio, home, and gallery here at the end of the 19th century. It quickly became a salon for Catalan bohemians and Rusiñol's base for proselytizing his theories of art as the new religion. His striking studio-home, now the **Museu Cau Ferrat,** contains the artist's own work and that of his contemporaries (including a great 1900 Picasso bullfight painting), as well as glass, ceramics, and wrought-iron sculpture. Broader in scope, the adjacent **Museu Maricel** displays the historic art collection of Doctor Jesús Pérez Rosales, which spans Romanesque, Gothic, and Renaissance periods but is especially strong in modern Catalan sculpture. Chiringuito: Paseo de la Ribera, s/n. ☎ 938-947-596. Tapas 3€–6€. AE, MC, V. Lunch & dinner daily. Museu Cau Ferrat and Maricel: ⏱ 45 min each. C/Fonollar, s/n. ☎ 938-940-364. www.mnac.es/museus/mus_ferrat.jsp. Each museum 3.50€, 2€ students and seniors. Oct–June Tues–Sat 9:30am–2pm and 3:30–6:30pm, Sun 10am–3pm; July–Sept Tues–Sat 9:30am–2pm and 4–7pm; Sun 10am–3pm.

> *Artist Santiago Rusiñol combined two 16th-century cottages to make the house that became Museu Cau Ferrat.*

> *Wild flamingos dot a lagoon in the Parque Natural del Delta de l'Ebre.*

Follow C-32 southwest 30km (19 miles). Pick up AP-7 southwest 40km (25 miles) to Salou.

2 Salou. The largest beach town of the Costa Daurada, Salou has managed to compartmentalize its attractions and retain the early-20th-century elegance of its main **beach.** The Passeig de les Palmeres, a broad promenade lined with towering palms, is said to have been modeled on the promenade in Nice. An impressive sculpture celebrates the departure of Jaume I from Salou in 1229 to recapture the island of Mallorca. Modernista villas lining the promenade attest to Salou's long-standing wealth and good taste.

Nonetheless, Salou also boasts one of Spain's biggest amusement parks on its outskirts, the sprawling kids **Port Aventura.** Polynesia, Aztec Mexico, China, and the Wild West theme areas each have their own thrill rides and dance spectacles. Port Aventura: 1–2 days. AP-7, exit 35. ☎ 902-202-220. www.portaventura.es. 44€, 35€ seniors and kids 4–10, free for kids 3 & under. Mid-Mar to early Jan. Call for days and hours.

Follow A-7 south 12km (7½ miles) to Cambrils.

3 ★ Cambrils. Stunning beaches stretch north and south of Cambrils, but the heart of the community is the marina and fishing port—a favorite activity for vacationers is watching the boats unload their catch from 4 to 5pm. **Creuers Costa Daurada** offers catamaran cruises along the coast.

Young Joan Miró spent summers in the hills above Cambrils, and an easy **walking trail** climbs from Pixerota beach for 8km (5 miles) to the hilltop chapel of La Mare de Déu de la Roca. Benches along the trail, which extends into the village of **Mont-roig del Camp,** are placed where Miró painted. Creuers Costa Daurada: Avinguda Diputació, 15. ☎ 977-363-090. www.creuerscostadaurada.com. Cruises 10€–41€.

Follow AP-7 south 56km (35 miles). At exit 41, follow N-340 for 5km (3 miles), taking the exit for Amposta. Continue 7km (4⅓ miles) on TV-3405 to Delta de l'Ebre.

4 Delta de l'Ebre. The magical water world of the Riu Ebre delta is one of Spain's principal rice-growing regions and an important haven for water birds, including breeding flamingos. The ★ **Parque Natural del Delta de l'Ebre** covers much of the region, and its **Ecomuseu del Parque Natural** has exhibits explaining both the human and the natural features. The information desk can also advise on boat trips and bicycle rentals. Ecomuseu: C/ Doctor Martí Buera, 22, Deltebre. ☎ 977-489-679. www.parcsdecatalunya.net. 1.20€ for museum. Oct–Apr Mon–Sat 10am–2pm and 3–6pm, Sun 10am–2pm; May–Sept open until 7pm Mon–Sat.

Where to Stay & Dine

> El Xalet (pronounced like "chalet").

El Xalet SITGES

This Modernista landmark from 1882 became an elegant small hotel in 2002. Its high style justifies the long walk to the beach. C/ Illa de Cuba, 35. ☎ 938-110-070. www.elxalet.com. 12 rooms. 60€–90€ with breakfast. AE, MC, V.

Hotel Calipolis SITGES

The well-maintained beachfront tower hotel has the sleek curves of an ocean liner. It's worth the extra euros for an oceanfront balcony. C/ Sofia, 2–6. ☎ 938-941-500. www.hotelcalipolis.com. 170 rooms. 98€–200€. MC, V.

★★ Joan Gatell Restaurant CAMBRILS SEAFOOD

From baby eels in spring to tuna roe in fall, Gatell gets the best seasonal fish and has the elegant presentation to match. A pricey gastronomic menu (from 65€) offers four grand fish courses. Passeig Miramar, 26. Entrees 18€–43€. AE, MC, V. Lunch Tues-Sun, dinner Tues-Sat.

L'Estrella de Xaimar SITGES CATALAN

Meats and herbs from the mountains meet fish from the sea here, and the result is value-packed, well-cooked meals in a handsomely modern dining room. C/ Major, 52. ☎ 938-947-054. Entrees 11€–26€. MC, V. Lunch daily; dinner daily in summer, Fri-Sat in winter.

Magnolia Hotel SALOU

This contemporary-design hotel just a block from the beach was created as an adult getaway—only two guests per smart and spacious room. C/ Madrid, 8. ☎ 977-351-717. www.magnoliahotelsalou.com. 72 rooms. 90€–190€ with breakfast. MC, V.

kids Monica Hotel CAMBRILS

Set at the juncture of the beach and fishing port, Monica offers a variety of rooms to accommodate both parents and children. Lovely grounds include a playground and swimming pool. C/ Galcerán Marquet, 1. ☎ 977-791-000. www.hotelmonica.com. 100 rooms. 97€–177€ with breakfast. MC, V.

Rull Hotel DELTEBRE

This contemporary, international-style small hotel is an ideal base for exploring the natural world of the delta. Its restaurant, El Garxal, specializes in regional rice and seafood dishes. Avenida Esportiva, 155. ☎ 977-487-728. www.hotelrull.com. 47 rooms. 69€–105€. Entrees 13€–20€. MC, V. Lunch Mon-Sun, dinner Mon-Sat.

★ Villa Alexander Restaurant SALOU CONTEMPORARY

The rising-star chef here prepares striking versions of Catalan and Spanish classics (wild boar with red fruits, veal tartare with violet jam) in the stunning modern dining rooms of a late-19th-century villa. Passeig de Jaume 1, 3. ☎ 977-353-683. Entrees 18€–25€. AE, MC, V. Lunch & dinner daily.

Penedès for Wine Lovers

The Penedès wine region southwest of Barcelona and northeast of Tarragona is one of Europe's oldest viticultural areas. It has been producing wine for more than 15 centuries, uninterrupted even during the Moorish occupation. The rolling plains are framed by the coastal Garraf hills and the rugged mountains of the Catalan interior, where some vineyards are planted at an altitude of 800m (2,625 ft.). Hundreds of small producers dot the countryside, although the area is also home of some of Spain's largest wine houses. This tour focuses on the Penedès Central, which has the greatest concentration of fine wineries open for visits and the best infrastructure for travelers. Plan on at least 3 days.

> Penedès, less well known than its neighbor, La Rioja, produces more than 95% of all the Cava made in Spain.

START Vilafranca del Penedès. **TRIP LENGTH** 22km (14 miles).

1 Vilafranca del Penedès. Wine warehouses circle this town of 35,000 that governs the Penedès wine producers. Founded in the mid-12th century, Vilafranca held a regional Aragonese court late into the 14th century, and its old quarter dates from that period. The arrival of rail in the 1800s cemented its position as a wine shipping center. The **Plaça de la Vila,** where the tourist office is located, and the nearby promenade of **La Rambla** overflow with food and flea markets on Saturdays from 8am to 2pm.

Vilafranca is also home to the ★ **Vinseum: Museu de les Cultures del Vi de Catalunya.** As the name promises, the multimedia experience here is as much anthropological as viticultural, focusing on Penedès history and cultural traditions as much as on the process of making and

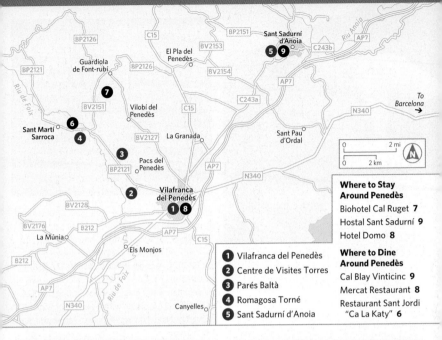

Where to Stay Around Penedès
Biohotel Cal Ruget **7**
Hostal Sant Sadurní **9**
Hotel Domo **8**

Where to Dine Around Penedès
Cal Blay Vinticinc **9**
Mercat Restaurant **8**
Restaurant Sant Jordi "Ca La Katy" **6**

1 Vilafranca del Penedès
2 Centre de Visites Torres
3 Parés Baltà
4 Romagosa Torné
5 Sant Sadurní d'Anoia

> The Torres winery was established in 1870 by native brothers Jamie and Miguel Torres.

Stack 'Em Up

Like most civic plazas, Plaça Jaume I, in front of the wine museum, has its share of statues depicting local heroes. The most prominent is the rendition in bronze of a *casteller,* or human tower (literally "castle")—usually built during Catalan cultural festivals—composed of Els Castellers de Vilafranca, a local organization of more than 400 members and one of Catalunya's most successful *colles castelleres* (*casteller* teams). The group holds a number of modern records for building the highest towers and for towers with the largest number of human "bricks" at each level.

selling wine. The museum occupies a small palace on the historic **Plaça Jaume I** and will expand into a larger additional palace now under restoration. In a refreshing break from the didactic nature of such museums, Vinseum poses questions about wine and wine culture and leaves the visitor free to decide on the answers. Vinseum: ⏱ 1½ hr. Plaça Jaume I, 1–5. ☎ 938-900-582. www.vinseum.cat. 5€, 3€ seniors and kids 13–17, free for kids 12 & under. Tues–Sat 10am–2pm and 4–7pm; Sun 10am–2pm.

> The soil in Penedès, mostly limestone, sand, and clay, along with the Mediterranean climate, is well suited to viniculture.

View from the Top

While you're in the neighborhood, continue into the village of Sant Martí Sarroca and watch for signs to the **Castell de Sant Martí Sarroca**. The 10th-century fortress is rarely open, but its hilltop setting overlooks miles and miles of vineyards stretching all the way to the jagged peaks of Montserrat on the blue horizon. The castle played a small role in several Spanish wars, including the War of the Spanish Succession, but it has been undergoing restoration since 1963.

To maximize your touring time, head northwest from Vilafranca on BP-2121 for 2km (1 mile) toward Pacs del Penedès and Sant Martí Sarroca.

② ★ **Centre de Visites Torres (Pacs del Penedès).** The Torres family has been a leader in Penedès wines since establishing its first winery in Vilafranca in 1870, and it controls some of the region's top vineyards. It's also the best organized for touring, offering a short video, a minitrain trip through a vineyard, and a brief explanation of the high-tech winery. The shop stocks most of the company's still wines, from its inexpensive Viña Sol to its pricey Perpetual Salmos. Tastings, however, focus on mid-priced reds and excellent brandy. ⏱ 1½ hr. BP-2121, Pacs del Penedès. ☎ 938-177-568. www.torres.es. Tour 6€, 3.50€ seniors and kids 17 & under, with 1 glass of wine. Tasting tour 12€, 3.50€ kids 17 & under, with 2 glasses of wine and a brandy. Mon–Fri 9am–5pm; Sat 9am–6pm; Sun 9am–1pm.

Continue on BP-2121 about 2km (1 mile) toward Sant Martí Sarroca, watching for signs on right to Parés Baltà.

③ ★★ **Parés Baltà (Pacs del Penedès).** This family operation has been making largely chemical-free fine wines and Cavas since 1790, and its five vineyard estates have been certified organic since 2004. The company keeps its own flock of sheep to fertilize the vines and beehives to encourage pollination. Intimate 2-hour tours visit vineyards, the winery, and Cava cellars, concluding with a taste of at least

> The Torres family now controls some of the region's top vineyards, making it a logical stop for a tour.

two wines and a Cava. Ask about the family's garage winery project in the Priorat. ⏱ 2 hr. Masia Can Balta, s/n (off BP-2121), Pacs del Penedès. ☎ 938-901-399. www.paresbalta.com. Tours 10€, must bearranged in advance. Open daily.

Continue on BP-2121 5km (3 miles) toward Sant Martí Sarroca. Romagosa Torné is on the left.

❹ **Romagosa Torné (Sant Martí Sarroca).** This moderate-sized operation between Vilafranca and Sant Martí Sarroca is a splendid example of trends in local winemaking. Its reds include both traditional *tempranillo* and cabernet sauvignon, as well as merlot, and chardonnay is blended into many of the whites. Cava production is extensive, with an increasing emphasis on environmentally friendly wines that have an appealing freshness. ⏱ 1 hr. Finca la Serra, Sant Martí Sarroca. ☎ 938-991-353. www.romagosatorne.com. Tour 1.50€, reserve a week ahead for a tour in English. Mon–Sat 10am–1pm and 4–7pm.

Vineyards line the C-243a on the 13km (8 miles) from Vilafranca to Sant Sadurní d'Anoia, and most of the grapes are destined to become sparkling wines.

❺ ★★★ **Sant Sadurní d'Anoia.** What Vilafranca is to still wines, Sant Sadurní is to Cavas—it produces no less than 75% of all Penedès's output. Thick-walled 19th-century Cava cellars fill the town, and the tourist office provides a brochure of about 40 cellars open for visits and tastes, usually for a token fee or no charge. Most ask that you call ahead, but the office will assist. Some are small operations making a few hundred cases of Cava; some are much bigger. Many close on Friday and Saturday afternoons and all day Sunday.

You'll need a snack between tastings. At **Cafe de la Plaça,** you'll find everyone from the guy selling lottery tickets to wine salesmen to city officials. Stand at the ancient marble bar and order the local trout on toast with your *café con leche.*

> *The alcohol that escapes the barrels during the aging process is called the "angels' share."*

> *The Codorníu's winery in Sant Sadurnì is considered a "cathedral of Cava."*

> *A tour of Codorníu includes its museum-cellar, where Cava was created.*

Located at the edge of town, the massive **Freixenet** operation pioneered U.S. distribution of Cava as a less expensive alternative to champagne. Since the winery gets large groups, much of the tour is via video and includes a heavy dose of marketing, complemented by a quick trip into the deep cellars to see aging bottles and—finally—a tasting.

The other giant of Sant Sadurní Cava production is ★★ **Codorníu,** worth visiting just to see the cathedral of Cava built from 1895 to 1915 and designed by Modernista architect Josep Puig i Cadafalch. Here, the much sought-after fizzy beverage—Codorníu is the top seller in all Spain—is stored and aged in 15km (9 miles) of subterranean tunnels. If you know Codorníu from its entry-level Cava, the tasting will open your eyes (and palate) to some extraordinary high-end selections. Cafe de la Plaça: Plaça de l'Ajuntament. ☎ 938-910-427. Trout toasts 3€. AE, DC, MC, V. Daily 8am–6pm. Freixenet: ⊙ 2 hr. C/ Joan Sala, 2. ☎ 938-917-096. www.freixenet.es. enotourism@freixenet.es. Tours 6€, 4€ seniors, 2€ kids 9–17, free for kids 8 & under, reservation recommended. Daily 10am–2:30pm and Mon-Thurs 4–7pm (3:30–4:30pm in winter). Codorníu: ⊙ 2 hr. Avinguda Jaume Codorníu, s/n. ☎ 938-913-342. www.codorniu.es. reserves@codorniu.es. Tours 6€, reservation recommended. Mon-Fri 9am–5pm; Sat-Sun 9am–1pm.

Where to Stay & Dine

> Artichokes at Mercat.

★★★ **Biohotel Cal Ruget** VILOBI DEL PENEDÈS
It's the ultimate wine stay in Catalunya for the slow tourist. Cal Ruget sits on a 19th-century wine estate transformed into a bed-and-breakfast compound by design-conscious Florian Porsche and Veronica Grimal (he German, she Spanish), both veterans of international hotel companies. Wake up to vineyards, go to sleep to vineyards, sop your bread with olive oil from the trees outside. Porsche also prepares lunch and dinner, if you like, and the couple seems to know every local winemaker, cheese maker, and culinary artisan. Masia Cal Ruget off BV-2151 in midst of vineyards. ☎ 938-979-342. www.calrugetbiohotel. com. 9 rooms. 100€–136€ with breakfast. MC, V.

★★ **Cal Blay Vinticinc** SANT SADURNÍ CATALAN
This self-styled "enogastronomic" restaurant in a 1905 Modernista wine cellar carries nearly all the several hundred wines and Cavas made in Sant Sandurnì, and pairs dishes to match them. Fast the day before; then order either the full 60€ tasting menu (two appetizers, two light courses, fish, meat, cheese, and dessert) with a different wine for each dish, or the "lighter" 45€ *cupatges* menu (two appetizers, three courses, and dessert) with four Cavas. Either is a crash course in the gastronomy of the Alt Penedès. C/ Josep Rovira, 27. ☎ 938-910-032. Entrees 15€–19€, tasting menus 45€–60€. MC, V. Lunch daily, dinner Fri–Sat.

Hostal Sant Sadurní SANT SADURNÍ
Sant Sadurní has long suffered from "day-trip syndrome," where most visitors leave before sundown. The chic, if small, rooms at Hostal Sant Sadurní, which opened in 2006, provide good reason to stay. Rare in Spain, the entire premises are strictly nonsmoking. C/ Sant Antoni, 99. ☎ 938-914-335. http://hostalsantsadurni. iespana.es. 10 rooms. 60€–72€. Cash only.

Hotel Domo VILAFRANCA DEL PENEDÈS
An industrial town, Vilafranca is short on lodging with character. The **Hotel Domo**, a 5-minute walk from the center of town, is your best bet, with large rooms as well as its own parking garage. But skip the spaghetti restaurant. Francesc Macià, 2. ☎ 938-172-426. www. domohotel.com. 44 units. 95€–135€. MC, V.

★★ **Mercat Restaurant** VILAFRANCA DEL PENEDÈS *CATALAN* Before leaving Vilafranca, experience the synergy of local food and wine at this foodies' haven that opened at the end of 2008. Its open kitchen and two seating areas overlook the Mercat Municipal de la Carn (meat market), giving fresh resonance to the term "market" cuisine. The inexpensive (10€) lunch menu is served at communal tables, while those desiring a more elegant a la carte meal dine off white tablecloths in the adjacent dining room. Plaça de l'Oli, 1. ☎ 938-905-609. Entrees 13€–19€. MC, V. Breakfast, lunch & dinner Tues–Sun.

★ **Restaurant Sant Jordi "Ca La Katy"** SANT MARTÍ SAROCCA *CATALAN* This excellent tiny restaurant looks like a roadside diner from the outside—except for the tethered sheep and goats, which signal that the owners take the concepts of fresh and local very seriously. They also maintain a fantastic wine cellar. The 10€ light midday menu is a steal, and the evening three-course menu of Alt Penedès cuisine is a gastronome's delight. The hillside lamb and fish from the nearby ocean are the stars. Reserve wines only boost the price a few euros. Carretera Vilafranca-Pontons, km 8. ☎ 938-991-326. Entrees 17€–21€, evening menu 19€–26€. AE, MC, V. Lunch daily, dinner Mon–Sat.

Monastic Catalunya

As a buffer state between France and often Islamic Spain, medieval Catalunya espoused a particularly fierce and intense Christian faith that reached its apogee in the cult of the Virgin of Montserrat, one of the legendary "dark" virgins of Iberian Catholicism. For a driving tour of deep faith in rugged environments, visit the Basilica of Montserrat and the three 12th-century Cistercian settlements in the hills north of Tarragona. Plan on a day for Montserrat alone and 2 to 3 days for the Cistercian triangle.

> The Basilica de Montserrat is a pilgrimage site for thousands every year.

START From Barcelona, follow the N-2 highway southwest to the junction with the N-11 and follow signs to Montserrat. **TRIP LENGTH** 117km (73 miles).

① ★★★ **Basilica de Montserrat.** An impressive complex has grown up around this mountainside pilgrimage site to La Moreneta ("The Dark One"), a 12th-century polychrome carving of the Virgin and Child said to possess miraculous properties. The 1m-high (3¼-ft.) statue is ensconced in a silver altar in a chapel high above the main altar. Head to the right

of the main entrance to climb winding stairs and wait your turn to parade past the image. She's encased in thick Plexiglas, but a cutout lets pilgrims kiss her extended hand holding the world. ⏱ 1 hr. Monte Montserrat. ☎ 938-777-701. www.montserratvisita.cat. Free. Daily 8:30am–7pm.

② **Museu de Montserrat.** An auxiliary attraction, the museum is filled with art that ranges from a few selections from medieval Catalan churches to a large number of mountaintop landscapes and devotional

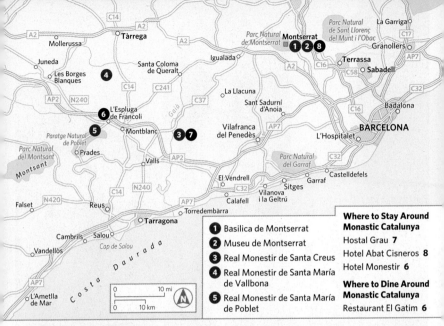

1. Basilica de Montserrat
2. Museu de Montserrat
3. Real Monestir de Santa Creus
4. Real Monestir de Santa María de Vallbona
5. Real Monestir de Santa María de Poblet

Where to Stay Around Monastic Catalunya

Hostal Grau **7**
Hotel Abat Cisneros **8**
Hotel Monestir **6**

Where to Dine Around Monastic Catalunya

Restaurant El Gatim **6**

> *Legend has it that the monks couldn't move La Moreneta, so they built around her.*

images from the late 19th century. All of it has been donated by the faithful. ⏱ 1 hr. Monte Montserrat. Mon–Fri 10am–5:45pm. 6.50€, 3.50€ kids 6–12, free for kids 5 & under.

Travel Tip

Rock slides can close the twisty 10km (6¼-mile) road and more direct cog railways to Montserrat, but the **Aeri de Montserrat** cable car, on C-55 at km 11.5 (☎ 938-350-005; www.aeridemontserrat.com), always operates. And the ascent of 544m (1,785 ft.) in 6 minutes makes the aerial route an attraction in its own right. The cost is 8.50€ adults, 7€ seniors, 4.50€ kids 4 to 13, free for kids 3 and under; cash only. It runs daily 9:40am to 2pm, and March to October from 2:45 to 7pm. The cable car also connects to the R-5 train (which goes to Manresa), run by Ferrocarrils de la Generalitat de Catalunya (☎ 932-051-515; www.fgc.cat).

> *Cistercian nuns have cared for Santa María de Vallbona since it was founded over 8 centuries ago.*

From Montserrat, follow the A-2 west toward Lleida to exit 559. Connect to C-37 for 37km (23 miles) to Santa Creus, first of the 12th-century monasteries of the Cistercian triangle—a tour of tiny villages and rugged hillsides terraced with olive trees, wine grapes, and wind turbines.

❸ ★ Real Monestir de Santa Creus (Aiguamúrcia).

The only monastery of the Cistercian triangle without an active community, Santa Creus is the best museum of monastic life in the area. Established in 1160, it was disbanded in 1835. Visit the tomb of Aragón king Pere el Gran (1239–85), where the gaudy red porphyry contrasts sharply with the spare architecture known as Cistercian Gothic. ⏲ 1–2 hr. Plaça Jaume el Just, s/n, Aiguamúrcia. ☎ 977-638-329. 4.50€, 3€ seniors and students, guide 2.10€ extra, audio guide 0.60€. Mar 16–Sept 15 Tues–Sun 10am–1:30pm and 3–7pm; Sept 16–Jan 15 Tues–Sun 10am–1:30pm and 3–5:30pm; Jan 16–Mar 15 Tues–Sun 10am–1:30pm and 3–6pm.

It's about 50km (31 miles) to Vallbona de les Monges. The unnamed and unnumbered back roads of La Ruta del Cister are well-signed for the monasteries and more interesting than main highways. They're also much faster. Vallbona is about a 1½-hr. drive from Santa Creus. Close to Vallbona, the road follows a mountain crest topped with wind turbines.

❹ ★ Real Monestir de Santa María de Vallbona.

Apart from a few hiatuses during wartime, this austere little convent has maintained a working community of nuns since at least 1176. The cloister captures the architectural development of Romanesque into Cistercian Gothic and finally into a warm Renaissance style. Simple tombs in the chapel preserve the remains of abbesses over the centuries. ⏲ 1 hr. Vallbona de les Monges. ☎ 973-330-266. www.vallbona.com. 3.50€, 2€ seniors and students. Nov–Feb Tues–Sat 10am–1:30pm and 4:30–6pm, Sun noon–1:30pm and 4:30–6pm; Mar–Oct Tues–Sat 10am–1:30pm and 4:30–6:45pm, Sun 4:30–6pm.

> *The Cistercian Royal Monastery of Santa María de Poblet, a UNESCO World Heritage Site, was founded in 1151.*

The 30km (19-mile) back-road drive to Poblet passes through the rich wine country of the Concha de Barberà and concludes in the famed wine district of Poblet.

❹ ★★ **Real Monestir de Santa María de Poblet.** Now surrounded by vineyards as far as the eye can see, this largest Cistercian community in Europe was reestablished in 1940 after lying vacant from 1835. Containing a pantheon of the kings of Aragón, the entire complex is a mass of religious and secular power embodied in stone. Along with medieval religious art, the small museum also chronicles the restoration of this UNESCO World Heritage Site. ⊙ 1½ hr. Plaça Corona d'Agaro, 11, Poblet. ☎ 977-870-254. www.poblet.cat. 6.50€, 3€ seniors and students. Oct 13–Mar 15 Mon–Sat 10am–12:45pm and 3–5:30pm, Sun 10am–12:30pm and 3–5:30pm; Mar 16–Oct 12 Mon–Sat 10am–12:45pm and 3–6pm, Sun 10am–12:30pm and 3–5:30pm (June 15–Sept 14 until 6pm).

Where to Stay & Dine

Hostal Grau AIGUAMÚRCIA
Just outside the Real Monestir de Santa Creus monastery gates, this modern hotel has fresh and comfortable small rooms. The rustic cooking of its **restaurant** uses fresh local products with gusto and finesse. Rabbit roasted with wild herbs is a specialty. Entrees are 9€ to 20€; breakfast, lunch, and dinner are served daily (closed Dec 15–Jan 15 and first full week after June 24). Pere el Gran, 3. ☎ 977-638-311. 14 rooms. Doubles 65€. Entrees 9€–20€. MC, V.

Hotel Abat Cisneros MONTSERRAT
Few pilgrims stay on the mountain overnight, but it's the best way to appreciate the stern beauty of the serrated hills at all hours. The small basic rooms here have private bathrooms, and the hotel's **restaurant** serves simple if pricey local food. Monte Montserrat. 938-777-701. www.montserratvisita.cat. 86 rooms. Doubles 68€–112€ with breakfast. AE, DC, MC, V.

Hotel Monestir L'ESPLUGA DE FRANCOLI
Founded in 1860, Monestir provides modern comforts in antique decor. Most doubles have two single beds. Les Masies, s/n. ☎ 977-870-058. www.hotelmonestir.com. 29 rooms. Doubles 78€–98€ with breakfast. MC, V.

Restaurant El Gatim L'ESPLUGA DE FRANCOLI
CATALAN This place specializes in Catalan dishes that complement local wines: snails, salt cod, and game birds of the high country. Avinguda Catalunya, 33. ☎ 977-870-765. Entrees 14€–23€. MC, V. Lunch & dinner Wed–Sat.

Tales of the Black Virgin

Montserrat's Black Virgin statue is shrouded in mystery. One explanation of the figure's origins is that it was carved by Luke in 50 A.D., then brought to Spain and hidden until shepherds found it 200 years later. Another more fanciful version suggests that two boys exploring the area in the 12th century saw a strange light descending the mountain and discovered the statue on the spot.

Tarragona

Just north of town, an arched Roman aqueduct bears witness to Tarragona's antiquity. In the 3rd century B.C., Rome made Tarragona, then called Tarraco, a regional capital and the military base for expansion into the Iberian Peninsula. The defensive walls, along with ruins of a circus and amphitheater, are among Spain's most impressive Roman remains. Fragmentary ruins that would be cordoned off as civic treasures elsewhere are simply part of a cityscape that is equal parts modern, ancient, and medieval. *Note:* Public transit is of little use in the compact heart of the Old City—plan on walking everywhere.

> *The ancient amphitheater in Tarragona, once a Roman regional capital, was used for gladiator battles.*

START Rambla Nova.

❶ Rambla Nova. A broad pedestrian strip divides the main thoroughfare of modern Tarragona and is the site of a flea market on Fridays and Saturdays from 10am to 4pm. Behind a simple facade, the **Teatre Metropol** contains an exquisite Modernista interior built in 1908 and still used for live theater, dance, and concerts. Metropol: Rambla Nova, 46. ☎ 977-244-795.

❷ Rambla Vella. Start drilling into Tarragona's past by crossing the city's strolling street, once part of the Via Augusta—with a pause to see the Modernista chapel at **L'Església de Sant Francesc.** L'Església: ⊕ 5 min. Rambla Vella, 28. No phone. Free. Mon–Sat 11am–1pm and 5–8pm.

❸ Plaça de La Font. You have to love a city square where a lively cafe scene coexists with municipal government offices. Pop into the Ajuntament (the town hall; open daily 8am–10pm) to see the Modernista ship-shaped tomb of Jaume I of Aragón (1208–76). Ajuntament: ⊕ 5 min. Plaça de la Font, 1. ☎ 977-296-100. www.tarragona.cat.

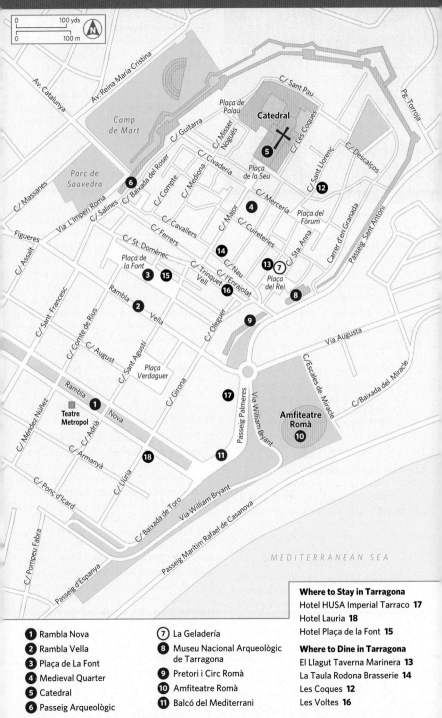

Where to Stay in Tarragona

Hotel HUSA Imperial Tarraco **17**

Hotel Lauria **18**

Hotel Plaça de la Font **15**

Where to Dine in Tarragona

El Llagut Taverna Marinera **13**

La Taula Rodona Brasserie **14**

Les Coques **12**

Les Voltes **16**

① Rambla Nova

② Rambla Vella

③ Plaça de La Font

④ Medieval Quarter

⑤ Catedral

⑥ Passeig Arqueològic

⑦ La Geladería

⑧ Museu Nacional Arqueològic de Tarragona

⑨ Pretori i Circ Romà

⑩ Amfiteatre Romà

⑪ Balcó del Mediterrani

> La Rambla Nova is Tarragona's main pedestrian thoroughfare.

④ Medieval Quarter. The streets narrow as you climb into medieval Tarragona, erected atop the battlements of the Roman city of Tarraco. The 14th-century arched arcade at C/ Mercería, at the foot of the stairs into the Plaça de la Seu, long served as Tarraco's marketplace.

⑤ Catedral. Begun in the mid-12th century and consecrated in 1331, the cathedral spans the transition from Romanesque to Gothic architecture. The immense rose window of the main facade is balanced by the Gothic upper tier of the octagonal bell tower, where windows flood the interior with light. ⏲ 30 min. Plaça de la Seu. ☎ 977-238-685. 3.50€. Mar 16–Oct 15 daily 10am–7pm; Oct 16–Nov 15 daily 10am–5pm; Nov 16–Mar 15 daily 10am–2pm.

⑥ ★ Passeig Arqueològic. About 1km (⅔ mile) of Tarragona's original 4.5km (2¾-mile) Roman walls remain, and this archaeological promenade traces half their length through landscaped grounds and along the old ramparts. At several points you can climb into 1709 Spanish battlements, where cannons still stand sentinel. ⏲ 45 min. C/ Catalunya, s/n. ☎ 977-245-796. 3.50€, 1.50€ seniors and students; 10€ combined entry with Pretori i Circ Romà, Amfiteatre Romà, and several smaller sites, 5€ seniors and students. Summer Tues–Sat 9am–9pm, Sun 10am–3pm; winter Tues–Sat 9am–7pm, Sun 10am–3pm.

⑦ 🍦 La Gelateria. Enjoy an ice cream on the plaza before entering the archaeology museum and Roman Circus. Plaça del Rei, 6. ☎ 690-315-767. $.

⑧ ★★ Museu Nacional Arqueològic de Tarragona. The sunlit galleries of Catalunya's oldest archaeology museum are filled with statues and mosaics, including an arresting head of Medusa and an astonishing 3rd-century-A.D. mural composed of 47 depictions of marine life. More humble objects such as toys, jewelry, and kitchen utensils evoke the daily life of ancient Tarraco. ⏲ 1 hr. Plaça del Rei, 5. ☎ 977-236-209. www.mnat.cat. 2.40€, 1.20€ students, free for seniors 65 & over and kids 17 & under. June–Sept Tues–Sat 9:30am–8:30pm, Sun 10am–2pm; Oct–May Tues–Sat 10am–1:30pm and 3:30–7pm, Sun 10am–2pm.

⑨ ★★ Pretori i Circ Romà. Study the wooden model on display to grasp how the Romans built this hillside complex on three levels: the top for worship, the central portion for government buildings, and the lowest for the circus. Three original 6.4m-high (21-ft.) semicircular arches of the circus facade still stand. Chills may run down your spine as you walk through the long, arched Porta Triumphalis, where the victor of a chariot race would exit. ⏲ 1 hr. Plaça del Rei, s/n. ☎ 977-230-171. 3.50€, 1.50€ seniors and students; 10€ combined entry with Pretori i Circ Romà, Amfiteatre Romà, and several smaller sites, 5€ seniors and students. Summer Tues–Sat 9am–9pm, Sun 10am–3pm; winter Tues–Sat 9am–7pm, Sun 10am–3pm.

⑩ ★★ Amfiteatre Romà. The last of the monumental Roman structures, the 2nd-century-A.D. theater above the crashing ocean was used for battles between gladiators and wild beasts, and as the execution site for such enemies of the state as Sant Fructuosus and his deacons (A.D. 259). A Visigothic church erected to mark his martyrdom was succeeded by the medieval Santa María del Miracle. ⏲ 30 min. Parc del Miracle. ☎ 977-242-501. 3.50€, 1.50€ seniors and students; 10€ combined entry with Pretori i Circ Romà, Amfiteatre Romà, and several smaller sites, 5€ seniors and students. Summer Tues–Sat 9am–9pm, Sun 10am–3pm; winter Tues–Sat 9am–7pm, Sun 10am–3pm.

⑪ Balcó del Mediterrani. The best seaward views in Tarragona are along this strip-park promenade that connects Rambla Vella and Rambla Nova.

Where to Stay & Dine

> *The awning says it all.*

El Llagut Taverna Marinera *CATALAN/SEAFOOD*
Specializing in rice dishes with seafood, this unpretentious spot with rough stone walls and blue-and-white tablecloths also has outdoor tables on Plaça del Rei. C/ Natzaret, 10. ☎ 977-228-938. Entrees 11€–20€. V. Lunch & dinner Tues–Sun.

Hotel HUSA Imperial Tarraco
The crescent shape gives many rooms at this large modern business hotel sweeping views of the sea and/or the Roman ruins. Passeig Palmeres, s/n. ☎ 977-233-040. www.husa.es. 170 rooms. Doubles 70€–200€ with parking. AE, DC, MC, V.

Hotel Lauria
Unpretentious but modernized rooms on the tree-lined central artery make a convenient base to explore the Roman ruins and the medieval Old Town. Rambla Nova, 20. ☎ 977-236-712. www.hlauria.es. 72 rooms. Doubles 64€–80€. MC, V.

Hotel Plaça de la Font
This cozy hotel with rooms in spare, contemporary style opened in 2004 on one of the Old City's most pleasant, cafe-filled plazas. Plaça de la Font, 26. ☎ 977-246-134. www.hotelpdelafont.com. 20 rooms. Doubles 55€–70€. MC, V.

★ **La Taula Rodona Brasserie** *CATALAN*
Local students, courting couples, and entire large families crowd this tavern for fabulous cuts of meat expertly grilled over an open fire. A great value in a casual setting dominated by the towering chimney. C/ La Nau, 4. ☎ 977-242-592. Entrees 9€–17€. MC, V. Lunch Tues–Sun, dinner Tues–Sat.

★★ **Les Coques** *CATALAN*
Massive stone walls, wood-beamed ceilings, and ancient stone arches lend an air of permanence to this old-city favorite since 1984. Abundant fresh seafood and an authoritative handling of Catalan classics, such as lamb chop glazed with red wine, justify the higher-than-average prices. C/ Sant Llorenç, 15. ☎ 977-228-300. Entrees 17€–28€. AE, MC, V. Lunch Mon–Sat, dinner Mon–Tues and Thurs–Sat.

Les Voltes *CATALAN/SEAFOOD*
This splashy modern restaurant in the vaults of the Roman circus serves meats from the nearby hills but excels at seafood. For a splurge on shrimp, lobster, and langostinos, opt for the shellfish assortment at 40€ per person, minimum of two people. C/ Trinquet Vell, 12. ☎ 977-230-651. Entrees 8€–20€. MC, V. Lunch Mon–Sat, dinner Tues–Sat.

Girona

Built by the Romans on a hill crouching above the Riu Onyar, Girona has been the gateway to Catalunya for 2 millennia. It lacks Barcelona's sprawling hurry-scurry but more than compensates with the intimate charm of its medieval quarter and the relaxed grace of its riverbank neighborhoods. *Note:* The L11 bus circles the Old City, but the bus is of little use for sightseeing. The sites here are laid out on a simple walking route beginning at the main municipal parking lot/train station.

> *Thank the Romans for Girona's charming pastel riverfront property.*

START Pont de Sant Feliu.

❶ Riu Onyar & Pont de Sant Feliu. As you cross the pedestrian footbridge from Girona's main parking lot to the Old City, pause to watch the Riu Onyar undulate through town, reflecting the muted pastel houses on its embankments. The Romans built Girona to control the river crossing.

❷ Plaça de Sant Feliu. Note the statue of a lioness mounted on a stone column. In a city rife with legends, tradition holds that a Gironan

returning from a journey must kiss the statue's hindquarters to prove his good citizenship. Tourists do it too.

❸ Església de Sant Feliu. Eight Roman and early Christian sepulchers are the main attractions of this Romanesque church with Gothic flourishes. A chapel contains the remains of city patron Sant Narcís. During the 1285 siege of Girona, legend says that flies escaping from his tomb drove away the French armies. ⏱15 min. Pujada de Sant Feliu. ☎ 972-201-407. Free. Mon-Sat 7am-12:30pm and daily 4-6:30pm.

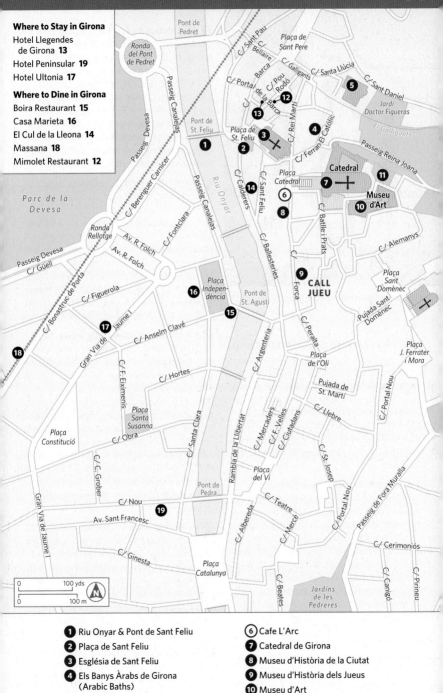

Where to Stay in Girona

Hotel Llegendes
de Girona **13**

Hotel Peninsular **19**

Hotel Ultonia **17**

Where to Dine in Girona

Boira Restaurant **15**

Casa Marieta **16**

El Cul de la Lleona **14**

Massana **18**

Mimolet Restaurant **12**

1 Riu Onyar & Pont de Sant Feliu

2 Plaça de Sant Feliu

3 Església de Sant Feliu

4 Els Banys Àrabs de Girona
(Arabic Baths)

5 Museu d'Arqueologia
de Catalunya

6 Cafe L'Arc

7 Catedral de Girona

8 Museu d'Història de la Ciutat

9 Museu d'Història dels Jueus

10 Museu d'Art

11 Jardins de la Francesa

> *The impassioned high relief carvings of the Església de Sant Feliu.*

④ Els Banys Àrabs de Girona (Arabic Baths). Built in 1194, after the Moors had been expelled, these baths follow a Roman rather than Arabic model. Nuns used them as a laundry in the 17th century, but they've been restored to show the ingenuity of medieval hygiene. ⏱ 20 min. C/ Ferran el Catòlic, s/n. ☎ 972-190-797. www.banysarabs.cat. 2€. Apr–Sept Mon–Sat 10am–7pm and Sun 10am–2pm; Oct–Mar daily 10am–2pm.

⑤ ★ Museu d'Arqueologia de Catalunya. Ostensibly dedicated to archaeology, this fine museum in a Romanesque Benedictine monastery would be called an art museum—except that all the work is more than 2,000 years old and the artists are anonymous. ⏱ 30 min. Plaça de Santa Llúcia, s/n. ☎ 972-202-632. www.mac.es. 2.30€, 1.65€ seniors. June–Sept Tues–Fri 10:30am–1:30pm and 4–7pm, Sat–Sun 10am–2pm; Oct–May Tues–Fri 10am–2pm and 4–6pm, Sat–Sun 10am–2pm.

⑥ 🍷 Cafe L'Arc. The arc in the name of this classic bar refers to the old Roman gate to the city on the Via Augusta. Enjoy a chorizo sandwich as you watch insane joggers scale the cathedral's 89 steps. Plaça Catedral, 9. ☎ 972-203-087. $.

⑦ ★★ Catedral de Girona. Boasting Europe's widest Gothic nave (23m/75 ft.), this church is known for its medieval Creation tapestry that includes a rare portrait of Jewish citizens. The carved capitals of the cloister are treasures of 12th-century Catalan sculpture, vividly narrating moral tales in intricate twists of stone. ⏱ 45 min. Plaça de la Catedral, s/n. ☎ 972-214-426. www.catedraldegirona.org. 5€ with audio guide, 3€ students and seniors. Apr–Oct daily 10am–8pm; Nov–Mar daily 10am–7pm.

⑧ Museu d'Història de la Ciutat. Even the building, with its 2nd-century cellars, recapitulates Girona's past. Apart from the Capuchin cemetery, where dead friars decayed on seats notched into the walls, the most interesting rooms deal with the artistic bloom of the early 20th century, subsequent repression under Franco, and the rebirth of Catalan identity. ⏱ 45 min. C/ Força, 27. ☎ 972-222-229. www.ajuntament.gi/museuciutat. 3€, 2€ seniors and students. Daily 10am–2pm; Tues–Sat also 5–7pm.

⑨ ★★ Museu d'Història dels Jueus. This modern museum relates the prominent role of the Jewish quarter, or Call, from the 12th century until Jews were expelled in 1492. Exhibits in interconnected medieval buildings take great pains to explain an unfamiliar faith and tradition to Spaniards, but go beyond basic education to explore Jewish artistic and cultural traditions specific to Catalunya, including exquisitely carved sepulchers. ⏱ 45 min. C/ Força Vella, 8. ☎ 972-216-761. www.ajuntament.gi/call. 2€, 1.50€ seniors and students. May–Oct Mon–Sat 10am–8pm and Sun 10am–3pm; Nov–Apr Mon–Sat closes 6pm.

⑩ ★★ Museu d'Art. The Romanesque vaults of the Episcopal Palace house this superb museum of Catalan art that ranges from powerful murals and altarpieces of the 12th century to the expressive art of the region's early-20th-century innovators. ⏱ 1 hr. Pujada de la Catedral, 12. ☎ 972-209-536. www.museuart.com. Mar–Sept Tues–Sat 10am–7pm and Sun 10am–2pm; Oct–Feb Mon–Sat closes 6pm.

⑪ kids Jardins de la Francesa. From the shaded gardens behind the art museum, you can ascend a staircase to walk Girona's ancient city walls.

Where to Stay & Dine

> The Moroccan meatballs at El Cul de la Lleona.

Boira Restaurant *MEDITERRANEAN/MARKET*
Climb the flight of stairs from the bustling plaza to a tranquil dining room with a strong emphasis on seasonal local food. Ask for a table overlooking the river. Plaça Independencia, 17. ☎ 972-219-605. Entrees 13€–17€. AE, MC, V. Lunch & dinner daily.

★ Casa Marieta *CATALAN*
More than a century of patina gives character to this dining room with wood-beamed ceilings and hay rakes on the walls. Try the signature Catalan seafood stew, *suquet*, on the city's liveliest eating and drinking plaza. Plaça Independencia, 5–6. ☎ 972-201-016. Entrees 7€–15€. MC, V. Lunch & dinner Tues–Sun.

kids El Cul de la Lleona *MOROCCAN*
Warm aromas of saffron, cumin, and coriander should be enough to entice you into this colorful Moroccan eatery near the cathedral for chickpea couscous or roasted lemon chicken. C/ Calderera, 8. ☎ 972-203-158. 8€–13€. MC, V. Lunch & dinner Mon–Sat.

★★ Hotel Llegendes de Girona
A modern renovation of a medieval building next to Sant Feliu celebrates the storied history of the city with reliefs and carvings recounting Girona legends. It's an ideal location for exploring the Old City from a sleekly high-tech, very comfortable room. Portal de la Barca, 4. ☎ 972-220-905. www.llegendeshotel.com. 15 rooms. Doubles 109€–150€. AE, DC, MC, V.

Hotel Peninsular
A good bet in the commercial shopping district near the train station, this recently refreshed but traditional hotel is handy for tapas hopping around the Pont de Pedra, and a 10-minute walk to the warren of the Old City. C/ Nou, 3 (at Avinguda Sant Françesc, 6). ☎ 972-203-800. www.novarahotels.com. 48 rooms. Doubles 74€–85€. AE, MC, V.

Hotel Ultonia
Less convenient to the Old City but still within walking distance, the Ultonia fits like a well-worn sport coat—comfortable but not too fancy. Avinguda Jaume I, 22. ☎ 972-203-850. www.husa.es. 45 rooms. Doubles 70€. AE, DC, MC, V.

★★★ Massana *CATALAN*
Pere Massana started running a simple roasted meat restaurant 2 decades (and numerous accolades) ago. He's transformed the space into a model of artful elegance and reinvented simple Catalan food as sparely modern dishes with explosive flavors and winning textures. Massana is the best fine dining in Girona and among the best in Catalunya. Bonastruch de Porta, 10. ☎ 972-213-820. Entrees 23€–30€. AE, DC, MC, V. Lunch Mon–Sat, dinner Mon and Wed–Sat.

Mimolet Restaurant *CATALAN/FRENCH*
The stylish dining room in this ancient building excels at such comfort fare as cassoulet, roast duck, or sea bream with roasted vegetables. Pou Rodó, 12. ☎ 972-202-124. Entrees 17€–25€. AE, MC, V. Lunch Tues–Sun, dinner Tues–Sat.

Catalunya Fast Facts

> A pharmacy in Girona's Old Town.

Arriving & Getting Around

BY PLANE Most overseas travelers reach Catalunya via Barcelona, but flights from all over Spain and Europe also service **Aeropuerto Girona-Costa Brava** (☎ 972-186-600; www.aena.es), just 12km (7½ miles) outside Girona. Buses run hourly to Girona and the Costa Brava.

BY TRAIN Again, Barcelona is the hub for rail service in Catalunya, with frequent connections northeast to Girona (service provided by **Renfe Girona,** Plaça d'Espanya, s/n; ☎ 902-240-202; www.renfe.es) and southwest to Tarragona (**Renfe Tarragona,** Plaza Pedrera, s/n; ☎ 902-240-202; www.renfe.es). Rail connections from Barcelona are also the best bet for reaching Montserrat, Vilafranca del Penedès, and the Costa Daurada. **BY BUS** Getting around by bus means using Girona as a hub for the Costa Brava and Tarragona for the Costa Daurada. From Girona to Costa Brava, the main services are provided by **SARFA** (☎ 972-201-796; www.sarfa.com). Between Tarragona, Costa Daurada, and Penedès, services are provided by **Plana** (☎ 977-354-445; www.autocarsplana.com).

BY CAR The **AP-7 toll road** links Figueres, Girona, Barcelona, and Tarragona with side roads to the beaches. The nontoll **N-II and A-2** highways parallel the toll road from the north to just outside Tarragona, where they turn inland. The **AP-2 toll road** runs west out of Barcelona through the Penedès, with good connections to Montserrat.

Booking Services

iPunt de Benvinguda, C/ Berenguer Carnicer, 3, Girona (☎ 972-211-678), arranges lodging and tours in Girona. (The office is open mid-Sept to June daily 9am–2pm and Mon–Sat 3–5pm; July to mid-Sept daily 9am–8pm.) **Turisme Sitges,** C/Sinia Morera, 1, Sitges (☎ 902-103-428 or 938-109-340), also books accommodation in Sitges.

Doctors & Hospitals

For emergency medical or dental attention, go to the *centro de urgencia* (emergency room) of the nearest hospital. Non-E.U. residents can consult national health service doctors for a relatively small fee; ask at your hotel for a list of doctors. Large-city hospitals with emergency rooms can be found in the following cities. **TARRAGONA** **Hospital Universitari De Tarragona Joan XXIII,** C/ Doctor Mallafre Guasch, 4 (☎ 977-295- 800). **GIRONA** **Hospitalitat de la Mare de Deu de Lourdes,** C/ Santa Eugènia, 25

(☎ 972-244-806). FIGUERES **Hospital de Figueres,** Ronada Rector Aroles, s/n (☎ 972-501-400). VILAFRANCA **Hospital Comarcal De l'Alt Penedes,** C/ Espirall, s/n (☎ 938-180-440).

Internet Access
Wi-Fi has become common in most hotels and is increasingly offered as a free amenity except in business hotels. Hotels without in-room Internet connections may provide access through a public computer. Internet cafes are common.

Pharmacies
To find an open pharmacy outside normal business hours, check the list of stores posted on the door of any drugstore. By law, there's always a drugstore open somewhere. Drugstores are called *farmacías*. When open, they display a neon green cross.

Police
Call ☎ **088** for the national police or ☎ **092** for the local police.

Post Office
GIRONA The main post office is at Avinguda Ramón Folch, 2 (☎ 972-222-111). TARRAGONA The main post office is on Plaça Corsini, s/n (☎ 977-240-149). VILAFRANCA The post office is at Avinguda Tarragona, 89 (☎ 938-903-106). All three are open Monday to Saturday 8am to 9pm.

Visitor Information
COSTA BRAVA **Oficina de Turisme Girona-Costa Brava** provides information about the entire Costa Brava and Figueres. It's at C/ Berenguer Carnicer, 3 (☎ 972-211-678; http://en.costabrava.org), and is open Monday to Saturday 9am to 2pm and 3 to 5pm, Sunday 9am to 2pm. CADAQUÉS **Oficina de Turisme** is at Cotxe, 1 (☎ 972-258-315; www.cadaques.cat), and is open Monday to Saturday 9am to 1pm and 3 to 6pm; Sunday 10am to 1pm. CAMBRILS **Turisme de Cambrils** is at Passeig de Cambrils, 1 (☎ 977-792-307; www.cambrils-tourism.com), and is open Monday to Friday 9:30am to 2pm and 4:30 to 6pm; Saturday 9:30am to 2pm. FIGUERES **Oficina de Turisme** is at Plaça de Sol

(☎ 972-503-155; www.figueresciutat.com), and is open mid-June to mid-September Monday to Saturday 9am to 8pm and Sunday 10am to 2pm; mid-September to mid-June Monday to Friday 10am to 2pm and 4 to 7pm, Saturday 10am to 2pm. PALAMÓS **Oficina de Turisme** is at Passeig de Mar, s/n (☎ 972-600-550; www.palamos.org), and is open Tuesday to Saturday 10am to 2pm and 3:30 to 7:30pm. POBLET **Oficina Comarcal de Turisme** offers information on wine tourism, agri-tourism, and hiking: It's at Paseo Abat Conill, 9 (☎ 977-871-247; www.concadebarbera.info), and is open Monday to Saturday 10am to 2pm and 3 to 6pm; Sunday 10am to 2pm. ROSES **Oficina de Turisme** is at Avinguda de Rhode, 77–79 (☎ 972-257-331; www.roses.cat), and is open mid-June to mid-September daily 9am to 9pm daily; mid-Sept to mid-June Monday to Friday 9am to 6pm, Saturday 10am to 2pm and 3 to 6pm, Sunday 10am to 1pm. SALOU **Patronato de Turisme** is at Passeig de Jaume, 1 (☎ 977-350-102; www.salou.org), and is open Monday to Friday 9:30am to 2pm and 4 to 6pm; Saturday 10am to 2pm and 4 to 6pm; Sunday 10am to 2pm. SANT FELIU DE GUÍXOLS **Oficina Municipal de Turisme** is at Passeig del Mar, 8–12 (972-820-051; www.guixols.cat), and is open Monday to Saturday 10am to 1pm and 4 to 7pm; Sunday 10am to 2pm. SANT SADURNÍ D'ANOIA **Oficina de Turisme** is at C/ Hospital, 26 (☎ 938-913-188; www.turismesantsadurni.cat), and is open Monday to Saturday 10am to 2pm and 4 to 7pm. SITGES **Oficina de Turisme** is at C/ Sinia Morera, 1 (☎ 902-103-428; www.sitgestur.com), and is open Monday to Friday 9am to 2pm and 4 to 6:30pm. TARRAGONA **Oficina de Turisme** is at C/ Major, 39 (☎ 977-250-795; www.tarragonaturisme.es), and is open Monday to Saturday 10am to 2pm and 4 to 7pm; Sunday 10am to 2pm. TOSSA DE MAR **Oficina Municipal de Turisme** is at C/ del Pelegrí, 25 (☎ 972-340-108; www.infotossa.com), and is open Monday to Saturday 10am to 2pm and 4 to 7pm. VILAFRANCA DE PENEDÈS **Oficina de Turisme,** C/ Cort, 14 (☎ 938-181-254; www.vilafranca.cat), is open Tuesday to Saturday 9am to 1pm; Monday to Saturday 4 to 7pm.

14
Barcelona

Our Favorite Moments

It's hardly a shock that Barcelona has become such a hot destination. What's surprising is how long it took the world to discover the thriving Catalan capital's diverse charms, which draw architecture and design fanatics, foodies, culture hounds, history buffs, and those merely in search of an all-night party.

❶ Wandering the Barri Gòtic. Barcelona's Gothic Quarter is a mesmerizing labyrinth of medieval buildings and narrow streets; it's a joy to take a stroll and discover a quiet square or picturesque patio. Meander down Sant Sever and slip into Plaça Sant Felip Neri, or along C/ dels Banys Nous. See p. 434.

❷ Breathing in La Boquería. Barcelona's wonderfully redolent food market is a feast for the senses, with hundreds of colorful stalls overflowing with fresh seafood, wild mushrooms, meats, and vegetables. For a special treat, pop into Bar Pintxo or El Quim for breakfast or lunch. See p. 410, ❽.

❸ Tuning in to El Palau de la Música. This spectacular 1908 Modernista museum piece draws hordes for its architectural tours. But there's nothing quite like experiencing a concert here; the spine-tingling monument to Art Nouveau excess takes a back seat to no musician. See p. 418, ❻.

❹ Gawking at La Sagrada Família. Gaudí's legendary, futuristic church remains a work in progress, but its soaring spires—like melting candles—never fail to amaze. Try to take in all its dense symbolism and grasp that this singular vision was begun a century ago. See p. 406, ❶.

❺ Grooving to jazz at La Pedrera (Casa Milà). The dreamlike rooftop of Antoni Gaudí's finest building is topped by surreal-looking chimneys, but it really comes to life during a summer eve's music program of jazz, swing, flamenco, or tango. Tap your toes, sip Cava (Catalan sparkling wine), and watch the Passeig de Gràcia turn to night. See p. 408, ❷.

❻ Biking along the beach. Only 20 years ago Barcelona turned its back on the Mediterranean and its polluted port; today the revitalized waterfront is lined with leisurely bike paths and immaculate beaches. Take a pit stop at a traditional seafood haunt in Barceloneta. See p. 414, ❼.

❼ Joining the throngs on La Rambla. Barcelona's pedestrian-only boulevard is the epicenter of life in the capital, and even though it's touristy, joining the vibrant street parade is the best way to immerse yourself in the city. Pick up fresh flowers and come face-to-face with outrageous human statues. See p. 410, ❼.

❽ Reveling in Santa Maria del Mar. This Gothic church is architectural perfection, a model of graceful, soaring dimensions. A sublime sanctuary on a quiet afternoon, it's also thrilling if you catch a society wedding spilling out onto the steps—which you can watch from a wine bar across the plaza. See p. 411, ⓫.

❾ Marveling at Modernista masterpieces. Beyond the must-sees La Pedrera and La Sagrada Família, Barcelona's L'Eixample neighborhood is full of spectacular Modernista buildings. Start on Passeig de Gràcia and see the Manzana de la Discòrdia, and then fan out to see innumerable examples of the Modernista craze that took over Barcelona in the late 19th and early 20th centuries. See p. 424.

❿ Sampling cutting-edge Catalan cuisine. Led by the likes of Ferran Adrià, Catalan cooking has exploded, making Barcelona the hottest dining scene in Europe. From chic tapas bars to minimalist haunts known for their celebrity chefs, Barcelona is a destination for gastronomic pilgrimages. See p. 430.

⓫ Dipping into old-school Barcelona. Unfazed by today's fashions and fast pace are authentic, time-stopping treasures in the Old City,

> PREVIOUS PAGE Antoni Gaudí's Casa Milà, or
La Pedrera (The Quarry). THIS PAGE Strollers
on C/ del Bisbe in the Barri Gòtic.

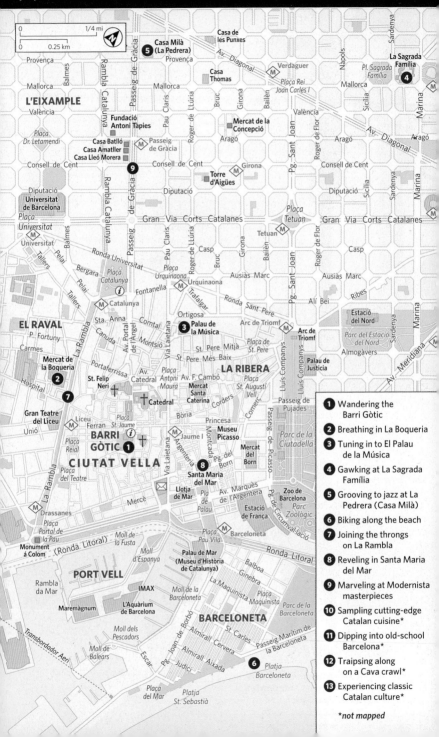

1 Wandering the Barri Gòtic

2 Breathing in La Boqueria

3 Tuning in to El Palau de la Música

4 Gawking at La Sagrada Família

5 Grooving to jazz at La Pedrera (Casa Milà)

6 Biking along the beach

7 Joining the throngs on La Rambla

8 Reveling in Santa Maria del Mar

9 Marveling at Modernista masterpieces

10 Sampling cutting-edge Catalan cuisine*

11 Dipping into old-school Barcelona*

12 Traipsing along on a Cava crawl*

13 Experiencing classic Catalan culture*

*not mapped

> *There's been a food market on the site of La Boquería since the Middle Ages; the current structure was finished in 1914.*

portals to an earlier era: a 1920s Modernista chocolate shop; a *granja,* or milk bar, serving thick chocolate drinks as it has for 125 years; or a gourmet food and wine shop in the same family for four generations. See p. 430.

⓬ **Traipsing along on a Cava crawl.** You can do a tapas crawl anywhere in Spain, but in Barcelona premeal snacks are washed down by glasses of Cava. *Xampanyerías* (Cava bars) are friendly spots where good cheer bubbles over. See p. 479.

⓭ **Experiencing classic Catalan culture.** La Mercé, Barcelona's signature folklore festival, has something for everyone: *castellers* (human "towers"); *gigants* and *cab grosses* (massive costumed royal figures parading the streets); and devils running, chasing each other down with fireworks in *correfocs* (fire parades). It's a blast and a quintessential expression of Catalan pride. See p. 368.

> *Quimet i Quimet, known for its tapas and wide selection of cheeses.*

The Best of Barcelona in 1 Day

This very full day, a "greatest hits" tour, begins with the best of Barcelona's Modernista architecture in the morning, followed by a stroll down the epic Rambla. It ends with the highlights of the Ciutat Vella, or Old City. You'll need your walking shoes.

> The spires of the handsome Catedral de Barcelona can be seen from all over the Old City.

START Metro to Sagrada Família.

1 ★★★ kids **La Sagrada Família.** Antoni Gaudí's unfinished legacy, the soaring 1882 "Holy Family" church, is a testament to his singular vision: the art of the impossible. This mind-altering creation—the best known, if not necessarily the best example, of Modernista architecture—has

become Barcelona's calling card. Its eight bejeweled spires drip like melting candlesticks, and virtually every square inch of the surface explodes with intricate spiritual symbols. Gaudí was run over by a tram long before it could be finished, and at present it remains only an otherworldly facade. Though many once hoped it would be left unfinished, a private foundation

1. La Sagrada Família
2. La Pedrera (Casa Milà)
3. tapaç 24
4. Casa Batlló
5. Casa Amatller
6. Casa Lleó Morera
7. La Rambla
8. Mercat de La Boqueria
9. Catedral de Barcelona
10. Museu Picasso
11. Santa Maria del Mar
12. La Vinya del Senyor

> *The sandcastlelike spires of La Sagrada Família drip with symbolism.*

Travel Tip

With a single ticket from **ArticketBCN Discounts** (www.articketbcn.org), you can visit seven top art museums in Barcelona, including the Museu Picasso, Museu Nacional d'Art de Catalunya (MNAC), Fundació Joan Miró, and the Museu d'Art Contemporani de Barcelona (MACBA). Purchase the ticket (20€; good for 6 months) at individual museum ticket offices, the Plaça de Catalunya Tourist Information Office, branches of Caixa Catalunya bank, online at www.barcelonaturisme.com, or from Tel-Entrada (☎ 902-10-12-12, or 34-93-326-29-46 from abroad; www.telentrada.com).

warriorlike chimneys that look like the inspiration for Darth Vader. ⏰ 1 hr. Passeig de Gràcia, 92 (at Provença). ☎ 902-40-09-73 or 902-10-12-12 for advance tickets. www.lapedreraeducacio.org. 9.50€ adults, 5.50€ students, part of ArticketBCN joint admission. Nov–Feb daily 9am–6pm; Mar–Oct daily 9am–7:30pm. Closed Dec 25–26 and Jan 1–6. Tours in English, Spanish, and Catalan. Metro: Diagonal or Provença.

③ 🍴 ★★ **tapaç 24.** The informal tapas bar of acclaimed chef Carles Abellan is a good-looking pit stop just off Passeig de Gràcia. Grab a snack or lunch of tantalizing small bites with big flavors, and wine and Cava by the glass. C/ Diputaciò, 269. ☎ 93-488-09-77. www.comerc24.com. $$.

④ ★★★ **Casa Batlló.** The centerpiece of the so-called Manzana de la Discordia (Block of Discord), Casa Batlló owes its extraordinary facade to Antoni Gaudí (1852–1926), who completed a remodeling in 1906. Thought to represent the legend of Saint George (patron saint of Catalunya) and his dragon, the house glimmers with fragments of colorful ceramics, while the roof curves like the blue-green scales of a dragon's back, and balconies evoke Carnivalesque masks or menacing monster jaws. The sinuous interior, full of custom Gaudí-designed furniture, is similarly stunning (though tours are a bit pricey). ⏰ 30 min. Passeig de Gràcia, 43. ☎ 93-488-06-66. www.casabatllo.es. Admission 17€ adults, 14€ kids and students, free for kids 4 & under. Daily 9am–8pm. Metro: Passeig de Gràcia.

is working furiously to finish the church—now projected for 2026, the centennial of Gaudí's death (with the vaults of the interior finished by 2010). ⏰ 1 hr. C/ Mallorca, 401. ☎ 93-207-30-31. www.sagradafamilia.org. 11€ adults, 15€ guided tour. Oct–Mar daily 9am–6pm; Apr–Sept daily 9am–8pm. Metro: Sagrada Família.

② ★★★ kids **La Pedrera (Casa Milà).** Thought by many to be the crowning glory of the Modernista movement, Antoni Gaudí's avant-garde apartment building Casa Milà is better known as La Pedrera (The Quarry) for its wavy mass of limestone. The exterior seems carved out of nature: It undulates like ocean waves along Passeig de Gràcia. The fascinating roof, what most people come to see, is guarded by a set of

> *The undulating lines of Gaudí's Casa Batlló suggest the dragon in the legend of St. George.*

⑤ ★★ Casa Amatller. Josep Puig i Cadafalch (1867–1956), a Gaudí contemporary, created this brilliant house—the first building on the Manzana de la Discordia block of Passeig de Gràcia—in 1900. It has a medieval-looking, ceramics-covered facade, topped by a distinctive Flemish-inspired roof. The carved stone and ironwork are related to the chocolate business and the hobbies of the original owners. ⏱ 10 min. Passeig de Gràcia, 41. ☎ 93-488-01-39. Ground floor open to public Mon–Sat 10am–7pm. Metro: Passeig de Gràcia.

⑥ ★ Casa Lleó Morera. This gorgeously ornate corner house (1905), the final member of the Block of Discord triumvirate, is the work of Lluís Domènech i Montaner (1853–1920), who designed El Palau de la Música Catalana and Hospital Sant Pau. Especially appealing when illuminated at night, the building is now home to the upscale leather-goods purveyor Loewe, which lamentably destroyed a good part of the lower facade and sumptuous interior of the ground floor. Passeig de Gràcia, 35. Except for the Loewe store, the house cannot be visited. Metro: Passeig de Gràcia.

> *Like no other apartments in the world, Casa Milà is Gaudí's best known work after the Sagrada Família.*

> A mosaic by Catalan artist Joan Miró underfoot on La Rambla, Barcelona's great commercial thoroughfare.

7 ★★★ kids **La Rambla.** Barcelona's great strolling boulevard is the centerpiece of life in the Catalan capital. It throbs with activity, as crowds at all hours of the day file past vendors, food markets, cafes, and historic buildings. The main avenue of La Rambla—with a lively succession of newspaper kiosks, fresh flower stands, bird sellers, and crowd-friendly human statues in elaborately conceived costumes and face paint—is actually composed of five smaller streets (Rambla de Canaletes, Rambla dels Estudis, Rambla de Sant Josep, Rambla dels Caputxins, Rambla de Santa Monica), each with a different character. About halfway down the boulevard, to the left as you face the port, is the Plaça Reial, a grand square with cafes, palm trees, arcades, and lampposts designed by Antoni Gaudí. Although it's now pretty touristy and you really have to watch your valuables, La Rambla is a must-experience. ⏱ 30 min. Begin at Plaça de Catalunya. Metro: Plaça de Catalunya.

8 ★★★ kids **Mercat de la Boquería.** Europe's largest food market, this dynamic, Catalan classic is the foundation of Barcelona's fascination with food. Wander among the more than 300 stalls and several small bar/restaurants to see and smell an amazingly lively gastronomic scene: the slicing, dicing, and selling of fresh fish, meats, produce, and more. Keep an eye out for *bolets* or *ceps* (wild mushrooms), massive prawns, eels, and octopus. The colorful bounty is a testament to the fertile region and Catalans' desire for the freshest and tastiest

foodstuffs available. ⏱ 30 min. La Rambla, 91–101. ☎ 93-318-25-84. Mon–Sat 8am–8pm. Metro: Liceu.

9 ★★ **Catedral de Barcelona.** The cathedral, the focal point of the Old City and a splendid example of Catalan Gothic architecture, was begun in 1298 but largely completed in the 14th and 15th centuries. Don't miss the carved choir and surprisingly lush cloister—a welcome oasis with its pond, magnolias, orange and palm trees, and white geese. ⏱ 45 min. Plaça de la Seu, s/n. ☎ 93-342-82-60. www.catedralbcn.org. Cathedral free; museum 1€; ticket for 1–4:30pm guided visit to museum, choir, rooftop terraces, and towers 4€; elevator to roof 2€. Cathedral daily 8am–1pm and 4:30–7:30pm; cloister museum daily 10am–1pm and 4:30–6:30pm; elevator 10:30am–1:30pm and 5–6pm. Metro: Jaume I.

10 ★★★ **Museu Picasso.** Pablo Picasso (1881–1973) was born in southern Spain, but he spent much of his youth and early creative years in Barcelona on his way to becoming the most famous artist of the 20th century. The museum houses the largest collection of his works in his native country: 2,500 paintings and sculptures, many of them early works, including several from his blue period. The highlight of the collection is *Las Meninas*, a series of 59 interpretations of Velázquez's masterpiece. The Picasso museum occupies several exquisite 15th-century palaces on a pedestrian-only street lined with medieval mansions. ⏱ 1 hr. Montcada,

15–23. ☎ 93-256-30-00. www.museupicasso.bcn. es. 9€ adults, 6€ students and youths 16–24, free for kids 15 & under, free Sun after 3pm and 1st Sun of the month, part of ArticketBCN joint admission. Tues–Sun 10am–8pm. Metro: Jaume I.

⑪ ★★ Santa Maria del Mar. A stunning 14th-century Catalan Gothic church that's neither opulent and jewel-encrusted nor home to a fabulous art collection. Instead, it's a simple and solemn but wholly inspired space—the kind of place about which architects understandably wax poetic, with perfect proportions in its three soaring naves, wide-spaced columns, and handsome stained-glass windows. 🕐 15 min. Plaça de Santa María. ☎ 93-215-74-11. Free. Mon–Sat 9am–1:30pm and 4:30–8pm; Sun 9am–2pm and 5–8:30pm. Metro: Jaume I.

⑪ 🍷 ★★ La Vinya del Senyor. A hip little wine bar with much-coveted tables on a terrace at the lovely square across from Santa Maria del Mar, it features an excellent selection of 100 or so wines from across Spain, including two dozen by the glass, as well as Spanish ham, salami, and cheeses. Plaça de Santa María, 5. ☎ 93-310-33-79. $$.

> *The Mercat de la Boquería is a feast for the eyes.*

> *The much-loved Santa Maria del Mar is one of the purest examples of Catalan Gothic architecture in Barcelona.*

The Best of Barcelona in 2 Days

After a very full first day in Barcelona, it's time for a more leisurely pace. Begin the day in the Gothic Quarter to get a feel for the city's ancient foundations before moving on to enjoy the revitalized waterfront, which has been a popular outdoor leisure destination since the 1992 Olympics. Stroll along the harbor, stop for lunch in the beachside district of Barceloneta, and hit the sands in the afternoon for sunbathing or a sunset cocktail, topped off by dinner at the new harbor, Port Olímpic.

> *An esplanade along Moll de la Fusta, between the Plaça Portal de la Pau and Plaça Antonio López.*

START Metro to Jaume I.

1 ★★ kids **Conjunt Monumental de la Plaça del Rei.** In one of the old quarter's most handsome squares, the stately Plaça del Rei, hemmed in by a remaining section of the old Roman city walls, is the fine **Museu d'Història de la Ciutat**—where the main attraction is underground walkways over the exposed foundations (1st c. B.C.–7th c. A.D.) of Barcino, the ancient city of the Romans and Visigoths. The **Palau**

Reial Major, an 11th-century royal palace and the residence of the Kings of Catalunya and Aragón, is also here. According to legend, Fernando and Isabel received Columbus at the Palau after he returned from the New World. ⏱ 1½ hr. Plaça del Rei, s/n. ☎ 93-315-11-11. www.museuhistoria.bcn.es. 6€ adults, 3€ students, free for kids 15 & under. June–Sept Tues–Sat 10am–8pm; Oct–Mar Tues–Sat 10am–2pm and 4–7pm; year-round Sun 10am–3pm. Metro: Jaume I.

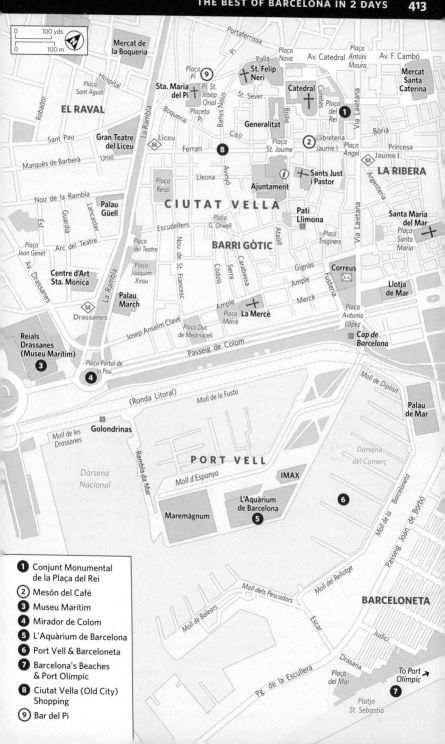

0 100 yds
0 100 m

Mercat de
la Boqueria

Portaferrissa

Plaça
Nova

Av. Catedral

Plaça
Antoni
Maura

Plaça
A. F. Cambó

Pi

Palla

Mercat
Santa
Caterina

Hospital

Plaça
Sant Agustí

Plaça
Pi

St. Felip
Neri

Catedral

Comtes

Plaça
del
Rei

EL RAVAL

Robador

Sta. Maria
del Pi

Pl. St.
Josep
Oriol

St. Sever

Plaça
del Rei

Via Laietana

Bòria

Boqueria

Placeta
Pi

Generalitat

Bisbe

Princesa

Gran Teatre
del Liceu

Liceu

Ferran

Plaça
St. Jaume

Llibreteria

Plaça
Jaume I

Jaume I

LA RIBERA

Sant Pau

Call

Lleona

Argenteria

Marquès de Barberà

Unió

Avinyó

Ajuntament

Sants Just
i Pastor

Nou de la Rambla

Plaça
Reial

CIUTAT VELLA

Pati
Llimona

Santa Maria
del Mar

Palau
Güell

Guàrdia

Lancaster

Escudellers

Plaça
G. Orwell

Ataülf

Plaça
Traginers

Plaça
Santa
Maria

Plaça
Jean Genet

Arc del Teatre

Plaça
del Teatre

BARRI GÒTIC

Serra

Carabassa

Gignàs

Correus

Centre d'Art
Sta. Monica

Plaça
Joaquim
Xirau

Nou de St. Francesc

Còdols

Ample

Mercè

Fusteria

Llotja
de Mar

Palau
March

Plaça
Duc
de Medinaceli

Ample

La Mercè

Plaça
Mercè

Plaça
Antonio
López

Drassanes

Josep Anselm Clavé

Passeig de Colom

Cap de
Barcelona

Reials
Drassanes
(Museu Marítim)

Plaça Portal de
la Pau

Moll de Dipòsit

Palau
de Mar

(Ronda Litoral)

Moll de la Fusta

Golondrinas

Moll de les
Drassanes

PORT VELL

Dàrsena
del Comerç

Dàrsena
Nacional

Rambla da Mar

Moll d'Espanya

IMAX

L'Aquàrium
de Barcelona

Moll de la Barceloneta

Maremàgnum

Passeig Joan de Borbó

Moll dels Pescadors

Moll del Rellotge

BARCELONETA

Moll de Balears

Escar

Judici

Drasana

To Port
Olímpic

Pg. de l'Escullera

Plaça
del Mar

Platja
St. Sebastià

① Conjunt Monumental
   de la Plaça del Rei

② Mesón del Café

③ Museu Marítim

④ Mirador de Colom

⑤ L'Aquàrium de Barcelona

⑥ Port Vell & Barceloneta

⑦ Barcelona's Beaches
   & Port Olímpic

⑧ Ciutat Vella (Old City)
   Shopping

⑨ Bar del Pi

> *Plaça del Rei stands over the old Roman city of Barcino.*

② 🍵 ★★★ **Mesón del Café.** This tiny 100-year-old place is probably one of the best cafes in the world. Locals drop in at all hours for superb *café con leche, café solo, cortado,* or a mean *picardía* (coffee with layers of condensed milk and whiskey). And while the coffee's great, there's something just ineffably cool about the place. Llibreteria, 16. ☎ 93-315-07-54. $.

❸ ★★ kids **Museu Marítim.** Barcelona's seafaring past comes to life in this rich maritime museum, located in the Reials Drassanes, or former Royal Shipyards. The medieval shipyards, a collection of evocative arches, columns, and vaults that was once at water's edge and today remains magnificently intact, is where the kingdom's ships were constructed, repaired, and dry-docked. Don't miss the glorious replica of a massive 16th-century vessel, the *Galería Reial.* ⏱ 1 hr. Avenida de les Drassanes, s/n. ☎ 93-342-99-20. www.mmb.cat. 6.50€ adults, 3.25€ kids 7–16. Daily 10am–8pm. Metro: Drassanes.

❹ kids **Mirador de Colom.** Though this monument to Christopher Columbus, built in 1888, has him pointing the wrong direction to the New World, it's a focal and meeting point, dividing the lower end of La Rambla from the waterfront. An elevator takes visitors inside to a *mirador* (lookout) for nice panoramic views of the harbor. ⏱ 30 min. Portal de la Pau, s/n. ☎ 93-302-52-24. 2.50€ adults, 1.50€ kids 4–12, free for kids 3 & under. June–Sept 9am–8:30pm; Nov–Apr 10am–6:30pm. Metro: Drassanes.

❺ kids ★★ **L'Aquàrium de Barcelona.** At Port Vell (the old port), and across the Rambla del Mar, a stylish drawbridge, is Europe's second-largest aquarium, with 21 glass tanks featuring different marine habitats. The highlight is a long, glass-enclosed underwater tunnel, where wide-eyed visitors can commune with fish, eels, and sharks. ⏱ 1 hr. Moll d'Espanya-Port Vell. ☎ 93-221-74-74. www.aquariumbcn.com. 17€ adults, 14€ seniors, 12€ kids 4–12 and students, free for kids 3 & under. July–Aug daily 9:30am–11pm; Sept–June Mon–Fri 9:30am–9pm, Sat–Sun 9:30am–9:30pm. Metro: Drassanes.

❻ **Port Vell & Barceloneta.** Moll de la Fusta, a very popular place for a *paseo,* or stroll, is a boardwalk and series of esplanades along Passeig Colom and the old harbor. It begins at the Columbus statue at the bottom of La Rambla and stretches to a giant Javier Mariscal sculpture of a playful crayfish and a colorful Pop-Art work by the American artist Roy Lichtenstein. Continuing past the harbor and along Passeig Joan de Borbó takes you to Barceloneta, a colorful old beachfront neighborhood that got a controversial makeover for the '92 Olympics, displacing many longtime residents. It's still known for its longtime *chiringuitos,* or informal seafood restaurants, which makes it a perfect place to stop for lunch, especially on weekends. ⏱ 45 min. Metro: Drassanes or Barceloneta.

❼ ★★ kids **Barcelona's Beaches & Port Olímpic.** It wasn't long ago that no self-respecting Barcelonan would venture down to the city's beaches, much less dream of wading into the polluted waters. Preparations for the 1992 Olympics dramatically reopened the city to the Mediterranean and cleaned up the urban beaches, vastly improving water quality. Today the long stretches of sand are a playground for city dwellers. The beaches (*platges*) are lined with palm trees, public sculptures, bars, and restaurants, as well as paths for biking, in-line skating, and walking. The first major beach is Barceloneta, followed to the north by Nova Icària (the most popular beach, near the Port Olímpic marina and Vila Olímpica district), Bogatell, and Mar Bella (an unofficial nudist beach). ⏱ 2 hr. Metro: Barceloneta or Ciutadella/Vila Olímpica.

> *The Mediterranean has since receded, but the site of the Museu Marítim was once at water's edge.*

8 Ciutat Vella (Old City) Shopping. Dozens of fashion boutiques, bars, and souvenir shops line bustling, pedestrian-only C/ Ferran, while dark, atmospheric C/ dels Banys Nous is home to some of the city's best antique shops. Shopaholics should continue across Vía Laetana to La Ribera and El Born, the site of some of the chicest boutiques in old Barcelona. See p. 452 for the box on "Prime Shopping Zones." ⏱ 2 hr. Metro: Liceu or Jaume I.

⑨ 🍺 ★ **Bar del Pi.** On one of the prettiest squares in the Ciutat Vella, or Old City, is one of the finest spots in town to linger at an outdoor cafe. Of the several cafes clustered around the square, Bar del Pi is the most traditional. People-watching opportunities abound, and on weekends artists and artisans set up booths in the plaza. Plaça Sant Josep Oriol. ☎ 93-302-21-23. $

> *Javier Mariscal, a Valencian artist who got his start in comics, designed the happy crayfish at Port Vell.*

The Best of Barcelona in 3 Days

This tour spends the morning on Montjuïc hill before making a brief stop in the Eixample district for one big Modernista highlight, finishing the day with a gorgeous bird's-eye view of the city from Tibidabo. (The first couple of days should be spent following "The Best of Barcelona in 2 Days.") The tour includes some of Barcelona's best stops for kids—open spaces that are particularly great after visiting museums.

> Lovers Playing with Almond Blossoms *(1975), a maquette for the sculptural group at La Défense, at the Fundació Joan Miró.*

START Metro to Espanya (though visitors who wish to take the aerial cable car from the port or funicular to Montjuïc should begin at Fundació Miró before working their way down to Poble Espanyol and MNAC).

❶ ★★★ Museu Nacional d'Art de Catalunya (MNAC). At the base of Montjuïc, within the domed Palau Nacional, this museum is anything but a stale repository of religious art. Its medieval collection, which includes Romanesque works salvaged from churches all over Catalunya, is unequaled; many of the superb altarpieces, polychromatic icons, and treasured frescoes are displayed in apses, just as they were in the country churches where they were found. These include the mesmerizing Apse of Santa María de Taüll, where a serene, doe-eyed Christ is surrounded by the apostles, who stand against an intense lapis lazuli–hued background. Other highlights are paintings by some of Spain's most celebrated Old Masters, including Velázquez, Ribera, and Zurbarán. The MNAC's more recently acquired exhibits cover the neoclassical, Modernista, and Noucentista (or *fin de siècle*) periods. ⏱ 1½ hr. Palau Nacional, Parc de Montjuïc.

1 Museu Nacional d'Art de Catalunya (MNAC)
2 El Poble Espanyol
3 La Font de Gat
4 Estadi Olímpic
5 Fundació Joan Miró
6 El Palau de la Música Catalana
7 Parc Güell

> One of the spectacular altarpieces at the Museu Nacional d'Art de Catalunya.

☎ 93-622-03-60. www.mnac.es. 8.50€ adults, 6€ students and youths 15–21, free for seniors and kids 14 & under and 1st Sun of the month, part of ArticketBCN joint admission. Tues–Sat 10am–7pm; Sun 10am–2:30pm. Metro: Espanya.

② ★ kids **El Poble Espanyol.** Erected for the 1929 Barcelona International Exhibition, this ambitious re-creation of a Spanish village presents more than 100 styles of emblematic architecture from across Spain, re-creating individual mansions, churches, streets, and squares, all reduced to scale. Though some adults and purists find it well-meaning kitsch, it's a fun and instructive place for families to visit and a great introduction to the country's architectural diversity. For those who haven't had the opportunity to travel the breadth of Spain and see its whitewashed Andalusian alleyways, small-town plazas, or Renaissance palaces, it's a godsend. ⏱ 1 hr. Avenida Marqués de Comillas, s/n, Parc de Montjuïc. ☎ 93-508-63-00. www.poble-espanyol.com. 8.50€ adults, 6.50€ seniors and students, 5.50€ kids 4–12, free for kids 3 & under, 30€ family ticket, 5€ night ticket. Mon 9am–8pm; Tues–Thurs 9am–2am; Fri–Sat 9am–4am; Sun 9am–midnight. Metro: Espanya, then 10-min walk uphill, or bus 13 or 50 from Plaça de Espanya.

③ 🍴 **La Font de Gat.** This resurrected Modernista cafe and restaurant, built by the acclaimed architect Josep Puig i Cadalfach, is ensconced in gardens of the Montjuïc hillside and makes for a relaxing spot for a coffee or beer, or even an inexpensive fixed-priced lunch. Passeig Sta. Madrona, 28. ☎ 93-289-04-04. $.

④ **Estadi Olímpic.** The setting for the majority of events during Barcelona's hosting of the 1992 Summer Olympics was Montjuïc. The park contains the Olympic Stadium, originally built in 1929 for the World's Fair, and Arata Isozaki's (b. 1931) sleek Palau d'Esports Sant Jordi, the indoor stadium that hosted the gymnastics and volleyball events (and now also hosts concerts). Nearby are a small sports museum, Galería Olímpica, and the outdoor pool and diving pavilion, which overlooks the city below. ⏱ 30 min. Avenida del Estadi, s/n, Parc de Montjuïc. Metro: Espanya (then take the escalator from Palau Nacional), bus 50 at Plaça d'Espanya, or Funicular de Montjuïc.

⑤ ★★ **Fundació Joan Miró.** Miró (1893–1983), a resolutely Catalan surrealist painter and sculptor, created a unique, whimsical artistic language—which to the uninitiated may look like colorful doodles—on his way to becoming one of the 20th century's most celebrated artists. In minimalist galleries bathed in natural light are several hundred of Miró's canvases, as well as a wealth of his drawings, graphics, and sculptures. A rooftop terrace and sculpture garden provide lovely views of Barcelona below. ⏱ 1½ hr. Parc de Montjuïc, s/n. ☎ 93-443-94-70. fundaciomiro-bcn.org. 8€ adults, 6€ students, free for kids 13 & under, part of ArticketBCN joint admission. July–Sept Tues–Wed and Fri–Sat 10am–8pm; Oct–June Tues–Wed and Fri–Sat 10am–7pm; year-round Thurs 10am–9:30pm and Sun 10am–2:30pm. Bus 50 at Plaça d'Espanya or Funicular de Montjuïc.

⑥ ★★★ **El Palau de la Música Catalana.** Lluís Domènech i Montaner's magnificent 1908 music hall is over-the-top ornate but indisputably one of Barcelona's Modernista masterpieces. The relatively sedate exterior is just a tease of what's inside: a riotous fantasy of ceramics, colored glass, and carved pumice, crowned by an enormous yellow, blue, and green stained-glass dome that looks like a swollen raindrop. It's surely the most exuberant music hall you'll ever see. A daytime guided tour addresses the architecture, but there's nothing like experiencing a concert here. ⏱ 1 hr. C/ de Sant Francesc de Paula, 2. ☎ 902-44-28-82 or 93-295-72-00 for information. www.palaumusica.org. Tour 12€ adults, 10€ students and seniors. Advance tickets at box office or online. Guided tours daily every 30 min. 10am–3:30pm (in English on the hour 10am–3pm). Metro: Urquinaona.

7 ★★★ kids **Parc Güell.** Yet another of Gaudí's signature creations, this open-air park on the outskirts of the Eixample district is pure whimsy. Resembling an idiosyncratic theme park, it features a mosaic-covered lizard fountain, Hansel and Gretel pagodas, and undulating benches swathed in broken pieces of ceramics, called *trencadis*. Gaudí carved part of the park out of a hillside, fashioning a forest of columns like tree trunks. A planned housing development that was never fully realized, Parc Güell is home to but a single house (where the ascetic architect lived while working on the project), now the **Casa-Museu Gaudí,** a small museum about Gaudí's life and work. On clear days, you can see much of Barcelona laid out beneath your feet, including the spires of La Sagrada Família and the twin towers on the beach. ⊙ 1 hr. **Carretera del Carmel, 28. ☎ 93-213-04-88.** Parc free, Casa-Museu Gaudí 4€. Dec–Feb daily 10am–6pm; Mar and Nov daily 10am–7pm; Apr and Oct daily 10am–8pm; May–Sept daily 10am–9pm. Metro: Lesseps (then a 15-min. walk uphill). Bus: 24 or 28.

> *The mosaic lizard at Gaudí's trippy Parc Güell, which spreads over several wooded acres above Barcelona.*

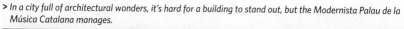

> *In a city full of architectural wonders, it's hard for a building to stand out, but the Modernista Palau de la Música Catalana manages.*

Ancient Barcelona

Barcelona is one of Spain's most historic cities. Founded as Barcino by the Romans in A.D. 15, it expanded outside the ancient walls—sections of which still remain—in the 11th century. Much of medieval Barcelona lives on gloriously in the Ciutat Vella (Old City) quarters of Barri Gòtic and La Ribera. The Barri Gòtic walking tour (see p. 434) provides additional details of the Roman and medieval city, including El Call, the old Jewish Quarter.

> *Sections of the old Roman walls, 2m (6½ ft.) thick in places, still remain in parts of the city.*

START Metro to Jaume I.

❶ ★★ Santa Maria del Mar. Designed by the architect Berenguer de Montagut in the mid–14th century and completed in just 5 decades, Santa Maria del Mar is a soaring Catalan Gothic church that once faced the Barcelona waterfront; its name, St. Mary of the Sea, refers to its history as a place of worship for ship owners, merchants, and sailors (and wives left behind) who came to pray for safe returns. ⏱ 30 min. See p. 411, **❶❶**.

❷ C/ de Montcada. At the back entrance to Santa Maria del Mar is this narrow, pedestrian-only lane through the La Ribera quarter, one of the most handsome medieval streets in Barcelona. From its origins in 1148, the street became an epicenter of commercial life. From the 14th to the 17th century, Montcada's *palaus*, or mansions, were.home to wealthy and noble families, many of whom were patrons of Santa Maria del Mar. While many *palaus* are private, a few are occupied by museums and galleries (including the famous Museu Picasso; see p. 410, **❶⓪**), giving visitors a chance to see their gorgeous courtyards and massive central stone staircases. ⏱ 45 min. Metro: Jaume I.

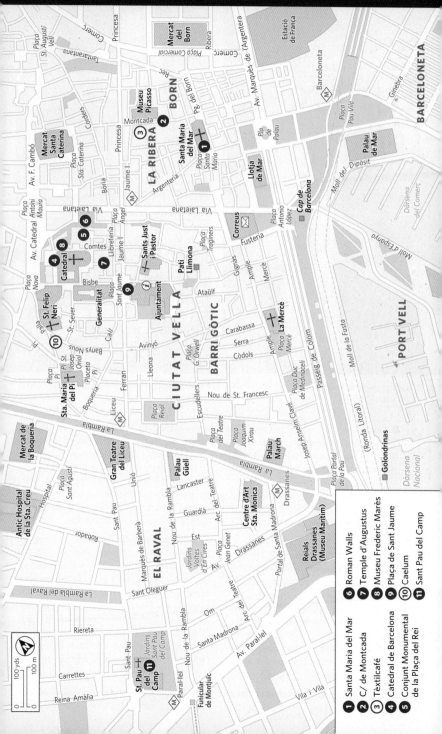

1 Santa Maria del Mar
2 C/ de Montcada
3 Textilcafé
4 Catedral de Barcelona
5 Conjunt Monumental de la Plaça del Rei
6 Roman Walls
7 Temple d'Augustus
8 Museu Frederic Marès
9 Plaça de Sant Jaume
10 Caelum
11 Sant Pau del Camp

> *Captains and their sailors once prayed seaside at Santa Maria del Mar.*

> *Guard geese still roam the cloister of Barcelona's cathedral.*

③ 🍴 **Tèxtilcafé.** This unexpected retreat, in the splendid medieval courtyard of the palace that houses the **Museu Tèxtil i d'Indumentària** (a small textiles museum), is a perfectly relaxed spot for coffee and a croissant at an outdoor table or a full, fixed-priced value lunch inside. C/ de Montcada, 12–14. ☎ 93-268-25-98. $.

④ ★★★ **Catedral de Barcelona.** A Roman temple and later a mosque once stood on this site in the heart of the Gothic Quarter. The lush cloister, built between 1350 and 1448, continues to be home to white geese, which in the Middle Ages functioned as guard dogs, their squawks alerting priests to intruders. Beneath the ancient slabs of the stone floor lie the remains of members of the Barri Gòtic's ancient guilds. ⏲ 30 min. See p. 410, ❾.

⑤ ★★★ kids **Conjunt Monumental de la Plaça del Rei.** Plaça del Rei abuts a remaining section of the old Roman walls, and in the 1930s, archaeologists unearthed ruins of Barcino, the old Roman city. (The subterranean ruins can be visited by the public.) The five-story tower Mirador del Rei Martí, which rises above the square, dates to 1555, when it was built as a lookout for foreign invasions—and peasant uprisings. ⏲ 45 min. See p. 412, ❶.

⑥ ★ kids **Roman Walls.** Barcino was a small settlement, comprising just 10 hectares (25 acres). Perhaps the biggest thing about Barcino was its 2m (6½-ft.) thick walls. Several sections of the Roman walls, enlarged in the 3rd and 4th centuries A.D., remain; some of the best examples are on Plaça Ramon Berenguer, parallel to Via Laietana. To the right of the front entrance to the Catedral de Barcelona, the Portal de l'Angel's twin semicircular towers frame the entrance to C/ del Bisbe. ⏲ 15 min. Metro: Jaume I.

⑦ ★ **Temple d'Augustus.** Three massive Corinthian columns, the best-preserved relics of the Roman city, are all that remain of the Temple d'Augustus, the principal temple built in the 1st century B.C. Hidden from view and lower than Barcelona's modern street level, they are one of the Barri Gòtic's great secrets. The temple once formed part of the Roman Forum dedicated to the emperor Caesar Augustus. ⏱ 10 min. C/ del Paradis, 10 (inside Centre Excursionista de Catalunya). ☎ 93-315-23-11. Free. June–Sept Tues–Sat 10am–8pm, Sun 10am–2pm; Oct–May Tues–Sat 10am–2pm and 4–8pm, Sun 10am–2pm. Metro: Jaume 1.

8 ★★ **Museu Frederic Marès.** Marès, a 20th-century sculptor and evidently obsessive collector, amassed one of Spain's finest private collections of medieval sculpture, from the pre-Roman to the Romanesque, Gothic, baroque, and Renaissance eras. The collection is housed in a palace—itself worthy of study, with its handsome interior courtyards, carved stone, and expansive ceilings—just behind the Catedral de Barcelona. ⏱ 45 min. Plaça de Sant Iú, 5–6. ☎ 93-310-58-00. www.museumares.bcn.cat. 4€ adults, free for kids 11 & under and Wed 3–7pm. Tues–Sat 10am–7pm; Sun 10am–3pm. Metro: Jaume I.

9 ★ **Plaça de Sant Jaume.** The site of the city and regional governments, this stately plaza is also a popular gathering place for Barcelonans during holiday celebrations and political demonstrations. The **Palau de la Generalitat,** home to the autonomous Catalan government, dates to the 15th century, while across the square, the 14th-century **Casa de la Ciutat,** built around a central courtyard, houses the municipal government. The **Saló de Cent** (Room of 100 Jurors) features immense arches, typical of the Catalan Gothic style. ⏱ 30 min. Casa de la Ciutat: Plaça de Sant Jaume, s/n. ☎ 93-402-70-00. Free. Sun 11am–3:30pm. Metro: Jaume I.

10 🍮 ★ **Caelum.** On the surface this appears to be simply an appealing shop selling teas, jams, olive oil, sweets, and other products made by nuns and religious orders in Spain and Europe. But downstairs in the cafe (where you can have tea, coffee, pastries, and sandwiches), in a space referred to as "the crypt," is another treat altogether: the exposed foundations of 14th-century Jewish baths, or *mikva'ot.* C/ de la Palla, 8. ☎ 93-302-69-93. $.

11 ★★ **Sant Pau del Camp.** The oldest church in Barcelona, dating back to the 9th century, Saint Paul of the Countryside used to sit far beyond the city walls, though today it is surrounded by the Raval barrio. The formerly rural church and monastery remains remarkably intact, with original Romanesque capitals and bases of the portal complementing sections from a rebuilding in the 11th and 12th centuries. The chapter house holds the tomb—which dates to A.D. 912—of Count Guífre Borrell, son of Wilfred the Hairy. ⏱ 30 min. C/ de Sant Pau, 101 (El Raval). ☎ 93-441-00-01. Cloister 2€. Mon–Fri 5–8pm; Tues–Sat 10am–1:30pm. Metro: Paral·lel.

> *The Catalan, Spanish, and Barcelonese flags fly proudly above Casa de la Ciutat.*

Modernista Barcelona

Barcelona is renowned for Modernisme, or Catalan Art Nouveau, a wildly original style of architecture that flourished in the late 19th and early 20th centuries. Best known are the stunning works of Antoni Gaudí, but so many talented Modernista architects left their mark on Barcelona that it's a big task to see them all. Still, this tour will attempt to hit the major landmarks in a day.

START **Metro to Lessep, then a taxi or 15-min. walk uphill to Parc Güell.**

❶ ★★★ kids **Parc Güell.** Although this visionary real estate development was never completed, the project bears Gaudí's stamp and reflects the naturalism that was beginning to flower in his work. The architect set out to design every detail in the park, but a disciple, Josep María Jujol (1879–1949), was responsible for the park's colorful splashes of *trencadis* (designs of broken shards of ceramics). At the main entrance are fairy tale-like gatehouses topped with chimneys resembling wild mushrooms. The covered marketplace, with an extraordinary tiled lizard fountain at the entrance, is supported by 86 Doric columns (not the 100 planned). Most famous are the sinuous, mosaic-covered benches that trace the perimeter of the plaza above. ◷ 45 min. See p. 419, ❼.

❷ ★★★ kids **La Sagrada Família.** Gaudí's most famous work is a landmark of unbridled ambition. He dedicated 4 decades of his life to it, and though the architect left behind no detailed plans, he expected that the cathedral—the world's largest if completed—would take several generations to finish. Gaudí envisioned 12 spires (one for each of the Apostles), a massive dome over the apse, and four additional higher spires, as well as one central bell tower. Biblical elements, such as the Tree of Calvary, pack the dense surface. ◷ 45 min. See p. 406, ❶.

❸ ★★ **Hospital de Santa Creu i Sant Pau.** Just a few blocks' walk from La Sagrada Família, this hospital campus reveals that Lluís Domènech i Montaner, like Gaudí, also thought in grand terms. Begun in 1902, it too was left unfinished at the time of its architect's death, with just 18 of a planned 48 pavilions completed (12 of those are by Domènech i Montaner, and all are classified as World Heritage monuments). The fanciful brick-and-tile pavilions feature gorgeous vaulted ceilings and decorative mosaics and sculpture. ◷ 45 min. Sant Antoni María Claret, 167-171. ☎ 902-076-621 or 93-256-25-04. www.santpau.es. Free; guided tours as part of Ruta del Modernisme 5€ adults, 3€ students, free for kids 14 & under. Guided tours daily at 10:15am and 12:15pm in English, 1:15pm in Spanish. Metro: Hospital de San Pau or Sagrada Família (then 10-min. walk along Avenida de Gaudí).

> *A whimsical pinnacle on the Sagrada Família.*

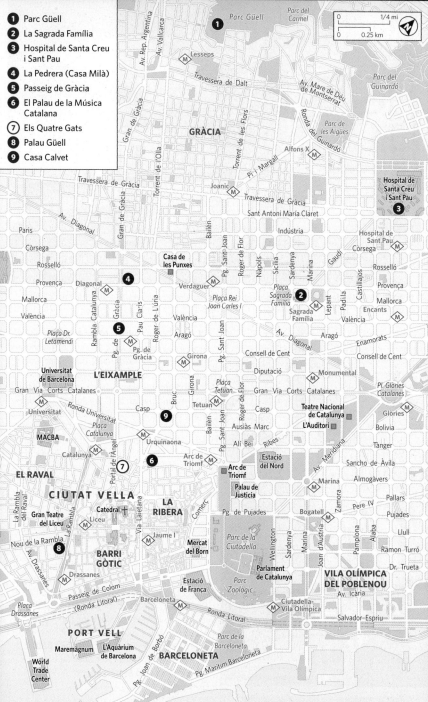

1. Parc Güell
2. La Sagrada Família
3. Hospital de Santa Creu i Sant Pau
4. La Pedrera (Casa Milà)
5. Passeig de Gràcia
6. El Palau de la Música Catalana
7. Els Quatre Gats
8. Palau Güell
9. Casa Calvet

MEDITERRANEAN SEA

> In 2008, the Palau de la Música Catalana celebrated its hundredth anniversary as home to the Catalan Choral Society.

> A fanciful pavilion of the Hospital de Sant Pau.

④ ★★★ kids **La Pedrera (Casa Milà).** Gaudí's most inspired civic work, this sinuous landmark apartment block is for many the pinnacle of Modernisme. The rooftop chimneys (which some claim represent Christians and Moors battling for Spanish turf) are spectacular, but those with an interest in architecture will be fascinated by the museum, **Espai Gaudí,** which exposes the splendid arches of the attic and delves into the life, times, and techniques of the architect. His restored original apartment, El Pis, shows off peculiar shapes, handcrafted doorknobs, and period furniture—all of Gaudí's design. ⏱ 1 hr. See p. 408, ②.

⑤ ★★★ **Passeig de Gràcia.** This elegant shopping boulevard is ground zero for Modernista architecture. In fact, on a single block are pivotal buildings by Gaudí and the other two architects that make up the movement's great troika, Doménech i Montaner and Josep Puig i Cadalfalch. The competing proximity of these landmarks earned the block the nickname Manzana de la Discordia ("Block of Discord"). Don't miss Gaudí's spectacular **Casa Batlló** (see p. 408, ④), **Casa Amatller** (see p. 409, ⑤), or **Casa Lleó Morera** (see p. 409, ⑥). ⏱ 45 min.

6 ★★★ **El Palau de la Música Catalana.** Lluís Domènech i Montaner designed this audacious concert hall as a home for the Catalan Choral Society. The interior is hallucinatory, from colored-glass canisters on staircases and a ceiling dominated by a colossal teardrop of stained glass, to a stage framed by pumice busts of the composers Bach, Beethoven, and Wagner by the sculptor Pau Gargallo. The Palau was given some breathing space when the noted Barcelona architect Oscar Tusquets completed a tasteful extension in 2003. ⏱ 45 min. See p. 418, **6**.

⑦   🍽 ★★ **Els Quatre Gats.** A favorite hangout of Pablo Picasso, Ramón Casas, and other turn-of-the-century Modernista bohemian intellectuals, this restaurant and cafe—one of the first commissions for the architect Josep Puig i Cadalfalch and site of Picasso's first exhibition—is the perfect stop on a Modernisme tour of Barcelona for either a late lunch or coffee and a pastry. C/ Montsió, 3. ☎ 93-302-41-40. $–$$.

8 ★★ **Palau Güell.** This 1888 mansion, not in the Eixample but in the much less fashionable district of El Raval, was Gaudí's first big commission from Eusebi Güell, the textile magnate who would become a lifelong patron. It's heavier and less whimsical than Gaudí's later

> *Casa Calvet, Gaudí's first commission, was designed for Pere Calvet, a local textile magnate.*

Ruta del Modernisme

You could easily spend days visiting Modernista landmarks in Barcelona. If your appetite has been whetted, check out the **Ruta del Modernisme de Barcelona** (Modernisme, or Catalan Art Nouveau, route) promoted by the city (☎ 93/317-76-52; www.rutadelmodernisme.com; 12€). A self-guided tour of 115 sites, it offers discounted admissions of up to 50% at both major and lesser-known buildings—everything from palaces to pharmacies. Information and discount vouchers are available at a desk in the entry of the main tourist information office on Plaça de Catalunya. Besides the highlights listed in this chapter, several other of the route's top 30 sites are also included in the Eixample walking tour (see p. 442), such as Casa Thomas, Casa de les Punxes, and Palau de Baró de Quadras.

works—on the outside it looks like a fortress—but the architect's early genius is evident in the underground stables and Moorish-style decorative skylights. On the roof is the building's crowd-pleasing surprise, a preview of what would later come with La Pedrera: a small contingent of colorful, *trencadis*-covered chimneys. ⏱ 1 hr. C/ Nou de la Rambla 3–5. ☎ 93-317-39-74. 3€, free for kids 6 & under. Mon–Sat 10am–6:15pm. Metro: Drassanes.

9 ★★ **Casa Calvet.** The best place to cap a day of touring Modernista landmarks is dinner at this upscale restaurant in one of Gaudí's earliest (and best-preserved) apartment buildings. The 1899 house features one of Barcelona's first elevators and elegant Modernista details throughout, making for a unique dining experience—the only way you'll be able to get a good look at the interior. See p. 460.

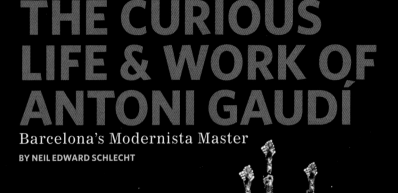

THE CURIOUS
LIFE & WORK OF
ANTONI GAUDÍ

Barcelona's Modernista Master

BY NEIL EDWARD SCHLECHT

THE VISIONARY ARCHITECT Antoni Gaudí i Cornet (1852–1926) was the most visible of a cadre of forward-looking architects working during the turn of the 20th century. They transformed Barcelona with an aesthetic revolution called Modernisme that left it looking like no other city. And Gaudí's life was every bit as eccentric as his work: An ardent Catalan nationalist and pious Catholic who became a religious zealot, Gaudí had a devil of an imagination but lived an ascetic life. After 1910, he devoted himself entirely to building the church of La Sagrada Família, living in the workshop of the temple for 44 years—but he left few plans to guide its completion. He died ignominiously, run over by a street trolley; at the time he was destitute, and because of his pauper's rags, taxis refused to take him to a hospital.

Gaudí's Visions

Most of Gaudí's buildings are in Barcelona—where eight have been declared UNESCO World Heritage Sites—though others can be found in his native Tarragona and farther afield, in Santander, León, and Palma de Mallorca. In 1910, Gaudí was commissioned to design a stunning futuristic hotel in New York City, but his plans were never realized.

CASA MILÁ/ LA PEDRERA (1905–10)
Topped by warrior-like chimneys, with an undulating limestone exterior that wraps around a corner lot, this wild apartment building is Gaudí's most complete work. Today it's nearly as great a symbol of Barcelona as La Sagrada Família.

LA SAGRADA FAMILIA (1883–p.)
Gaudí's master work (above and left), which many argue should be left unfinished; the temple's sculptural

additions remain despised by some even as the city races toward its completion (theoretically in 2026, the centenary of Gaudí's death).

PARC GÜELL (1900–14)
An open-air park envisioned by Gaudí and his patron, Eusebi Güell, as a housing development; never finished but loved for its flights of fancy (including support structures that look like trees and undulating benches and dragon fountains swathed in colorful broken tiles).

CASA BATLLÓ (1904–06)
One of Gaudí's most attention-getting buildings, though he only renovated the facade. But what a re-model: Elements evoke dragons, carnival

masks, and the patron saint of Catalunya, Sant Jordi.

COLÒNIA GÜELL (1908–15)
Designed as part of a worker's colony (for Güell's textile factory employees) just

outside Barcelona, in Santa Coloma de Cervello; the church was never completed, though the vaulted crypt is thought by

some to be Gaudí's purest work of technical genius.

Elements of Modernisme

Catalan Modernisme (a movement that extended beyond architecture to art and literature) was a unique take on Art Nouveau. The Catalan Modernista movement's signature elements, employed in private and public buildings across the district of L'Eixample in Barcelona, include:

▶ **trencadis,** shards of decorative ceramics.

▶ abundant **wrought iron,** including highly decorative balconies.

▶ **Gothic** and **Islamic** references.

▶ stained **glass.**

▶ decorative and structural parabolic **arches** and **spirals.**

Gourmet Barcelona

With its rise as a foodie capital in the past decade,

Barcelona now rivals San Sebastián as one of the top eating cities in Europe. In addition to haute cuisine restaurants and chef-driven tapas bars, there are scores of both old-school and innovative *colmados* (grocery stores), chocolatiers, and wine shops. Don't worry—this isn't a daylong tasting menu unless you choose to make it one! Note that Monday isn't the best day for this tour, as several shops are closed.

> There are over 300 stalls at La Boqueria, Spain's largest food market and one of the best in Europe.

START Metro to Liceu.

① ★★★ **El Quim de la Boqueria.** Chef Quim Márquez Durán has been at the helm of this bustling *taburete* (kiosk bar) within Mercat de la Boqueria for the past 21 years. Prized by fellow chefs and foodies in the know, it's a place for fresh grilled seafood and tapas of the highest order. Your best bet is breakfast at the counter; try the fried eggs topped by a heaping pile of *chipirones* (baby squid). Mercat de la Boqueria, parada no. 584/585. ☎ 93-301-98-20. www.boqueria.info. $$.

② ★★★ **Mercat de la Boqueria.** Spain's largest food market is a gastronomic paradise. The market, just off La Rambla, dates to 1840; today it has more than 300 stalls stocked with eye-popping displays of salted fish, exotic fruits, wild mushrooms (*ceps* and *bolets*), and more. You can eat, too, at El Quim, Bar Pintxo, and a couple of restaurants in the back. Buffet & Ambigú (parada no. 437), a shop toward the rear, features cookbooks by some of Spain's best-known chefs. ⏱ 1 hr. See p. 410, ❽.

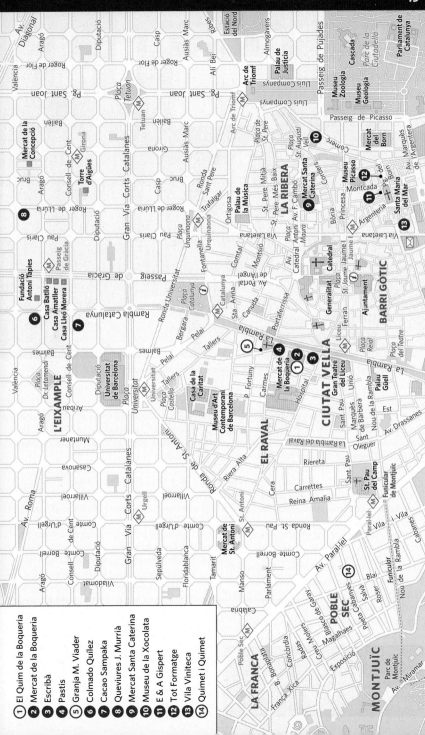

1. El Quim de la Boqueria
2. Mercat de la Boqueria
3. Escribà
4. Pastis
5. Granja M. Viader
6. Colmado Quílez
7. Cacao Sampaka
8. Queviures J. Murrià
9. Mercat Santa Caterina
10. Museu de la Xocolata
11. E & A Gispert
12. Tot Formatge
13. Vila Viniteca
14. Quimet i Quimet

> *Booze and beef: liquor and charcuterie for sale at the old-school grocery Colmado Quílez.*

❸ ★ Escribà. Talk about eye candy. One of Barcelona's oldest and best-known chocolatiers is this little shop on La Rambla with a shimmering Modernista exterior of colorful broken glazed tiles, à la Gaudí, and a tea salon within. Its traditional chocolates now have lots of competition from designer chocolate shops such as Oriol Balaguer and the small chains Xocoa and Cacao Sampaka, but a stop here is essential. ⏱ 20 min. La Rambla, 83. ☎ 93-221-07-29. www. escriba.es. Metro: Liceu or Plaça de Catalunya.

❹ Pastis. Another venerable chocolate seller in Modernista surroundings, this place began as a coffee roaster, Cafés Garriga, in 1890. Formerly a branch of the small chain Xocoa, it has now gone independent. Check out the lovely stained-glass design at the rear of the shop and the elegant carved-wood ceiling. ⏱ 20 min. C/ Carme, 3. ☎ 93-304-23-60. Metro: Liceu or Plaça de Catalunya.

⑤ ☕ ★ Granja M. Viader. Although the old neighborhood of El Raval has seen a huge amount of upheaval, this place with marble-topped tables has resisted change. A gloriously authentic *granja,* or milk bar (the oldest in Barcelona, open since 1870), it's known for thick chocolate drinks such as *xocolata desfeta* and the original *Cacaolat,* a bottled chocolate drink famous throughout Spain. C/ Xuclà, 4–6. ☎ 93-318-34-86. www. granjaviader.cat. $.

❻ ★★ Colmado Quílez. Another charming throwback is this 1908 grocery store and wine shop, the most famous *colmado* in Barcelona. Its floor-to-ceiling shelves are stocked with gourmet packaged goods, while backrooms stock wines from across Spain—as well as 300 types of beer. ⏱ 30 min. See p. 454.

Travel Tip

For information on other spots to buy your favorite gourmet items, see p. 454. For a list of restaurants, see p. 456.

7 Cacao Sampaka. The pastry-chef brother of Ferran Adrià, the world-famous chef of elBulli (see p. 56), started this hip shop that features both traditional and avant-garde chocolates, as well as a cafe-restaurant (menu items are both sweet and savory). With great packaging, the chocolates here make excellent gifts. ⏱ 20 min. Consell de Cent, 292. ☎ 93-272-08-33. www.cacao sampaka.com. Metro: Passeig de Gràcia.

8 ★★ Queviures J. Murrià. Even older and more old-school than Quílez (see above), this food-and-wine shop has been in the same family since the late 19th century. Its handsome exterior, the work of the Modernista artist Ramón Casas, is only a prelude to the 200 types of cheese, 300 wines, Iberian *jamón* (ham), and canned goods inside. ⏱ 30 min. C/ Roger de Llúria, 85. ☎ 93-215-57-89. www.murria. cat. Metro: Passeig de Gràcia.

9 ★★ Mercat Santa Caterina. This gorgeously redesigned covered food market (in operation since 1848) has a nice casual restaurant, **Cuines de Santa Caterina,** tucked inside. ⏱ 30 min. Avinguda de Francesc Cambó, 16. ☎ 93-319-57-40. www.mercatsantacaterina.net. Daily 8am–11:30pm. Cuines: ☎ 93-268-99-18. www. cuinessantacaterina.com. Entrees 10€–20€. AE, MC, V. Breakfast, lunch & dinner daily.

10 kids Museu de la Xocolata. A small chocolate museum, with exhibits about the history of chocolate and chocolate-making classes. The large-scale chocolate sculptures of cartoon figures and Barcelona landmarks, including Gaudí's La Sagrada Família and La Pedrera, are fun. ⏱ 30 min. C/ del Comerç, 32. ☎ 93-268-78-78. www.pastisseria.com. 3.80€ adults, 3.20€ seniors and kids. Mon–Sat 10am–7pm; Sun 10am–3pm. Metro: Arc de Triomphe.

11 ★★ E & A Gispert. One of the oldest continuously running shops in Barcelona (since 1851) sells coffee and teas, dried fruits and nuts, honey and jams, and traditional Catalan *torron* (nougat made with honey and almonds), as well as gift baskets and other artisanal and organic products. One of the most redolent places you'll ever poke your nose into, the shop retains the original one-piece counter and wood shelves and still uses a spectacular 150-year-old, wood-burning nut roaster—the only one of its kind in Europe. ⏱ 30 min. See p. 454.

12 ★ Tot Formatge. This cute little cheese shop (the name means "All Things Cheese") on stylish Passeig del Born is another place to overwhelm your nose. ⏱ 15 min. See p. 455.

13 Vila Viniteca. From cult wines such as Pingus to small-yield Priorats, including plenty of bottles you can't get outside Spain, this is Barcelona's wine temple, with more than 6,000 choices. Check out scheduled *catas* (wine tastings) at www.vilaviniteca.es. ⏱ 30 min. See p. 455.

14 🍴 Quimet i Quimet. In the Poble Sec neighborhood, off the beaten track, this incredible little joint is packed with hungry patrons and drinkers, the walls lined to the ceiling with liquor bottles and canned foods. Foodies come for the stunningly creative and delicious *montaditos* (little gourmet sandwiches). C/ Poeta Cabanyes 25. ☎ 93-442-31-42. Metro: Paral·lel. $$.

> E & A Gispert, with its 150-year-old nut roaster and timeless storefront, has beome a Barcelona institution.

The Barri Gòtic

The Barri Gòtic, or Gothic Quarter, is where Barcelona was born, and it remains the heart of the city. It includes remnants of the medieval Jewish district, El Call, as well as Barcelona's 2,000-year-old Roman past, and is a joy to wander. Anything but a time-forgotten museum, its lively labyrinth of narrow, cobblestone streets is lined with both important monuments—including palaces, convents, and churches—and a thriving collection of popular bars, hot restaurants, and chic shops.

> *Eduardo Chillida's 1986 iron sculpture* Topos V (Moles V) *in the Plaça del Rei.*

START Metro to Jaume I.

① ★★ **Catedral de Barcelona.** The Barri Gòtic has long been known as the Cathedral Quarter, so this is the logical place to start. Locals gather at the **Plaça Nova** (new square, dating from 1358) in front of the cathedral to perform the *sardana,* a Catalan folk dance (Sun mornings and national holidays). To the right of the main entrance of the cathedral is the **Portal de Bisbe,** semicircular twin towers and one of three gateways to the walled settlement of Roman Barcino (4th c. A.D.). ⏱ 1 hr. See p. 410, **⑨**.

② ★★ **Plaça de Ramon Berenguer el Gran.** In this square is one of largest surviving sections of the second Roman wall, dating to the 4th century A.D. The equestrian statue is of the 12th-century hero who extended the reign of independent Catalunya. Rising above the wall are the 14th-century Palau Reial Major (Royal Palace), Santa Agata chapel, and a Gothic tower. These are all best seen from Plaça del Rei (see below). Vía Laietana, s/n.

③ 🍺 ★★ **Mesón del Café.** A tiny, charming cafe that dates back to 1909, this is the kind of good-vibes spot where some neighborhood folks stop by every day for some of the city's best coffee. Belly up to the bar or see if you can score a table in back. C/ Llibretería, 16. ☎ 93-315-07-54. $.

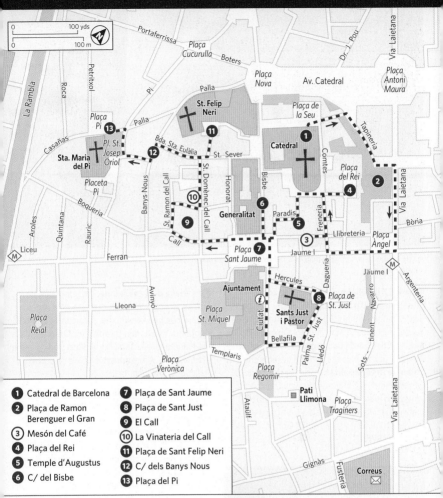

0 | 100 yds
0 | 100 m

1 Catedral de Barcelona
2 Plaça de Ramon Berenguer el Gran
3 Mesón del Café
4 Plaça del Rei
5 Temple d'Augustus
6 C/ del Bisbe
7 Plaça de Sant Jaume
8 Plaça de Sant Just
9 El Call
10 La Vinateria del Call
11 Plaça de Sant Felip Neri
12 C/ dels Banys Nous
13 Plaça del Pi

4 ★★★ **Plaça del Rei.** This noble and austere square is the most beautiful part of the Barri Gòtic. Here you'll find subterranean Roman ruins and the medieval royal palace where the *reyes Católicos* (Catholic monarchs, aka Fernando and Isabel) are said to have received Columbus on his return from the New World in 1493. The sculpture in the square, *Topos V,* is by the Basque sculptor Eduardo Chillida (1924–2002), one of Spain's great 20th-century artists. See p. 412, **1**.

5 ★★ **Temple d'Augustus.** ⏱ 10 min. See p. 422, **7**.

> A Gothic gargoyle contemplates the narrow passage of C/ del Bisbe.

> *The medieval cellarlike synagogue below the Call was discovered in 1995 and restored by the Associació Call de Barcelona.*

❻ ★★ C/ del Bisbe. One of the loveliest streets in the Barri Gòtic, the former principal artery of the Roman city connects Catedral de Barcelona to Plaça Sant Jaume. On one side are the **Cases dels Canonges,** a series of 14th-century Gothic palaces. On the other is the **Palau de la Generalitat,** home to the Regional Government of Catalunya. Notice the rooftop gargoyles watching over the street action below. Arching over the lane is a bridge of carved stone, which only looks Gothic; it was added in 1928.

El Caganer in a Manger

Barcelona's annual nativity crafts fair and Christmas market in the square in front of the cathedral features one traditional folk-loric figure that in recent years has taken on all kinds of modern permutations. It is *el caganer*. Placed in nativity scenes, the small figure, traditionally donning a red peasant's cap, is depicted squatting and defecating. *El caganer* symbolizes Catalans' ties to the land and the hope for continued fertility. With an eye toward young consumers and tourists, today *el caganer* is not limited to peasant figures. You'll also see figurines of priests, nuns, Bart Simpson, local and international politicians, and more—all squatting and fertilizing the earth. See p. 369.

❼ ★ Plaça de Sant Jaume. An important crossroads during the Roman era, this broad square has been the political epicenter of Barcelona for more than 5 centuries. On one side is the Palau de la Generalitat. Across from it is the 14th-century **Ajuntament,** Barcelona's Town Hall. See p. 423, ❾.

❽ ★★ Plaça de Sant Just. This quiet, diminutive square is one of the most representative and unadulterated of medieval Barcelona. The **Església dels Sants Just i Pastor,** a church begun in 1342, features a single nave in the Catalan Gothic style. It's usually open only for Sunday Mass. The Gothic fountain in the square dates to 1367. **Palau Moxó,** a seigniorial mansion across the square, was added in 1700. Església: Plaça de Sant Just, 6. ☎ 93-301-73-33. Free. Open for Mass Mon–Fri 7pm, Sat 8pm, Sun 11am. Palau: Plaça de Sant Just, 4. ☎ 93-315-22-38. Open for special events only.

❾ ★ El Call. C/ del Call leads into the warren of small streets that once composed the Call, or Jewish Quarter, in medieval Barcelona (until the Jews were expelled from Spain in 1492). Only a few important vestiges of the community remain. The **Sinagoga Medieval de Barcelona** claims to be the oldest synagogue in Spain (based on a royal document from 1267). A nearby medieval Hebrew inscription marking a death in A.D. 692 reads, RABBI SAMUEL HAS-SARERI, MAY HIS LIFE NEVER CEASE. ⊙ 30 min.

> *The pocked walls surrounding Plaça de Sant Felip Neri are a reminder of the Civil War.*

Sinagoga: C/ Marlet, 5. ☎ 93-317-07-90. www.calldebarcelona.org. 2€. Mon–Fri 10:30am–2:30pm and 4–7pm; Sat–Sun 10:30am–3pm.

⑩ 🍴 **La Vinateria del Call.** This romantic little spot in the heart of the old Jewish Quarter serves up local wines and Catalan tapas, such as cured meats and cheese. C/ de Sant Domènec del Call, 9. ☎ 93-302-60-92. $.

⑪ ★★★ **Plaça de Sant Felip Neri.** Down a tiny passageway off C/ Sant Sever is one of the most tranquil and poetic spots in the Ciutat Vella. It was once the site of a cemetery, and the specter of the dead lingers. Behind the gurgling fountain is a reminder of Spain's not-too-distant violence: The walls of the 17th-century church are scarred by Civil War bombs that killed 42 people in 1938.

⑫ ★ **C/ dels Banys Nous.** This atmospheric street (named for the location of the "new baths," dating from the 12th century) follows the line of the old Roman wall and today is

> *There's always something happening on Plaça del Pi, recognizable for its sgraffito facades.*

known as *el carrer dels antiquaris*—the street of antiques dealers.

⑬ ★★ **Plaça del Pi.** A trio of pretty, contiguous plazas surrounds the 15th-century church of **Santa María del Pi,** known for its rose window. **Plaça de Sant Josep Oriol** adjoins Plaça del Pi and, behind the church, tiny **Placeta del Pi.** The squares are recognized for the unusual *sgraffito* decorative technique on the plaster facades of several buildings, an 18th-century style imported from Italy. But the leafy squares are also popular for the weekend artisans' market and open-air cafe-bars, making this an excellent place to while away the hours and finish a walking tour. Santa María: C/ del Cardenal Casañas, 16. ☎ 93-318-47-43. www.parroquiadelpi.com. Free. Daily 9am–1pm and 4–9pm.

La Ribera

As maritime commerce grew in the 13th and 14th centuries, Barri de la Ribera ("neighborhood of the waterfront," reflecting a time when the shoreline reached this far) became a populous residential district for the merchant class. Until recently, the quarter was known principally for its great church, Santa Maria del Mar, and the much-frequented Museu Picasso. But in the past decade, La Ribera (and particularly the zone within it called El Born) has become the city's most fashionable district, exploding with chic bars, restaurants, and boutiques. Though it can get rowdy late at night, it still retains its medieval character.

> The nave of Santa Maria del Mar soars to a simple ribbed vault, allowing plenty of light and air in the church.

START **Metro to Jaume I.**

❶ **C/ de l'Argenteria.** Leave behind the congestion of Vía Laeitana, a thoroughfare cut through the Ciutat Vella in the 1930s, for the foot traffic of the "Street of Silversmiths," a name dating to the 16th century. Fashion boutiques, bars, tapas restaurants, and hotels have taken over, but take a detour onto C/ Grunyí or Rosic, for example, and you'll glimpse the old Ribera district.

❷ ★★★ **Santa Maria del Mar.** You'll be powerless to pass by without taking at least a quick spin through this extraordinarily graceful 14th-century Catalan Gothic church. It's the kind of contemplative place that should clear your head before you continue through this bustling neighborhood. ⏱ 20 min. See p. 411, ⓫.

❸ **Fossar de les Moreres.** An eternal flame burns on a small square around the right side of the main entrance to Santa Maria del Mar. It commemorates the royal sacking of Barcelona

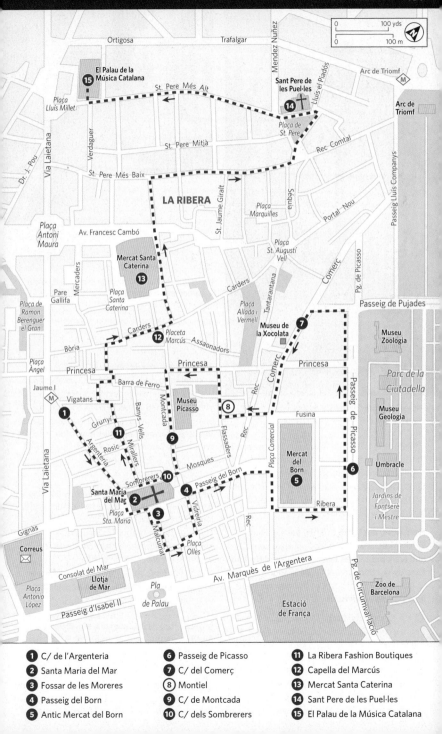

1 C/ de l'Argentería
2 Santa María del Mar
3 Fossar de les Moreres
4 Passeig del Born
5 Antic Mercat del Born
6 Passeig de Picasso
7 C/ del Comerç
8 Montiel
9 C/ de Montcada
10 C/ dels Sombrerers
11 La Ribera Fashion Boutiques
12 Capella del Marcús
13 Mercat Santa Caterina
14 Sant Pere de les Puel·les
15 El Palau de la Música Catalana

> *The Passeig del Born once hosted jousts; now it hosts cyclists.*

> *Designer boutiques and posh apartments lend a fashionable sheen to La Ribera.*

on September 11, 1714, which marked the end to the Spanish War of Succession. The king, Felipe V, then outlawed Catalan culture and its institutions, including the Catalan language. The date, 9/11 (or 11/9 in Spain), is now celebrated as the National Day of Catalunya.

From here, duck into the tiny passageway C/ de Malcuinat (literally, "poorly cooked") and walk out to Plaça de les Olles and back to Passeig del Born, along C/ de la Vidreria, just to get a feel for this part of the quarter that leads to the waterfront.

❹ ★★ **Passeig del Born.** This wide and elegant tree-lined *passeig* (*paseo* in Castilian, meaning "promenade"), with its stone benches, is a good place for a breather. Once the site of medieval jousting tournaments, it became the main square and heart of the city during Barcelona's seafaring heyday (13th–18th c.). Today apartment dwellers in its Gothic mansions are more commonly up in arms about the busy boutiques, outdoor cafes, and bars that populate the ground floors and every neighboring side street.

❺ **Antic Mercat del Born.** At the end of Passeig del Born is the old Ribera covered market, with its distinctive wrought-iron roof. Constructed in 1876, it has been abandoned for years, as authorities have deliberated its potential uses. However, because it was found to sit on medieval archaeological remains, it's most likely that it will soon become a museum and/or cultural center.

❻ **Passeig de Picasso.** This avenue borders the western edge of Parc de la Ciutadella, the largest green space in downtown Barcelona. Here you'll find Antoni Tàpies's 1981 sculpture, *Homenatge a Picasso,* a glass cube containing a cubist-like assemblage of running water and furniture. A bit farther up are the **Museu de Geologia** and **Museu Zoologia,** the latter designed by Domènech i Montaner, and L'Hivernacle, a 19th-century greenhouse. Museus: Parc de la Ciutadella, s/n. ☎ 93-319-68-95. www.museugeologia.bcn.es. 5.30€, free for kids 16 & under. Tue–Fri 10am–6pm, Sat–Sun 10am–8pm.

❼ **C/ del Comerç.** This street, bending around the edges of La Ribera, is one of many that have been inundated with shops and restaurants—

not surprisingly, given its name, Commerce Street. The **Museu de la Xocolata** (see p. 433, **10**) is found at Comerç, 36. The street parallel to Comerç, **C/ del Rec,** is flush with designer clothing and furniture boutiques.

8 🍴 ★ **Montiel.** This attractive little gourmet food store–cum–informal restaurant serves Catalan and Spanish standards, including *jamón de Jabugo* (Iberian ham), *pa amb tomaquet* (peasant bread with rubbed tomatoes and olive oil), Catalan sausages, and local wines. Have a selection of tapas or the inexpensive fixed-price lunch. C/ Flassaders, 19. ☎ 93-268-37-29. $.

9 ★★★ **C/ de Montcada.** Famous for its collection of stately Gothic mansions and the **Museu Picasso** (see p. 410, **10**), this elegant avenue is a joy to stroll. Don't miss the narrow and poetically named C/ de les Mosques (Street of the Flies). See p. 420, **2**.

10 **C/ dels Sombrerers.** Just off C/ de Montcada, and flanking **Santa Maria del Mar** (see p. 411, **11**), is this small street, formally named St. Anthony of the Hat Makers. **E & A Gispert** (see p. 454), at no. 23, is a wonderful old epicurean shop with a 150-year-old roasting oven.

11 ★ **La Ribera Fashion Boutiques.** Off C/ de la Princesa is a series of alleyways that have given over to a handful of chic designer boutiques, typifying the neighborhood's stunning transformation. Make a brief detour along C/ Carassa and C/ Vigatans before returning to Princesa.

12 ★ **Capella del Marcús.** Worth a look is this small Romanesque chapel, built in 1166 next to what was once the main thoroughfare in and out of the Roman city (today C/ dels Carders). Plaza Marcús, s/n.

13 ★★ **Mercat Santa Caterina.** This colorfully reimagined covered market has become a hit with foodies and architecture fans. See p. 433, **9**.

14 **Sant Pere de les Puel·les.** Little remains of the original pre-Romanesque church and Benedictine monastery, although you can still see a section of the 10th-century Greek-cross floor plan, the Romanesque bell tower, and a few Corinthian capitals beneath the 12th-century dome. ◷ 10 min. C/ Lluís el Piadós, 1. ☎ 93-268-07-42. Free. Tues and Thurs 6:30–8:30pm.

15 ★★★ **El Palau de la Música Catalana.** If you haven't already had a chance to tour this extraordinary concert hall, Domènech i Montaner's masterpiece, this would be the time to do it. See p. 418, **6**.

> *The technicolor patchwork roof of the Mercat Santa Caterina evokes the rainbow of fruits and vegetables sold inside.*

L'Eixample

L'Eixample is an area best known for its extraordinary collection of late-19th- and early-20th-century Modernista buildings, which earned it the nickname El Quadrat d'Or (The Golden Square). This tour takes you off the Eixample's well-trodden path. If you have time and energy at the end of this tour, you should tack on a stroll down Passeig de Gràcia (see p. 426, ❺) or Rambla de Catalunya.

> Josep Puig i Cadafalch incorporated some Moorish elements into his Palau de Baró de Quadras.

START Metro to Urquinaona.

❶ **Casa Calvet.** Antoni Gaudí's 1899 apartment building, one of his first commissions, is best appreciated for its wrought-iron and sculptural details. The building also saw the installation of Barcelona's first elevator. A top-flight restaurant, Casa Calvet, inhabits the first floor, allowing architectural and gastronomic enthusiasts an enticing look up close at an important early work of Gaudí. See p. 460.

❷ ★ **Passatge de Permanyer.** You'll find this lovely side street off Roger de Llúria, between Diputació and Consell de Cent. It is home to a small community of impeccable town houses and English-style gardens, tucked behind an engraved iron gate.

❸ **Pati de les Aigües.** In the next block along Diputació, between Roger de Llúria and Bruc, this inner courtyard has been reclaimed and opened to the public, allowing a view of the central courtyards and green public spaces of the original Eixample plan that the designer, Ildefons Cerdà, had in mind for the district. Most have been appropriated by private interests. C/ Roger de Llúria, 56.

❹ ★★ **Queviures J. Murrià.** This wonderful, old-school *colmado* (grocery store) has remained in the same family for 150 years. The decorative storefront is the work of Modernista painter Ramón Casas. See p. 433, ❽.

❺ ★★ **Casa Thomas.** Just down C/ Mallorca is this spectacular house (1895–98) by Lluís Domènech i Muntaner. Originally just two floors, it was expanded in 1912. It is now home to a furniture store. Feel free to enter and wander the two floors of this important building. C/ Mallorca, 291–293. ☎ 93-476-57-21.

> *Exquisite wrought-iron details distinguish Gaudí's Casa Calvet.*

⑥ 🍴 **Cor Caliu.** An attractive corner restaurant-bar, this surprisingly elegant spot is perfect for coffee, a beer, or tapas in the front bar, or a full meal in the restaurant at back. It's a longtime neighborhood favorite. C/ Roger de Llúria, 102. ☎ 93-208-20-29. $$.

❼ **Casa de les Punxes.** Also called Casa Terrades, or "House of Spikes," for its sharp turrets, this massive and eccentric 1905 house is one of Josep Puig i Cadafalch's and Modernisme's most prized buildings. It's a neo-Gothic and fairy tale mansion with distinctive features, such as three separate entrances (built for the family's daughters) and outer walls facing all four points of the compass. Avenida Diagonal, 416–420.

❽ **Palau de Baró de Quadras.** This 1904–06 mansion, also by Puig i Cadafalch, is a great example of the architect's creativity. Now owned by Casa Asia, an Asian cultural foundation, it is open to visitors. Although the imported Asian themes, incense, and modern light fixtures seem out of place, the interior, with its Moorish-style ceiling, carved wood, and leaded glass, is extremely handsome. From the top-floor terrace are terrific views of Casa de les Punxes, echoing the spires of La Sagrada Família in the background. ⏱ 45 min. Avenida Diagonal, 373. ☎ 93-368-73-37. www.casaasia.es. Free. Mon–Sat 10am–8pm; Sun 10am–2pm.

❶ Casa Calvet
❷ Passatge de Permanyer
❸ Pati de les Aigües
❹ Queviures J. Murrià
❺ Casa Thomas
⑥ Cor Caliu
❼ Casa de les Punxes
❽ Palau de Baró de Quadras

Montjuïc

The largest green space in Barcelona, this gentle hill overlooking the city and the Mediterranean is treasured by locals for its serene parkland—popular with families on weekends—as well as its museums and cultural attractions. First settled by Iberian Celtic peoples and then used by the Romans for ceremonies, Montjuïc has continued to play a central role in modern celebrations in Barcelona, including the 1929 International Exhibition and the 1992 Olympic Games. For other attractions in Montjuïc, see "The Best of Barcelona in 3 Days," on p. 416.

> The cheery gardens of Montjuïc's Castell may make you forget this was once a fortress and prison.

START Aerial cable car or funicular to Montjuïc.

1 ★ kids **Transbordador Aeri.** The best way to get to the green expanse of Montjuïc is to soar over the city in this aerial cable car that travels from the harbor up to the hill (dropping you off among the pine trees and cactus gardens of Costa i Llobera, a public park). Passeig Joan de Borbó, s/n. ☎ 93-225-27-18. 7.50€ one-way, 9€ round-trip. Runs daily every 15 min from 10:30am–7pm.

2 **Castell de Montjuïc.** Pass the Plaça de la Sardana (marked by a sculpture of the folkloric Catalan group dance) and through the Miramar and Mirador gardens in Parc de Montjuïc. Then head up Carretera Montjuïc to **Mirador de l'Alcalde,** a viewpoint overlooking the sea. Just beyond is a *castell* (fortress) built in the 18th century to defend Barcelona. The courtyard is open to the public, and inside the castle is a military museum. The views of the sea, though, are the star attraction. Carretera de Montjuïc, 66. ☎ 93-256-44-45. Free. Oct–Mar Tues–Sun 9am–7pm, Apr–Sept Tues–Sun 9am–9pm.

3 ★ kids **Jardí Botànic.** The Botanic Gardens of Barcelona, originally inaugurated in 1930, reopened as a new and improved, and beautifully landscaped, green space in 1999. The gardens show off Mediterranean-climate plants from all over the globe, including Africa, Australia, California, the Canary Islands, and Chile. The 71 zones are connected by paths and feature walkways over ponds. ⏱ 1 hr. Dr. Font i Quer, 2 (Parc de Montjuïc). ☎ 93-256-41-60. www.jardi botanic.bcn.es. Nov–Jan, Apr–May, and Sept daily 10am–5pm; Feb–Mar and Oct daily 10am–6pm; June–Aug daily 10am–8pm. 3.50€, 1.70€ seniors

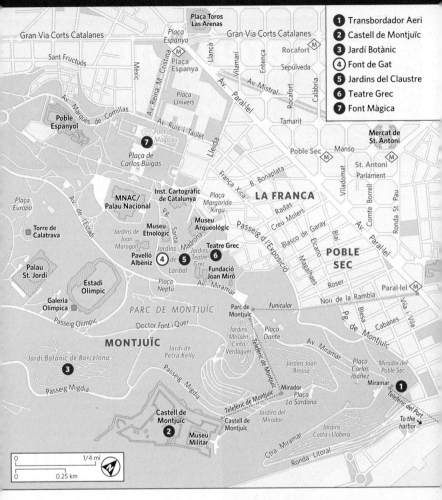

Map legend:

1. Transbordador Aeri
2. Castell de Montjuïc
3. Jardí Botànic
4. Font de Gat
5. Jardins del Claustre
6. Teatre Grec
7. Font Màgica

and students, free for kids 15 & under and last Sun of the month.

④ 🍽 **Font de Gat.** Down a path from the Fundació Joan Miró (see p. 418, ⑤) is this historic Modernista cafe, now revived as a cafe and restaurant surrounded by gardens. It's a nice, open-air spot for a breather and refreshments, which might even include a fixed-price lunch. Passeig de Santa Madrona, 28. ☎ 93-289-04-04. $

⑤ **Jardins del Claustre.** The Cloister Garden is one of the prettiest spots on Montjuïc, with a tree-lined pond, pergola, and sculpture by the Catalan artist Antoni Alsina for the 1929 International Exposition. Passeig de Santa Madrona, 2. Free. Daily 10am–dark.

⑥ **Teatre Grec.** This replica of a bowl-shaped Greek theater, built for the 1929 World's Fair, continues to host open-air concerts and dance performances. It's a focal point of the Festival Grec summer music and arts festival held every summer. Passeig de Santa Madrona, 36. ☎ 93-413-24-00.

⑦ ★ kids **Font Màgica.** The waters of the Magic Fountain dance to a light and pop-music show at the center of a plaza in front of the Palau Nacional. Parc de Montjuïc.

The Waterfront

For much of the 20th century, Barcelona's Mediterranean waterfront was a polluted, industrial, and marginalized sector. But the Catalan capital took advantage of the 1992 Olympic Games to completely revamp the old port and beaches and create new areas for leisure. Today it's Barcelona's outdoor playground, an essential part of the city.

> *The Transbordador Aeri runs every 15 minutes between Barceloneta and Montjuïc.*

START Metro to Drassanes.

1 kids **Las Golondrinas.** You'll see these double-decker "swallow boats" lined up across from the Mirador de Colom, boarding passengers for short cruises around the old harbor. ⏱ 35 min. Plaça Portal de la Pau, s/n. ☎ 93-442-31-06. www.lasgolondrinas.com. Mon–Fri 11:45am–7pm; Sat–Sun and holidays 11am–6pm. 6€–13€ adults, 2.60€–5€ kids 4–14.

2 **Moll de la Fusta.** The tree-lined boardwalk in front of Port Vell (the Old Port) extends from the Golondrinas to the Barceloneta district. It's popular with locals on weekend strolls. At the eastern end of the promenade are massive Pop Art sculptures of a giant crayfish and a head by Roy Lichtenstein (1923–97).

3 ★ **Barceloneta.** Barcelona's fishermen and their families inhabited this picturesque beachfront neighborhood for decades before it received a stylistic makeover in 1992. It was a traditional haunt for low-key seafood restaurants called *chiringuitos,* several of which have survived.

④ 🍽 ★ **La Bombeta.** This authentic tapas joint serves great seafood snacks, including mussels and fried calamari. The *bombas* are the house take on *patatas bravas* (fried potatoes with a spicy sauce). C/ Maquinsta, 3. ☎ 93-319-94-45. $–$$

5 ★ kids **Transbordador Aeri.** The aerial cable car that climbs from the port to Montjuïc starts out at Passeig de Joan de Borbó in Barceloneta. It stops at the World Trade Center and soars above the harbor. See p. 444, **1**.

6 ★★ kids **Platges & Port Olímpic.** Barcelona's urban *platges,* or beaches, have been amazingly transformed, and the water quality is now excellent. Popular with families, topless sunbathers, and surfers, the beaches are lined with public sculptures, bars and restaurants, and paths for biking, in-line skating, and walking. In order: Barceloneta, Nova Icària, Bogatell, and Mar Bella (unofficially a nudist beach). Nova Icària is the most popular, the best spot for people-watching, and has the most bars and

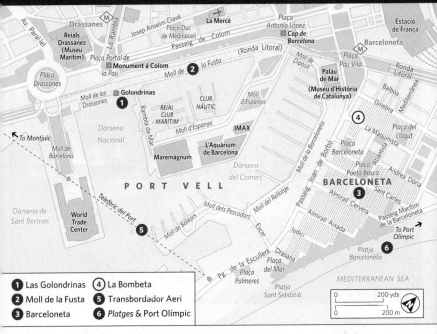

1 Las Golondrinas
2 Moll de la Fusta
3 Barceloneta
4 La Bombeta
5 Transbordador Aeri
6 *Platges* & Port Olímpic

> *A bicycle-friendly esplanade overlooks the Mediterranean waters lapping at the sands of Nova Icària Beach.*

restaurants in easy reach, while Bogatell and Mar Bella are even prettier and less populated. The Port Olímpic marina between the first two beaches is full of chic sailboats and trendy restaurants and bars.

Biking the Waterfront

The Old City of Barcelona is not always conducive to bike riding, but the waterfront is: Starting out at Barceloneta, take Passeig Marítim and head northeast along the beach to Port Olímpic. Cycle along the paths that line the beaches. You can continue as far north as Fòrum Park.

Barcelona Shopping Best Bets

Best Dreamy Antiques
L'Arca de l'Avia, C/ dels Banys Nous, 20 (see p. 450)

Best Men's Designer Clothing
Antonio Miró, C/ Consell de Cent, 349 (see p. 451)

Best Women's Designer Clothing
Josep Font, C/ Provença, 304 (see p. 452)

Most Creative Leather Goods
Lupo Barcelona, C/ Mallorca, 257, bajos (see p. 452)

Best Shop for Slaves to Design
Vinçon, Passeig. de Gràcia, 96 (see p. 453)

Best-Smelling Gourmet Foods
E & A Gispert, C/ dels Sombrerers, 23 (see p. 454)

Best Wine-Cellar Fantasy Shop
Vila Viniteca, C/ Agullers, 7 (see p. 455)

Best Dip into Old-World Barcelona
Herboristeria del Rei, C/ del Vidre, 1 (see p. 455)

Best Old-City Spot for an Antiques Stroll
C/ de la Palla (see p. 452)
C/ dels Banys Nous (see p. 437, ⑫)

Best Mall for Kids
Maremàgnum, Moll d'Espanya, 5 (see p. 451)

Most Theatrical Clothing Boutique
Natalie Capell Atelier de Moda, Carassa, 2 (see p. 453)

Best Products by Nuns & Priests
Caelum, C/ de la Palla, 8 (see p. 454)

Best Unpronounceable T-Shirt Shop
Kukuxumusu, C/ L'Argenteria, 69 (see p. 454)

Best One-Stop Shopping
El Corte Inglés, Plaça de Catalunya, 14 (see p. 450)

> *Vinçon, a temple of high design.*

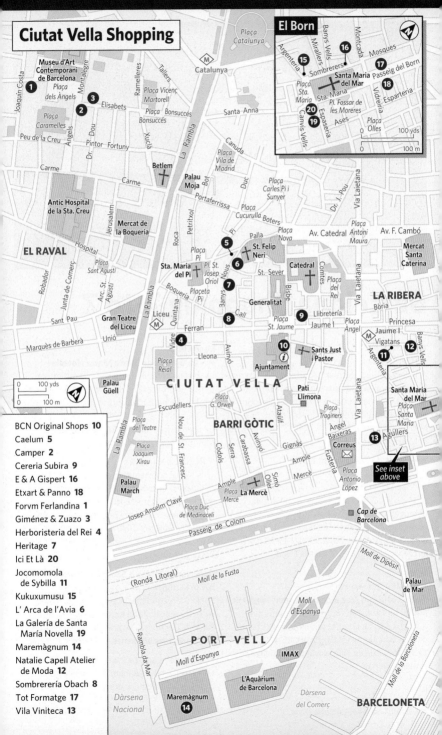

Ciutat Vella Shopping

El Born

Museu d'Art Contemporani de Barcelona ①

Plaça dels Àngels

Joaquín Costa

Montalegre

Talers

Ramelleres

M Catalunya

Plaça Catalunya

Argentería

Miralles

Banys Vells

Montcada

Mosques

⑮

Sombrerers

⑯

Santa Maria del Mar

⑰

Passeig del Born

⑱

Espartería

Plaça Sta. Maria

Sta. Maria

Pl. Fossar de les Moreres

Plaça Olles

Canvís Vells

Espasería

Ases

⑳

⑲

0   100 yds
0   100 m

Plaça Vicenç Martorell

Elisabets

③

②

Plaça Caramelles

Plaça dels Àngels

Dr. Dou

Pintor Fortuny

Xuclá

Plaça Bonsuccés

Bonsuccés

Santa Anna

Peu de la Creu

Angels

Carme

Carme

Jerusalem

Betlem

Palau Moja

La Rambla

Canuda

Plaça Vila de Madrid

Duc

Plaça Carles Pi i Sunyer

Dr. J. Pou

Av. F. Cambó

Antic Hospital de la Sta. Creu

Plaça Sant Agustí

Mercat de la Boqueria

Portaferrissa

Petritxol

Roca

Plaça Cucurulla

Boters

Palla

Plaça Nova

Av. Catedral

Plaça Antoni Maura

Mercat Santa Caterina

EL RAVAL

Hospital

Robador

Junta de Comerç

Arc St. Agustí

Plaça Pi

⑤

St. Felip Neri

Sta. Maria del Pi

Pl. St. Josep Oriol

⑥

⑦

St. Sever

Catedral

Comtes

Plaça del Rei

Via Laietana

LA RIBERA

Bòria

Sant Pau

Gran Teatre del Liceu

Banys Nous

Boqueria

Placeta Pi

Bisbe

Generalitat

Llibretería

Princesa

Marquès de Barberá

Unió

M Liceu

Quintana

Ferran

Call

⑧

Plaça St. Jaume

⑨

Jaume I

Plaça Àngel

M Jaume I

Vigatans

Banys Vells

Argentería

CIUTAT VELLA

Vidre

④

Lleona

Avinyó

⑩

i

Ajuntament

Sants Just i Pastor

Plaça Traginers

⑪

⑫

Palau Güell

Escudellers

Plaça G. Orwell

Pati Llimona

Santa Maria del Mar

Plaça Santa Maria

BARRI GÒTIC

Plaça del Teatre

Nou de St. Francesc

Ataúlf

Plaça Traginers

Angel Baixeras

Aguilers

⑬

Plaça Joaquim Xirau

Serra

Carabassa

Avinyó

Gignàs

Correus

See inset above

Palau March

Codols

Ample

Fustería

Plaça Antonio López

Cap de Barcelona

Simó Oller

La Mercè

Ample

Plaça Mercè

Mercè

Josep Anselm Clavé

Plaça Duc de Medinaceli

Passeig de Colom

Palau de Mar

Rambla de Mar

(Ronda Litoral)

Moll de la Fusta

Moll de Dipòsit

Moll d'Espanya

Moll d'Espanya

PORT VELL

IMAX

L'Aquàrium de Barcelona

Moll de la Barceloneta

Dàrsena Nacional

Maremàgnum

⑭

Dàrsena del Comerç

BARCELONETA

Barcelona Shopping A to Z

Antiques & Art
★ **Heritage** BARRI GÒTIC
A theatrical-looking shop, stuffed with old costumes, jewelry, and Spanish shawls. You have to buzz to be let in, but it's worth it to snoop around a bit under the proprietor's watchful eye. C/ dels Banys Nous, 14. ☎ 93-317-85-15. MC, V. Metro: Jaume I.

★★ **L'Arca de l'Avia** BARRI GÒTIC
Antique lace, linens, and curtains, as well as handkerchiefs, and other textiles from the 18th to the early 20th century are found at this uniquely lovely shop, where some of the period clothing for the movie *Titanic* was purchased. C/ dels Banys Nous, 20. ☎ 93-302-15-98. www. larcadelavia.com. MC, V. Metro: Liceu.

Books
★★ **LAIE** L'EIXAMPLE
With a cafe and nice stock of English-language books, including literature, travel maps, and guides, LAIE's a favorite with foreigners resident in Barcelona. C/ Pau Claris, 85. ☎ 93-318-17-39. www.laie.es. MC, V. Metro: Catalunya or Urquinaona.

Cosmetics
★★ **La Galería de Santa María Novella**
LA RIBERA This is the Barcelona outlet of a famed apothecary in Florence, the oldest in the world. The perfumes and soaps are extraordinary and the packaging delightfully antiquated. C/ Espaseria, 4–8. ☎ 93-268-02-37. MC, V. Metro: Jaume I or Barceloneta.

★ **Regia** L'EIXAMPLE
This high-end cosmetics shop has a treat: a museum (free admission) with 5,000 examples of perfume bottles and flasks dating back as far as ancient Greece, including a cool bottle by Salvador Dalí. Passeig de Gràcia, 39. ☎ 93-216-01-21. www.regia.es. AE, MC, V. Metro: Passeig de Gràcia.

Department Stores & Shopping Centers
El Corte Inglés PLAÇA DE CATALUNYA
Spain's largest department store chain sells everything from food to furnishings to fashion. Plaça de Catalunya, 14. ☎ 93-306-38-00. AE, DC, MC, V. www.elcorteingles.es. Metro: Catalunya.

El Triangle PLAÇA DE CATALUNYA
This large white elephant occupies a good chunk of Plaça de Catalunya at the head of La

> *A vintage corset at L'Arca de l'Avia.*

Antonio Miró **6**
Colmado Quílez **4**
El Corte Inglés **9**
El Triangle **10**
Josep Font **2**
LAIE **8**
Lupo Barcelona **3**
Regia **5**
Vinçón **1**
Zara **7, 11**

L'Eixample Shopping

Rambla. It may stick out, but it's convenient for hitting such shops as Sephora, FNAC, Camper, and Habitat. C/ Pelai, 39. ☎ 93-318-01-08. www.eltriangle.es. Metro: Plaça de Catalunya.

Maremàgnum WATERFRONT
This mall is perched out in the old harbor, near L'Aquarium. It has plenty for the whole family, from toy stores to high-end fashion. Moll d'Espanya, 5. ☎ 93-225-81-00. www.maremagnum.es. Metro: Drassanes.

Fashion & Accessories
★★ Antonio Miró L'EIXAMPLE
The designs of the Catalan Antonio Miró are chic and sleek, with a retro edge. Men's and

women's clothing, including a less expensive Miró Jeans line. C/ Consell de Cent, 349. ☎ 93-487-06-70. www.antoniomiro.es. AE, MC, V. Metro: Passeig de Gràcia.

★★ Etxart & Panno EL BORN
Unabashedly sexy fashions for women with style and money to burn, in a cool little shop in the heart of the chic Born district. Passeig del Born, 14. ☎ 93-310-37-24. www.etxartpanno.com. MC, V. Metro: Jaume I or Barceloneta.

★★ Giménez & Zuazo EL RAVAL
These quirky and cutting-edge creations with audacious prints, interesting fabrics, and contrasting cross-stitches represent Barcelona at

> *Haute couture at Natalie Capell Atelier de Moda.*

Prime Shopping Zones

Barcelona's elegant Passeig de Gràcia is home to some of the most fashionable and expensive retail space in Spain. **La Rambla de Catalunya,** which runs parallel to Passeig de Gràcia, is like an open mall of stores, perfect for strolling, and the cross streets between the two are loaded with interesting shops of all kinds—particularly València, Provença, and Consell de Cent, the last known for its art galleries. The long boulevard **Diagonal** is the site of many high-end furnishings and fashion boutiques. In **Ciutat Vella,** the main streets of Portal d'Angel, Portaferrisa, and Ferrán are packed with clothing stores and young shoppers. Small boutiques and one-of-a-kind retailers are tucked in the neighborhoods **El Born** and **Barri Gòtic,** and increasingly in **El Raval.** Antiques dealers, meanwhile, are largely clustered around the labyrinth of streets near C/ de la Palla, Banys Nous, and Plaça del Pi in the **Barri Gòtic.**

its most fashion-conscious. C/ Elisabets, 20. ☎ 93-412-33-81. AE, MC, V. Metro: Plaça de Catalunya or Liceu. A 2nd location is at C/ Rec, 42, in El Born.

★★ Jocomomola de Sybilla EL BORN
The brightly colored, informal women's fashions from this Madrileña designer have a retro bent, with a jaunty, funky European sensibility. C/ Vigatans, 6 (off Princesa). ☎ 93-310-66-66. www.larobanostra.com. AE, MC, V. Metro: Jaume I.

★★★ Josep Font L'EIXAMPLE
This original Catalan designer, whose gorgeous shop shows off Modernista details, creates women's clothes that are timeless, sleek, and bold, with a dramatic feel for luxurious materials. C/ Provença, 304. ☎ 93-487-21-10. www.josepfont.com. MC, V. Metro: Passeig de Gràcia.

★★★ Lupo Barcelona L'EIXAMPLE
Lupo is the hottest name in stylish leather goods. Bags and belts mold and fold leather into unexpected shapes and feature vivid colors. C/ Mallorca, 257, bajos. ☎ 93-487-80-50. www.lupo.es. AE, DC, MC, V. Metro: Passeig de Gràcia.

> *Attention to detail at clothier Antonio Miró.*

★★★ Natalie Capell Atelier de Moda EL BORN
Timeless, handmade, high-fashion designs for women in a dark boutique that looks like a theater set. Carassa, 2 (off Princesa). ☎ 93-319-92-19. www.nataliecapell.com. MC, V. Metro: Jaume I.

Zara BARRI GÒTIC
This ubiquitous shop makes men's, women's, and kids' fashions (and now home design) accessible. For trendy, seasonal items, it's tough to beat Zara (pronounced "*Thah*-duh"). C/ Pelai, 58. ☎ 93-301-09-78. www.zara.com. AE, DISC, MC, V. Metro: Plaça de Catalunya. Many other locations, including Passeig de Gràcia, 16. ☎ 93-318-76-75. Metro: Passeig de Gràcia.

Furnishings
★ Ici Et Là LA RIBERA
A good indication of Barcelona's individualistic,

> *A one-of-a-kind shopping experience at Josep Font.*

design-crazy personality is this stylish shop. You'll find quirky and limited editions by local artists and designers, as well as interesting "world" pieces, such as African baskets and Indian textiles. Plaça de Sant Maria, 2. ☎ 93-268-11-67. www.icietla.com. MC, V. Metro: Jaume I or Barceloneta.

★★★ Vinçón L'EIXAMPLE
Fernando Amat's temple of good design, Vinçón features more than 10,000 products—everything from household items to the finest Catalan and Spanish contemporary furnishings. It's housed in the former home of Modernista

> *A little bit of everything at Colmado Quílez.*

painter Ramón Casas (1866–1932). The singular window displays alone are always a conversation piece. Passeig de Gràcia, 96. ☎ 93-215-60-50. www.vincon.com. AE, MC, V. Metro: Diagonal or Passeig de Gràcia.

Gifts

★ BCN Original Shops BARRI GÒTIC

If you're after particularly Barcelona-themed gifts and souvenirs, this is your place. Art and architecture books, mugs, ceramics, jewelry, T-shirts, notebooks, and more. Citutat, 2. ☎ 93-270-24-29. AE, MC, V. Metro: Jaume I.

★★ Kukuxumusu LA RIBERA

Don't even try to pronounce the name of this shop, originally from Navarra but now all over Spain. Do pop by for witty, hip T-shirts and accessories. With a fun take on Spanish cultural traditions, they make great souvenirs. L'Argentaria, 69. ☎ 93-310-36-47. www.kukuxumusu.com AE, MC, V. Metro: Jaume I.

Gourmet Food Shops

★★ Caelum BARRI GÒTIC

Cloistered nuns and religious orders produce everything in this shop, including jams and preserved fruit, biscuits, marzipan, and liquors, all handsomely packaged. In the cafe downstairs are the remains of ancient Jewish baths. C/ de la Palla, 8. ☎ 93-302-69-93. MC, V. Metro: Jaume I.

> *Nuts about nuts at E & A Gispert.*

★★★ Colmado Quílez L'EIXAMPLE

An old-school *colmado,* or packaged-goods store, with great Catalan and Spanish cheeses, canned goods, and a huge selection of wines. A real throwback. Rambla de Catalunya, 63. ☎ 93-215-23-56. www.lafuente.es. MC, V. Metro: Passeig de Gràcia.

★★★ E & A Gispert LA RIBERA

Follow your nose to this fantastic, century-old food shop, where coffee and nuts are roasted daily (in a 150-year-old oven). Also: dried fruit, olive oils, and much more. C/ dels Sombrerers, 23. ☎ 93-319-75-35. www.casagispert.com. MC, V. Metro: Jaume I.

Travel Tip

For a tour of Barcelona's best gourmet eating, see p. 430.

> *Vila Viniteca stocks over 4,000 wines.*

★ Tot Formatge EL BORN

Cheese hounds should beeline to this cute little shop with terrific smells and a cornucopia of cheeses from Catalunya and across Spain. Passeig del born, 13. ☎ 93-319-53-75. MC, V. Metro: Jaume I or Barceloneta.

★★★ Vila Viniteca LA RIBERA

Barcelona's best wine shop started as a food shop in 1932, and it maintains a gourmet locale just across the alley. Connoisseurs of Spanish wines will be in heaven, especially because among its 4,000-plus wines the shop stocks a number of hard-to-find, small-production bottles, several not available outside Spain. C/ Agullers, 7. ☎ 902-32-77-77. www.vilaviniteca.es. AE, MC, V. Metro: Jaume I or Barceloneta.

Jewelry

★★ Forvm Ferlandina PLAÇA DE CATALUNYA

The unique works of several dozen contemporary jewelry designers are on view in this gallery-like shop. C/ Ferlandia, 31. ☎ 93-441-80-18. AE, DC, MC, V. Metro: Liceu or Plaça de Catalunya.

Old World Emporiums

★★ Cereria Subira BARRI GÒTIC

The oldest continuous shop in Barcelona, this iconic store specializes in candles, from those used at Mass to more creative and colorful numbers. Baixada de Llibretería, 7. ☎ 93-315-26-06. MC, V. Metro: Jaume I.

★★ Herboristeria del Rei EL RAVAL

A purveyor of herbs, natural remedies, cosmetics, and teas since 1823, this atmospheric shop

> *Euro-chic Camper.*

looks the part. C/ del Vidre, 1. ☎ 93-318-05-12. MC, V. Metro: Plaça de Catalunya or Liceu.

★ Sombrerería Obach BARRI GÒTIC

Proudly old-fashioned, this shop in the old Jewish quarter sells nothing but hats, including classic Spanish berets *(boinas)*. C/ del Call, 2. ☎ 93-318-40-94. MC, V. Metro: Jaume I.

Shoes

★★ Camper EL RAVAL

Camper shoes, originally from Mallorca, are now famous across the globe. You can get the latest models of this hipster shoemaker, in unusual colors and shapes, in Barcelona. The shop interior is quirky, just like the shoes. Plaça dels Àngels, 4. ☎ 93-342-41-41. www.camper.com. AE, DISC, MC, V. Metro: Universitat.

Barcelona Restaurant Best Bets

Best Old-School Catalan Dining
Agut d'Avignon $$$ C/ Trinitat, 3 (see p. 457)

Most Worth the Wait
Cal Pep $$ Plaça des les Olles, 8 (see p. 460)
Quimet i Quimet $ C/ Poeta Cabanyes, 25 (see p. 463)

Best-Value Foodie Restaurant
Hisop $$ Passeig Marimón, 9 (see p. 461)
Restaurant Embat $$ C/ Mallorca, 304 (see p. 463)

Best Designer Tapas
Comerç 24 $$$ C/ Comerç, 24 (see p. 460)

Best Classic Tapas
Inopia $ C/ Tamarit, 104 (see p. 461)

Best Seafood
Els Pescadors $$$ Plaça Prim, 1 (see p. 461)
Cal Pep $$ Plaça des les Olles, 8 (see p. 460)

Best Family Meal
7 Portes $$ Passeig d'Isabel II, 14 (see p. 464)

Best Comfort Food
Senyor Parellada $$ C/ L'Argenteria, 37 (see p. 463)

Best Modernista Digs
Casa Calvet $$$ C/ Casp, 48 (see p. 460)

Best Lunch Deal
Restaurant Embat $$ C/ Mallorca, 304 (see p. 463)

Most Relaxed Beachfront Dining
Agua $$ Passeig Marítim de la Barceloneta, 30 (see p. 457)

Biggest Portions
7 Portes $$ Passeig d'Isabel II, 14 (see p. 464)

Best Upstart Foodie Destination
Cinc Sentits $$$ C/ Aribau, 58 (see p. 460)

Best for Impatient Kids
La Paradeta $$ C/ Comercial, 7 (see p. 462)

Best Terrace Dining
Café de L'Academia $ C/ Lledó, 1 (see p. 457)

> *The secret's out: Cal Pep.*

Barcelona Restaurants A to Z

★ **kids Agua** WATERFRONT/VILA OLÍMPICA
MEDITERRANEAN A casually cool spot with great beach views off its terrace, Agua is popular for simply prepared fresh fish, rice dishes, and vegetarian items. It's a great spot for families with boisterous and picky young ones. Passeig Marítim de la Barceloneta, 30. ☎ 93-225-12-72. www.aguadeltragaluz.com. Entrees 9€–21€. AE, DC, MC, V. Lunch & dinner daily. Metro: Ciutadella.

★★ **Agut d'Avignon** BARRI GÒTIC CATALAN
A classic revered among locals for its consistently fine, traditional Catalan cooking, this rustic spot is one of the best places in the city to sample the down-to-earth ingredients of *cuina catalana*, such as duck with figs and langostinos (prawns) *all-i-oli* (in garlic and olive oil). C/ Trinitat, 3 (alley off Avinyó, 8). ☎ 93-302-60-34. Entrees 19€–44€. MC, V. Lunch & dinner daily. Closed last 3 weeks in Aug. Metro: Jaume I or Liceu.

kids Bestial WATERFRONT/VILA OLÍMPICA
MEDITERRANEAN/ITALIAN This cool, futuristic spot is hip but relaxed, with large picture

> *The vibrant interior of Senyor Parellada.*

windows looking out to a very attractive outdoor space and views of the beach. The Mediterranean menu has an Italian bent, offering pastas, risottos, and individual pizzas with fresh ingredients. C/ Ramón Trias Fargas, 2-4. ☎ 93-224-04-07. Entrees 10€–22€. AE, DC, MC, V. Lunch & dinner daily. Metro: Ciutadella-Vila Olímpica.

★ **Café de L'Academia** BARRI GÒTIC CATALAN
This dark, ancient-looking little restaurant sits on a lovely medieval square and is usually packed for lunch, when it offers a superb fixed-price menu. In warm weather, tables are set out on the terrace, a perfect place to drink in this quintessential Barri Gòtic corner. C/ Lledó, 1. ☎ 93-315-00-26. Entrees 10€–18€. AE, MC, V. Lunch & dinner Mon–Fri. Metro: Jaume I.

Travel Tip

Catalans generally have lunch from 1 to 4pm, with "rush hour" at 2pm. A *tapeo*, or stroll from tapas bar to tapas bar, may start in the early evening, but dinner begins after 9pm. Most kitchens stay open until 11:30pm.

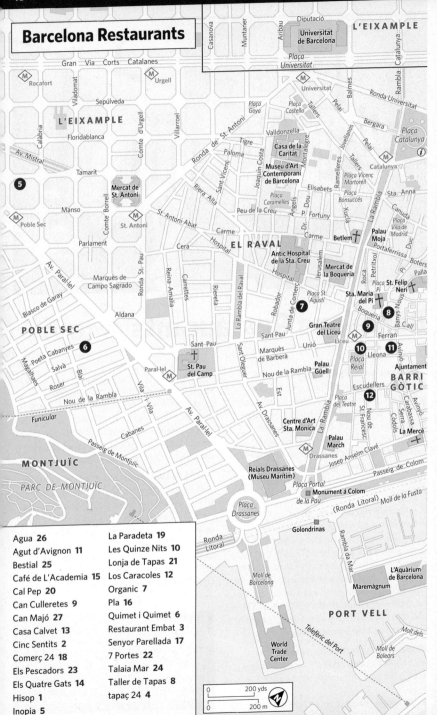

Barcelona Restaurants

L'EIXAMPLE

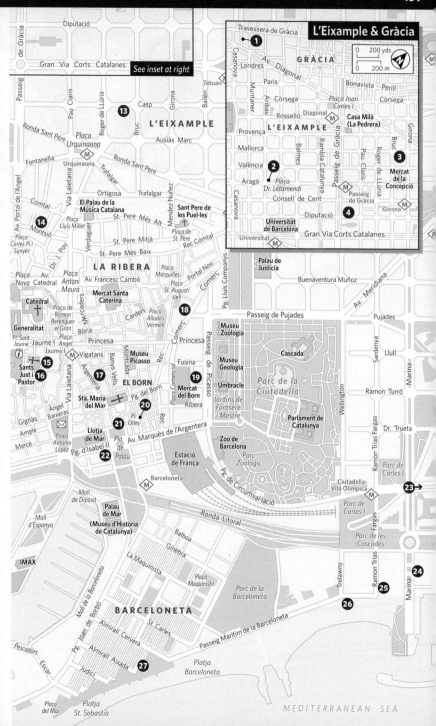

> *Tapas are for sharing at Inopia.*

> *Artful cuisine at Cinc Sentits.*

★★ **Cal Pep** LA RIBERA/WATERFRONT *SEAFOOD*
This tiny place used to be a secret, but local foodies and those from abroad now know that it serves some of the most succulent seafood in town. Cal Pep doesn't take reservations, so you have to wait until a seat at the counter opens up. There's no menu, either, but Pep and his boys will set you up with the works. **Plaça des les Olles, 8.** ☎ 93-310-79-61. Entrees 14€–24€. AE, DC, MC, V. Lunch Tues–Sat, dinner Mon–Sat. Closed Aug. Metro: Barceloneta or Jaume I.

Can Culleretes BARRI GÒTIC *CATALAN*
Barcelona's oldest restaurant has been serving traditional Catalan cooking since 1786. It's down-home and old-school, a good place to try standards such as *espinacas a la catalana* (spinach with pine nuts and raisins) and *butifarra* (white sausage). C/ Quintana, 5. ☎ 93-317-64-85. www.culleretes.com. Entrees 8€–18€. MC, V. Lunch Tues–Sun, dinner Tues–Sat. Closed Aug. Metro: Liceu.

★★ **Can Majó** WATERFRONT/PORT VELL *SEAFOOD*
Insiders know that this tavern-style, harborfront restaurant is one of the top seafood places in Barcelona. Try the excellent *sopa de pescado y marisco* (fish and shellfish soup), sautéed squid, or paellas. C/ Almirall Aixada,

23. ☎ 93-221-58-18. www.canmajo.es. Entrees 14€–27€. AE, DC, MC, V. Lunch Tues–Sun, dinner Tues–Sat. Metro: Barceloneta.

★★ **Casa Calvet** L'EIXAMPLE *CATALAN/ MEDITERRANEAN* Casa Calvet is housed within one of Antoni Gaudí's first Modernista apartment buildings, with a gorgeous white-brick and stained-glass decor. The contemporary Catalan cuisine doesn't take a back seat to the surroundings. C/ Casp, 48. ☎ 93-412-40-12. www.casacalvet.es. Entrees 23€–31€, tasting menus 49€–75€. AE, DC, MC, V. Lunch & dinner Mon–Sat. Closed last 2 weeks in Aug. Metro: Passeig de Gràcia.

★★★ **Cinc Sentits** L'EIXAMPLE *MEDITERRANEAN*
Haute cuisine, but also family-run—this recent arrival is a unique synthesis of the Barcelona dining scene. Chef Jordi Artal's innovative fusion cuisine is best sampled on the eight-course tasting menu. Prepare yourself for monkfish sprinkled with bacon "dust" or a soft poached egg with tomato jam. C/ Aribau, 58. ☎ 93-323-94-90. www.cincsentits.com. Entrees 18€–36€, tasting menu 45€–65€. AE, DC, MC, V. Lunch Mon–Sat, dinner Tues–Sat. Closed Easter week and Aug 8–31. Metro: Passeig de Gràcia.

★★★ **Comerç 24** LA RIBERA/EL BORN
CATALAN/INTERNATIONAL The small plates of celebrity chef Carles Abellan are so creative that it's a disservice to call them tapas. The theatrical dishes offer a visionary take on Catalan classics. C/ Comerç, 24. ☎ 93-319-21-02.

> *Casual beachside dining at Agua.*

> *Picasso once hung his work at Els Quatre Gats.*

www.comerc24.com. Entrees 12€–28€, tasting menu 48€. AE, DC, MC, V. Lunch & dinner Tues–Sat. Closed Christmas week and last 3 weeks in Aug. Metro: Jaume I.

★★ **Els Pescadors** WATERFRONT/POBLE NOU SEAFOOD Family-run, "the Fishermen" focuses, naturally, on providing superb fresh fish and seafood, with just a hint of new-school preparations. Plaça Prim, 1. ☎ 93-225-20-18. www.els pescadors.com. Entrees 15€–35€. AE, DC, MC, V. Lunch & dinner daily. Closed Easter week. Metro: Poble Nou.

★ **Els Quatre Gats** BARRI GÒTIC CATALAN A cafe that's become legend, this place was the turn-of-the-20th-century hangout of Picasso and other bohemian intellectuals. The "Four Cats" today is on the Modernista tourist circuit, but it's a surprisingly good spot for simple, homey Catalan fare using fresh market ingredients. C/ Montsió, 3. ☎ 93-302-41-40. www.4gats. com. Entrees 14€–24€, fixed-price lunch menu

14€. AE, DC, MC, V. Breakfast, lunch & dinner daily. Metro: Plaça de Catalunya.

★★ **Hisop** GRACIA *CONTEMPORARY CATALAN* Less intimidating than some of Barcelona's chicest restaurants featuring *cocina de autor* (creative haute cuisine), Hisop is small, inviting, and dynamic. Although difficult to find on a tiny side street just north of the Diagonal boulevard, it's worth the hunt for subtly complex dishes, such as scallops with figs and Jabugo ham, and scrumptious desserts. Passeig Marimón, 9. ☎ 93-141-32-33. www.hisop.com. Entrees 22€–24€. AE, DC, MC, V. Lunch & dinner Tues–Sat. Closed last 2 weeks in Aug. Metro: Hospital Clinic.

★★ **Inopia** L'EIXAMPLE/ESQUERRA *TAPAS* People hear that this tapas joint is by the brother of the legendary chef Ferran Adrià and expect all kinds of funky foams. But it's a classic tapas bar serving up superb Spanish and Catalan tapas. The standards, such as *patatas bravas* (spicy fried potatoes) and *croquetas de jamón ibérico* (croquettes stuffed with Spanish ham), are rarely this tasty elsewhere. C/ Tamarit, 104. ☎ 93-424-52-31. Tapas 3€–12€. MC, V. Lunch Sat, dinner Tues–Sat. Metro: Poble Sec.

Travel Tip

For a structured tour of eating well in Barcelona, see p. 430.

Lonja de TAPAS

- PERNIL de QLA "JOSELITO" do GUIJUELO • OLIVES KALA
- GRAELLADA de VERDURETES A LA PLANXA AMB ROME
- OU ESCLAFAT AMB PATATA i XORICET de BURGOS
- CAMEMBERT FREGIT AMB SALSA de FRUITS VERI
- FOIE D'ANEC a la PLANXA AMB PA D'ESPECIES i MAN
- LES NOSTRES PATATES "BRAVES" • BUNYOLS de BACALL
- FRESH de "ARRÒS" de CALAMAR A LA MALAGUENYA o TRUIT

> *Cava and a tapas spread at Quimet i Quimet.*

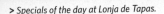

> *Specials of the day at Lonja de Tapas.*

kids La Paradeta LA RIBERA *SEAFOOD* You can pick your own seafood and *mariscos* (shellfish) from large plastic tubs; it's then weighed and served on a platter. Kids should love it, and parents can pair dinner with a nice selection of wines. C/ Comercial, 7. ☎ 93-268-19-39. Entrees (cost is per kilogram) 12€–24€. No credit cards. Dinner Tues–Sat. Closed Dec 22–Jan 22. Metro: Arc de Triomf.

Les Quinze Nits LA RAMBLA/BARRI GÒTIC *MEDITERRANEAN* This attractive, bargain-priced restaurant with a few tables under the arches on Plaça Reial, draws long lines of people looking for a solid meal and great deal. The Catalan and Mediterranean dishes are simple and straightforward but surprisingly well prepared. Plaça Reial, 6. ☎ 93-317-30-75. www.lesquinzenits.com. Entrees 5€–15€. MC, V. Lunch & dinner daily. Metro: Liceu.

★ **Lonja de Tapas** WATERFRONT *TAPAS* A bright and easygoing tapas restaurant in a good-looking space, this new place is solid, especially if you're just in the mood for grazing or don't quite know what you want. Tapas cover the Spanish standards, from Iberian ham and steamed cockles to paellas and monkfish with wild mushrooms. Pla del Palau, 7. ☎ 93-268-72-58. www.lonjadetapas.com. Tapas 3€–20€, tasting menu 26€. AE, DC, MC, V. Lunch & dinner daily. Metro: Barceloneta or Jaume I.

Los Caracoles BARRI GÒTIC *CATALAN* Popular with tourists, this restaurant is one of those only-in-Spain places. You're first greeted by an open spit roasting chickens; inside is an ancient, atmospheric labyrinth of cluttered dining rooms. "The Snails" is all about Catalan comfort food, such as *arroz negre* (rice cooked in squid ink), grilled squid, and roast chicken. C/ Escudellers, 14. ☎ 93-302-31-85. Entrees 9€–28€. AE, DC, MC, V. Lunch & dinner daily. Metro: Liceu or Drassanes.

> *The dining room at 7 Portes.*

★ **Organic** RAVAL *VEGETARIAN*
It's taken a while for vegetarian restaurants to catch on, but this cool, laid-back place with large communal tables really fills a void. There's a help-yourself soup-and-salad bar, organic tapas, and main courses that include vegetarian pizza, pasta, and stir-fries. C/ Junta de Comerç, 11. ☎ 93-301-09-02. www.antoniaorganickitchen. com. Main courses 6€–14€. AE, DC, MC, V. Lunch & dinner daily. Metro: Liceu.

★ **Pla** BARRI GÒTIC *MEDITERRANEAN*
Popular with locals and visitors alike for its well-prepared dishes at exceedingly fair prices, this attractive restaurant serves excellent carpaccios, tasty salads, and gently exotic main courses, such as Thai curry or Moroccan couscous. C/ Bellafila, 5. ☎ 93-412-65-52. www.pla-repla.com. Entrees 15€–22€. DC, MC, V. Dinner daily. Closed Dec 25–27. Metro: Jaume I.

★★ **Quimet i Quimet** POBLE SEC *TAPAS*
In the Poble Sec neighborhood, this incredible hole-in-the-wall—the walls lined to the ceiling with liquor bottles and canned foods—is always jampacked with hungry patrons and drinkers in the know, who come for the stunningly creative and delicious *montaditos* (little gourmet sandwiches). C/ Poeta Cabanyes, 25. ☎ 93-442-31-42. Tapas 3€–10€. MC, V. Metro: Paral·lel.

★★ **Restaurant Embat** L'EIXAMPLE *CONTEMPORARY CATALAN* This smart little restaurant, part of the "bistronomic" wave in Barcelona, does clever Catalan cuisine at an extremely reasonable price. The dining room is relaxed, rustic chic, with rough-hewn tables and brown linens. Lunch, whether a la carte or from the daily *menú*, is one of the best deals in the city. C/ Mallorca, 304. ☎ 93/458-08-55. www. restaurantembat.es. Entrees 9€–22€. AE, DC, MC, V. Lunch Mon–Fri, dinner Thurs–Sat. Metro: Jaume I.

★ **Senyor Parellada** LA RIBERA *CATALAN/ MEDITERRANEAN* One of the best values in Barcelona is this cheery, stylish restaurant carved out of an old mansion. The colorful dining rooms look photo ready, so it's a surprise to get such dependably executed, fresh preparations of authentic Catalan fare—including baked monkfish with mustard and garlic sauce—at bargain prices. C/ L'Argenteria, 37. ☎ 93-310-50-94. www.senyorparellada.com. Entrees 8€–21€. AE, DC, MC, V. Lunch & dinner daily. Metro: Jaume I.

> *"Bar food" at tapaç 24.*

★★ kids 7 Portes WATERFRONT *CATALAN*

A favorite of large dining parties since 1836, this elegant but unassuming place really does have seven doors under porticoes (hence the name). It's famous for its rice dishes, such as black rice with squid in its own ink; portions are enormous and reasonably priced. **Passeig d'Isabel II, 14. ☎ 93-319-30-33. www.7portes.com. Entrees 15€–35€. AE, DC, MC, V. Lunch & dinner daily. Metro: Barceloneta or Drassanes.**

★★ Talaia Mar WATERFRONT/PORT OLÍMPIC

MEDITERRANEAN The Olympic Port teems with restaurants, but none of them is as good as this one. The innovative chef has created a seafood-dominated menu, featuring grilled fresh fish and more audacious dishes that tempt the senses, including barnacles with a seawater sorbet. **Marina, 16. ☎ 93-221-90-90. www.barcelona-comercio.com/talaia. Entrees 18€–32€, fixed-price menu 51€. AE, DC, MC, V. Lunch & dinner Tues–Sun. Metro: Ciutadella–Vila Olímpica.**

★ Taller de Tapas BARRI GÒTIC *TAPAS*

This pleasant, modern "Tapas Workshop" simplifies the ordering of tapas, which are prepared fresh in an open kitchen. You'll find delightful small dishes from across Spain: marinated anchovies, prawns with scrambled eggs, and sizzling chorizo cooked in cider. **Plaça Sant Josep Oriol, 9. ☎ 93-301-80-20. www.tallerdetapas. com. Tapas 3€–14€. AE, DC, MC, V. Lunch & dinner daily. Metro: Liceu. A 2nd location is at C/ L'Argenteria, 51. ☎ 93-268-85-5. Metro: Jaume I.**

★★ tapaç 24 L'EIXAMPLE *CREATIVE TAPAS*

Ultracool Comerç 24 does upscale tapas, while this below-street-level bar is the more informal offshoot. But it shares an interest in fresh ingredients and just the right touch of creativity. **C/ Diputació, 269. ☎ 93-488-09-77. Tapas 2.50€–14€. MC, V. Breakfast, lunch & dinner Mon–Sat. Metro: Passeig de Gràcia.**

Barcelona Hotel Best Bets

Most Romantic Hotel
Hotel Neri $$$ C/ Sant Sever, 5 (see p. 472)

Best Business Hotel
Hotel Arts $$$$ C/ de la Marina, 19–21 (see p. 469)

Best Cutting-Edge Design
Hotel Omm $$$$ C/ Rosselló, 265 (see p. 472)

Best Service
Hotel Arts $$$$ C/ de la Marina, 19–21 (see p. 469)

Best In-House Restaurant
Hotel Omm $$$$ C/ Rosselló, 265 (see p. 472)

Best Gay Hotel
Hotel Axel $$$ C/ Aribau, 33 (see p. 470)

Best Boutique Hotel
Duquesa de Cardona $$$ Passeig Colom, 12 (see p. 466)

Most Affordable Design
Hotel Banys Orientals $$ C/ L'Argenteria, 37 (see p. 470)

Best Sea Views
Hotel Arts $$$$ C/ de la Marina, 19–21 (see p. 469)

Best for Families
Hispanos Siete Suiza $$ C/ Sicilia, 255 (see p. 469)

Best Rooftop Pool
Grand Hotel Central $$$ Vía Laietana, 30 (see p. 468)

Best Step Up from a Hostel
Gat Xino $ C/ Hospital, 155 (see p. 468)

Best Spa Pampering
Hotel Arts $$$$ C/ de la Marina, 19–21 (see p. 469)

Best Modernista Hotel
Hotel Casa Fuster $$$$ Passeig de Gràcia, 132 (see p. 471)

> *Rooftop views at Duquesa de Cardona.*

Barcelona Hotels A to Z

★★ **Casa Camper** RAVAL

If you're a fan of funky Camper shoes, this idiosyncratic, design-trippy place, where all rooms have sitting rooms, is probably for you. The hotel's aesthetics are as playful as the company's shoe stores, though it's a little pricey for the transitional neighborhood and the young, design-obsessed crowd it courts. The roof terrace beckons with its hammocks for siesta-taking, and there's also a cafeteria with round-the-clock snacks. C/ Elisabets, 11. ☎ 93-342-62-80. www.camper.com/web/en/casacamper.asp. 25 units. Doubles 179€–255€. AE, DC, MC, V. Metro: Catalunya or Liceu.

★ **Ciutat Barcelona Hotel** LA RIBERA

A bargain hotel that offers a lot of cool design and comfort for a great price, this new addition to the hip neighborhood, just steps from the Picasso Museum, is a winner. Rooms are crisply contemporary and clean, and there's a nice little rooftop pool and deck. C/ de la Princesa, 35. ☎ 93-269-74-75. www.ciutatbarcelona.com. 78 units. Doubles 105€–125€. AE, DC, MC, V. Metro: Arc de Triomf or Jaume I.

★★★ **Constanza** L'EIXAMPLE

Travelers looking for affordable Barcelona style will be pleased with this small boutique hotel. Although rooms aren't large, they are modern and comfortable, and the hotel's very well located, within walking distance of Plaça de Catalunya. A room with its own private terrace is a real bargain. C/ Bruc, 33. ☎ 93-270-19-10. www.hotelconstanza.com. 20 units. Doubles 120€–130€. AE, MC, V. Metro: Urquinaona.

★★★ **Duquesa de Cardona** WATERFRONT A

sedate boutique hotel across the street from the marina, this restored 19th-century palace is elegant and intimate. It also has something unique: a large rooftop solarium terrace with a pool and great views of the port. This place is ideal for honeymooners, with views of Montjuïc, though you should pay the extra euros for the harborfront rooms. Passeig Colom, 12. ☎ 866-376-7831 in the U.S., or 93-268-90-90. www.hduquesadecardona.com. 44 units. Doubles 265€–305€. AE, DC, MC, V. Metro: Jaume I or Drassanes.

> *The lobby at Casa Camper.*

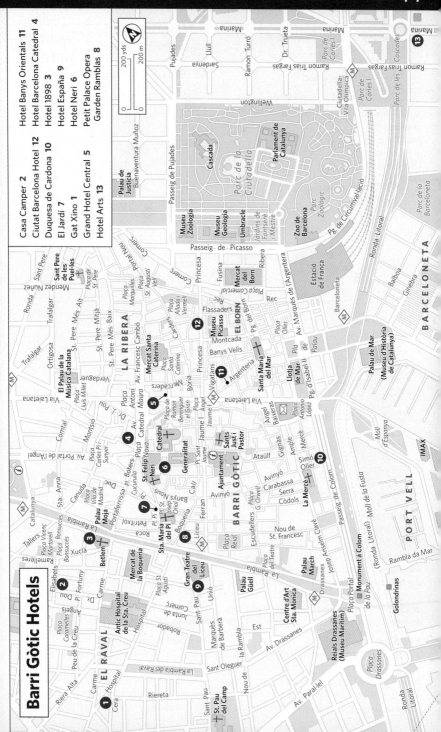

Barri Gòtic Hotels

Casa Camper **2**
Ciutat Barcelona Hotel **12**
Duquesa de Cardona **10**
El Jardí **7**
Gat Xino **1**
Grand Hotel Central **5**
Hotel Arts **13**
Hotel Banys Orientals **11**
Hotel Barcelona Catedral **4**
Hotel 1898 **3**
Hotel España **9**
Hotel Neri **6**
Petit Palace Opera
Garden Ramblas **8**

L'Eixample Hotels

El Jardí BARRI GÒTIC

Simple and easygoing, this small hotel has an extraordinary location, overlooking two of the prettiest plazas in the heart of Ciutat Vella. Rooms are somewhat austere with bright lighting, but they're clean and cheap, and five have private terraces. Plaça Sant Josep Oriol, 1. ☎ 93-301-59-00. www.hoteljardi-barcelona.com. 40 units. Doubles 40€–85€. MC, V. Metro: Liceu.

★★ Kids Gat Xino RAVAL

Just because you don't want to spend a lot of money doesn't mean you don't want some style. A major step up from hostels, this groovy place is popular with hipsters, design sorts, young families, and travelers with more style

than cash. Rooms are spare, with a bright green, white, and black aesthetic, and there's a cool rooftop terrace. A sister hotel, Gat Raval, C/ Joaquín Costa, 4 (☎ 93-481-66-70), in the same 'hood, is similar in style but cheaper and a tad plainer (not all rooms have en suite bathrooms). C/ Hospital, 155. ☎ 93-324-88-33. www.gatrooms.es. 35 units. Doubles 95€–110€, with breakfast. MC, V. Metro: Liceu.

★★ Grand Hotel Central LA RIBERA

In a palatial 1926 mansion owned by an old Catalan family, this new property has been beautifully converted to a contemporary luxury hotel. Rooms are warmly decorated in rich creams and chocolates. Use of the rooftop infinity pool,

> *Gat Xino's modern breakfast room.*

> *The Modernista Hotel Casa Fuster.*

surrounded by wood decking and views of the Gothic Quarter and the sea, is a privilege. Vía Laietana, 30. ☎ 93-295-79-00. www.grand hotelcentral.com. 147 units. Doubles 185€–275€. AE, DC, MC, V. Metro: Arc de Triomf or Jaume I.

★★ kids Hispanos Siete Suiza L'EIXAMPLE

An apartment hotel with the comforts of a top-flight resort, the Suiza is perfect for families and long-term stays. Apartments in the historic house are two-bedroom, two-bath, with a living room and kitchen. Incredibly, the in-house restaurant is overseen by a famed Catalan chef, Carles Gaig. But best of all, some of the hotel's profits go toward a cancer foundation established by the original owner of the house. C/ Sicilia, 255. ☎ 93-208-20-51. www.hispanos 7suiza.com. 19 units. Doubles (2-bedroom apt) 130€–210€, with breakfast. AE, DC, MC, V. Metro: Sagrada Família.

★ Hostal Goya L'EIXAMPLE

A refreshingly smart, centrally located *hostal* and an extremely good value, this small inn is clean and friendly. The best and quietest rooms are in the recently renovated Principal wing; others are small and dark. Most who stay here are young people in Barcelona to have a good time. C/ Pau Claris, 74. ☎ 93-302-25-65. www. hostalgoya.com. 19 units. Doubles 70€–90€. MC, V. Metro: Urquinaona or Catalunya.

★★★ Hotel Arts WATERFRONT

One of only three skyscrapers in Barcelona, this sleek, high-tech luxury hotel is on the beach and enjoys sweeping beach views. Service is personable and efficient, as you'd expect from a Ritz-Carlton property, making this a favorite of business travelers and celebs. The outdoor pool, swanky new spa overlooking the marina, and restaurant by star chef Sergi Arola only add to the allure. C/ de la Marina, 19–21. ☎ 800-241-3333 in the U.S., or 93-221-10-00. www. ritzcarlton.com/hotels/barcelona. 482 units. Doubles 265€–250€. AE, DC, MC, V. Metro: Ciutadella–Vila Olímpica.

> *A room with a loft at Hotel Claris.*

★ **Hotel Axel** L'EIXAMPLE

Filling a niche in Barcelona is this midsize hotel serving an international gay population. It's confident enough to call the surrounding neighborhood the "Gayxample" and decorate rooms with erotic art, but it's also "hetero-friendly." Rooms are stylish, with top-quality bedding, and the hip cocktail bar, rooftop pool, and sun deck are prized. C/ Aribau, 33. ☎ 93-323-93-93. www.hotelaxel.com. 66 units. Doubles 150€– 225€. AE, DC, MC, V. Metro: Universitat.

★★ **Hotel Banys Orientals** LA RIBERA

A pioneer leading the way for stylish but inexpensive boutique hotels, this cool place is immensely popular, as much for its bargain rates and hip style as its terrific location near El Born. Rooms are small but chic, though noise-sensitive guests should seek one in the back; the area is full of late-night revelers. C/ L'Argenteria, 37. ☎ 93-268-84-60. www.hotel banysorientals.com. 43 units. Doubles 100€. AE, DC, MC, V. Metro: Jaume I.

Apartments & B&Bs in Barcelona

As Barcelona's popularity with visitors has grown, so has its inventory of alternative accommodations, including bed & breakfasts (which only a few years ago didn't really exist in Barcelona) and private apartments for rent. For long-term stays especially, either alternative might be a comfortable and good-value choice. For inexpensive B&Bs, try **Bed andBreakfast.com** (www.bedandbreakfast. com/barcelona-spain.html), with a dozen or so offerings, including photo albums and reviews; and **International Bed & Breakfast Pages** (www.ibbp.com/europe/spain/ barcelona.html), which usually lists about three dozen centrally located B&Bs with reviews and photos. One particularly good B&B is **Fashion House B&B,** C/ Bruc, 13 (☎ 93-790-40-44; www.bcn-fashionhouse.com; doubles 55€–102€; MC, V; Metro: Urquinaona), run like a hotel in a nicely restored 19th-century town house with a leafy communal terrace and a self-catering apartment that's great for families.

The city's tourism bureau, **Barcelona Turisme** (www.barcelonaturisme.com), maintains a long list of tourist apartments rented by either the day or the week. Private online brokers include **www.visit-bcn.com**, which offers everything from Barri Gòtic town houses to loft-style apartments; **www. friendlyrentals.com**, offering stylish properties at a surprisingly good value; and **www.oh-barcelona.com**, which lists more than 300 apartments for rent. Two buildings with 13 chic, modern apartments for rent in the Old City (both Born and waterfront) can be found at **La Casa de les Lletres** (☎ 93-226-37-30; www.cru2001.com), while **Chic & Basic** (www.chicandbasic.com), with hip, minimalist hotels in Barcelona and several other European cities, also offers a nice selection of a half-dozen apartments with a modern aesthetic similar to their hotels in the old part of town.

★ kids **Hotel Barcelona Catedral** BARRI GÒTIC

One of Barcelona's newest hotels is in the oldest part of town, right across from the Cathedral. It's stylishly modern but affordably priced. Unexpected bonuses are the pool, terrace, and

> *Hotel 1898's subterranean pool.*

wireless Internet access, as well as cooking lessons, wine tastings, and guided tours around the Old City. C/ Capellans, 4. ☎ 93-304-22-55. 80 units. Doubles 179€. AE, DC, MC, V. Metro: Jaume 1.

★★★ Hotel Casa Fuster GRACIA

Converted into a luxury hotel in 2004, Casa Fuster, which occupies one of the city's more significant Modernista buildings, has made a splash. No expenses were spared, giving it a feel of period indulgence with every modern amenity, including a pool, restaurant, bar, lounge, and business center. Passeig de Gràcia, 132. ☎ 93-255-30-00. www.hotelcasafuster.com. 105 units. Doubles 210€–375€. AE, DC, MC, V. Metro: Diagonal.

★★★ Hotel Claris L'EIXAMPLE

This is one of the most interesting hotels in Barcelona, where modern design commingles with a landmark 19th-century palace facade and a for-guests-only museum of Egyptian art. Rooms, many of which are split-level and even two-story, are a mix of cool chic and warm sophistication. On the top-floor terrace is a small pool and lovely views of the surrounding Eixample neighborhood. C/ Pau Claris, 150. ☎ 90-099-00-11 or 93-487-62-62. www.derbyhotels.es. 120 units. Doubles 190€–345€. AE, DC, MC, V. Metro: Passeig de Gràcia.

★★ Hotel 1898 LA RAMBLA

This large hotel occupies a late-19th-century building that was once the Philippine Tobacco Co. headquarters. It has been strikingly converted, with bold artwork, stripes, and colors; most spectacular is the underground pool beneath brick arches. La Rambla, 109 (entrance on Pintor Fortuny). ☎ 93-552-95-52. www.hotel 1898.com. 169 units. Doubles 275€–460€. AE, DC, MC, V. Metro: Catalunya or Liceu.

Hotel España RAVAL

Off the lower part of La Rambla, this classic old hotel is known primarily for its foyer and dining room, the work of the preeminent Modernista architect Lluís Domènech i Montaner. Guest rooms are comparatively bland, but clean; the neighborhood, though, continues to be transitional and may give some guests pause, especially at night. C/ Sant Pau, 11. ☎ 93-318-17-58. www.hotelespanya.com. 60 units. Doubles 110€, with breakfast. AE, DC, MC, V. Metro: Liceu or Drassanes.

★ Hotel Jazz L'EIXAMPLE

Around the corner from La Rambla, Hotel Jazz aims, by name and middle-of-the-road contemporary design, for a wide international clientele (many of whom appear to be young

> *Splendid comfort at Hotel Neri.*

people on group junkets). The impressive lobby has plenty of glass and bleached wood floors; the soundproofed rooms are attractive if a bit generic. The star of the show, however, is the rooftop pool and wood-deck terrace. C/ Pelai, 3. ☎ 93-552-96-96, 0870-120-1521 in the U.K., or 207-580-2663 in the U.S. www.nnhotels.es. 180 units. Doubles 110€–165€. AE, DC, MC, V. Metro: Catalunya or Universitat.

★★★ Hotel Neri BARRI GÒTIC
A sumptuous Gothic palace discretely tucked away on charming Plaça Felip Neri, this small, upscale hotel is romance incarnate, all velvet drapes and soft-lit rooms. Rooms are luxurious, with fine linens, and the restaurant and cafe on the square are unexpected bonuses. A true find in the Old City, it's the kind of place you won't want to leave. C/ Sant Sever, 5. ☎ 93-304-06-55. www.hotelneri.com. 22 units. Doubles 265€–280€. AE, DC, MC, V. Metro: Jaume I.

★★★ Hotel Omm L'EIXAMPLE
The hotel with the most buzz in Barcelona is this sleek temple of hip, Zen-like design and an even cooler clientele. Its restaurant, **Moo,** is one of the city's best. Design freaks will be in heaven—the place was created for them. The rooftop lap pool and deck have views of La Pedrera. C/ Rosselló, 265. ☎ 93-445-40-00. www.hotelomm.es. 59 units. Doubles 240€–360€. AE, DC, MC, V. Metro: Diagonal.

★★ Hotel Palace Barcelona L'EIXAMPLE
Though this 1919 Art Deco hotel has changed names, many still refer to it as the Ritz, and the grace and old-money elegance remain. It's white-glove treatment all the way here; public rooms are grand and aristocratic, guest rooms are large and formal. The restaurant, **Caelis,** with a new chef, is getting a lot of attention. Gran Vía de les Corts Catalanes, 668. ☎ 93-510-11-30. www.hotelpalacebarcelona.com. 122 units. Doubles 380€–585€. AE, DC, MC, V. Metro: Passeig de Gràcia.

★★ Hotel Pulitzer L'EIXAMPLE
Sleek and trendy, but affordable for a hotel of its design and amenities, this relative newcomer to the scene is understandably popular. With a stylish cocktail bar and alluring candlelit rooftop terrace, the hotel is bound to win a design prize or two. C/ Bergara, 8. ☎ 93-481-67-67. www.hotelpulitzer.es. 91 units. Doubles 180€–250€. AE, DC, MC, V. Metro: Catalunya.

★ Petit Palace Opera Garden Ramblas
LA RAMBLA This is a member of a successful, value-priced Spanish chain. It's near, though not on, La Rambla and just seconds from La Boquería food market. Rooms have laptop computers with free Wi-Fi connections. C/ La Boquería, 10 (at Rambla, 78). ☎ 93-302-00-92. www.hthoteles.com. 69 units. Doubles 140€–245€. AE, DC, MC, V. Metro: Liceu.

Barcelona Nightlife & Entertainment Best Bets

Best Spot for Outlaw Liquor
Marsella, C/ Sant Pau, 65 (see p. 474)

Best Wine Bar
La Vinya del Senyor, Plaça Santa Maria, 5 (see p. 479)

Best *Xampanyería* (Cava Bar)
El Xampanyet, C/ de la Montcada, 22 (see p. 479)

Best Latin Dance Club
Antilla Latin Club, C/ Aragó, 141 (see p. 475)

Best Yesteryear Dance Hall
La Paloma, C/ Tigre, 27 (see p. 475)

Best Drag Show
Café Dietrich, C/ Consell de Cent, 255 (see p. 478)

Best Lounge for Beautiful People
CDLC (Carpe Diem Lounge Club) Passeig Marítim, 32 (see p. 474)

Best Jazz Club
Harlem Jazz Club, Comtessa de Sobradiel, 8 (see p. 478)

Best Flamenco
Tablao Flamenco Cordobés, La Rambla, 35 (see p. 478)

Best Opera House
Gran Teatre del Liceu, La Rambla, 51–59 (see p. 475)

Best Sporting Event
Fútbol Club Barcelona, Avenida del Papa Joan XXIII (see p. 479)

Best Concert Hall
El Palau de la Música Catalana, C/ Sant Francesc de Paula, 2 (see p. 475)

Best Live Music
Luz de Gas, C/ Muntaner, 246 (see p. 478)

Best Classic Cocktails
Gimlet, C/ Rec, 24 (see p. 474)

> *The ballroom at La Paloma attracts young and old.*

Barcelona Nightlife & Entertainment A to Z

Casinos
Casino Barcelona WATERFRONT
Hugely popular, this casino also contains a disco, a restaurant, and all the gaming opportunities you could want. Don't forget to bring your passport. C/ Marina, 19–21. ☎ 93-225-78-78. Admission 5€. Metro: Ciutadella/Vila Olímpica.

Cocktail Bars, Pubs & Lounges
★ **CDLC (Carpe Diem Lounge Club)** WATERFRONT This trendy place is all attitude and *gente bella* (beautiful people). If you want to see and be seen, it's appropriately swanky, and right on the edge of the beach. To chill on the luxe white beds, you'll have to pony up for a pricey bottle of whiskey. Better yet, have a drink on the outdoor terrace. Passeig Marítim, 32. ☎ 93-224-04-70. Metro: Vila Olímpica/Ciutadella.

★★★ **Gimlet** LA RIBERA
People who know their cocktails frequent this sophisticated, retro-style bar, where excellent

bartenders and cool jazz on the stereo complete the scene. Perfect for predinner drinks. C/ Rec, 24. ☎ 93-310-10-27. Metro: Arc de Triomf.

★ **Luz de Gas Port Vell** WATERFRONT
A summer-only lounge bar on a boat in the marina, this sister bar of the very cool nightspot Luz de Gas is ideal in warm weather for evening cocktails. Candlelit tables and a dance floor overlook the pier. Moll de Diposit, s/n (in front of Palau de Mar). ☎ 93-209-77-11. Metro: Drassanes or Barceloneta.

★★★ **Marsella** RAVAL
This dusty joint—around since 1820—is *the* place to try *absenta* (absinthe), the wickedly strong anise-flavored liqueur distilled from wormwood, said to be hallucinogenic and still banned in some countries. They say that Picasso, Dalí, and Hemingway were regulars here. C/ Sant Pau, 65. ☎ 93-442-72-63. Metro: Liceu.

Travel Bar BARRI GÒTIC
The name says it all: This bar is a refuge for on-the-cheap travelers and backpackers to meet

> *On a boat: Luz de Gas Port Vell.*

> Opera fans at Gran Teatre del Liceu.

> A glass of the green fairy at Marsella.

up, gather information, dial up the Internet, grab some cheapo grub, and, of course, pound back beers. C/ Boquería, 27. ☎ 93-342-52-52. Metro: Liceu.

Concert Venues

★★★ **El Palau de la Música Catalana** LA RIBERA This 1908 concert hall, designed by Lluís Domènech i Montaner, is a Modernista masterpiece. Concerts are primarily classical, though the administration has sought to widen exposure to the hall by adding jazz, world, and alternative rock. For daily guided tours of the building, see p. 418, ➏. A new extension called Petit Palau includes a luxury restaurant and rehearsal space. C/ Sant Francesc de Paula, 2. ☎ 93-295-72-00. www.palaumusica.org. Tickets 20€–70€. Metro: Urquinaona.

★★★ **Gran Teatre del Liceu** LA RAMBLA Barcelona's great opera house, founded in 1874, is one of the grandest theaters in the world. Though it burned in 1994, it was quickly rebuilt with donations, preserving the look and feel of the original. The Liceu has long been the home

turf of the international opera stars José Carreras and Montserrat Caballé, both from Barcelona. In addition to opera, you'll find concerts, as well as recitals and chamber music, in the smaller **El Petit Liceu.** La Rambla, 51–59. ☎ 93-485-99-13 or 93-485-99-00. www.liceubarcelona.com. Tickets 20€–85€. Metro: Liceu.

Dance Clubs

★★★ **Antilla Latin Club** L'EIXAMPLE A fixture among Barcelona's large Latin American and Caribbean community, this happening *salsateca* is a great place to shake it if you know what you're doing. (And if you don't, check out the club's dance school, Mon and Wed–Fri 9–11:30pm, 120€ for a package of lessons, free on Tues with cover.) It also gets some big-name Latino performers. C/ Aragó, 141. ☎ 93-451-21-51. Cover 10€. Metro: Urgell.

★★★ **La Paloma** RAVAL A historic, lavish ballroom, more than a century old, this theater, with its red-velvet entry, murals, and glimmering chandeliers, is an extraordinary place to dance. In the early evening, that means fox trot, tango, and bolero, accompanied by live orchestras. Late night Thursday to Sunday, it morphs into a much younger and hipper nightclub. Note that it was closed temporarily at press time, so call ahead. C/ Tigre, 27. ☎ 93-301-68-97. Cover 5€–10€. Metro: Universitat.

Barcelona Nightlife & Entertainment

See inset at right

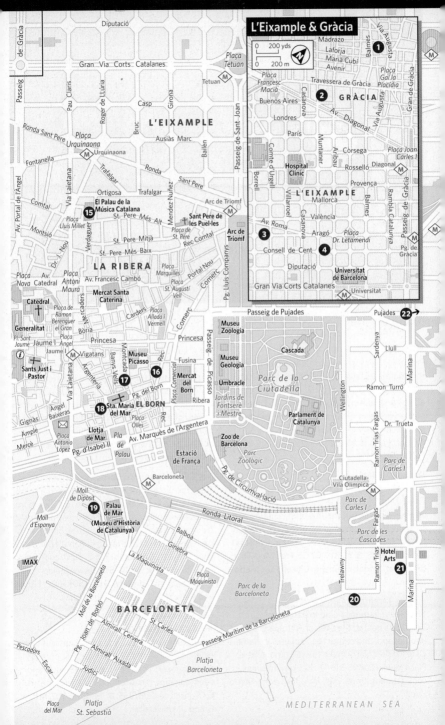

L'Eixample & Gràcia

0   200 yds
0   200 m

GRÀCIA

L'EIXAMPLE

Madrazo
Laforja
Marià Cubí
Avenir
Plaça Gal.la Placídia

Travessera de Gràcia
Buenos Aires
Londres
París

Av. Diagonal

Hospital Clínic

Còrsega
Rosselló
Provença
Mallorca
València
Aragó
Consell de Cent
Diputació
Gran Via Corts Catalanes

Plaça Joan Carles I
Diagonal

Plaça Dr. Letamendi

Plaça de Gràcia

Universitat de Barcelona
Universitat

Av. Roma

Diputació
Gran Via Corts Catalanes
Plaça Tetuan
Tetuan

L'EIXAMPLE
Ausiàs Marc
Casp

Plaça Urquinaona
Ronda
Urquinaona
Fontanella

Ronda Sant Pere
Trafalgar
Ortigosa
Trafalgar
El Palau de la Música Catalana
St. Pere Més Alt
Sant Pere de les Puel·les
St. Pere Mitjà
St. Pere Més Baix

Arc de Triomf
Arc de Triomf

Passeig de Pujades
Passeig de Sant Joan
Passeig de Picasso

LA RIBERA
Av. Francesc Cambó
Mercat Santa Caterina

Plaça Marguilles
Portal Nou
Comerç
Plaça St. Augustí Vell

Museu Zoologia
Museu Geologia
Umbracle
Cascada
Parc de la Ciutadella
Jardins de Fontseré i Mestre
Parlament de Catalunya

Catedral
Generalitat
Pl. Sant Jaume
Jaume I
Princesa
Vigatans
Museu Picasso
Fusina
Mercat del Born
Princesa
Ribera

Plaça de Ramon Berenguer el Gran
Boria
Carders
Plaça Allada i Vermell

Sants Just i Pastor
Argenteria
Banys Vells
Pg. del Born
EL BORN
Sta. Maria del Mar
Plaça Olles
Av. Marquès de l'Argentera

Zoo de Barcelona
Parc Zoològic

Llotja de Mar
Pla de Palau
Estació de França

Àngel
Baixeras
Gignàs
Ample
Mercè
Plaça Antonio López
Pg. d'Isabel II

Barceloneta
Moll de Dipòsit
Moll d'Espanya
Palau de Mar (Museu d'Història de Catalunya)
Ronda Litoral
Balboa
Ginebra
IMAX
La Maquinista
Plaça Maquinista
Parc de la Barceloneta

Moll de la Barceloneta
Pg. de Joan de Borbó
Almirall Cervera
St. Carles
Almirall Aixada
Judici
BARCELONETA
Passeig Marítim de la Barceloneta

Pescadors
Escar
Plaça del Mar
Platja St. Sebastià
Platja Barceloneta

Wellington
Sardenya
Llull
Ramon Turró
Dr. Trueta
Ramon Trias Fargas
Parc de Carles I
Parc de les Cascades
Ciutadella-Vila Olímpica
Marina
Pujades
Trelawny
Hotel Arts
Pg. de Circumval·lació

MEDITERRANEAN SEA

> *A performance at Tablao Flamenco Cordobés.*

★★★ Otto Zutz GRACIA
Probably the most famous club in Barcelona, this multilevel favorite still draws trendsetters, the rich, the famous, and the wannabes. With eight bars, four main dance areas, and spanning a variety of musical genres, you're bound to find something—or someone—you like. C/ Lincoln, 15. ☎ 93-238-07-22. Cover 10€–15€. Metro: Gràcia.

Flamenco & Jazz
★★ Harlem Jazz Club BARRI GÒTIC
One of Barcelona's oldest and finest jazz clubs was remodeled, but the tiny spot remains intimate and the music wide-ranging, covering bebop, blues, bossa nova, and more. Comtessa de Sobradiel, 8. ☎ 93-310-07-55. Free Mon–Thurs, 6€ Fri–Sat; 1-drink minimum. Closed Aug. Metro: Jaume I.

★★ Los Tarantos BARRI GÒTIC
The oldest flamenco club in Barcelona (since 1963) has hosted the likes of Antonio Gades and Rosario, and respected Andalucían flamenco artists regularly make the pilgrimage here. Plaça Reial, 17. ☎ 93-319-17-89. www.masimas.com/tarantos. Cover 20€, includes 1 drink. Metro: Liceu.

★★★ Luz de Gas L'EIXAMPLE
For years, this glamorous turn-of-the-century music hall has reigned supreme in Barcelona for its stylish looks (chandeliers and thick red curtains) and programming of live music, which is very often Latin jazz. The lineup covers jazz, pop, folk, R&B, and salsa. C/ Muntaner, 246. ☎ 93-209-77-11. www.luzdegas.com. Cover 15€–25€, includes 1 drink. Metro: Diagonal.

★★ Tablao Flamenco Cordobés LA RAMBLA
Near the waterfront, this Andalucían-style club has been around since 1970. The upstairs room hosts traditional *cuadro flamenco,* performances by singers, dancers, and a guitarist. Shows are perhaps the most authentic in Barcelona. Three shows nightly with dinner at 7, 8:30, and 10pm. La Rambla, 35. ☎ 93-317-57-11. www.tablaocordobes.com. Dinner and show 50€–60€, 1 drink and show 30€–35€. Metro: Drassanes.

Gay & Lesbian Bars
★★ Café Dietrich L'EIXAMPLE
For a great drag show, you can't beat this glam cafe, one of the city's most enduring popular gay hangouts. The bartenders wear little and seem to enjoy the attentions of their patrons. C/ Consell de Cent, 255. ☎ 93-451-77-07. Metro: Gràcia or Universitat.

★ Metro LA RAMBLA/RAVAL

Cruisy, with two dance floors, Metro remains one of the most popular gay discos in Barcelona. The crowd ranges from pretty fashionistas to handlebar-mustache, macho types. One dance floor even spins traditional Spanish music and Spanish pop. The back room isn't for the meek. C/ Sepulveda, 185. ☎ 93-323-52-27. Cover 10€. Metro: Universitat.

Pop & Rock Clubs

★ Sala Apolo POBLE SEC

This 1940s dance hall covers the bases: On Tuesday it programs alternative cinema; Wednesday is for Latin music; Thursday it's funk night; Sunday is gay night; and on Friday and Saturday it becomes a dance club, Nitsa. And they fit in rock shows, too. Nou de la Rambla, 113 (Poble Sec). ☎ 93-318-99-17. Admission varies. Metro: Poble Sec.

★ Sala Razzmatazz PORT OLÍMPIC/POBLE NOU

This sprawling, young-skewing club—with five separate music spaces within—is also a concert venue. Its "Pop Club" hosts Spanish and international pop, alternative, hip-hop, and rock acts, such as Arctic Monkeys and LCD Soundsystem. C/ dels Almogavers, 122 (at Pamplona). ☎ 93-320-82-00. Admission varies. www.sala razzmatazz.com. Metro: Bogatell/Marina.

Spectator Sports

★★ Fútbol Club Barcelona SANTS

Barcelona's immensely popular football, or soccer, team—perennially one of the best in Europe—plays at Camp Nou, a 120,000-seat stadium. To see "Barça" (*Bar*-sa), as the locals affectionately refer to the team, take on one of its chief rivals, such as Real Madrid, is a treat that transcends sport and approaches social anthropology. Although many games are sold out long in advance, individual tickets are frequently available. How popular is the team? The **Museu del Fútbol Club Barcelona,** devoted to the F.C. Barcelona soccer team, is one of the most-visited museums in Spain. Avenida del Papa Joan XXIII; ticket office C/ Aristides Maillol, 12-18. ☎ 93-496-36-00. www.fcbarcelona.com. Tickets start at 25€. Museum: C/ Aristides Maillol, 7-9. ☎ 93-496-36-08. 7€–11€. Metro: María Cristina, Palau Reial, or Collblanc.

> *Cava barrels line the wall at El Xampanyet.*

Wine & Cava Bars

★★★ El Xampanyet LA RIBERA

A revered institution, as comfortable as an old tweed jacket, this is one place worth popping into every time you're wandering through La Ribera, for a fizzy *copa de Cava* and some excellent snacks. Family-owned since the 1930s, it is as authentic as they come, with colored tiles, marble tables, an old zinc bar, and wine barrels. C/ de la Montcada, 22. ☎ 93-319-70-03. Closed Aug. Metro: Jaume I.

★★ La Vinya del Senyor LA RIBERA

Across from Santa Maria del Mar, this tiny wine bar with a gorgeous terrace draws hordes of tourists and local wine connoisseurs with its spectacular list of Spanish wines and Cavas, and a yummy selection of tapas. Plaça Santa Maria, 5. ☎ 93-310-33-79. Metro: Barceloneta or Jaume I.

Barcelona Fast Facts

> *The Liceu metro stop on La Rambla.*

Arriving & Getting Around

BY PLANE From Barcelona's **El Prat** airport (13km/8 miles from the city center), there are several ways to get into town: **Aerobús** (4.25€, or round-trip 7.30€), which leaves from just outside all three terminals every 15 minutes from 6am to midnight; rail service (2.20€) that departs between 6:15am and 11:15pm from El Prat to Estació Sants (with connections with the Metro); and taxi (about 20€). **BY CAR** Highway **A-7** leads to Barcelona from France and northern Catalunya (Costa Brava and Girona). The **A-2** leads to Barcelona from Madrid, Zaragoza, and Bilbao. From Valencia or the Costa del Sol, take the **E-15** north. Look for one of two signs into downtown Barcelona: CENTRE CIUTAT takes you downtown into the Eixample district, while RONDA LITORAL is a beltway that takes you quickly to the port area. **BY TRAIN** Most national RENFE (www.renfe.es) and international trains arrive at **Estació Sants,** Plaça dels Països Catalans, s/n (☎ 93-495-62-15; Metro: Sants).

ATMs

Maestro/MasterCard, Cirrus, and Visa cards are readily accepted at all ATMs, which are plentiful throughout the city. Most banks offer 24-hour ATMs. Spain uses four-digit PINs; if you have a six-digit number, change it at your bank before you leave.

Doctors, Dentists & Hospitals

DOCTORS Dial ☎ **061** to find a doctor. For hospitals, the **Centre d'Urgències Perecamps** (☎ 93-441-06-00), located near La Rambla at Avenida de las Drassanes, 13–15, is a good, centrally located choice. **DENTISTS** For a dentist, try **Dental Clinic Center,** Passeig de Gràcia, 8 (☎ 93-412-16-95).

Emergencies

For an ambulance or medical emergencies, dial ☎ **061;** for fire, ☎ **080.** For other emergencies, call ☎ **112.**

Internet Access

Internet access is plentiful, both in cybercafes (*cafés Internet*) and frequently in hotels, most of which now offer Wi-Fi. The **Internet Gallery Cafe** is down the street from the Picasso Museum, Barra de Ferro, 3 (☎ 93-268-15-07). To find other cybercafes in Barcelona, check **www.cybercaptive.com** and **www.cybercafe.com**.

Pharmacies

Pharmacies (*farmacías*) operate during normal business hours, and one in every district remains open all night and on holidays. The location and phone number of this *farmàcia de guàrdia* is posted on the door of all the other pharmacies. A very central pharmacy open 24/7 is **Farmàcia Alvarez,** Passeig de Gràcia, 26 (☎ 93-302-11-24). You can also call ☎ 010 or ☎ 93-481-00-60 to contact all-night pharmacies.

Police
The national police emergency number is ☎ **091.** For the local police, call ☎ **092.**

Post Office
Spanish post offices are called *correos* (koh-*ray*-os), identified by yellow-and-white signs with a crown and the words *CORREOS Y TELÉGRAFOS*. Major post offices are open Monday through Friday from 9am to 8pm and Saturday 9am to 7pm. The **Central Post Office** is at Plaça de Antoni López, s/n, at the end of Vía Laietana (☎ 902-19-71-97).

Public Transportation
The **Metro** (☎ 010 or 93-298-70-00; www.tmb. net) is Barcelona's excellent, modern, and clean subway. Its five lines are by far the fastest and easiest way to navigate the city. Red diamond symbols mark stations. Single-ticket fares (*senzill,* or *sencillo*) are 1.35€, although you can get a T10 pass (good for 10 trips) for 7.70€. You can also get free rides on all public transport with purchase of the Barcelona Card discount pass (www.barcelonacard.com). The Metro runs Monday to Thursday 5am to 11pm, Friday and Saturday 5am to 2am, and Sunday 6am to midnight.

Safety
Violent crime in Barcelona is a rarity, but criminals frequent tourist areas and major attractions such as museums, restaurants, hotels, beaches, train stations, airports, subways, and ATMs. Exercise care around major tourist sights, especially La Rambla (in particular, the section closest to the waterfront), Barri Gòtic, Raval district, and La Sagrada Família. You shouldn't walk alone at night in either the Barri Gòtic or the Raval district. **Turisme Atenció** (Tourist Attention Service), La Rambla, 43 (☎ 93-256-24-30), has English-speaking attendants who can aid crime victims in reporting losses and obtaining new documents. The office is open 24/7.

Taxis
Black-and-yellow taxis are plentiful and reasonably priced; few journeys within the city limits cost more than 8€. There's no negotiating over fares; you pay what the meter reads (it starts at 2€). Most locals round up the fare to the next half- or full euro, if they tip at all. Note that fares will include special supplements for airport trips, as well as luggage. Night fares are also higher. You can either hail a cab in the street (the green light on the roof means it's available) or grab one where they're lined up (usually outside hotels). Reliable taxi companies include **Servi Taxi** (☎ 93-330-03-00) and **Barna Taxi** (☎ 93-357-77-55). For more information about taxi fares and policies, see www.taxibarcelona.cat.

Telephones
For national telephone information, dial ☎ 1003. For international telephone information, call ☎ 025. You can make international calls from booths identified with the word *INTERNACIONAL*. To make an international call, dial ☎ 00, wait for the tone, and dial the country code, area code, and number. If you're making a local call, dial the two-digit city code first (**93** in Barcelona) and then the seven-digit number. To make a long-distance call within Spain, the procedure is exactly the same—the only difference being that you dial the individual two-digit city code first (in the case of Madrid, for example, it's 91).

Toilets
In Catalunya, public toilets are called *aseos, servicios,* or *lavabos,* and are labeled *caballeros* for men and *damas* or *señoras* for women.

Visitor Information
The office for **Turisme de Barcelona,** Plaça de Catalunya, 17 (underground; ☎ 93-285-38-34; www.barcelonaturisme.com), is open daily 9am to 9pm. **Informació Turística de Catalunya** has information on Barcelona and the entire region; it's located in Palau Robert, Passeig de Gràcia, 107 (☎ 93-238-40-03). Tourism information offices are also at Sants train station and the airport. Call ☎ 010 for general visitor information, or visit the very helpful website www. barcelonaturisme.com.

The Balearic Islands

The Best of Mallorca in 1 Week

With 1 week in Mallorca, you'll have time to see a good cross section of the island and some of its stunning, varied landscapes. This tour takes in the best of the capital, Palma, as well as the scenic northwest coast, the wide bays and capes of the northeast coast, and a couple of the interior's highlights.

> PREVIOUS PAGE *A day of fun near Platja d'en Bossa on Ibiza.* THIS PAGE *An outdoor cafe in the Old Town of Palma.*

START Palma de Mallorca. TRIP LENGTH 238km (148 miles).

1 ★★★ **Palma de Mallorca.** Palma, fronting a wide bay and the beaches that made Mallorca famous, has a sultry, Mediterranean air, but a **Centre Históric** (historic old quarter) makes it feel like a laid-back version of Barcelona. You'll need 2 days to see a good portion of both the Old City and its modern 19th- and 20th-century expansion, home to Modernista buildings and the city's best shopping. Start with the mesmerizing **Catedral La Seu** and the **Palau de l'Almudaina** (royal palace) before moving on to the city's ancient **Banys Àrabs** (Arab baths), narrow streets hiding palatial courtyards, and the stately **Basílica de Sant Francesc** on the first day. On the second, visit **Mercat de l'Olivar,** the city's principal food market; wander through two outstanding art spaces (**Fundació La Caixa** and **Es Baluard,** the contemporary art museum); and stroll

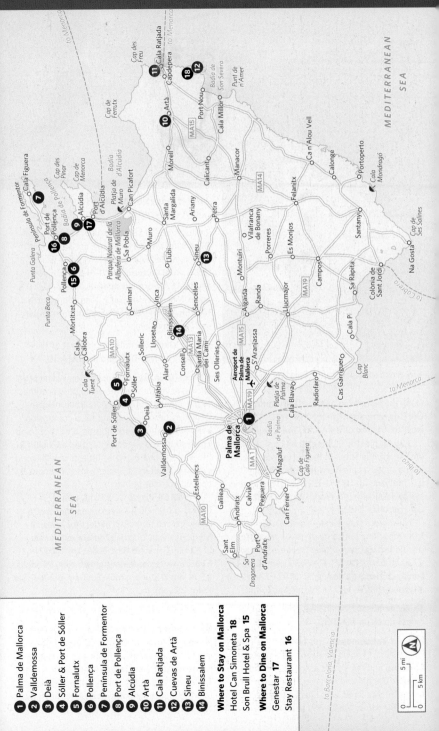

1. Palma de Mallorca
2. Valldemossa
3. Deià
4. Sóller & Port de Sóller
5. Fornalutx
6. Pollença
7. Península de Formentor
8. Port de Pollença
9. Alcúdia
10. Artà
11. Cala Ratjada
12. Cuevas de Artà
13. Sineu
14. Binissalem

Where to Stay on Mallorca
Hotel Can Simoneta **18**
Son Brull Hotel & Spa **15**

Where to Dine on Mallorca
Genestar **17**
Stay Restaurant **16**

> *One of Europe's oldest railways travels between Sóller and Palma.*

> *Frédéric Chopin and George Sands once stayed at Valldemossa's 14th-century monastery.*

along the waterfront and the **Dalt Murada,** the Old City ramparts with their gorgeous late-day views of the Bay of Palma and the cathedral.

A great pit stop—though a bit hard to find on a small side street in the old quarter—is Palma's oldest cafe, **Ca'n Joan de S'Aigó,** C/ Can Sanç, 10 (☎ 971-71-07-59), founded in 1697. Classically Old World, it's known for its hot chocolate and pastries.

Finish your stay in Palma with a night on the town, checking out some of its ★★ **nightlife** in the old fishing quarter near Sa Llotja. **Abaco,** C/ Sant Joan, 1 (☎ 971-71-49-39), and **Café La Lonja,** C/ de Llotja de Mar, 2 (☎ 971-72-27-99), are good choices for a night out. See p. 490.

To Valldemossa from Palma, drive 24km (15 miles) north on MA-1130.

❷ ★★★ **Valldemossa.** This pretty and storied village is best known for its monastery, **Reial Cartoixa,** and the town's associations with Frédéric Chopin and his lover, the French writer George Sand, who spent a memorably miserable winter (1838–39) here, later

immortalized in Sand's book, *A Winter in Mallorca.* Sand disparaged locals as "barbarians" and dismissed Mallorca as "Monkey Island." ⏱ 2 hr. Reial Cartoixa: ☎ 971-61-21-06. 8.50€ adults, 4€ seniors and students, free for kids 9 & under. Mar–Oct Mon–Sat 9:30am–6pm and Sun 10am–1pm; Nov–Feb Mon–Sat 9:30am–4:30pm and Sun 10am–1pm.

Deià is 10km (6¼ miles) northeast of Valldemossa on MA-1130 and then MA-10.

❸ ★★★ **Deià.** Famous for its literary and artistic associations over the years (it was home to the English writer and poet Robert Graves), Deià is incomparably beautiful, a composition of honey-colored stone houses, tiled roofs, and green shuttered windows perched on a hill. On the way to a nearby, rocky little cove with good swimming waters is Graves's longtime house, now open to the public.

★★ kids **Sa Vinya,** C/ Sa Vinya Vella, 3 (☎ 971-63-95-00), a welcoming spot with a lovely garden terrace, is perfect for a casual Mediterranean lunch. ⏱ 2hr. Graves's home: ⏱ 20 min. Carretera Deià–Soller, km 1. ☎ 971-63-61-85. www.lacasaderobertgraves.com. 5€ adults, 2.50€ kids 11 & under. Mon–Fri 10am–4:20pm; Sat 10am–2:20pm.

Sóller is 11km (6¾ miles) east of Deià on MA-10.

❹ ★★ **Sóller & Port de Sóller.** A historically prosperous town nestled amid citrus groves in a mountain valley, Sóller boasts handsome Modernista architecture, a 1912 train to Palma, and an equally vintage tram that travels down to an attractive harbor with beaches lined by cafes and restaurants. ⏱ 3 hr.

> *The spectacular view from a mirador off the Formentor Peninsula, Mallorca's fjord country.*

Fornalutx is 4km (2½ miles) east of Sóller on MA-2121.

5 ★★ **Fornalutx.** A gem of a little mountain town a relatively short walk from Sóller, this is one of Mallorca's most enchanting towns, with clean mountain air and relaxing medieval beauty. ⏲ **2 hr.**

Travel northeast 50km (31 miles) on MA-10 to reach Pollença.

6 ★★ kids **Pollença.** A delightful and historic resort town, Pollença is convenient for visiting the wide beaches of the Pollença and Alcúdia bays as well as the spectacular scenery of Formentor. The town is famed for its **El Calvari** (Way of the Cross), a long climb of 365 stone steps leading to a chapel and great panoramic views.

There's great people-watching on Pollença's main square from **Café Espanyol**, Plaça Major, 2 (☎ 971-53-42-14), a local favorite day and night right next to the church. ⏲ **3 hr.**

Travel northeast 13km (8 miles) on MA-2210 to get to Formentor.

7 ★★★ kids **Península de Formentor.** One of the most photographed sights on Mallorca is the otherworldly scenery of the Formentor Cape jutting out into the Mediterranean. Beyond the *mirador* (viewpoint) is a lovely beach, Platja de Formentor, and the storied 1929 Hotel Formentor. ⏲ **2 hr.**

Port de Pollença is 7km (4⅓ miles) southwest of Formentor on MA-2210.

8 ★ kids **Port de Pollença.** This family-friendly beach resort, which grew out of an old fishing village, has a nice wide swath of white sand, but it feels laid-back even in summer. ⏲ **2 hr.**

Drive 8km (5 miles) southwest on MA-2220 to reach Alcúdia.

9 ★★ kids **Alcúdia.** This historic town goes all the way back to the Phoenicians and Romans, who left behind stony elements of their settle-ment, **Pol·lèntia,** including a Roman amphi-theater. ⏲ **3 hr.** Pol·lèntia: Avenida Prínceps d'Espanya, s/n. ☎ 971-89-71-02. www.pollentia.net. 3€ adults, 2€ seniors and students (ticket good for all Roman ruins). Oct-Apr Tues-Fri 10am-4pm, Sat-Sun 10am-2pm; May-Sept Tues-Sun 9:30am-8:20pm.

On Island Hopping

The Balearic Islands (other than Mallorca) are small, but it would be next to impossible to try to visit all four islands on a single trip. Most people visit one island at a time; at the most, your best bet would be to approach them in tandem: Mallorca and Menorca (by plane or ferry) or Ibiza and Formentera (by ferry). For this reason, there is no "Best of the Balearics in 1 Week" tour.

> *Pollença Bay offers some of the island's finest beaches, as well as excellent sailing and windsurfing.*

Artà is 33km (21 miles) southeast of Alcúdia on MA-12.

⑩ ★ Artà. A former Moorish stronghold, this unassuming town is distinguished by a fortified 14th-century castlelike church on a hilltop, **Santuari de Sant Salvador.** Like Pollença, it has a **Vía Crucis** (Way of the Cross) leading to it and great views of the surrounding countryside and coast.

Grab a cappuccino at ★ **Café Parisien,** C/ Ciutat, 18 (☎ 971-83-54-40), a little French bistro that has tables along Artà's restaurant row and a garden patio out back. ⏱ 45 min. Santuari: C/ de San Salvador. ☎ 971-83-61-36. Free. Daily 8am–8pm.

Cala Ratjada is 11km (6¾ miles) east of Artà on MA-15.

⑪ ★ kids Cala Ratjada. The first of many beach resorts lining the east coast, this popular spot has a couple of nice sandy beaches, the prettiest being **Cala Gat,** a protected cove. ⏱ 2 hr.

From Capdepera, travel south along MA-4040 before turning off east 1km (⅔ mile) north of Canyamel.

⑫ ★★ kids Cuevas de Artà (Capdepera). These incredible, 300-million-year-old caves are dramatically lit, with oddly shaped formations said to have inspired Jules Verne to write *Journey to the Center of the Earth.* ⏱ 1 hr. C/ de Las Cuevas, s/n. ☎ 971-84-12-93. www.cuevasdearta.com. 10€ adults and students, free for kids 4 & under. May–Oct 10am–6pm; Nov–Apr 10am–5pm.

Sineu is 46km (29 miles) west on MA-15 and MA-3310.

⑬ ★★ Sineu. This historic market town south of Inca is perhaps interior Mallorca's most attractive, the site of a 14th-century royal palace, 16th-century waymarking stone cross, and lively traditional market. ⏱ 1 hr.

Binissalem is 20km (12 miles) northwest on MA-3240.

⑭ ★ Binissalem. The area around this small town is the epicenter of the resurgent Mallorcan wine industry. If you're interested in tasting excellent local wines and unique grapes harvested nowhere else, visit a handful of friendly, down-to-earth wineries. For more information, see www.binissalemdo.com. ⏱ 3 hr.

Travel Tip

For hotels and restaurants in Palma, see p. 493. For hotels and restaurants along the northwest coast of Mallorca (including Deià, Sóller, and Fornalutx), see p. 497.

Where to Stay & Dine

> *Son Brull Hotel & Spa was once a monastery.*

★★★ **Genestar** ALCÚDIA *MEDITERRANEAN*

One of the best-value gourmet meals to be had in Mallorca. You can have a five-course tasting menu for a song, every item prepared from scratch by the chef-owner Juanjo. **Plaça Porta de Mallorca, 1, baixos.** ☎ 971-54-91-57. www.genestarestaurant.com. Fixed-price menu 18€–25€. AE, MC, V. Lunch Mon–Tues and Thurs–Sat, dinner Mon–Tues and Thurs–Sun.

★★★ **Hotel Can Simoneta** CANYAMEL

Perched at the edge of a cliff with astounding panoramic Mediterranean views, this rural luxury hotel in a 15th-century estate ensures privacy. **Carretera Artà a Canyamel, km 8.** ☎ 971-81-61-10. www.cansimoneta.com. 17 units. Doubles 185€–320€ with buffet breakfast. AE, DC, MC, V.

★★★ **Son Brull Hotel & Spa** POLLENÇA

A converted Jesuit monastery and rural estate is now an incredibly chic but relaxed country hotel, with a magnificent outdoor pool, full spa, and gourmet restaurant. **Carretera Palma–Pollença (MA-2200), km 50.** ☎ 971-53-53-53. www.sonbrull.com. 23 units. Doubles 262€–465€ with buffet breakfast. AE, DC, MC, V. Closed Dec–Jan.

★★ 🄺🄸🄳🄢 **Stay Restaurant** PORT DE POLLENÇA

SEAFOOD/MEDITERRANEAN With great views of Pollença Bay from a pier, this contemporary glass jewel box serves excellent fresh seafood. **Port de Pollença marina.** ☎ 971-86-40-13. www.stayrestaurant.com. Entrees 11€–41€. AE, DC, MC, V. Breakfast, lunch & dinner daily.

Mallorca's Best Beaches

Mallorca's vast coastline includes everything from long white-sand beaches with every kind of facility to secluded coves not yet defiled by human intervention, where it's necessary to hike or arrive by boat. For additional information on beaches (including opening and closing hours, daily swimming conditions, and transport), visit **www.platgesdebalears.com**.

Counterclockwise from Palma, some of the best beaches are ★ **Platja de Palma,** one of the island's longest stretches of fine-grained sand, comprising several crowded beaches and run-on resorts, all popular with the young, tan, and minimally clothed; ★★ **Platja des Coll Baix,** one of the north coast's most secluded beaches, backed by high cliffs and with perfectly translucent water; ★★★ **Platja de Formentor,** one of Mallorca's loveliest beaches, shaded by pine trees and with stunning views of Alcúdia bay; ★★★ **Platja del Port de Pollença,** a nice wide beach on a bay, popular with families and good for watersports; ★★ **Platja de Muro,** a long, pleasant sweep of fine-grained golden sand sheltered by Alcúdia bay; and ★★ **Cala de Mondragó,** a pretty, clean cove sheltered by pine woods and beautiful rock formations within the Mondragó Nature Park.

The Best of Palma in 2 Days

Though the Romans founded Palmaria around the 1st century B.C., the Moors transformed the Mediterranean settlement into a *casbah,* or walled city. Its foundations are still visible, though obscured by the high-rise hotels that have cropped up. Today it's a bustling tourist destination with a vibrant old quarter. Palma is the largest of the Balearic ports, and arrival by sea is the most impressive, the skyline characterized by the Catedral's bulk.

> *Catedral La Seu is a phantasmagoric masterpiece combining Modernista additions with Gothic architecture.*

START Centre Históric.

❶ ★★★ Catedral La Seu. Constructed during the 13th and 14th centuries on the site of the Great Mosque, the centerpiece of Moorish Mallorca, this graceful Gothic cathedral is one of Europe's great churches, with magnificent stained-glass rose windows, Antoni Gaudí's iron canopy suspended over the altar, and Miquel Barceló's equally unexpected ceramic mural covering an entire chapel. ⏱ 1 hr. Palau Reinal, s/n. ☎ 971-723-130. www.catedralde mallorca.org. 4€. Apr–May and Oct Mon–Fri 10am–5:15pm; June–Sept Mon–Fri 10am–6:15pm; Nov–Mar Mon–Fri 10am–3:15pm. Year-round Sat 10am–2:15pm. Bus: 2.

❷ ★★ Palau de l'Almudaina. The official summer residence of the King and Queen, constructed on the site of a former Moorish royal palace and fortress, retains vaulted Arab baths and has a soaring stone-vaulted 13th-century Gothic Room. ⏱ 1 hr. Palau Reinal, s/n. ☎ 971-214-134. www.patrimonionacional.es. 4€ guided tours, 3.20€ unguided, 2.30€ seniors and students, free on Wed for E.U. citizens. Apr–Sept Mon–Fri 10am–

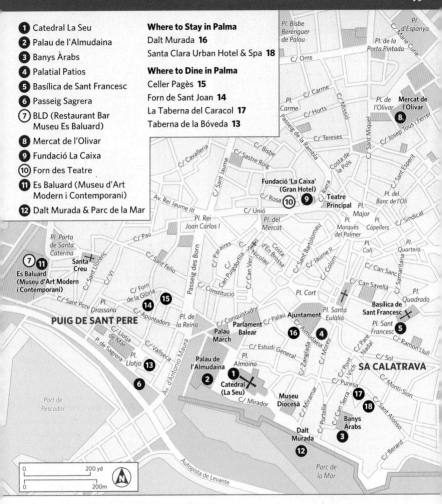

1. Catedral La Seu
2. Palau de l'Almudaina
3. Banys Àrabs
4. Palatial Patios
5. Basílica de Sant Francesc
6. Passeig Sagrera
7. BLD (Restaurant Bar Museu Es Baluard)
8. Mercat de l'Olivar
9. Fundació La Caixa
10. Forn des Teatre
11. Es Baluard (Museu d'Art Modern i Contemporani)
12. Dalt Murada & Parc de la Mar

Where to Stay in Palma
Dalt Murada **16**
Santa Clara Urban Hotel & Spa **18**

Where to Dine in Palma
Celler Pagès **15**
Forn de Sant Joan **14**
La Taberna del Caracol **17**
Taberna de la Bóveda **13**

5:45pm; Oct–Mar Mon–Fri 10am–1:15pm and 4–5:15pm, Sat and holidays 10am–1:15pm. Bus: 2.

③ ★ kids **Banys Àrabs.** These 12th-century Arab baths, set amid lovely gardens, are an evocative reminder of Mallorca's Muslim past. Slender columns (with capitals recycled from Roman buildings) support the domed ceiling of the main chamber. ⏱ 20 min. C/ Serra, 7. ☎ 971-72-15-49. www.bisbatdemallorca.com. 2€. Daily 9am–6pm, summer closes 7:30pm. Bus: 2.

④ ★★ **Palatial Patios.** A significant number of 17th- and 18th-century baronial mansions, built around majestic interior courtyards, remain in old Palma. Peek in at **Can Oleza,** C/ d'en Morey, 9, a 16th-century palace with large arches and a

grand staircase; **Can Bordils,** C/ de l'Almudaina, 33, one of Palma's oldest mansions, with Gothic features dating to the 13th century; and **Can Vivot,** C/ de Can Savellà, 4, a spectacular 18th-century mansion often open during the day and showing off antique cars in the patio, where coaches were once parked. ⏱ 45 min. Bus: 2.

⑤ ★★★ **Basílica de Sant Francesc.** A Gothic basilica begun in the 13th century and enlivened by a Plateresque portal has an impressive altarpiece and massive organ, but the real highlight is the ethereal Gothic cloisters. ⏱ 45 min. Plaça de Sant Francesc, s/n. ☎ 971-71-46-25. 1€. Mon–Sat 9:30am–12:30pm and 3:30–6pm; Sun 9:30am–12:30pm. Bus: 2.

> *Palma's Arab baths are a reminder of the island's Moorish history.*

6 ★ kids **Passeig Sagrera.** Directly across from the port is this delightful promenade dotted with tall, leafy palm trees and lined by walking and cycling paths. Between Avenida Antoni Maura and Avenida d'Argentina. Bus: 1.

⑦ ★★ kids **BLD (Restaurant Bar Museu Es Baluard).** This expansive terrace cafe-restaurant, attached to the Es Baluard Art Museum (see below), is one of the most relaxing spots in the city, with panoramic views of Palma and the sea. Perfect for a late-afternoon bottle of wine as the sun sets. Plaça Porta de Santa Catalina, 10. ☎ 971-90-81-99. $$.

8 ★★ **Mercat de l'Olivar.** The city's fresh fish, meat, and produce market is at its most boisterous early in the morning. The covered Mercat, dating to 1941, is a cook's dream, teeming with beautiful vegetables, fruit, and an amazing array of exotic fish still nearly wriggling, brought in straight from the harbor. Plaça Olivar, s/n. ☎ 971-72-03-14. Daily 7am–2pm. Bus: 2.

9 ★★ **Fundació La Caixa.** Of all Palma's Modernista buildings, this is the most ornate and probably the greatest. One of Gaudí's Barcelona contemporaries, Lluís Domènech i Montaner, built it in 1903 as the Gran Hotel; today it houses a terrific art museum. ⏱ 30 min. Plaça Weyler, 3. ☎ 971-17-85-00. www.fundacio.lacaixa. es. Free. Mon–Sat 10am–9pm; Sun 10am–2pm. Bus: 2.

> *Forn des Teatre bakery recently expanded to a cafe next door.*

⑩ ★ kids **Forn des Teatre.** One of Mallorca's most famous products is a delicate spiral pastry called an *ensaïmada*. And this landmark Modernista bakery is reportedly the King of Spain's favorite spot to pick up his. Plaça de Weyler, 9. ☎ 971-71-52-54. $.

11 ★★ kids **Es Baluard (Museu d'Art Modern i Contemporani).** This architecturally adventurous contemporary art museum has a nice collection of outdoor sculptures and a smashing cafe (see above) with sweeping views of the bay and much of Palma. ⏱ 1 hr. Plaça Porta de Santa Catalina, 10. ☎ 971-90-82-00. www.es baluard.org. 6€ adults, 4.50€ seniors and students, free for kids 11 & under, Fri pay what you wish. Oct to mid-June Tues–Sun 10am–8pm; mid-June to Sept Tues–Sun 10am–10pm. Bus: 1.

12 ★★ kids **Dalt Murada & Parc de la Mar.** As night falls, stroll along Dalt Murada, the Renaissance-era wall alongside the Catedral, illuminated at night and reflected in the pools of the city's seaside park. Avenida Antoni Maura at Avenida Gabriel Roca. Bus: 1.

Where to Stay & Dine

> *Spanish celebrity sightings are common at Forn de Sant Joan.*

★★ **kids Celler Pagès** SA LLOTJA *MALLORCAN* A charmingly old-school Mallorcan restaurant, this inexpensive, family-style venue has been serving first-rate hardy Mallorcan fare since 1956. Specialties include *sopas mallorquinas* (vegetable soup), *croquetas* (fried rolls) with seared peppers, and squash stuffed with shellfish. Felip Bauza, 2. ☎ 971-72-60-36. Main course 11€–18€. MC, V. Lunch Mon–Sat, dinner Tues–Sat. Bus: 2.

★★★ **Dalt Murada** CENTRE HISTÒRIC This boutique hotel in a handsome 17th-century mansion brims with old-world charm. Rooms are huge and elegant, and a good deal. C/ Almudaina, 6A. ☎ 971-42-53-00. www.daltmurada.com. 8 units. Doubles 159€–199€, with buffet breakfast. AE, DC, MC, V. Bus: 2.

★★ **Forn de Sant Joan** SA LLOTJA *TAPAS/ MEDITERRANEAN* This stylish four-level tapas-oriented restaurant is also unpretentious, and thus very popular. It has four intimate dining spaces and lies in the heart of Palma's hottest nightlife zone. C/ Sant Joan, 4. ☎ 971-72-84-22. www.forndesantjoan.net. Entrees 13€–28€. AE, MC, V. Dinner daily. Bus: 2.

★★ **La Taberna del Caracol** CENTRE HISTÒRIC *TAPAS/SPANISH* Tucked away among the warren of narrow alleyways of the old Jewish quarter, this warm and rustic tavern with impossibly high arched ceilings and wooden beams is a real crowd pleaser. It does a host of Spanish tapas very well, from *pimientos de padrón* (fried green peppers) and aubergine with honey to *boquerones fritos* (fried small whitefish). C/ Sant Alonso, 2. ☎ 971-71-49-08. www.taberna.name. Main courses 7€–18€. AE, MC, V. Lunch & dinner Mon–Sat. Bus: 2.

★★★ **Santa Clara Urban Hotel & Spa** CENTRE HISTÒRIC This stylish, design-conscious new hotel has bold modern furnishings, a spa, and a rooftop deck. C/ Sant Alonso, 16. ☎ 971-72-92-31. www.santaclarahotel.es. 16 units. Doubles 160€–180€, with breakfast buffet. AE, DC, MC, V. Bus: 2.

★★ **Taberna de la Bóveda** SA LLOTJA *TAPAS/ SPANISH* This great tapas spot with a sunny terrace is right on Palma's waterfront promenade—irresistible on a nice afternoon or warm evening. C/ Sagrera, 3. ☎ 971-72-00-26. www.tabernadelaboveda.com. Entrees 8€–18€. MC, V. Lunch & dinner Mon–Sat. Bus: 1.

The Northwest Coast of Mallorca in 2 Days

Mallorca's northwest coast is worlds removed from the island's popular image of high-rise hotels and sun worshipers. What it's lacking in beaches, it more than makes up for with picturesque mountain villages, the forested Serra de Tramuntana range, and dramatic high cliffs slicing into the sea.

> The natural port of Andratx brings boaters, fishermen, and those who "summer" together.

START MA-1 (coastal road) from Palma to Andratx (28km/17 miles). **TRIP LENGTH** 144km (89 miles).

➊ ★ Port d'Andratx. Yachts bob in the marina, and elegantly dressed summer-home owners sip cocktails in waterfront cafes in this genteel, sheltered, and pretty natural harbor. ⏱ 30 min.

➁ ★★ **Café Es Grau.** At the edge of a cliff, this simple cafe has unrivaled panoramic views. **Carretera Andratx-Estellencs/MA-10, km 98.** ☎ 971-61-85-27. $

From Andratx, travel 14km (8⅔ miles) northeast along MA-10.

➌ ★★★ kids MA-10's *Miradores*. The northwest's coastal road, MA-10, climbs dizzily into the rugged Tramuntana mountains. Luckily, you

Travel Tip

A tour of the northwest coast of Mallorca is easily combined with 1 or 2 days in Palma; an ideal 3-day trip would include stop nos. 1 to 7 from the Palma tour (see p. 490), plus this entire tour.

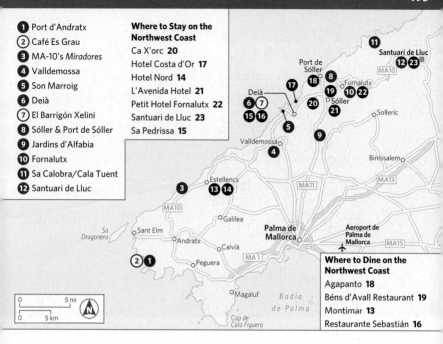

1. Port d'Andratx
2. Café Es Grau
3. MA-10's *Miradores*
4. Valldemossa
5. Son Marroig
6. Deià
7. El Barrigón Xelini
8. Sóller & Port de Sóller
9. Jardins d'Alfabia
10. Fornalutx
11. Sa Calobra/Cala Tuent
12. Santuari de Lluc

Where to Stay on the Northwest Coast
Ca X'orc **20**
Hotel Costa d'Or **17**
Hotel Nord **14**
L'Avenida Hotel **21**
Petit Hotel Fornalutx **22**
Santuari de Lluc **23**
Sa Pedrissa **15**

Where to Dine on the Northwest Coast
Agapanto **18**
Béns d'Avall Restaurant **19**
Montimar **13**
Restaurante Sebastián **16**

can pull over at *miradores,* viewpoints with mesmerizing vistas of the cliffs and a flat horizon of the sea in all directions. This first is **Mirador de Ricardo Roca,** next to Café Es Grau (see above). Farther east (11km/6¾ miles) is **Mirador de Ses Animes,** a 16th-century tower.

Valldemossa is another 18km (11 miles) east on MA-10.

❹ ★★★ **Valldemossa.** See p. 486, ❷.

Son Marroig is 7km (4⅓ miles) northeast of Valldemossa on MA-10.

❺ ★ **Son Marroig.** A 19th-century Austrian aristocrat, Archduke Ludwig Salvator, had an enduring love affair with Mallorca and bought several properties on the northwest coast. Just outside of Deià, **Son Marroig,** his mansion perched on the cliff, has stunning views of the jagged coast and the famous rock promontory **Sa Foradada,** which juts out into the sea. (The walk out to it is less than an hour.) ⏱ 1 hr. MA-10, s/n. ☎ 971-63-91-58. www.sonmarroig.com. 3€. Tues–Sat 9:30am–6pm.

Deià is 5km (3 miles) northeast on MA-10.

❻ ★★★ kids **Deià.** See p. 486, ❸.

> *A 16th-century tower mans the Mirador de Ses Animes on Mallorca's MA-10 coastal road.*

> *A series of hairpin turns have given this Mallorcan stretch of road the nickname "Sa Calobra" (The Snake).*

⑦ 🍴 ★★ kids **El Barrigón Xelini.** Sit in the cellarlike 130-year-old dining room or sunny terrace overlooking Deià and enjoy *montaditos* (tapa-like sandwiches), salads, and dozens of different tapas. C/ Archiduque Luis Salvador, 19, Deià. ☎ 971-63-91-39. $$.

13km (8 miles) east on MA-10.

⑧ ★★ **Sóller & Port de Sóller.** See p. 486, ④.

The Jardins d'Alfabia are south of Sóller on MA-11, on the other side of Coll de Sóller, next to the tunnel entrance. Or take the longer but much more scenic old road, full of hairpin turns and cyclists—the turnoff is to the left just before the tunnel entrance.

⑨ ★ kids **Jardins d'Alfabia.** An oasis among the Tramuntana mountains, these lush gardens, towering palm trees, and fountains are part of a country estate that once belonged to a 12th-century Moorish viceroy. ◷ 1 hr. Carretera Palma–Sóller, km 17. ☎ 971-61-31-23. www.jardinesdealfabia.com. 4.50€. Nov–Mar Mon–Fri 9:30am–5:30pm, Sat 9:30am–1pm; Apr–Oct Mon–Sat 9:30am–6:30pm; closed Dec.

Backtrack to Sóller. Follow signs to Fornalutx along MA-10 for 3km (1¾ miles).

⑩ ★★ **Fornalutx.** See p. 487, ⑤.

MA-10 continues 13km (8 miles) toward Pollença and past the Mirador de Ses Barques, with a detour toward the coast to Sa Calobra and Cala Tuent.

⑪ ★ kids **Sa Calobra & Cala Tuent.** A notoriously twisty road of hairpin turns called Sa Calobra (The Snake) wends its way to the coast. After the harrowing drive, arrive at Cala Tuent, a pretty beach with turquoise waters, and the tiny beach at a river gorge, **Torrent de Pareis.** ◷ 2 hr.

Santuari de Lluc is 30km (19 miles) east on MA-10.

⑫ ★★ **Santuari de Lluc.** A revered place of pilgrimage and the spiritual center of Mallorca, the monastery of Lluc dates to the 13th century. The highlights are the baroque basilica and the Escolonia de Lluc boys' choir. The first and second floors also make up a small museum. ◷ 30 min. Lluc, s/n. ☎ 971-87-15-25. www.lluc.net. Monastery: Free. Daily 8am–8pm. Museum: 4€. Daily 10:30am–1pm and 2:30–5pm.

Where to Stay & Dine

> The boutique Sa Pedrissa hotel in Deià.

★ **Agapanto** PORT DE SÓLLER *MEDITERRANEAN*
The port's most stylish restaurant, with a great terrace overlooking the harbor, Agapanto serves nicely prepared Mediterranean fare. Camino del Faro, 2. ☎ 971-63-38-60. Entrees 30€–45€. AE, DC, MC, V. Lunch & dinner Tues–Sun.

★★★ **Béns d'Avall Restaurant** SÓLLER *HAUTE MEDITERRANEAN* Off the beaten track and renowned for its coastal views and creative cuisine, this makes an unforgettable restaurant stop. Arrive early in the evening for sunset. Carretera Sóller–Deià (near Sóller). ☎ 971-63-23-81. www.benetvicens.com. Entrees 30€–45€. MC, V. Lunch & dinner Tues–Sun. Closed Nov–Mar.

★★ **Ca X'orc** SÓLLER
Adjoining 200-year-old *fincas* (farmhouses) form a sophisticated and rustic country hotel, with a sexy infinity pool, terraces with distant mountain and coastal views, and a chic restaurant. Carretera de Deià, km 56.1. ☎ 971-63-82-80. www.casxorc.com. 12 units. Doubles 195€–315€, with buffet breakfast. Closed Nov to mid-Mar. AE, DC, MC, V.

★★ kids **Hotel Costa d'Or** LLUCALCARI
In a tiny village just around the bend from Deià, with a gorgeous setting above the Mediterranean coastline and a pool, this hotel is plenty stylish but remains low-key. C/ Luc Alcari, s/n. ☎ 971-63-90-25. www.epoquehotels.com. 41 units. Doubles 160€–240€, with buffet breakfast. MC, V.

★ kids **Hotel Nord** ESTELLENCS
This charming, good-value country hotel has eight stylish rooms in a delightful old stone building. Plaça d'es Triquet, 4. ☎ 971-14-90-06. www.hotelruralnord.com. 8 units. Doubles 88€–130€, with buffet breakfast. AE, DC, MC, V.

★★ **L'Avenida Hotel** SÓLLER
This new boutique hotel in a century-old mansion in the heart of town is hip and urbane, with an elegant courtyard pool and bistro restaurant. Gran Via, 9. ☎ 971-63-40-75. www.avenida-hotel.com. 8 units. Doubles 225€–245€, with buffet breakfast. Closed Nov–Feb. AE, DC, MC, V.

★ kids **Montimar** ESTELLENCS *MALLORCAN*
A homey restaurant with a lovely covered terrace and great views overlooking town, this is a super spot for lunch, with a 15€ midday menu. Plaça de la Constitució, 7. ☎ 971-61-85-76. Entrees 8€–17€. MC, V. Lunch & dinner Tues–Sun.

★ **Petit Hotel Fornalutx** FORNALUTX
This small hotel in a former convent couples contemporary accents with great views and an infinity pool overlooking the mountains and orange groves. C/ Alba, 22. ☎ 971-63-19-97. www.fornalutxpetithotel.com. 8 units. Doubles 141€–152€, with buffet breakfast. AE, DC, MC, V.

★★★ **Restaurante Sebastián** DEIÀ *MEDITERRANEAN* This romantic gourmet restaurant serves exquisitely prepared fresh fish and meat dishes. C/ Felipe Bauza, s/n. ☎ 971-63-94-17. www.restaurantesebastian.com. Entrees 7€–18€. AE, DC, MC, V. Dinner Thurs–Tues. Closed Dec–Feb.

★ kids **Santuari de Lluc** LLUC
This is a favorite of both the faithful and hiking fanatics, who come to stay in the austere but thrifty former monks' cells surrounded by mountains and great trekking. Monasteri de Lluc. ☎ 971-87-15-25. www.lluc.net/eng/ahostatg. html. 129 units. Doubles 25€. MC, V.

★★★ kids **Sa Pedrissa** DEIÀ
A charming, family-owned boutique hotel just outside Deià, this place has commanding views of the coast from its perch on a hill, a stunning pool, and a breakfast terrace. Carretera de Valldemossa, s/n. ☎ 971-63-91-11. www.sapedrissa.com. 8 units. Doubles 120€–327€, with buffet breakfast. AE, DC, MC, V.

SPANISH SURREALISTS

Eccentric Personalities & Revolutionary Art

BY NEIL EDWARD SCHLECHT

	MEDIUM	CLAIM TO FAME	CAREER
LUÍS BUÑUEL 1900–83	Film.	Provocative, existential films infused with disturbing images, such as a razor slowly slicing a woman's eyeball.	One of the greatest film directors of all time, known for *Un Chien Andalou* (1929), and *Belle de Jour* (1967).
SALVADOR DALÍ 1904–89	Primarily painting, but also sculpture, photography, fashion, and film.	Surreal imagery, such as soft pocket watches (*The Persistence of Memory*); the fanciful, self-designed Teatre-Museu Dalí (see p. 373, ❹); flamboyant mustache.	Achieved new heights of celebrity for an artist; detractors claimed his greatest skill was self-promotion (André Breton called him Avida Dollars, or "Eager for Dollars," an anagram of his name).
FEDERICO GARCÍA LORCA 1898–1936	Poetry, plays, and literature.	Considered the greatest Spanish poet and playwright of the 20th century, thanks to his trilogy of "folk tragedies": *Bodas de Sangre, Yerma,* and *La Casa de Bernarda Alba*.	Created indelible portraits of his native Andalucía, its Moorish legacies, gypsies, and bullfighters; often considered the first author to introduce surrealism into literature.
JOAN MIRÓ 1893–1983	Painting and sculpture, as well as ceramics and illustrations for children's books.	Large paintings of whimsical and brightly colored squiggles, biomorphic shapes, balloons, and constellations; seemingly childlike images replete with graphic sexual symbols.	He was modest, diligent, and serious—hardly the mark of an avant-garde artist; grouped with surrealists for his free associations and dreamlike images.
PEDRO ALMODÓVAR b. 1949	Film.	Operatic and daring comedy-melodramas about women, including *All About My Mother* (1999), which won the Academy Award for best foreign film.	Though more of a provocateur and absurdist, several of his films contain surreal situations, especially his early, transgressive films like *Matador* (1986), a surrealist sex comedy.

SURREALISM ORIGINATED in Paris at the end of World War I, but artists in tradition-bound Spain took the movement to new heights in the 20th century. It began as an exploration of Freudian ideas, with dreamlike imagery tied to the subconscious, and became infused with antibourgeois, Marxist ideals. Luis Buñuel founded the surrealist cinema; Salvador Dalí revolutionized and scandalized the art world; Federico García Lorca revived Spanish theater and poetry; and Joan Miró created an entirely new abstract language in painting. Their direct descendant may be Pedro Almodóvar, the filmmaker who's exhibited a similar flair for generating shock and publicity.

PERSONAL LIFE	POLITICAL VIEWS	LITTLE-KNOWN FACT	QUINTESSENTIAL QUOTE
In 1949 became a citizen of Mexico; was a college friend of Dalí (with whom he cowrote *Un Chien Andalou* but later split acrimoniously) and García Lorca.	Known for overt attacks on the Catholic Church and bourgeoisie; was exiled after the Spanish Civil War; ultimately denounced by Dalí as a communist and an atheist.	After exile from Spain, worked briefly in the film archives of the Museum of Modern Art in New York and later in Hollywood dubbing hit films.	"I am still, thank God, an atheist."
Married a Russian immigrant named Gala, his temperamental muse; lived in a castle with her, receiving guests on a throne.	An anarchist and communist in youth, he became a devout Catholic after World War II and supported Franco, drawing the ire of surrealists; in 1934, was formally expelled from the group.	Iconic mustache modeled after 17th-century Spanish master Diego Velázquez (see p. 20).	"There is only one difference between a madman and me. I am not mad."
Was conflicted about his homosexuality, especially since his close friend Dalí rejected his erotic advances.	Supported leftist Popular Front; was executed by Franco's Nationalists (and presumably dumped in a mass grave) and his work was banned until 1953.	In 1929, studied briefly at Columbia University in New York; became enamored of African-American spirituals, which recalled the *cante jondo* ("deep song") of his native Andalucía.	"In Spain, the dead are more alive than the dead of any other country in the world."
Married a Mallorcan woman, Pilar Juncosa, and relocated to Mallorca, where he built a home-studio and museum and stayed from 1956 until his death in 1983.	Not an overtly political artist, but a fervent Catalan nationalist, as expressed in images of the Catalan countryside (such as the famous painting *The Farm*).	Miró's 1974 tapestry for New York's World Trade Center was one of the most expensive works of art destroyed in the September 11, 2001, terrorist attacks.	"I want to assassinate painting."
Grew up poor in rural La Mancha, where his village did not have a movie house; openly gay and has frequently featured gay, lesbian, and transgendered characters in his films.	While not known for political commitment, has occupied a leading role in progressive Spain's La Movida cultural movement and international queer cinema.	Worked for a decade as an administrative assistant at Spain's national phone company, Telefónica, and played in a glam-punk parody band before writing his first film in 1980.	"I was born at a bad time for Spain, but a really good one for cinema."

Menorca from End to End

Just 45km (28 miles) from one end to the other, Menorca can be seen in 3 days. The island is largely flat and unusually serene, with rolling green agricultural landscapes and idyllic beach coves with aquamarine waters. The British-influenced capital, Maó, possesses one of the deepest natural harbors in the world, while the Old Town of Ciutadella is the most beguiling city in the Balearics.

> *The city of Ciutadella, with its narrow port on the west of the island, was once the capital of Menorca.*

START From Maó, head north in the direction of ME-7 (toward Es Grau) and then west toward Cala Llonga on ME-3; follow signs to La Mola. **TRIP LENGTH** 94 km (58 miles).

① ★★★ kids **Fortaleza La Mola.** This massive architectural marvel was built by the Spanish to protect the Maó port against resumed British or French incursions in the Mediterranean. Unfortunately, by the time it was completed in 1875, its weaponry was already obsolete. ⏱ 2 hr. Carretera de la Mola, Maó. ☎ 971-36-40-40. www.fortalesalamola.com. 7€, free for kids 11 & under. June–Sept daily 10am–8pm; May and Oct daily 10am–6pm; Nov–Apr Tues–Sun 10am–2pm.

② ★ **Maó.** Menorca's capital is a low-key, English-influenced port city known for its spectacularly deep natural harbor, which attracted the Spanish, French, and British to it as a strategic military point in the Mediterranean (best seen by glass-bottom boat tour). Among the city's highlights are the **Museu de Menorca,** the island's largest museum, and **Xoriguer Gin Distillery,** which dates back to the British occupation. Museu: ⏱ 45 min. Plaça des Monestir, s/n. ☎ 971-35-09-55. 2.40€, free Sat 6–8pm and Sun 10am–2pm. Apr–Oct Tues–Sat 10am–2pm and 6–8pm, Sun 10am–2pm; Nov–Mar Mon–Fri 9:30am–2pm, Sat–Sun 10am–2pm. Xoriguer:

🕐 1 hr. Costa des Muret, s/n. ☎ 971-36-21-97. Free.
June–Sept Mon–Fri 8am–7pm, Sat 9am–1pm; Oct–
May Mon–Fri 9am–1pm and 4–7pm.

Binibèquer Vell is 11km (6¾ miles) south of
Maó on ME-8 and then ME-5.

3 ★★ kids Binibèquer Vell. Although this
cluster of houses and alleyways coated with
thick white paint looks like an authentic, old
Menorcan fishing village, it's actually a 1970s
architectural re-creation. 🕐 30 min.

Travel 13km (8 miles) north on Carretera de
Sant Climent a Bintda to reach Talatí.

4 ★★ kids Talatí de Dalt. Menorca is littered
with the remnants of ancient megalithic sites;
this settlement just outside Maó, dating to
around 1300 B.C., is one of the best preserved
on the island. 🕐 30 min. 4€ adults, 3€ students
and seniors, free for kids 7 & under. Apr–Oct
daily 10am–7pm; Nov–Mar open access and free
admission.

Monte El Toro is 21km (13 miles) west on ME-1.

5 ★ kids Monte El Toro. From Menorca's highest peak (357m/1,171 ft.), there are great views
from the top of the entire island, from coast to
coast. 🕐 30 min.

> A late Bronze Age megalith from an ancient
settlement just outside of Maó.

> *Cala en Turqueta, on Menorca's southern coast, is a sheltered cove with fine white sand and clear, blue water.*

Drive 9km (5⅔ miles) north of Es Mercadal on ME-15.

6 ★★★ kids **Fornells.** The picturesque fishing village built around a marina on a sheltered inlet is a gourmet favorite for its seafood restaurants. **Es Cranc,** in the center of the village, is the best of them, with an unbeatable lobster stew. ⏲ 2 hr. Es Cranc: See p. 503.

Head 15km (9⅓ miles) southwest on ME-15 and west on CF-3.

7 ★★★ kids **Cala Pregonda.** At least for dramatic scenery, no beach on Menorca has Cala Pregonda beat. It has deep red sands and sea stacks, completely unlike the gentle white sands, limestone, and pine trees of the southern coast. **Note:** It's a 20-minute hike along a trail from the car park. 9km (5⅔ miles) north of Es Mercadal along CF-3.

Head back to Es Mercadal; then travel west on ME-1. Naveta des Tudons is 13km (8 miles) west of Ferreries on ME-1 and about 20km (12 miles) from Es Mercadal.

8 ★★ kids **Naveta des Tudons.** One of Menorca's best-known ancient structures, this burial chamber, which looks something like an upside-down ship, is early Bronze Age. ⏲ 30 min. ME-1, km 40. 1.80€ adults, 1.10€ seniors and students.

Mid-Apr to Sept Tues–Sat 10am–9pm, Sun–Mon 9am–3pm; Oct Tues–Sun 9am–3pm; Nov to mid-Apr open hours and free admission.

Ciutadella is 5km (3 miles) west on ME-1.

9 ★★★ kids **Ciutadella.** The gorgeous limestone Old Town and picturesque, slender port make Ciutadella the most captivating city in the Balearic Islands. The one-time capital of Menorca until the early 18th century (when the British moved it to Maó) is a delight to stroll, as locals do, especially in the early evening. Among the highlights are the 14th-century **Catedral** and the magnificent 17th- and 18th-century **manor houses.**

If you need a break, the 1893 ★ **Restaurante Aurora** on the edge of the old quarter spills into the genial square, with tables under an awning for people-watching. ⏲ 3 hr. Restaurante: Plaça Alfons III, 3. ☎ 971-38-00-29. Entrees 13€–22€. AE, MC, V. Lunch & dinner daily.

Drive 7km (4½ miles) south along Camí Sant Joan de Missa after the Son Vivó fork, for about 10km (6 miles) total.

10 ★★★ kids **Cala en Turqueta.** This cove about 10km (6¼ miles) south of Ciutadella is pretty much the perfect beach, with limpid turquoise waters and brilliant white sand protected by pine woods.

Where to Stay & Dine

> *Lobster stew is a Menorcan specialty.*

★★★ Alcaufar Vell SANT LLUIS

A grand stone manor house—in the same family since the 14th century—has been converted into a truly elegant country hotel, with a warm minimalist aesthetic, huge bathrooms, and a gourmet restaurant in the old carriage house. Carretera Cala Alcaufar, km 8. ☎ 971-15-18-74. www.alcaufarvell.com. 21 units. Doubles 130€–240€, with buffet breakfast. AE, MC, V.

★★★ Café Balear CIUTADELLA SEAFOOD

A terrific old-school restaurant with a terrace at the edge of the port, Café Balear specializes in fresh, market-priced seafood and shellfish, with a great midweek lunch menu. Pla de Sant Joan, 15. ☎ 971-38-00-05. www.cafe-balear.com. Entrees 14€–45€. AE, DC, MC, V. Lunch & dinner Tues–Sun.

★★★ Ca Na Xini FERRERIES

This handsome farmhouse estate, a 1919 manor house, is very modish and modern inside, with chic white-and-chrome rooms, lovely gardens, and a pool. Camí de Sant Patrici, s/n. ☎ 971-37-37-02. www.canaxini.com. 8 units. Doubles 140€–290€, with buffet breakfast. AE, DC, MC, V.

★★★ Es Cranc FORNELLS SEAFOOD

One of the premier dining destinations on Menorca, this down-to-earth restaurant serves maybe the finest fresh seafood—and, specifically, *caldereta de llagosta* (lobster stew)—on the island. C/ Escoles, 31. ☎ 971-37-64-42. Entrees 15€–73€. AE, DC, MC, V. Mid-Mar to Oct lunch & dinner Thurs–Tues.

★ kids Hotel Hesperia Patricia CIUTADELLA

A smart and conveniently located good-value hotel just a short walk from the port and Old Town, this is a good choice for travelers of all types. Passeig Sant Nicolás, 90–92. ☎ 971-38-55-11. www.hesperia-patricia.com. 44 units. Doubles 64€–118€, with buffet breakfast. AE, DC, MC, V.

★ JM Café FERRERIES MEDITERRANEAN

This breakfast and lunch-only cafe serves up a mean three-course lunch *menú* (13€), including a glass of wine. ME-1, Poligono Industrial. ☎ 971-37-38-37. AE, DC, MC, V. Breakfast & lunch daily.

★★ Ses Forquilles MAÓ HAUTE MEDITERRANEAN

Maó's top restaurant features adventurous tasting menus (from six to nine courses), an excellent value three-course lunch menu, and a chalkboard of tapas. Rovellada de Dalt, 20. ☎ 971-35-27-11. www.sesforquilles.com. Tasting menus 27€–50€. AE, DC, MC, V. Lunch & dinner Mon–Sat.

Menorca's Best Beaches

Menorca's southern coast is characterized by high limestone cliffs and pine forests, with a number of small, protected coves but also open sea along the middle of the island. The north coast is much wilder, buffeted by sharp northerly winds, with an abundance of sandstone; reddish, earthy sands; and more secluded coves. Two favorite beaches, ★★★ **Cala en Turqueta** (southwest coast) and ★★★ **Cala Pregonda** (north coast), are already stops on the tour of Menorca (see p. 502). Other great beaches include ★★★ **Cala Macarella** and **Cala Macarelleta,** a pair of alluring beach coves surrounded by high cliffs and covered by thick pine trees. (Macarelleta, a 10-min. walk around the bend, is unspoiled and considered a nudist or seminudist beach.) ★★ **Cala Mitjana** and **Cala Mitjaneta** are another twin set of secluded coves on the south coast with fine-grained white sand and calm, crystal-clear water. Finally, ★ **Cala de Biniparratx** and **Cala Binidalí,** two attractive small beach coves along the southeast coast, are sheltered and good spots for swimming.

Ibiza & Formentera

Ibiza became world-famous for its hippie scene in the 1960s and more recently for its crazed, all-night clubbers, but it also has some of the Balearics' finest beaches and pretty rural areas, as well as the spectacular walled Old Town of Eivissa. Tiny Formentera, reachable only by boat, is remarkably undeveloped; it has little more than beaches but a special allure all its own. The two islands together can be seen in 3 days (2 for Ibiza and 1 for Formentera).

> *Many Ibiza beaches offer lounge chairs and parasols; some have showers, toilets, and changing rooms.*

START Eivissa (Ibiza).

❶ ★★★ **Eivissa (Ibiza). Dalt Vila,** the medieval Upper Town of Eivissa, was founded 2,600 years ago by the Phoenicians. Today the well-preserved walled city of narrow cobblestone streets and ancient, blinding-white houses is a UNESCO World Heritage Site. Its imposing Renaissance-era defense walls were begun in the 16th century to defend the island against attacks by the French and Turks. The principal gate into the walled city is the Portal de Ses Taules, with a drawbridge and inscription from 1585.

Near the Portal de Ses Taules and inhabiting an 18th-century arsenal, the **Museu d'Art Contemporani** contemporary art museum has underground exhibition spaces within the old-town fortifications.

The Catalan Gothic ★★ **Catedral** of Eivissa was begun in the 14th century on a hilltop at the site of a Moorish mosque and, prior to that, temples dating to Punic times. It has a soaring Gothic tower but was given a heavily baroque renovation in the 18th century. More of Ibiza's storied past is revealed at the ★ **Museo Arqueològic,** housed in the 13th-century building of Ibiza's governing body. It covers everything from Carthaginian burial artifacts and Roman glass bottles to a spectacular collection of Punic pottery and figurines.

For a change of pace, head to ★ **Sa Penya,** the hip district overlooking Eivissa's harbor. It's full

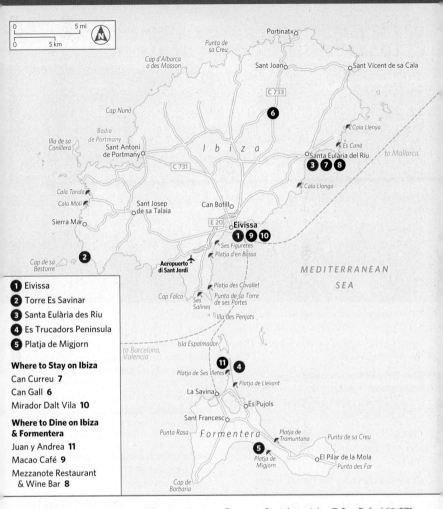

1 Eivissa
2 Torre Es Savinar
3 Santa Eulària des Riu
4 Es Trucadors Peninsula
5 Platja de Migjorn

Where to Stay on Ibiza

Can Curreu **7**
Can Gall **6**
Mirador Dalt Vila **10**

Where to Dine on Ibiza & Formentera

Juan y Andrea **11**
Macao Café **9**
Mezzanote Restaurant & Wine Bar **8**

of art galleries, trendy fashion and furniture boutiques, and stylish bars and cafe terraces, perfect for people-watching (and the best spot to start your evening). And, of course, your evening will probably involve the ★ **club scene.** Ibiza is internationally renowned—or infamous—for its hedonistic nightclubs (those sex- and drug-induced dens of iniquity where dancers lose their inhibitions in thick plumes of fog and foam). If you're up for it (literally, since they don't get going until after 1am, and cover charges are steep), check out famous clubs like **El Divino,** Port Deportivo, Ibiza Nova (☎ 971-31-83-38; www.eldivino-ibiza.com); **Pachá,** Avenida 8 de Agosto, s/n (☎ 971-31-36-12; www.pacha.com); and **Privilege,** Carretera Sant Antoni, km 7, San Rafael (☎ 971-19-80-86; www.privilegeibiza.com). Dalt Vila: ◷ 1 hr. Walking entrance at Portal de Ses Taules. Museu: ◷ 45 min. Ronda Narcís Puget, s/n. ☎ 971-30-27-23. www.eivissa.org. 1.20€, free Sun. Nov-Apr Tues-Fri 10am-1:30pm and 4-6pm, Sat-Sun 10am-1:30pm; May-Oct Tues-Fri 10am-1:30pm and 5-8pm, Sat-Sun 10am-1:30pm. Catedral: ◷ 30 min. C/ Major. ☎ 971-31-27-74. Free. Mon-Sat 10am-1pm; Sun 10:30am-noon. Museo: Plaza de la Catedral, 3. ☎ 971-30-12-31. 2.40€ adults, 1.20€ students, free for kids 17 & under, free on Sun. Oct-Mar Tues-Sat 9am-3pm, Sun 10am-2pm; Apr-Sept Tues-Sat 10am-2pm and 6-8pm, Sun 10am-2pm. Sa Penya: C/ de Barcelona.

> *What happens in Ibiza stays in Ibiza—the island's nightclub scene.*

Travel 6km (3¾ miles) southwest on E-20 to reach Torre Es Savinar.

2 ★ **Torre Es Savinar (Ibiza).** This ancient defense tower has dazzling views of the islets of Es Vedrà and Es Venadrell, just offshore. ⏱ 20 min. Near Cala d'Hort.

To reach Santa Eulària, travel 36km (22 miles) east on PM-803 and northeast on C-733 and PM-810.

3 **Santa Eulària des Riu (Ibiza).** Ibiza's third-largest town is crowned by a fortified 16th-century church, **Es Puig de Missa,** on a hilltop. The small resorts just north, **Es Canar** and **Sant Carles,** are known primarily for their hippie markets (Wed and Sat, respectively), which have become steadily less authentic but are still a big deal. **Las Dalias,** Carretera Sant Carles, km 12 (☎ 971-32-68-25; www.lasdalias. es), in Sant Carles, is another hippie market with cool boho fashions. This stretch of coastline was once hippie headquarters of Ibiza in the '60s.

Return to Eivissa, 16km (10 miles) southwest on PM-810 to C-733, for the ferry to Formentera.

4 ★★★ **Es Trucadors Peninsula (Formentera).** This slender strip of land jutting into the Mediterranean, just north of the port, counts a couple of the most spectacular beaches in all the Balearics: **Ses Illetes** and long **Platja de Llevant,** with fine-grained white sand and translucent waters. They're popular with both divers and nude sunbathers.

Platja de Migjorn is 8km (5 miles) south on PM-V-820-2.

5 ★ **Platja de Migjorn (Formentera).** Formentera's longest (5km/3 miles) beach is framed by pine woods and is largely undeveloped, though there are a few bars and hotels. The beach is quite popular with nudists.

Travel Tip

Tiny Formentera—just 83 sq. km (32 sq. miles) and a world removed from Mallorca and Ibiza, with stunning beaches and solitude—is visited by most people on an easy day trip from Ibiza. The fast ferry from Eivissa takes just 25 minutes. Once on Formentera, the best thing to do is rent a motor scooter, the most popular means of getting around the island.

Where to Stay & Dine

★★ kids Can Curreu SANTA EULÀRIA (IBIZA)
This handsome *finca* (farmhouse) set amid orange groves on the northeast coast is a terrific getaway; it features a spa, a large pool, an attractive terrace restaurant, and horse stables. Rooms are cozy and elegant but unfussy. Private sun terraces are a nice bonus. Carretera Sant Carles, km 12. ☎ 971-33-52-80. www.cancurreu.com. 10 units. Doubles 220€–275€, with buffet breakfast. AE, MC, V.

★★★ kids Can Gall SANT LLORENÇ (IBIZA)
A 200-year-old farmhouse on a large estate, this friendly, family-run *agroturismo* (rural hotel) has elegantly rustic rooms with exposed stone walls, rough-hewn wood-beam ceilings, and private balconies. The grounds have a lovely infinity pool. Carretera Sant Joan, km 17.2. ☎ 971-33-70-31. www.agrocangall.com. 9 units. Doubles 165€–255€, with buffet breakfast. AE, MC, V.

★★ Juan y Andrea PLATJA ILLETES (FORMENTERA)
SEAFOOD A Formentera institution so close to stunning Illetes beach that you literally dine with your toes in the sand. For more than 25 years, this pricey spot has catered to the beautiful people and yacht owners who are fetched for lunch by raft. Carretera Sa Savina, s/n. ☎ 971-18-71-30. www.juanyandrea.com. Entrees 22€–40€. AE, MC, V. Lunch & dinner Tues–Sun.

★ Macao Café EIVISSA (IBIZA) *MEDITERRANEAN*
With an open kitchen specializing in fresh fish and pasta dishes, this casual seaside restaurant in the thick of Eivissa's nightlife scene doesn't try too hard to be trendy or cool, though it has a cool vibe (and its own music label). Plaça de Sa Riba, 11. ☎ 971-31-47-07. www.macaocafe.com. Entrees 14€–25€. MC, V. Dinner daily May–Oct.

★ Mezzanote Restaurant & Wine Bar SANTA EULÀRIA (IBIZA) *ITALIAN* An intimate restaurant with just a dozen tables inside and a few more on an interior patio and the sidewalk, this charming place serves good Italian specialties with fresh ingredients, such as linguine with jumbo shrimp. At lunch, the prix-fixe menu is a deal. Passeig de s'Alamera, 22. ☎ 971-31-94-98. Entrees 12€–22€. AE, MC, V. Lunch & dinner Tues–Sun.

★★★ Mirador Dalt Vila EIVISSA (IBIZA)
Within the walled Old Town, this property—in a 1905 colonial-style manor house—has style to burn. Rooms are crisp and modern, with gorgeous views of the Old Town, harbor, and sea. The hotel even has its own boat for charters. No children. Plaça d'Espanya, 4. ☎ 971-30-30-45. www.hotelmiradoribiza.com. 13 units. Doubles 285€–475€, with buffet breakfast. AE, DC, MC, V.

Ibiza's Best Beaches

The hugely popular beaches just south of Eivissa are **Ses Figueretes, Platja d'en Bossa, Platja des Cavallet,** and **Ses Salines** (near salt pans that are a haven for birds). The beaches, all accessible by city bus, can be very crowded, and it's not unusual to see nude sunbathers.

Some of Ibiza's finest beaches—the reason sun seekers flock here in summer—are located along the western coast. The pick of the litter are the largely secluded and not overcrowded small coves **★★ Cala Molí** and **★★ Cala Tarida.**

Just south of Santa Eulària, **★ Cala Llonga** is a long stretch of white sand on a wide bay and is popular with families, while just north, **★ Cala Llenya** and **★ Es Canà** are two of the finest beaches on the island.

The Balearic Islands Fast Facts

> The Balearic Islands ferry.

Arriving & Getting Around

BY PLANE **To Mallorca:** Palma de Mallorca's **Sant Joan Airport** (☎ 971-78-90-00) is the busiest in Spain, with hundreds of flights arriving daily from mainland Spain, as well as the U.K., Germany, and many other points across Europe, including those of many low-cost carriers and charters. From the airport (11km/6¾ miles southeast of the city center), Bus Line 1 (Aeroport–Ciutat–Port; ☎ 971-431-024; 2€) leaves every 15 minutes for central Palma; taxis (about 15€) leave from outside all terminals. **To Menorca:** There are direct flights to Maó from Palma, as well as from the U.K. and other parts of Europe, though many require stops in either Barcelona or Palma. The **Aeropuerto de Menorca,** Carretera de San Climent, s/n (☎ 971-15-71-15), is 5km (3 miles) southeast of the capital, with transport by bus (☎ 902-07-50-66) or taxi (about 2€ to Maó). **To Ibiza:** As

with Menorca, there are direct flights to Eivissa from the U.K. and other parts of Europe, though many require stops in either Barcelona or Palma. **Aeropuerto de Sant Jordi** (☎ 971-80-99-00) is 7.5km (4⅔ miles) southeast of Eivissa. A taxi into Eivissa is about 15€, and Lines 9 and 10 of **Ibizabus** (☎ 971-34-04-12; ibizabus.com) travel to Eivissa and other points on the island. For additional information, dial ☎ 902-40-47-04 or visit www.aena.es. BY FERRY From Barcelona and Valencia, ferries go to Palma, Maó, and Ciutadella (Menorca); Eivissa (Ibiza); and Sant Antoni (Formentera). Check schedules and fares with **Acciona Trasmediterranea** (☎ 902-45-46-45; www.trasmediterranea.es); **Baleària Eurolínies Marítimes** (☎ 902-16-01-80; www.balearia.com); and **Iscomar** (☎ 902-11-91-28; www.iscomar.com). Ferry is the only way to get to Formentera (from Ibiza). **Mediterranea Pitiusa** (☎ 971-32-24-43; www.medpitiusa.net)

and **Trasmapi** (☎ 917-31-44-33; www.trasmapi. com) travel between Ibiza and Formentera. **BY TRAIN** Two train lines operate in Mallorca. The narrow-gauge 1912 **Ferrocarril de Sóller** leaves from Estació Plaça Espanya, Eusebio Estada, 1, Palma (☎ 971-75-20-51; www.trendesoller. com), and makes seven trips daily to Sóller (10€ one-way, 17€ round-trip). The modern **Ferro-carril Inca-Manacor** also leaves from Estació Plaça Espanya, Palma (☎ 971-75-22-45), but travels to Inca and Sa Pobla or Manacor. **BY TAXI In Mallorca:** Reliable taxi companies include **Fono Taxi** (☎ 971-72-80-81) and **Radio Taxi** (☎ 971-76-45-45). **In Menorca:** In Maó, dial ☎ 971-36-71-11 for a taxi, or ☎ 971-38-28-96 in Ciutadella. **In Ibiza:** Call **Teléfono Radiotaxi** (☎ 971-80-00-80). **In Formentera:** Dial ☎ 971-32-23-42. **BY BUS** Bus lines crisscross the three largest islands, but their limited services can make traveling through the islands a challenge. For more information on Mallorcan bus schedules (five lines fan out from Palma to each major coast), visit www.caib.es or call ☎ 971-17-77-77. On Menorca, call ☎ 902-07-50-66 or visit www.e-torres.net.

Doctors & Hospitals
Dial ☎ **061** to find a doctor or an ambulance. **MALLORCA** The main hospital is **Hospital Universitari Son Dureta,** C/ Andrea Doria, 55, Palma de Mallorca (☎ 971-17-50-00; www.hsd.es).

Emergencies
For an ambulance or medical emergencies, dial ☎ **061.** For other emergencies, call ☎ **112.**

Internet Access
Internet access is plentiful, both in *cafés Internet* (cybercafes) and frequently in hotels, many of which offer Wi-Fi. The **Azul Computer Group** operates an Internet cafe in Palma de Mallorca at C/ Soledad, 4, bajos (☎ 971-71-29-27). To find additional cybercafes, check www.cyber captive.com and www.cybercafe.com.

Pharmacies
Pharmacies operate during normal business hours, and one in every district remains open all night and on holidays. The location and phone number of this *farmacía de guàrdia* is posted on the door of all the other pharmacies. A central pharmacy in Palma is **Plano,** C/ de la Volta de la Mercè, 4 (☎ 971-22-88-88).

Police
The national police emergency number is ☎ **091.** For local police, call ☎ **092.**

Post Office
The Central Post Office in **Palma de Mallorca** is at C/ de la Constitució, 6, Palma. It is open from 9am to 8pm Monday through Friday and Saturday 9am to 1pm.

Safety
Violent crime in the Balearics is a rarity, but pickpockets frequent tourist areas and major attractions such as restaurants, hotels, beach resorts, train stations, airports, and ATMs. Exercise care with your belongings around major tourist sights and on beaches. The club scene and drugs in Ibiza have fostered some muggings, so partiers should take precaution to not let things get too far out of control, to have transportation back to their hotels, to go with a group, and to not trust every stranger they meet.

Visitor Information
MALLORCA There are **tourist information offices (OITs)** scattered across the island, beginning with the Sant Joan airport in Palma (☎ 971-78-95-56); Passeig des Born, 27, Palma (☎ 902-10-23-65); and Can Bordils, C/ de l'Almudaina, 9, Palma (☎ 971-22-59-63). Other offices are in Valldemossa, Sóller, Pollença, Port d'Alcúdia, Cala Ratjada, Portocolom, Colònia de Sant Jordi, and other resorts along the east and south coasts. **MENORCA** There are OITs at the airport in Maó, downtown Maó, Fornells on the north coast, and Ciutadella. **IBIZA** The main OIT is in Eivissa, at Passeig Vara de Rey, 1 (☎ 971-30-19-00; www.ibiza.travel). **FORMENTERA** The OIT is at Port de la Savina (☎ 971-32-20-57; www.formentera.es).

The Best of the City of Valencia in 3 Days

You could spend weeks in the city of Valencia, doing something new every day. But in 3 days you can at least touch on the highlights, from the late medieval Old Town to the gleaming educational park of the City of Arts & Sciences. And you'll have plenty to eat along the way. For a more complete tour, see p. 530.

> PREVIOUS PAGE *Benidorm's azure bay.* THIS PAGE *The Puerta de los Apóstoles, a 14th-century addition to Valencia's cathedral.*

START Colón Metro station to Plaza Mercado.

❶ Mercado Central. Get an early start on the day as fruit vendors lay out still-life displays and fishmongers artfully layer the gleaming-eyed catch. Valencia's 1928 Modernista building is said to be Europe's oldest market site and its largest covered market. More than 400 stalls on two levels sell almost every fresh or preserved food you can imagine, along with spices and kitchen equipment. Every neighborhood in Valencia has a market, but chefs, foodies, and even vendors from other markets shop at Mercado Central. ⏱ 1–2 hr. See p. 520, ❶.

② 🥤 **Horchatería El Siglo.** En route to the Catedral, stop for a refreshing drink of *horchata* at the famous El Siglo, founded in 1836. In Latin America, *horchata* is a rice-based drink, but in Spain it's made from tiger nuts and is often served with *churros* (fried dough). See p. 522, ❼.

❸ Plaza de la Reina. If the avenues of the Old City were spokes, this plaza would be the hub. Not only is it central for many restaurants and bars, but it's right in front of the Catedral. See p. 530, ❶.

1. Mercado Central
2. Horchatería El Siglo
3. Plaza de la Reina
4. Catedral
5. El Miguelete
6. Museo Nacional de Cerámica
7. Antiguo Cauce del Río Túria
8. Instituto Valenciano de Arte Moderno
9. Torres de Serranos
10. Museo de Bellas Artes de Valencia
11. Playa de Malvarossa
12. City of Arts & Sciences

> *The light-filled atrium of Valencia's impressive Mercado Central.*

❹ **Catedral.** When Jaume I recaptured Valencia from the Moors in 1238, one of his first acts was to order the mosque razed and a cathedral built in its place. Work finally got underway in 1252, and dragged on for another 230 years. Further additions, including an 18th-century baroque facade, muddle the stylistic purity, but the cathedral nonetheless achieves a kind of warrior majesty. Renaissance frescoes that had been covered for centuries were recently restored, and the cathedral also displays two superb paintings by Goya. It is said to be the home of the Holy Grail, but the cathedral's most unusual relic is the mummified left arm of St. Vincent Martyr, Valencia's patron saint killed here in A.D. 304. ⏱ 30 min. See p. 530, ❸.

❺ **El Miguelete.** The bell tower of the Catedral has been an iconic image of Valencia for the past 600 years. The top level, reached by climbing 207 stairs, provides panoramic views over the city. The nickname refers to the largest bell of the carillon, a 10-ton behemoth called "Miguel" that was cast in 1532. ⏱ 1 hr. See p. 530, ❹.

❻ **Museo Nacional de Cerámica.** Many visitors simply snap a photo of the extravagantly baroque 18th-century alabaster facade of the **Palacio del Marqués de Dos Aguas.** But it's worth going inside to see a museum that marries simplicity and baroque decoration in both its architecture and its subject matter. The lower level of the structure, filled with rooms in French Second Empire style, serves as a reminder of how well the nobility lived here in the 19th century. Upper levels are devoted to decorative and functional ceramics, with an emphasis on the Valenciana tradition. ⏱ 45 min. See p. 532, ❻.

❼ **Antiguo Cauce del Río Túria.** The Río Túria was diverted after major flooding of the city in 1957, and in the past quarter century, the old riverbed has been transformed into a series of parks, walkways, and playgrounds, as well as sites for performance centers and museums.

❽ **Instituto Valenciano de Arte Moderno.** Valencia began its cultural renaissance when this striking contemporary art museum opened in 1989. Central to its collections are many works by Barcelona-born Julio González, one of the artists who used to hang out with Picasso at Els Quatre Gats coffeehouse in Barcelona (see p. 427, ❼). The cubist painter turned to iron sculpture after learning how to weld while working at the Renault factory in France in 1918. The museum is noted for its challenging temporary exhibitions. ⏱ 1–2 hr. See p. 533, ❿.

❾ **kids Torres de Serranos.** These 14th-century Gothic towers functioned as the main gate to the Christian city from the beleaguered countryside. Constructed as secure fortress towers, they never saw battle but were

In the China Shop

Once you've seen the range of Spanish ceramics at Dos Aguas (see above), walk across the street to the flagship store of **Lladro,** C/ Poeta Querol, 9 (☎ 963-511-625; www.lladro.com), the country's best-known maker of ceramic figurines. Show an interest and you'll be invited to visit the factory.

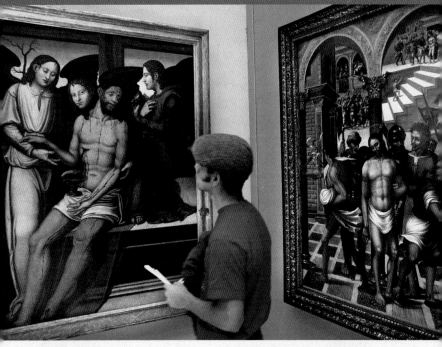

> *Its collection of 14th- and 15th-century Valencian "primitives" distinguishes the city's Museo de Bellas Artes.*

sometimes used to imprison nobility. Local art treasures were stored here for protection during the Spanish Civil War. Views from the top sweep across the city and the riverbed park. ☺ 30 min. Plaza de los Fueros, s/n. ☎ 963-919-070. 2€. Tues–Sat 10am–2pm and 4:30-8:30pm; Sun 10am–3pm. Bus: 1, 6, 8, 11, 16, 26, 29, 36, 80, 95.

🔟 **Museo de Bellas Artes de Valencia.** Set in a former seminary building at the edge of the lovely Real Viveros park, this large art museum tends to emphasize art from elsewhere in Spain and Europe, often at the expense of its terrific holdings in Gothic and primitive art from Valencia itself. Be sure to seek out the medieval altarpieces. ☺ 1 hr. See p. 533, 🔟.

⓫ **Playa de Malvarrosa.** It's easy to catch a Metro from Bellas Artes to this beach, chief among Valencia's swimming, sunbathing, and socializing beaches. New construction is knitting the beachside community together with the adjacent old fishermen's quarter of **El Cabanyal.** Next to the revitalized port (now called **Port America's Cup,** in honor of its role

in the 2007 and 2009 competitions), **Paseo Neptuno** serves as a long block of dining and other entertainment. If you are going to eat paella only once in Valencia, plan to feast at the legendary **La Pepica** (see p. 523, ⓬). It is one place that has *not* gone downhill since Ernest Hemingway ate there. See p. 533, ⓬.

⓬ **City of Arts & Sciences.** You'll want to spend a whole day at the dynamic **Ciudad de las Artes y las Ciéncias,** the artistic and educational complex where "entertainment" is not a dirty word. Native son Santiago Calatrava designed most of the complex, save the cool aquariums and dolphin performing center of L'Oceanogràfic. ☺ 1 day. See p. 533, ⓭.

Get Rolling

Explore the riverbed parks and gardens of Valencia on a bicycle: Located near the Mercado Central, **Orange Bikes,** C/ Editor Manuel Aguilar, 1 (☎ 963-917-551; www.orange bikes.net), rents and services mountain bikes, city bikes, and motor-assisted bikes.

The Best of Valencia in 1 Week

For the first 3 days of this tour of the Autonomous Community of Valencia, spend your time in the city of Valencia following "The Best of the City of Valencia in 3 Days." For the next 4 days, head south down the N-332 to the sun-drenched beaches of the Costa Blanca, a promotional term coined in 1957 by a British airline to advertise its London–Valencia flights. Resort developers took it seriously, and lounge chairs swiftly replaced fishing boats on the beaches. Better known to European vacationers, Costa Blanca remains relatively unexplored by Americans.

> A peaceful evening row near El Saler in the Parque Natural de L'Albufera.

START N-332 south from Valencia to El Saler (about 13km/8 miles). TRIP LENGTH 221km (137 miles).

❶ **Parque Natural de L'Albufera.** Rice farmers have labored in the flooded fields around L'Albufera lake for centuries, but the 21-sq.-km (8-sq.-mile) ecosystem of lagoons, barrier

beaches, and dunes was declared a natural reserve only in 1986. Rice fields still cover about two-thirds of the area, and produce the bulk of the tall, hard-to-cultivate *bomba* strain that's optimal for paella.

Nowhere is the contrast of built and natural environments so striking as at **El Saler beach.** Look east to see giant cargo ships and tankers in Valencia's industrial port. Yet the beach itself, which consists of smooth flat stones like giant lentils, is covered with shorebirds, and the brush on the dunes hides the nests of quail and several species of songbirds.

Travel Tip

While individual points are served by bus or train, a car is best for following this entire itinerary.

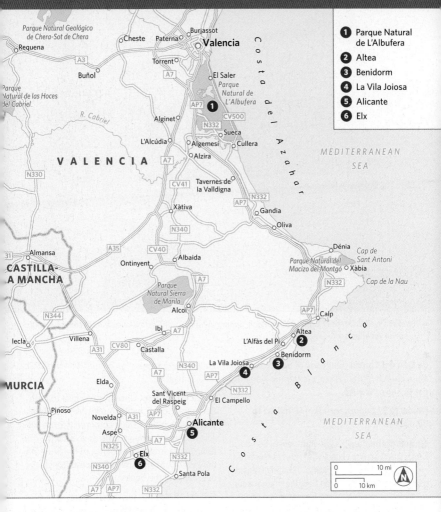

1. Parque Natural de L'Albufera
2. Altea
3. Benidorm
4. La Vila Joiosa
5. Alicante
6. Elx

The thriving town of **El Saler**—a favorite weekend escape for Valencianos—sits between the sea and the freshwater lake formed millennia ago by sedimentation of the deltas of the Túria and Zùquer rivers. You may see fishermen in small, flat-bottomed boats on the lake, mostly catching mullet or collecting American red crayfish, a crustacean introduced in the 1970s that is prized for paella.

The wetlands between fresh and salt water rank among the Iberian Peninsula's most important breeding grounds for night, squacco, and purple herons (there are currently more than 5,000 breeding pairs) and four varieties of terns. For details on birding in the park, see the exhibits and bird checklist at the **Racó de l'Olla Centre d'Interpretación.** See p. 524, ❶.

Pick up AP-7 south for 133km (83 miles) to Altea.

❷ **Altea.** Although the Costa Blanca begins at Dénia (the northern terminus of the beach tram), it's worth skipping the towering resorts of Cabo de Sant Antoni and Cabo de la Nau to reach this slow-paced beach resort that sits below an atmospheric white village. The nearby Serra Bernia hills shelter Altea from continental winds, creating a microclimate where palm trees flourish along the seafront esplanade. The blue-and-white-tiled domes of **La Mare**

> *Thanks to well-advertised flights from London, Spain's White Coast (Costa Blanca) has become a favorite European vacation spot.*

de **Déu del Consol** (Our Lady of Solace), the main church of the village, are unique along the coast. See p. 525, **❸**.

Follow N-332 south for 13km (8 miles) to Benidorm.

❸ Benidorm. Barely a generation ago, Benidorm was a small fishing village with houses clustered on the rocky Canfali promontory that divides the beach in half. Its fishermen had been famous for centuries as masters of the *almadrabas,* a cooperative way of catching tuna with weirs when they migrated between the Mediterranean and the Atlantic. Today Benidorm is the largest beach resort on the Costa Blanca—and arguably the best organized and most user-friendly. The **Playa Levante,** east of Canfali, was the first section to be developed and has a denser concentration of hotel towers and street-level bars and trinket shops. When you tire of playing beach volleyball, consider a boat trip to **Benidorm Island.** There are many boat services, but select one that shuttles back and forth regularly so you can spend as long as you want snorkeling or hiking the small island. A huge population of peacocks and hens gives Benidorm the local nickname Peacock Island. See p. 525, **❹**.

Follow N-332 south for 15km (9⅓ miles) to La Vila Joiosa.

❹ La Vila Joiosa. Since it is so close to both Benidorm and Alicante, most travelers merely pass through the fishing community of La Vila Joiosa. Pay attention on the drive though—the town spreads along the banks of the Riu Amadorio with beautiful pastel-colored houses overhanging the banks.

Follow AP-7 south for 17km (11 miles) to AP-70. Continue 7km (4⅓ miles) to N-332 and follow that 4km (2½ miles) to Alicante.

❺ Alicante. Look at Alicante from the shore and you see a city straining toward the sea with outstretched wharves and piers. View it from the ocean, and Alicante's buildings seem to cling to the skirts of a mountain topped by a fierce castle.

Locals claim to see a protective spirit outlined on Benacantil mountain: La Cara del Moro, or

Travel Tip

For detailed coverage of hotels and restaurants on the Costa Blanca, see p. 528.

> *Candy-colored houses hang over the bank of the Riu Amadorio in La Vila Joiosa.*

"Face of the Moor." It's an appropriate moniker: The sprawling **Castell de Santa Bárbera** grew from a 9th-century Moorish castle into one of Spain's largest medieval fortresses. (In typical Spanish fashion, the Moors built on a Roman fort, the Romans on a Carthaginian one.) It now covers the entire top of the hill, standing 166m (545 ft.) above sea level.

The Old City boasts two landmark buildings in the high baroque style known as Churrigueresque (see p. 231), usually associated with Castilla y León: the plain-faced Gothic **Santa María** church and the Renaissance palace of the **Ayuntamiento,** both redone in baroque style in the early 18th century. The sculptor in charge, Juan Bautista Borja, had been trained by a disciple of the Churriguera family in Salamanca.

Although Alicante is headquarters for the heavily staffed European Union's Office for Harmonization in the Internal Market (the trademark police), it is also a beach town. Cross the **Explanada de España** (the wave-pattern promenade formed of 6.6 million tiles) to get to the water. As bureaucrats combat pretend Prada and other faux fashion, you can romp on the sands of **Playa de Postiguet** below

the castle, or hop the tram to ride 5km (3 miles) to the 8km (5 miles) of golden sands at **Playa de Sant Joan.** See p. 526, **5**.

Follow N-332 south for 3km (1¾ miles) to the A-7 and continue 13km (8 miles) to CV-85 for 3km (1¾ miles) to Elx.

6 Elx. The pride of Elx (Elche in Spanish) is its palm grove, the largest in Europe and a UNESCO World Heritage Site. The usually tropical trees thrive in the arid microclimate sheltered from the continental cold. Brought by the Arabs and cultivated for more than a millennium, the date palms now number more than 200,000. See p. 527, **6**.

Calling All Shoe Lovers

Shoe manufacturing is the largest industry in Elx, and the Elx Parque Industrial east of town sports 24 shoe and clothing manufacturer outlets. If you have time for only one, choose **Pikolinos Tienda Museo,** C/ Germán Bernacer, 4 (☎ 965-681-488; www. pikolinos.com), for bargains on the stylish and highly coveted shoes.

Gastronomic Valencia

The adage that "you are what you eat" could have been coined for the city of Valencia. If you're a Valenciano, you eat a variety of fish and fresh oranges and other fruits grown in the gardens and truck farms outside the city. And you eat rice, rice, rice. This foray into the gastronomic corners of the city should take at least 2 days. Your palate will never be the same.

> Gabi Serrano incorporates both coastal favorites and inland specialties into Cervecería Maipi's menu.

START Colón Metro station to Plaza Mercado.

❶ ★★★ kids Mercado Central. As you enter this Modernista cathedral of food, you'll be overwhelmed by rich aromas. At stall no. 457, Antonio Catalán piles up mounds of sweet, hot, and smoked paprika (pimenton ahumado). He also sells reasonably priced saffron. Want bomba rice for paella? See La Pista Pastor, stall no. 43. At stall no. 51, Ceramicas Terriols sells iron and stainless-steel paella pans and ceramic casseroles for the soupier rice dishes. ⏱ 1–2 hr. Plaza Mercado, s/n. ☎ 963-829-101. www.mercado centralvalencia.es. Free. Mon–Sat 7:30am–2:30pm. Metro: Colón.

❷ kids Cacao Sampaka. The Valencia outpost of this revolutionary Barcelona-based chocolatier is the best place to chill out with a chocolate granizado (a Spanish frozen dessert) in the cafe. Or try a breakfast of hot chocolate, pastries, and freshly squeezed Valencia orange juice for just 4€. C/ Conde Salvatierra, 19. ☎ 963-534-062. www.cacaosampaka.com. Mon–Fri 9am–9pm; Sat 10am–9pm. MC, V. Metro: Colón.

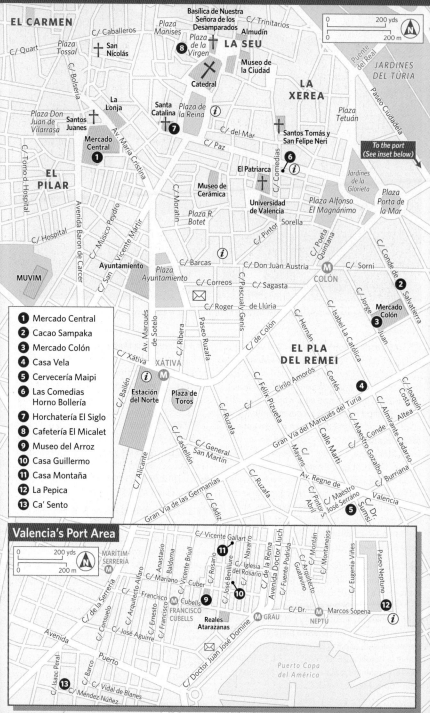

EL CARMEN

C/ Quart
Plaza Tossal
C/ Caballeros
San Nicolás
Plaza Manises
Basílica de Nuestra Señora de los Desamparados
C/ Trinitarios
Almudín
LA SEU
Museo de la Ciudad
Plaza de la Virgen
Catedral
LA XEREA
Puente del Real
JARDINES DEL TÚRIA
Paseo Ciudadela
Plaza Tetuán

C/ Bolsería
Plaza Don Juan de Vilarrasa
Santos Juanes
La Lonja
Santa Catalina
Plaza de la Reina
C/ del Mar
Santos Tomás y San Felipe Neri

C/ Toma d. Hospital
Mercado Central
Av. María Cristina
C/ Paz
C/ Comedias
To the port (See inset below)
Jardines de la Glorieta
Plaza Porta de la Mar

EL PILAR
Av. Músico Peydro
Avenida Baron de Carcer
C/ Moratín
Museo de Cerámica
Plaza R. Botet
El Patriarca
Universidad de Valencia
Sorella
Plaza Alfonso El Magnánimo
C/ Poeta Quintana

C/ Hospital
MUVIM
Ayuntamiento
C/ San Vicente Mártir
Plaza Ayuntamiento
C/ Barcas
C/ Pintor
C/ Don Juan Austria
COLÓN
C/ Sorni
C/ Conde de Salvatierra

C/ Correos
C/ Sagasta
C/ Jorge
Mercado Colón

C/ Roger
de Llúria
C/ Pascual y Genis
C/ Isabel La Católica
Juan

C/ Marqués de Sotelo
Paseo Ruzafa
C/ de Colón
C/ Hernán
EL PLA DEL REMEI
C/ Joaquín Costa

C/ Xátiva
XÁTIVA
C/ Ribera
C/ Bailén
Estación del Norte
Plaza de Toros
Cirilo Amorós
Cortés
C/ Félix Pizcueta
Gran Vía del Marqués del Turia
Calle Marti
C/ Maestro Conde
C/ Almirante Cadarso
Altea

1. Mercado Central
2. Cacao Sampaka
3. Mercado Colón
4. Casa Vela
5. Cervecería Maipi
6. Las Comedias Horno Bollería
7. Horchatería El Siglo
8. Cafetería El Micalet
9. Museo del Arroz
10. Casa Guillermo
11. Casa Montaña
12. La Pepica
13. Ca' Sento

C/ Ruzafa
C/ Castellón
C/ General San Martín
Mayans
Av. Regne de Valencia
C/ Maestro Gozalbo
C/ Burriana
C/ Pintor S. Abril
C/ José Serrano
C/ Dr. Sumsi

Gran Vía de las Germanias
C/ Cádiz

Valencia's Port Area

MARÍTIM-SERRERÍA
C/ Vicente Gallart
Casa Montaña
C/ Navarro
C/ Iglesia del Rosario
Avenida Doctor Lluch
C/ Fuente Podrida
C/ Montán
C/ Montanejos
C/ Arquitecto Guatavino
Paseo Neptuno

C/ de la Serrería
C/ Anastasio
C/ Baldoma
C/ Mariano
C/ Vicente Brull
C/ Cuber
C/ Rosario
C/ José Benlliure
Cubells
Museo del Arroz
Casa Guillermo
C/ de la Reina
C/ Eugenia Viñes
La Pepica

C/ Arquitecto Alfaro
C/ Francisco
C/ Ernesto
C/ Francisco
FRANCISCO CUBELLS
Reales Atarazanas
GRAU
C/ Dr.
Marcos Sopena
NEPTÚ

C/ Consuelo
C/ José Aguirre
C/ Doctor Juan José Domine
Puerto Copa del América

Avenida
Puerto
C/ Isaac Peral
C/ Barco
C/ Vidal de Blanes
C/ Méndez Núñez
Ca' Sento

> *Seemingly ancient wine barrels line the walls of Casa Montaña, a local favorite since 1836.*

❸ ★ **Mercado Colón.** The cafe-filled ground level of this soaring glass-and-steel Modernista structure is the city's snazziest food court, with free concerts at noon on Sundays (Sept–June). Sushi-to-go anchors one end, while at the other, locals slurp *horchata*—a cooling, milky drink as popular as Coca-Cola—from plastic cups at **Món Orxata** (☎ 963-527-307). On the lower level, **Manglano,** stall no. 5 (☎ 963-528-854), was named best gastronomic boutique in Spain in 2009. Primarily a butcher shop with a wide selection of Spanish wines, Manglano also carries small-production artisanal cheeses, such as Heretat de Pere, a semisoft goat cheese. ⏱ 45 min. C/ Jorge Juan, 19. Free. Cafes open daily 8am–9pm. Metro: Colón.

❹ Casa Vela. The food is as traditional as ever in this 1908 *charcutería* (delicatessen). Hams hang on the walls, meats gleam in the cases, and the bar does a brisk business all day. Head to the tables in back to enjoy pâté-and-cheese sandwiches or a combination plate of a small steak, squash, asparagus, and eggplant. C/ Isabel la Católica, 26. ☎ 963-516-734. Sandwiches 3€–7€, combination plates 10€–16€. Mon–Sat 7am–10pm. MC, V. Metro: Colón.

❺ ★★ **Cervecería Maipi.** Valencianos aren't big on barhopping for tapas. They pick one place, such as Maipi, and share plates—a practice known locally as *la picaeta.* Gabi Serrano, the flamboyant owner here, is the master of *manitas* (pig's feet) and other hearty mountain dishes from inland Valencia. (In spring, inquire about the baby goat chops.) Don't let the soccer trappings make you think this is just a sports bar—Serrano is a gourmet as well as a fan. C/ Maestro José Serrano, 1. ☎ 963-735-709. Entrees 6€–30€. MC, V. Lunch & dinner Mon–Fri. Metro: Colón.

❻ kids **Las Comedias Horno Bollería.** This small bakery is known for inventing a dish sold all over town: the *empanadilla* filled with oil-preserved anchovies and fresh tomato. Other specialties include sweet *carquinyols,* an almond cookie. C/ Comedias, 11. ☎ 963-517-141. Mon–Sat 8am–2:30pm and 5–8pm. Metro: Colón.

❼ kids ★ **Horchatería El Siglo.** Valencianos will never agree on who makes the city's best *horchata.* But they do agree that no place has been making the drink pressed from tiger nuts longer than this delightful establishment, founded 1836. Plaza de Santa Catalina, 11. ☎ 963-918-466. Horchata 1.70€–2.40€. Sun–Fri 8am–9pm. Metro: Colón.

> Stop in for a charcuterie plate from Casa Vela.

> You haven't had paella until you've had it in Valencia.

8 Cafetería El Micalet. If *horchata* is Valencia's soft drink of choice, its preferred cocktail is Agua de Valencia, first served in 1959 at the Cafe Madrid de Valencia. El Micalet's version mixes orange juice, orange liqueur, gin or vodka, and Cava. Plaza de la Virgen, s/n. ☎ 963-922-874. Agua de Valencia 10€ for small pitcher, 19€ for large pitcher. Daily 9am–10pm or later. Metro: Colón.

9 kids Museo del Arroz. Located in the old fishermen's quarter of El Cabanyal, this museum occupies an early-1900s rice mill that has been restored to show how the grain used to be processed. ⏱ 30 min. C/ Rosario, 1. ☎ 963-676-291. www.museoarrozvalencia.com. 2€; 1€ kids, students, and seniors. Tues–Sat 10am–2pm and 4:30–8:30pm; Sun 10am–3pm. Metro: Neptú.

10 ★★ Casa Guillermo. With his deft salt–and-olive oil cure for small fish, Guillermo Madrigal called himself the "king of anchovies." He passed on in 1998, but his daughter Amparo continues the tradition—delicately filleting each order using two tiny forks. C/ José Benlliure, 26. ☎ 963-673-825. Raciones 3€–24€. MC, V. Lunch Tues–Sat, dinner Mon–Sat. Metro: Marítim–Serrería.

11 ★★ Casa Montaña. Hungry Valencianos have bellied up to the bar here since 1836. It's hard to see the beautifully tiled walls behind the giant barrels of wine, but proprietor Emiliano García favors wine in the bottle over wine in the cask. Casa Montaña usually has 800 to 1,000 wines available, along with a nearly encyclopedic choice of tapas. Some seafood dishes, such as *clóchinas al vapor* (tiny steamed mussels), are seasonal, but you can always order *bacalao* (salted cod) in a creamy béchamel casserole. C/ José Benlliure, 69. ☎ 963-672-314. Raciones 3€–22€. AE, MC, V. Lunch & dinner daily. Metro: Dr. Lluch.

12 ★★★ La Pepica. This palace of paella opened on the beachfront in 1898. Hemingway liked the food, but who doesn't? Waiters in white shirts and black vests bring each pan of paella to the table for approval, then retire to a serving station to dole it out on individual plates. Enter from the street, rather than the beach side, so you can walk through the dynamic kitchen. Paseo Neptuno, 2–8. ☎ 963-710-366. Entrees 13€–30€. AE, DC, MC, V. Lunch Mon–Sun, dinner Mon–Sat. Metro: Neptú.

13 ★★ Ca' Sento. When chef Raul Alexandre returned from a stint under Ferran Adrià, his parents put their celebrated seafood restaurant in his hands. Alexandre strikes a balance between his radical mentor and traditional mother. For example, he serves his *fideua* (a variation on paella) of thin noodles with cuttlefish and baby squid with a side of aioli and squid ink. C/ Méndez Núñez, 17. ☎ 963-301-775. Entrees 18€–36€. AE, MC, V. Lunch & dinner Tues–Sat.Metro: Marítim–Serrería.

Costa Blanca

The light along the coast between Valencia and Alicante is some of the brightest in Spain—a trick of arid air and peninsular geography. That, combined with the luminous nature of the chalky landscape, has earned the area the nickname the "White Coast." High-rise development has swamped some of the former fishing villages here, but others retain their ancient rhythms while still welcoming beachgoers. Allow 5 days for this tour.

> *Most of Spain's bomba rice is cultivated in the rice paddies of the Parque Natural de L'Albufera.*

START From Valencia, follow CV-500 south to El Palmar. **TRIP LENGTH** 190km (118 miles).

1 ★★ kids **Parque Natural de L'Albufera.** Only 10km (6¼ miles) south of Valencia, this wetlands park surrounds the largest lake in Spain. (L'Albufera is Arabic for "Little Sea.") Most of Spain's *bomba* rice (the best for paella) is cultivated here. An observation tower at the **Racó de l'Olla Interpretation Center** gives an overview of the dynamic interplay of beach, dunes, rice fields, and lake. Two walking trails explore the immediate environs, and you can pause in a natural blind to observe ducks, geese, egrets, and herons in a lagoon. To explore on your own, pick up maps of cycling and driving routes—a dedicated bicycle path from the City of Arts & Sciences (see p. 533, **13**) leads to the amazing beach at El Saler at the north end of the park. ⏱ 1 day. Interpretation Center: ⏱ 20 min. El Palmar turnoff from CV-500. ☎ 961-627-345. http://parquesnaturales.gva.es. Daily 9am–2pm, also Oct–May Tues and Thurs 4–5:30pm.

Follow N-332 south for 54km (34 miles) to Gandia.

2 Gandia. For a break from the casual coast, visit this old inland city, where the **Palau Ducal dels Borja** hides extraordinary Renaissance and

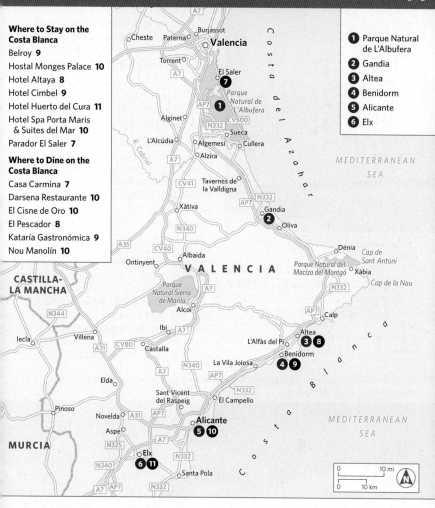

Where to Stay on the Costa Blanca

Belroy **9**

Hostal Monges Palace **10**

Hotel Altaya **8**

Hotel Cimbel **9**

Hotel Huerto del Cura **11**

Hotel Spa Porta Maris & Suites del Mar **10**

Parador El Saler **7**

Where to Dine on the Costa Blanca

Casa Carmina **7**

Darsena Restaurante **10**

El Cisne de Oro **10**

El Pescador **8**

Kataría Gastronómica **9**

Nou Manolín **10**

1 Parque Natural de L'Albufera

2 Gandia

3 Altea

4 Benidorm

5 Alicante

6 Elx

baroque architecture inside its plain exterior. When Cardinal Rodrigo de Borja bought Gandia's dukedom in 1485, the palace became the family residence. Rodrigo became infamous as Pope Alexander VI, the most secular of the Borgia (the Italian spelling of Borja) popes. His descendents by his mistress held onto the Gandia title until 1740. The palace is now a Jesuit-owned museum. ⏱ 1 day. Palau: ⏱ 45 min. C/ Duc Alfons el Vell, 1. ☎ 962-871-465. www.palauducal.com. 6€, 5€ students and seniors. Mid-June to mid-Sept Mon–Sat 10am–1:30pm and 4–7:30pm (closes 6:30pm mid-Sept to mid-June).

Follow AP-7 south 63km (39 miles) to Altea.

3 kids **Altea.** There's no mistaking Altea, even from a distance. Whitewashed houses run up the hill to **La Mare de Déu del Consol,** a church crowned with blue-and-white-tiled cupolas. The foot of the hill used to be the fishermen's quarter, though these days they share the beach with vacationers. Its relatively short, boulder-strewn beach saved Altea from overdevelopment, making it one of the most laid-back spots on the coast. ⏱ Half-day.

Follow N-332 south for 13km (8 miles) to Benidorm.

4 kids **Benidorm.** By contrast, Benidorm has a gorgeous 5km (3-mile) stretch of beach—and

> The Carthaginians built the Castell de Santa Bárbera.

rooms for 200,000 vacationers. Some of these vacationers, usually on package tours, can get a bit rowdy, but Benidorm has made efforts to rebrand itself as an upmarket destination. Get an overview of the sweep of sea and sand from the "Balcony of the Mediterranean," the plaza atop the rocky Canfali hill that divides the beach in two. Grab an outdoor table at **El Castell**, Plaça del Castell, s/n (☎ 965-860-939), to relax with a *granizado de cafe*. ⏱ Half-day.

Follow the AP-7 south 30km (19 miles) to AP-70. Continue 7km (4⅓ miles) to N-332, and follow it 4km (2½ miles) to Alicante.

❺ ★★ **Alicante.** Most of Costa Blanca is lined with beaches to which towns are attached. Alicante is a city that happens to have terrific beaches (**Playa de Postiguet** downtown, **Playa de Sant Joan** a quick tram ride away). It also has an ancient castle atop the chalky hill of Benacantil, built by Carthaginians as a fortress 2,400 years ago and expanded by Romans, Arabs, and Aragonese. An elevator ascends to the **Castell de Santa Bárbera,** where you can explore the maze of ramparts, breastworks, and dungeons—or simply enjoy the view.

The Old Town, or **Vila Vella,** crouches around the hill's flanks and centers on the **Concatedral de San Nicolás de Bari.** This spare Cistercian Gothic church celebrated its 500th anniversary as a cathedral in 2009.

> Benidorm's Playa de Levante is well prepared for the estimated 180,000 people a day who visit the town's beaches during high season.

A marker on the bottom step of the staircase of the **Ayuntamiento** (town hall) used to be Spain's reference point for measuring heights above sea level. A painting in the stairwell shows carvers creating the remarkable twisted-rope columns on the front facade. The best paintings in town, however, are housed in the **Museo Bellas Artes Gravina,** which chronicles art from the Alicante region over the past 400 years.

Alicante is a delight for walkers, from its palm-shaded, tiled promenade by the sea, the **Explanada de España,** to such banyan-tree-filled squares as **Plaza Gabriel Miró** and **Portal de Elche.** Gaudí-esque benches in colored mosaic tile tempt you to sit in **Plaza Dr. Balmis.** Even the docks are made for walking: The avenue of **Muelle de Levante,** home to the casino and restaurant complex known as El Puerto, reaches into the harbor. Amid the glamour, fishermen still cast from the rocks day and night in a rhythm as old as the tides. Women in caftans and peddlers hawking carvings from Senegal or elsewhere also often populate the waterfront. ⏱ 1 day. Castell: ⏱ 2 hr. Elevator at Avenida Jovellanos, s/n (across from Playa Postiguet). ☎ 965-162-128. Elevator 2.40€, castle free. Oct–Apr daily 10am–8pm; May–Sept 10am–10pm. Concatedral: ⏱ 30 min. Plaza Abad Penalva, s/n. ☎ 965-212-662. Free. Daily 7:30am–12:30pm and 5:30–8:30pm. Ayuntamiento: Plaza Ayuntamiento, 1. ☎ 965-149-100. Free. Mon–Fri 9am–2pm. Museo: C/ Gravina, 13–15. ☎ 965-146-780. www.mubag.com. Free. Mon–Sat 10am–2pm and 4–8pm (closes 9pm May–Sept); Sun 10am–2pm.

Follow N-332 south for 3km (1¾ miles) to the A-70 and continue 13km (8 miles) to CV-85. It's another 3km (1¾ miles) to Elx.

⑥ Elx. The inland city of Elx (Elche in Castilian) is one of the cradles of Iberian civilization. (The 4th-century-B.C. *La Dama d'Elche* statue, discovered in 1897 and now in the National Archaeological Museum in Madrid, rewrote the book on the sophistication of the peninsula's earliest indigenous cultures.) To get a fix on Elx through the millenniums, visit the ★ **Museu Arqueològic i d'Història d'Elx** (MAHE), which tunnels underground from a modern structure to emerge in a historic palace.

La Dama isn't Elx's only madonna. The medieval mystery play about the Assumption known as **Misteri d'Elx** is performed every year (Aug 14–15) in the **Basilica de Santa María,**

> *Gandia's Palau Ducal dels Borja was Pope Alexander VI's family residence.*

complete with flying angels and a liturgy sung in medieval Catalan. Reserve seats in the church far in advance.

Elx is perhaps best known for the extraordinary forest of 200,000 date palms that runs through the city. A walking tour of the historic palm groves extends 2.5km (1½ miles). The **Museu del Palmerar** details how the palms are grown and offers weekday demonstrations of palm-frond weaving. ⏱ 1 day. MAHE: ⏱ 2 hr. Diagonal del Palau, s/n. ☎ 966-658-203. 3€, 1.50€ seniors, 1€ students, free for kids 5 & under, free Sun. Tues–Sat 10am–1:30pm and 4:30–8pm; Sun 10:30am–1:30pm. Basilica: Plaça del Congrés Eucaristic. Daily 7am–1:30pm and 5:30pm–9pm. Palmerar: ⏱ 30 min. Porta de la Morera, 12. ☎ 965-422-240. 1€. Tues–Sat 10am–1:30pm and 4:30–8pm; Sun 10am–1:30pm.

Where to Stay

> A room at Hostal Monges Palace in Alicante.

Belroy BENIDORM
This sleek new facility rethinks the Benidorm hotel model with spacious white rooms, lush baths, and all the high-tech amenities. Avenida Mediterráneo, 13. ☎ 965-850-203. www.belroy. es. 125 rooms. Doubles 115€–210€, with breakfast. MC, V.

Hostal Monges Palace ALICANTE
A family-run hotel, its stylish small rooms are in the heart of historic Alicante, just around the corner from city hall and a 5-minute stroll to the beach. San Agustin, 4. ☎ 965-215-046. www.lesmonges.es. 22 rooms. Doubles 45€–58€. MC, V.

Hotel Altaya ALTEA
This charming small hotel with an excellent dining room stands across the street from Altea's beach. The four superior rooms have balconies facing the ocean. First-come, first-served parking is free. C/ Sant Pere, 28. ☎ 965-840-800. www.hotelaltaya.com. 24 rooms. Doubles 63€–139€. MC, V.

Hotel Cimbel BENIDORM
The classic tower hotel on Playa de Levante was fully renovated in 2006. All the double rooms feature balconies looking at the beach. Avenida Europa, 1. ☎ 965-852-100. www.hotel cimbel.com. 157 rooms. Doubles 108€–185€, with breakfast. AE, DC, MC, V.

★★ **Hotel Huerto del Cura** ELX
Spread out in duplex and triplex bungalows in a palm-forest park, this central Elx (Elche) lodging is quiet and private, and the rooms are, by Spanish standards, huge. Porta de la Morera, 14. ☎ 966-612-050. www.huertodelcura.com. 81 rooms. Doubles 90€–140€. MC, V.

★★★ **Hotel Spa Porta Maris & Suites del Mar**
ALICANTE These two sister properties share a roof and a reception area on the pier next to the cruise port walkway, a 5-minute stroll from Old Town. Porta Maris rooms and suites are a steal for space, comfort, and views. Guests who step up to the Suites del Mar also enjoy an exclusive lounge, a cafe, a pool, and a spa. These are the finest luxury accommodations in Alicante. Plaza Puerta del Mar, 3. ☎ 965-147-021. www.hotelspa portamaris.com. Hotel Spa: 113 standard rooms, 13 junior suites; Suites del Mar: 47 suites. Hotel Spa doubles 80€–145€, suites 116€–185€; Suites del Mar 150€–250€, with breakfast. AE, MC, V.

★★ **Parador El Saler** L'ALBUFERA
This environmentally sensitive low-rise luxury hotel with a superb 18-hole golf course snuggles up to the sea in the middle of L'Albufera Nature Reserve. Avenida Pinares, 151 (km 13 off CV-500), El Saler. ☎ 961-611-186. www.paradores. es. 58 rooms. Doubles 225€–259€. AE, DC, MC, V.

Where to Dine

★ **Casa Carmina** L'ALBUFERA *VALENCIAN*
With only a dozen tables, this in-town eatery
is jammed daily for its fabulous selection of
paellas and other rice dishes featuring shellfish
from the lagoon and fish from the lake.
C/ Embarcadero 4, El Saler. ☎ 961-830-049.
Entrees 14€–22€. MC, V. Lunch Tues–Sun.

★ **Darsena Restaurante** ALICANTE *VALENCIAN*
When locals want a big night out with great
views, they head to Darsena to choose among
170 different rice dishes, including popular duck
and vegetables. Reservations are essential on
weekends. Muelle de Levante, 6. ☎ 965-207-589.
13€–30€. AE, MC, V. Lunch & dinner Mon–Sat,
lunch Sun.

★ **El Cisne de Oro** ALICANTE *SPANISH*
The spectacular old-fashioned tapas bar
decorated with tiles and hung with hams uses
roasted-garlic mayonnaise on many house specialties, including small rolls with sliced pork
and mushroom, or the roasted potato salad.
C/ César Elguezábal, 23. ☎ 965-141-427. Tapas
1.20€–5.10€. Cash only. Lunch & dinner Mon–Sat.

★★ **El Pescador** ALTEA *SEAFOOD*
Paellas, rice soups, and shellfish may top the
menu at this casual eatery across the street from
the beach playground, but the wood-fired grill
also turns out superb hake, tuna, and even beef
steaks. C/ Sant Pere, 24. ☎ 965-842-571. Entrees
10€–19€. MC, V. Lunch & dinner Tues–Sat, lunch Sun.

Kataría Gastronómica BENIDORM *SPANISH*
The contemporary plates are as flavorful as
they are pretty. Basque accents are sprinkled
throughout the menu, such as the pairing of
Gernika peppers with smoked duck or the
addition of salt cod to fried artichokes. The
wine list is extensive, embracing local whites
and roses as well as Jumilla's hearty reds.
Avenida Europa, 5. ☎ 966-831-372. 15€–24€. AE,
DC, MC, V. Lunch Mon–Sun, dinner Mon–Sat.

★★★ **Nou Manolín** ALICANTE *VALENCIAN*
Ferran Adrià of elBulli and French superchef Joël
Robuchon are of the opinion that Nou Manolín
has the best tapas in Spain. Follow their lead
and order the fresh-caught grilled shrimp and
gazpacho—or wait for dinner to enjoy a thick

> *Straight from the sea at El Pescador.*

slab of roasted red tuna or the baked monkfish
and rice. The adjacent fancy cocktail bar (called
NiC) may be even more popular than the
restaurant, thanks to its emphasis on American
cocktails and mixed drinks. C/ Villegas, 3. ☎ 965-
200-368. Entrees 12€–19€. AE, DC, MC, V. Lunch &
dinner daily.

The City of Valencia

This capital of a medieval Mediterranean trade empire emerged from decades of repression under Franco to reimagine itself with some of the world's most exciting civic buildings, a literal river of museums and parks, and a 21st-century transport system. Yet forward-looking Valencia has also cherished its past while building anew. This tour covers the best of both worlds in a week, expanding on "The Best of the City of Valencia in 3 Days" (see p. 512).

> Jaume I's Catedral only took 230 years to finish.

START Colón Metro station to Plaza de la Reina.

1 Plaza de la Reina & Plaza Catalina. These squares in front of the Catedral are the heart of the Old City, and a good place to start exploring. **Off C/ La Paz. Bus: 4, 5b, 6, 8, 9, 11, 16, 28, 36, 70, 71.**

2 Plaza de la Virgen. This square sits on the site of the old Roman forum. People congregate at the cafes ringing the over-the-top Túria fountain. **Off C/ Bailia. Metro: Colón.**

3 Catedral. Built from 1252 to 1482 on the site of the Great Mosque, this Gothic structure has a lovely 18th-century baroque facade. *The Da Vinci Code* aside, the church houses the purported Holy Grail, an agate-and-gold chalice that Christ is said to have used at the Last Supper. Spirited to Spain during the crusades, it was deposited here in the 15th century. ⏱ **30 min. Plaza de la Reina, s/n. ☎ 963-918-127. www.archivalencia.org. Free. Guided visits 4€, 2.70€ students and seniors. Daily 8am–8:30pm; guided visits Mon–Sat 10am–5:30pm, Sun 2–5:30pm. Bus: 4, 5b, 6, 8, 9, 11, 16, 28, 36, 70, 71.**

4 kids El Miguelete. The left door at the main facade of the Catedral leads to El Miguelete, the cathedral's iconic bell tower. Climbing the 207 spiral stairs 51m (167 ft.) to the top rewards you with panoramic views of the city, the port, and the nearby tower of Santa Catalina. ⏱ **1 hr. 2€, 1€ kids 13 & under. Mon–Sat 10am–7pm; Sun 10am–1:30pm and 7–9pm. Bus: 4, 5b, 6, 8, 9, 11, 16, 28, 36, 70, 71.**

5 Plaza Redonda. This 1840 arcaded square slowly undergoing renovation contains ceramics and souvenir shops during the week. The Sunday craft and flea market based here

C/ Manyá

C/ Llano de la Zaidia

C/ Mauro Guillem

Puente
San José

JARDINES
DEL TÚRIA

PONT DE
FUSTA

C/ Cronista Rivelles

Puente de
las Artes

Casa Museo
Benlliure

Puente de
Serranos

Real Monasterio
de la Trinidad

C/ Guillem de Castro

Iglesia del
Carmen

C/ Blanquerias

Museo de
Bellas Artes

C/ Na Jordana

Plaza
Carmen

Torres de
Serranos

Plaza
Fueros

C/ Conde de Trénor

Puente
Trinidad

C/ San Pío V

10   IVAM

9

C/ Salvador Giner

C/ Corona

Centro Cultural
la Beneficencia

C/ Alta

Plaza
Cisneros

LA SEU

C/ Pintor López

11

12
26

C/ Dr. Beltrán Bigorra

C/ Baja

C/ Portal
d. Valldigna

Basílica de Nuestra
Señora de los
Desamparados

C/ Trinitaris

14

EL CARMEN

C/ Caballeros

Plaza
la Virgen

Almudín

Plaza
del Temple

13

C/ Quart

Plaza
Tossal

San
Nicolás

2

Museo de
la Ciudad

25

Torres
de Quart

C/ Murillo

C/ Serranos

Catedral

LA
XEREA

18

C/ Pinto Domingo

C/ Bolsería

15

3

Plaza
Tetuán

C/ Carniceros

16

La
Lonja

Santa
Catalina

Plaza de
la Reina

4

C/ Guillem de Castro

Plaza Don
Juan de
Vilarrasa

Santos
Juanes

7

1

C/ del Mar

17

Santos Tomás y
San Felipe Neri

C/ Balmes

Mercado
Central

5

C/ de la Paz

Jardines
de la
Glorieta

C/ Camarón

Av. María Cristina

20

El Patriarca

C/ Bany

EL
PILAR

6

Museo de
Cerámica

Universidad
de Valencia

19

Iglesia
del Pilar

C/ Tomo d. Hospital

Avenida Barón de Carcer

C/ Músico Peydró

C/ Moratin

Plaza R.
Botet

Plaza Alfonso
El Magnánimo

21

23

C/ Pintor Sorella

C/ Poeta Quintana

COLÓN

C/ Hospital

Vicente Mártir

22

C/ Barcas

C/ Don Juan Austria

C/ Sorni

MUVIM

Ayuntamiento

Plaza
Ayuntamiento

24

C/ Guillén
de Castro

San
Agustín

C/ San

C/ Correos

C/ Sagasta

EL PLA
DEL REMEI

C/ Xátiva

C/ Marqués de Sotelo

C/ Roger
de Llúria

Hernán Cortés

XÁTIVA

C/ Ribera

Paseo Ruzafa

C/ Pascualy Genís

C/ de Colón

Estación
del Norte

C/ Bailén

C/ Alicante

Where to Stay in Valencia
Astoria Palace **23**
40 Flats **25**
Hostal Venecia **22**
Hotel Neptuno **26**
Hotel Petit Palace Bristol **20**
Vincci Palace Valencia **19**

Where to Dine in Valencia
Chust Godoy Restaurante **14**
La Masia del Vino **21**
La Riuà **17**
La Sardinería **15**
Palace Fesol **24**
Restaurante De Ana **18**
Tapa 2 **16**

1 Plaza de la Reina
   & Plaza Catalina

2 Plaza de la Virgen

3 Catedral

4 El Miguelete

5 Plaza Redonda

6 Museo Nacional
   de Cerámica

7 Lonja de la Seda

8 Antiguo Cauce
   del Río Túria

9 Bioparc

10 Instituto Valenciano
   de Arte Moderno

11 Museo de Bellas Artes
   de Valencia

12 Playa de Malvarossa

13 City of Arts & Sciences

0   200 yds
0   200 m

N

> *Near the cathedral, vendors hawk crafts, ceramics, and souvenirs at the "round square," Plaza Redonda.*

spreads into adjacent streets. C/ Derechos. Metro: Colón.

6 ★ **Museo Nacional de Cerámica.** The jaw-dropping alabaster baroque entrance of this museum in the **Palacio del Marqués de Dos Aguas** was carved in the 18th century, while rooms were created in 1867 for the seventh Marqués de Dos Aguas. Half the museum is a reverential showcase of 19th-century noble life, including the marquis's gilded Cinderella carriage. Upper levels contain extensive ceramic collections. The high point is a Valencian kitchen, where tiles depict the chores that would be performed at each station. ⏱ 45 min. C/ Poeta Querol, 2. ☎ 963-516-392.

http://mnceramica.mcu.es. 3€, free for students and seniors, free to all Sat afternoon and Sun. Tues-Sat 10am–2pm and 4–8pm; Sun 10am–2pm. Metro: Colón. Bus: 4, 6, 8, 9, 11, 16, 26, 27, 36, 70, 71.

7 **Lonja de la Seda.** Built in 1492 under master mason Pere Compte as Valencia's silk exchange, this seeming fortress in the heart of the city ranks as one of Europe's finest examples of Gothic civic architecture and is a UNESCO World Heritage Site. The transaction hall is supported by a forest of beautiful twisted-wheat columns, and orange trees and a fountain fill the central courtyard. Children on field trips are invariably amused by the gargoyles flaunting bodily functions. ⏱ 15 min. Plaza Mercado, s/n. ☎ 963-525-478. Free. Tues-Sat 10am–2pm and 4:30–8:30pm; Sun 10am–3pm. Metro: Xàtiva.

8 **Antiguo Cauce del Río Túria.** The Río Túria had circled Valencia for centuries, but the catastrophic floods of 1957 led the city to divert the river underground. The dry bed, in turn, was transformed into a 10km (6¼-mile) parkland around the city center.

9 ★ kids **Bioparc.** Valencia's zoo wins plaudits, even from zoo critics. Still under development, the Bioparc replicates natural habitats of equatorial Africa, the African savannas, and the biologically diverse island of Madagascar. (No

> The grand old silk exchange speaks to Valencia's one-time mercantile wealth.

talking lions or scheming penguins, thank you.) Natural barriers keep big animals and humans safely apart, while permitting comfortably close observation of elephants, giraffes, and lions. There's no keeping playful lemurs at bay—they have the run of the place. ⏱ 3 hr. Avenida Pío Baroja, 3. www.bioparcvalencia.es. 21€, 17€ seniors, 16€ kids. Daily 10am–8pm. Metro: Nou D'Octubre. Bus: 7, 17, 29, 61, 81, 95.

⑩ ★ Instituto Valenciano de Arte Moderno. Spain's first contemporary art museum, IVAM opened in 1989. Paintings and welded iron sculptures by abstract/cubist artist Julio González (1876–1942) anchor the permanent collection, but IVAM's strength lies in temporary exhibitions of the highest quality, displayed in galleries luminous with filtered daylight. Use a separate entrance for the **Sala Muralla,** so-called because it preserves a section of the city's medieval walls.

⏱ 1–2 hr. C/ Guillém de Castro, 118. ☎ 963-889-000. www.ivam.es. 2€, 1€ students, free for seniors, free to all Sun. June–Sept Tues–Sun 10am–10pm; Oct–May Tues–Sun 10am–8pm. Metro: Túr.

⑪ Museo de Bellas Artes de Valencia. This large art museum is strongest in Spanish and Flemish painters, but its local artists are what distinguish the collections—from the so-called "Valencian primitives" of the 14th and 15th centuries to the winsome 20th-century landscapes and portraits by Joaquín Sorolla. ⏱ 1 hr. C/ San Pio V, 9. ☎ 963-870-300. Free. Mon–Sat 10am–8pm. Bus: 1, 6, 8, 11, 16, 26, 29, 36, 80, 95.

⑫ Playa de Malvarossa. Malvarossa is Valencia's most popular summer beach—crowded with swimmers and sunbathers by day, with partygoers at night. Waves are gentle and light brown sands stretch into the distance. Restaurants and bars line the beach at **Paseo Neptuno,** including the legendary **La Pepica** (see p. 523, ⑫). The adjacent **Port America's Cup** was constructed to host Spanish competition for the 2007 and 2009 America's Cup. The striking Veles e Vents building is the work of U.K. architect David Chipperfield. Bus: 1, 2, 19, 20, 21, 22, 23, 32. Metro: Eugenia Viñes.

SITE GUIDE
PAGE 534

⑬ City of Arts & Sciences. Valencia was in luck when it decided to create the dynamic **Ciudad de las Artes y las Ciéncias** on the southern end of the former riverbed of the Río Túria. Native son and renowned architect/engineer Santiago Calatrava outdid himself as the lead designer of the futuristic complex that vaulted Valencia onto the world stage of architecture. The engrossing site includes a planetarium, an aquarium complex, a science museum, and an opera house. ⏱ 1 day.

Travel Tip

The City of Arts & Sciences is located at Avinguda Autopista del Saler (☎ 902-100-031; www.cac.es). Combined admission to the most popular attractions—L'Hemisfèric, L'Oceanogràfic, and Museu de las Ciéncias—is 32€ adults, 24€ seniors and kids 4 to 12. To get to the City, take buses 19, 35, 40, or 95 from the city center, or walk for 30 minutes along the riverbed.

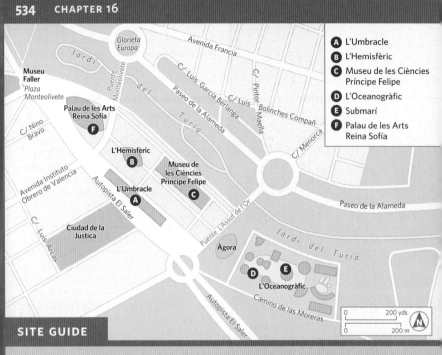

A L'Umbracle
B L'Hemisfèric
C Museu de les Ciències Príncipe Felipe
D L'Oceanogràfic
E Submarí
F Palau de les Arts Reina Sofía

SITE GUIDE

13 City of Arts & Sciences

Tempting as it may be to simply wander the 35-hectare (86-acre) gardenlike site to marvel at the futuristic buildings, Valencia's City of Arts & Sciences is first and foremost a place of "intelligent entertainment," equally engrossing for adults and children. You know you're about to be dazzled when you walk through **A L'Umbracle** (right), an 18m-high (59-ft.) rib cage that functions as the ceremonial entrance. Pause on the garden terrace for an overview of the complex.

Since **B L'Hemisfèric** is partly a planetarium, Santiago Calatrava designed the glass and metal exterior shell of the giant eye-shaped structure to blink like an eyelid—a real eye on the sky. When the "Eye of Wisdom" opened in 1998 as the first structure in the City, it set a high standard of art in the service of science. You'll also find a Laserium and an IMAX cinema where headphones play the soundtrack in your language of choice. Not that you need the words—the panoramic screen speaks for itself.

The largest building of the complex, the **C Museu de les Ciències Príncipe Felipe** science museum could exhaust you (or your kids)

with the number of interactive exhibits. Most are so entertaining that you won't notice you're actually learning principles of science and technology. Imagine flight with a model of Leonardo's flying machine, or let the kids play with insects.

Replicating ocean and shore environments of the poles, the Mediterranean, deep seas, islands, and wetlands, **D** **L'Oceanogràfic,** a cluster of buildings arranged around a lake, is largely underground and air-conditioned, making it a favorite with Valencianos on hot summer days. Even with stiff competition from beluga whales, walruses, and giant ocean sunfish, the bottlenose dolphins make the biggest splash, performing for crowds of more than 2,000 spectators. The magical complex is the final work of Spanish-Mexican architect Félix Candela.

If you want to dine in the Oceanogràfic complex, make reservations at **E** **Submarí,** where tables set with fine linens and crystal are surrounded by eight tanks holding 10,000 fish. Fortunately, the menu has good nonfish dishes such as roasted shoulder of lamb.

With four halls suitable for every kind of performance—from chamber music to theatrical spectacles—Calatrava's 14-story **F** **Palau de les Arts Reina Sofía** performance center is the 2005 capstone to the City of Arts & Sciences, putting the arts front and center. A 230m-long (755-ft.) plumelike roof arches over two steel shells that encase the building, evoking both a giant egg and the wings of a bird. State-of-the-art performance facilities make the center especially suited to grand opera productions, which tend to sell out shortly after the season is announced in the fall. ⏱ 1 day. L'Hemisfèric: ⏱ 2 hr. 7.50€ adults, 5.80€ seniors and kids 4-12. Daily 10am–start of last film. Museu: ⏱ 3 hr. 7.50€ adults, 5.80€ seniors and kids 4-12. Jan-June and mid-Sept to Dec daily 10am-7pm; July to mid-Sept daily 10am-9pm. L'Oceanogràfic: ⏱ 4 hr. 24€ adults, 18€ seniors and kids 4-12. Mid-July to Aug daily 10am–midnight; mid-June to mid-July and early Sept daily 10am-8pm; mid-Sept to mid-June Mon–Fri and Sun 10am-6pm, Sat 10am-8pm. Submarino: ☎ 961-975-565. Entrees 17€-30€. AE, MC, V. Lunch & dinner daily. Palau: Autopista del Saler, 1. ☎ 902-202-383. www.lesarts.com. Box Office: Daily noon-8pm and Sat, Sun, and holidays 3 hr. prior to performance.

Where to Stay

> *Convenience and style at Hotel Petit Palace Bristol.*

Astoria Palace CENTRO
As you might expect from one of Valencia's oldest hotels, the traditional style is a bit faded. But the rooms are large and the location on a quiet plaza near the Ayuntamiento is a good base for exploring. The rooftop gym with sauna and whirlpool is a plus. Plaza de Rodrigo Botet, 5. ☎ 963-981-000. www.hotelastoriapalace.com. 169 rooms. Doubles 135€–250€, with breakfast. AE, DC, MC, V. Bus: 4, 6, 10, 13, 16, 36, 62, 72, 81. Metro: Xátiva.

★ kids **40 Flats** CITY OF ARTS & SCIENCES
The friendly staff and a location just 100m (328 ft.) from the City of Arts & Sciences make these modern apartments a good choice for families. Fully furnished units sleep two to six people. Avenida Instituto Obrero, 20. ☎ 963-356-793. www.40flats.com. 101 rooms. Doubles 50€–145€. AE, DC, MC, V. Bus: 35, 95.

Hostal Venecia CENTRO
This modernized but modest lodging occupies a striking building on one of the city's most beautiful plazas. In fact, some rooms have bird's-eye views of the Plaza del Ayuntamiento. For the price, the location can't be beat. Family rooms are available. C/ En Llop, 5. ☎ 963-524-267. www.hotelvenecia.com. 54 rooms. Doubles 65€–120€. AE, DC, MC, V. Bus: 8, 9, 11, 70, 71. Metro: Xátiva.

★ **Hotel Neptuno** MALVARROSA
The clean lines of the facade hint at the simple and stylish decor of the rooms, all with views of the beach or the Marina Juan Carlos I. A rooftop sun terrace with a tiny pool makes a nice break from the beach. Paseo de Neptuno, 2. ☎ 963-567-777. www.hotelneptunovalencia.com. 48 rooms. Doubles 120€–240€. AE, DC, MC, V. Metro: Neptú.

★ **Hotel Petit Palace Bristol** CENTRO
So that guests can exercise both mind and body, Bristol provides a computer with Internet access in every room and loans bicycles free of charge. The modern sensibility of the hotel fits comfortably into a renovated 19th-century palace right in the heart of the Old City. C/ L'Abadía de San Martín, 3. ☎ 963-945-100. www.hotelpetitpalacebristol.com. 43 rooms. Doubles 75€–140€. AE, DC, MC, V. Bus: 31, 36, 70, 71. Metro: Colón.

★ **Vincci Palace Valencia** CENTRO
Dark, rich fabrics and shiny surfaces create sleek rooms in this ornate in-town palace turned hotel. It's only a 5-minute walk to the Catedral. The lobby coffee and tea bar is a good place to take a break. C/ La Paz, 42. ☎ 962-062-377. www.vinccihoteles.com. 76 rooms. Doubles 80€–130€. AE, MC, V. Metro: Alameda.

Where to Dine

★★ Chust Godoy Restaurante CARMEN
CREATIVE MEDITERRANEAN Star chef Vicente
Chust veers between idiosyncratic versions
of classic dishes (including paella) and sheer
inventions (venison ragout with chocolate and
hazelnuts). Patrons are well-dressed, well-
heeled, and well-fed. C/ Boix 6. ☎ 963-913-815.
Entrees 15€–30€, tasting menus 47€–55€. AE,
DC, MC, V. Lunch Mon–Fri, dinner Mon–Sat. Bus:
2, 80, 95.

La Masia del Vino CENTRO *VALENCIAN*
Hardwood coals make all the difference in this
small spot that is half wine bar, half meat grill.
The *parrillada* (mixed grill) is always a good bet.
C/ Hospital, 16. ☎ 963-921-566. Entrees 11€–19€.
MC, V. Lunch & dinner Mon–Sat. Bus: 5b, 7, 13,
28, 60.

La Riuà CENTRO *VALENCIAN*
This handsome, traditional restaurant is favored
by locals and tourists for its rice dishes, including vegetarian paella. For a change, try the fish
baked in salt. C/ Del Mar, 27. ☎ 963-917-172.
Entrees 10€–25€. MC, V. Lunch & dinner Tues–Sat.
Bus: 31, 36, 70, 71.

★ La Sardinería CENTRO *SEAFOOD*
Who knew sardines could be so big or so tasty?
This small spot has imagined almost every way
to serve them, from steamed with orange and
cinnamon to grilled and served on red peppers
with a fried egg. C/ Bordadores, 10. ☎ 963-914-
313. 7€–12€. AE, MC, V. Lunch & dinner daily. Bus:
4, 5b, 6, 8, 9, 11, 16, 28, 36, 70, 71.

Palace Fesol COLÓN *VALENCIAN*
The century-old "bean palace" has evolved into
an elegant room specializing in time-honored
dishes. That includes rice and, yes, even a few
fava bean dishes. But the waiter will rightly
suggest the catch of the day. C/ Hernán Cortés,
7. ☎ 963-529-323. Entrees 15€–26€. AE, DC, MC,
V. Lunch daily, dinner during Fallas and Féria festivals (see p. 686). Bus: 5. Metro: Colón.

Restaurante De Ana CENTRO *VALENCIAN*
This bright dining room near the Alameda, next
to the city's old granary, makes it a point of

> *The catch of the day at Palace Fesol.*

pride to include traditional fresh snails in the
paella Valenciana. Grilled beef and veal are also
specialties. Plaza Tetuán, 18. ☎ 963-509-109.
Entrees 14€–22€. AE, MC, V. Lunch & dinner daily.
Metro: Alameda.

★ Tapa 2 CARMEN *CREATIVE MEDITERRANEAN*
The hip young chef-owner divides his menu
of imaginative tapas and *raciones* (large-scale
tapas) into vegetarian, meat, and fish plates—
all made from that day's best offerings at
Mercado Central. Open *very* late. C/ Cardá 6.
☎ 963-921-470. 7€–15€. MC, V. Lunch & dinner
daily. Bus: 7, 60, 81.

Travel Tip

For more dining options, see "Gastronomic
Valencia," p. 520.

Valencia Fast Facts

> *Valencia's beaches are easily reached by highway and smaller access roads.*

Arriving & Getting Around

BY PLANE Flights from Spain, the United Kingdom, and other European countries service **Valencia Airport** (☎ 961-598-500), which is located about 8km (5 miles) from the city center. Two subway lines connect to Estación del Norte train station. The Aérobus route concludes at Gran Via Fernando el Católico behind the Estación del Norte. European and Spanish carriers also service the **Alicante Airport** (☎ 966-919-000) in nearby L'Altet, with frequent bus service to downtown Alicante.

BY TRAIN Trains from throughout Spain service the city of Valencia, which is the hub for rail service in the autonomous region. The stunning Modernista **Estación del Norte** (☎ 963-528-573) is located at C/ Xàtiva, 24. Many lines also service Alicante, where the **main station** is located at Avenida Salamanca, 1. BY BUS Buses from throughout Spain, including Barcelona,

Madrid, and Málaga, arrive at Valencia's **Estación de Autobuses** (☎ 963-466-266), located at Avenida Menéndez Pidal, 13. The city of Valencia is well-covered by the five metro lines of **MetroValencia** (☎ 900-461-046; www.metrovalencia.es) and the system's **Tranvia,** or tram service. Metro stations are located throughout the city. The service is supplemented by the extensive **EMT** bus routes (☎ 963-158-515; www.emtvalencia.es). You can pick up most bus lines at Plaza del Ayuntamiento. The Metro normally stops running at 2am but operates continuously during the weeks of the Fallas and Féria festivals (see p. 686). The **Llorente Bus system** (☎ 965-854-322; www.llorentebus.com) provides in-town bus service in the communities of the Costa Blanca, as well as frequent tram service between the beaches of Alicante, Benidorm, and Altea. BY CAR The **AP-7** toll road runs north-south along the coast of the region of Valencia, providing easy connections to Catalunya and France on the north and to Murcia on the south. Well-marked access roads service the beach towns. The newly enlarged **A-23** highway shoots inland from Valencia to Teruel and Zaragoza, while the **A-3** runs between Valencia and Madrid. The **A-31** connects Alicante to Madrid.

ATMs

You'll find 24-hour ATMs throughout the region, even in the smallest villages. Most accept Maestro/MasterCard, Cirrus, and Visa.

Booking Services

The online **Valencia City Guide** (www.valencia-cityguide.com) has an extensive list of hotels and hostels and facilitates online booking.

Doctors & Hospitals

For emergency medical or dental attention, go to the *centro de urgencia* (emergency room) of the nearest hospital. VALENCIA **Hospital Clínico Universitario,** Avenida Blasco Ibáñez, 17 (☎ 963-862-600). Non-E.U. residents can consult national health service doctors for a relatively small fee; ask at your hotel for a list of doctors.

Emergencies

The all-around emergency number in Spain is ☎ **112.** For an ambulance, call ☎ **061.** For national police, call ☎ **091;** for local police, call ☎ **092.**

Internet Access

Wi-Fi has become common in most hotels and is increasingly offered as a free amenity except in business hotels. Hotels without in-room Internet connections may provide access through a public computer. Internet cafes are common; look for a sticker in the window. Long-distance phone shops, called *locutorios,* also usually offer Internet access.

Pharmacies

To find an open pharmacy outside normal business hours, check the list of stores posted on the door of any drugstore. By law, there's always a drugstore open somewhere. Drugstores are called *farmacías.* When open, they display a green neon cross.

Police

Call ☎ **091** for the national police or ☎ **092** for the local police.

Post Office

VALENCIA The main branch in the city is at Plaza Ayuntamiento, 24 (☎ 902-197-197). ALICANTE The main branch is at C/ Arzobispo Loaces, 10 (☎ 902-197-197). Both are open Monday to Friday 8am to 8pm and Saturday 8am to noon. You can also purchase stamps at tobacconist shops, called *estancos.*

Safety

The city of Valencia and the region's other tourist destinations are generally quite safe. Use common sense and avoid deserted streets at night and during afternoon closing hours. Be especially mindful of your belongings when you are in large crowds. Take care not to leave anything visible in a parked car, especially overnight.

Visitor Information

VALENCIA The extremely helpful **Oficina de Turismo** at C/ Paz, 48 (☎ 963-986-422; www.comunitatvalenciana.com), provides information about both the city and the broader region. It's open Monday to Friday 9am to 8pm, Saturday 10am to 8pm, and Sunday 10am to 2pm. ALICANTE **Tourist Info** at Avenida Rambla de Méndez Núñez, 23 (☎ 965-200-000; www.comunitatvalenciana.com), is open Monday to Friday 9am to 8pm, Saturday 10am to 8pm, Sunday 10am to 2pm. ALTEA **Tourist Info** at C/ Sant Pere, 9 (☎ 965-844-114; www.ayuntamiento altea.es), is open Monday to Friday 9:30am to 2pm and 5 to 7:30pm, Saturday 10:30am to 1pm. BENIDORM **Tourist Info** at Avenida Martínez Alejos, 16 (☎ 965-851-313; www.benidorm.org), is open Monday to Friday 9am to 8:30pm, Saturday 10am to 1pm. ELX The excellent regional **Tourist Info** at Plaça del Parc, 3 (☎ 966-658-196; www.comunitatvalenciana.com), is open Monday to Friday 9am to 7pm, Saturday 10am to 7pm, and Sunday 10am to 2pm. GANDIA **Oficina de Turismo** at Avenida Marqués de Campo, s/n (☎ 962-877-788; www.gandiaturismo.com), is open Monday to Friday 9:30am to 1:30pm and 3:30 to 7:30pm, Saturday 9:30am to 1:30pm.

**17
Andalucía**

The Best of Andalucía in 5 Days

In popular imagination, it seems the vast region of Andalucía will forever remain the Moorish world of al-Andalus—no matter that the Christian kings of northern Spain drove the Muslims from it 5 centuries ago. With only 5 days, you owe it to yourself to experience the regal power of Sevilla, the inspirational faith of Córdoba, and the final flowering of Moorish art and architecture that is Granada. The three main cities are well-connected by train service; drivers can easily add a quick en-route visit to the Renaissance city of Jaén.

> PREVIOUS PAGE *A long view of Arcos de la Frontera.* THIS PAGE *La Giralda once called Sevilla's Muslims to prayer.*

START Sevilla. TRIP LENGTH 327km (203 miles).

❶ Sevilla. With 2 days in Sevilla, you'll want to follow the city tour outlined later in this chapter. Perhaps the most symbolic sight in the city is **La Giralda** (see p. 590, ❸): The minaret of the city's great mosque was appropriated to serve as the bell tower for the Christian cathedral and has become the iconic image of the city. The **Catedral** (see p. 590, ❷) itself—the third-largest Gothic cathedral in Europe—was built on the site of the mosque to leave no doubt who the winner was in the epic struggle between Christian and Muslim kings. Yet even the conquering kings couldn't bring themselves to obliterate the beautiful Patio de Naranjas:

The mosque's ablution courtyard, where the faithful washed before prayer, remains an integral and evocative part of the cathedral. The **Real Alcázar** (see p. 591, ❹), however, was the last word about the power and might of the victorious Christian kings. Europe's oldest royal residence still in use (King Juan Carlos stays here when he's in Sevilla) consists of two distinct palaces, several connecting structures, and extensive and beautiful gardens. Focus your time in the Palacio Mudéjar, constructed at the end of the 14th century in much the same style—and, tradition says, by many of the same artisans—as the Alhambra in Granada (see p. 624). Its elaborate decoration and

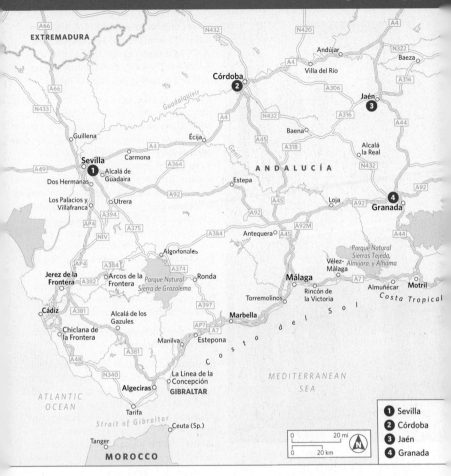

graceful construction hint of things to come. You should still have time to explore the colorful streets of the **Barrio Santa Cruz** (see p. 592, ❻).

Sevilla moved on from its Moorish past more decisively than the other cities of this tour. Since it held a monopoly on trade with the Spanish colonies of the New World, Sevilla grew rich enough from the 16th to the 18th century to practically sink beneath the weight of gold and silver. Great wealth meant a building boom, with plenty of cash left over to patronize the arts. Do not miss the rooms of master paintings, especially those of Francisco Zurbarán, in the **Museo de Bellas Artes** (see p. 593, ❾). And take in the exuberance of Spanish baroque architecture at the **Basílica de Nuestra Señora de la Macarena** (see p. 593,

❿) and the church of **San Luis de los Franceses** (see p. 594, ⓬). ⏱ 2 days. See p. 588.

From Sevilla, follow the A-4 east 130km (81 miles) to Córdoba.

❷ **Córdoba.** The Old City of Córdoba is actually much smaller than it was 1,000 years ago, when it was the most cultured and learned city in Europe and the capital of the Caliphate that ruled al-Andalus. One can only wonder what has been lost, but there is still plenty to see in a very packed day. Start at **La Mezquita** (see p. 630, ❹), the largest mosque ever built in western Europe. The forest of red and white arches vanishing into the distance evokes the ascetic spirituality of a desert people, and it is easy to imagine the majesty of 40,000 worshipers bowing as one toward Mecca.

> THIS PAGE *Córdoba's geranium-scented Calleja de las Flores, "Little Street of Flowers."* OPPOSITE PAGE *A bird's eye view of Jaén.*

The best parts of the **Alcázar de los Reyes Cristianos** (see p. 630, ❺), a palace for the caliphs given a questionable gut renovation by Fernando and Isabel, are the Arabic baths in the cellars (which they left alone) and the grand formal gardens, constructed long after their time. Concentrate instead on wandering the twisting narrow alleys of the **Judería,** where several sites evoke the heyday of Córdoba, when philosophers like Moses Maimonides and Averroes walked these same streets. Quick visits to the **Casa de Sefarad** (see p. 631, ❾) and its counterpart, the **Casa Andalusí** (see p. 631, ❿), will illuminate daily life in the 12th century for Córdoban Jews and Muslims, respectively. ⏱ 1 day. See p. 628.

From Córdoba, follow the E-5/A-4 east for 53km (33 miles) to exit 346. Go south on A-6175 for 16km (10 miles), then east on A-306 for 27km (17 miles), until it merges with A-316. Jaén is just 13km (8 miles).

❸ **Jaén.** Jaén was transformed in the late 15th to 17th centuries into a showpiece of Renaissance architecture. It's worth taking a couple of hours to stop over on your way to Granada to see the **Catedral de Jaén** (see p. 586, ⓫), the greatest surviving work of Andrés Vandelvira, arguably the greatest Spanish architect of the Renaissance. He inherited a work in progress that was not finished until centuries after his death. Yet Vandelvira's inspirational handling of harmonious space and his penchant for full, soft light stamp the building with his genius. It's also worth driving uphill to the **Castillo de Santa Catalina** (see p. 587, ⓬), a largely Christian fortress high on the mountain overlooking Jaén. It was the vanguard defense on the border between Christian Spain and Moorish Granada for more than 2 centuries. ⏱ 2 hr.

From Jaén, follow the A-44 south for 88km (55 miles) to Granada.

❹ **Granada.** It is no coincidence that modern Granada joyfully embraces its native son, poet Federico García Lorca, and his composer friend, Manuel de Falla. Easily the most lyrical city in Andalucía, it is also the city of what might have been: Through the 5-century battle of the Christian Reconquista, Muslim Granada outlasted the rest of al-Andalus by more than 250 years, falling finally on January 2, 1492, when Fernando and Isabel entered the city and Boabdil (Mohammed XII) left for exile in North Africa. Boabdil took his ancestors' bones with him, but he left behind the magnificent palaces and fortress of the **Alhambra and Generalife** (see p. 624), one of the most beautiful castles in the world. (You should reserve at least a day to see it.) The winners of the religious war, Fernando and Isabel, are entombed in considerable splendor in the **Capilla Real** (see p. 612, ❸), adjacent to the hulking **Catedral** (see p. 610, ❷). You should still have part of your second day in Granada left to stroll up **Carrera del Darro** (see p. 613, ❼), visit the **Baños Árabes** (see p. 613, ❽), and wander the magically medieval Arabic warren of the **Albaicín** (see p. 614, ⓬). ⏱ 2 days. See p. 610.

The Best of Andalucía in 10 Days

No doubt your head is spinning from those first 5 days touring the Moorish highlights of Spain. For the next 5 days, you'll get some R&R on the beach by spending 2 days in ancient Almuñécar with a side visit to Nerja, a day in Málaga to shop and see the Picasso sights, and 2 days on the Costa del Sol working on your tan.

> The view from Punta de la Mona, near Almuñécar, to the bay of La Herradura (The Horseshoe) on the Costa Tropical.

START From Granada, follow A-44 south for 55km (34 miles) to the A-7, in the direction of Málaga. Watch for signs to N-340 and follow it 10km (6N miles) to Almuñécar. **TRIP LENGTH** 524km (326 miles), including "The Best of Andalucía in 5 Days."

1 Almuñécar. The first thing you might notice about the beach at Almuñécar is that it rattles. Waves set its smooth and rounded stones tumbling one over the other. Yet the stoniness of the strand deters neither sunbathers nor swimmers. Nor does it stop the *churrerías* (*churro*, or

fried dough, sellers) from setting up shop early in the morning when only fishermen and the odd insomniac British pensioner are around. By the time the beachgoers arrive, the air is sizzling with the aroma of hot oil and great hoops of *churros*.

Almuñécar has a grace unmatched by Andalucía's other beach resorts, perhaps because it has built parks and promenades around its historic ruins just steps from the beach. Between stretches of sunning or walking the beach, visit the **Castillo San Miguel** to

Map legend:
1. Almuñécar
2. Cueva de Nerja
3. Nerja
4. Málaga
5. Fuengirola
6. Mijas Pueblo

understand the Moorish history; then dig back into the Phoenician and Roman eras at the **Museo Arqueológico.** You can't help but notice the adjacent pits of the Roman-period factory for making fermented fish paste, an industry the Phoenicians launched in Almuñécar. See p. 573, ②.

Nerja is just 24km (15 miles) west of Almuñécar on the A-7 highway, the Autopista Mediterráneo.

② Cueva de Nerja. Nerja makes a good half-day excursion from Almuñécar. Before you enter the village, stop east of town to visit this interpretive center for one of the more spectacular geological discoveries in recent years. Inside the series of subterranean chambers, it's hard to tell if the natural rock formations or the archaic human art on the walls is the more remarkable. See p. 557, ⑥.

③ Nerja. Visitors to Nerja say it looks and feels different than the rest of Andalucía, and they're right. An earthquake leveled most of the town in 1884, so Nerja is not overburdened by the ancient past. Think "Victorian" and you'll understand the tidy, rather formal plaza known as the **Balcón de Europa** that is perched

> The massive stalactites and stalagmites of Nerja's caves were discovered by spelunkers in 1959.

on a hill overlooking the sea. The square also serves as a handy meeting place for parties that split up to go shopping in the narrow, pre-earthquake streets. Among the stones on the tiny beach below the Balcón are almost gemlike pieces of polished sea glass. See p. 574, ③.

Málaga is just 75km (47 miles) west of Almuñécar on the A-7 highway, the Autopista Mediterráneo.

4 Málaga. Málaga's fine beaches are often overshadowed by the Costa del Sol, easily accessible by bus or train. But the buses and trains run both ways, and visiting this compact city can add a touch of urban sophistication to a beach vacation. Pablo Picasso was born here and spent many of his formative years in Málaga. Start stalking the giant of 20th-century art by visiting the **Casa Natal de Picasso** (see p. 652, **2**), the home where he was born. Looking at his swaddling clothes in a glass case tends to cut the legend down to size. The major attraction, of course, is the **Museo Picasso Málaga** (see p. 654, **4**), one of the institutions established by his heirs and endowed with a core collection drawn from works that Picasso had withheld from sale over the decades. Few artists were so prolific that their works could fill as many dedicated museums, but every piece here maintains Picasso's high standard. Excavations in the cellar during renovations uncovered Phoenician and Roman ruins, now conserved as their own exhibition.

What Picasso loved about Málaga was its rhythm. Indeed, as you walk from neighborhood to neighborhood, the beat changes. Plaza de la Merced, where the **Picasso statue** (see p. 652, **1**) sits, has a formal clip-clop pace as people stride purposefully across it. C/ Granada and C/ San Agustín, which link Merced to Plaza Constitución, call for a stutter-step to navigate around fellow pedestrians in narrow passages. But **C/ Marqués de Larios** (see p. 656, **10**) calls for a strut. The broad promenade is lined with the city's best boutiques and features its best street performers. Every few strides there's a side street with a little cafe where you can duck in for coffee, chocolate, or tapas. See p. 652.

From Málaga, follow the A-7 west for 33km (21 miles) to Fuengirola.

5 Fuengirola. Every community on the Costa del Sol has a beautiful beach, so it can be hard to choose where to base yourself for the last 2 days of this leg of your trip. Fuengirola's advantages include easy public transportation to Málaga and to the nearby striking mountain village of Mijas. The harbor is also a center for watersports: Head to the Puerto Deportivo to book a sightseeing cruise along the coast, zoom around in a powerboat, or parasail. It's also worth strolling the promenade to the cable-stay bridge leading to **Castillo Sohail**

> *Málaga is the cultural capital of the Costa del Sol, and C/ Marqués de Larios is its social center.*

fortress. You should definitely make time to visit the **Fuengirola Zoo** (see p. 571, ❼), one of the best zoo facilities in Europe. The Costa del Sol's warm climate allows the zoo to focus on tropical rainforest habitats in Africa and Asia. See p. 566, ❸.

Save the aggravation (and time) of driving. Buses from the Fuengirola bus station run every 30 min. between Fuengirola and Mijas Pueblo.

❻ **Mijas Pueblo.** You'll barely leave the beach behind before you arrive in Mijas Pueblo, a small community perched high on the mountainside. The picturesque town with buildings so old that whitewash has rounded their corners is an attraction in itself—a welcome contrast to the sprawl of the beach communities. Enjoy Mijas Pueblo by visiting the **Ermita de la Virgen de la Peña** church (see p. 571, ❾) and strolling along the edges of the village belvedere. You could even spring for a **donkey taxi** (see p. 571, ❽) to haul you around the village to see the sights. Unless you've already purchased bullfight tickets in advance, don't plan on visiting Mijas on a Saturday between May and October, when buses from all over the Costa del Sol bring in fans for the *corridas* (fights). On any other day, tour the **oval bullring,** built in 1900. Bullring: Plaza de Toros. ☎ 952-485-852. 3€. Sun–Fri 10am–2pm and 5–7pm.

> ABOVE *The Museo Picasso in the artist's home-town, Málaga.* BELOW *Better than a cab in Mijas.*

The Best of Andalucía in 15 Days

For your final 5 days, you'll complete the trifecta of

Andalucían attractions. You've toured the haunting Moorish glories and enjoyed the sun-splashed beaches. Now it's time to investigate the mountain villages of Ronda and the Pueblos Blancos, or White Towns. Then return to sea level to spend your last 3 days on the dry plains, where sherry springs from tough vines, and in the watery world of the beautiful bay that surrounds the ancient city of Cádiz.

> *The white town of Ronda, overlooking a deep river gorge, was once a hide-out for smugglers and bandits.*

START From Fuengirola, follow the AP-7, in the direction of Algeciras, for 41km (25 miles) to exit 172. Continue 45km (28 miles) on A-397 to Ronda. **TRIP LENGTH** 766km (476 miles), including the previous two tours.

1 Ronda. Because Ronda is so close to the Costa del Sol, most people make it a day trip. The outdoor tables of its restaurants are generally buzzing on a warm afternoon, then only half full at dinnertime. You should treat yourself to an overnight stay to experience the changing faces of Ronda. It's only a slight exaggeration to say that the entire city is one big belvedere. It stands 120m (394 ft.) above the valley floor on a limestone escarpment that is sliced in two by the Río Guadalevín. On one side, streets twist like ancient vines around the escarpment to form La Ciudad, the ancient Iberian settlement modified by the Romans and built to medieval glory by the Moors. The other side of **El Tajo gorge** (see p. 636, **1**) is a post-16th-century

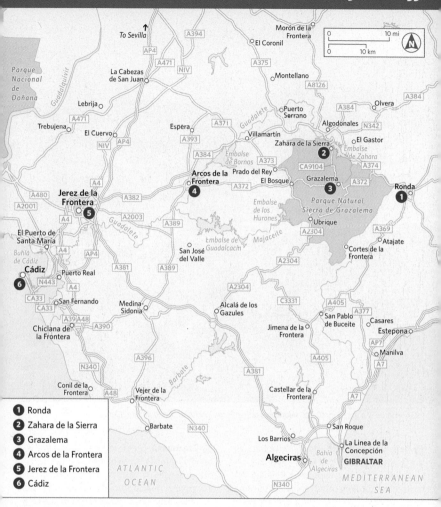

1 Ronda
2 Zahara de la Sierra
3 Grazalema
4 Arcos de la Frontera
5 Jerez de la Frontera
6 Cádiz

district laid out on a grid and known as **El Mercadillo.** On either side, you are never far from an overlook with long vistas of rich farmland stretching toward distant mountains.

Two palaces in La Ciudad recapture Ronda's long history. The **Casa Palacio del Gigante** (see p. 638, ❼) is a cultural-history museum emphasizing the Moorish period—appropriate in a Nasrid palace roughly contemporaneous with the Alhambra in Granada. City Hall operates out of the elegant **Palacio de Mondragón** (see p. 638, ❽), but you're less likely to run into politicians than brides and grooms posing happily in this stunning setting perched at the edge of the gorge.

Ronda is also revered among bullfight aficionados for its historic bullring, the **Plaza de Toros** (see p. 639, ❾), where you can walk on the sands of the arena and imagine the air charged with adrenaline. Finally, don't miss the **Museo del Bandolero** (see p. 640), which tells the tale of bandits who ruled the mountains west of town until they were largely exterminated during the Civil War. (The last bandit died in 1934 after serving 2 decades in jail.) See p. 636.

Follow the A-374 northwest for 34km (21 miles) to Algodonales; then follow signs to CA-9104. It's a twisting drive south for 9km (5⅗ miles) to Zahara de la Sierra.

> *Grazalema is a gateway to the mountains of the Parque Natural Sierra de Grazalema.*

2 Zahara de la Sierra. Today's drive through the Sierra de Grazalema Natural Park is a chance to experience southwest Andalucía's most dramatic landscapes, ending at the small town of Zahara, perched high above the upland plateau. You'll want to stop at the edge of the reservoir beneath it to take a photograph of the whitewashed buildings huddling around a peak, with the ruins of a forbidding brown castle towering above it all. It's a perfect example of a typical Pueblo Blanco, or White Town. Once you actually enter the town, it's a 15-minute uphill walk on a zigzag trail to reach the **Castillo.** You'll be happy to have a small flashlight to negotiate the stone stairs of its tower, but once you reach the top, you'll have a commanding panorama of the surrounding mountain passes. See p. 559, **3**.

Continue south on CA-9104 for 16km (10 miles) to Grazalema.

3 Grazalema. Green and wet, Grazalema is an anomaly among the White Towns, as it sprawls in a river valley instead of clinging to a hillside. Principally a staging ground for hikers heading into the **Parque Natural Sierra de Grazalema** (see p. 557, **4**), the genial small town also has a substantial population of artists, artisans, and New Age farmers. Stop for a coffee or a beer in one of the cafes on Plaza Andalucía or Plaza España, and you'll almost certainly overhear hikers recounting their latest adventures in the surrounding hills. See p. 560, **5**.

Follow the A-372 west for 30km (19 miles) to Arcos de la Frontera.

4 Arcos de la Frontera. The western gateway between the Sierra de Grazalema and the plain leading down to Jerez de la Frontera, Arcos is another unusual community. It was nearly leveled by the Lisbon earthquake of

1755. Unable to anticipate the need for roads wide enough to accommodate automobiles, the nobles simply rebuilt, placing neoclassical palaces on the medieval street plan. The main square at the top of the town, **Plaza del Cabildo,** has it all—an ancient church, a castle turned into a private residence, a *mirador* (vantage point) with long views, and the historic palace turned into the beautiful *parador* (state-run hotel) where you should spend the night. See p. 561, ❻.

From Arcos, follow the A-382 west for 33km (20 miles) to Jerez de la Frontera.

❺ **Jerez de la Frontera.** It is amazing that the dry plains around Jerez can produce enough grapes to fill the bodegas and warehouses that produce the wine named for the place. Don't leave Jerez without seeing the sherry production, by visiting either the industrial giant **González Byass** (see p. 648, ❹) or the upmarket boutique producer **Bodegas Tradición.** The area around Jerez is also famous for breeding the Andalucían horse, or Pura Raza Española, as it is called in Spain. These magnificent creatures (and their riders)

are trained at the **Fundación Real Escuela Andaluza del Arte Ecuestre** (see p. 649, ❽). If you aren't in town for one of the performances of the dancing horses on a Tuesday or Thursday, try to catch the training sessions. Since you'll spend 2 nights in Jerez, be sure to explore the Plaza Arenal and side streets for the lively bar and tapas scene, and perhaps a little impromptu flamenco. See p. 646.

From Jerez de la Frontera, take the A-2004 toward the AP-4 for 5km (3 miles). Follow the AP-4 toward Cádiz for 25km (16 miles), connecting to the N-433 to Cádiz. You'll enter the city in 9km (5⅔ miles).

❻ **Cádiz.** Because it sits on a thin peninsula, the sea surrounds graceful Cádiz. Stroll its busy port district with enticing restaurants and perambulate the promenades and parks that line the seafront. Be sure to see the Phoenician sarcophagi in the **Museo de Cádiz** (see p. 644, ❼). After all, the Phoenicians founded the town 3,100 years ago, making Cádiz the oldest city in Europe. See p. 642.

> *Enjoy the oldest city in Europe with a stroll along Cádiz's leafy Alameda Marqués de Comillas.*

Andalucía's Natural Landscapes

Andalucía's gentle hills and great mountain ranges are mute testimony to the tectonic collision between North Africa and Europe 20 million years ago. You are never far from a mountain or a rocky outcrop—and wherever you travel, the landscape always seems larger than life. But if you really want to be wowed, check out these natural areas with some of the region's most distinctive geological marvels.

> The almost lunar landscape of El Torcal, Andalucía's first natural park, is a great day trip from Málaga.

START From Málaga, follow A-357 west for 49km (30 miles) to the exit for MA-444. Turn left and continue 5km (3 miles) to MA-448. Turn right and follow signs to Garganta del Chorro. Continue past the dam and lake and turn left to the parking lot. Follow the right side of the lake on foot. There is no visitor center. TRIP LENGTH 287km (178 miles).

① ★ **Garganta del Chorro.** Over the eons, wind and water have eroded the limestone hills northwest of Málaga, creating a series of striking rock formations. The Río Guadalhorce

has cut the most dramatic gash of all: a 4km (2½-mile) gorge that reaches 400m (1,312 ft.) deep yet is only 10m (33 ft.) wide in places. The walls of the Chorro are nearly sheer verticals, making it Andalucía's premier rock-climbing destination. Nonclimbers can walk along the river, observing both the geology and the railroad trestles and tunnels of the Málaga–Sevilla line. A decaying concrete catwalk about 100m (328 ft.) above the river is known as Camino del Rey because Alfonso XIII walked it in 1921. The walkway was officially closed in 1992 but daredevils still use it. ⏱ 1 hr.

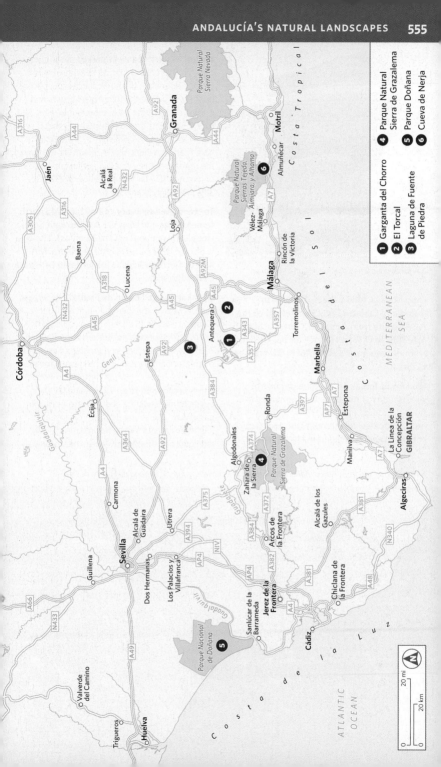

> *A precarious limestone formation at El Torcal.*

From Málaga, follow the A-45 north to Antequera (about 52km/32 miles), then the A-343 south from Antequera, then local road MA-3310 to El Torcal (watch for brown signs). From Antequera, it's about 16km (10 miles) to El Torcal.

❷ ★★★ El Torcal. These bone-dry hills of wind-sculpted limestone were protected as Andalucía's first natural park in 1929. An excellent road winds through the landscape of twisted and serrated forms to the **visitor center,** where three well-marked paths circle through the rocks. Some 30 species of wild orchids flourish in the harsh landscape, falcons hunt for lizards in the thin desert brush, and griffin vultures float on overhead thermals. The rock formations are so otherworldly that it's no surprise that more UFO sightings are reported here than anywhere else in Spain. Do *not* leave the marked paths—you can get lost in a matter of minutes. ⏱ 2 hr. Visitor Center: ☎ 952-031-389. Free. Daily 10am–5pm.

To reach the sanctuary, follow the A-45 north from Malaga and then the A-92 toward Sevilla (for a total of about 60km/37 miles). The lake is next to the exit for Fuente de Piedra. MA-454 to Sierra de Yeguas from Fuente de Piedra circles the lake.

❸ ★ Laguna de Fuente de Piedra. The largest natural lake on the Iberian Peninsula, Fuente de Piedra stretches 16 sq. km (6 sq. miles) when swollen by winter rains. Brine shrimp flourish in the hypersaline water, nourishing thousands of greater flamingos that come from Africa to breed. The birds construct flattened muddy cones in the knee-deep waters and lay their eggs on these nesting posts in late April and early May. The young fledge in August and join their parents for the return to Africa. By late summer, the shallow lake is nearly dry.

> *After a long trip from Africa, flamingos wade in the shallow waters of Laguna de Fuente de Piedra.*

Although a high fence surrounds the sanctuary, the sight of the sea of pink birds is stunning. Bring binoculars or a long telephoto camera lens to observe the flamingos or any of 170 species of wading birds and waterfowl. ⏱ 2 hr. Interpretation Center: Cerro del Palo, off MA-454 outside Fuente de Piedra village. ☎ 952-111-715. Free. Tues–Sun 9am–2pm and 4–7pm.

From Málaga, follow MA-5404 south 7km (4⅓ miles) to A-384 west. In 50km (31 miles), turn south on A-2300 to Zahara de la Sierra.

❹ ★★ **Parque Natural Sierra de Grazalema.** Botanists are particularly fascinated by the reserve of *Abies pinsapo,* an Ice Age Spanish fir once thought extinct. The towering trees grow at the uppermost reaches of the tree line, and guided hikes to this part of the park (about 6 hr. round-trip) can be arranged in Grazalema and Zahara de la Sierra. Heavy rainfall has carved the limestone mountains of the 534-sq.-km (206-sq.-mile) park to create rocky ridges, green valleys, gorges, waterfalls, and deep underground caverns—terrain for virtually any type of activity. Hiking trails are detailed on the topographic map available at information centers. Staff can advise on other outdoor adventures. These knowledgeable outposts should be your first stop before venturing into the wilderness: **Centro de Visitantes Zahara Catur,** Zahara de la Sierra (see p. 559, ❸); **Pinzapo,** Grazalema (see p. 560, ❺); and **Horizon Aventura,** C/ Corrales Terceros, 29, Grazalema (☎ 956-132-363; www.horizonaventura.com), which is a more extreme outfitter that can arrange hikes and canoe trips in the reserve area as well as rock climbing, cycling, and caving expeditions elsewhere in the park. ⏱ 6 hr.

From Grazalema, continue west on A-372 to Arcos de la Frontera and pick up A-382 west for 24km (15 miles). Merge onto A-4, and then take exit 641 onto A-480, continuing 20km (12 miles) to Sanlúcar de la Barrameda.

❺ ★★ **Parque Doñana.** The estuarine system at the mouth of the Río Guadalquivir is more than just pretty marshes. It sustains the Bay of Cádiz shellfishery, creates the climate for making sherry, and literally keeps millions of birds alive on their annual migrations between Europe and Africa. It is also rich with resident storks, egrets, herons, and songbirds. On Bajo

> *The Cueva de Nerja has galleries up to 60m (200 ft.) high, some featuring prehistoric drawings.*

de Guia beach in Sanlúcar de la Barrameda (see p. 583, ❸), the interpretive center at the **Fábrica de Hielo** explains the marshes, shifting sands, and stabilized dunes of the complex ecosystem. The center books 2½-hour riverboat trips into the park with two stops for guided walks. ⏱ 2½ hr. Fábrica de Hielo: ☎ 956-381-635. Free. Daily 9am–8pm. Riverboat trips Nov–Feb daily 10am; Mar–May and Oct daily 10am and 4pm; June–Sept daily 10am and 5pm. 16€ adults, 8.10€ seniors and kids, 33€ families.

Take the exit from A-7/N-340 Autopista Mediterráneo, 4km (2½ miles) east of Nerja.

❻ ★ **Cueva de Nerja.** Visit this complex of deep caves to see the gigantic stalactites and stalagmites formed by subterranean mineral deposits. The underground complex, discovered in 1959, holds other treasures: A few chambers contain human drawings of horses, deer, handprints, dancing stick figures, and other graffiti, apparently painted over tens of thousands of years. All visits are guided, and the wait between groups can be long. Fortunately, the cafe on the grounds has superb views of the ocean. ⏱ 2 hr. Carretera de Maro (4km/2½ miles east of town). ☎ 952-529-520. www.cuevadenerja.es. 8.50€ adults, 4.50€ kids 6–12. July–Aug daily 10am–7:30pm; Sept–June daily 10am–2pm and 4–6:30pm.

Ronda & the White Towns

Perched high above a river gorge, Ronda is the starting point for a driving trip through the Sierra de Grazalema mountain range—an outsized crumple of planetary crust where Europe and Africa last danced the tectonic bump. One mountain ridge rises behind another, and most of the whitewashed villages cling to the rough security of their peaks. For 2 millennia, these mountains were the place of legend: the realm of warlords and highwaymen, the frontier of the epic struggle between Moors and Christians, and a rare Republican stronghold during the Spanish Civil War.

> *The Puente Nuevo is one of three bridges that span the Guadalevín River gorge that divides Ronda.*

START **Ronda.** TRIP LENGTH **55km (34 miles).**

1 ★★★ **Ronda.** The largest of the White Towns, Ronda clings to a high escarpment split in two by the Río Guadalevín. On one side, the narrow medieval streets of the Old Town twine around the massif like a strangler fig tree. On the other, a high plateau supports the "new" town. You get a stomach-dropping view

from the **Centro de Interpretación del Puente Nuevo** (see p. 637, **6**), suspended 120m (394 ft.) above the gorge. Visit the restored Nasrid-style **Casa Palacio del Gigante** (see p. 638, **7**) for background on Moorish Ronda, then the elegant **Palacio de Mondragón** (see p. 638, **8**) to get a sense of just how graceful a palace on the edge of the gorge can be. Exhibits at the **Museo del Bandolero** (see p. 640) tell

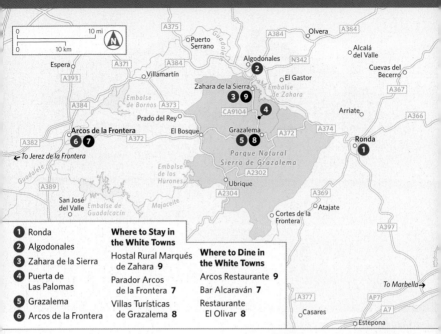

Ronda
1. Ronda
2. Algodonales
3. Zahara de la Sierra
4. Puerta de Las Palomas
5. Grazalema
6. Arcos de la Frontera

Where to Stay in the White Towns
Hostal Rural Marqués de Zahara 9
Parador Arcos de la Frontera 7
Villas Turísticas de Grazalema 8

Where to Dine in the White Towns
Arcos Restaurante 9
Bar Alcaraván 7
Restaurante El Olivar 8

the exploits of the brigands who roamed the hills west of Ronda from the Roman era into the early 20th century. When you hit the road, you'll encounter motorcycle drivers who channel that untamed spirit by leaning into hairpin turns at lightning speed. ⏱ 1 day. See p. 636.

Follow the A-374 northwest for 34km (21 miles) to Algodonales. (The road becomes the A-384 at Algodonales.)

2 **Algodonales.** The village calls itself Puerta de la Sierra (Gateway to the Mountains), but for one group of adventurers it's the gateway to the sky. Windy Algodonales was discovered by paragliders about a decade ago and has become Spain's paragliding capital. Residents of the small, traditional community are quite amused by the daredevils. **Fly Spain** runs beginner and advanced paragliding courses here. Fly Spain: C/ Sierra, 41. ☎ 651-736-718. www.flyspain.co.uk. 5-day beginner course with lodging and airport transfer 846€–960€. Tandem flights from 120€ for 30–60 min.

Travel Tip

For additional information on sights, shops, and recommended hotels and restaurants in Ronda, see p. 636.

> Fountains and horseshoe arches grace the Moorish courtyards of Ronda's Palacio de Mondragón.

Follow signs to CA-9104 and twist southward 9km (5⅔ miles) to Zahara de la Sierra.

3 ★★ **Zahara de la Sierra.** Easily one of Spain's most picturesque villages, Zahara circles the peak of a high mountain with the romantic ruins of a 13th- to 15th-century Nasrid castle at the top. The **Torre del Homenaje,** the central tower of the **Castillo,** stands 605m (1,985 ft.) above sea level. From the village,

> *A Nasrid castle crowns the hill above Zahara de la Sierra like a wedding cake topper.*

a graded track leads to the castle, where the massive iron door is usually closed but rarely locked. Once you climb the stone stairs to the top, you'll appreciate the location: You can see your enemies approaching from a day's march away in every direction.

Zahara is one of the chief access points for hikes in the **Parque Natural Sierra de Grazalema** (see p. 557, ❹). The **Centro de Visitantes Zahara Catur** provides information on the park and can arrange a variety of outings, including all-terrain vehicles (from 40€), canoeing (from 11€), hiking (from 13€), and horseback riding (from 18€).

Just south of the village, the modern-looking **El Vínculo** oil mill actually dates from 1755. Displays explain how olive oil is produced from picking to pressing to bottling. In harvest season you can see the milling; any time of year you can taste distinctive extra-virgin oils pressed from the Manzanillo and Lechín varieties. Castillo: ⌚ 1 hr. Zahura Catur: Plaza del Rey, 3. ☎ 956-123-114. www.zaharacatur.com. Daily 9am–2pm and 4–7pm. El Vínculo: ⌚ 45 min. Carretera Zahara-Grazalema, s/n. ☎ 956-123-002.

Continue south on CA-9104 for 16km (10 miles) toward Grazalema.

❹ **Puerta de Las Palomas.** The route from Zahara to Grazalema is possibly the most dramatic stretch of road in these dramatic mountains. The road climbs swiftly to the Puerta de Las Palomas, or Pass of the Doves, at 1,356m (4,450 ft.). Just as your ears pop, you start spiraling downhill to Grazalema.

❺ ★★ **Grazalema.** The wettest town in Spain, receiving 2,160 millimeters (85 in.) of rain a year, Grazalema nestles in a green valley—suddenly appearing out of nowhere when you round a curve. The Berber farmers who settled here in the 8th century never fortified their town, so warring Moorish and Christian armies simply passed it by. That live-and-let-live attitude still persists, and a substantial backpacker contingent shows up here in the summer. So do serious hikers bound for the high-altitude preserve of *Abies pinsapo,* an Ice Age fir tree once thought extinct. Guided walks for more casual nature lovers are available through **Pinzapo Interpretación Ambiental Grazalema.**

Grazalema's main square, **Plaza Andalucía,** is lined with cafes and bars that make good spots to kick back after a gnarly day on the trails. As you might expect in a town where hippies flocked a generation ago, Grazalema is full

> *Restaurants, shops, and hikers occupy Plaza España, one of Grazalema's two main squares.*

of artisans and back-to-the-land farmers. One of the best artisan shops is **Taller de Cerámica La Jara,** C/ Agua, 19 (☎ 956-132-075), which sells ceramics decorated with images of the flora of Sierra Grazalema park. **Panadería Todo Sierra,** Plaza Andalucía, 23 (☎ 956-132-415), offers one-stop shopping for local mountain foods, including sheep and goat cheeses, fresh bread and pastries, local olive oil, and bulk sherry from the cask. Pinzapo Interpretación: C/ Las Piedras, 11. ☎ 956-132-166. Guided hikes July–Aug Tues–Sun; May–June and Sept Sat–Sun. Group hikes 10€–15€. Also issues permits for restricted areas of park.

Follow the A-372 west through deep forest for 10km (6¼ miles) to El Bosque, where it becomes open road over the outwash plain for another 20km (12 miles) west to Arcos de la Frontera.

⑥ ★★ Arcos de la Frontera. As the name suggests, Arcos spent 5 centuries on the disputed borderland between Christian and Muslim Spain. The fortress city sits atop a rocky peak surrounded by the Río Guadalete. Author González Ruano (1903–65) observed that Arcos's steep maze of streets opening

into orderly squares "embody the essence of all Andalucía." The families who built the in-town palaces were nobles (Alfonso X knighted the whole village in 1255 to keep them in the Christian fold), but only a few current buildings predate the 1755 earthquake. When disaster struck, the wealthy cork and wine merchants maintained the medieval street plan but rebuilt the city with stately neoclassical palaces. The resulting old quarter exudes sheer lyrical beauty, making Arcos a city of interior patios cool with shade and bright with flowers.

Plaza del Cabildo at the summit is surrounded by beautiful buildings that are testaments to wealth, power, and faith. A 15th-century Arabic fortress is now a private ducal residence, while the 1635 duke's residence has been turned into the Ayuntamiento (Town Hall) and tourist office. A striking statue of patron saint San Miguel (archangel Michael) stands above the town hall door. The massive **Santa María de la Asunción** church, closed indefinitely for repairs, is a classic example of building on the bones of one's enemies. The 13th-century church sits on the ruins of a mosque which sits in turn on a 7th-century Latin-Byzantine church. One of Spain's loveliest *paradores* (see p. 563) rounds out the

> *ABOVE The Muslim fortress of Arcos de la Frontera sits high above the former border town. BELOW The Plaza del Cabildo.*

architecture. One side of the plaza remains open to the **Balcon de Arcos,** also called **Mirador de la Peña Nueva,** which looks across the river valley far below the city. Stunning at any hour, it turns magical at dusk when swallows dart along the cliff walls.

From the plaza, follow C/ Escribanos past the **Convento de las Mercedarías Descalzas** (where you can buy cookies from a *retorno,* or revolving window, weekdays 10am–2pm) to Plaza Boticas, site of the city market. Turn down C/ Oliveras Veras to reach the head of **C/ Maldonado,** a street celebrated by poets for its beautiful courtyards. You can finally get a look at some of those courtyards at the **Palacio de Mayorazgo.** Behind the palace are the **Jardines Andalusí,** formal plantings amid beautiful tilework and fountains. If you follow C/ Abades steeply downhill, you will wind up at the **Mirador de Abades,** a scenic overlook where you can look across the countryside or crane your neck to see ancient Arcos towering on the hill above. Mayorazgo: ◷ 30 min. C/ Núñez del Prado. Free. Mon–Sat 10am–2pm and 5–8pm; Sun 11am–2pm. Andalusí: ◷ 20 min. Summer Mon–Fri 10am–2pm and 7–10pm, Sat–Sun 11am–2pm; winter Mon–Fri 10am–2pm and 5–8pm, Sat–Sun 10am–2pm.

Where to Stay & Dine

★ **Arcos Restaurante** ZAHARA DE LA SIERRA
ANDALUCÍAN You can gaze at the mountains
while you tuck into delicious sierra dishes like
herb-stuffed quail or grilled trout. Hotel Arco
de la Villa, C/ Paseo Nazarí, s/n. No phone.
Entrees 5€–16€. MC, V. Breakfast, lunch &
dinner daily.

Bar Alcaraván ARCOS DE LA FRONTERA
ANDALUCÍAN Vaulted rooms in this atmospheric bar were carved from the cellars of
palaces on the plaza above. Your best bets are
spicy local sausages, stewed pork, or chicken
casseroles. If you're lucky, local flamenco
artists might perform. C/ Nueva, 1. ☎ 956-703-
397. Raciones 3.50€–7€. MC, V. Lunch & dinner
Tues–Sun.

Hostal Rural Marqués de Zahara ZAHARA DE
LA SIERRA Traditionally furnished rooms on the
upper levels of this historic village-center house
are arrayed around a beautiful patio. Six rooms
overlooking the street have balconies hung
with geraniums. No elevator. Breakfast is down
the street at Los Naranjos bar. C/ San Juan, 3.
☎ 956-123-061. www.marquesdezahara.com. 11
rooms. Doubles 50€, with breakfast. MC, V.

★★★ **Parador Arcos de la Frontera** ARCOS DE
LA FRONTERA The former palace at the top of
Arcos has spectacular panoramic views and
large rooms with traditional decor. There's
parking on the plaza, but be forewarned that
extremely narrow streets make for difficult
driving. The restaurant features cuisine of the
local mountains and Bay of Cádiz fish. Plaza del
Cabildo, s/n. ☎ 956-700-500. www.paradores.es.
24 rooms. Doubles 103€–186€. Entrees 12€–24€.
AE, DC, MC, V. Breakfast, lunch & dinner daily.

★ **Restaurante El Olivar** GRAZALEMA
ANDALUCÍAN The sophisticated dining at
backcountry prices here emphasizes local lamb,
wild boar, trout, and foraged mushrooms. The
wine list is strong on Cádiz and Huelva region
whites. Villas Turísticas de Grazalema, Carretera
Olivar, s/n. ☎ 956-132-213. Entrees 8€–20€. MC,
V. Breakfast, lunch & dinner daily.

> *Tasty tapas at the subterranean Bar Alcaraván.*

★★ kids **Villas Turísticas de Grazalema**
GRAZALEMA A 5-minute walk from the village
center, this bargain complex has a hotel with
spacious rooms and a cluster of buildings with
modern one- and two-bedroom apartments
with wood-burning fireplaces. Carretera Olivar,
s/n. ☎ 956-132-213. www.tugasa.com. 24 rooms,
38 apts. Double rooms 60€, with breakfast; apts
70€ for 1-bedroom, 120€ for 2-bedroom. MC, V.

Costa del Sol

High-density resorts form a nearly continuous beachfront strip from Torremolinos through Benalmádena and Fuengirola, but the 85km (53-mile) coast west of Málaga is much more than a concrete jungle. Each of these communities has a Casco Antiguo (Old Town) and harbors a vestigial fishing fleet. Like a gem-spangled belt buckle, Marbella and Puerto Banús create a luxurious middle to the coast. To the west, Estepona remains the least developed outpost. Linking them together is the stop-and-go coastal highway of the N-340, with inland options of the faster A-7 and the even faster limited-access AP-7. With 325 days of annual sunshine, the region is indeed the "coast of the sun."

> *The next generation of rich and famous find space to play in Marbella.*

START Torremolinos. **TRIP LENGTH** 86km (53 miles).

❶ Torremolinos. "Torrie" lies so close to Málaga (12km/7½ miles) that Fernando and Isabel staged their siege of the city from the spring-riddled hillside. Proximity to a big city and airport—and 7km (4⅓ miles) of beautiful beaches—made Torrie Spain's first major resort in the 1950s. Today its hotels and apartments accommodate about 50,000 sun lovers.

The prototypical Costa del Sol vacation was born here: Settle into a resort hotel, cross the street to lie on the beach, dine in the neighborhood, and sleep soundly to the rhythmic whoosh of surf. When you get restless, stroll along the palm-lined Paseo Marítimo, explore

Travel Tip

For attractions suitable for kids on the Costa del Sol, see p. 570.

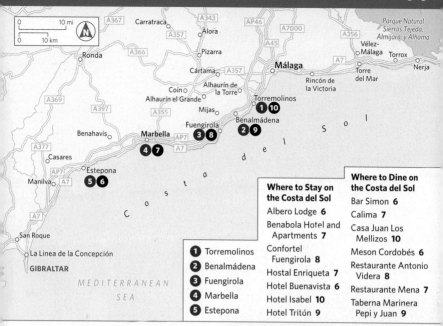

Where to Stay on the Costa del Sol

Albero Lodge **6**

Benabola Hotel and Apartments **7**

Confortel Fuengirola **8**

Hostal Enriqueta **7**

Hotel Buenavista **6**

Hotel Isabel **10**

Hotel Tritón **9**

Where to Dine on the Costa del Sol

Bar Simon **6**

Calima **7**

Casa Juan Los Mellizos **10**

Meson Cordobés **6**

Restaurante Antonio Videra **8**

Restaurante Mena **7**

Taberna Marinera Pepi y Juan **9**

1 Torremolinos

2 Benalmádena

3 Fuengirola

4 Marbella

5 Estepona

the boutiques and souvenir shops of the old town, and visit the fishing port. Torrie's Casco Antiguo is one of the busiest, and its main pedestrian street, **C/ San Miguel,** has been paved with marble. In the old town, the airplane-shaped **Centro Cultural Pablo Ruíz Picasso,** C/ de la Cruz, 42 (☎ 952-053-835) stages concerts, lectures, and cinema.

★ **La Carihuela,** the lively port, has more restaurants than fishermen. One block back from the beach, the streets of Carmen, Mar, and San Ginés constitute a bustling shopping district studded with small bars and cafes.

Go south 9km (6 miles) on N-340 to Benal-mádena.

2 Benalmádena. This shore town is distinguishable from Torremolinos only by the change in street signs, but it does offer another 9km (5⅔ miles) of coves and beaches. The best is the brown crescent of **Playa Malapesquera,** bracketed on the east by the lively **Puerto Deportivo,** a district of pleasure boats, attractions, and restaurants. (★ **Dolphin Cruises** offers 1-hr. cruises on a modest sailboat out of Puerto Deportivo. In addition to dolphins, you might also see giant sunfish and sea turtles. The crew encourages passengers to help with the sails and even take the wheel.)

> The idea of the Costa del Sol vacation was born on beaches like Torremolinos's Bajondillo and Playamar.

> *Marbella purchased a series of sculptures by Salvador Dalí for the newly redeveloped Alameda Park.*

Benalmádena Pueblo, the original town, is about 2.4km (1½ miles) from the beach. At the west end, **Plaza Solymar**—nicknamed the "24-Hour Square"—is surrounded by bars and discos that attract many young northern European vacationers to dance, flirt, and let off steam. Dolphin Cruises: Puerto Deportivo. ☎ 669-665-844. 15€ adults, 10€ kids. Daily 11am–5pm.

From Benalmádena, go south 10km (6 miles) on N-340 to Fuengirola.

❸ **Fuengirola.** Similarly overgrown with resort hotels, Fuengirola offers some intriguing variations on the Costa del Sol model. It is a center for watersports and boasts a truly wonderful zoo (see p. 571, ❼) and a very cool castle. At the Puerto Deportivo, **Local 62** (☎ 952-581-861), a storefront operated by Brits, serves as the clearinghouse for local cruises (from 8€), extreme powerboating (from 25€), and parasailing (from 36€).

★ **Castillo Sohail** surmounts the hill above the beach where Carthaginians and Romans both settled, so it's hard to miss if you walk along Paseo Marítimo toward the elegant cable-stay bridge over the Río Fuengirola. The

castle was built by the Almohad dynasty in the 12th century and modified many times since it fell into Christian hands in 1485. Restored by Fuengirola students, it is surrounded by beautiful green lawns. Castillo: ☎ 685-855-246. 3€ adults, 2€ seniors and kids. Spring and fall daily 10am–6:30pm; summer daily 9:30am–9pm; winter daily 10:30am–6pm.

The E-15/AP-7 connects Fuengirola with Marbella (to the southeast), for a total distance of 34km (21 miles).

❹ **Marbella.** The glamorous heart of the Costa del Sol, Marbella boasts upscale luxury boutiques, moorings for block-long yachts, and parking lots for Rolls-Royces and Bentleys. From the beachfront, the **Avenida del Mar** promenade is filled with sculptures by Salvador Dalí. It rises to the beautiful **Parque Paseo de la Alameda,** where you can find a shady spot for quiet meditation on one of the tiled benches. Cross a major avenue and you suddenly enter the warren of the Old Town. The **Plaza de Los Naranjos,** where you'll find jewelry and fashion shops, is the heart of the district, but it's fun to wander the side streets. Don't miss the

> *The fishing village of Estepona hasn't been developed as much as its neighbors on the Costa del Sol.*

Museo del Grabado Español Contemporáneo, ensconced in a 16th-century hospital. The excellent museum specializes in lithographs, engravings, silk-screens, and other prints of 20th-century artists, including works by Picasso, Dalí, and Miró.

Underneath the glitz, Marbella is another former fishing village. The **Paseo Marítimo** connects the Old City to **Puerto Banús,** an erstwhile fishing harbor. You'd be hard-pressed to find a fishing boat among the gleaming white speedboats and yachts, but the compact harbor does have a lively cafe culture. Museo: C/ Hospital Bazán, s/n. ☎ 952-765-741. 3€. Mon and Sat 9am–2pm; Tues–Fri 9am–2pm and 6–9pm.

The E-15/AP-7 continues on another 33km (21 miles) southeast to Estepona.

5 Estepona. Seven **watchtowers,** or *almenaras,* dot Estepona's 21km (13-mile) shoreline. Built by Muslim and Castilian rulers alike, they operated into the 19th century to warn of North African pirates who would capture and sell villagers into slavery. No pirates roam the two main beaches these days. **Playa de la Rada** fronts the village, with a 3km (1¾-mile) Paseo Marítimo shorefront promenade. Smaller **Playa del Cristo,** in a cove near the marina, is popular with families because its waves are gentle and trees along the beach provide a shady respite.

Although resort developments have sprung up at both ends of Estepona's beaches, the town itself has the preresort demeanor of a tight community where everyone knows everyone else. The Casco Antiguo, which rises up a slight hill from Playa de la Rada, retains traces of the 10th-century Muslim village in modest **Arabic ruins,** including a well, on Plaza del Cabildo. Evidence of the 15th-century Castilian fort, **Castillo San Luis,** is equally subtle—a rusty cannon in the flower garden at Plaza Casa Cañada and traces of stone walls on C/ Castillo. The most enchanting square is **Plaza de las Flores,** where cafes surround a burbling fountain.

Travel Tip

All public beaches in Spain are free, but don't expect changing or other facilities.

Where to Stay

> Hostal Enriqueta is a more modest choice in pricey Marbella.

★★ Albero Lodge ESTEPONA
This charming complex features rooms decorated in chic styles from around the world. Each has its own patio, terrace, or garden, while all share a gleaming silver pool in quiet, mature gardens. The beach is adjacent, but you may never want to leave your patio chair. Located 4km (2½ miles) east of town. C/ Támesis, 16, Urbanización Finca La Cancelada, km 165 on the A-7. ☎ 952-880-700. www.alberolodge.com. 9 rooms. Doubles 90€–120€, suites 100€–155€. AE, DC, MC, V.

★ kids Benabola Hotel and Apartments
MARBELLA Apartments in the heart of upscale Puerto Banús are huge and contemporary—and a bargain. Pasaje de la Alhambra, s/n, Puerto Banús. ☎ 952-815-000. www.benabola.com. 98 suites. 1-bedroom apt 79€–300€. AE, DC, MC, V.

Confortel Fuengirola FUENGIROLA
Ultracontemporary style follows the new paradigm of tech-friendly rooms with a limited but dramatic color palette. Even better, the beach is across the street. Paseo Marítimo Rey de España, 87. ☎ 952-910-100. www.confortelhoteles.com. 180 rooms. Doubles 75€–110€. AE, DC, MC, V.

Hostal Enriqueta MARBELLA
This friendly family-run hotel sits on a small plaza in the Old City, about a 5-minute walk to the beach. Many rooms overlook a flower-filled courtyard, which is reserved for the owners. C/ de los Caballeros, 18. ☎ 952-827-552. 20 rooms. Doubles 50€–60€, triples 70€–80€. Cash only.

Hotel Buenavista ESTEPONA
Twenty rooms here have killer sunrise views of Estepona's wonderful village beach. Rooms are small but well maintained. But they can sometimes be noisy in summer due to heavy traffic nearby. Paseo Marítimo, 180. ☎ 952-800-137. www.buenavistaestepona.com. 38 rooms. Doubles 50€–70€. MC, V.

★ Hotel Isabel TORREMOLINOS
Set away from the high-rise part of Torrie, the Isabel has airy rooms, comfortable lounges, and a lovely pool and gardens—all just across the street from lively Playamar beach. Paseo Marítimo, 47, Playamar. ☎ 952-381-744. www.hotel isabel.net. 70 rooms. Doubles 70€–130€, corner rooms higher, with breakfast. AE, MC, V.

Hotel Tritón BENALMÁDENA
Next to the marina on one of the best stretches of Benalmádena's beach, this 1961 tower hotel has been completely renovated, keeping the balconies and beach views but adding a spa. Avenida Antonio Machado, 29. ☎ 952-443-240. www.besthotels.es. 373 rooms. Doubles 48€–98€, with breakfast. MC, V.

Where to Dine

> *A typical Costa del Sol seafood spread.*

★ Bar Simon ESTEPONA *SEAFOOD*
Estepona is as much a fishing port as a resort, and the best local catch ends up on ice here. Point to a fish—usually a choice of bass, bream, red mullet, mackerel, or sardines—and get it grilled in minutes. Don't miss the *almejas Esteponas,* a local clam that's tiny, smooth, and tasty. Avenida San Lorenzo, 40. ☎ 952-791-455. Entrees 9€–18€. MC, V. Lunch & dinner Mon–Sat.

★★★ Calima MARBELLA *CONTEMPORARY/ ANDALUCÍAN* Chef Dani García may be one of Spain's leading culinary innovators, but he always puts taste ahead of showmanship. His flavors are Andalucían (gazpacho, grilled fish, mountain ham, Córdoban olive oil), but he surprises and delights by playing soft against firm, hot against cold, sweet against salty. Reservations essential. Hotel Gran Meliá Don Pepe, Avenida José Meliá, s/n. ☎ 952-764-252. Entrees 22€–40€. AE, DC, MC, V. Lunch & dinner daily.

★★ Casa Juan Los Mellizos TORREMOLINOS *SEAFOOD* This fried seafood empire sprawls through an entire plaza in the former fishing village of La Carihuela, with many dining rooms sharing a single kitchen. Walk by and watch the cooks through the window and you won't be able to resist going in. Plaza San Ginés, s/n. ☎ 952-373-512. Entrees 9€–19€. MC, V. Lunch & dinner daily.

Meson Cordobés ESTEPONA *ANDALUCÍAN* Wood-grilled pork and beef steaks are the specialties of the house, though fried seafood is also good. Plaza de los Flores, 15. ☎ 952-800-737. Entrees 7€–16€. MC, V. Lunch & dinner Tues–Sun.

kids Restaurante Antonio Videra FUENGIROLA *SEAFOOD* This beachfront restaurant is a good place to treat yourself to sardines cooked on a stake *(pez espeto)* over an open fire built in a sand-filled boat. Paseo Marítimo Los Boliches. ☎ 952-119-193. Entrees 9€–19€. MC, V. Lunch & dinner daily.

Restaurante Mena MARBELLA *SEAFOOD* Beat the paella blues of the resort scene by ordering fish baked in salt, stewed monkfish, or sautéed clams. There is an excellent choice of regional wines. Plaza de los Naranjos, 10. ☎ 952-771-597. Entrees 10€–22€. MC, V. Lunch & dinner daily.

★ Taberna Marinera Pepi y Juan BENAL-MÁDENA *SEAFOOD* More than 25 rice dishes highlight the menu at this yachting center dining room. Try *"humillante"*-style rice with pork, red peppers, chorizo, and a fried egg. Centro Náutico, Avenida Capitanía, s/n. ☎ 952-441-578. Entrees 9€–20€. MC, V. Lunch & dinner Tues–Sun.

Costa del Sol with Kids

The Costa del Sol has plenty of surf, sand, and sun.
If that's not enough to keep the kids amused on vacation, there's no shortage of diversions for children of all ages.

> A dolphin show at Selwo Aventura in Estepona.

START Torremolinos. **TRIP LENGTH** 84km (52 miles), not including the bus trip to Mijas.

❶ ★ Parque de la Batería (Torremolinos). Small children can have bargain-priced fun in this city park with a large playground and a lake in the center. Rowboats rent for 1€ per 30 minutes. ⏱ 45 min.

❷ Crocodile Park (Torremolinos). Between the guided tour and live demonstrations, you could see as many as a few hundred crocodiles ranging from purse-sized babies to a half-ton Nile behemoth. You can even have your picture taken holding a croc. ⏱ 1½ hr. C/ Cuba, 14.

☎ 952-051-782. www.crocodile-park.com. 11€ adults, 9€ seniors, 8.50€ kids, free for kids 3 & under. June–Sept daily 10am–7pm; Oct and Mar–May closes 6pm; Nov–Feb closes 5pm.

Go south 9km (6 miles) on N-340 to Benalmádena.

❸ ★ Sea Life Benalmádena. This aquarium and minigolf complex is right at Malapesquera Beach, so you and the kids can take a break from swimming. Several ecosystems are featured, but Sea Life has especially good displays of octopus. ⏱ 2 hr. Puerto Deportivo. ☎ 952-560-150. www.sealife. es. 6.50€–13€; buy tickets online for best price. Nov–May 10am–6pm; June and Sept–Oct 10am–8pm; July–Aug 10am–midnight.

❹ Selwo Marina (Benalmádena). Now that you've seen the fish, visit this inland marine park where children are delighted by penguins and South American marine mammals. Dolphins and sea lions perform several times daily. ⏱ 2 hr. Parque de la Paloma, s/n. ☎ 902-190-482. www.selwo marina.com. 17€ adults, 13€ kids 3–7 and seniors. Mid-Feb to May and Oct daily 10am–6pm; June and Sept daily 10am–7pm; July–Aug 10am–9pm; Nov Fri–Sun 10am–6pm; closed Dec to mid-Feb.

❺ Tivoli World de Cine (Benalmádena). Live spectacles of singing, dancing, and acrobatics punctuate the day here, but the youngsters are usually too busy on the amusement park rides to catch the performers. ⏱ 2–3 hr. Arroyo de la Miel, s/n. ☎ 952-577-016. www.tivoli.es. 6€ general admission, 12€ admission with unlimited rides, free for kids under 1m (3¼ ft.) tall. July to mid-Sept daily 6pm–midnight or later; Oct–June Sat–Sun noon–7pm, some later hours in May and June.

From Benalmádena, go south 10km (6 miles) on N-340 to Fuengirola.

1. Parque de la Batería
2. Crocodile Park
3. Sea Life Benalmádena
4. Selwo Marina
5. Tivoli World de Cine
6. Parquelandia
7. Fuengirola Zoo
8. Mijas Pueblo Donkey Taxi
9. Ermita de la Virgen de la Peña
10. Casa Museo Ayuntamiento de Mijas
11. Selwo Aventura

6 Parquelandia (Fuengirola). If the beach and the castle don't suffice for young children, the go-karts, trampolines, and rides at this old-fashioned marina amusement park might. ⏱ 2 hr. Parcel C-2, Puerto Deportivo. ☎ 609-447-768. 2€–4€. Daily 1:30–9:30pm.

7 ★★★ Fuengirola Zoo. Since a 2001 turn-around that made it one of Europe's model facilities, the Fuengirola Zoo has become the top attraction of the Costa del Sol. The full-immersion zoo (no cages) replicates the tropical rainforests of Madagascar, equatorial Africa, and southeast Asia with 1,300 animals. ⏱ 3 hr. C/ Camilo José Cela 8–10. ☎ 952-666-301. www.zoofuengirola.com. 16€ adults, 11€ kids 3–9 and seniors. Winter daily 10am–6pm; summer daily 10am–8pm.

Don't bother driving to Mijas. A bus running from the Fuengirola station runs every 30 min. between Fuengirola and Mijas Pueblo.

8 ★ Mijas Pueblo Donkey Taxi. Even though Mijas is a steep little village, it's easy to cover on foot. But for 30 minutes of sightseeing, kids will love riding in a cart pulled by a donkey decked out in ribbons. ⏱ 30 min. 15€.

9 Ermita de la Virgen de la Peña (Mijas Pueblo). Kids also tend to get a kick out of this cave next to a *mirador* with views all the way to the sea. A Carmelite monk dug the cave in the 17th century to hold a carved image of the Virgin Mary that had been hidden from the Moors for 500 years. ⏱ 15 min. Free. Daily sunrise–sunset.

10 Casa Museo Ayuntamiento de Mijas. The town museum focuses on how Mijans used to make a living, so it has a fun if funky working olive press and lots of old agricultural tools. ⏱ 20 min. Plaza de la Libertad, 2. ☎ 952-590-380. Free. Daily 10am–2pm and 4–7pm.

Return on the bus to Fuengirola, then go south 65km (40 miles) on AP-7 to Estepona.

11 Selwo Aventura (Estepona). Roughly 2,000 creatures from five continents—including lions, tigers, giraffes, and American bison—roam this wildlife park east of town. Visitors usually tour the park in safari vehicles; camel rides are also available. ⏱ 1 hr. A-7, km 162.5. ☎ 902-190-482. ww.selwo.es. 25€, 17€ kids 3–7 and seniors. Mid-Feb to June and Sept to early Dec daily 10am–6pm (Apr–Jun and Sept open 1 hr later Sat–Sun); July–Aug daily 10am–8pm; closed Jan to mid-Feb.

Costa Tropical & Axarquía

The stretch of ocean from Almuñécar west toward Málaga is one of the most scenic coastal drives in southern Spain. The N-340a twists and turns along the shore, sometimes following high ridgelines above the ocean coves and passing ancient watchtowers. The route begins on the Costa Tropical, where the microclimate makes it possible to grow avocados, mangoes, and papayas all year. The weather doesn't change west of Almuñécar, but the political boundaries do. The coast from Nerja to Málaga belongs to the Axarquía region of Málaga province and is sometimes called the Costa del Sol Oriental.

> By day, tourists line up on Nerja's Balcón de Europa for stunning Mediterranean views; by night, street performers appear.

START Take the A-44 55km (miles) south from Granada to the N-340a; it's another 5km (3 miles) west into Salobreña. TRIP LENGTH 57km (35 miles), not including the trip from Granada.

1 Salobreña. From a distance, Salobreña appears as a mirage of a 13th-century hilltop castle with houses tumbling down the slope like so many sugar cubes. Indeed, sugar cane has been the town's main crop for hundreds of years. If you visit between March and June, the air may be full of smoke as the stubble is burned to restore nutrients to the soil. The town is about 2km (1¼ miles) from the beach, which is a mass of modern congestion, most of it built in the past decade. You can visit the partially restored castle, **Castillo Arabe,** which is mostly an open keep but displays some superb medieval stonework. Castillo: ⏱ 20 min. ☎ 958-610-314. 3€. Daily 9:30am–2pm and 4–6:30pm.

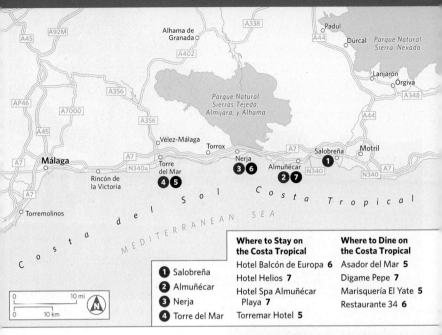

Where to Stay on the Costa Tropical	Where to Dine on the Costa Tropical
Hotel Balcón de Europa **6**	Asador del Mar **5**
Hotel Helios **7**	Digame Pepe **7**
Hotel Spa Almuñécar Playa **7**	Marisquería El Yate **5**
Torremar Hotel **5**	Restaurante 34 **6**

1 Salobreña
2 Almuñécar
3 Nerja
4 Torre del Mar

Continue west 13km (8 miles) on N-340.

2 ★★ **Almuñécar.** Called Sexi by the Phoenicians who founded it in the 8th century B.C., the town was a major producer of fermented fish paste, or *garum,* for both Phoenicia and then Rome for more than a millennium. Most visitors come for the long stony beach dotted with *churrerías,* but an extensive complex of parks and ruins in Barrio San Miguel near the beach explains Almuñécar's rich history. Stop at what might be Spain's most beautiful tourist office, the neo-Mudéjar **Palacete de la Najarra,** for a map. The office also serves as the visitor center for the adjacent castle, botanical park, and aviary.

Ceramics date the **Castillo San Miguel,** Almuñécar's first fortress, to the Carthaginian occupation in the 3rd century B.C. Evidence of a Roman fort has also been uncovered. But the castle as it now stands is largely a 13th-century Nasrid structure that was famous for its prison and dungeon used for political prisoners. Modified under the Spanish monarchy, the castle was partly destroyed by English bombardment in 1808.

The botanic park, **Parque Botánico El Majuelo,** next to the ruins of the Roman fish-paste factory, is rich in tropical and subtropical

> *Salobreña's Castillo Arabe watches over the white-washed town and its sugar cane fields.*

> *Plants from as far afield as India, Polynesia, and South America thrive in the Parque Botánico El Majuelo.*

species that flourish in the warm microclimate. The nearby **Parque Ornitológico Loro-Sexi** houses more than 1,500 birds representing about 200 species, which fly in large caged areas inside this modern aviary. Scarlet macaws, toucans, and peacocks provide colorful splendor.

Located in the vaulted basements of Roman ruins (La Cueva de los Siete Palacios), the **Museo Arqueológico** displays Roman and Moorish artifacts as well as Phoenician materials recovered from a necropolis on the northwest side of town. The most remarkable (and mysterious) piece in the museum is an Egyptian glass sculpted from solid quartz and inscribed with hieroglyphics that date from the 17th century B.C. Palacete: Avenida de Europa, s/n. ☎ 958-631-125. www.almunecar.info. Nov–Mar daily 10am–2pm and 4:30–7pm; Apr–June and Sept 16–Oct daily 10am–2pm and 5–8pm; July–Sept 15 daily 10am–2pm and 6–9pm. Castillo: ⊕ 45 min. Barrio San Miguel. ☎ 958-631-125. www.almunecar.info. 2.35€ adults, 1.60€ seniors and kids. Tues–Sat 10:30am–1:30pm and 4–6:30pm; Sun 10:30am–2pm. Parque Botánico: ⊕ 20 min. Barrio de San Miguel. Daily sunrise–sunset. Parque Ornitológico: ⊕ 30 min. Barrio de San Miguel. ☎ 958-631-125. www. almunecar.info. 4€ adults, 2€ seniors and kids. Daily 11am–2pm and 4–6pm. Museo: ⊕ 45 min. C/ San Joaquín, s/n. ☎ 651-588-030. www.almunecar.info. 2.35€, 1.60€ seniors and kids. Tues–Sat 10:30am–1:30pm and 4–6:30pm; Sun 10:30am–2pm.

Continue west 23km (14 miles) on N-340.

❸ **Nerja.** Travelers are not drawn to Nerja by the small beaches of El Salón and Calahonda, but by the promontory that separates them. The famous 19th-century belvedere plaza is known as the ★ **Balcón de Europa.** Horse-drawn carriages line up here to take visitors around the picturesque village (20 min. for 30€), which has some of the coast's better boutique shopping. The natural wonder, the **Cueva de Nerja** (see p. 557, ❻), is east of town.

Continue west 21km (13 miles) on N-340.

❹ **Torre del Mar.** Vélez-Málaga is a community with two faces—a staid business center 4km (2½ miles) inland, and the roaring beachside apartment-tower resort of Torre del Mar. The long brown-sand beach lined with bars and cafes is by far the main attraction, but you can also see three lighthouses and the old sugar factory, **Casa de Larios,** Plaza Larios, Urbanización Pueblo del Rocio (no phone), that now serves as the mayor's office. Torre del Mar also has an excellent fresh food market, the **Mercado Municipal,** C/ Río, 28 (Mon–Sat 9am–2pm).

Where to Stay & Dine

> Fresh food fast at Digame Pepe.

★ **Asador del Mar** TORRE DEL MAR *GRILL*
With both charcoal and wood grills, the kitchen here is ready to make succulent steaks and chops as well as whole grilled fish. Paseo Maritimo de Levante at C/ San José. ☎ 951-283-032. Entrees 11€–19€. MC, V. Lunch & dinner Tues–Sun.

★ **Digame Pepe** ALMUÑÉCAR *SEAFOOD*
The fishermen can't unload their catch fast enough for the cooks here, who turn out some of the biggest, least expensive plates of fried and grilled fish on the Costa Tropical. Paseo de los Flores, s/n. ☎ 958-349-315. Entrees 8€–20€. MC, V. Breakfast, lunch & dinner daily.

Hotel Balcón de Europa NERJA
This grande dame of Nerja has classic old-world ambience and some of the greatest views on the coast. Paseo Balcón de Europa, 1. ☎ 952-520-800. www.hotelbalconeuropa.com. 110 rooms. Doubles 98€–168€. AE, DC, MC, V.

Hotel Helios ALMUÑÉCAR
The city's pioneer resort hotel has pleasant, well-kept rooms across the street from the beach. The smart, helpful staff are a big plus. Paseo San Cristóbal, 12. ☎ 958-634-459. www.heliosalmunecar.com. 230 rooms. Doubles 75€–117€, with breakfast and parking. MC, V.

Hotel Spa Almuñécar Playa ALMUÑÉCAR
Spacious rooms in this salmon-hued giant all have ocean views. The hotel augments the beach with an excellent sun terrace and spa. Paseo San Cristóbal, s/n. ☎ 958-639-450. www.playasenator.com. 227 rooms. Doubles 86€–200€, with breakfast and parking. AE, DC, MC, V.

★★ **Marisquería El Yate** TORRE DEL MAR
SEAFOOD You might have to elbow through the crowd at Torre's best casual fish house, but it's worth it for fried anchovies (a Torre specialty), sweet steamed prawns, and grilled fish. C/ Saladero Viejo at C/ del Mar. ☎ 952-540-774. Most food is market price, about 15€–20€ per person. MC, V. Lunch & dinner Thurs–Tues.

★★ **Restaurante 34** NERJA *SPANISH/FUSION*
Chef Fernando Diaz Padial does creative turns on classics like monkfish wrapped in pancetta or confit of pork cheeks served with cauliflower purée. Dine inside or in the garden under the stars. C/ Carabeo, 34. ☎ 952-525-444. Entrees 16€–26€. MC, V. Dinner Tues–Sun.

Torremar Hotel TORRE DEL MAR
This new hotel in a traditional style is just 2 blocks from the beach. The knowledgeable staff will help you find great dining and activities. C/ Saladero Viejo, 15. ☎ 952-547-057. www.hoteltorremar.com. 83 rooms. Doubles 60€–125€. AE, DC, MC, V.

La Alpujarra de Granada

It's hard to believe that it's only an hour's drive from the Moorish splendor of Granada to the rustic mountain villages on the south side of the Sierra Nevada. Isolated by bad roads until the 1950s, the district of La Alpujarra has retained a Moorish mien. Even the architecture echoes Berber houses in northern Morocco. The green valleys and rugged hills terraced with olives and vines are spectacularly scenic, and the drive will delight fans of twisting mountain roads.

> Secaderos *dominate the mountain town of Trevélez, whose serrano hams are famous throughout Spain.*

START A-44 south from Granada, exit 164.
TRIP LENGTH 43km (27 miles).

❶ A-348 East. From the superhighway, you enter the Parque Natural Sierra Nevada and the narrow road begins climbing and twisting around the mountainsides. The drop-off is precipitous—making for both scary moments and grand vistas. At one point the road runs parallel with the blades of giant wind turbines that suddenly appear when you round a corner. ⏱ 30 min.

❷ ★ Lanjarón. After the 5km (3-mile) thrill ride on A-348, this ancient spa town seems pretty tame, even quaint. Eight mineral springs, each purported to have a different healing property, pour from the rocks. The Romans came here to take the cure, and Europe's afflicted follow in their footsteps. The town revolves around the spa, the **Balneario de Lanjarón,** and twice a day you'll encounter residents and visitors lining up in the lobby to fill bottles with water from a flowing spring.

Where to Stay in the Alpujarra de Granada
Hostal Pampaneira **6**
Hotel Nuevo Palas **5**

Where to Dine in the Alpujarra de Granada
Jamones Gustavo Rubio **5**
Mesón Alberto **6**
Mesón Joaquin Restaurante **7**

1 A-348 East
2 Lanjarón
3 Pampaneira
4 Trevélez

Whether or not you subscribe to the healing properties of the waters, this is a great place for a relaxing retreat, taking advantage of spa services that range from thermal baths to massage and reflexology. The spa also arranges weeklong therapy programs with lodging and meals. Balneario de Lanjarón: Avenida Andalucía, s/n. ☎ 958-770-137. www.balneariodelanjaron.com. Daily 9am–2pm and 5–8pm. Treatments 11€–56€.

Follow A-348 east for 8km (5 miles), then A-4132 northeast for 14km (8⅔ miles) to Pampaneira.

Take a Hike

Hikers interested in a good afternoon excursion are usually encouraged to follow well-marked trails from **Pampaneira** to the nearby ridgeline villages of **Bubión** and **Capileira.** The distance is only about 3km (1¾ miles), with an elevation rise to 1,250m (4,101 ft.) on switchback trails. The last stretch to Capileira follows the asphalt road, as the historic trail is washed out. A more ambitious hike across the valley leads to a Zen Buddhist monastery.

> *This style of colorful, shaggy cotton rug sold across La Alpujarra has been made since the 15th century.*

> *Fountain of youth? The purportedly healing waters of Lanjarón.*

❸ ★★ **Pampaneira.** As both the tourist and the hiking center for the High Alpujarra, Pampaneira is a village for the fit. The steep climbs between streets, at an elevation of 1,000m (3,281 ft.), can tax less athletic visitors, while gung-ho hikers run up and down just to stay loose. The small mountain village supports numerous shops selling colorful, shaggy, woven cotton rugs (called *jarapes de Alpujarra*), as well as jewelry and other handcrafts. Two ham producers also sell their wares, and the village even has an artisanal chocolate maker. But the main reason to come here is to hike. Do *not* set out on a trail without first visiting **Punto de Información Parque Natural de Sierra Nevada.** The center has interpretive displays about the Sierra Nevada park, sells trail guides and gear, and will arrange guides for ambitious excursions. Most important, staff can fill you in on exact current trail conditions. **Punto de Información:** Plaza de la Libertad, s/n. ☎ 958-763-127. www.nevadensis.com. Guided hikes 25€–120€. Tues–Sat 10am–2pm and 4–6pm; Sun–Mon 10am–3pm.

Continue on A-4132 on steep, winding road for 21km (13 miles) to Trevélez.

❹ ★ **Trevélez.** At an elevation of 1,500m (4,921 ft.), Trevélez is the highest year-round community on the Iberian Peninsula. The dry, rarefied mountain air makes it the ideal place to cure ham, and *jamón de Trevélez* (a controlled designation) is considered one of the two best serrano hams in Spain. Big warehouses with open windows, called *secaderos,* or drying rooms, dominate the village. The cure uses no preservatives or additives and takes 14 to 24 months, resulting in a delicate ham. Most visitors come to buy (or eat) ham close to the source. The town is also a base to scale nearby peaks from July to mid-August. Check with the center in Pampaneira on trail conditions to the shrine of the Virgen de los Nieves, and be prepared to spend the night on the mountain.

Where to Stay & Dine

> *No frills but fantastic views at Hostal Pampaneira.*

Hostal Pampaneira PAMPANEIRA

To hikers returning from camping in the outback of the Sierra Nevada, this charming small *hostal* (inexpensive hotel) could seem like the Ritz. For everyone else, it's a cozy spot for an overnight in the mountains. All rooms have televisions and heat—air-conditioning is never needed. Views from the windows are sweeping, and there's a good bar-restaurant on the ground level. Avenida de la Alpujarra, 1. ☎ 958-763-002. www.hostalpampaneira.com. 15 rooms. Doubles 40€. MC, V.

Hotel Nuevo Palas LANJARÓN

Because Lanjarón is the western gateway to the Alpujarra, it is rich with hotels. Nuevo Palas is one of the nicest—a spa resort hotel founded in 1941 and completely overhauled a few years ago. Guest rooms are cozy but comfortable and are furnished in pale-wood furniture with pastel walls. Avenida de la Alpujarra, 24. ☎ 958-770-086. www.hotelnuevopalas.com. 32 rooms. Doubles 65€–76€, with breakfast. MC, V.

★ Jamones Gustavo Rubio LANJARÓN *DELI*

Alpujarran hams hang everywhere, and huge casks of mostly local wines line the back walls. Principally a deli selling sliced meat and cheeses to go, Rubio also has a half dozen tables in the back where he serves plates of ham and cheese and a changing assortment of tapas—including excellent seasonal salads. It's a good place to sample the surprisingly fresh wines. Avenida Andalucía, 38. ☎ 958-771-124. Entrees 9€–14€ (26€ for the top hams). MC, V. Mar–Oct lunch & dinner daily.

★ Mesón Alberto PAMPANEIRA *ALPUJARRAN*

With a wood-burning oven and grill, Antonia Alonso Pérez serves a lot of roasted and grilled meats, but she also cooks up a special casserole, such as stewed partridge or rabbit pie, each day. The kitchen is wide open behind the bar, so you can watch your meal being prepared. C/ Real, 9. ☎ 958-763-003. Entrees 6€–12€. MC, V. Lunch & dinner Fri–Wed.

★★ Mesón Joaquin Restaurante TREVÉLEZ

ALPUJARRAN Mesón Joaquin is one of the larger producers of Trevélez hams and maintains a sales room and deli on this square in the lower town. They also have this fine restaurant that offers both the fantastic hams and the spectacular farmed trout for which the mountain village is justly acclaimed. Outdoor tables let you enjoy the intense high-altitude sun. Glorieta de Arabial, 4. ☎ 958-858-514. Entrees 7€–14€. MC, V. Summer lunch & dinner daily, winter lunch daily.

The Sherry Triangle

Roughly 3,000 years ago, Phoenicians planted the first wine grapes in the chalky soil between the mouth of the Río Guadalquivir and the Bahía de Cádiz. Romans, Visigoths, and even teetotaling Moors followed suit. Warm temperatures, meager rainfall, and moisture-trapping soil have proven ideal growing conditions for *palomino* and Pedro Ximénez grapes, making the triangle formed by Jerez, El Puerto de Santa María, and Sanlúcar the only place in the world that makes sherry.

> On a self-guided audio tour, visitors can watch Bodegas Pedro Romero's sherry masters at work.

START Jerez de la Frontera. **TRIP LENGTH** 40km (25 miles).

1 Jerez de la Frontera. Settled by Iberians and colonized by Phoenicians and Romans, Jerez came into its own as a border town between Muslim and Christian Spain over the course of 5 centuries. The name for its wine, sherry, is an English corruption of Xèrès, as the city was spelled until the 20th century. It is the capital of the sherry-producing area and the **tourist office** can advise on touring bodegas.

★ **González Byass** (see p. 648, **4**), maker of the world's top-selling fino sherry, Tío Pepe, gives a thorough tour from vineyard to *soleras* (aging barrels) to tasting room. For an intimate look inside the sherry aristocracy, visit ★★ **Bodegas Tradición,** which specializes in

Travel Tip

For additional information on recommended hotels and restaurants in Jerez, see p. 650.

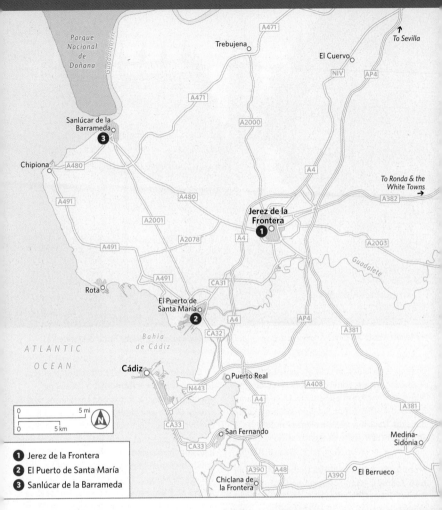

To Sevilla

Parque Nacional de Doñana

Trebujena

El Cuervo

Sanlúcar de la Barrameda **3**

Chipiona

Jerez de la Frontera **1**

To Ronda & the White Towns

Rota

El Puerto de Santa María **2**

ATLANTIC OCEAN

Cádiz

Bahía de Cádiz

Puerto Real

San Fernando

Medina-Sidonia

Chiclana de la Frontera

El Berrueco

0   5 mi
0   5 km

1 Jerez de la Frontera
2 El Puerto de Santa María
3 Sanlúcar de la Barrameda

blending and cellaring the rarest and most expensive sherries. Founder Joaquín Rivero is a leading collector of Spanish art, and part of his 15th- to 19th-century collection (including two Goyas) is displayed at the bodega.

The armed outpost of the ★ kids **Alcázar** (see p. 646, **1**) helped preserve the vineyards during Muslim rule. When the caliph of Córdoba ordered the destruction of all vineyards in 966, Jerez grape growers argued that their vines also produced raisins for the imperial armies. The caliph relented and spared two-thirds of the plantings. The country fort, where the gardens and baths are bigger than the military portion, must have been a choice

> The rare sherries at Bodegas Tradición have been aged more than 20 or 30 years.

> *Manuel María González Ángel watches over the Tío Pepe bodega, still operated by his descendants.*

posting for a Moorish soldier. **Tourist Office:** Alameda Cristina, Edificio Los Claustros. ☎ 956-338-874. www.turismojerez.com. Mon–Fri 9am–3pm and 4:30–6:30pm; Sat–Sun 9:30am–2:30pm. Bodegas Tradición: ◷ 1½ hr. Plaza Cordobeses, 3. ☎ 956-168-628. www.bodegastradicion.com. 15€. Tours by reservation Mon–Fri 9:30am–5:30pm.

From Jerez, take the N-IVa to the A-4. At exit 646, follow C-31 to El Puerto de Santa María, a total of 15km (9⅓ miles).

❷ El Puerto de Santa María. This deep-water port just a short ferry ride from Cádiz has a long and storied history. Columbus's flagship, the *Santa María*, hailed from here, and a plaque on the 12th-century castle in the heart of town honors local mariners who took part in the 1492 journey. Today, Santa María is primarily a fishing port filled with small shrimpers and deep-water tuna boats. The town's cavernous warehouses are filled with sherry.

Bodega de Mora produces manzanilla (see below) for Osborne, the company whose giant silhouettes of black bulls dot the Spanish hillsides. Reserve ahead for a tour in English Monday to Friday at 10:30am and Saturday at 11am.

Food lovers from Cádiz often hop the ferry just to eat at ★★★ **Romerijo,** a sprawling shellfish market with bar and restaurant. The choice of fish and shellfish on ice is almost overwhelming. Best bet is to order one of the sampler plates that might include three or four kinds of shrimp and a few types of saltwater crayfish or members of the lobster family. Bodega de Mora: ◷ 1 hr. C/ Los Moros, s/n. ☎ 956-869-100. www.osborne.es/rrpp. Reserve tours by e-mail: visitas.bodegas@osborne.es. 3€. Romerijo: C/ José Antonio Romero Zarazaga, 1 (at

Manzanilla vs. Fino

Light, pale, and almost astringently dry, fino is the most popular sherry in Spain. After fermentation, a layer of yeast *(flor)* settles on top of the wine in the cask. In Jerez the cold winter kills the *flor,* so the wine continues oxidizing. But the yeast survives the sea-moderated winters of El Puerto de Santa María and Sanlúcar de la Barrameda, creating the more delicate and nutty manzanilla. You might even detect a hint of salt from the sea air and coastal soil.

> *Romerijo is one of the best seafood bars on Puerto de Santa María's Ribera del Marisco (Shellfish Way).*

Ribera del Río). ☎ 956-543-353. www.romerijo. com. Market prices, usually 13€–30€ per person. AE, DC, MC, V. Lunch & dinner daily.

Follow the A-2001/Carretera de Sanlúcar 25km (16 miles) southeast from El Puerto de Santa María.

③ Sanlúcar de la Barrameda. Sanlúcar's harbor at the mouth of the Guadalquivir was once so deep that Columbus launched his third voyage to America here. But centuries of silting have made the river shallower, creating lovely in-town beaches and protecting the upstream wetlands of **Parque Doñana** (see p. 557, **⑤**). The healthy estuarine system is a fisherman's delight. Look for extraordinary shrimp, king prawns, and rock lobster on restaurant menus. Most visitors gravitate to the sandy strand at Bajo de Guia or to restaurant-lined Plaza del Cabildo.

When Magellan sailed from Sanlúcar in 1519 to circumnavigate the globe, he reportedly spent more on manzanilla than he did on armaments. Many of the town's sherry producers offer guided tours, but only ★ **Bodegas Pedro Romero** offers a free audio-guide tour whenever the shop is open. You'll get a key and a map so you can enter each building to observe the sherry-making process.

The marques emblazoned on cafe umbrellas on **Plaza del Cabildo** signal who owns each bar.

Order a plate of shrimp and a manzanilla at **Casa Balbino,** Plaza del Cabildo, 11 (☎ 956-360-513), and enjoy the sunshine. Pedro Romero: ⏱ 45 min. C/ Trasbolsa, 84. ☎ 956-360-736. www.pedroromero.es. Daily 9am–8pm. Audio-guide tour free, guided tours 6€. Guided tours in English Sept–May Tues–Fri noon and 6pm, Sat noon only; July–Aug Tues–Fri noon and 8:30pm, Sat noon only.

Spending the Night in Sanlúcar

Sanlúcar is a city of great restaurants and charming hotels. If you're spending the night, **Hotel Los Helechos** has light-filled, high-ceilinged rooms around a patio with a burbling fountain. It's a 10-minute walk to either the beach or Plaza del Cabildo. Plaza Madre de Dios, 9. ☎ 956-361-349. www.hotel loshelechos.com. Doubles 58€–76€. AE, MC, V.

★★ **Restaurante Mirador de Doñana** is arguably the best seafood restaurant in the city. The upstairs dining room has sweeping views of the bay, but the beachside tables are the most coveted. Spectacular shrimp are augmented by tuna and swordfish caught south of Cádiz. Bajo de Guia. ☎ 956-364-205. www.miradordonana.com. Lunch & dinner daily. Entrees 9€–30€. AE, MC, V.

The Renaissance Cities

In a region known for Moorish design, the cities of Úbeda, Baeza, and Jaén are showpieces of Renaissance architecture. In the 16th century, wealth from olives and textiles met its match in the talents of self-taught architect Andrés de Vandelvira, who translated the lessons of Italy into the vernacular of Spain. His work transformed the high-country cities into examples of Renaissance principles of harmony, grace, and light.

> Renaissance architect Andrés de Vandelvira's magnum opus was the Catedral de Jaén.

START Plaza Vásquez de Molina in Úbeda.
TRIP LENGTH 57km (35 miles).

❶ ★★★ Plaza Vásquez de Molina (Úbeda). Also known as Plaza Monumental, this square defined by two churches and four palaces is often cited as the most beautiful in Spain. Vandelvira learned his trade as master builder of **Sacra Capilla del Salvador** and as designer of Renaissance facades for the old **Santa María church** here. (He knew how to flatter—the chapel facade features an image of his patron as a stand-in for Christ.) With those lessons under his belt, he turned out two original masterpieces: The **Palacio de las Cadenas,** commissioned as a private palace, now serves as town hall; walk in to see the elegant courtyards. The **Palacio de Condestable Dávalos,** now a *parador,* is the most graceful of all. A modern statue of the quintessential Renaissance architect stands on the plaza. He looks satisfied. ⏱1 hr. El Salvador: 3€ adults, 1€ kids. Mon–Sat 10am–2pm and 4–6:30pm; Sun 11:15am–2pm and 4–7pm.

❷ Mirador Santa Lucía (Úbeda). Just a block past the El Salvador church, this scenic overlook at the high medieval walls of Úbeda provides sweeping views of the rolling upland plain, practically covered in olive trees. ⏱20 min.

❸ La Casa del Aceite (Úbeda). The Jaén province of Andalucía produces a tenth of the world's olive oil. The best and most distinctive is made from the region's signature Picual olive. This shop carries an excellent selection, including organic and biodynamic producers. C/ Juan Ruiz González, 19. ☎ 953-753-337. www.casadel aceite.com. MC, V.

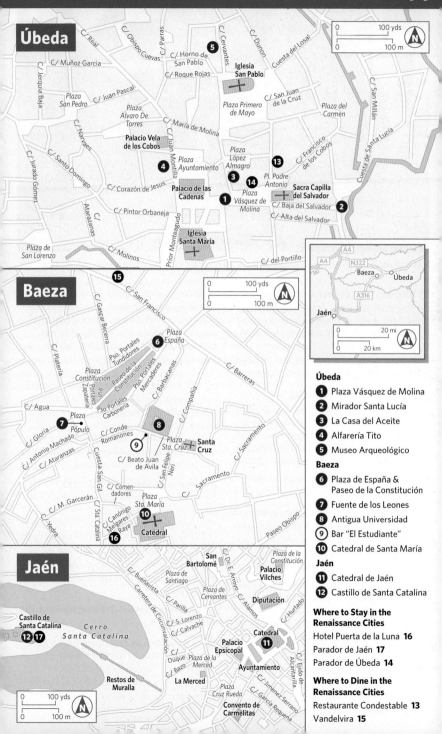

Úbeda

1 Plaza Vásquez de Molina
2 Mirador Santa Lucía
3 La Casa del Aceite
4 Alfarería Tito
5 Museo Arqueológico

Baeza

6 Plaza de España &
  Paseo de la Constitución
7 Fuente de los Leones
8 Antigua Universidad
9 Bar "El Estudiante"
10 Catedral de Santa María

Jaén

11 Catedral de Jaén
12 Castillo de Santa Catalina

**Where to Stay in the
Renaissance Cities**

Hotel Puerta de la Luna 16
Parador de Jaén 17
Parador de Úbeda 14

**Where to Dine in the
Renaissance Cities**

Restaurante Condestable 13
Vandelvira 15

> *Master potter Juan Martínez Villacañas ("Tito") throws classic Úbeda ceramics at his namesake shop.*

❹ Alfarería Tito (Úbeda). Úbeda's traditional pottery often features a distinctive dark green glaze with curves and decorative carving that evoke Moorish ceramics. Potter Juan Martínez Villacañas—aka "Tito"—is a nationally celebrated master of the style. Plaza Ayuntamiento, 12. ☎ 953-751-302. www.alfareriatito.com. MC, V.

❺ Museo Arqueológico (Úbeda). Set in a 14th-century Mudéjar house with a simple patio and pointed arches, this small museum focuses largely on the local Roman-era history. ⏱ 30 min. C/ Cervantes, 6. ☎ 953-779-432. 1.50€. Tues 2:30–8:30pm; Wed–Sat 9am–8:30pm; Sun 9am–2pm.

To reach Baeza, follow A-316 west for 9km (5⅔ miles).

❻ Plaza de España & Paseo de la Constitución (Baeza). Few of Vandelvira's buildings in Baeza have survived, but even the "modern" downtown displays a Renaissance ideal of proportion and formal rhythm with its parks and arcaded streets.

❼ ★ Fuente de los Leones (Baeza). The lions and female figure of this 16th-century fountain are nearly eroded away—not surprising given that the Iberian carvings date from at least 500 B.C. The fountain marks Plaza del Pópulo and the stairs into Baeza's old town.

❽ Antigua Universidad (Baeza). Much of the university was built after Vandelvira's time, but in his signature Renaissance style. The reddish-brown graffiti comes from the tradition of students painting their names on the buildings as a graduation ritual. Step inside to visit the classroom where poet Antonio Machado taught French from 1914 to 1919. ⏱ 30 min. C/ Beato Juan de Ávila, s/n. ☎ 953-740-150. Free. Daily 10am–2pm and 4–7pm.

⑨ 🍺 Bar "El Estudiante" (Baeza). Directly opposite the university, this cafe-bar offers the perfect refresher: a *caña* (glass) of beer with a plate of local olives and a miniroll filled with *tortilla española* (potato omelet). C/ Conde Romanones, 3. No phone. $.

❿ Catedral de Santa María (Baeza). In all the centuries of makeovers of this church accreted atop a Roman temple, the style that finally stuck was Renaissance. See the Capilla Dorada, or Golden Chapel, as the purest example. ⏱ 20 min. Plaza de Santa María, 2. ☎ 953-744-157. 2€ adults, 1€ students and seniors. Daily June–Sept 10:30am–1pm and 5–7pm; Oct–May 10:30am–1pm and 4–6pm.

To reach Jaén, follow A-316 west for 48km (30 miles).

⓫ ★★★ Catedral de Jaén. Cheerful orange trees on the plaza set the tone for this graceful church where Vandelvira turned Gothic arches into Renaissance monumentality. Considered his greatest surviving work, it wasn't finished until centuries later. Vandelvira's handling of

> The elaborate high altar of Baeza's Catedral de Santa María.

light and space combines with Pedro Roldán's humanistic carvings and statues to make this one of Spain's most upbeat cathedrals. **Plaza Santa María, s/n. ☎ 953-234-233. www.catedral dejaen.org. 3€. Tues–Sat 10:30am–1pm and 4–7pm; Sun 10:30am–1pm and 5–7pm.**

⑫ ★★ Castillo de Santa Catalina (Jaén).

Originally a Moorish castle, this fortress high above Jaén served as the front line against the Muslim kingdom of Granada for 200 years. Walk the path to the Cross Mirador for dizzying views of the valley below. Exhibits inside the keep detail Jaén's complex military history. ⏱ 1 hr. ☎ 953-120-733. Apr–Oct Tues–Sun 10am–2pm and 5–9pm; Nov–Mar Tues–Sun 10am–2pm and 3:30–7:30pm. 3.50€ adults, 2.50€ seniors and students, 1.50€ kids.

Where to Stay & Dine

Hotel Puerta de la Luna BAEZA

The Renaissance grace of a 16th-century building is the perfect backdrop to this clean, modern boutique hotel. The hotel's restaurant, **La Pintada,** serves contemporary market cuisine in a beautiful, formal room. C/ Canónigo Melgares Raya, s/n. ☎ 953-747-019. www.hotelpuerta delaluna.es. 44 rooms. Doubles 79€–129€. Entrees 12€–21€. AE, DC, MC, V. Lunch Tues–Sun, dinner Tues–Sat.

Parador de Jaén JAÉN

Parts of the castle of Santa Catalina are now this *parador,* where soaring ceilings in the dining room and salons, wrought-iron lights, and massive doors play up its medieval origins. Rooms look out on a patchwork of olive groves on the surrounding hills. Castillo de Santa Catalina, s/n. ☎ 953-230-000. www.parador.es. 45 rooms. Doubles 148€–160€. Entrees 13€–25€. AE, MC, V. Breakfast, lunch & dinner daily.

★★★ Parador de Úbeda ÚBEDA

This majestic and stately *parador* was built by Vandelvira for the dean of the adjacent El Salvador church. There's no better way to immerse yourself in the distinctive architecture of Úbeda than by booking a room, ideally one of six overlooking the plaza. Plaza Vázquez Molina, s/n. ☎ 953-750-345. www.parador.es. 36 rooms. Doubles 160€–171€. AE, DC, MC, V.

★ Restaurante Condestable ÚBEDA ANDA-LUCÍAN

Úbeda has a distinct local cuisine, well represented here. Try roast kid with fried garlic cloves, or *andrajos* soup, a local chowder with vegetables, pasta, shrimp, and cod cooked in fish broth. C/ Horno de Contador, 11. ☎ 953-750-278. Entrees 14€–22€. MC, V. Lunch & dinner Tues–Sun.

★Vandelvira BAEZA ANDALUCÍAN

This 16th-century former convent has been converted into a citadel of good cooking. Milk-fed lamb is the way to go, but if you're willing to experiment, try the pigs' knuckles. Calle de San Francisco, 14. ☎ 953-748-172. www.vandelvira.es. Entrees 12€–25€. AE, DC, MC, V. Lunch & dinner Tues–Sat; lunch only Sun.

Sevilla

An ancient and storied city, Sevilla has been the center of wealth and power in Andalucía since the 12th century, first as the capital of al-Andalus under the Almohad dynasty, then as the southern Christian capital under the kings of Castilla. Start with the monumental structures that embody the struggle of faith and power—the cathedral and its iconic bell tower, and the sprawling palace complex of the Alcázar. There often seem to be two religions in Sevilla: an ardent form of Roman Catholicism that finds its full expression in the baroque architecture and decoration of the churches, and the dark blood faith in *duende* (spirit) voiced in the deep song and passionate dance of flamenco. Peek in on a flamenco museum founded by one of the top dancers of the late 20th century, and visit two cherished parish churches—while pondering the mysticism of Sevilla master painters Bartholomé Esteban Murillo (1617–82) and Francisco de Zurbarán (1598–1664) in the city's fine arts museum.

> *The Patio de las Doncellas, perhaps a reference to the Reconquista myth that Spain's Muslim rulers required an annual tribute of 100 virgins from Iberia's Christian kings.*

START Plaza Virgen de los Reyes.

1 Plaza Virgen de los Reyes. At some point, you'll find yourself standing in this crossroads of Sevilla tourism as you keep backing up to squeeze the cathedral and La Giralda into a picture. Turn around and any side street will lead you into the Barrio Santa Cruz. Turn another direction and you'll face the Plaza del Triunfo, the entry to the Real Alcázar. In the early morning, carriage horses clip-clop into the plaza as they come to work, and flocks of pigeons startle to the sudden buzz of a Spanish mosquito, or motor scooter. By evening, travelers gather around the fountain to share their experience as water burbles from gargoyles.

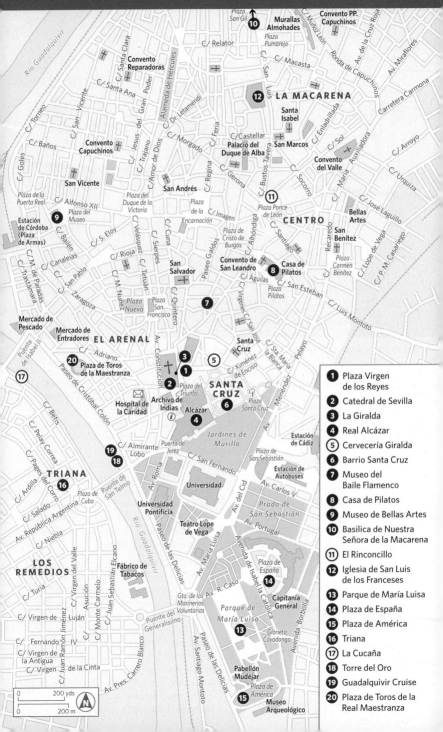

Río Guadalquivir

Plaza San Gil

Convento PP. Capuchinos

Murallas Almohades

C/ Relator

C/ Macasta

Ronda de Capuchinos

Av. de la Cruz Roja

Av. Miraflores

Convento Reparadoras

C/ Santa Clara

C/ Santa Ana

C/ San Vicente

C/ Torneo

C/ Baños

C/ Goles

Alameda de Hércules

C/ Jesús del Gran Poder

C/ Trajano

C/ Amor de Dios

C/ Morgado

C/ Feria

Plaza Pumarejo

C/ San Luis

LA MACARENA

C/ Muñoz León

C/ Castellar

Santa Isabel

San Marcos

C/ Enladrillada

C/ Sol

Carretera Carmona

Convento Capuchinos

San Vicente

Plaza de la Puerta Real

C/ Alfonso XII

Plaza del Museo

Estación de Córdoba (Plaza de Armas)

C/ Bailén

C/ M. de Paradas

C/ Trastámara

C/ Canalejas

C/ San Pablo

C/ Zaragoza

C/ S. Eloy

C/ Velázquez

C/ Rioja

C/ Sierpes

C/ Cuna

C/ Tetuán

C/ M. Núñez

Plaza del Duque de la Victoria

Plaza de la Encarnación

San Andrés

San Salvador

Plaza de Cristo de Burgos

Plaza Nueva

Plaza San Francisco

C/ Quintero

Paseo Galdós

Convento de San Leandro

Casa de Pilatos

C/ Águilas

Plaza Pilatos

C/ Virgenes

C/ San Esteban

C/ Luis Montoto

Palació del Duque de Alba

C/ Gerona

C/ Regina

C/ Imagen

C/ Bustos Tavera

Plaza de la Alhóndiga

C/ Socorro

C/ Santiago

Plaza Ponce de León

CENTRO

Convento del Valle

C/ María Auxiliadora

C/ Arroyo

C/ Urquiza

C/ José Laguillo

Bellas Artes

San Benítez

Recaredo

Plaza Carmen Benítez

C/ Lope de Vega

C/ P. M. Casariego

C/ Luis Montoto

Mercado de Pescado

Mercado de Entradores

EL ARENAL

Plaza de Toros de la Maestranza

Puente de Isabel II

Paseo de Cristóbal Colón

C/ Adriano

Av. Constitución

Santa Cruz

C/ Ximénez de Enciso

SANTA CRUZ

C/ Sta. María la Blanca

C/ San José

Pelayo

Menéndez

Estación de Cádiz

Hospital de la Caridad

Archivo de Indias

Alcázar

Plaza del Triunfo

Plaza Santa Cruz

Jardines de Murillo

Puerto de Jerez

C/ Almirante Lobo

C/ San Fernando

Av. Roma

TRIANA

C/ Betis

C/ Pelay Correa

C/ Pagés del Corro

C/ Ardilla

C/ Salado

Av. República Argentina

C/ Niebla

Plaza de Cuba

Puente de San Telmo

Universidad

Universidad Pontificia

Teatro Lope de Vega

Río Guadalquivir

Paseo de las Delicias

Estación de Cádiz

Plaza de San Sebastián

Estación de Autobuses

Av. Carlos V

Prado de San Sebastián

Av. Portugal

Capitanía General

Plaza de España

LOS REMEDIOS

C/ Turia

C/ Virgen de Luján

C/ Asunción

C/ Monte Carmelo

C/ Virgen de

C/ Fernando IV

C/ Virgen de la Antigua

C/ Virgen de la Cinta

Fábrico de Tabacos

C/ Juan Sebastián Elcano

C/ Juan Ramón Jiménez

Av. María Luisa

Av. del Cid

Av. de Isabel la Católica

Gta. de los Marineros Voluntarios

Puente del Generalísimo

Parque de María Luisa

Glorieta Covadonga

Pabellón Mudéjar

Plaza de América

Museo Arqueológico

Av. Pres. Carrero Blanco

Av. Santiago Montoto

Paseo de las Delicias

Av. R. Caso

Avenida Borbolla

0   200 yds
0   200 m

N

1 Plaza Virgen de los Reyes
2 Catedral de Sevilla
3 La Giralda
4 Real Alcázar
5 Cervecería Giralda
6 Barrio Santa Cruz
7 Museo del Baile Flamenco
8 Casa de Pilatos
9 Museo de Bellas Artes
10 Basílica de Nuestra Señora de la Macarena
11 El Rinconcillo
12 Iglesia de San Luis de los Franceses
13 Parque de María Luisa
14 Plaza de España
15 Plaza de América
16 Triana
17 La Cucaña
18 Torre del Oro
19 Guadalquivir Cruise
20 Plaza de Toros de la Real Maestranza

> *A 2006 DNA analysis assured Sevillanos that the remains of Columbus do in fact rest in their cathedral.*

❷ ★ **Catedral de Sevilla.** Determined to prove that bigger is better, the cathedral was begun in 1402 on the site of the Almohad mosque. "We shall have a church of such kind that those who see it built will think we were madmen," an anonymous clergyman wrote. Just over a century later (1506), the largest Gothic church in Europe (third in size only to St. Peter's in Rome and St. Paul's in London) opened to worshipers. Its altarpiece, the world's largest, was the life's work of Fleming Pieter Dancart, who carved and gilded 45 scenes from the life of Christ. But despite lavish gold decoration throughout, the cathedral remains wholly Gothic, its spaces soaring into the darkness above. Only some side altars exhibit Sevilla's typical baroque style.

If you see young women praying before Murillo's atmospheric rendering of the *Vision de San Antonio,* they are likely seeking the intercession of the patron saint of the lovelorn.

Visitors exit through the **Patio de Naranjas,** originally the ablutions court of the mosque, where the faithful washed before prayer. It is a haunting reminder of the grandeur that was lost when the mosque was leveled in 1401.

The modern tomb of Christopher Columbus (his remains retrieved from Cuba in 1899) was installed in 1902, just inside the Puerta San Cristóbal. A debate raged for many years about whether the remains were in fact Columbus's, since he had been successively buried at several sites. DNA analysis finally concluded in 2006 that the body is indeed the explorer. ⏲ 1 hr. Puerta San Cristóbal. ☎ 954-214-971. www. catedraldesevilla.es. 8€ adults, 2€ students and seniors, free for kids 15 & under. July–Aug Mon-Sat 9:30am–4pm, Sun 2:30–6pm; Sept–June Mon-Sat 11am–5pm, Sun 2:30–6pm.

❸ ★★ kids **La Giralda.** When the Catedral de Sevilla's original architects reused the old mosque's minaret as the cathedral's bell tower, called La Giralda, a symbol of Moorish Sevilla was transformed into an emblem of Christianity. When four globes on top fell in an earthquake, they were replaced in 1582 with a belfry containing 25 bells and crowned by a weather vane of a woman depicting Faith—the herald of La Giralda. The summit is reached by a series of 34 ramps installed so the muezzin could ride his horse to the top to call the faithful to prayer.

Only from the top can you truly appreciate the cathedral's bulk and its dominance over the city. ⏱ **45 min. Combined admission with cathedral; see above.**

④ ★★★ kids Real Alcázar. The last Moorish rulers of Sevilla and the Castilian kings who ousted them thought a lot alike. The Almohads built their palace next to the mosque, and the conquerors followed suit, creating a complex of gardens and palaces that rivals the Alhambra and Generalife in Granada (see p. 624). Spanish kings have lived here since the 13th century, making it the oldest royal palace in Europe still in use.

The **Palacio Mudéjar** is the architectural tour de force of the Alcázar. Pedro I (aka "the Cruel") ordered it built in 1362, and tradition says he employed some of the same artisans who worked simultaneously on the Alhambra in Granada. The carved plaster and stone, the delicate arches, and the calligraphic friezes all echo the Nasrid style of the Alhambra, and interior rooms feature carved wooden ceilings and decorative tiles. The sunny **Patio de las Doncellas** (Courtyard of the Damsels) sits at the center. Some ground-level rooms contain a scholarly exhibit on the history of Sevilla tile making, but wander through to find the **Patio de las Muñecas** (Courtyard of the Dolls), where the royal children once played. Its cool overhangs and fish pond offer tranquil respite from the crowds elsewhere in the Alcázar.

The more austere **Palacio Gótico** was built in the 13th century by Alfonso X ("the Wise"). In the early 16th century, the plain structure underwent a decorative makeover to mark the achievements of Holy Roman Emperor Carlos V, the first Hapsburg king of Spain. The Great Hall is hung with tapestries depicting his 1535 conquest of Tunis. The Sala de Fiestas room was covered with painted tiles to celebrate his wedding in March 1526 to Isabella of Portugal, his first cousin, a union that triggered the genetic problems that afflicted the Hapsburg line.

The Alcázar gardens are a mix of Moorish, Renaissance, and baroque styles, but all of them have prominent water features, including a spouting waterfall where visitors crowd the railing to take group pictures. ⏱ **2 hr. Patio de Banderas. ☎ 954-502-324. www.patronato-alcazarsevilla.es. 7€, free for students and seniors. Apr–Sept Tues–Sun 9:30am–7pm; Oct–Mar Tues–Sun 9:30am–5pm.**

> *The Palacio Mudéjar at Sevilla's Real Alcázar, on par with Granada's Alhambra for Nasrid craftsmanship.*

> It may be worth getting lost in the charming Barrio Santa Cruz, Sevilla's former Jewish quarter.

⑤ 🍺 **Cervecería Giralda.** Before you plunge into the Barrio Santa Cruz, stop here for a beer and maybe a tapa of duck-breast slices on mushrooms. This place is a hangout for tourists and Sevillanos alike. Unlike most bars, it serves food continuously from morning until midnight. C/ Mateos Gago, 1. ☎ 954-228-250. $.

❻ **Barrio Santa Cruz.** When Fernando III (San Fernando) captured Sevilla in 1248, he installed a large contingent of Jews to run the royal palace and business matters, settling them in this neighborhood close to the cathedral. Today the twisting narrow streets are filled with shops and cafes. Every visitor has a tale of getting delightfully lost, only to stumble into a plaza where flower boxes overflow with geraniums, a fountain trickles at the center, and a waiter stands by a table, ready to bring a drink.

❼ ★★ 🧒 **Museo del Baile Flamenco.** "Queen of Flamenco" Cristina Hoyos is among the vanguard of flamenco artists responsible for the new golden age of their art form. Best known to international audiences for her soulful performances in Antonio Gades's "flamenco trilogy" of films—*Bodas de Sangre, Carmen,* and *El Amor Brujo*—she founded this museum in 2006 to introduce outsiders to an art where music and dance are inseparable. While most museums treat flamenco as a pantheon of great, usually dead performers, the Museum of Flamenco Dance treats the art as eternal sound and movement—a tradition that outlives individual performers. You can go as deep as you want here, delving into the subtle influences a dozen cultures have exerted on flamenco, or you can simply enjoy video clips that clarify the various styles. The museum often features up-and-coming flamenco artists in weekend concerts. ⊙ 1 hr. C/ Manuel Rojas Marcos, 3. ☎ 954-340-311. www.museoflamenco.com. 10€, 8€ students, 6€ kids. Apr–Oct daily 9am–7pm; Nov–Mar daily 9am–6pm.

❽ **Casa de Pilatos.** The ducal families that built, inherited, and renovated this lovely palace at the edge of Barrio Santa Cruz represented the cutting edge of Spanish nobility. They were always just a cousin or two away from the throne and hence enjoyed lucrative grants of lands and privileges. The governor of Andalucía had the house built when his son, the Marqués de Tarifa, returned from a pilgrimage to the Holy Land in 1519. Tarifa created a Way of the Cross in Sevilla that would parallel the route Jesus took to Golgotha from the house of Pontius Pilate. This palace, naturally, represented the house of Pilate. During Holy Week, religious brotherhoods still follow the path in their penitential processions.

The house is neither Roman (as the connection to Pilate would suggest) nor reverentially austere. When the Medinaceli family reclaimed their ancestral home after the Civil War, they restored it to a Renaissance elegance, paying special attention to the gardens. (Gardens are always a sign of great wealth in a desert climate like Andalucía.) Bougainvillea bloom in magenta profusion on the arched entry to the property, and the statuary and shade trees in the patios frame lush greenery and fountains. Skip the optional house tour unless you have a strong interest in the evolution of decorating styles among Spanish nobility. ⏱ 1 hr. Plaza de Pilatos, 1. ☎ 954-225-298. www.fundacionmedina celi.org. 5€; inquire for hours of guided house tours, which cost 3€ extra. Apr–Oct daily 9am–7pm; Nov–Mar daily 9am–6pm. Bus: C3, C4, 21–23.

⑨ ★★ Museo de Bellas Artes. Second only to Madrid's Prado in holdings of Spanish art, Sevilla's fine arts museum is especially rich in religious paintings seized from convents closed in the 19th century when the government disenfranchised the church. The museum, in fact, occupies the former Merced Calzadas convent, with its astounding tiled courtyard. It is crowded with religious paintings by Sevillano artist Bartolomé Esteban Murillo, including a gigantic rendering of his favorite subject, the Immaculate Conception. Francisco Polanco's 1640 portraits of saints created for the Convento de Capuchinos include a rendering of St. Paul in

the throes of god-ridden madness. But the best paintings in the museum are portraits of monks and saints by Francisco de Zurbarán, another Sevillano. Zurbarán painted in an autobiographical tone. His early works show the holy men imbued with vigor, while his late works give their corruptible flesh a deathly pallor. If this seems just too dark and mystical, head to the 19th-century galleries for sunny images of society ladies in parks and carnal cigar rollers at the tobacco factory. ⏱ 2 hr. Plaza del Museo 9. ☎ 954-786-500. www.museosdeandalucia.es. 1.50€, free for students. Tues–Sat 9am–8:30pm; Sun 9am–2:30pm. Bus: B2.

⑩ ★ Basilica de Nuestra Señora de la Macarena. Possibly the best-loved parish church in Sevilla, the Macarena sits just inside the ruins of the 12th-century Moorish walls on the north end of the Old City. The great dome is covered with beautiful Sevilla tiles—a colloquial manifestation of the baroque impulse afoot in the city when the church was built in the late 17th century. The namesake of the church (and the neighborhood) is the 17th-century carving of the Esperanza Macarena, mounted in a silver altar. The parade of this statue through the streets is one of the highlights of Holy Week, but the church is perhaps

> La Visita de San Bruno al Papa Urbano II *(1630–1635) in a Zurbarán gallery at Sevilla's Museo de Bellas Artes.*

> *Each tiled alcove of the Plaza de España highlights a Spanish city or province—an architectural travel guide.*

at its best on Saturdays, when wedding parties in flamenco-inspired fashion wait their turn for nuptial masses. ⏱ 20 min. C/ Becquer 1. ☎ 954-901-800. Free. Mon–Sat 9am–2pm and 5–9pm; Sun opens 9:30am.

⑪ 🍺 **El Rinconcillo.** This classic *tasca*, or pub, where your tab is marked with chalk on the bar, is a perfect crib course in Sevillano tapas. Regulars favor the spinach and chickpeas and slices of *caña de lomo Ibérico*, a sausage made from the same pigs that provide the most expensive ham. Vintage posters of Sevilla's annual Feria de Abril festival (see p. 609) cover the dining room walls. C/ Gerona 40. ☎ 954-223-183. Daily 1pm–1:30am. $.

⑫ **Iglesia de San Luis de los Franceses.** San Luis, a 1731 church built for Jesuit novices, is hardly the gaudiest of Sevilla's baroque religious sights. Several Zurbarán paintings flank the main altar, but the paintings of heaven inside the cupola are the main reason to visit. A table-height round mirror on the floor below reflects the magical image of muscular angels romping through the hereafter. ⏱ 15 min. C/ San Luis. ☎ 954-550-207. Free. Tues–Thurs 9am–2pm; Fri–Sat 9am–2pm and 5–8pm.

⑬ ★★ 🧒 **Parque de María Luisa.** When Spain's princess María Luisa de Borbón graciously gave the city some of her lands in 1914, the stage was set to transform a royal retreat into a public amenity. Landscape architect Nicolas Forestier quickly fashioned the district into Parque de María Luisa, one of the most beautiful and tranquil neighborhoods in central Sevilla. The green oasis was chosen as the site for the Exposición Ibero-Americana of 1929, King Alfonso XIII's scheme to showcase Spain's newfound modernity while bolstering Andalucía's flagging economy. Former colonies (as well as trade partners like the U.S., Morocco, and Portugal) constructed neo-Mudéjar palaces and pavilions throughout the park. The collapse of the U.S. stock market and ensuing worldwide depression put a damper on the festivities, and Sevilla was saddled with debt for the next half century. But the trees and gardens remain, as do the pavilions, now mostly foreign consulates or university buildings. ⏱ 3 hr. Bus: AC, B2, C4, 5, 21, 22, 23. Tram: Universidad.

> *Visitors can thank the 1929 Spanish-American Exposition for the verdant paths and pavilions of the Parque de María Luisa.*

> *The painted cupola of the Iglesia de San Luis de los Franceses once urged Jesuit novices to look heavenward.*

14 ★★ **kids Plaza de España.** Built as Sevilla's own pavilion for the 1929 Expo, architect Anibel González anchored this grand semicircle with baroque towers on each end and covered almost every surface in bright Sevilla tiles. Each of the 54 enclosures depicts a scene from a Spanish city or province—enduring enticements to see the whole country. On weekends, you can navigate the surrounding canal in a rented rowboat.

15 ★ **kids Plaza de América.** Three Expo pavilions surround the broad Plaza de America, where vendors sell cracked corn to feed the flocks of white pigeons, and small children delight in flushing them into flight. Two of these pavilions now contain museums.

The brightly colored Mudéjar Pavilion of the **Museo de Artes y Costumbres Populares** seems an appropriate setting for exhibits of traditional Andalucían costumes and traditional crafts such as ceramics and leatherwork. The best displays are of flamenco garb and old Feria de Abril (see p. 609), Semana Santa, and bullfight posters.

> *On nice days, bars and seafood joints along the Guadalquivir in Sevilla's Triana neighborhood set out tables.*

Set in a more staid Gothic-style pavilion, the **Museo Arqueológico** focuses primarily on Sevilla's Roman heritage. Don't miss the copy of the Tesoro Carambola—a hoard of 6th-century-B.C. gold jewelry from the Tartessian civilization unearthed near Sevilla in 1958. Artes: ◷ 30 min. ☎ 954-232-576. 1.50€. Tues 3–8pm; Wed–Sat 9am–8pm; Sun 9am–2pm. Archeológico: ◷ 1 hr. ☎ 954-232-401. 1.50€. Tues 2:30–8:30pm; Wed–Sat 9am–8:30pm; Sun 9am–2:30pm.

16 Triana. This neighborhood across the Río Guadalquivir is the traditional *gitano*, or Gypsy, quarter of Sevilla, and it remains perhaps the most colorful barrio in the city. The district around C/ San Jorge continues Sevilla's 2,000-year tradition of tile making. Brightly painted blue, white, yellow, and green *azulejo* tiles were introduced during the Moorish period, and the tiles remain popular for entryways and decorative walls, even in new construction (see "Sevilla Shopping," p. 601). Triana has also produced many bullfighters (tiled plaques note their birthplaces) and flamenco musicians and dancers. Many Triana tailors specialize in flamenco

clothing worn by both performers and ordinary Sevillanos during Feria (see p. 609). In warm weather, bars and *marisquerías* (seafood shops) set up outdoor tables along the riverbank from Puerta de Triana, at the foot of Puente Isabel II, all the way to Puente San Telmo, where fancier restaurants own the waterfront property. Bus: B2, C3, 5, 40–43.

17 🍴 **La Cucaña.** Waterfront tables in the shade of decorative Sevilla orange trees at this bar-restaurant near Puente Isabel II have splendid views of the Sevilla skyline. A chilled bowl of gazpacho is the perfect refresher. Just watch out for falling fruit. C/ Betis, 9. ☎ 954-340-131. $$.

18 Torre del Oro. Built in 1220 as an Almohad tower to protect the city from Christian invaders, the "tower of gold" houses a small naval museum with old cannons, sextants, and even a model of one of the caravels in Columbus's 1492 expedition. ◷ 30 min. Paseo de Colón. ☎ 954-222-419. 2€, free Tues. Mon–Fri 10am–2pm; Sat–Sun 11am–2pm.

> *An hour's boat tour along the Guadalquivir River will get you acquainted with Sevilla.*

19 kids **Guadalquivir Cruise.** It's hard to beat a cruise to get a feel for how the river undulates through the city. You'll see 900 years of skyline, from the Torre del Oro (see above) to Santiago Calatrava's harp-shaped Puente del Alamillo, the artful bridge he built for the 1992 Expo. Boats run by **Cruceros Torre del Oro** depart every 30 minutes. Narrated in six languages, the trip lasts 1 hour. Paseo Alcalde Marqués del Contadero. ☎ 954-561-692 or 954-211-396. www.cruceros torredeloro.com. 16€, free for kids 13 & under. Nov–Feb daily 11am–7pm; Mar–Oct daily 11am–11pm.

20 **Plaza de Toros de la Real Maestranza.** Built in the 18th century, this bullring seats 14,000—and it's full for almost every *corrida*. The theatrical pageant of the modern bullfight evolved here. The ring has an unsettling intimacy and

> *The Torre del Oro lost its* oro *years ago when thieves made off with the gold tiling that covered it.*

Two-Wheel Sevilla

Tangled networks of one-way medieval streets and the near-absence of parking garages make driving a car in Sevilla challenging. But there's a good alternative for covering a lot of ground quickly: The municipal bicycle rental program, **SEVICI** (☎ 902-011-032; www.sevici.es), provides access to bikes for a 5€ weekly "subscription" charge plus an even smaller hourly fee (.50€–1€ per hour). The snazzy red bikes are parked in 250 areas all over the city, each with a kiosk where you can subscribe by credit card as well as pick up or deposit bikes. Cities all over Europe have been copying the Sevilla program. For your first outing, try the broad paths in Parque de María Luisa.

acoustics that allow spectators to hear every snort of the bull or gasp of the matador. A 20-minute tour puts a human side on the sport, especially in the *enfermería,* where wounded bullfighters are treated. Unless there's a special festival going on, bullfights occur on Sundays; the best are staged during the Feria de Abril de Sevilla (see p. 609). Tickets tend to be pricey and should be purchased in advance at the ticket office on C/ Adriano. ⏱ 1 hr. Paseo de Colón, 18. ☎ 954-224-577. 4€. Daily 9:30am–7pm by guided tour; tour departs every 40 min. Bus: B2, C4.

THE SPANISH SOUNDTRACK

Flamenco's Gypsy Blues Echo from Every Corner

BY PATRICIA HARRIS & DAVID LYON

THE ART FORM of flamenco is much more than women in high heels and polka-dot dresses. It's a fusion music born of North African, Iberian, Celtic, and Romany (Gypsy) roots. The traditional Andalucían art was discouraged by the Franco government but exploded into popularity with the 1971 album *Entre Dos Aguas,* by guitarist Paco de Lucía and singer Camarón de la Isla. Even revived popularity hasn't changed the basics: Music, rhythm, and dance are so interdependent that even the dancers get credit on the studio recording sessions.

The Essential Flamenco Playlist

1. *Entre Dos Aguas*
Paco de Lucía,
Camarón de la Isla
2. *La Lleyenda del Tiempo* Camarón de la
Isla, Tomatito

3. *Palma y Cornoa*
Carmen Linares
4. *Barrio Negro*
Tomatito
5. *Mira Que Bonita Es*
Ramón El Portugués

6. *Habichuela en Rama* Ketama, Pepe
Habichuela
7. *Nostalgia Granadina* Niño Ricardo
8. *Calles de Cádiz*
Enrique Morente

Meet the Stars

CARMEN AMAYA
(1913–63)
This Gypsy dancer fled Spain during the Civil War and popularized *flamenco pura* in Latin America and the U.S. before returning to Spain as an international star. Her descendants preserve her fiery performance style.

PEPE HABICHUELA
(b. 1944)
Hailing from the Gypsy caves of Sacromonte, the guitarist and band leader introduced modern harmonies to flamenco and explored collaborations with jazz and Indian music.

CRISTINA HOYOS
(b. 1946)
The principal dancer from 1968 to 1988 with the Antonio Gades troupe, Hoyos starred in three seminal flamenco films by Carlos Saura and founded the Museo del Baile Flamenco in Sevilla.

PACO DE LUCÍA
(b. 1947)
The virtuoso guitarist began touring with José Greco at age 11 and spurred the flamenco revival; today he's the acknowledged technical and stylistic master of modern flamenco guitar.

CAMARÓN DE LA ISLA
(1950–92)
This fair-haired Gypsy vaulted from singing at bus stops to stardom at age 16, recording 10 albums with Paco de Lucía. His unfettered emotional style remains the benchmark of flamenco singing.

CARMEN LINARES
(b. 1951)
Arguably the greatest *cantaora* (woman flamenco singer) of her era, her encyclopedic repertoire embraces virtually all styles and forms of flamenco. She remains a popular recording and television star.

TOMATITO
(b. 1958)
This Málaga-born guitarist rose to fame as an accompanist for Camarón de la Isla but became a concert star after Camarón's death. He often sacrifices flashy technique in favor of brilliant, even minimal phrasing.

Keeping the Beat

While the singer, guitarist, and lead dancer often draw all the attention in flamenco performances, a complete troupe may have several musicians solely devoted to maintaining the complex rhythms. The basic beat (usually 11–13 beats per measure) is kept by the *cajón*, a wooden drum with bass tones. Hand claps are the key rhythmic device, and different musicians may perform three interwoven rhythms at a time. Castanets, rarely used in authentic flamenco, sometimes fill in for hand claps in large venues.

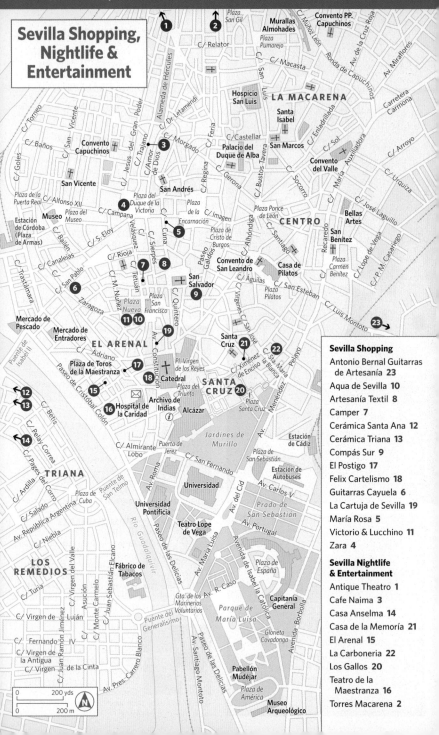

Sevilla Shopping, Nightlife & Entertainment

Sevilla Shopping

Antonio Bernal Guitarras de Artesanía **23**

Aqua de Sevilla **10**

Artesanía Textil **8**

Camper **7**

Cerámica Santa Ana **12**

Cerámica Triana **13**

Compás Sur **9**

El Postigo **17**

Felix Cartelismo **18**

Guitarras Cayuela **6**

La Cartuja de Sevilla **19**

María Rosa **5**

Victorio & Lucchino **11**

Zara **4**

Sevilla Nightlife & Entertainment

Antique Theatro **1**

Cafe Naima **3**

Casa Anselma **14**

Casa de la Memoria **21**

El Arenal **15**

La Carboneria **22**

Los Gallos **20**

Teatro de la Maestranza **16**

Torres Macarena **2**

Sevilla Shopping

Ceramics

Cerámica Santa Ana TRIANA

This tile-encrusted building might be its own best advertisement. The factory and show-room, which opened in 1870, has the broadest and most tempting selection of painted tiles, pots, tableware, and decorative items in Sevilla's *azulejo* tradition. C/ San Jorge, 31. ☎ 954-333-990. MC, V. Bus: B2, C3, 43.

Cerámica Triana TRIANA

An olive dish with an attached holder for the pits makes a great souvenir. This smaller ceramics showroom is a good place to find one. C/ Antillane Campos, 3–4. ☎ 954-33-179. MC, V. Bus: B2, C3, 43.

El Postigo ARENAL

Many individual ceramics artists display at this arts-and-crafts market that also carries leather, jewelry, and even silver hair combs. C/ Arfe. ☎ 954-560-013. AE, MC, V. Bus: C5. Tram: Archivo de Indias.

> *Everything ceramic at Cerámica Santa Ana.*

La Cartuja de Sevilla CENTRO

If you prefer fine china in the English style to the Moorish earthenware, check the outlet for this factory that dates from 1839. Avenida de la Constitución, 16. ☎ 954-214-155. www.lacartuja desevilla.es. V. Tram: Archivo de Indias.

Fashion

Aqua de Sevilla CENTRO

This shop stocks women's clothing, but the real specialties are fragrances derived from sweet flowers of the bitter Sevilla orange. Plaza Nueva, 9. ☎ 954-213-145. AE, DC, MC, V. Bus: C5. Tram: Plaza Nueva.

Artesanía Textil CENTRO

Hand-embroidered silk shawls are iconic in Sevilla fashion. They run as high as 1,500€ here, but machine-made synthetics are available for as low as 35€. C/ Sierpes, 70. ☎ 954-562-840. www.artesania-textil.com. MC, V. Bus: B2, C5.

Camper CENTRO

Ultracomfortable shoes for men and women have a funky charm and a cult following.

> *Embroidered silk shawls at Artesanía Textil.*

C/ Tetuán, 24. ☎ 954-222-811. AE, DC, MC, V. Bus: C5. Tram: Plaza Nueva.

María Rosa CENTRO
Just lift the weighted hem on a flamenco dress and you'll appreciate the muscles behind the artistry. The shop outfits men, women, and children. C/ Cuna, 13. ☎ 954-217-293. www.maria rosa-sevilla.com. AE, DC, MC, V. Bus: B2, C5.

Victorio & Lucchino CENTRO
It doesn't cost anything to look in the boutique of Sevilla's top international fashion designers. Plaza Nueva, 10. ☎ 954-227-951. www.victorioy lucchino.com. AE, DC, MC, V. Bus: C5. Tram: Plaza Nueva.

Zara CENTRO
This Spanish company is queen of the knock-offs, producing up-to-the-minute styles at affordable prices. Plaza Duque, 1. ☎ 954-214-875. www.zara.es. MC, V. Bus: B2, C5.

Music
Antonio Bernal Guitarras de Artesanía SANTA JUSTA Valeriano Bernal has made the family name one of the most respected brands in classical and flamenco guitars. His nephew, Antonio, carries on the legacy. C/ Hernando del Pulgar, 20. ☎ 954-582-679. www.antoniobernal. com. MC, V. Tram: Santa Justa.

Compás Sur CENTRO
The store's name refers to the percussive clapping of flamenco and Andalucían folk music—specialties of this independent store that carries CDs, sheet music, and rhythm instruments. Cuesta del Rosario, 7-F. ☎ 954-215-662. www.compas-sur.com. MC, V. Bus: C5.

Guitarras Cayuela ARENAL
Four generations of luthiers have been making classical and flamenco instruments for discerning musicians since the 1950s. C/ Zaragosa, 4. ☎ 954-224-557. www.juanluiscayuela.com. AE, DC, MC, V. Bus C5.

Posters
Felix Cartelismo CENTRO
This antiques dealer specializes in all sizes of vintage posters promoting Semana Santa, Feria de Abril, bullfights, and Spanish tourism destinations. Avenida Constitución, 26. ☎ 954-218-026. MC, V. Tram: Archivo de Indias.

Open-Air Markets

Nothing quite beats the fun of surveying the goods at an open-air market to discover something you didn't know you were looking for—and haggling over the price.

For **collectibles,** head to the Plaza del Cabildo; vendors flood the market with stamps and coins, pins, old watches, medals, and other "smalls" on Sunday mornings. Some are shop owners on the plaza whose stores are open the rest of the week.

Paintings, prints, sketches, and other **art,** mainly by locals, form an outdoor gallery on Sunday mornings on the Plaza del Museo, by the Museo de Bellas Artes. The work varies in style and quality.

Also known as "Jueves" because it takes place on Thursday mornings, the **antiques** street market on C/ Feria is one of the city's oldest. "Antiques" is a loose term, as some vendors offer antique computer games and CDs. Others have picture frames, furniture, and vintage jewelry.

The **hippie markets,** more kindly called "crafts" markets, are Thursday-to-Saturday street markets on Plaza del Duque and Plaza de la Magdalena. They overflow with belts, scarves, beadwork, tooled leather, and carved wooden boxes. Magdalena has many African vendors, some selling folk art.

Sevilla Restaurants

Egaña-Oriza SANTA CRUZ *BASQUE*
Great game dishes, such as pigeon with rice, top the exquisite menu of one of Sevilla's classiest restaurants. Formal dinner is best in the fine dining room, but summer meals under the orange trees in the garden are magical. C/ San Fernando, 21. ☎ 954-227-211. www.restauranteoriza.com. Entrees 25€–50€. AE, DC, MC, V. Lunch Mon–Fri, dinner Mon–Sat. Closed Sat July–Aug. Bus: C3, C4, 21, 23. Tram: Prado de San Sebastian.

Enrique Becerra ARENAL *ANDALUCÍAN* The downstairs dining room is wonderfully old-fashioned, while the upstairs room is more intimate and casual. Both serve the same great Andalucían dishes, including authentic gazpacho and thick slabs of tuna steak in season. C/ Gamazo, 2. ☎ 954-213-049. www.enriquebecerra.com. Entrees 12€–22€. AE, DC, MC, V. Lunch & dinner Mon–Sat. Closed Aug. Bus: 21, 25, 30, 40.

Mesón Don Raimundo SANTA CRUZ *ANDALUCÍAN* With its handsome carved wood and elaborate tiles, this is one of the most atmospheric dining rooms in the Old City. Deeply flavored dishes, such as wild duck cooked in sherry, pay homage to Sevilla's Mozarabic past. Save room for the Arab-inspired desserts featuring nuts and honey. C/ Argote de Molina, 26. ☎ 954-223-355. www.mesondonraimundo.com. Entrees 16€–25€. DC, MC, V. Lunch & dinner daily. Bus: C5.

Poncio Cartuja TRIANA *ANDALUCÍAN* The Paris-trained chef here gets inventive with Andalucían cuisine, serving such dishes as salt-baked sea bass with olive "caviar" or baby fava beans with speckled quail eggs and diced serrano ham. One look at the perfectly chosen wine list will tell you why it's a popular hangout for folks in the sherry trade. C/ Victoria, 8. ☎ 954-340-010. www.ponciorestaurantes.com. Entrees 12€–26€. AE, DC, MC, V. Lunch Mon–Sat, dinner Tues–Sat. Closed Aug. Bus: C3.

> *Hams and bullfighting sum up Sol y Sombra.*

> *A classic dining room at Taberna del Alabardero.*

Restaurante Casa Modesto SANTA CRUZ
ANDALUCÍAN Inventive treatments of
Andalucía's wonderful fruits and vegetables
characterize the light cooking at Modesto. This
is an unusually seasonal kitchen for Sevilla,
with a strong emphasis on seafood from the
mouth of the Guadalquivir and rosemary-
studded lamb from the hills west of the city.
C/ Cano y Cueto, 5. ☎ 954-416-811. www.
modestorestaurantes.com. Entrees 12€–25€. AE,
MC, V. Lunch & dinner daily. Bus: C3, C4, 21, 23.
Tram: Prado de San Sebastian.

Río Grande TRIANA *ANDALUCÍAN*
Sure, you could order the roast chicken or the
rabo de toro (braised oxtail), but the specialties
of the house are the fish. Ask about the catch
of the day—usually either hake or bream—
and enjoy it *a la plancha* (simply grilled). The
riverfront room has great views of La Giralda.
C/ Betis. ☎ 954-273-956. Entrees 15€–21€. AE,

DC, MC, V. Lunch & dinner daily (dinner only July–
Aug). Bus: C3.

Sabina ARENAL *ANDALUCÍAN*
Set in a former shipyard building with soaring,
vaulted ceilings, Sabina specializes in hearty
Andalucían country fare, such as braised pork
trotters, stewed partridge, and squid cooked in
their own ink. If it's available, choose the leg of
lamb roasted with rosemary. C/ Dos de Mayo, 4.
☎ 954-562-547. Entrees 10€–18€. MC, V. Lunch &
dinner Mon–Sat. Bus: C5. Tram: Archivo de Indias.

Sol y Sombra TRIANA *ANDALUCÍAN*
The name, which refers to the choice of seats
in the sun or the shade at the bullring, is your
first hint that this *taberna* (pub) has a bullfight
theme. Colorful posters of *corridas* cover the
walls. Nets hang from the ceiling, holding wine
bottles and braids of garlic, and customers
hunch knee-to-knee at tables with bottles of
Rioja as they wait for plates of garlic shrimp
to arrive. C/ Castilla, 151. ☎ 954-333-935. www.
tabernasolysombra.com. Entrees 10€–13€. MC, V.
Lunch & dinner daily. Bus: C3.

Taberna Coloniales ALFALFA *TAPAS*
Maybe the best deal on great tapas in Sevilla,
Coloniales is usually jammed with locals
enjoying small dishes of chicken in almond
sauce or pork loin with garlic, serrano ham, and
mushrooms. To score an outside table, put your
name on the inside chalkboard. Plaza Cristo de
Burgos, 19. ☎ 954-214-191. Tapas 2€–3.50€. MC,
V. Lunch & dinner Mon–Sat. Bus: C5.

Taberna del Alabardero ARENAL *ANDALUCÍAN*
Enjoy seasonal market cuisine in the elegant
dining rooms in this 19th-century town
house as master chef Juan Manuel Marcos
orchestrates student talent of the hospitality
and culinary school. Marcos overhauls the
menu four times a year, and tweaks it daily
depending on what pleases him at the market.
The 13€ midday menu is a real bargain, but
you'll have to compete for a table. C/ Zaragoza,
20. ☎ 954-502-721. www.tabernadelalabardero.
com. Entrees 12€–24€. AE, DC, MC, V. Lunch &
dinner daily. Closed Aug. Bus: C1, C5.

Travel Tip

For a map denoting the locations of Sevilla's
restaurants and hotels, see p. 606.

Sevilla Hotels

Casa Romana CENTRO
This boutique hotel sports bright and spacious rooms, where daily fresh flowers are part of the maid service and marble lines the bathrooms. A sun deck and Jacuzzi on the roof are a bonus. C/ Trajano, 15. ☎ 954-915-170. www.newhotel. hotelcasaromana.com. 26 rooms. Doubles 120€–275€. AE, DC, MC, V. Bus: 13, 14.

★★ EME Fusion Hotel SANTA CRUZ
This exclusive luxury design hotel may have the best location in town—literally across the street from the cathedral. The facade, which covers several historic buildings, seamlessly unites a complex with many different room configurations, from avant-garde doubles to suites with private terraces. A spa, wellness center, hip bar, and four restaurants round out Sevilla's newest and most futuristic hotel. C/ Alemanes, 7. ☎ 954-560-000. www.emehotel. com. 60 rooms. Doubles 150€–350€. AE, DC, MC, V. Bus: 1, C3, C5.

Hotel Alcántara SANTA CRUZ
The owners of this former convent have transformed monastic simplicity into stylish modernity with rooms decked out in white linens and low-key striped upholstery. All the comforts are here, including Wi-Fi in the lobby and free parking for bicycles, the ideal form of transit in this neighborhood. C/ Ximemez de Enciso, 28. ☎ 954-500-595. www.hotelalcantara. net. 21 rooms. Doubles 73€–112€. AE, DC, MC, V. Bus: 1, C3, C5.

★★★ Hotel Alfonso XIII PARQUE MARIA LUISA
This opulent Mudéjar Revival palace was built as a showpiece in 1928 in anticipation of the 1929 Ibero-American Exposition. Guest rooms with authentic antiques and silk and linen wallcoverings recapitulate Moorish, baroque, and Castilian styles. This octogenarian remains Sevilla's most luxurious hotel. C/ San Fernando, 1. ☎ 954-917-000. www.starwoodhotels.com. 147 rooms. Doubles 245€–598€. AE, DC, MC, V. Bus: AC, B2, C4, 5, 21, 22, 23. Tram: Universidad.

> *Rooftop views of the Catedral at EME Fusion.*

Sevilla Restaurants & Hotels

Sevilla Restaurants

Egaña-Oriza **18**

Enrique Becerra **14**

Mesón Don Raimundo **7**

Poncio Cartuja **17**

Restaurante Casa Modesto **10**

Río Grande **16**

Sabina **15**

Sol y Sombra **1**

Taberna Coloniales **3**

Taberna del Alabardero **4**

Sevilla Hotels

Casa Romana **2**

EME Fusion Hotel **13**

Hotel Alcántara **11**

Hotel Alfonso XIII **19**

Hotel Alminar **6**

Hotel and Apartments Murillo **9**

Hotel Inglaterra **5**

La Hostería del Laurel **12**

Las Casas de la Judería **20**

YH Giralda **8**

> *Eclectic style with the expected Moorish accents at Hotel Murillo.*

★ Hotel Alminar CENTRO

Set in a historic building a stone's throw from the cathedral, this ultramodern boutique hotel doesn't put its best foot forward with the tiny lobby. But head upstairs and you'll find spacious, soothing guest rooms equipped with Wi-Fi and satellite TV. C/ Alvarez Quintero, 52. ☎ 954-293-913. www.hotelalminar.com. 12 rooms. Doubles 95€–155€. AE, DC, MC, V. Bus: C5.

kids Hotel and Apartments Murillo SANTA CRUZ

The suits of armor and carved woodwork in the lobby give way to modern, marble-laden hotel rooms and apartments. The street is strictly pedestrian, but a cab can get you close. Studio apartments are only about 5€ more than double rooms and include a rudimentary kitchen. Ask about discounts for stays of a week or more. Hotel: C/ Lope de Rueda, 7–9. ☎ 954-216-095. Apartments: C/ Reinoso, 6. ☎ 954-210-959. www.hotelmurillo.com. 94 hotel rooms, 17 apartments. 70€–120€. AE, DC, MC, V. Bus: 1, C3, C4, 21.

Hotel Inglaterra CENTRO

The Inglaterra is Sevilla's oldest hotel, but its recently renovated rooms are comfortable and spacious, if formal. The Plaza Nueva location is steps from the shopping on C/ Sierpes and a few minutes' walk from the cathedral and Alcázar. Plaza Nueva, 7. ☎ 954-224-970. www.hotelinglaterra.es. 108 rooms. Doubles 130€–220€. AE, DC, MC, V. Bus: C5. Tram: Plaza Nueva.

★ La Hostería del Laurel SANTA CRUZ

When author José Zorrilla stayed at this venerable inn in 1844, the romantic atmosphere apparently inspired him to create his now-immortal character, the tragic womanizer Don Juan Tenorio. The inn retains a lot of its original character, but the modern and cheerful rooms contain no hint of that licentious past. The bar-restaurant, where breakfast is served, has classic low ceilings hung with Spanish hams. Plaza de los Venerables, 5. ☎ 954-220-295. www.hosteriadellaurel.com. 22 rooms. Doubles 78€–104€. AE, DC, MC, V. Bus: 1, C3, C4, 21.

★★★ Las Casas de la Judería SANTA CRUZ

This hotel has transformed several 15th-century houses into a luxury complex where the rooms are arrayed around no fewer than 30 patios. Every room is different, and some are downright opulent. Amazingly, the hotel even squeezes a rooftop pool and a spa into the old buildings. Callejon de Dos Hermanas, 7. ☎ 954-415-150. www.casasypalacios.com. 118 rooms. Doubles 140€–275€. AE, DC, MC, V. Bus: 1, C3, C4, 21.

YH Giralda SANTA CRUZ

Less than the length of a soccer field from La Giralda, this 18th-century former residence of abbots distributes its intimate rooms on three levels around a picturesque little courtyard. Cheerful, whitewashed rooms and modern bathrooms create an illusion of spaciousness. Note that the hotel has no elevator. C/ Abades, 30. ☎ 954-228-324. www.yh-hoteles.com. 14 rooms. Doubles 71€–88€. AE, DC, MC, V. Bus: 1, C3, C5.

Sevilla Nightlife & Entertainment

Disco

Antique Theatro CARTUJA

If you're seeking the hard-edged international disco scene, head to Cartuja. Actors, soccer players, and other celebrities are often spotted at Antique Theatro, a cavernous club fitted out to please the most avid discogoer. Dress sharp and look attractive to improve your chances of getting in. C/ Mathemáticos Rey Pastor y Castro. ☎ 954-462-207. www.antiquetheatro.com. Bus: C1, C2.

Flamenco

Casa Anselma TRIANA

Named for the flamboyant owner, who just might be an even bigger attraction than the music, this bar is the epicenter of the Triana flamenco scene. Regulars often dance *sevillanas* (a folk dance that has been "flamenco-ized"), which is quite an accomplishment, given the close quarters. Not for the claustrophobic, but you're bound to make some new friends. C/ Pagés del Corro, 49. No phone. Bus: B2, C3.

> *The fashionable crush at Antique Theatro.*

Casa de la Memoría SANTA CRUZ

Young and emerging artists are the headliners at this *tablao* in the intimate patio of an ancient Andalucían house. Organizers are self-conscious of their role as keepers of traditional culture and often preface performances with a short, informative lecture. The price is right, and the audience often includes large numbers of young Spaniards, including schoolchildren. C/ Ximénez de Enciso, 28. ☎ 954-560-670. www.casadelamemoria.es. Tickets 15€, students 13€. Bus: 1, C3, C4, 23.

El Arenal ARENAL

Many a visitor to Sevilla has first seen authentic flamenco at this *tablao* that's been operating for decades in this atmospheric 17th-century building. Management will strongly suggest a rather expensive dinner with the show, but the better

Travel Tip

For a map denoting the locations of Sevilla's nightlife and entertainment, see p. 600.

bet is to opt for the show only with a drink. The intimate surroundings mean you're never far from the stage. C/ Roda, 7. ☎ 954-216-492. www.tablaoelarenal.com. Bus: B2, C4, C5.

La Carboneria SANTA CRUZ

The question isn't "who's here?"—it's "who's not?" Spaniards and tourists, young and old, hipsters and Birkenstock wearers all show up to enjoy free flamenco on the back patio. The rustic bar in front is snug and cozy, with a couple of fireplaces—a good spot on a winter night. C/ Leviés, 18. ☎ 954-229-945. Bus: C5.

Los Gallos SANTA CRUZ

Ever since this small club opened in 1966, it has fostered the careers of dozens of singers, musicians, and dancers who went on to major careers. Nightly shows begin at 8 and 10:30pm, and each lasts for 2 hours, featuring 12 performers per night. Flamenco purists hail Los Gallos as the most authentic *tablao* in Sevilla. Plaza de Santa Cruz, 11. ☎ 954-216-981. www.tablaolosgallos.com. Bus: 1, C3, C4, 23.

Torres Macarena MACARENA

The *peñas,* or clubs of flamenco aficionados, kept the art form alive through decades of unpopularity—and downright hostility from the Franco government. Torres Macarena is one of the most important in Andalucía, and the often impromptu shows either in the bar or out on the patio are old-style flamenco at its purest. C/ Torrijiano, 29. ☎ 954-372-384. Bus: C1-C4, 13, 14.

Jazz

Cafe Naima ALAMEDA

Live bebop, progressive jazz, and (of course) flamenco-inspired guitar fusion jazz hold forth from the stage of this relaxed small corner bar in the Alameda. As you might expect of a venue named for John Coltrane's first wife, photos of jazz legends cover the walls. C/ Trajano, 47. ☎ 954-382-485. www.naimacafejazz.com. Bus: B2, 13, 14.

Opera & Classical Music

Teatro de la Maestranza ARENAL

Sevilla's spectacular opera house was completed in 1991 in anticipation of Expo '92. It was acclaimed from the start as one of the world's premier venues for opera, thanks to both its sightlines and its extraordinary acoustics. Programming often focuses on works inspired

> *Free flamenco at the popular La Carboneria.*

by the city, such as Mozart's *The Marriage of Figaro.* The hall also hosts the major concerts of the Sevilla Symphony Orchestra and occasional jazz performances, and even stages *zarzuelas,* a particularly Spanish blend of operetta and music hall. Paseo de Colón, 22. ☎ 954-226-573. www.teatromaestranza.com. Bus: B2, C4.

Party Time

Originally a cattle-trading fair, Sevilla's **Feria de Abril** usually takes place about 2 weeks after Easter. The riverbank fairground is set up with tents, called *casetas,* that are hosted by aristocratic families, trade unions, political parties, clubs, and business associations. Admission is by invitation only. Flamenco rings out from about 9pm until dawn. Most women put on Gypsy-inspired flamenco dresses and everyone consumes copious quantities of sherry. Sometimes described as "2,000 cocktail parties to which you're not invited," Feria is colorful and exciting, but hotel rooms are scarce and pricey.

Granada

Granada provides a tantalizing glimpse of the ghosts of al-Andalus, the medieval Moorish empire that briefly stretched from Toledo through all of Andalucía and east through Valencia. When Fernando and Isabel took the capital city in 1492, they left the Alhambra intact, and the palace-city still conveys long-lost grandeur—Granada is as much a tale of endurance as a story of power. The Albaicín, or Moorish quarter, remains a medieval hillside warren of narrow cobbled streets. Gypsy *zambras* (feasts) still echo from the caves of Sacromonte. And an air of poetic grief continues to hang over the green parkland and sunny summer home where literary genius Federico García Lorca dreamed the fiery verses of *Romancero Gitano*, the *Gypsy Ballads*.

> *Legend has it the Patio de los Cipreses at the Generalife was the secret rendezvous point for the sultan's wife and her lover.*

START Bus 30 or 32 from Plaza Isabel la Católica to Alhambra ticket office.

❶ ★★★ **Alhambra & Generalife.** Buy a ticket in advance (see p. 627) so you can spend a leisurely day appreciating the subtleties of this huge complex of palaces and gardens. The high points are the Nasrid palaces, built largely at the end of the 14th century, when Granada reached the apex of wealth, power, influence,

and culture. But don't neglect the museum, which teases out the development of Moorish artistry and technology, or the beautiful Generalife, a hilltop retreat far from the city's cares. ⏲ 1 day. See p. 624.

❷ ★ **Catedral.** The Reconquista was as much holy war as power grab, and Fernando and Isabel drove home that point in 1501 when they destroyed the Great Mosque and ordered this

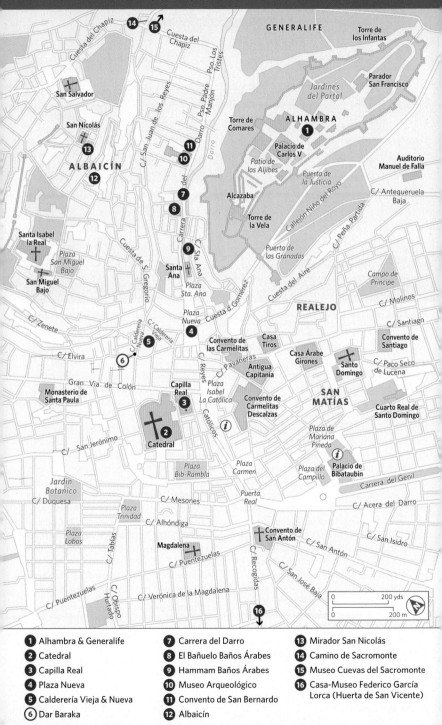

1 Alhambra & Generalife
2 Catedral
3 Capilla Real
4 Plaza Nueva
5 Calderería Vieja & Nueva
6 Dar Baraka
7 Carrera del Darro
8 El Bañuelo Baños Árabes
9 Hammam Baños Árabes
10 Museo Arqueológico
11 Convento de San Bernardo
12 Albaicín
13 Mirador San Nicolás
14 Camino de Sacromonte
15 Museo Cuevas del Sacromonte
16 Casa-Museo Federico García Lorca (Huerta de San Vicente)

> *Making a statement even in death: Fernando and Isabel lie in repose at Granada's purpose-built Royal Chapel.*

massive cathedral built in its place. Work didn't begin until 1518 and sputtered along until 1721, but the Catholic kings succeeded in creating a massive temple charged with the fierce power of their Christian god, which left no question who won the war. (The reverberating deep tones of the organ contribute substantially to the effect.) Santiago the Moorslayer, a peculiarly Spanish representation of St. James the Apostle, has the most prominent side chapel, where he is depicted on horseback decapitating his enemies with a broad sword. In at least a half dozen other spots, archangel San Miguel brandishes his sword to defeat a squirming snakelike Satan. For all its dated anti-Moorish propaganda, the cathedral also boasts some artistic high points: the majestic high altar, the polychrome wooden statue of the Immaculate Conception by native Granadino painter and sculptor Alonso Cano, and the bold and unusually graceful baroque west facade, also the work of Cano. In 1658, he took vows as a priest to ensure he got the job. ⏱ 1 hr. Gran Vía de Colón. ☎ 958-222-959. 3.50€ adults, 2.50€ seniors, free for kids 9 & under. Mar–Oct Mon–Sat 10:45am–1:30pm and 4–8pm, Sun 4–8pm; Nov–Feb Mon–Sat 10:45am–1:30pm and 4–7pm, Sun 4–7pm. Bus: 6, 9, 11.

③ ★★ **Capilla Real.** To emphasize the importance of the Reconquista, Fernando and Isabel commissioned the Royal Chapel next to the Catedral to serve as their burial site and ultimately the tomb of their daughter Juana la Loca (Juana the Mad) and her husband, Felipe el Hermoso (Philip the Handsome). The main attractions are the mausoleums with carved likenesses of the royals, but the attached museum is more rewarding. It displays Isabel's scepter and crown, Fernando's sword and robes, and their collection of religious paintings. Ironically, the best works were painted by Flemish, not Spanish, masters. ⏱ 1 hr. Gran Vía de Colón. ☎ 958-229-239. 3.50€ adults, 2.50€ seniors, free for kids 9 & under. Apr–Oct Mon–Sat 10:30am–1pm and 4–7pm, Sun 11am–1pm and 4–7pm; Nov–Mar Mon–Sat 10:30am–1pm and 3:30–6:30pm, Sun 11am–1pm and 3:30–6:30pm. Bus: 6, 9, 11.

④ **Plaza Nueva.** This square was reconstructed under the Catholic kings as the new city center. The **Real Chancillaría** courthouse, the stately golden Renaissance building, is headquarters of Andalucía's justice system. Tourist buses use Plaza Nueva as a rendezvous point, and at night the steps around the perimeter serve a similar social function. Bus: 31, 32.

> *A stone bridge across the Río Darro looks worse for wear but does the trick.*

5 Calderería Vieja & Nueva. These steep, tiny streets behind the Real Chancillaría bustle with entrepreneurial merchants largely selling tourist wares in a setting both claustrophobic and atmospheric. See p. 617.

6 🍵 Dar Baraka. Inexpensive and unpretentious, near the foot of Calderería Vieja, this is a friendly spot to enjoy Arabic specialties such as exquisite baklava, almond tarts, and freshly brewed mint tea. Cash only. C/ Elvira, 20. ☎ 649-114-171. $.

7 ★ Carrera del Darro. The Río Darro flows west from Sacromonte (see p. 615, 14) until it disappears under Plaza Nueva. This narrow riverside street lined with boutiques, restaurants, and small lodgings is the most romantic walk in the city. You can crisscross the river at several half-crumbled bridges and enjoy the view of the Alhambra high above. (It's even better at night, when the fortress is floodlit.) Bus: 31, 32.

8 El Bañuelo Baños Árabes. Pop into this modest historic site to see the 11th-century Moorish baths, among the best preserved in Spain. Star-shaped skylights illuminate the vaulted subterranean rooms, where it's easy to imagine soaking off the day's grit. ⏱ 20 min. Carrera del Darro, 31. ☎ 958-027-800. Free. Tues–Sat 10am–2pm. Bus: 31, 32.

> *Granada's 11th-century Arab baths predate even the Alhambra.*

⑨ Hammam Baños Árabes. Stop imagining and do it. Just across the river from its historic counterpart, this complex of Arabic baths established in 1998 offers both traditional hot and cold pools, as well as a steam room, massage, and aromatherapy. ⏱ 2–3 hr. Santa Ana, 16. ☎ 902-333-334. www.hammamspain.com. 19€–38€. Daily 10am–11:30pm. Bus: 31, 32.

⑩ ★ kids Museo Arqueológico. The best, and maybe least noticed, aspects of this museum are the Roman, Visigothic, and Moorish columns and capitals of its Renaissance palace. They're not excavated artifacts—they've simply been continually recycled over the millennia. Zip through the Paleolithic display cases to get to the ancient Iberians, who brought a surprisingly sophisticated culture to Spain in the 6th through 1st centuries B.C. The circa-500-B.C. stone bull suggests that the *corrida,* or bullfight, is hardly a modern invention. ⏱1 hr. Carrera del Darro, 43. ☎ 958-575-408. 1.50€. Tues 2:30–8:30pm; Wed–Sat 9am–8:30pm; Sun 9am–2:30pm. Bus: 31, 32.

⑪ kids Convento de San Bernardo. On your way into the narrow mazes and warrens of the Albaicín, you have the chance to touch Granada's shadow world at this nondescript building at the corner of C/ Gloría. Step inside the alcove and mark an order slip, and then set it into the *retorno*. Inside, a nun will take your money and fill your order for confections made with honey and/or almonds. It is her only interaction with the outside world. ⏱5 min. Gloría, 2. Cookies 6.50€ per .5kg (1.1 lb.). Bus: 31, 32.

⑫ Albaicín. The labyrinthine streets of the Albaicín retain a distinctly Islamic character (Granada's mosque is here), making it a neighborhood for wandering and marveling. Even the best map will be of little aid. Just know that the best views are up, and the city is at the bottom of the hill. Most residents live in traditional *carmens,* postage-stamp estates where flower-bedecked walls surround the house and gardens. If the gate is open, peek inside. ⏱2 hr. Bus: 31, 32.

> *Shops and vendors crowd C/ de la Calderería Nueva and C/ de la Calderería Vieja in the Albaicín.*

> *The Museo Cuevas del Sacromonte sheds some light on the reclusive Roma community that inhabits the area's whitewashed cave dwellings.*

⑬ Mirador San Nicolás. Try to conclude your Albaicín stroll late in the day at this scenic overlook with multiple cafes. At sunset, the reflection of the setting sun makes the Alhambra gleam like gold. With luck, a guitarist will be playing flamenco. Bus: 31, 32, 34.

⑭ Camino de Sacromonte. After the Reconquista, Granada's citizens often made a great show of Christian piety, and the discovery of religious artifacts on the mountain facing the Alhambra led to the creation of Stations of the Cross and regular pilgrimages to the summit of the Sacromonte, or sacred mountain. By the late 19th century, the pilgrimage path was lined by more than 1,000 crosses, few of which have survived. But the road became a haven for Granada's Gypsies, who established their own tight-knit community in houses dug from the hard-packed limestone soil of the hillside. In 1950, Sacromonte had more than 3,600 inhabited caves, though many were abandoned after a 1963 flood. One cluster along the road, Las Cuevas El Abanico, functions as a hotel (see p. 620). Other caves have been converted to restaurants with nightly flamenco spectacles of *zambra* (see p. 623). ⏰ 2 hr. Bus: 34 from Plaza Nueva, or walk from Bus 31 stop at corner of Cuesta del Chapíz and Camino de Sacromonte.

⑮ ★ kids Museo Cuevas del Sacromonte. Travelers have always been frustrated by the hermetic nature of the tight-knit Gypsy community. But this interpretive center signals a new spirit of openness and ethnic pride, and the exhibitions dispel many misconceptions about Granada's largely self-sufficient Roma (Gypsy) community. You walk in and out of a sequence of tidy cave dwellings with tile or packed-earth floors, whitewashed walls, and low ceilings. Several caves are set up as studios for traditional weaving, metalwork, pottery, and basketry, and artisans may be demonstrating their skills. ⏰ 1½ hr. Barranco de los Negros. ☎ 958-215-120. www.sacromontegranada.com. 5€. Apr–Oct Tues–Sun 10am–2pm and 5–9pm; Nov–Mar Tues–Sun 10am–2pm and 4–7pm. Bus: 34.

⑯ Casa-Museo Federico García Lorca (Huerta de San Vicente). Artistic polymath Federico García Lorca (1898–1936) is best remembered as a poet (*Gypsy Ballads* and *Poet in New York*) and playwright (*Mariana Pineda* and *Blood Wedding*). The San Vicente farm was his family's summer home from 1926 to 1936, and he took refuge here at the outset of the Civil War—only to be arrested and killed by Falangists for his outspoken democratic views and homosexuality. Only a handful of artifacts are his, yet the museum evokes the lyric contemplation of Granada's greatest poet. ⏰ 1½ hr. Virgen Blanca, Parque Federico García Lorca. ☎ 958-258-466. www.huertadesanvicente.com. 3€ adults, 1€ seniors and kids, free Wed. Oct–Mar Tues–Sun 10am–12:30pm and 4–6:30pm; Apr–June and Sept Tues–Sun 10am–12:30pm and 5–7:30pm; July–Aug 10am–2:30pm. Bus: 6.

Granada Restaurants

★★ Cunini Restaurante & Marisquería CENTRO
SEAFOOD Restaurants in Granada are extraordinarily generous with free tapas, and Cunini is no exception. You can sample much of the menu here by ordering drink after drink standing at the undulating marble bar. (The tapas get better with each drink.) If you want to enjoy the best seafood in Granada, have a seat in the restaurant or on the plaza for the likes of monkfish in white wine or a heaping plate of fried red mullet. **Plaza de Pescadería, 14.** ☎ 958-250-777. http://cunini granada.iespana.es. Entrees 13€–33€. MC, V. Lunch & dinner Mon–Sat. Bus: 23, 30, 31, 32.

★ Paprika ALBAICÍN *SPANISH FUSION*
Far from the madding crowds at the west end of the Albaicín, Paprika is literally a hole in the city wall. Bebop jazz and changing art exhibits only hint at the culinary sophistication of such dishes as cashew-studded vegetarian paella or codfish in thick lemon sauce. Very vegetarian-friendly. **Cuesta de Abarquares, 3.** ☎ 958-804-785. www.

> *Cafe Botánico (see p. 621): cafe and nightspot.*

paprika-granada.com. Entrees 8.50€–17€. MC, V. Lunch Tues–Sun, dinner Tues–Sat. Bus: 30, 31, 32.

Restaurante Arrayanes ALBAICÍN *NORTH AFRICAN* It feels like the Moors won and the Catholic kings lost when you sit down on a low padded bench surrounded by pillows at this halal couscous house in the heart of the Albaicín. (There are regular-height tables for stiff-kneed tourists.) Best bets are chicken or lamb couscous, or a vegetarian tagine. Don't miss the dessert of almond and honey crepes. No alcohol. **Cuesta Marañas, 4.** ☎ 958-228-401. www.rest-arrayanes.com. Entrees 12€–16€. MC, V. Lunch & dinner Wed–Mon. Bus: 31.

★ Restaurante Ruta del Azafràn ALBAICÍN *NORTH AFRICAN/SPANISH FUSION* Contemporary Spanish cooking with a decidedly North

Travel Tip

For a map denoting the locations of Granada's restaurants, see p. 619.

African accent is only half the attraction here. There are also stunning views (looking up) of the Alhambra, and a range of choices from inexpensive couscous to pricey but elegant veal steaks with foie gras. The excellent wine list includes some bargains on local white table wines, as well as a great selection of bottles from Spain's emerging wine regions, such as Jumilla. **Paseo del Padre Manjón, 1.** ☎ 958-226-882. www.rutadel azafran.es. Entrees 9€–22€. AE, MC, V. Lunch & dinner daily. Bus: 31.

★ **Restaurante Sevilla** CENTRO *ANDALUCÍAN* This longtime favorite is located on a tiny street near the Catedral. In fact, you might hear the guitarist playing a Manuel de Falla tune before you find the door. But Restaurante Sevilla has been Granada's see-and-be-seen venue since the 1930s, when composer de Falla and poet Federico García Lorca used to eat here. The staff will push the gazpacho, but we recommend the *cordero a la pastoril,* Andalucían lamb with mountain herbs. Reservations are a good idea. C/ Oficios, 12. ☎ 958-221-223. ww.restaurantesevilla. es. Entrees 12€–24€. AE, DC, MC, V. Lunch & dinner Mon-Sat. Bus: 32, 39.

★★ **San Nicolás Restaurante.** ALBAICÍN *ANDALUCÍAN* This bastion of innovative Andalucían cuisine is 20m (66 ft.) from the Mirador San Nicolás, and you'll still enjoy the view from the upstairs dining rooms. It is also a serious foodie stop. Simple *salmorejo* (a cold soup similar to gazpacho) is reinvented with a tuna confiture, quail eggs, and prosciutto chips. Grilled bonito is accompanied by watermelon and an avocado purée, and other classic dishes serve as starting points for delicious *nuevo cocina* (contemporary cuisine). San Nicolás, 3. ☎ 958-804-262. www. restaurantesannicolas.com. Entrees 16€–23€. AE, MC, V. Lunch & dinner Thurs–Tues. Bus: 31, 32, 34.

Shopping in Granada

The shopping districts of Granada are mainly confined to the Albaicín, Alcaicería, and Centro districts. When you wander the steep alleyways of Calderería Vieja and Calderería Nueva off C/ Elvira in the **Albaicín,** you can be forgiven for imagining that you've been transported to a Moroccan souk. There's a stall every few feet offering hookahs, painted tea glasses, plaited leather, embroidered pillows and wall hangings, silvery teapots, and other clichés of North African culture. Feel free to haggle for a souvenir-grade checked scarf, woven bag, or brass bracelet. The best bargains are with cash.

Turn down C/ Rubio from Avenida Reyes Católicos and you'll plunge into the **Alcaicería,** the historic market streets around the cathedral. They're jammed with tiny shops hawking souvenirs, silver jewelry, decorated fans, and other crafts. In contrast to the Caldererías, the goods here are more Spanish and less North African and the streets have a little more breathing room.

The **Centro** has more mainstream shopping: Look for name boutiques, home-goods stores, jewelry stores, and department stores on the major arteries of Gran Vía de Colón, Avenida Reyes Católicos, and Avenida Recogidas. Calle Navas, leading east behind the Ayuntamiento (Town Hall) is dotted with small boutiques, antiques shops, and excellent gourmet stores.

Granada Hotels

Alhambra Palace ALHAMBRA

In keeping with its era, public areas in this grand 1910 hotel are lush and ceremonial, which can make the rather small and basic bedrooms seem disappointing. But the location directly across the street from the Alhambra is perfect for getting a quick start on your visit, and some exterior rooms have sweeping city views. Plaza Arquitecto García de Paredes, 1. ☎ 958-221-468. www.hotelalhambra palace.com. 126 rooms. Doubles 115€–130€, with breakfast and parking. AE, DC, MC, V. Bus: 30.

★★ Casa Morisca ALBAICÍN

Located at the foot of the Alhambra, this house dates from the end of the 15th century. In the patio you can still see the remains of a Moorish pool and galleries supported by pilasters and columns. Bedrooms are individually decorated in an old style but with all the modern comforts. Cuesta de la Victoria, 9. ☎ 958-221-100. www.hotelcasamorisca.com. Doubles 90€–148€. AE, DC, MC, V. Bus: 31 or 32.

> *Granada's parador is just a stone's throw from the Alhambra.*

★★ Gar-Anat Hotel CENTRO

These spectacular contemporary rooms—each themed—opened at the end of 2008 in a historic central courtyard building across from the Cate-dral. Even the smallest room (in the attic) is spacious, and boasts a modest view of the Alhambra to boot. Placeta del los Peregrinos, 1. ☎ 958-225-528. www.gar-anat.es. 15 rooms. Doubles 110€–175€, with breakfast. AE, MC, V. Bus: 6, 9, 11.

★ kids Hotel Los Tilos CENTRO

The top-floor balcony open to guests often becomes a place for quiet parties while gazing on the floodlit Catedral at night. Many rooms overlook the pretty, tranquil plaza. The decor is cheerful if modest, but the location in the heart of the city and the availability of triple rooms (good for families) are big pluses. Book three or more nights to get free breakfast. Plaza Bib-Rambla, 4. ☎ 958-266-712. www.hotellostilos.com. 30 rooms. Doubles 55€–80€. MC, V. Bus: 23, 30, 31, 32.

★★ Hotel Palacio de los Navas CENTRO

This historic in-town palace of limestone and

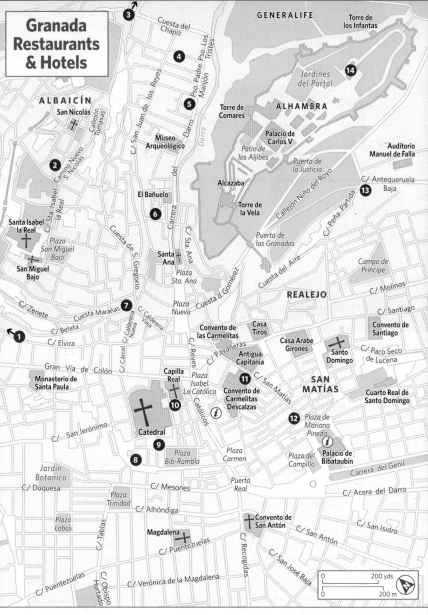

Granada Restaurants & Hotels

GENERALIFE

Torre de los Infantas

Cuesta del Chapiz

ALBAICÍN

San Nicolás

Callejón Tomasas

C/ San Juan de los Reyes

Pso. Padre Manjón

Pso. Los Tristes

Jardines del Partal

Camino Nuevo S. Nicolás

Museo Arqueológico

Darro

Torre de Comares

ALHAMBRA

Palacio de Carlos V

Auditorio Manuel de Falla

C/ Sta. Isabel la Real

Patio de los Aljibes

Puerta de la Justicia

C/ Antequeruela Baja

Santa Isabel la Real

El Bañuelo

Carrera

Alcazaba

Callejón Niño del Royo

C/ Peña Partida

Plaza San Miguel Bajo

Torre de la Vela

Cuesta de S. Gregorio

C/ Sta. Ana

San Miguel Bajo

Cuesta de Marañas

Puerta de las Gránadas

Campo de Príncipe

C/ Zenete

Santa Ana

Plaza Sta. Ana

Cuesta del Aire

REALEJO

C/ Molinos

C/ Beteta

Plaza Nueva

Cuesta d. Gomérez

C/ Santiago

C/ Elvira

Cuesta Marañas

C/ Calderería Vieja

C/ Calderería Nueva

Convento de las Carmelitas

Casa Tiros

Convento de Santiago

C/ Reyes

C/ Pavaneras

Casa Arabe Girones

Santo Domingo

C/ Paco Seco de Lucena

Gran Vía de Colón

C/ Cárcel

Antigua Capitanía

C/ San Matías

SAN MATÍAS

Monasterio de Santa Paula

Capilla Real

Plaza Isabel La Católica

Convento de Carmelitas Descalzas

Cuarto Real de Santo Domingo

C/ San Jerónimo

C/ Reyes Católicos

Plaza de Mariana Pineda

Catedral

Plaza Bib-Rambla

Plaza Carmen

Plaza del Campillo

Palacio de Bibataubín

Jardín Botánico

Carrera del Genil

C/ Duquesa

C/ Mesones

Puerta Real

C/ Acera del Darro

Plaza Trinidad

C/ Alhóndiga

Convento de San Antón

C/ San Antón

C/ San Isidro

Plaza Lobos

Magdalena

C/ Puentezuelas

C/ Recogidas

C/ Tablas

C/ Puentezuelas

C/ Obispo Hurtado

C/ Verónica de la Magdalena

C/ San José Baja

0   200 yds
0   200 m

Granada Restaurants

Cunini Restaurante
& Marisquería **8**

Paprika **1**

Restaurante Arrayanes **7**

Restaurante Ruta
del Azafràn **5**

Restaurante Sevilla **10**

San Nicolás Restaurante **2**

Granada Hotels

Alhambra Palace **13**

Casa Morisca **4**

Gar-Anat Hotel **11**

Hotel Los Tilos **9**

Hotel Palacio
de los Navas **12**

Hotel Palacio
de Santa Inés **6**

Las Cuevas El Abanico **3**

Parador de Granada **14**

> *Stay in a Gypsy cave with modern trappings at Las Cuevas El Abanico.*

marble has been transformed into a modestly priced luxury hotel with truly sumptuous rooms. Although it's at the end of a busy shopping street, the setting is as peaceful as it gets in Granada. All you're likely to hear is the water burbling quietly in the central fountain. C/ Navas, 1. ☎ 958-215-760. www.palaciodelosnavas.com. 19 rooms. Doubles 125€–145€, with breakfast. AE, DC, MC, V. Bus: 30.

★★ Hotel Palacio de Santa Inés ALBAICÍN

The stunning boutique hotel nestled into a pair of 16th-century Mudéjar buildings in the Albaicín takes its design cues from the fragmentary 16th-century frescoes in the reception area. Decorated throughout with bold hues of Tuscan plaster, rooms and public areas alike are visual delights. Interior balconies with wooden spindles circle the glass-roofed central courtyard. Cuesta de Santa Inés, 9. ☎ 958-222-362. www.palaciosantaines.com. 34 rooms. Doubles 80€–250€. AE, MC, V. Bus: 31.

★ kids Las Cuevas El Abanico SACROMONTE

As much an adventure as a place to sleep, these one- and two-bedroom units in the Gypsy quarter of Sacromonte are fully modernized cave dwellings with whitewashed walls, tiny bathrooms, and a corner equipped for minimal cooking. The kids won't be able to wait to tell their friends they stayed in a Gypsy cave. You too. Just be aware that the caves are a real uphill schlep from the road. C/ Verea de Enmedio, 89. ☎ 958-226-199. www.el-abanico.com. 5 rooms. Doubles 70€. MC, V. Bus: 31, 34.

★★★ Parador de Granada ALHAMBRA

You can't stay any closer to the Nasrid palaces of the Alhambra than this repurposed 15th-century convent on the site of the former palace mosque. Just look out your window to the fountains, gardens, and buildings of the Alhambra grounds. Modern conveniences complement the classical ambience. Space is limited, so book far ahead. The only shortcoming is that you'll ride the bus a lot to see the rest of the city. Real de Alhambra. ☎ 958-221-440. www.parador.es. 36 rooms. Doubles 244€–311€, with parking. AE, DC, MC, V. Bus: 30.

Granada Nightlife & Entertainment

Bars

Al Pié de la Vela ALBAICÍN

Don't let the wild-animal theme freak you out. This trendy bar draws many young professionals, especially early in the evening, and an increasingly exotic crowd as the night stretches on. Technically, it's a pub with inexpensive draft beer, though the thumping music makes it feel more like a club. It's a very popular place to hook up, straight or gay. Go before 9:30pm and the doors will probably be locked. **Carrera del Darro, 135.** ☎ 958-228-539. Bus: 31.

Cafe Botánico UNIVERSITY

Located on a small plaza west of the Catedral near the university's law school, Botánico wears many different hats through the day and night. Most of the time it's a bright and cheery cafe-bar where you can get tapas and a beer or a coffee, though it also serves a full, inexpensive dinner menu that includes a lot of the vegetarian fare favored by the students. Around 11pm, the lights go down and the techno music comes up, and folks start dancing. **C/ Málaga, 3.** ☎ 958-271-598. Bus: 30, 31, 32, 34.

Reca CENTRO

Plaza Trinidad is one of the hot spots for gay nightlife in Granada (a famously gay-friendly city), and the smiles don't get much warmer than at this trendy tapas bar favored by university faculty and local fashionistas. Tapas here are bold and flashy (goat cheese with fried eggs and blood sausage), and the progressive jazz and contemporary flamenco on the sound system is deliberately loud. That way you have to lean a little closer to talk. **Plaza Trinidad.** ☎ 958-228-826. Bus: 30, 31, 32, 34.

> A zambra *show in an authentic Sacromonte cave at Venta El Gallo.*

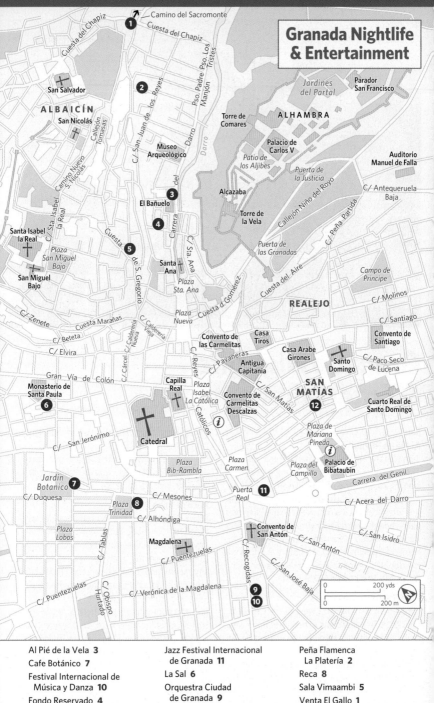

Granada Nightlife & Entertainment

Dance Clubs

Fondo Reservado ALBAICÍN

If you've wondered why all those hot young people are standing in line on the street, it might be because Reservado doesn't even open the doors until midnight or later. In theory it's a beer bar, but with frequent cabaret performances and a whole lot of shaking going on to recorded music, it's one of Granada's most popular dance destinations. Cuesta de Santa Inés, 3. ☎ 958-221-024. 5€ cover. Bus: 31.

La Sal CENTRO

Where the girls are. This pioneer lesbian dance club is also a favorite with clean-scrubbed Spanish boys dressed in chinos and button-down shirts. It's a genial, mellow crowd, with a minimum of annoying come-ons. Drinking and socializing continues until about 11pm, when the house music comes on and everybody dances. C/ Santa Paula, 11. No phone. No cover. Bus: 30, 31, 32, 34.

Perfíl CENTRO

Everyone really dresses up for Granada's leading hard-core dance club, where the pretty people get hot and sweaty to postmidnight rave music and go home with each other at dawn. The youthful crowd is evenly split between straight and gay, but everyone has a good time. C/ Rosario, 10. No phone. 4€ cover. Bus: 23.

Flamenco Music & Dance

Peña Flamenca La Platería ALBAICÍN

The oldest flamenco enthusiasts' club in Spain opens to nonmembers on Thursday nights (Feb–July) to showcase up-and-coming artists of flamenco music and dance. Club members are friendly, and while the space feels a little like a church hall with a raised stage on one end, the performances are utterly without touristy flourishes. This is the real thing, as fostered by aficionados. Placeta Toqueros 7. ☎ 958-210-650. http://www.laplateria.org.es. 8€. Bus: 31.

Sala Vimaambi ALBAICÍN

Flamenco is just part of the programming at this artists' cooperative, founded by a poet, which also produces cinema retrospectives, poetry readings, music, and various spectacles too imaginative to pigeonhole. Friday and Saturday nights are usually devoted to flamenco. Cuesta de San Gregorio, 30–38. ☎ 958-227-334. www.vimaambi.com. Prices vary; flamenco 15€. Bus: 31.

Venta El Gallo SACROMONTE

Many caves in Sacromonte offer flamenco shows of varying authenticity, but the moody, comfortable hillside cave of El Gallo puts on first-rate spectaculars of Granada *zambra*. This more primitive form of flamenco goes through three stages, corresponding to the three parts of a Gypsy wedding. Make your reservation for the show without dinner (unless you *must* sit up front), but do pay the extra charge for transportation via minibus. City buses stop running at 11pm, when the musicians and dancers will just be hitting their stride. Barranco Los Negros, 5. ☎ 958-228-476. www.ventaelgallo.com. 22€ show, 52€ for show and dinner, additional 6€ for transportation from hotel. Bus: 34.

Jazz & Classical Music

Festival Internacional de Música y Danza

CITYWIDE Since 1950, Granada has held an international festival of opera, classical music, ballet, modern dance, and flamenco performed everywhere from city streets to the plazas in the Alhambra to small bars and big performance halls. The festival runs from the last week of June to mid-July. Many events are free. The full schedule is announced each year in late April. Box Office: C/ Mariana Pineda s/n. ☎ 958-221-844. www.granadafestival.org.

Jazz Festival Internacional de Granada CENTRO

Granada may be a flamenco city, but a lot of jazz fans are lurking in the wings. In November, both established and up-and-coming jazz artists perform in this month-long festival, one of Europe's oldest and best-established jazz fests. Official concerts are at the Teatro Municipal Isabel La Católica, but many bars and cafes also feature jazz all month. Teatro Municipal Isabel La Católica. C/ Almona del Campillo, 2. www.jazzgranada.es.

Orquestra Ciudad de Granada ALHAMBRA

This city's symphonic orchestra plays an ambitious schedule from September to June in its home venue, the **Auditorio Manuel de Falla.** Blockbuster concerts move to the **Palacio de Exposiciones & Congresos,** Paseo Violón, s/n (☎ 958-246-700). Auditorio: Paseo de los Mártires, s/n. ☎ 958-220-022. www.orquestaciudadgranada.es.

The Alhambra & Generalife

Granada's hilltop fortress-palace complex of the Alhambra and Generalife distills the artistry, power, and wealth of Moorish Spain. Left intact when the city was conquered in 1492, it has been restored to its 14th-century grandeur. You came to Granada to see the Alhambra before you die. Plan on spending a full, stupendous day.

> The Patio de los Arrayanes, with its placid reflecting pool surrounded by myrtle, was a place of contemplation for Nasrid royalty.

START Plaza San Agustín.

① 🛒 **Mercado San Agustín.** Plan your lunch ahead of time by visiting the municipal market to buy picnic fixings of fruit, bread, cheese, and sausage. You'll eat them in the Jardines del Partal (see p. 626, ⑦). Plaza San Agustín. No phone. $.

Walk to Plaza Isabel la Católica to catch Bus 30 or 32 to the Alhambra.

② ★★★ **Nasrid Palaces.** Each of the three buildings in the royal complex is organized around a stunning patio and linked by passageways. The last Moorish king of Granada, Mohammed XII (known as Boabdil; 1460–1533), handed over the city to Fernando and Isabel in January 1492. On his way to the coast to sail to North Africa, he wept when he looked back on Granada; once you've seen the palace, you'll understand why. Previous Nasrid rulers laid the basic plans for the Alhambra, but the three buildings now standing are the work of sultans Yusef I (1318–54) and his son, Mohammed V (1338–91). The Arabic inscription on the wall frieze as you enter the square reception hall of the **Mexuar,** the first of the three palace buildings, sets the tone. It

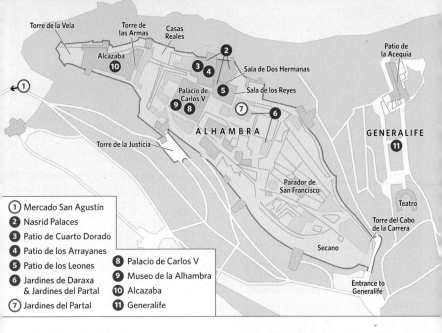

Torre de la Vela
Torre de las Armas
Casas Reales
Alcazaba
10
1
2
3 **4**
Sala de Dos Hermanas
5
Sala de los Reyes
Palacio de Carlos V
7
9 **8**
6
ALHAMBRA
GENERALIFE
Patio de la Acequia
11
Torre de la Justicia
Parador de San Francisco
Teatro
Torre del Cabo de la Carrera
Secano
Entrance to Generalife

1 Mercado San Agustín
2 Nasrid Palaces
3 Patio de Cuarto Dorado
4 Patio de los Arrayanes
5 Patio de los Leones
6 Jardines de Daraxa & Jardines del Partal
7 Jardines del Partal
8 Palacio de Carlos V
9 Museo de la Alhambra
10 Alcazaba
11 Generalife

translates as EVERYTHING THAT YOU OWN COMES FROM GOD. Yusef I saw himself as the lawgiver, and made the formal **Hall of Justice** the first grand room of his palace complex. Behind it stands the more intimate **Oratory,** or prayer room, where windows overlook the Albaicín. Yusef I also established a religious school in Granada. ⏱ 2 hr minimum for palaces. ☎ 902-441-221. www.alhambradegranada.org. 12€ adults, 9€ seniors and students, free for kids 11 & under, 6€ for gardens only. Mar–Oct daily 8:30am–8pm, also Tues–Sat 10–11:30pm Nasrid palaces and Generalife only; Nov–Feb daily 8:30am–6pm, also Fri–Sat 8–9:30pm Nasrid palaces and Generalife only. Bus: 30, 32.

3 Patio de Cuarto Dorado. The Golden Room Courtyard is the heart of the **Palacio Comares,** the administrative area. Study the south wall of the patio, which exhibits all the artistic elements of the Alhambra: geometric tiles, borders of Arabic inscriptions, a carved-plaster frieze, and panels ornamented with leaves and vines. Walk into the Cuarto Dorado to complete the decorative perfecta with a carved and painted wooden ceiling that gives the room its name. ⏱ 30 min.

> Moorish architectural craftmanship in Spain reached its apogee with the Alhambra.

> *Visitors explore the mazelike remains of the Alhambra's Alcazaba, the oldest part of the compound.*

4 **Patio de los Arrayanes.** Welcome to the private royal quarters, where the slender reflecting pool in the Courtyard of the Myrtles served as a spot for quiet contemplation. Pass through to the **Sala de Barca,** where Nasrid coats of arms and Arabic inscriptions cover the walls. Beyond stands the most beautiful room in the most beautiful palace in Spain: the ★ **Salon de Embajadores,** or Hall of Ambassadors. The intricate wooden marquetry dome represents the seven heavens of the Koran. The colored tiles and carved plaster of the walls are the apex of Moorish decorative art. The Arabic inscription offers good advice to diplomats: SPEAK BRIEFLY AND YOU WILL LEAVE IN PEACE. The windows are placed so that the sun would blaze behind the sultan's throne, all but blinding any minister who gained an audience. ◷ 45 min.

5 **Patio de los Leones.** Named for the recently restored 14th-century stone lions supporting the central fountain, this courtyard manifests the Moorish precept that private living quarters should surround a hidden garden. The **Sala de Dos Hermanas** was the daytime living room of the sultan's wives and favorites from the harem. An unusual star-shaped lantern cupola based on the philosophy of Pythagoras

distinguishes the **Sala de los Abencerrajes,** named for the Abencerrajes clan. They were slaughtered by Boabdil, who piled their heads in the fountain upon learning that his wife was meeting secretly with one of them. ◷ 30 min.

The palace tour continues through the baths and other utilitarian rooms before exiting to the gardens. Make sure you've spent as much time as you want before leaving—guards will prevent you from going back inside.

6 **Jardines de Daraxa & Jardines del Partal.** The Nasrid palaces tour deposits you at a tranquil post-Moorish garden of orange trees (Daraxa). The terraced flower gardens beyond (Partal) are a charming 19th-century addition in place of palace outbuildings destroyed in the 17th and 18th centuries. The Partal's sweeping views of the battlement towers and Granada below make it a favorite spot for taking "I was here" photos. ◷ 30 min.

⑦ 🍴 **Jardines del Partal.** There's nowhere to eat inside the Alhambra, but it's fine to picnic on the grounds. Grab a bench in the Jardines del Partal. Make sure you've gone to the **Mercado San Agustín** (see p. 624, ①) to stock up on supplies first.

8 ★ **Palacio de Carlos V.** Started in 1527 for Carlos V (1500–58), this soaring palace with its interior circular plaza designed by Michelangelo protégé Pedro Machuca is often cited as one of the most important Renaissance buildings in Spain. The pure lines and monumental dimensions are a strong contrast to the overwhelming visual patterning of the adjacent Nasrid palaces. ⏱ 30 min.

9 ★★ **Museo de la Alhambra.** In the lower level of the Palacio de Carlos V, this superb museum chronicles the evolution of art and technology in Moorish pottery, tiles, wood and plaster carving, and work in stone, bronze, and gold. English signage is limited—a dictionary would help to distinguish which pieces were salvaged from the Alhambra ruins and which represent Moorish artistry in other parts of Granada province. ⏱ 1 hr. Palacio de Carlos V. ☎ 958-027-900. www.alhambra-patronato.es. Entrance fee included in Alhambra admission. Tues–Sat 9am–2:30pm. Bus: 30, 32.

10 kids ★ **Alcazaba.** The original fortress dates from the early years of Moorish occupation,

> *Running water is never out of earshot at the Generalife.*

though the current configuration is the work of Mohammed I (1191–1273), founder of the Nasrid dynasty. Climb into the late-8th-century **Torre de la Vela** for a panoramic view of the Nasrid palaces and the city. The bell of the watchtower rings every January 2 to mark the date that the Catholic kings took the city. ⏱ 1 hr.

11 ★ **Generalife.** Up the hill through a well-manicured patch of woods, the Generalife was the modest "summer palace" and hunting lodge for the Nasrid dynasty. A desert culture, the Moors prized the sound of running water, and the landscape is designed so that you're never out of earshot from a burbling fountain or the trickle of irrigation. Water for the complex flows from the delightful **Patio de Acequia,** where crisscrossing jets arch over a pond. The **Patio de los Cipreses** is a sunken garden, sometimes called the Patio de la Sultana because, legend says, Boabdil discovered his wife entertaining one of the Abencerrajes clan here. ⏱ 1 hr. Included in Alhambra admission.

Getting into the Alhambra & Generalife

Only 1,500 visitors at a time are allowed into the Alhambra. The best time to visit the Nasrid palaces is at 8:30am before fellow tourists clog the halls. Once inside, you can spend all day. But if you wait until the day of your visit, you may have to buy a ticket early in the morning for late-afternoon entry, if tickets are available at all.

You can get your preferred time in advance. Order up to 3 months ahead with a credit card (☎ 934-923-750 from abroad, or 902-888-001 from Spain; www.alhambra-tickets.es). Each ticket has a 1€ surcharge. You'll get a reservation number to use when you pay for and pick up the actual tickets at ServiCaixa machines throughout Spain (see p. 686) or at the Alhambra. Skip the box office line and walk swiftly to the entry point for the Nasrid palaces to be on time. Once inside, don't dawdle; the palaces are a 15-minute walk and your ticket is stamped with a 30-minute window. You have no choice of how you tour the palaces. Follow the arrows.

Córdoba

A thousand years ago Córdoba was Europe's brightest city—a center of music, philosophy, science, medicine, and scholarship where Muslims, Christians, and Jews lived and worked in peace. Scholars from the corners of the known world came here to study the ancient texts of Greece and Rome and puzzle over the newly invented algebra. Córdoba was the glorious capital of al-Andalus and, until the late 11th century, the capital of western Islam—its mosque was the largest in Europe. Córdoba's influence waned as Andalucía disintegrated into regional kingdoms, but the streets and whitewashed buildings of the medieval city center endure.

> Fernando and Isabel governed from Córdoba's Alcázar as they plotted to reconquer Granada.

START Across the Río Guadalquivir from Córdoba's center.

❶ ★ Torre de la Calahorra. This 14th-century defensive tower along the Río Guadalquivir houses an excellent cultural and historical interpretation center. A 1-hour audio tour (available in English) traces the city's rise and fall between the 9th and 14th centuries, with an emphasis on native Córdoban thinkers. Listen to the wisdom of Averroes (1126–98), the Muslim philosopher, mathematician, and astronomer who was the father of secular philosophy in Europe. His near contemporary, the great Torah scholar Moses Maimonides (1135–1204), gets equal time. ⏱ 1½ hr. Puente Romano. ☎ 957-293-929. www.torrecalahorra.com. 4.50€ adults, 3€ seniors and students. May–Sept 10am–2pm and 4:30–8:30pm, Oct–Apr 10am–6pm.

❷ Puente Romano. Constructed during the reign of Julius Caesar, the Roman bridge over the Guadalquivir has been rebuilt many times, but always on its Roman footings. Halfway across the bridge, you might see Christian believers leaving sprigs of wild rosemary at the shrine of archangel San Rafael. Below, herons and egrets wade in the shallows.

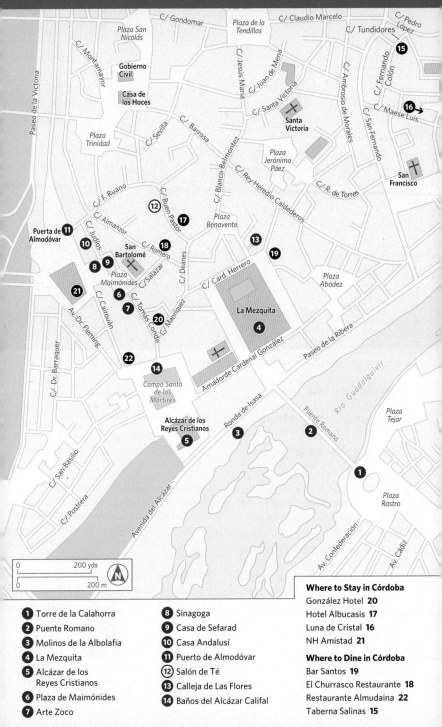

0 — 200 yds
0 — 200 m

1. Torre de la Calahorra
2. Puente Romano
3. Molinos de la Albolafia
4. La Mezquita
5. Alcázar de los Reyes Cristianos
6. Plaza de Maimónides
7. Arte Zoco
8. Sinagoga
9. Casa de Sefarad
10. Casa Andalusí
11. Puerto de Almodóvar
12. Salón de Té
13. Calleja de Las Flores
14. Baños del Alcázar Califal

Where to Stay in Córdoba

González Hotel **20**
Hotel Albucasis **17**
Luna de Cristal **16**
NH Amistad **21**

Where to Dine in Córdoba

Bar Santos **19**
El Churrasco Restaurante **18**
Restaurante Almudaina **22**
Taberna Salinas **15**

> *Córdoba prospered under Roman rule; the Puente Romano was built under Julius Caesar.*

3 Molinos de la Albolafia. This restored Moorish mill and water wheel on the city side of the river not only ground flour, but also pumped water to the Alcázar (see below).

4 ★★★ La Mezquita. Córdoba is known chiefly for this crowning Muslim landmark. A UNESCO World Heritage Site, the Great Mosque has been an architectural wonder for 1,000 years. ⊕ Half-day.

SITE GUIDE PAGE 632

5 ★★ kids Alcázar de los Reyes Cristianos. Constructed for the caliphs of Córdoba, this palace-fortress was refashioned by Fernando and Isabel, who lived here for 8 years. Their makeover left the spa (the Arabic baths) intact but changed everything else. The gardens contain statues of all the monarchs associated with the Alcázar, though the most famous shows Columbus in an audience with Fernando and Isabel. Over the centuries the Alcázar served as the base for the Inquisition, and Franco used it as a political prison. But children will still enjoy having the run of the ramparts. ⊕ 1 hr. C/

Caballerizas Reales, s/n. ☎ 957-297-567. 4€ adults, 2€ students, free Fri. Tues-Sat 10am-2pm and 4:30-6:30pm; Sun 9:30am-2:30pm.

6 Plaza de Maimónides. When the Almohads captured Córdoba in 1148, they expelled the Jews. One 13-year-old forced into exile would become philosopher and physician Moses Maimonides, a seminal thinker of medieval Judaism. Although his career is more associated with Morocco, Córdoba proudly reclaimed him and erected a statue in his honor. Pilgrims touching the feet of the bronze for luck have polished them to a high sheen. C/ Judíos.

7 Arte Zoco. About a dozen artisans working in leather, wood, ceramics, and jewelry sell their wares in stalls arranged around a central patio—sort of a minisouk. Several also maintain studios, though hours when they demonstrate their crafts vary. It's a good spot to find one-of-a-kind work instead of mass-produced souvenirs. C/ Judíos, s/n. ☎ 957-204-033. May-Sept daily 10am-8pm; Oct-Apr Mon-Fri 9:30am-8pm, Sat-Sun 9:30am-2pm.

> *The Casa de Sefarad tells the story of the Judeo-Iberian communities that settled around the Mediterranean during the Diaspora.*

⑧ ★ Sinagoga. One of only three medieval synagogues remaining in Spain, this house of worship was built in 1315. (The Nasrid dynasty invited Jews back to al-Andalus after defeating the Almohads in 1212.) The synagogue was discovered only in 1884 during renovations to the building. Its carved plaster employs the same decorative techniques as carvings in Granada's Alhambra palace—except that the script is Hebrew from the Torah, not Arabic from the Koran. ⏱ 20 min. C/ Judíos, 20. ☎ 957-202-928. .30€. Tues–Sat 9:30am–2pm and 3:30–5:30pm; Sun 9:30am–1:30pm.

⑨ Casa de Sefarad. Córdoba was the de facto capital of Sephardic Jewry, and this small museum re-creates the ambience of 11th- to 12th-century daily Jewish life. Many exhibits explain basic precepts of Judaism in a country where Jews were expelled 5 centuries ago. Visitors more familiar with the culture nonetheless enjoy the rooms explaining the traditional craft of making golden thread and those highlighting the musical and literary traditions of the Sephardim. ⏱ 30 min. C/ Judíos at C/ Averroes. ☎ 957-421-404. www.casadesefard.com. 4€ adults, 2€ seniors and students. Mon–Sat 11am–8pm; Sun 11am–2pm.

⑩ Casa Andalusí. Get a taste of how the Muslim neighbors lived across the street at this other new cultural museum, which re-creates daily life during the 12th-century Caliphate. There's a bit of disconnect between the didactic exhibits and their sensual presentation. Enjoy the rose-strewn fountain in the ivy-draped main patio, and don't worry if you don't quite grasp details on how Córdobans manufactured paper. ⏱ 30 min. C/ Judíos, 12. ☎ 957-290-642. www.lacasaandalusi. com. 2.50€. Daily 10:30am–7:30pm.

City of Flowers

Córdobans are so proud of their flowers that every mid-May they open their patios to visitors for the **Concurso Popular de Patios Cordobeses**, or Córdoba Patio Festival (www.amigosdelospatioscordobeses. es). Pick up a map of participants from the tourist office. You will enter people's homes to see their patios and fountains and whitewashed walls hung with pots of blazing geraniums, or *gitanillas* (little Gypsies). Admission is free, but it's customary to leave a few coins in a tip tray to help with upkeep. If you miss the festival, local etiquette dictates that it's okay to peek into patios where the gate is left open. You can also visit the **Palacio de Viana,** Plaza de Don Gome, 2 (☎ 957-496-741), about a 15-minute stroll outside the Judería. Skip the house tour to simply visit the 12 patios, each with a different style of garden. A full visit is 6€; patios only are 3€. It's open Monday to Friday 10am to 1pm and 4 to 6pm, Saturday 10am to 1pm.

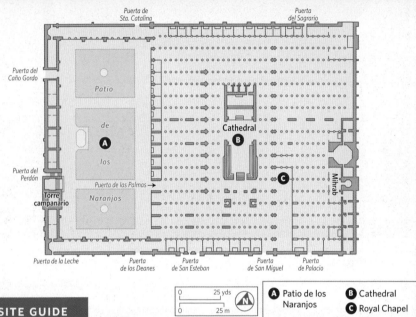

Puerta de Sta. Catalina

Puerta del Sagrario

Puerta del Caño Gordo

Patio

de

A

los

Cathedral

B

Puerta del Perdón

Puerta de las Palmas →

Naranjos

C

Mihrab

Torre campanario

Puerta de la Leche   Puerta de los Deanes   Puerta de San Esteban   Puerta de San Miguel   Puerta de Palacio

| 0 | 25 yds |
| 0 | 25 m |

A Patio de los Naranjos   **B** Cathedral   **C** Royal Chapel

SITE GUIDE

❹ La Mezquita

In its heyday, 40,000 worshipers would gather inside this Great Mosque as light flooded through its open doors. Admission to the **A Patio de los Naranjos,** where worshipers performed ritual ablutions, is free. The shade of the orange trees, sound of running water, and rhythmic patterns of the gardens still work their magic. The building itself is immense—nearly the length of three football fields—and the horizontal forest of red and white arches inside is as impressive as the soaring heights of a Gothic cathedral. Author Nikos Kazantzakis called La Mezquita "a triumphant, wholehearted paean to God." When Fernando III conquered Córdoba in 1236, he left the mosque intact. But a 16th-century archbishop ripped out the heart of the building to construct a **B Cathedral** and **C Royal Chapel.** When Carlos V saw it in 1523, he upbraided the cleric for desecrating one of the world's great artistic buildings. If you look at the cathedral (which has magnificent carved choir stalls) as engaged in a dialogue with the mosque, Islam gets the last word. ⏱ Half-day. C/ Cardenal Herrero, 1. ☎ 957-470-512. 8€ adults, 4€ kids. Mon–Sat 10am–7pm; Sun 2–7pm.

> *The tradition of the Arab bath is experiencing a small modern revival, but at one point, Córdoba could boast over 500 baths.*

⓫ Puerto de Almodóvar. This northwest gate to the Judería is perhaps the best preserved part of the old Moorish walls and a handsome example of a structural horseshoe arch.

⑫ 🍵 **Salón de Té.** Sample the sybaritic side of Andalucían life in Córdoba's heyday by settling onto a padded bench at this flower- and fruit-filled courtyard for a pot of tea and an assortment of pastries made with figs, almonds, honey, dates, and pistachios. C/ Buen Pastor, 13. ☎ 957-487-984. MC, V. $.

⓭ Calleja de las Flores. One of the narrowest streets in the Catedral neighborhood, the "Flower Street" is also one of the most photographed. Just don't try walking two abreast.

⓮ Baños del Alcázar Califal. This restoration (and re-creation) of the original baths of the Alcázar recounts the philosophy, aesthetics, techniques, and even engineering involved in this institution so central to Moorish culture. ⏰ 1 hr. Campo Santo de los Mártires. ☎ 957-420-151. 2€ adults, 1€ students. Mid-June to mid-Sept Tues–Sat 8:30am–2:30pm, Sun 9:30am–2:30pm; mid-Sept to mid-June Tues–Sat 10am–2pm and 5:30–7:30pm, Sun 9:30am–2:30pm.

> *An artisan handpaints ceramic tiles at one of the Arte Zoco studios.*

Where to Stay & Dine

> *The courtyard dining room at Restaurante Almudaina.*

★ **Bar Santos** JUDERÍA *ANDALUCÍAN*
You can get a full range of tapas at this narrow bar near the Mezquita. But don't leave without trying the unusually thick and creamy *tortilla española*. C/ Magistral González Frances, 3. ☎ 957-476-360. Tapas 1.40€–2.50€. Cash only. Lunch & dinner Fri–Wed.

El Churrasco Restaurante JUDERÍA *ANDALUCÍAN*
Grilled and stewed pork and beef are the highlights here, especially when served with *salsas árabes* (dipping sauces) spiked with cumin and cinnamon. C/ Romero, 16. ☎ 957-290-819. Entrees 14€– 20€. MC, V. Lunch & dinner daily.

★ kids **González Hotel** JUDERÍA
The friendly staff and owner make this budget lodging a fun stay. The location is ideal, and triple and quad rooms are good for families or groups. Not all rooms are serviced by the elevator. C/ Manríquez, 3. ☎ 957-479-819. www.hotel-gonzalez.com. 16 rooms. Doubles 44€–71€, triples 60€–110€, quads 80€–130€. MC, V.

Hotel Albucasis JUDERÍA
This hotel is set back from the street as its own private oasis. Spacious digs and a walled courtyard with wrought-iron furniture are luxuries in the crowded Judería. C/ Buen Pastor, 11. ☎ 957-478-625. www.hotelalbucasis.com. 15 rooms. Doubles 85€. MC, V.

★★ **Luna de Cristal** NEW CITY
Steps outside the Judería walls, this beautiful building on a quiet plaza holds six contemporary studio apartments. Kitchens are tiny, beds are big, charm is huge. Plaza de las Cañas, 1. ☎ 957-492-353. www.lunadecristal.com. 6 units. 100€–130€ per night, 650€ per week. MC, V.

NH Amistad JUDERÍA
Classic details like the Mudéjar-style courtyard and ornate woodwork ceilings maintain a sense of grace and history in this otherwise modern lodging set conveniently at the edge of Judería. Plaza de Maimónides. ☎ 957-420-335. www.nh-hotels.com. 83 rooms. Doubles 99€–230€. AE, DC, MC, V.

★ **Restaurante Almudaina** ALCÁZAR *CONTINENTAL* An elegant dining room set into one of the Old City walls serves some local classics (fritters stuffed with ham), but it really excels at fancier plates like pork steak with truffles. Jardines de los Santos Mártires, 1. ☎ 957-474-342. Entrees 14€–28€. AE, DC, MC, V. Lunch & dinner daily.

★ **Taberna Salinas** NEW CITY *ANDALUCÍAN*
A fixture since 1879 near Plaza de Corredera, Salinas serves only full plates of tapas dishes, including the signature orange and cod salad drizzled with olive oil. C/ Tundidores, 3. ☎ 957-480-135. Raciones 6€–12€. MC, V. Lunch & dinner Mon–Sat, closed Aug.

Ronda

"Ronda the glorious" is how Pliny the Elder described the city nearly 2,000 years ago—and his quip still fits. Its whitewashed buildings sit like a snowcap on a high limestone shelf that rises suddenly from the surrounding plain. The mountain, and hence the city, is cleaved in two by a deep gorge cut by the Río Guadalevín. Locals call the old Moorish city—a warren of twisting hillside streets—La Ciudad, while the post-1500 market district on the opposite side of the gorge is called El Mercadillo. In *Death in the Afternoon*, Ernest Hemingway wrote, "The entire town and as far as you can see in any direction is romantic background . . . if a honeymoon or an elopement is not a success in Ronda it would be as well to start for Paris and both commence making your own friends." Ronda's proximity to the Costa del Sol (45 min. on the bus) makes it a popular day trip. To experience the full magic, stay the night. All sights in town are in close walking proximity.

> *Stand in the middle of Pedro Romero's home field, the Plaza de Toros, and imagine tangling with a 2-ton bull.*

START In the valley at Puente Romano, aka Puente San Miguel.

❶ ★★★ El Tajo. Ronda rises high above you from this cliffside vantage point. Farmland stretches into the upriver distance, while the downriver banks of the Guadalevín are buried in the deep shadow of El Tajo gorge. These depths always gave invading armies a disadvantage in taking the town, but it was conquered nonetheless by the Romans in 200 B.C., by the Berber armies of Tariq in 711, and by the relentless forces of Fernando and Isabel in 1485.

❷ Puente Romano. The oldest of three bridges spanning the Guadalevín has been rebuilt many times, but its support structure still consists of arches laid by Roman engineers.

❸ Baños Árabes. Only recently restored as a museum, these 13th-century baths are among the best preserved in Andalucía, still boasting intact brick columns, horseshoe arches, and barrel vaults with star-shaped skylights. They are located close to the river, below the Old City that the Moors called Madinat Runda. ⏱ 30 min. Barrio de Padre Jesús. ☎ 656-950-937.

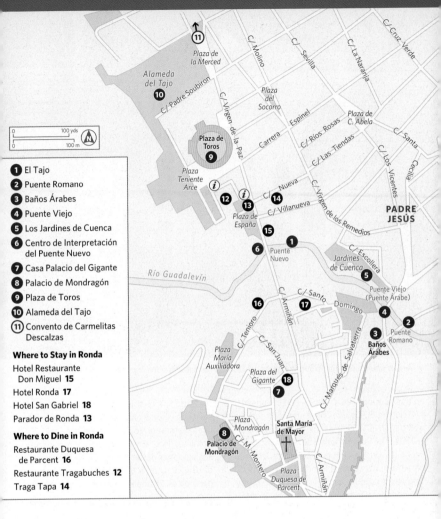

1 El Tajo
2 Puente Romano
3 Baños Árabes
4 Puente Viejo
5 Los Jardines de Cuenca
6 Centro de Interpretación del Puente Nuevo
7 Casa Palacio del Gigante
8 Palacio de Mondragón
9 Plaza de Toros
10 Alameda del Tajo
11 Convento de Carmelitas Descalzas

Where to Stay in Ronda

Hotel Restaurante Don Miguel **15**
Hotel Ronda **17**
Hotel San Gabriel **18**
Parador de Ronda **13**

Where to Dine in Ronda

Restaurante Duquesa de Parcent **16**
Restaurante Tragabuches **12**
Traga Tapa **14**

3€ adults, 1.50€ seniors and students, free Sun. Mon–Fri 10am–6pm; Sat 11am–1:45pm and 3–6pm; Sun 10am–3pm.

4 **Puente Viejo.** If you walk up the steps from the baths to the edge of the Old City, you can exit through the ceremonial **Puerta de Felipe V,** constructed in 1742, and cross the river on the Puente Viejo, aka the **Puente Árabe.** This bridge represented a significant engineering advance over the Puente Romano, as it crosses high above the river. It was built in the 15th century on the ruins of an earlier Moorish bridge.

5 ★ **Los Jardines de Cuenca.** These terraced gardens rising from the Puente Viejo to Plaza de España in El Mercadillo afford some of the best views of the Tajo cliffs and of the Old City on the opposite side. Walk through the gardens on the lip of the gorge, pausing to peer down into the depths. ⏱ 20 min.

6 ★ kids **Centro de Interpretación del Puente Nuevo.** Ronda's citizens successfully petitioned for a new bridge in 1542, but 2 centuries passed before technology advanced enough to attempt to span the top of the gorge. The first bridge

> *The star-shaped skylights in Ronda's Baños Árabes were modeled after the more famous bath at the Alhambra.*

on this spot opened in 1739—and collapsed in 1741, killing 50 people. The current structure was begun in 1759 and finally inaugurated in 1793. The interpretation center is located inside the bridge's support structure. Exhibits provide an overview of Ronda's geography (El Tajo gorge is 120m, or 394 ft. deep) and the engineering achievements necessary to construct the bridge. As always in Ronda, the view is the thing, and windows give the sensation of being suspended in the open air. Plaza de España, s/n. ☎ 649-965-338. 2€ adults, 1€ seniors and students, free for kids 13 & under. Mon–Fri 10am–7pm; Sat 10am–1:45pm and 3–6pm; Sun 10am–3pm.

❼ ★ Casa Palacio del Gigante. This palace was named for the Phoenician stone sculpture in the courtyard. Displays in the small Nasrid castle from the 13th to the 15th century race through Ronda's formation from the geological forces that created the gorge to the Iberian settlement of the city, the Roman occupation, and then the Moorish urban explosion of the 10th and 11th centuries that shaped the city you see today. Some exhibits deal with the building's restoration to become a museum in 2004, detailing decorative features that are small-scale echoes of the Alhambra. ⏱ 30 min. Plaza del Gigante, s/n. ☎ 678-631-445. www.turismo deronda.es. 2€ adults, 1€ seniors and students.

❽ ★★ Palacio de Mondragón. Power has gravitated to this beautiful palace since the 14th century. Legend says it was built for the son of a Moroccan sultan. When Fernando stormed the city in 1485, he dispossessed the last Moorish governor of Ronda from the building so he and Isabel could move in. Today it is Ronda's city hall. Beautiful tiled walls, carved Mudéjar ceilings, fountains, gardens, and arched doorways make it a favorite setting for wedding photos. Upstairs rooms contain exhibits on city history, ethnography, and the Ronda-area environment. ⏱ 1 hr. Plaza Mondragón. ☎ 952-187-119. www.turismoderonda.es. 3€ adults, 1.50€ seniors and students. Mon–Fri 10am–7pm; Sat 10am–1:45pm and 3–6pm.

9 ★★ **Plaza de Toros.** Skipping Ronda's bullring because you disapprove of bullfighting would be like skipping Chartres cathedral because you're a nonbeliever. Aficionados of the *corrida* consider it one of the most important in the history of the sport. Legendary matador Pedro Romero, who dispatched more than 5,000 bulls before dying of natural causes in 1839, made Ronda his home base. His formal and, by modern standards, austere style is the model for the "Goyesca" bullfight. These September contests, named for Goya's depiction of them, have been an annual event in Ronda since 1954. On the unguided tour, you can stand in the ring and imagine facing an enraged 2-ton beast. Photographs and memorabilia in the **Museo Taurino** conjure the adrenaline of the matadors and their inevitably diminutive size. They may be rock stars to their fans, but most are short and slender. They look especially small in photos with longtime resident Orson Welles, a lover of the *corrida* who once wrote of Ronda, "A man does not belong to the place where he was born, but where he chooses to die." ⏱ 1 hr. C/ Virgen de la Paz, 15. ☎ 952-871-539. www.rmcr.org. 6€ adults, 5€ college students, 4€ kids 15 & under. Nov–Feb 10am–6pm; Mar and Oct 10am–7pm; Apr–Sept 10am–8pm.

> *Sultans, Fernando and Isabel, and now the city hall have inhabited the Palacio de Mondragón.*

> *Most matadors are "compact," as illustrated by their uniforms on display at the Museo Taurino.*

> *The ceremonial Puerta de Felipe V leads to Ronda's Old City from the Puente Viejo.*

⑩ Alameda del Tajo. Rondenses gather in this tree-filled park behind the bullring to socialize, show off their children, and enjoy the shade. The edge of the park is one of the city's best scenic overlooks, providing views of the spreading countryside below and the mountains in the distance. Off C/ Virgen de la Paz.

⑪ 🍴 Convento de Carmelitas Descalzas. A small door in the left corner of the convent facing the plaza contains a *retorno,* or revolving window, where you can purchase the luxurious butter cookies known as *mantecadas,* baked and sold by the cloistered nuns. Plaza Merced, 2. No phone. Retorno open 10:15am–1:15pm and 4:45–6:45pm. $.

Bold Deceivers

Ronda has always been a frontier town at the edge of an often lawless wilderness. From the time of the Romans into the early 20th century, the rugged mountains between Ronda and the Straits of Gibraltar harbored thieves, bandits, rebels, and brigands who preyed on travelers and trade caravans. By the late 19th century, many of these thugs had achieved folk-hero status, complete with such colorful names as "Cabeza Torcida," or "Twisted Head." Their exploits were exaggerated for newspaper stories, comic books, and pulp novels. Using yellowed copies of those sources and sometimes hokey dioramas, the ★ kids **Museo del Bandolero,** or Banditry Museum, C/ Arminar, 65 (☎ 952-877-785), both romanticizes the outlaws and addresses the issue of crime. One of the most famous bandits was José Maria Hinojosa Cabacho, known as "El Tempranillo" ("The Early One"). Born in 1805 and killed in 1833, he specialized in stickups but was acclaimed in ballads for his gallantry toward women. The museum also chronicles how the Civil War was meant to bring law to the mountains in 1844. The last of the famous Ronda bandits, José Mingolla Gallardo ("Pasos Largos," or "Longshanks"), died in 1934. The museum's signage is almost entirely in Spanish. Cost is 3€ adults, 2€ students; open daily 10am to 8pm.

Where to Stay & Dine

> *Ronda's parador clings to the edge of the gorge.*

★ **Hotel Restaurante Don Miguel** EL MERCA-DILLO Two-thirds of the tasteful rooms have windows on El Tajo—confirming the adage about location, location, location. Some rooms have private balconies. Plaza de España, 4–5. ☎ 952-877-722. www.dmiguel.com. 30 rooms. Doubles 85€–100€. AE, DC, MC, V.

★ **Hotel Ronda** LA CIUDAD
Family photos decorate the lobby of this home transformed into a delightful hotel. Guests can use the rooftop deck for vistas of the Sierra Nieves. Ruedo Doña Elvira, 12. ☎ 952-872-232. www.hotelronda.net. 5 rooms. Doubles 65€–90€. MC, V.

★★ **Hotel San Gabriel** LA CIUDAD
This romantic hotel with sumptuous rooms even has a tiny movie theater. Doubles are cozy love nests; the spacious Luna de Miel (Honeymoon) suite is a luxury bargain. C/ Marqués de Moctezuma, 19. ☎ 952-190-392. www.hotelsangabriel.com. 21 rooms. Doubles 82€–92€, honeymoon suite 150€. AE, MC, V.

★★★ **Parador de Ronda** EL MERCADILLO
Only the facade of Ronda's historic town hall remains, but the stunning hotel behind it—Ronda's best—features top-notch contemporary design in large rooms with all the amenities. Most rooms overlook El Tajo. Plaza España,
s/n. ☎ 952-877-500. www.paradores.es. 78 rooms. Doubles 102€–274€. AE, DC, MC, V.

★ **Restaurante Duquesa de Parcent** LA CIUDAD *ANDALUCÍAN* The marvelously formal dining room has great traditional food and spectacular countryside views. Time it right and you can enjoy sea bass baked in salt as the sun sets. The bargain menu is available all day. C/ Tenorio, 12. ☎ 952-871-965. Entrees 9€–22€. MC, V. Lunch & dinner daily.

★★★ **Restaurante Tragabuches** EL MERCADILLO *CONTEMPORARY SPANISH* Chef Benito Gómez is so inventive that deciding what to order is like trying to choose your favorite pictures in a Picasso exhibition. If you can afford it, take the tasting menu and let Gómez decide for you. C/ José Aparicio, 1. ☎ 952-190-291. Entrees 11€–25€, tasting menu 90€. AE, DC, MC, V. Lunch Tues–Sun, dinner Tues–Sat.

★★ **Traga Tapa** EL MERCADILLO *ANDALUCÍAN* Fortunately, Gómez is also a pioneer in reinventing tapas, and this minimalist bar lets you sample his artistry for a pittance. A single spear of grilled asparagus with grated cheese and quince paste may sound precious, but you'll remember the taste forever. C/ Nueva, 4. ☎ 952-877-209. Tapas 1.50€–4€, raciones 4€–12€. AE, DC, MC, V. Lunch & dinner daily.

Cádiz

The earthquake of 1755 destroyed most of the buildings, so while Cádiz is the oldest continuously inhabited city in western Europe, it follows an Enlightenment plan with streets laid out in a grid. Most of the Old City of pastel houses sits on a long peninsula guarded by now-abandoned fortifications. Cádiz turns every face to the ocean, and its waterfront promenades and graceful parks make a seamless transition between urban center and timeless sea.

> *The gilded dome of the Catedral Nueva gleams across the city's waterfront.*

START Playa La Caleta.

1 ★ kids **Castillo de Santa Catalina.** Thank the English for the forts of Cádiz, which were constructed to fend off their ships. Sir Francis Drake attacked Cádiz in 1587, and Anglo-Dutch invaders stormed the city in the 1590s. Santa Catalina is the most intact of the forts, and children enjoy having the run of the ramparts. Its rooms serve as a cultural exhibition space and studios for artisans. ⊕ 30 min. C/ Antonio Burgos at La Caleta beach. Free. Mar–Oct 10am–8:30pm; Nov–Feb 10am–7:45pm.

2 ★ **Catedral Nueva.** Bridging both baroque and neoclassical styles, the "new" cathedral replaced one burned by Anglo-Dutch forces in 1596. Started in 1720, it wasn't finished until the 1850s. The shining gilded tiles of its main dome and the beautifully carved choir stalls, moved here from a Carthusian church in Sevilla, are its artistic highlights. Composer Manuel de Falla (1876–1946) lies interred in the crypt. ⊕ 30 min. Plaza de la Catedral. ☎ 956-286-154. 4€ adults, 2.50€ seniors and kids. Mon–Fri 10am–6:30pm; Sat 10am–4:30pm; Sun 1–6:30pm. Bus: 1.

3 ★ kids **Torre de Poniente.** The cathedral's bell tower, constructed during the late-18th-century golden age of Cádiz, is accessible via a ramp for outstanding overviews of both city and coastline. ⊕ 20 min. 3.50€ adults, 2.50€ seniors and kids. June 15–Sept 15 10am–8pm; Sept 16–June 14 10am–7pm.

1/8 mi
1/8 km

A T L A N T I C

O C E A N

Baluarte de la Candelaria

Antiguos Cuarteles

Parque Genovés

Antiguo Hospicio

Playa de la Caleta

Paseo Fernando Quiñones

Castillo de Santa Catalina

Plaza de la Hispanidad

Disputación Provincial

Plaza España

Av. del Puerto

Paseo de Canalejas

Plaza de San Juan de Dios

Av. Ramón de Carranza

Catedral

Iglesia de San Francisco

Plaza de la Mina

Plaza San Antonio

Plaza Topete

Mercado Central

Gran Teatro Falla

Plaza Mentidero

Plaza Fragela

1 Castillo de Santa Catalina
2 Catedral Nueva
3 Torre de Poniente
4 Torre Tavira
5 Freiduría Las Flores
6 Oratorio de Santa Cueva
7 Museo de Cádiz

Where to Stay in Cádiz
Hotel de Francia y Paris 9
Hotel Las Cortes de Cádiz 10
Parador Hotel Atlántico 8

Where to Dine in Cádiz
La Leyenda 13
Marisquería Joselito 11
Sopranis 12

④ ★ kids Torre Tavira. In the late 18th century, the port of Cádiz handled three-quarters of Spain's trade with the Americas, and more than 150 watchtowers monitored the passage of ships in the harbor. The last remaining watchtower has two levels of exhibits about New World trade. Rooftop views of the city, harbor, and shipping lanes make the long climb up the stairs worth the effort. There's a demonstration of the camera obscura every 30 minutes. Its rotating aperture creates an ever-changing panorama of the city on the chamber's circular walls. ⏱ 1 hr. C/ Marqués Real Tesoro, 10. ☎ 956-212-910. 4€ adults, 3.30€ students and seniors. May 15–Sept 15 10am–8pm; Sept 16–May 14 10am–6pm.

⑤ 🍤 Freiduría Las Flores. Located on the plaza of the flower market, this shop sells paper cones, or *cartuchos,* of breaded seafood quickly deep-fried in olive oil. Order a *cartucho* of *gambas* (tiny shrimp) and join the Gaditanos—as the people of Cádiz are called—snacking on benches in the plaza. Plaza Topete, 4. ☎ 956-226-112. $.

⑥ Oratorio de Santa Cueva. This private religious site happens to own a few of the most important paintings in Cádiz. Most of its canvases are typically dark and sentimental works by artists you never had to study in school. But just as you despair, you reach the unusual egg-shaped Capilla Alta, or upper chapel, to discover three striking frescoes by Goya. His version of the Last Supper has Christ and his disciples sprawled on cushions on the floor. ⏱ 30 min. C/ Rosario, 10. ☎ 956-222-262. 2.50€ adults, 1.50€ seniors and students. Thurs–Fri 10am–1pm and 4:30–7:30pm; Sat–Sun 10am–1pm.

> *Tía Norica marionette theater has been a tradition in Cádiz for over 200 years.*

⑦ ★★★ Museo de Cádiz. Julius Caesar's first public office was in Cádiz, but centuries earlier the Phoenicians held sway. This museum owns the best collection of Phoenician artifacts in Europe, including sarcophagi of a man and a woman, excavated in 1887 and 1987, respectively. Move quickly through the Roman statuary to reach upstairs art galleries with masterful Zurbarán portraits of rouge-cheeked angels and haunted saints. Another gallery is devoted to the scenery and marionettes from the city's witty Tía Norica puppet theater. ⏱ 1 hr. Plaza de Mina, s/n. ☎ 956-203-368. 1.50€. Tues 2:30–8:30pm; Wed–Sat 9am–8:30pm; Sun 9:30am–2:30pm.

> *The Castillo de Santa Catalina was built to fend off "piratas" like Sir Francis Drake.*

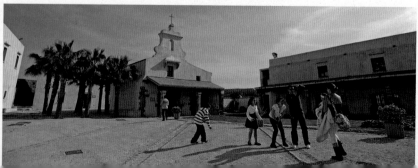

Where to Stay & Dine

> Get up close and personal with your meal at Marisquería Joselito.

Hotel de Francia y Paris HARBOR
Large rooms have high ceilings and modern Spanish decor with cherry-toned furniture. The sweet scent of orange trees wafts in the windows of rooms on the plaza side. Ask for a balcony—there's no extra charge. **Plaza de San Francisco, 6.** ☎ 956-212-319. www.hotelfrancia.com. 56 rooms. Doubles 75€–100€. AE, MC, V.

★ **Hotel Las Cortes de Cádiz** HARBOR
Each tile-and-marble room in this deluxe hotel is named for a person or an event associated with the Constitution of 1812, proclaimed in Cádiz. Warm wall colors and Victorian spindle headboards contribute an airy grace to rooms. **C/ San Francisco, 9.** ☎ 956-212-668. www.hotellascortes.com. 36 rooms. Doubles 80€–140€, with breakfast. AE, MC, V.

★ **La Leyenda** PLAYA VICTORIA SEAFOOD/
ANDALUCÍAN This formal dining room at the beach gives innovative twists to market ingredients—duck and *langostino* salad, for example, or Mediterranean corvina roasted with artichokes and clams. Desserts are widely acclaimed. **Paseo Marítimo, 20.** ☎ 956-262-185. Entrees 9€–14€, gourmet menu 24€. MC, V. Lunch Tues–Sun, dinner Tues–Sat.

★★ **Marisquería Joselito** HARBOR SEAFOOD
Every great fishing port in Spain has a place like Joselito—the fishmonger who cooks the catch and serves it indoors at the bar or outside at cafe tables. Fish is freshest, prices are lowest, enjoyment is tops. **C/ San Francisco, 38.** ☎ 956-266-548. Entrees market price, usually 4€–12€. MC, V. Lunch daily, dinner Mon–Fri.

★★ **kids Parador Hotel Atlántico** PARQUE
GENOVES Possibly the easiest Cádiz hotel to reach if you're driving, this sprawling 1980s complex is beautifully maintained and decorated in a low-key international style. Sandwiched between a park and a beach, it's great for families and handy for walking everywhere in the central city. **Avenida Duque de Nájera, 9.** ☎ 956-226-905. www.parador.es. 132 rooms. Doubles 105€–192€. AE, DC, MC, V.

Sopranis HARBOR CONTEMPORARY SPANISH
Zen minimalism is the aim of the raised communal tapas table with steel bar stools in this stylish restaurant with a young clientele. You can also claim a table for full-sized dishes like roast *bacalao* served on a bed of ratatouille. The unusually good wine list departs from the usual "sherry or Rioja?" routine. **C/ Sopranis, 5.** ☎ 956-284-310. Entrees 11€–17€. MC, V. Lunch Tues–Sun, dinner Tues–Sat.

Jerez de la Frontera

Sleepy farmland for the first 2 millennia after the Phoenicians colonized it, Jerez blossomed in the 17th century, when winemakers began producing oxidized, fortified wines that shipped well and were named "sherry" after their hometown. Cafe umbrellas in Plaza Arenal are emblazoned with the most popular marques—Tío Pepe, Don Patricio, El Gallo—and several major producers offer tours and tastings. But don't while away all your hours sipping fino in the plazas to the ubiquitous soundtrack of flamenco guitar. Jerez is also Spain's equestrian center, and even if you miss the Feria del Caballo in May, you can still thrill to the artistry of dressage. All sights in town are in close walking proximity.

> *The famous Andalucían "dancing horses" perform a veritable equine ballet adapted from classical dressage.*

START Alameda Vieja.

1 ★ **kids** **Alcázar.** Constructed as a rural fort in the 12th century, this compound contains an austerely beautiful mosque, lovely gardens, and Moorish baths. Although the mosque was converted to a church in 1264, the *mihrab*, or prayer niche, was preserved—as was the boiler system of the baths, enabling you to see how they operated. Side by side with these reminders of the Moorish era, the Alcázar also functions as a local history museum. In the 1700s, the city had 32 active olive mills, and two of

them are on display. An unusual addition to the fortress is the Palacio Villavicencio, a noble palace constructed from the late 1600s to 1927. Its history paintings are mostly remarkable for their immense size. A tower room contains a camera obscura, which projects images of the city in a darkened room. ⏲ 1 hr. Alameda Vieja, s/n. ☎ 956-326-923. www.turismojerez.com. Alcázar only 3€ adults, 1.80€ students; with camera obscura 5.40€ adults, 4.20€ students. May 1–Sept 15 Mon-Sat 10am-8pm, Sun 10am-3pm; Sept 16–Apr 30 Mon-Sat 10am-6pm, Sun 10am-3pm.

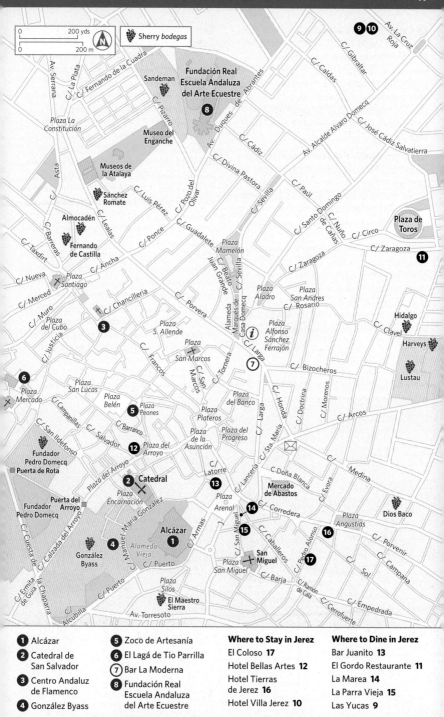

200 yds
200 m

Sherry *bodegas*

Av. La Cruz Roja

C/ Gibraltar

C/ Caldas

9 10

Av. Serrana

Av. La Plata

C/ Fernando de la Cuadra

Sandeman

Fundación Real
Escuela Andaluza
del Arte Ecuestre
8

Av. Duques de Abrantes

Plaza La
Constitución

C/ Pizarro

Museo del
Enganche

Av. Alcalde Alvaro Domecq

C/ José Cádiz Salvatierra

Museos de
la Atalaya

C/ Cádiz

C/ Divina Pastora

C/ Paúl

C/ Sevilla

C/ Santo Domingo

Plaza de
Toros

Sánchez
Romate

C/ Luis Pérez

C/ Pozo del Olivar

C/ Nuño
de Cañas

C/ Circo

Almocadén

C/ Leales

C/ Ponce

C/ Guadalete

Plaza
Mamelón

C/ Zaragoza

C/ Barreras

Fernando
de Castilla

C/ Taxdirt

C/ Ancha

Plaza
Aladro

Plaza
San Andres

C/ Zaragoza

C/ Nueva

Plaza
Santiago

C/ Merced

C/ Chancillería

C/ Porvera

C/ Rosario

Plaza
Alfonso
Sánchez
Ferrajón

Hidalgo

C/ Clavel

Harveys

C/ Muro

Plaza
del Cubo

3

Plaza
S. Allende

C/ Larga

i

Plaza
San Marcos

C/ Bizocheros

Lustau

C/ Justicia

C/ Francos

C/ San
Marcos

7

6

Plaza
Mercado

Plaza
San Lucas

Plaza
Belén

Plaza
Peones

5

Plaza
del Banco

C/ Honda

C/ Doctrina

C/ Morenos

C/ Arcos

C/ San Ildefonso

C/ Campanillas

C/ Salvador

C/ Barranco

12

Plaza del
Arroyo

Plaza
Plateros

Plaza
de la
Asunción

Plaza del
Progreso

C/ Larga

C/ Sta. María

Fundador
Pedro Domecq
Puerta de Rota

Plaza del Arroyo

2 Catedral

Plaza
Encarnación

C/ Latorre

13

C/ Lancería

Mercado
de Abastos

C Doña Blanca

C/ Evora

Medina

Puerta del
Arroyo

Fundador
Pedro Domecq

María González

Alcázar
1

Plaza
Arenal

14

C/ Corredera

Plaza
Angustias

16

Dios Baco

C/ Armas

González
Byass

4

Alameda
Vieja

C/ Manuel

C/ Puerto

15

San
Miguel

C/ San Miguel

C/ Caballeros

C/ Pedro Alonso

17

C/ Porvenir

C/ Campana

C/ Cuesta de la Chaparra

C/ Ermita de Guía

C/ Puerto

Plaza
Silos

Plaza
San Miguel

C/ Barja

C/ Sol

C/ Alcubilla

El Maestro
Sierra

Av. Torresoto

C/ Ramón de Cala

C/ Cerrofuerte

C/ Empedrada

---

1 Alcázar

2 Catedral de
San Salvador

3 Centro Andaluz
de Flamenco

4 González Byass

5 Zoco de Artesanía

6 El Lagá de Tío Parrilla

7 Bar La Moderna

8 Fundación Real
Escuela Andaluza
del Arte Ecuestre

Where to Stay in Jerez

El Coloso **17**

Hotel Bellas Artes **12**

Hotel Tierras
de Jerez **16**

Hotel Villa Jerez **10**

Where to Dine in Jerez

Bar Juanito **13**

El Gordo Restaurante **11**

La Marea **14**

La Parra Vieja **15**

Las Yucas **9**

2 **Catedral de San Salvador.** It's worth trying to visit this heavy baroque edifice during its limited hours to see Zurburán's touching painting of the Virgin Mary as a sleeping child. During the fall harvest, the first sherry grapes are crushed with great ceremony on the stone steps of the entrance. ⏱ **20 min. Plaza de la Encarnación, s/n. ☎ 956-348-482. Free. Mon–Fri 11am–1pm.**

3 **Centro Andaluz de Flamenco.** Jerez proclaims itself a birthplace of flamenco, and this academic center possesses the art's largest public archive of books, musical scores, and performance videos. Flamenco engravings and paintings line the walls of the central courtyard, and free videos are screened daily in the auditorium. You'll always hear flamenco in the background—the center features a different performer every week. Staff are immersed in the local scene; ask about upcoming performances at Jerez *peñas* (clubs of aficionados). ⏱ **30 min. Plaza de San Juan, 1. ☎ 956-814-132. www.centroandaluzdeflamenco.es. Free. Mon–Fri 10am–2pm.**

4 ★ **González Byass.** There are many smaller bodegas in Jerez, but González Byass produces Tío Pepe, the top-selling sherry in the world (available in 115 countries on 6 continents). The Tío Pepe bodega tour is one of the most comprehensive. You see a small vineyard of Palomino grapes and observe the stacked barrels of the *solera* system that blends wine from several decades. The tour verges on a sales pitch, but it's hard not to appreciate the vast operation that began modestly in 1835 when 23-year-old Manuel María González Angel left his bank job to make wine. You get a glimpse of the grand bodega designed by Gustave Eiffel and a look at the brandy factory, where you can smell the "angel's share" (the alcohol lost to evaporation). In 1844, González bought Arab stills to make brandy from year-old sherry—the same year that he named his best fino Tío Pepe after his uncle. The now-classic logo of the bottle with hat, jacket, and guitar was designed in the 1930s. ⏱ **1½ hr. C/ González Byass at Manuel María González, 12. ☎ 956-357-046. www.bodegastiopepe.com. 10€, or 15€ with tapas served with tasting. English tours Mon–Sat 11:30am–5:30pm; Sun 11:30am–2pm.**

> *The Alcázar features an octagonal mosque, ancient Arab baths, and two former municipal olive mills.*

> *Stacked sherry barrels used in the* solera *aging process are seen in Tío Pepe's tasting room.*

5 ★ **Zoco de Artesanía.** This large, light-filled space is a welcome relief from tacky souvenir shops. As you browse the wares in more than 20 small stalls, you might also encounter artisans sewing flamenco apparel, making wooden sherry casks or silver jewelry, sculpting in clay, or even crafting violins. Plaza Peones, s/n. No phone. Mon–Fri 10am–2pm and 5–8:30pm; Sat 10:30am–2:30pm.

6 ★★ **El Lagá de Tío Parrilla.** Unless you got a hot lead on a *peña* at the Centro Andaluz de Flamenco, this flamenco club offers the least sensationalized, most authentic *tablao* (flamenco nightclub) in town—the legacy of legendary guitarist Tío Parrilla. His son, master guitarist and recording artist Juan Parrilla, operates the show. Dinner is pricey; opt for tickets for the show and a drink. Plaza Mercado, s/n. ☎ 956-338-334. Show 24€. Mon–Sat 10:30pm.

7 🍷 **Bar La Moderna.** This ancient local is the perfect spot for a glass of fino with a tapa of *carne con tomate* (beef with grated fresh tomato). C/ Larga, 67. No phone. Cash only. $.

8 ★★★ **Fundación Real Escuela Andaluza del Arte Ecuestre.** Even non-horse lovers will be fascinated by this Royal School that was founded in 1973 to train horses and riders and to operate a breeding farm of the Andalusian horse. A beautifully filmed video celebrates the bond between horse and man, while a more didactic museum traces military and civil horsemanship from the Middle Ages to the present. Performances of the so-called "dancing horses" (usually noon Tues and Thurs) are a great spectacle. But it's equally interesting to visit on nonperformance days, when you can observe trainers and horses working in the arena from 11am to 1pm to learn and polish their routines. Arrive early to screen the video, visit the museum, and stop in at the saddlery to see leather artisans working on the tack. ⏱ 1½ hr. Avenida Duque de Abrantes, s/n. ☎ 956-318-015. www.realescuela.org. Nonperformance tour 10€, tour with performance 18€–24€. Mon–Sat 10am–2pm.

El Caballo Andaluz

Historians can date the Spanish love affair with the *caballo*, the horse, to the equine images painted in caves outside Ronda some 20,000 years ago. But it wasn't until the late medieval period that breeders in the Carthusian monasteries around Jerez worked with bloodlines of the compact, muscular Iberian horse to develop the Pura Raza Española ("pure Spanish race"), known in English as the Andalusian horse.

Where to Stay & Dine

> *A meal at El Gordo Restaurante.*

★ **Bar Juanito** CENTRO ANDALUCÍAN
Famous as a tapas bar in the colorful district of the old fish market, Juanito actually serves full-sized plates of local specialties like pork meatballs in a rich sweet oloroso sherry sauce or fresh tuna loin in a salad dressed with sherry vinegar. If you enjoy organ meats, don't miss the dark, juicy sweetbreads *al Jerez*. C/ Pescadería Viejo, 8–10. ☎ 956-334-838. Raciones 4.50€–7€. MC, V. Lunch & dinner daily.

★ kids **El Coloso** CENTRO
Owned and operated by the same family for more than 40 years, El Coloso is a bargain hunter's dream. The hotel rooms are very traditional—white stucco walls, white tile floors, typical Spanish furnishings—but restful and cool, thanks especially to new and efficient air-conditioners. The four apartments are a great bet for families who also want to save on dining costs, as they have well-equipped kitchens. (That includes a clothes washer, a standard in Spanish apartments.) The ground-level units seem more spacious because they open to an outdoor patio. C/ Pedro Alonso, 13. ☎ 956-349-008. www.elcolosohotel.com. 25 hotel rooms. Doubles 55€–95€. 4 apts. 65€, 350€ per week. MC, V.

El Gordo Restaurante PLAZA DE TOROS
ANDALUCÍAN The city bullring may be a block away, but El Gordo eschews the usual bulls-and-hams decor in favor of a pretty room lined with blue and white tiles and tables set with matching blue and white linens. Owner Manuel García López is justly acclaimed for his baked rice dishes, such as the *arrroz negro* (black rice) made with squid ink, and the quality of his Bay of Cádiz fish and crustaceans. C/ Zaragoza, 38. ☎ 956-169-080. Entrees 11€–13€. MC, V. Lunch Tues–Sat, dinner Tues–Sun.

★ **Hotel Bellas Artes** CENTRO
The great rooftop terrace with hot tub (you can soak and see the cathedral) is a nifty amenity at this small, romantic palace with airy rooms in soft pastels. No wonder wedding parties often book the entire premises for a weekend. Although decor varies, every room is warm and welcoming and has a modern tiled bathroom. Security is great—the hotel abuts the headquarters of the regional police. Plaza del Arroyo, 45. ☎ 956-348-430. www.hotelbellasartes.com. 18 rooms. Doubles 90€. AE, MC, V.

Hotel Tierras de Jerez CENTRO
This good business hotel on Plaza de las Angustias a few blocks from Plaza Arenal expanded into the adjacent building a few years ago, nearly doubling its size. The older rooms are perfectly adequate, but the new rooms are half again larger and boast contemporary decor, wood floors, and more updated baths. Room nos. 206 to 208 even have private patios. C/ Corredera, 58. ☎ 956-346-400. www.hotel tierrasdejerez.com. 50 rooms. Doubles 90€–95€. AE, DC, MC, V.

> *Enjoy a fino poolside at Hotel Villa Jerez.*

★★★ Hotel Villa Jerez CENTRO

This exquisite boutique hotel set in the middle of extensive gardens feels like a sherry baron's estate. Created from a private mansion at the edge of town, the hotel's rooms are each unique but share a common style of traditional, elegant Spanish furniture. Every room has a view of either the gardens or the pool. Best of all, a waiter will bring you a fino anywhere on the property. Staff are especially plugged into the wine and sherry makers and can make all arrangements for private tours. Avenida de la Cruz Roja, 7. ☎ 956-153-100. www.villajerez.com. 18 rooms. Doubles 130€–255€. AE, DC, MC, V.

★ La Marea CENTRO *ANDALUCÍAN*

Even though La Marea is immensely popular, you can usually find a table on the sidewalk or in the back dining room because locals prefer to stand at the bar to drink fino and share big plates of shrimp, crab legs, and goose barnacles. Grilled yellowfin tuna at roughly 15€ per kilogram (2.2 lb.) is a steal. C/ San Miguel, 3. ☎ 956-320-923. Entrees market price (average 25€ for meal). MC, V. Lunch & dinner daily.

La Parra Vieja CENTRO *ANDALUCÍAN*

Ever look at a bar with hams dangling from the ceiling and wonder what happened to the rest of the pig? Modestly calling itself "The Old Grill," this popular establishment almost within sight of Plaza Arenal treats pork steaks from Iberian black pigs as a specialty. It's also one of the few spots that serves a thick and juicy beef sirloin steak. C/ San Miguel, 9. ☎ 956-335-390. Entrees 9€–15€. AE, MC, V. Breakfast, lunch & dinner daily.

★★ Las Yucas CENTRO *INTERNATIONAL*

The chic restaurant of Hotel Villa Jerez is as gracious as the hotel—the kind of place that makes you enjoy dressing for dinner. Not surprising in Jerez, this is very sherry-friendly cuisine, with dishes like shrimp meatballs served with dual sauces of fino sherry and creamed cherries. Service is available in the dining room or outside in the gardens. Avenida de la Cruz Roja, 7. ☎ 956-153-100. Menus 25€–50€. AE, DC, MC, V. Lunch & dinner daily.

Málaga

Even though Málaga was founded around 1100 B.C. by Phoenicians, the city identifies more with modern art than its ancient past. The city is intensely proud that Pablo Ruiz Picasso was born here in 1881, and tracing his childhood is a great way to experience Málaga. Free audio tours offered by Málaga tourism (see p. 659) include a "Picasso Route," which you can also preview on the website.

> From the heights of the Castillo de Gibralfaro, visitors get a bird's-eye view of the harbor of Andalucía's largest coastal city.

START Plaza de la Merced.

❶ **Picasso Statue.** This 2008 bronze of the mature Picasso seated on a bench with pencil and drawing pad hints at how much of his native city he absorbed. In fact, his fond recollections of his hometown ultimately led to the creation of a Picasso museum (see p. 654, ❹). Go ahead—pose next to the artist for a photo. Look around the plaza and on side streets for blue and white tiles identifying sites associated with Picasso's youth. Plaza de la Merced.

❷ ★ kids **Casa Natal de Picasso.** The house where Picasso was born displays the artist's prints as well as photographs of him throughout his life. Baby Pablo's baptismal outfit and even his cloth umbilical band are displayed solemnly in glass cases. His father was an art teacher, and exhibits explain how the gifted boy began drawing and painting as a toddler. His mother was also a great supporter. Picasso later said, "When I was a child, my mother said to me, 'If you become a soldier, you'll be a general. If you become a monk, you'll end up as the pope.' Instead I became a painter and wound up as Picasso." ⏱ 1 hr. Plaza de la Merced, 15. ☎ 952-060-215. www.fundacion picasso.es. 1€ adults, free for seniors and kids 16 & under, free Sun. Daily 9:30am–8pm.

1 Picasso Statue
2 Casa Natal de Picasso
3 Iglesia de Santiago
4 Museo Picasso Málaga
5 Catedral
6 Teatro Romano
7 Alcazaba de Málaga
8 Castillo de Gibralfaro
9 Kelipe Centro de Arte Flamenco
10 C/ Marqués de Larios
11 Casa Aranda
12 Paseo del Parque
13 Antigua Casa de Guardia

Where to Stay in Málaga
Hotel del Pintor 16
Hotel Kris Tribuna 14
Room Mate Lola 20

Where to Dine in Málaga
Cafe Central 15
Cortijo de Pepe 17
El Pimpi 18
El Trillo 19

> *From the cradle to the grave, the Casa Natal de Picasso museum follows the artist's life.*

❸ Iglesia de Santiago. Picasso was baptized at this lovely parish church, which retains a Moorish horseshoe doorway from the mosque it replaced. The interior, especially the 18th-century main altarpiece, is ornately baroque. ⏲ 10 min. C/ Granada, 62. Free. Daily 9am–1pm and 6–8pm.

❹ ★★★ Museo Picasso Málaga. When excavations for the Picasso museum began at the 16th-century Palacio de Buenavista, builders discovered so many archaeological ruins that the museum was delayed nearly a decade. Now the basement preserves ruins from Phoenician, Roman, and Moorish eras. The dozen above-ground galleries are devoted to 155 timeless works by Picasso, donated by his daughter-in-law and grandson. The collection is just large enough to capture subtleties of the artist's talent, and the absence of the "famous" paintings focuses your attention more on the art than the art history. Two additional galleries host changing exhibitions of Picasso's work loaned by other institutions or art by his contemporaries—which includes most artists of the 20th century. ⏲ 1½ hr. C/ San Agustin, 8. ☎ 902-443-377. www.museopicassomalaga.org. Permanent collection 6€ adults, 3€ seniors and students, free for kids 18 & under; temporary exhibitions 4.50€. Tues–Thurs and Sun 10am–8pm; Fri–Sat 10am–9pm.

❺ ★ Catedral. Nicknamed *La Manquita,* or the "one-armed lady," because its second bell tower was never completed after work halted in 1782, Málaga's Catedral de la Encarnación was one of many symbolic power plays exercised by Fernando and Isabel. They captured Málaga from its Islamic ruler in August 1487 and promptly ordered the destruction of the mosque that sat more or less at the foot of the Alcazaba, the Moorish fortress-city. The cathedral to replace it was slow in coming. Work didn't begin until 1528 and was often interrupted. As a result, the basic plan is late Gothic, but the decorative style is baroque. The guided tour belabors the 18 paintings by Alonso Cano and 17 by Claudio Coello. Look around on your own, paying special attention to the 17th-century choir stalls carved from mahogany and cedar. The 40 images of saints are the work of Pedro de Mena (1628–88), one of Spain's greatest wood sculptors. ⏲ 30 min. C/ Molina Lario, s/n. ☎ 952-060-215. 3.50€. Tours Mon–Fri 10am–6pm, Sat 10am–5pm.

❻ Teatro Romano. Only uncovered in 1951, the Roman theater is the best preserved Roman ruin in Málaga province. It is enclosed behind bars, but the 1st-century-A.D. venue is still occasionally used for live theater. Antonio Banderas even performed here early in his career. ⏲ 30 min. C/ de la Alcazabilla, s/n. ☎ 686-130-978. Guided tour free. Apr–Sept Wed–Sat 10am–2:30pm and 5–8pm, Sun 10am–2pm; Oct–May afternoons closes 1 hr. earlier.

❼ ★ kids Alcazaba de Málaga. This Moorish fortress-city is a rarity in Andalucía because it represents the chaotic Taifa period, when the central Islamic empire had disintegrated into

> *Thanks to construction delays, Málaga's "one-armed" cathedral bears both late Gothic and baroque styles.*

small kingdoms and city-states often run by local warlords. Construction began shortly after the 711 conquest of Andalucía, but most of the Alcazaba was built from the 11th to the 14th century, when dynasty after dynasty held sway until the power structure fell apart. Just as Catholic churches throughout Andalucía freely reused columns and capitals from the mosques they displaced, this structure is filled with fluted Greek columns with acanthus capitals dating to 300 B.C., as well as blocks of Roman stones with still-visible Latin inscriptions. Archaeologists have even identified capitals and columns incorporated from the Teatro Romano. The fortifications are a study in creating a defensible city in the era before gunpowder, but domestic pleasures trump military details at every turn. Ultimately, it's more interesting to enjoy gurgling fountains in orange and palm gardens than to note how the battlements gave defending warriors an advantage over attackers. Visitors who have trouble climbing the long set of steps to the entrance can use the elevator behind the Ayuntamiento (city hall) at the corner of C/ Guillén Sotelo and C/ Francisco Bejarrano Robles. ⏱ 2 hr. C/ Alcazabilla, s/n. ☎ 952-128-860. 2€ adults or 3.30€ combined with Castillo de Gibralfaro; .60€ kids, students, and seniors; free after 2pm Sun. Tues–Sun 9:30am–8pm (closes 7pm in winter).

8 kids **Castillo de Gibralfaro.** Less preserved than the Alcazaba, this castle high on the hill was constructed in the early 14th century by King Yusef I of Granada. The heights are more impressive than the ruins themselves, as the view from the ramparts stretches all the way to the harbor. Although a bus runs up the hill, most visitors walk to the castle, following the long, slippery, and steep inclines on Paseo de Don Juan Tamboury. The effort is repaid with a great bird's-eye view of Málaga's bullring. ⏱ 1 hr. ☎ 952-227-230. 2€ adults or 3.30€ combined with Alcazaba; .60€ kids, students, and seniors; free after 2pm Sun. Daily 9am–8pm. Bus: 35 from Alameda Principal.

9 **Kelipe Centro de Arte Flamenco.** Classes in flamenco song, dance, and guitar are Kelipe's mainstay, but this tiny center near the Teatro de Cervantes also presents short performances on weekends—purist flamenco that's a good introduction to the real thing. ⏱ 10 min. C/ Peña, s/n. ☎ 692-829-885 for courses, 951-003-784 for performances. www.kelipe.net. Performances 10€ adults, 8€ students. Thurs–Sat 9pm.

> *The Moors who arrived in Málaga centuries after the Romans used their amphitheater for building materials for their Alcazaba.*

⑩ C/ Marqués de Larios. This broad pedestrian promenade stretching from Plaza de la Constitución down to the Alameda Principal is Málaga's main shopping street—and its social center, as people stop to watch musicians and other street performers. (Living statues on Larios often incorporate elaborate sets and costumes.) Side streets are jammed with tapas bars and cafes. Larios is elaborately decorated at holidays and often features sculpture exhibitions.

⑪ 🍴 **Casa Aranda.** Since 1932, Malagueños of all ages and social classes have swarmed this cafe for piping-hot *churros* and thick, rich cups of hot chocolate. C/ Herrería, 3. No phone. $

⑫ Paseo del Parque. This beautiful strip park flanked by promenades divides the harbor from the 18th-century Aduana palace (the former customs house) and the Ayuntamiento. A delightful stroll from C/ Larios to the end brings you to Málaga's bullring.

⑬ Antigua Casa de Guardia. The Málaga region has been making a fortified, oxidized wine—a first cousin to sherry—for thousands of years. This venerable tavern founded in 1840 carries about 20 Málaga wines in the cask. Sweet versions, such as the Pajarete 1908, are usually preferable to dry. Alameda Principal, 18. ☎ 952-214-680. MC, V. Mon–Sat 9am–10pm.

Where to Stay & Dine

> *Autographed wine barrels furnish El Pimpi.*

Cafe Central CENTRO *ANDALUCÍAN*
Enjoy simple, filling combo plates like pork filets in onion-mushroom-carrot sauce or grilled red mullet. Coffee is a passion—owner José Prado standardized the ordering slang (clarified on a tile plaque). Plaza de la Constitución, 11. ☎ 952-224-972. Plates 6€–10€. Cash only. Breakfast, lunch & dinner daily.

Cortijo de Pepe CENTRO *ANDALUCÍAN*
This bar diagonally across the plaza from the house where Picasso was born is a favorite with local artists, and the upstairs dining room does a great job with roasted meats and fish from Málaga bay. Plaza Merced, 2. ☎ 952-224-071. Entrees 8€–17€. MC, V. Lunch & dinner Wed–Mon; closed mid-Aug to mid-Sept.

El Pimpi CENTRO *ANDALUCÍAN*
Wine casks autographed by celebrities dominate the patio, but head to the bar to eat generous tapas and gaze at aging posters of the Málaga Feria and vintage ads for the then-new Costa del Sol. C/ Granada, 62; also enter via plaza on C/ Alcazabilla. ☎ 952-228-990. Entrees 6€–18€. MC, V. Lunch & dinner daily.

El Trillo CENTRO *ANDALUCÍAN*
This atmospheric restaurant just off C/ Larios offers intriguing twists on local cuisine, such as the grandmotherly roasted eggplant stuffed with hard-boiled egg, bread crumbs, and ham. C/ Don Juan Díaz, 4. ☎ 952-603-920. Entrees 13€–25€. MC, V. Lunch & dinner daily.

Hotel del Pintor CENTRO
Self-consciously modern and arty—it's not far from the Picasso sites, and the owner is a painter—this new small hotel a block from the Teatro Cervantes has used a bold color scheme of red, black, and white in each modest-sized room. Clientele is mostly under 40. C/ Álamos, 27. ☎ 952-060-980. www.hoteldelpintor.com. 17 rooms. Doubles 60€–80€. MC, V.

Hotel Kris Tribuna CENTRO
Set atop the remains of an 11th-century wall (visible in the cafe), the Tribuna is a short walk to Plaza de la Constitución. Rooms are small but attractive, with wrought-iron headboards and tiled bathrooms. C/ Carretería, 6–10. ☎ 952-122-230. www.krishoteles.com. 42 rooms. Doubles 70€–80€. MC, V.

Room Mate Lola ALAMEDA
Lola pioneered the gentrification of its neighborhood between the Alameda and the port. The fashion-forward boutique hotel is decorated in intense modern colors. A generous buffet breakfast is served until noon. C/ Casa de Campos, 17. ☎ 952-579-300. www.room-matehotels.com. 50 rooms. Doubles 85€–160€. AE, MC, V.

Andalucía Fast Facts

Arriving & Getting Around

BY PLANE Most overseas travelers reach Andalucía by flying into **Málaga Airport,** Avenida Garcia Morato (☎ 952-048-838), or into Sevilla's **Aeropuerto San Pablo** (☎ 954-449-000). BY TRAIN High-speed **AVE trains** from Madrid service Córdoba and Sevilla. Sevilla is a hub for Andalucían train service to all other communities. For details, visit www.renfe.es. BY BUS Most of Andalucía is serviced by bus lines under the umbrella of **Alsa,** which has a superb multilingual website with schedules and prices (www.alsa.es). BY CAR Coastal Andalucía is linked by the **N-340, A-7,** and **AP-7** highways. The **A-4** connects Cádiz, Jerez de la Frontera, Sevilla, and Córdoba. The **A-44** links Jaén and Granada to the coast. The **A-92** connects Sevilla and Granada.

Booking Services

Jerez de la Frontera has implemented a direct booking system, available in the tourism office at C/ Larga, 39 (☎ 956-149-863), or online at **www.turismojerez.com**.

Doctors & Hospitals

For emergency medical or dental attention, go to the *centro de urgencia* (emergency room) of the nearest city hospital. Non-E.U. residents can consult national health service doctors for a relatively small fee; ask at your hotel for a list of doctors. Hospitals with emergency rooms in the major cities of Andalucía are as follows. CÁDIZ **Hospital Universitario Puerta del Mar Centralita,** Avenida Ana de Viya, 21 (☎ 956-242-100). CÓRDOBA **Hospital Universitario Reina Sofia,** Avenida de Menéndez Pidal, 1 (☎ 957-217-000). GRANADA **Hospital de San Juan de Dios,** Avenida San Juan de Dios 19–29 (☎ 958-295-221). JEREZ DE LA FRONTERA **Servicio Andaluz de Salud,** Carretera Madrid-Cádiz, s/n (☎ 956-303-347). MÁLAGA **Hospital Civil,** Plaza Hospital Civil, s/n (☎ 952-287-500). RONDA **Hospital General Basico Centralita,** Carretera El Burgo, km 1 (☎ 952-871-540). SEVILLA **Hospital Universitario Virgen del Rocio Centralita,** Avenida Manuel Siurot, s/n (☎ 955-012-000).

Pharmacies

To find an open pharmacy outside normal business hours, check the list of stores posted on the door of any drugstore. By law, there's always a drugstore open somewhere. Drugstores are called *farmacias*. When open, they display a neon green cross. Some 24-hour pharmacies in Andalucía are as follows. CÁDIZ **Farmacia Afri,** Avenida Segunda Aguada, 13 (☎ 956-279-457). CÓRDOBA **Farmacia Mendez Picon,** Avenida América, 3 (☎ 957-472-095). GRANADA **Farmacia Tallón Padial,** C/ Recogidas, 48 (☎ 958-251-290). JEREZ DE LA FRONTERA **Farmacia Porvera,** C/ Porvera, 32 (☎ 956-342-323). MÁLAGA **Farmacia Caffarena,** Alameda Principal, 2 (☎ 952-212-858). SEVILLA **Farmacia Neto Del Río,** C/ Castillo de Constantina, 4 (☎ 954-610-437).

Police

Call ☎ **088** for the national police or ☎ **092** for the local police.

Post Office

Main post offices are marked on all maps available at tourist offices. They are generally open Monday to Saturday 9am to 6pm. You can also buy stamps at any tobacconist. The main post offices in the major cities of Andalucía are as follows. CÁDIZ Plaza Topete, s/n (☎ 956-210-511). CÓRDOBA C/ Jose Cruz Conde, 15 (☎ 957-496-342). GRANADA Puerta Real, 2 (☎ 958-221-138). JEREZ DE LA FRONTERA C/ Cerron, 2 (☎ 956-326-733). MÁLAGA Avenida Andalucía, 1 (☎ 952-364-380). RONDA C/ Virgen De La Paz, 20 (☎ 952-872-557). SEVILLA Avenida Constitución, 32 (☎ 954-224-760).

Safety

Andalucía's cities are generally quite safe. Avoid deserted streets at night and during the afternoon closing hours. Do not leave anything visible in a parked car, especially overnight.

Visitor Information

See below for the addresses and hours of tourism offices around Andalucía. ALMUÑECAR Avenida de Europa, s/n (☎ 958-631-125; www.almunecar.info). Open July to September 15 daily 10am to 2pm and 6 to 9pm; April to June daily 10am to 2pm and 5 to 8pm; October to March daily 10am to 2pm and 4:30 to 7pm. **ARCOS DE LA FRONTERA** Plaza del Cabildo, s/n (☎ 956-702-264). Open Monday to Saturday 10am to 2pm and 3:30 to 7:30pm, Sunday 10am to 2pm. **BAEZA** Plaza del Populó, s/n (☎ 953-740-444; www.andalucia.org). Open Monday to Friday 9am to 7:30pm; Saturday to Sunday 9:30am to 3pm. **BENALMÁDENA** Avenida Antonio Machado, 10 (☎ 952-441-295; www.benalmadena.com). Open in summer Monday to Friday 9am to 6:30pm, Saturday 9am to 3:30pm; winter Monday to Saturday 9am to 3:30pm. **CÁDIZ** Paseo de Canalejas, s/n (☎ 956-241-001). Open Monday to Friday 8am to 6pm; Saturday to Sunday 9am to 5pm. **CÓRDOBA** C/ Torrijos, 10 (☎ 957-355-179). Open Monday to Friday 9am to 7:30pm; Saturday to Sunday 9am to 3pm. **EL PUERTO DE SANTA MARIA** C/ Guadalete, s/n (☎ 956-542-475; www.turismoelpuerto.com). Open daily 10am to 2pm and 5:30 to 7:30pm. **ESTEPONA** Avenida Juan Carlos, s/n (☎ 952-802-002; www.estepona.es). Open Monday to Friday 9am to 2pm and 5 to 8pm; Saturday 10am to 2pm. **FUENGIROLA** C/ Jesús de Rein, 6 (☎ 952-467-457). Open Monday to Friday 9:30am to 2pm and 5 to 7pm; Saturday 10am to 1pm. **GRAZALEMA** Plaza España, 11 (☎ 956-132-225). Open in summer daily 10am to 2pm and 6 to 8pm; winter daily 10am to 2pm and 4 to 7pm. **JAÉN** C/ Ramón y Cajal, 4 (☎ 953-313-281; www.andalucia.org). Open Monday to Friday 9am to 7:30pm; Saturday to Sunday 9:30am to 3pm. **JEREZ DE LA FRONTERA** C/ Larga, 39 (☎ 956-331-150; www.turismojerez.es). Open Monday to Friday 8am to 3pm and 4:30 to 6:30pm; Saturday to Sunday 9:30am to 2:30pm. **LANJARÓN** Avenida de la Alpujarra, s/n (☎ 958-770-462). Open Thursday to Saturday and Tuesday 10am to 2pm and 4 to 8pm; Sunday 10am to 2pm. **MÁLAGA** Plaza de la Marina (☎ 952-122-020; www.malagaturismo.com). Open Monday to Friday

9am to 6pm; Saturday to Sunday 10am to 6pm. **MARBELLA** Plaza de los Naranjos, s/n (☎ 952-823-550; www.marbella.es). Open Monday to Friday 9am to 2pm and 5 to 8pm; Saturday 10am to 2pm. **MIJAS** Plaza Virgen de la Peña, s/n (☎ 952-589-034; www.mijas.es). Open daily 10am to 7pm. **NERJA** C/ Carmen, 1 (☎ 952-521-531; www.nerja.org). Open summer 10am to 2pm and 4 to 6pm; winter 10am to 2pm. **PAMPANEIRA** Punto de Información Parque Nacional de Sierra Nevada, Plaza de la Libertad, s/n (☎ 958-763-127; www.nevadensis.com). Open Tuesday to Saturday 10am to 2pm and 4 to 6pm; Sunday to Monday 10am to 3pm. **RONDA** Paseo de Blas Infante, s/n (☎ 952-187-119; www.turismoronda.es). Open Monday to Friday 10am to 2pm and 5 to 7pm; Saturday 10am to 2pm; Sunday 11am to 2pm. **SANLÚCAR DE BARRAMDEDA** C/ Calzada del Ejército, s/n (☎ 956-366-110; www.aytosanlucar.org). Open Monday to Friday 10am to 2pm and 5 to 7pm; Saturday 10am to 2pm; Sunday 11am to 2pm. **SALOBREÑA** Plaza Goya, s/n (☎ 958-610-314; www.ayto-salobrena.org). Open in winter Tuesday to Saturday 9:30am to 1:30pm and 4 to 7pm; summer Sunday to Monday 10:30am to 1:30pm and 6 to 9pm, Tuesday to Saturday 10:30am to 9pm. **TORRE DEL MAR** Paseo de Larios at Rotunda (☎ 952-541-104; www.ayto-velezmalaga.es). Open winter Monday to Friday 8am to 3pm; summer daily 9am to 2pm and 5 to 9pm. **TORREMOLINOS** Plaza de la Comunidades Autonomos, Playamar Beach traffic circle (☎ 952-371-909). Open Mid-September to April Monday to Friday 9:30am to 2:30pm; May to June 9:30am to 2:30pm and 6 to 8pm; mid-July to mid-Sept daily 10am to 2pm and 6 to 8pm. **ÚBEDA** C/ Baja del Marqués, 4 (☎ 953-779-204; www.andalucia.org). Open Monday to Friday 9am to 7:30pm; Saturday to Sunday 9:30am to 3pm. **ZAHARA DE SIERRA** Plaza del Rey, 3 (☎ 956-123-114; www.zaharacatur.com). Open daily 9am to 2pm and 4 to 7pm.

Spanish History & Culture

Spain: A Brief History

Beginnings

The first humanlike inhabitants of Spain crossed the land bridge from Africa into Andalucía roughly 1.8 million years ago. But archaeological evidence becomes scarce until the appearance of full-blown Neanderthal culture 40,000 years ago, followed by a sudden uptick in human activity as Homo sapiens fled the European glaciers into Iberia 30,000 years ago. After another 10,000 years, these hunters and gatherers began creating remarkable wall paintings of hands and game animals in the caves of Asturias, Cantabria, and the Basque Country.

Around 1300 B.C., the first Germanic migrations began as the Celts filtered into northern Spain, opening the rich tin mines of Galicia. Celtic culture persists in the northern fringe of Iberia to this day and gave modern Spanish one key word: cerveza, or beer. As the Celts expanded into the entire peninsula, a hybrid Celtiberian culture arose—recalled in the outstanding female sculptures from Baza (near Granada) and Elx (or Elche, near Alicante), now displayed in the archaeology museum in Madrid.

Phoenician traders appeared on the southern coasts about the same time as the Celts arrived in the north. Around 1100 B.C., they founded the cities of Cádiz and Málaga and may have played a role in the rise of Tartessos, a refined civilization at the mouth of the Guadalquivir river that was known in ancient times for its silver, gold, and tin, and for its dancers with castanets.

Roman Hispania

As Phoenician power waned, its outpost of Carthage on the North African coast began to colonize the Mediterranean coast of Iberia, often in conflict with Greek settlements such as Ampurion on the Costa Brava. In 228 B.C., Carthage began to recruit armies among the Iberians for an assault on Rome led by Hannibal. Rome countered by occupying Iberia, establishing its first forces at Tarragona. By 218 B.C., Rome had defeated Carthage in the Second Punic War. Over the next 200 years, Rome assimilated the entire Iberian Peninsula, either through warfare or by agreements with existing leaders that allowed them to retain power in return for tribute.

Under the Romans, Iberian plains were planted in wheat, river valleys in wine grapes, and dry hillsides in olive trees. Tarragona became the administrative capital of eastern Iberia, Mérida its counterpart in the west. The extensive Roman ruins in both cities demonstrate the full flowering of culture in Roman Hispania.

Rome invited the Visigoths into Iberia in 415 to drive out the Vandals, which they achieved by 429. The Visigoths established their own kingdom in Iberia in 484, with its capital at Toledo. Visigothic culture reached its height in the 7th century, but only fragments of its architecture have survived, serving as building material for succeeding cultures.

Al-Andalus

Spanish history and culture took an abrupt turn on April 30, 711, when a small Arabic and Berber army led by Tariq ibn Ziyad landed at Gibraltar. By July he had defeated the Visigothic armies at the Battle of Guadalete and, with reinforcements from North Africa, had managed to subjugate most of the Iberian Peninsula within 7 years. Only the Basques remained out of Tariq's reach; the Asturians threw off the Muslim yoke in 722.

Córdoba emerged as the capital of Muslim-controlled al-Andalus, which became an emirate independent from Damascus in 756. The declaration of the Córdoban Caliphate in 929 proved the high-water mark of Muslim rule in Spain, a golden age of prosperity and scholarship.

Although Spaniards later lumped all Muslim rulers under the generic term "Moors," a succession of dynasties controlled al-Andalus. The region broke up into independent city-states in 1031, then was reunited by Berber armies of the Almoravids by 1094. They were succeeded by the Islamic fundamentalist Berbers, the Almohads, less than a century later. With the loss of Córdoba and Sevilla to Christian forces, by 1248 al-Andalus was reduced to the kingdom of Granada, which survived for another 250 years as a trading conduit to the Muslim world, subject to the rule of the king of Castilla.

> *PAGE 660 A bison drawing from the Altamira cave. ABOVE A carving of Boabdil (Mohammed XII) relinquishing Granada to the Catholic monarchs in that city's Royal Chapel.*

Coalescing Christian Kingdoms

The Muslim conquest of Iberia was a stunning military feat, but the Muslims found it difficult to maintain control in the north. When Asturian warlord Pelayo defeated a small Muslim force at Covadonga in 722, the foundation of the kingdom of Asturias was established. Other mountain peoples followed suit, and the Muslim occupiers slowly withdrew to the Río Duero. The politics and dynasties of the various Christian kingdoms that arose are complex, but modern Spain began to come into focus around the end of the 12th century, thanks to the consolidation of kingdoms by either the sword or the wedding ring. By 1250, chroniclers refer to the Five Kingdoms of Spain: Portugal, Pamplona/Navarra (which included the Basque lands),

Castilla y León (which included Galicia, Asturias, and Cantabria), the Crown of Aragón (which included Catalunya and Valencia), and the Muslim kingdom of Granada.

Reconquista

The reconquest of Muslim-held lands—the *Reconquista*—became the driving force of geopolitics in Iberia. As Muslim influence waned, two great powers arose. On the north and west, Castilla led the charge into Andalucía. In 1085, Alfonso I and his troops (including El Cid) seized Toledo. On the east, Aragón took the county of Barcelona from the French and Valencia and the Balearics from the Muslims, reaching its greatest influence under Jaume I the Conqueror, who also controlled Sicily and Naples. (His stunning Modernista tomb is in the town hall in Tarragona.)

The marriage of Isabel of Castilla and Fernando of Aragón mustered the two greatest powers under a single flag. Abrogating the deal between Castilla and Granada, the "Catholic monarchs" (as the pope declared them) laid siege to Granada in 1491. On January 2, 1492, the city capitulated.

It was a singular year in Spanish history, as Columbus set sail from Andalucía and discovered the Americas, although word didn't reach Spain until 1493. Fernando and Isabel also took the occasion of capturing Granada to expel Jews and Muslims from the country.

Imperial Spain

Fernando and Isabel bound Spain together by force of personality and fierce Roman Catholic orthodoxy. They married their heir, Juana, to a

Hapsburg, and following her death in 1516, her son was crowned Carlos I, the first of the Hapsburg kings of Spain. Through his father's side, he brought Flanders into the empire. Three years later, Carlos was elected Holy Roman Emperor and assumed the title Carlos V, by which he is best known. He dispatched *hidalgos* (Spanish gentry) to conquer the peoples of Mexico and Peru and return their treasure to Sevilla and Toledo.

Yet Carlos V squandered much of the newfound wealth of the *hildalgos* fighting small wars in Europe and bigger wars in the Mediterranean as he tried to prove himself defender of the Catholic faith. In 1556, beset by gout, he retired and his son Felipe II came to the throne.

The reign of Felipe II was the apogee of the Spanish monarchy. Riches were pouring in from the New World, and Felipe managed to negotiate truces in some of his father's ongoing wars. In 1561, he moved the court from Toledo to Madrid but focused much of his attention on building El Escorial as a pantheon for the Hapsburgs. Felipe had been the king consort of England when his first wife, Mary Tudor, was queen. When Mary Queen of Scots was executed by order of Elizabeth I in 1587, Felipe pressed his case for the English throne. His Spanish Armada was soundly defeated when it tried to invade England, tipping the balance of power on the Atlantic to England.

By the time Felipe IV was crowned in 1621, the Spanish line of Hapsburgs was petering out, but he unwittingly

secured his legacy by appointing a genius as court painter, Diego Velázquez. When Felipe IV's son Carlos II died, he bequeathed his title to his half-sister's grandson—a Bourbon who was Duke of Anjou. All of Europe got involved in the War of Spanish Succession, which ended with the Bourbon duke taking the throne as Felipe V. The same dynasty sits on the throne today.

The early Bourbon kings proved effective monarchs. Well-versed in the advanced ways of the French court, they sought to modernize Spain. Carlos III, who came to the throne in 1759, is credited with bringing Enlightenment planning to Madrid, putting Francisco de Goya on the royal payroll, and supporting the American colonists in their revolution against England.

Chaotic Spain

Napoleon Bonaparte's 1808 invasion of Spain set off 167 years of instability and political oppression. Spaniards literally took to the hills to fight Napoleon in the War of Independence, finally driving his armies out in 1813. Francisco de Goya famously delineated the horrors of French occupation in a series of paintings now in the Prado, including scenes of French troops putting down a rebellion in Madrid. Fernando VII, who reassumed the throne, proved no friend of the freedom fighters and spent 2 decades putting down revolts. His death in 1833 prompted a civil war between supporters of his daughter (Isabel II) and the Carlists who favored a distant male heir to the throne. Two more Carlist wars were

fought, mostly in Navarra and the Basque Country, over the next 50 years, and Carlist sympathies festered up into the 20th century. (At the outset of the Civil War in 1936, Francisco Franco [see below] rejected the tentative support of the crown because many of his closest advisors and generals had Carlist roots.)

Isabel II ultimately was driven into exile in Paris, but the shaky monarchy was restored in 1874 when her son Alfonso XII became king. His sudden death in 1886 left his unborn son as monarch. The child was crowned Alfonso XIII at birth, but his mother, Queen María Cristina, served as regent until 1902. Her advisors botched both the Spanish economy and its international relations: During this period, Spain relinquished its remaining American colonies, suffering as much loss of national dignity as overseas riches. While enjoying immense personal popularity—he was the first celebrity king—Alfonso XIII exercised little real power. His chief legacy was to create the Real Madrid football team and the *parador* hotel system. In 1923, he allowed prime minister Primo de Rivera take over as dictator for the next 7 years.

Civil War & the Franco Years

Primo de Rivera was overthrown, and in 1931, Spain declared the Second Republic. Initially progressive and left wing in its politics, the new government broke into ever smaller factions. Conservative, fascist-minded parties gained ground in the elections. When a group of right-wing generals

> *General Francisco Franco visits the headquarters of the Northern Front in Burgos during Spain's Civil War.*

declared a coup in 1936, the Civil War was joined.

The world took sides, with Hitler and Mussolini backing Francisco Franco and the Nationalist generals and most of the rest of Europe nominally backing the Republicans. Germany and Italy sent weapons and military assistance to the right, while the rest of the world sent a few volunteer brigades to the left. Franco showed who held the cards by calling in the fire bombing of Gernika (Guernica) in 1937. By 1939, most of the fighting was over. Much of the country lay in ruins, and Franco stood atop the smoking pile.

Steering Spain clear of alliances, Franco continued to rule until his death in 1975. He brought order if not freedom, but he also isolated Spain from the rest of Europe. Only the U.S. had close relations, initiated in the 1950s to place air bases on Spanish soil.

Democratic Spain

Franco, who died in 1975, had made provisions for Juan Carlos de Borbón, the grandson of Alfonso XIII, to become king on his death. (Juan Carlos I remains on the throne today.) Under the terms of a 1978 constitution, Spain became a constitutional democracy with a reigning monarch who has no role as a ruler. It was a heady time, as Spain exploded with artistic and cultural energy, often called La Movida. In 1983, the constitution devolved much of its centralized powers to autonomous regions, addressing in part long-standing calls for self-government in the Basque Country, Catalunya, and Galicia. Spain had its coming-out party of sorts in 1992 when it hosted the World's Fair in Sevilla and the immensely successful summer Olympics in Barcelona.

Spain has taken a leadership position in art and architecture—creating the Guggenheim Bilbao Museum by Frank Gehry and Valencia's City of Arts & Sciences, designed in large part by Santiago Calatrava. It is catching up with France and Germany in high-speed rail service and added a stunning new terminal to Barajas International Airport in Madrid in 2006. Until the economic slump of 2008–09, Spain enjoyed the fastest growing major economy in Europe.

A Timeline of Spanish History

20,000 B.C.

20,000–12,000 B.C. Artists paint walls of caves in northern Spain.

1300 B.C. Celts arrive in Galicia, begin mining large tin deposits in Europe to make bronze weaponry.

1100 B.C. Phoenicians settle Cádiz and Málaga as trading posts.

600–400 B.C. Greeks establish colonies on Mediterranean coast, including Ampurion.

218–220 B.C. Rome defeats Carthage in Second Punic War and takes Carthaginian territories in Iberia. Tarragona becomes Roman capital of Hispania.

25 B.C. Mérida (left) founded as Augusta Emerita.

400 A.D.

415–429 Visigoths enter Iberia and drive out Vandals.

711 Tariq ibn Ziyad invades Iberia from North Africa, subjugates peninsula within 7 years.

722 Visigothic chieftain Pelayo leads revolt against Muslim army, establishes Kingdom of Asturias.

1212 Combined armies of Castilla, Navarra, Aragón, and Portugal defeat Berber Almohad forces in Battle of Las Navas Tolosa, crushing central Muslim control of al-Andalus.

1213 Jaume I (left) ascends to throne of Aragón, conquers Balearic Islands in 1229–35, Valencia in 1238.

1400

1469 Isabel of Castilla marries Fernando of Aragón; they jointly rule most of Spain.

1478 The Spanish Inquisition (left) begins expelling Jews.

1492 Armies of Fernando and Isabel enter Granada, completing the Reconquista. Columbus sets sail and makes New World landfall in October.

1513 Navarra joins Castilla, placing all of Spain under one government.

1516 Carlos I is crowned king, uniting all the Spanish crowns in one person. In 1519, he is elected Holy Roman Emperor.

1556 Felipe II ascends to Spanish throne.

1588 Claiming the English throne, Felipe II attacks England with the Spanish Armada, which is soundly thrashed.

1624 Diego Velázquez enters service of Felipe IV as court painter.

1701–04 War of Spanish Succession seats Bourbon dynasty on throne.

1759 Carlos III begins Enlightenment modernization of Spain.

1800

1808 Napoleon invades Spain; guerrilla warfare breaks out.

1812 Revolutionary parliament issues liberal constitution in Cádiz.

1833 Three-year-old Isabel II becomes queen, touching off the First Carlist War, a 6-year civil war over succession.

1846-49 Second Carlist War ruins Spanish economy.

1868 Isabel II (left) flees to exile in Paris.

1872-76 Third Carlist War leads to fierce crackdown on Basque rights.

1873-74 First Spanish Republic declared.

1898 Spanish-American War strips Spain of Cuba, Puerto Rico, Guam, and the Philippines.

1900

1914 With relatives on both sides, King Alfonso XIII declares Spain neutral in World War I.

1923-30 General Manuel Primo de Rivera rules Spain as dictator.

1931 Second Spanish Republic declared. Alfonso XIII goes into exile but does not abdicate.

1936 Civil War breaks out (left). Generalissimo Francisco Franco's Nazi-Fascist alliances give him the military advantage. Franco declares himself dictator in October 1936.

1937 Nazi planes bomb Gernika on April 26.

1939 Spanish Civil War concludes with Nationalist victory.

1975 Francisco Franco dies. Juan Carlos de Borbón, grandson of Alfonso XIII, becomes king.

1978 New constitution establishes Spain as constitutional democracy with reigning but not ruling monarch.

1980

1982 Spain joins NATO, ending its outcast status from Europe.

1986 Spain joins European Union.

1992 World's Fair is held in Sevilla, summer Olympics in Barcelona.

1997 Frank Gehry's innovative Guggenheim museum (left) opens in Bilbao.

2004 Madrid train bombings kill 191 and injure 2,050. Spain withdraws troops from Iraq.

2010 Spain emerges from a deep 2-year recession and promises budget cuts and belt-tightening, but still faces a long uphill battle to economic recovery.

Spain's Architectural Evolution

> Segovia's Roman aqueduct.

> Santiago de Compostela.

Roman (100 B.C.–A.D. 300)
Classical Roman structures still standing in Spain include the **aqueduct** in Segovia—constructed of fitted stone without mortar (see p. 218, ❶). Equally spectacular are the seaside amphitheater in Tarragona and the classical theater in Mérida.

Visigothic (A.D. 460–711)
Few Visigothic buildings survive, but their columns and capitals are often found in later buildings. The archaeological museums of **Granada** (see p. 614, ❿), **Mérida** (see p. 188, ❾), and **Cuenca** (see p. 154, ❶) have good examples of the delicate carvings.

Ummayyad (711–987)
Architecture under the Córdoban Caliphate drew its inspiration from Damascus, representing the natural world with evocative geometric forms. Perhaps the most famous example is **La Mezquita,** the Great Mosque of Córdoba (see p. 630, ❹), with

its forest of striped arches and horseshoe portals.

Almoravid & Almohad (1086–1237)
Berbers of both the Almoravid and Almohad dynasties used brick as the principal material and kept surface decoration to a minimum. Little Almoravid architecture exists today, while the best example of Almohad architecture is the tower of Sevilla's **La Giralda,** originally the minaret of the mosque (see p. 590, ❸).

Romanesque (10TH–13TH C.)
A primitive Italian Romanesque style, with thick load-bearing walls and rhythmic arches, came over the Pyrenees into Catalunya, though few examples remain. French-influenced Romanesque entered northern Spain along the Camino de Santiago. The **Capilla del Cristo Baja** beneath Santander's cathedral (see p. 284, ❸) exemplifies the style with its columns that rise like thick tree trunks

to support low vaults. The **24 churches of Zamora** (see p. 206, ❸)—all built within a century of each other—demonstrate Romanesque influence coupled with Visigothic ornament and Moorish multifoil arches. The **cathedral in Santiago de Compostela** (see p. 256, ❶) is an extreme adaptation of local stone carving to Romanesque ornamentation.

Nasrid (1237–1492)
Granada's Nasrid dynasty produced the richest Islamic architecture of its age. It adopted the horseshoe arch from Córdoba and the geometric representation of the palm tree from Almohad and Almoravid buildings, while forging new artistic expression in carved clay, plaster, and wood. Nasrid architecture also integrated gardens and flowing water into the design. The greatest remaining examples are the **Alhambra** palaces and **Generalife** in Granada (see p. 624).

> *The Nasrid Alhambra.*

> *Teruel's Mudéjar Catedral.*

Gothic (12TH–15TH C.)

Introduced into Spain in the 12th century, the Gothic style extended Romanesque construction upward to create higher vaults, as in the **Ávila cathedral** (see p. 224, ❸). High Gothic took root along the Camino de Santiago in the 13th century. Two of the finest examples are the cathedrals of **León** (encrusted with stained glass; see p. 208, ❼) and **Burgos** (see p. 209, ❽), perhaps the stateliest Spanish cathedral. The Gothic style persisted into the 15th century with two variants: Levantino and Isabelline Gothic. Levantino Gothic, found in Catalunya, Valencia, and Mallorca, is notable for unifying interior spaces. Good examples include **Santa Maria del Mar** in Barcelona (see p. 411, ⓫) and **La Seu** (see p. 490, ❶) in Palma de Mallorca. Isabelline Gothic was a late-15th-century reaction to the Italian Renaissance. This transitional style employs

commemorative banner inscriptions and shield decorations. The best example is the **Capilla Real** in Granada (see p. 612, ❸).

Mudéjar (12TH–16TH C.)

Spain's unique Mudéjar style arose from Muslim architects and artisans who remained on Christian turf after the Reconquista. Through geometric bricklaying augmented by painted tiles, carved wood, and shaped plaster, they reinterpreted Christian motifs via Islamic geometry and added color and texture to Romanesque, Gothic, and even Renaissance building plans. The style reached its apex from the 13th to the 15th century in **Teruel** in Aragón, where the cathedral is the finest surviving Mudéjar building (see p. 353, ❺). Other good examples include the cathedral in **Zaragoza** (see p. 350, ❷) and the **Sinagoga del Tránsito** in Toledo (see p. 170, ❿).

Renaissance/Plateresque (15TH–16TH C.)

Spanish architects learned Renaissance principles from engravings and secondhand accounts of Italian buildings. Combining the basic principles of rectilinear monumentality with Gothic vertical reach, they added elaborate surface decoration based on Spanish silversmithing, hence the term Plateresque (from *plata,* meaning "silver"). The finest early example of pure Renaissance construction was the **Palacio de Carlos V** in the Alhambra, designed in 1527 by Pedro Machuca (1485–1550), who may have trained in Michelangelo's atelier (see p. 627, ❽). The greatest of Spain's Renaissance architects, Andrés de Vandelvira (1509–75), almost singlehandedly designed the Renaissance palaces and churches of **Jaén** (see p. 586, ⓫), **Úbeda** (see p. 584, ❶), and **Baeza** (see p. 586, ❿). His masterpiece is the

> *Gaudí's Sagrada Família.*

> *Valencia's City of Arts & Sciences.*

cathedral of Jaén. **El Escorial** (see p. 90, ❹), built by Juan Bautista de Toledo (1515–67) and Juan de Herrera (1530–93), is the most sober structure of the Spanish Renaissance, reproducing classical form with minimal ornament.

Baroque (17TH–18TH C.)

Herrera's influence was so pervasive that Spanish architects followed his sober lead for more than a century. But in the late 1660s, Alonso Cano (1601–67) added Italian baroque ornament to the essentially Renaissance structure of the cathedral of Granada. The Italian baroque style was later hijacked by a vernacular baroque invented by the Churriguera family of Salamanca. The **Churrigueresque** style integrates the Salamanca stone-carving tradition with columns of inverted cones. From the Italians, they adapted the spiral, reinterpreting it as twisted rope. Among the

purest examples is the **Capilla Santisimo Sacramento,** a gold-encrusted side altar in the Segovia cathedral (see p. 220, ❸) designed around 1700 by José de Churriguera (1665–1725). Baroque's final phase, the exaggerated **Rococo,** was championed by Ventura Rodríguez (1717–85). His best work is the interior of the **Basílica de Nuestra Señora del Pilar** in Zaragoza (see p. 350, ❷).

Neoclassical (18TH–19TH C.)

Baroque remained the Spanish architecture of choice for a long time, though Carlos III's favorite architect, Juan de Villanueva (1739–1811), brought an intellectual neoclassicism to bear in his designs for the **Prado museum** (see p. 96) and the current design of the **Plaza Mayor** (see p. 81, ❾).

Catalan Modernisme (19TH–20TH C.)

When Barcelona expanded beyond its Old City in the late 19th century, the new

Eixample neighborhood became the playground of a radical architecture dubbed Modernisme. Superficially related to Art Nouveau and Jugendstil movements of the age, it was more concerned with organic structure than nature-inspired decoration. Modernisme's identifying features include an emphasis on the uniqueness of craft (it is a rebellion against the era of mass production); heavy use of organic motifs (asymmetrical designs were often based on plants and flowers); and varying mediums (including wrought iron, stained glass, tile, and handpainted wallpaper). The most extreme practitioner was Antoni Gaudí (1852–1926; see p. 428), who seemed as much to grow his buildings as construct them. His masterpiece, **La Sagrada Família** cathedral (see p. 406, ❶), integrates the impossibly soaring arches of High Gothic with a decorative style

> *The new terminal at Madrid's Barajas Airport.*

akin to melted candle wax. Several others worked in the Modernista vein, including Lluís Domènech i Montaner (1850–1923), known for the **Palau de la Música Catalana** in Barcelona (see p. 418, **❻**), and Josep Puig i Cadafalch (1867–1956), who designed the **Codorníu bodega** in Sant Sadurní d'Anoia (see p. 57, **❹**).

Modern Architecture
(20TH C.)

When the 1929 World's Fair was held in Barcelona, the German pavilion designed by Ludwig Mies van der Rohe electrified a generation of young architects. Among them was Catalan genius Josep Lluís Sert (1902–83), who later designed the Spanish pavilion for the 1937 World's Fair (where his friend Picasso's *Guernica* was first shown). Sert spent most of his career in the United States but returned to Barcelona in 1975 to design the **Fundació Joan Miró** museum building (see p. 418, **❺**). But Franco hated Modern architecture, and few Modern buildings were constructed in Spain during his dictatorship.

Contemporary Architecture
(20TH–21ST C.)

The death of Franco provided opportunities for a generation of innovative designers. Architect-engineer Santiago Calatrava (b. 1951) is known for the gestural flying curves of his bridges and roadways. Some of his best work is at the **City of Arts & Sciences** in his native Valencia (see p. 533, **⓭**). The thumbprint of the more cerebral Rafael Moneo (b. 1937) is all over Madrid, most notably in the recent expansion of the **Prado museum** (see p. 96). Antonio Lamela (b. 1926) was the rare Modern architect who worked in Spain during the Franco years. At age 80, his most daring design yet was unveiled: the futuristic **Terminal 4 of Barajas Airport** (see p. 150). Canadian architect Frank Gehry created the **Museo Guggenheim Bilbao** (see p. 312, **❷**), which opened in 1997. Bilbao's sudden ascent to the A-list of international cultural destinations has encouraged other cities to engage in similarly adventurous architectural commissions.

Picturing Spain

> The Martyrdom of St. Maurice *by El Greco (1580–83)*.

El Greco (1540–1614)

Crete-born Doménikos Theotokópoulos settled in Toledo in 1577 and spent the next 4 decades filling the city's churches with his singular style. His phantasmagoric color and action-filled application of paint made him an inspiration to 20th-century expressionists. His work is found extensively in Toledo and in the Prado in Madrid (see p. 96).

Francisco de Zurbarán (1598–1664)

The Spanish master of chiaroscuro concentrated on painting ascetic religious meditations for monastery walls, often using the monks as models for saints and martyrs. His forte was the struggle between passionate spirit and palpable flesh—hence his frequent rendering of St. Jerome. Many of his major works are in the Prado in Madrid (see p. 96) and the Museo de Bellas Artes in Sevilla (see p. 593, ➒).

Diego Velázquez (1599–1660)

Becoming Felipe IV's court painter at 25, Velázquez painted his greatest works— mostly portraits—in the royal employ. When the paintings were later deposited in the Prado (where they occupy several galleries; see p. 99, ⓫), his genius was rediscovered by critics and artists. His masterpiece, *Las Meninas* (1654; see p. 20), became one of the most influential paintings in the history of European art.

Francisco de Goya (1746–1828)

Capable of both giddy pictorialism—as in his bucolic scenes created for the tapestries hung at El Pardo (see p. 91, ➎)— and harrowing, nightmarish images, Goya stands with Velázquez and Picasso in the triumvirate of Spain's greatest artists. His late works painted during the French occupation carry a direct emotional force that was truly new in European art. The best of Goya's work is found in the Prado (see p. 98, ➒, ➓) and in the Real Academia de Bellas Artes de San Fernando (see p. 95, ➐), both in Madrid.

Joaquín Sorolla (1863–1923)

Born in Valencia, Sorolla was Spain's premier painter of light and saturated color. He made a career of painting nominally representational scenes that were more about the play of light than form. Adept at portraiture as well as landscape, his most heartfelt canvases depict his native Valencian

> Dona i Ocell *(1982) by Joan Miró.*

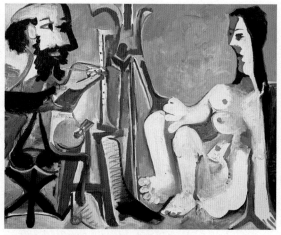

> Self Portrait with Model *(1963) by Pablo Picasso.*

shore of churning waves, sun-mottled rocks, and innocently erotic bathers.

Pablo Picasso (1881–1973)

The quintessential artist of the 20th century did it all, inventing new styles when he had exhausted old ones. (Yet even he remarked of Spain's Neolithic cave paintings, "After Altamira, everything is decadence.") Many of his early works are housed in Barcelona's Museu Picasso (see p. 410, **10**), and an abbreviated survey of his work can be found in the Museo Picasso Málaga (see p. 654, **4**). The Reina Sofía in Madrid (see p. 94, **4**) also displays many Picassos, most notably the iconic *Guernica* (1937; see p. 294).

Juan Gris (1887–1927)

Working with a brighter palette and more mordant wit than either Picasso or Georges Braque, Gris helped pioneer cubism. He never quit his day job drawing political satire for magazines, allowing him not to take himself too seriously. Recent reappraisals suggest that the approachable Gris influenced an entire generation of Spanish artists.

Joan Miró (1893–1983)

A poet of color and form, Miró is often categorized as a surrealist. He did sign the Surrealist Manifesto of 1924, but his sense of form derives more from Spain's Neolithic cave paintings than the formal classicism of most surrealism, and his lyrical celebration of color is unmatched in modern abstract art. His visionary art is best in large doses, available at the Fundació Joan Miró in Barcelona (see p. 418, **5**).

Salvador Dalí (1904–89)

The clown prince of Spanish painting, Dalí defines surrealism in popular culture.

Employing a hyper-realist style to explore a world of fantasy and nightmare, he will forever be associated with limp watches. Dalí lived for a good joke, as the Teatre-Museu Dalí in Figueres (see p. 373, **4**) demonstrates. Many of his works are in the Perrot–Moore Museum in Cadaqués and the Reina Sofía in Madrid (see p. 94, **4**).

Antoni Tàpies (B. 1923)

Nominally an abstract expressionist, the mercurial painter continuously experiments with new ideas. Among the first to incorporate marble dust and gravel into his compositions, he moved on to ever larger objects, including pieces of furniture. His works are characterized by boldly graphic composition and emotional immediacy. The best collection of his work is in the Fundació Tàpies in Barcelona.

Spanish Tales

PRIMERA PARTE
D'EL INGENIOSO
hidalgo don Quixote de
la Mancha.

*Capitulo Primero. Que trata de la condi-
cion, y exercicio del famoso hidalgo don
Quixote de la Mancha.*

> *First edition of Miguel de Cervantes's* Don Quixote de la Mancha *(1605).*

> *Lope de Vega.*

Spain's literary Golden Age. Breaking with the classical unities of time, place, and action, he redefined the three-act comedy in rollicking, politically pointed terms. His embrace of the Castilian vernacular made him second only to Cervantes in defining the Spanish tongue.

José Zorrilla y Moral (1817–93)

A florid Romantic poet as well as a playwright, Zorrilla's lasting fame rests on his vivid depiction of a rake driven from bed to bed by an insatiable desire for amorous conquest. First produced in 1844, *Don Juan Tenorio* is Spain's longest-running play. Theaters throughout the country present it annually on All Saint's Day.

Benito Pérez Galdós (1843–1920)

Considered Spain's second-greatest novelist after Cervantes, Pérez Galdós was a master of naturalism: realism where characters are at the mercy of their environment. *Fortunata y Jacinta* (1886–87), a novel of four characters

Miguel de Cervantes Saavedra (1547–1616)

The rough-and-tumble Cervantes could render the ridiculous with sympathetic tenderness, and his absurd hero Don Quixote remains one of the most memorable figures in Western literature. The novel, published in two installments a decade apart, proved so popular that it codified the Castilian language as Shakespeare codified English. Readily available everywhere, it deals with the conflict between the ideal and the real in human nature.

Lope de Vega (1562–1635)

Astonishingly prolific—425 of his estimated 1,800 plays survive—Lope de Vega was the lion of Madrid theater in

> *Miguel de Unamuno.*

> *Federico García Lorca.*

nearly as long as Tolstoy's *War and Peace,* is considered the masterpiece of his 31 novels.

Miguel de Unamuno (1864–1936)

The all-around man of letters wrote essays, novels, poetry, plays, and philosophy—often blurring the lines between genres. A strong pacifist strain runs through his work, in part from his childhood experiences in war-torn Bilbao. His mature novels prefigure existentialist themes. *San Manuel Bueno, Mártir* (1930), for example, concerns a priest who has lost his faith yet continues to minister to his parishioners.

Antonio Machado (1875–1939)

Combining social conscience with a lyrical sense of language, Machado was the seminal Spanish-language poet of the 20th century and a source of inspiration for Pablo Neruda and other Latin American poets. He spent most of his adult life as a professor of French in provincial universities.

Federico García Lorca (1898–1936)

Best known as a poet and playwright, Lorca has become the most widely read Spanish writer, even surpassing Cervantes. As a leader of the literary and artistic avant-garde, he engaged in wild flights of language and imagery in both plays and poetry. His *Bodas de Sangre (Blood Wedding)* is frequently produced in Spain and abroad, and his early poems, *Romancero Gitano (Gypsy Ballads),* remain a touchstone of Spanish lyric poetry.

Luis Buñuel (1900–83)

Pioneer Spanish filmmaker Buñuel rocketed to avant-garde fame with *Un Chien Andalou* (1929), a 16-minute short he co-wrote with Salvador Dalí. (Film students never forget the image of an eyeball being sliced with a razor.) No friend of Franco, he spent most of his career outside Spain. His final

film, *Cet Obscur Objet du Désir (That Obscure Object of Desire),* was released in 1977. It sets a shocking and dysfunctional love story against the backdrop of a terrorist insurgency.

Camilo José Cela (1916–2002)

Nobel laureate Cela is best remembered for his gripping 1951 novel, *La Colema (The Hive),* a grotesquely realistic account of gritty life in post–Civil War Madrid. His biting sarcasm and penchant for extensive descriptions of bodily functions kept his novels out of print in Spain during most of the Franco years.

Carlos Saura (B. 1932)

Saura's films have veered from documentary to fiction to combinations of the two. He is especially well remembered for the "flamenco trilogy" of *Bodas de Sangre, Carmen,* and *El Amor Brujo,* all produced in the 1980s.

Pedro Almodóvar (B. 1951)

One of the key figures of the Movida Madrileña, filmmaker Almodóvar has become almost a cult figure in Spanish popular culture. Self-taught (Franco had closed the film schools as too radical), Almodóvar combs through Spanish pop culture and family dynamics to find tragedy, disappointment, high comedy, and low farce—usually in difficult amorous relationships. His madcap *Woman on the Verge of a Nervous Breakdown* won an Academy Award nomination in 1989.

The Spanish Table

> You can get **tortilla española** *just about anywhere.*

> *Grilled sardines.*

The rhythm of life in Spain is the rhythm of mealtimes. If you want to understand the culture from the inside out, try eating like a Spaniard—or at least on a Spanish schedule. Spaniards usually eat lunch between 2pm and 4pm, and it's easier to adjust to this afternoon hiatus than you might think. (If you get hungry in the late morning, join the Spaniards in a cafe for a quick coffee and pastry.) Visitors often find it more difficult to adapt to the Spanish habit of eating dinner at 10pm or later. But tapas fill the gap—and can even make a fine meal if you really can't wait. Tapas time (usually 7–9pm) is an institution of peripatetic socializing— entertainment and sustenance rolled into one.

Just as Spain is a tapestry of independent-minded peoples, Spanish cuisine is an amalgam of regional dishes. You can find them all in Madrid—along with such Madrileño specialties

as **cocido,** a rich mixed-meat stew. Wherever you go around the country, you can always order **solomillo** (fried pork steak), **tortilla española** (potato omelet), or **ensalada mixta**—a green salad with crumbled tuna), but don't miss the local specialties listed below.

Castilla-La Mancha
When you see herds of sheep wandering the plains, you *know* the local cuisine has to feature cheese, in this case the famous **queso Manchego.** Restaurants also serve a lot of lamb and wild game, especially **perdiz** (partridge), **cordoniz** (quail), **conejo** (rabbit), and **venado** (venison). Bread from the local wheat is amazing, especially dabbed in olive oil from Toledo.

Extremadura
This hilly western region produces **pimentón,** the smoky ground paprika critical to so many Spanish dishes. It is the key flavor in **caldereta—**a stew made with small pieces of

lamb or kid fried with peppers and seasoned with raw garlic, mashed liver, and large quantities of **pimentón.**

Castilla y León
A Castilian likes nothing better than to light a wood fire and roast meat over it. Segovia is famous for **cochinillo** (whole roast suckling pig), while Ávila is known for its amazing **chuleta d'Ávila,** an entire rib of veal grilled like a steak. León is celebrated for pork, beef, and lamb sausages, jointly known as **embutidos.** León also produces the bovine equivalent of mountain ham, called **cecina de León**—salted, smoked, and air-dried beef.

The North Coasts
Bonito is the prized fish of the Cantabrian and Basque coasts, often served **escabeche** (fried, then marinated in vinegar with garlic and bay). Round the corner to Galicia, and the favorite is **atún rojo,** a rich dark tuna served as steak and flaked in

> *Hanging* jamón ibérico.

> Cochinillo *from the fire.*

empanadas de atún (pastries). Among crustaceans, look for **percebes** (goose barnacles) in Galicia and **txangurro** (spider crab) in the Basque Country. **Merluza** (hake) is popular and versatile, appearing poached with boiled onions, potatoes, and sweet red pepper sauce as **merluza gallego,** or pan-roasted with garlic, potatoes, and lots of parsley as **merluza en salsa verde.** Head inland and you encounter the intense blue cheese called **Cabrales,** dry hard apple cider called **sidra,** and the bean-and-pork casserole **fabada Asturiana.**

Navarra & Aragón

Lamb is ubiquitous throughout these regions, often as tiny chops, or **chuletillas.** Like the Castilians, the Navarrese and Aragonese are great fans of wood grills, or **asadors.** For a special treat, look for grilled **trucha,** or wild mountain trout. Rice is grown here, and **arroces**—vegetable and rice

casseroles—often appear on the menu.

Catalunya

Barcelona is the hotbed of **cuina de autor** (signature cuisine), where the chef is revered as if he were Picasso. Yet outside the city, the region often sticks to the tried and true, such as **pez espada,** a large sardine cooked on a stake over an open fire, ideally on the beach where it was caught. **Suquet,** a seafood stew finished with a garlic-almond paste, is sublime and complex. Few dishes are better or simpler than the Catalan snack of **pa amb tomate,** grilled country bread rubbed with tomato, drizzled with olive oil, and dusted with salt.

Valencia

Until you have eaten **paella** in Valencia, you have never had the real dish. The classic preparation involves garden vegetables, snails, chicken, and rabbit—not a shrimp or mussel

in sight. While you're here, eat anything that involves lemon or orange; the citrus fruit is incomparable.

Andalucía

Honey, nuts, and egg yolks in the pastries indicate a strong Moorish influence on the cuisine, but Andalucía also has many foods forbidden in the Koran. The finest **jamón ibérico** comes from the mountains west of Sevilla (Jabugo) and south of Granada (Trevélez). Similar to prosciutto but nuttier and more complex, it is produced from Iberian pigs fattened on acorns. The towns of the Bay of Cádiz are similarly famous for their shellfish, ranging from tiny **camarónes blancas** (glass shrimp), eaten shell and all, to **langostinos** (a large prawn nothing like the French *langoustine*), to the **cigala** (known in French as *langoustines* or in the Italian plural as *scampi*). They are all best accompanied by the local sherry.

19 The Best Special Interest Trips

Age-Appropriate Trips

Families

Independent-minded adults or families should consider **Untours,** a company that offers 1- or 2-week apartment-based vacations with just enough assistance (pretrip planning, an orientation session at the destination, a local expert to offer advice and assistance) to help travelers chart their own course. Options include city apartments in Barcelona and country digs in Andalucía. 415 E. Jasper St., Media, PA 19063 U.S. ☎ 888-868-6871. www.untours.com.

Seniors

The travel itineraries devised by **Exploritas** (formerly known as **Elderhostel**) are geared for mature adults and feature educational activities that flesh out the details of a place. Among the most popular Spanish programs are a 16-night trip that traces the "Pathways of Culture" through Madrid, Sevilla, and Granada; and a 16-night itinerary that explores the evolution of Spanish painting in Madrid, Bilbao, and Barcelona. Those who prefer less structured travel can opt for "Independent Explorations" in such Spanish cities as Barcelona or Madrid. 11 Avenue de Lafayette, Boston, MA 02111 U.S. ☎ 800- 454-5768. www.exploritas.org.

Students

Actually, anyone between the ages of 18 and 26 who wants to have a good time (while leaving the details to someone else) can book the 11-day "Spanish Fiesta" trip through Madrid, the Costa del Sol, and Barcelona offered by **EF College Break.** 1 Education St., Cambridge, MA 02141 U.S. ☎ 800-766-2645. www.efcollegebreak.com.

Travel Tip

Be sure to inquire about guided tours at local information offices. The Madrid tourism office, for example, offers a number of inexpensive walking and biking tours, such as "The Madrid of Cervantes." The Málaga tourist office has prepared several free audio tours, including one that traces Picasso's early years in the city. Santiago de Compostela offers an MP3 tour of the Old City as well as a number of guided walking tours focusing on gastronomy, architecture, and other themes.

Food & Wine Trips

A group of Spanish food professionals and foodies founded **A Taste of Spain** in 1999 to offer personalized food-oriented travel opportunities. They could range from a half-day cooking class in Valencia, Marbella, San Sebastián, or Madrid to a 2-night trip through La Rioja wine district or a 5-night tour of Andalucía to observe the olive harvest. C/ Alonso Cano, 8, Cádiz, Spain. ☎ 856-079-626. www.atasteofspain.com.

Located in a stone family house turned small hotel in the village of El Masroig, **Catacurian** offers a full immersion in Catalan cuisine with cooking classes, restaurant meals, visits to wineries, and wine and olive oil tastings. Harvest-season classes add grape picking or watching the olive harvest to the itinerary. 1717 5th St. N., St. Petersburg, FL 33704 U.S. ☎ 866-538-3519 or 941-870-5567. www.catacurian.com.

Cellar Tours began their luxury individualized tour programs in Spain and still have many offerings for wine and food touring in Andalucía, Catalunya, La Rioja, and Ribera del Duero. Some itineraries are as short as a weekend. C/ Monte Esquinza, 24, Madrid, Spain. ☎ 651-823-735. www.cellartours.com.

For a simpler introduction to Catalan cuisine, **Cook and Taste** offers two half-day cooking classes a day in their kitchen in Barcelona. Students can elect to add a visit to Barcelona's famous Boquería market before class. La Rambla, 58, Barcelona, Spain. ☎ 933-021-320. www.cookandtaste.net.

With Spanish cuisine the hottest in Europe and Spanish vineyards gaining worldwide recognition, it's not surprising that a number of tour companies focus exclusively on Spain. **Epicurean Ways** is yet another good option for individual travel itineraries and private cooking classes with a chef. 507 Nottingham Rd., Charlottesville, VA 22901 U.S. ☎ 866-642-2917 or 434-738-2293. www.epicureanways.com.

Letango Tours has knowledgeable guides in a number of cities (including Madrid, Barcelona, Bilbao, Málaga, and Pamplona) who take couples or small groups on an evening of tapas hopping with plenty of commentary on local cuisine. Spain. ☎ 913-694-752. www.letango.com.

Spain Taste offers 5-day food and wine jaunts to Michelin-starred Catalan restaurants. Can Valles de Moagueroles, Fogars de Montclus, Barcelona. ☎ 938-475-115. www.spaintaste.com.

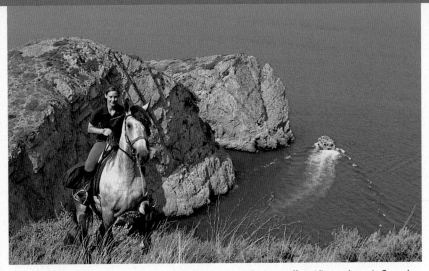

> *PAGE 678 The Sierra de Tramuntana on Mallorca.* THIS PAGE *Equitours offers riding packages in Granada and on the Catalunya coast.*

Language Classes & Trips

Don Quijote offers language study throughout Spain, but no place seems more appropriate than the great university city of Salamanca, where students fit right into the academic environment. Classes are open to students of all ages but tend to attract a younger clientele. C/ Placentinos, 2, Salamanca, Spain. ☎ 923-268-860. www.donquijote.org.

A small group of teachers owns and operates **Escuela Montalbán,** which is located in a historic home in a charming Granada neighborhood. Students tend to be a little older here and like to supplement their language courses with study of guitar, flamenco, or cooking. C/ Conde Cifuentes, 11, Granada, Spain. ☎ 958-256-875. www.escuela-montalban.com.

Family-run **Eureka Academia de Español** is a good option for students of all ages to study Spanish in Madrid. The school is based right in the heart of Puerta del Sol and augments language study with introductions to cooking, music, and dance. C/ Arenal, 26, Madrid, Spain. ☎ 915-488-640. www.eureka-madrid.com.

The intensive language courses at **Spanish Abroad** are designed to enable you to speak Spanish as soon as possible. Native Spanish teachers with university degrees are instructors. 5112 N. 40th St., Ste. 103, Phoenix, AZ 85018 U.S. ☎ 888-722-7623. www.spanishabroad.com.

Learning Trips

Archaeology

British archaeologists own and run **Andante Travels,** which specializes in visits to archaeological sites around the world. Spanish options might feature the caves of northern Spain or a visit to Catalunya, where various sites preserve the region's Iberian, Greek, and Roman roots. The Old Barn, Old Road, Alderbury, Salisbury SP5 3AR U.K. ☎ 1722-713-800. www.andantetravels.co.uk.

Not surprisingly, the caves of northern Spain might also be among the offerings of **Archaeological Tours.** Tours led by noted scholars might focus on ancient pilgrimage routes or an overview of the notable ruins and monuments from the various civilizations that have shaped Spain. 271 Madison Ave., Suite 904, New York, NY 10016 U.S. ☎ 866-740-5130. www.archaeologicaltrs.com.

Art

Creative types can draw inspiration from the natural beauty and small villages of Andalucía on specialized painting or photography trips from U.K.-based **Andalucian Adventures.** 15 Merretts Mill, Merrits Causeway, South Woodchester, Stroud, Gloucestershire GL5 5EU U.K. ☎ 1453-834-137. www.andalucian-adventures.co.uk.

Based in the charming Andalucían white town of Benarrabá, **Atelier Capelletes** offers 1- or 2-week painting courses with lodging in a rural hotel and daily excursions. Hotel Banu Rabbah, Benarrabá, Spain. ☎ 952-150-089. www. paint-in-holidays.com.

Barcelona is one of Spain's most striking cities, and **Barcelona Photographer** offers day or evening guided photography walks, as well as a weekend course that supplements the walks with studio work and the opportunity to shoot a flamenco performance. Rambla de Catalunya, 100, Barcelona, Spain. ☎ 645-968-417. www. barcelonaphotographer.com.

Flamenco

Students come from all over the world to study at Sevilla's **Taller Flamenco.** A 1-week course in flamenco dance is available, but many students opt for longer courses that specialize in dance technique, choreography, guitar, singing, or percussion. C/ Peral, 49, Sevilla, Spain. ☎ 954-564-234. www.tallerflamenco.com.

Gardens

There's no better place to appreciate the magic of a lush garden than in the parched landscape of Andalucía. Check **Brightwater Holidays** for availability of their 6-night tour of the gardens and architecture of Andalucía. Eden Park House, Cupar, Fife KY15 4HS U.K. ☎ 1334-657-155. www. brightwaterholidays.com.

Nature

Spain's diverse climate and geography offer lots of opportunities for nature lovers. **Naturetrek** tours might search for birds in Extremadura, whales in the Bay of Biscay, or butterflies in the Picos de Europa. Cheriton Mill, Cheriton, Alresford, Hampshire SO24 ONG U.K. ☎ 1962-733-051. www.naturetrek.co.uk.

Outdoor Activities & Trips

Biking

Many competitive cyclists train on Spain's hilly terrain, but options exist for more casual peddlers. **Ciclismo Classico** rates its 9-day trip through Andalucía for intermediate-level cyclists. 30 Marathon St., Arlington, MA 02474 U.S. ☎ 800-866-7314 or 781-646-3377.

The quiet country roads of the Penedès wine region are great for casual cycling—and wine tasting. **El Molí Tours** rents bikes for travelers to follow their 10 to 25km (6- to 16-mile) itineraries through vineyards and groves of almond and olive trees. C/ Baix, 19, Torrelles de Foix,

Barcelona 08737 Spain. ☎ 938-972-207. www. elmolitours.com.

While most pilgrims follow the route to Santiago de Compostela by foot, there's no reason not to tackle it by bike. **Santiago Reservas** offers a 9-day trip that starts in León and includes hotels, some meals, a knowledgeable guide, and van support. Santiago de Compostela, Spain. ☎ 902-190-160. www.santiagoreservas.com.

VBT Bicycling Vacations charts a 7-day Andalucían itinerary of easy to moderate peddling. 614 Monkton Rd., Bristol, VT 05443 U.S. ☎ 800-245-3868. www.vbt.com.

Horseback Riding

Spain is known for its horses and horsemanship. U.K. operator **Equestrian Escapes** offers a 6-night package based in a 16th-century hacienda near Sevilla. Daily instruction will prepare you for rural trail rides as well as a ride along the beach and into Donaña national park. Rose Cottage, Common Lane, Duddon, Tarporley, Cheshire CW6 0HG U.K. ☎ 1829-781-123. www. equestrian-escapes.com.

Equitours offers 8-day village-to-village horseback trips through the Moorish-tinged Alpujarra of Granada or along the stunning Catalan coast. 10 Stanlaker St., Dubois, WY 82513 U.S. ☎ 800-545-0019. www.ridingtours.com.

Paragliding

Fly Spain runs 5-day beginner paragliding classes in windy Algodonales in the Sierra de Grazalema. Instruction for more advanced fliers is also available. C/ Sierra, 41, Algodonales, Spain. ☎ 651-736-718. www.flyspain.co.uk.

Surfing

Spain Surf Holidays teaches small-group surf courses for beginner to intermediate surfers on one of the longest beaches in eastern Cantabria. The school was founded by Meco, one of Spain's surfing pioneers. Accommodations are arranged with area hotels. Bajada a La Playa, 22, Laredo, Spain. ☎ 636-595-571. http://spain-surf-holidays.eu.

Also on the Cantabrian coast, **Surf Spirit** calls its school "surf camp," and with good reason: Participants camp on the beach in tents. The school is primarily French speaking, and the off-season contact is in France. June–Aug: Avenida Miramar, 7, San Vicente de la Barquera, Spain. ☎ 669-588-772. Sept–May: 40 Avenue de la Rhune, 64500 Cibourne, France. ☎ 663-38-08-26. www.surfspirit.org.

> *Catacurian hosts a wine tasting.*

Walking, Hiking & Climbing

You can combine city walks with scenic hikes on the 8-day trip from Granada through Andalucía's white towns to Sevilla offered by **Country Walkers.** P.O. Box 180, Waterbury, VT 05676 U.S. ☎ 800-464-9255 or 802-244-1387. www.countrywalkers.com.

Horizon Aventura is an outfitter that arranges hikes and canoe trips in the *pinzapo* reserve area of the Parque Natural de Sierra de Grazalema, as well as rock climbing, cycling, and caving expeditions elsewhere in the park. C/ Corrales Terceros, 29, Grazalema, Spain. ☎ 956-132-363. www.horizonaventura.com.

The husband-and-wife team who operate **Ibex Trex** live in the Alpujarra de Granada and offer guided and unguided walking holidays of various lengths. Some of their itineraries focus on wildlife of the region. C/ Santa Rita, 8, Narila, Spain. ☎ 958-850-998. www.ibextrex.com.

For guided treks and walking holidays, **Mallorcan Walking Tours** offers 57 guided day hikes and several weeklong trekking itineraries in spring and autumn for groups of four or more. Port de Pollença, Mallorca, Spain. ☎ 609-708-026. www.mallorcanwalkingtours.puertopollensa.com.

Another option in the Balearic Islands are the 7-night holidays featuring five guided walks designed by **Menorca Walking Holidays.** Menorca, Spain. ☎ 0800-072-4832. www.menorca walkingholidays.com.

Mountain Travel Sobek concentrates on the Picos de Europa in 8-day trips based in the charming mountain village of Cangas de Onís. 1266 66th St., Emeryville, CA 94608 U.S. ☎ 888-831-7526 or 510-594-6000. www.mtsobek.com.

Punto de Información Parque Natural de Sierra Nevada is both the public information center for the mountain park and a central resource for guided hikes. You won't need a guide to follow the goat trails from Moorish village to Moorish village in the High Alpujarra, but consult here first to buy a map and learn about current trail conditions. Plaza de la Libertad, s/n, Pampaneira, Spain. ☎ 958-763-127. www.nevadensis.com.

Santiago Reservas (see p. 682) also offers the option of a 9-day walk along the pilgrimage route from Astorga to Santiago de Compostela. Luggage transport makes the walk a lot easier, as does the prospect of a hotel and hot meal waiting at the end of the day. Santiago de Compostela, Spain. ☎ 902-190-160. www.santiago reservas.com.

Watersports

The complex of **Club Náutico La Horadada,** right on Playa de la Magdalena in Santander, consists of a basic, beachy hostel and a facility that rents equipment and gives lessons in sailing, windsurfing, and kayaking. Avenida de la Reina Victoria, Santander, Spain. ☎ 942-273-013.

The waters off Barcelona are great for sailing, and **Lagoon Watersports** (a British company with an offshoot in Spain) offers a 5-day course in seamanship and helmsmanship for anyone who has ever dreamed of sailing a yacht. U.K.: Kingsway, Hove, East Sussex, BN3 4LX U.K. ☎ 1273-424-842. Spain: Lagoon Espana, Francisco Giner, 44, Barcelona, Spain. www.lagoonwater sports.co.uk. Picos de Europa. Cheriton Mill, Cheriton, Alresford, Hampshire SO24 ONG U.K. ☎ 1962-733-051. www.naturetrek.co.uk.

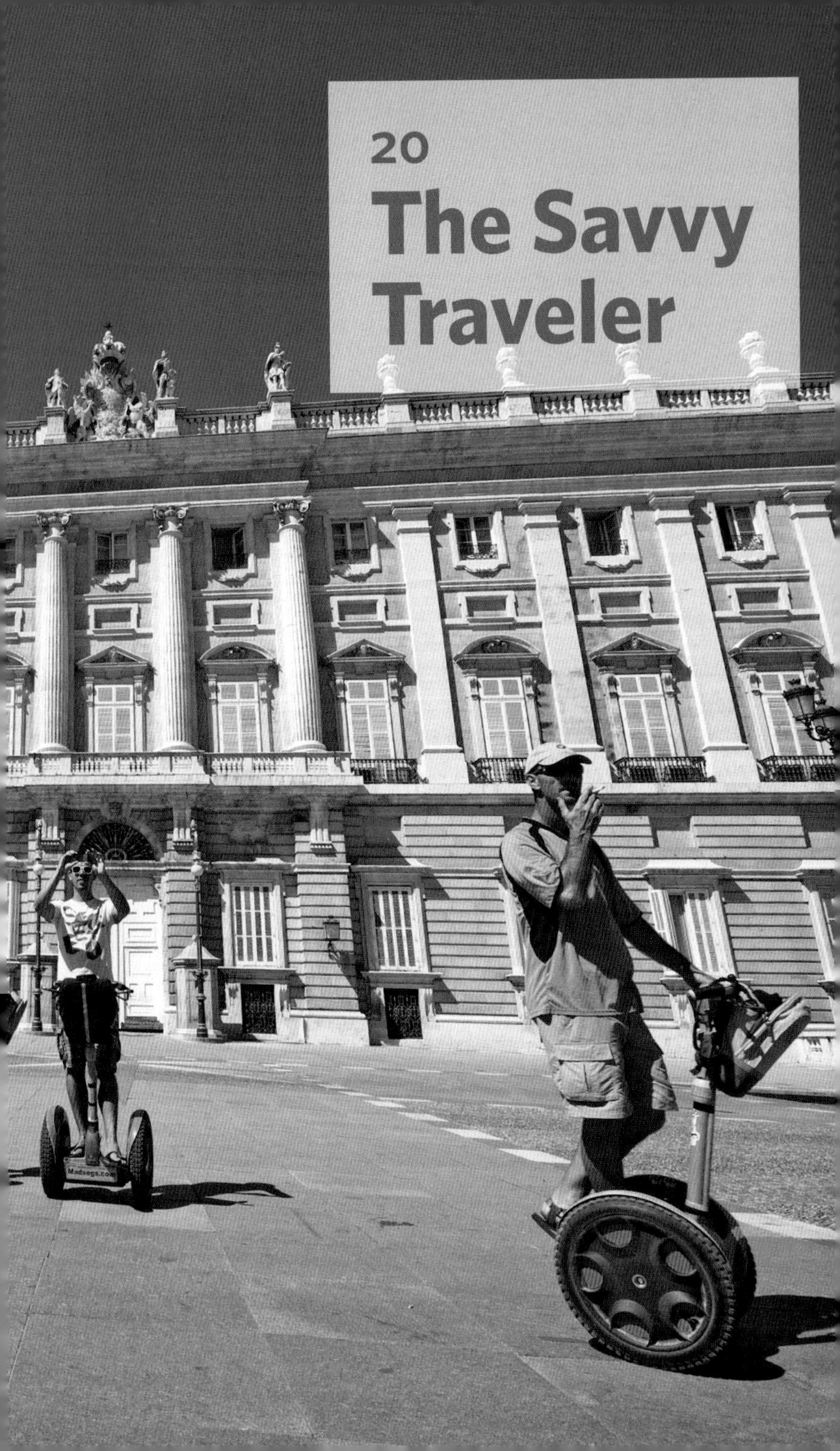

20 The Savvy Traveler

Before You Go

Government Tourist Offices

IN THE UNITED STATES

666 Fifth Ave., 35th Floor, New York, NY 10103 (☎ 212-265-8822); 8383 Wilshire Blvd., Suite 960, Beverly Hills, CA 90201 (☎ 323-658-7195); 845 N. Michigan Ave., Suite 915E, Chicago, IL 60611 (☎ 312-642-1992); and 1395 Brickell Ave., Suite 1850, Miami, FL 33131 (☎ 305-358-1992).

IN CANADA

2 Bloor St. W., Suite 3402, Toronto, Ontario M4W 3E2 (☎ 416-961-3131).

IN THE UNITED KINGDOM

79 New Cavendish St., 2nd Floor, London W1W 6XB (☎ 087-0850-6599).

Best Times to Go

The best months to visit Spain are April (after Easter), May, September, and October, when weather and crowds are moderate. The least desirable month is generally August, when the rest of Europe descends on Spanish beaches, making it hard to find a room or a seat at a restaurant. Many Spaniards also go on vacation in August, which means that some restaurants and shops (and even some sights) are closed or keep reduced hours. If August is your only free month, by all means make the trip—just be ready for a few inconveniences, higher prices, and hot weather in much of the country. If traveling in the spring, try to avoid Semana Santa (the week before Easter) unless you want to observe the activities. Most of the country comes to a standstill and hotel rates skyrocket.

Festivals & Special Events

To avoid disappointment, it's always a good idea to purchase tickets in advance for major events, as well as for theater, music, dance, and other performances. The Spanish agency **ServiCaixa** handles tickets for performing arts, sporting events, museum admission, and much more. The website (www.servicaixa.com) is available in English. The service charge varies but is usually worth it for convenience and peace of mind. Advance hotel reservations are essential for most of the events highlighted below.

For an exhaustive list of events beyond those listed here, check http://events.frommers.com, where you'll find a searchable, up-to-the-minute roster of what's happening in cities all over the world.

JANUARY

Spaniards love any excuse for a party, and one of the first of the year is the January 1–2 **Reconquest Festival** in Granada, to mark the city's recapture from the Moors in 1492. Cities throughout Spain, including Madrid, Sevilla, Barcelona, Cadiz, Málaga, and Palma de Mallorca, mark the religious holiday of Epiphany on January 6 with lively **Processions of the Three Kings,** usually the evening before. The event is a favorite with small children since the kings often hand out candy. Devil figures usually join the torch-lit processions in La Puebla on the island of Mallorca on the January 17 **Día de San Antonio,** in honor of town patron Saint Anthony of Padua. On January 29, Zaragoza honors its patron with the **Fiesta de San Valero,** when locals and visitors alike share pieces of a gigantic *roscón,* or fruitcake.

FEBRUARY

There's barely a city or town in Spain that doesn't celebrate **Carnival** during the week before Ash Wednesday, but Cádiz stages the oldest and most elaborate event. Other good bets are Sitges (popular with gay travelers), Madrid, Barcelona, Alicante, and Santiago de Compostela. Madrid is also the site of the much more sedate **ARCO** (www.ifema.es), a midmonth international contemporary art fair that's considered one of the top events in Europe. The **Jerez Flamenco Festival** (www.festivaldejerez.es), which usually begins in late February and runs into March, has similar international stature, with major performers from around the world.

MARCH

The city's great architecture is the backdrop for the **Barcelona Marathon** (www.barcelona marato.es) in early March. Nothing quite compares to **Las Fallas** in Valencia, a weeklong blur of parades and other activities leading up to the March 19 burning of giant papier-mâché figures to chase away the demons of winter. As many as two million people attend; for a smaller celebration also in honor of Saint Joseph, try **Las Fallas** in nearby Gandia. There's also no escaping the crowds during **Semana Santa** celebrations the week before Easter, when religious brotherhoods move through the streets bearing enormously heavy *pasos,* or floats, with images of Christ or the Virgin Mary. Some of the most moving and impressive processions take place in Sevilla, Málaga, Cuenca, Jerez, and Zamora.

APRIL

Things become considerably more lighthearted during the weeklong **Feria de Abril de Sevilla** (see p. 609), one of the most colorful events in Spain. It includes parades of horses and carriages, flamenco performances, bullfights, and dancing in the streets. Most women in Sevilla own at least one flamenco dress for the occasion. In Catalunya, many women are named for the **Virgin of Montserrat,** who is honored on April 27 with Masses in the basilica and processions and dances in the streets, including the traditional folk dance the *sardana.*

MAY

In early May, the **Feria Nacional del Queso** fills Plaza Mayor in Trujillo. In mid-May, the much anticipated **Feria del Caballo** in Jerez highlights the city's equestrian heritage with displays of horsemanship, performances by the famous Andalucían horses, flamenco, and bullfights. One of Spain's most welcoming and low-key events is the **Concurso de los Patios** (www. amigosdelospatioscordobeses.es) in Córdoba during the first 2 weeks in May. Many residents of the old quarter open their private family courtyards to visitors. In a much more public display, Madrileños take a week for the **Fiesta de San Isidro** with parades, music, dancing, and food fairs, leading up to the saint's May 15 feast day.

JUNE

Cities throughout Spain also observe the Christian holiday of **Corpus Christi,** which is usually in early June, depending on when Easter falls. Some of the largest processions are in Barcelona, Valencia, Toledo, Málaga, Sevilla, and Granada. Bonfires and fireworks are the traditional ways to celebrate the summer solstice and the feast day of San Juan. You can join in the fun at Alicante's **Las Hogueras de San Juan** (St. John's Bonfires), Zaragoza's **Noche de San Juan,** and Barcelona's **Verbena de Sant Joan.** Many events require careful planning, but it's easy to attend Madrid's **Los Veranos de la Villa,** which kicks off in late June with 2 months of concerts, dance, theater, *zarzuela,* and poetry—including many free events. Granada's

International Music and Dance Festival (www. granadafestival.org) stretches from late June to the first week in July.

JULY

A must-see for horse lovers is **La Rapa das Bestas,** the first weekend in July in San Lorenzo de Sabucedo. Wild horses of the Galician hills are rounded up, branded, and checked by veterinarians before being released back to their homes in the verdant green valleys. Guitar lovers head to Córdoba for the international lineup of artists at the **Festival de la Guitarra** during the first 2 weeks of the month. If you want to see Pamplona the way Ernest Hemingway saw it, the running of the bulls takes place each morning during the July 6–14 **Fiesta de San Fermín.** The Virgen de Carmen is the patron saint of sailors and fishermen, so you'll find the July 16 **Fiesta del Carmen** celebrated in coastal towns such as Nerja and Fuengirola in Andalucía. Politicians usually join pilgrims at the **Fiesta de Santiago** on July 24–25 in Santiago de Compostela, where the faithful watch the swinging of the giant *botafumeiro* (incense burner) in the cathedral and everyone gathers for astonishing fireworks. The **San Sebastián Jazz Festival** (www. jazzaldia.com) at the end of the month features numerous outdoor performances.

AUGUST

Some of the first **horse races** in Spain were held along Bajo de Guía beach in Sanlúcar de Barrameda, and the tradition continues with several dates in August (www.carrerassanlucar. es). The city of Alicante enacts battles between **Moros y Cristianos** (Moors and Christians) throughout the year, with the greatest frequency of these colorful events that mix history and fun in August. The highlight of the **Festival of the White Virgin** in Vitoria-Gasteiz is a human-sized puppet that soars above the crowd in Plaza de la Virgen Blanca, but other Basque folk traditions also hold sway during this event, held early in the month. The moving **Misteri d'Elx** (www.misteridelx.com), a sacred drama about the assumption of the Virgin, takes place in mid-August in the 17th-century basilica in Elx (Elche). You'll get a chance to observe the curious strongman competitions and sample lots of Basque food during Bilbao's **Aste Nagusia** festival that begins around August 15 and runs 9 days.

SPAIN'S AVERAGE DAILY TEMPERATURE & MONTHLY RAINFALL

MADRID	JAN	FEB	MAR	APR	MAY	JUNE	JULY	AUG	SEPT	OCT	NOV	DEC
Temp. (°F)	49	45	49	52	60	68	75	75	68	58	49	44
Temp. (°C)	5	7	9	11	15	20	24	24	20	14	9	6
Rainfall (in.)	1.8	1.7	1.5	1.8	1.6	1.0	0.4	0.4	1.2	1.8	2.5	1.9

SEVILLA	JAN	FEB	MAR	APR	MAY	JUNE	JULY	AUG	SEPT	OCT	NOV	DEC
Temp. (°F)	52	54	58	61	67	73	81	81	77	67	59	52
Temp. (°C)	11	12	14	16	19	23	27	27	25	19	15	11
Rainfall (in.)	2.6	2.1	1.5	2.2	1.3	0.5	0.1	0.2	0.9	2.4	3.3	3.7

BARCELONA	JAN	FEB	MAR	APR	MAY	JUNE	JULY	AUG	SEPT	OCT	NOV	DEC
Temp. (°F)	48	49	52	54	61	68	73	73	70	62	54	50
Temp. (°C)	8	9	11	12	16	20	22	23	21	16	12	10
Rainfall (in.)	1.3	0.9	0.9	1.1	1.4	0.9	0.5	1.6	2.4	2.3	1.6	1.3

BILBAO	JAN	FEB	MAR	APR	MAY	JUNE	JULY	AUG	SEPT	OCT	NOV	DEC
Temp. (°F)	49	51	52	54	60	65	68	68	67	61	54	51
Temp. (°C)	9	10	11	12	15	18	20	20	19	16	12	10
Rainfall (in.)	2.7	2.3	1.9	3.2	1.9	1.5	1.6	1.6	1.7	3.0	3.7	2.9

SEPTEMBER

The *senyera,* the red-and-yellow-striped Catalan flag, punctuates the ceremonies and celebrations of **Catalunya's National Day** on September 11 in Barcelona. Jerez celebrates the sherry grape harvest with the 9-day **Fiesta de la Vendimia** that begins midmonth. The highlight is the blessing and ceremonial crushing of a basket of grapes. **La Mercé** is Barcelona's classic celebration of Catalan folklore. It begins midmonth and features *castellers* (human towers as much as eight levels high), *els gigants* (massive, big-headed costumed figures parading the streets), and devils taking over the streets in fits of fireworks called *correfocs.* Hollywood heads to San Sebastián during the second week of September for the prestigious **San Sebastián International Film Festival** (www.sansebastianfestival.com). Sevilla's **Bienal de Flamenco** (www.bienal-flamenco.org) is held only in even-numbered years and packs every performance venue with the top artists and most enthusiastic fans.

OCTOBER

Big prize money is at stake in the **ASP World Tour-Billabong Pro** surfing competition when the big waves hit tiny Mundaka on the Basque coast in early October. October 12 is the **Dia de la Hispanidad,** or Spain's National Day, marked in Madrid with a military procession at Plaza de Colón. October 12 is also the **feast day of the Virgen del Pilar** and the highlight of Zaragoza's 10-day celebration featuring processions and flower offerings to the saint. Foodies flock to O Grove's **Exaltación del Mariscos,** a seafood festival that offers the chance to try goose barnacles as well as other delicious Galician shellfish. You'll have to settle for the rich aroma of saffron stamens toasting over wood fires at the **Saffron Rose Festival** in late October in Consuegra. Madrid's **Festival de Otoño** begins in mid-October and fills a month with contemporary arts performances and a program of contemporary circus.

NOVEMBER

On November 1, cities and towns throughout Spain commemorate Tosantos, or **All Saints' Day,** with one of the biggest celebrations in Cádiz. From late November into December, Alicante hosts **Festitíteres,** an international puppet festival that fills the performing venues. In late November, about 100 stalls are set up in Plaza Mayor for Madrid's **Christmas Market.** In addition to gifts and religious items, shoppers grab up wigs and crazy costumes for Día de los Santos Inocentes (see below).

DECEMBER

Be prepared for anything on **Día de los Santos Inocentes** on December 28. Spaniards take their equivalent of April Fools' Day very seriously! Good places to join the crowds of revelers on **New Year's Eve** are La Plaza Nueva in Sevilla or Puerta del Sol in Madrid.

Weather

Spain is a big country, and temperatures can vary dramatically from region to region. In the summer, daytime highs in inland Andalucía and central Spain often exceed 100°F (38°C). But, as they say, it's a dry heat. Coastal temperatures are more moderate, but high humidity guarantees steamy nights. By contrast, the Atlantic coast's daytime summer highs tend to bask in the temperate mid-70s (low 20s Celsius).

Winter in Spain can be surprising. Most travelers flock to the Costa del Sol, west of Málaga, where daytime temperatures reach the 60s (high teens Celsius). Madrid is known for cold winters, with nighttime temperatures sometimes dropping to freezing, but light-jacket weather with brilliant blue skies is common in January and February. Spring and fall are often the best times to visit central Spain and Andalucía since the temperatures are more moderate, but you run the risk of rain. Spring is also the rainy season in the north.

Useful Websites

www.okspain.org: The official U.S. site of the Tourist Office of Spain provides a good overview on destinations within Spain, offers planning advice, and gives current weather conditions. This U.S. portal will take you into the international site, **www.spain.info**. Links will sometimes switch to Spanish-language versions of a page. To see the English, change the last two letters of the URL from *es* to *en*. The site also facilitates online booking at about 2,000 hotels throughout the country.

www.munimadrid.es: At present, the information-packed website run by the city of Madrid is available in Spanish only.

www.barcelonaturisme.com: Barcelona's official tourism website has excellent information in English.

www.barcelona.com: A good option for one-stop tour, hotel, and activity booking.

www.illesbalears.es: The Balearic Islands' official site has information on all four islands.

www.platgesdebalears.com: This detailed compendium has information about beaches on all four Balearic Islands, with daily swimming conditions, transport, and more.

www.renfe.es: Although it is in Spanish only, it's fairly easy to navigate the official site for Spanish rail to research routes and schedules.

www.raileurope.com: You can also research train routes and schedules on the site of this U.S.-based commercial operator. Depending on your itinerary, some of the rail passes available could save money.

Regional Information

Once you've narrowed your itinerary, delve into more depth at the websites of Spain's autonomous regions: www.andalucia. org; www.turismodearagon.com (Aragon); www.infoasturias.com (Asturias); www. basquecountry-tourism.com; www. turismodecantabria.com (Cantabria); www. visitclm.com (Castilla-La Mancha); www. turismocastillayleon.com; www.gencat.cat (Catalunya); www.turismoextremadura.com; http://turgalicia.com (Galicia); www.esmadrid. com (Madrid province); www.turismo.navarra. es; www.lariojaturismo.com (La Rioja); and www.turisvalencia.es (Valencia).

Cellphones (Mobiles)

If your cellphone is on a GSM (Global System for Mobiles) system and offers multiband coverage, you can probably make and receive calls in Spain. Contact your phone company and request that international mobile roaming be activated. If you are coming from the U.S. or Canada, the cost could be prohibitive. It is often less expensive to purchase a cheap pay-as-you-go phone once in Spain, available from El Corte Inglés and FNAC stores everywhere. They start around 50€, but include about a 20€ credit for calls. North Americans can rent a GSM phone before leaving home from **InTouch USA** (☎ 800-872-7626; www.intouchglobal.com) or **Roadpost** (☎ 888-290-1606 or 905-272-5665; www.roadpost.com).

Ecotourism

Spain's excellent public transportation network makes it possible to limit automobile travel to reduce one's overall carbon footprint. The country's 10 national parks are managed jointly by state and regional governments and preserve habitats ranging from wetlands to mountain peaks. In every region, you'll find other protected areas under local control. As in other parts of Europe, an increasing interest in agritourism is encouraging more small farms, orchards, and vineyards to welcome lodgers who want to become involved in farm activities and enjoy food products at their source. Ironically, such rural travel usually requires an automobile. When renting, try to reserve a clean-diesel car for lowest emissions and least expensive (and least refined) fuel. A good general resource for tourism in the countryside is the **Asociación Española de Turismo Rural** (www.ecoturismorural. com), which helps to promote rural tourism throughout Spain.

Getting There

By Plane

The dates that you fly to Spain influence the cost of airfare more than your choice of airline. **Low season** on most flights between North America and Spain is from mid-November to March, while **shoulder season** is March to April and September to mid-November. **High season** runs May to August. You can sometimes get lower rates from North America by booking flights on U.S. carriers through their European codeshare partners, which have different seasonal pricing rules. When comparing airfares, make sure that you're including the add-ons for taxes, departure fees, fuel surcharges, checked luggage, and so on.

Spain's major overseas air gateways are Madrid, Barcelona, and Málaga, with the vast majority of North American flights going to or through Madrid. Flights from inside Europe also serve Santiago, Bilbao, Sevilla, and many other smaller Spanish airports.

FROM THE UNITED STATES

Most visitors traveling to Spain by air fly into Madrid (see p. 150) or Barcelona (see p. 480). Flying time to Madrid from New York, Newark, and Boston is 7 to 9 hours; from Chicago, 9 to 11 hours; and from Los Angeles, 11½ to 13½ hours. Flying time to Barcelona is up to 1 hour longer.

Iberia Airlines (☎ 800-772-4642; www.iberia.com) offers direct flights between the U.S. and Spain with service from Boston, New York (JFK), Washington (D.C.), Miami, and Los Angeles to Terminal 4 at Madrid Barajas, and service from New York to Barcelona. Occasionally, Iberia also offers direct flights from New York (JFK), Washington, and Miami to Málaga. Iberia offers the best connections from Madrid to other Spanish cities.

Discount carrier **Air Europa** (☎ 888-238-7672; www.air-europa.com) flies direct to Madrid from Newark and Miami, and Iberia's chief Spanish competitor **Spanair** (☎ 888-545-5757; www.spanair.com) offers its own flights from New York's La Guardia and through codeshares with Star Alliance airlines from all over North America. Both offer good connections in Madrid to the rest of Spain. Spanair in particular often has excellent prices for flights to Palma de Mallorca.

American Airlines (☎ 800-433-7300; www.aa.com) offers daily nonstop service to Madrid from its Miami hub (as well as codeshares on Iberia flights from Boston and New York's JFK). **Delta** (☎ 800-221-1212; www.delta.com) operates daily nonstop service from Atlanta and New York's JFK to both Madrid and Barcelona. **Continental Airlines** (☎ 800-231-0856; www.continental.com) flies nonstop from Newark to Madrid from spring to fall. **US Airways** (☎ 800-428-4322; www.usairways.com) also offers nonstop service between Philadelphia and Madrid. Flights on US Airways and other carriers connect with the Philadelphia hub, but those connecting flights can be more expensive than similar flights to New York airports.

FROM CANADA

Air Canada (☎ 888-247-2262; www.aircanada.ca) flies nonstop to Madrid from Toronto, but Canadian travelers often find it less expensive to fly US Airways, with a plane change in Philadelphia.

FROM THE UNITED KINGDOM

Spain is a popular destination for British travelers and airfares fluctuate wildly. Both **British Airways** (☎ 087-0850-9850; www.britishairways.com) and **Iberia** (☎ 087-0609-0500; www.iberia.com) fly several times a day to Madrid and Barcelona—and less frequently to Málaga—from London's Heathrow and Gatwick airports. The two carriers also fly to Madrid and

Barcelona from Manchester and Birmingham. Some of the least expensive flights are from Luton or non-London airports on discount carriers **Ryanair** (www.ryanair.com), **easyJet** (www.easyjet.com), and **Air Europa** (www.aireuropa.com). Check British Sunday newspapers for charter flights, which often leave from regional airports in Britain and go straight to Málaga for holidays on the Costa del Sol. One charter company with good Spanish packages is **Trailfinders** (☎ 084-5058-5858; www.trailfinders.com). Bucket shops around London's Victoria Station and Earls Court offer cheap fares, but many restrictions apply and cancellation penalties can be high.

FROM AUSTRALIA

Qantas (☎ 13-13-13 in Australia; www.qantas.com.au) flies from Sydney and Melbourne to Madrid. Qantas serves Spanish destinations from Auckland and Christchurch through connections in Sydney and Melbourne.

By Train

If you plan to travel heavily on the European rails, you'll do well to secure the latest copy of the *Thomas Cook European Timetable of Railroads.* It's available online at **www.thomascooktimetables.com**.

Getting to Spain from elsewhere in Europe is fairly straightforward, especially now that Spain's high-speed lines have adopted the same track specifications as neighboring France. Overnight sleeper trains are available from Paris, entering Spain along the north coast. Connections from Marseilles to Barcelona are slower and can involve changing trains. A luxurious **Trenhotel Elipsos** overnight train, the *Salvador Dalí,* connects Milan and Turin with Barcelona in Spain. For information on trains inside Spain, visit the **RENFE** website at www.renfe.es.

EURAIL GLOBAL PASS

Many North American travelers to Europe take advantage of one of the greatest travel bargains, the **Eurail Global Pass,** which allows you unlimited travel over a select period of time (from 15 days to 3 months) in 21 Eurail-affiliated countries. Unless you'll be traveling through Europe extensively before arriving in Spain, however, it's not a cost-effective option for you. Prices for first-class adult travel range from $687 for 15 days to $1,926 for 3 months. Children 4 to 11 pay half fare; those 3 and under travel for free.

Additional global pass options include the **Eurail Global Pass Saver,** which offers a special deal for two or more people traveling together; and the **Eurail Global Youth Pass** for those age 12 to 25, which allows second-class travel for $446 for 15 days to $1,255 for 3 months.

For those limiting their travel to Spain and the surrounding territory, Eurail does offer a host of discount passes that are cheaper and more flexible than the Eurail Global Pass. Check out www.raileurope.com for details.

By Car

If you're touring the rest of Europe in a rental car, ask if you can drop your vehicle in a major city such as Madrid or Barcelona. Highway approaches to Spain are across France on expressways. The most popular border crossing is near Biarritz, but there are 17 other border stations between Spain and France. If you plan to visit the north or west of Spain (Galicia), the Hendaye–Irún border is the most convenient frontier crossing. If you're going to Barcelona or Catalunya and down the coast to Valencia, take the expressway in France to Toulouse, then the A-61 to Narbonne, and then the A-9 toward the border crossing at La Junquera. You can also take the RN-20, with a border station at Puigcerdà.

By Ship/Ferry

Car and passenger ferry service to northern Spain is an option for travelers coming from the U.K. **Brittany Ferries** (☎ 0871-244-0871 in the U.K., or 942-36-06-11 in Spain; www.brittanyferries.co.uk) runs overnight service from Portsmouth and Plymouth to Santander, while **P&O Ferries** (☎ 0871-664-5645 in the U.K., or 902-02-04-61 in Spain; www.poferries.com) runs overnight service from Portsmouth to Bilbao.

Getting Around

Spain is bigger than it looks on many maps. While concentrating a visit on one small area can be a good strategy, you'll likely want to see two or three regions in a 2-week vacation. Most of the itineraries in this book are calculated to minimize transit time between points.

By Plane

Spanish domestic flights are inexpensive by European standards, and flying gets you there quickly, though it's worth calculating wait times in airports and getting to and from city centers when deciding whether to fly or take the train. **Iberia** (☎ 800-772-4642; www.iberia.com) has the most complete network of routes in Spain, but **Spanair** (☎ 888-545-5757; www.spanair.com) often offers cheaper fares. If you're planning to hop long distances frequently, both airlines offer very good-value air pass programs, though they must be purchased before arriving in Spain. The passes are sold only in conjunction with an intercontinental ticket and allow you to buy additional flights in continental Spain and the Canary and Balearic islands. The trick is you're not allowed to land at the same airport twice and can buy a maximum of four segments, priced by mileage. **Air Europa** (☎ 888-238-7672; www.aireuropa.com) offers a similar program that can also be purchased in Spain (☎ 902-401-501).

By Train

While Americans and Canadians were building more highways, the Spanish were building new rail lines. You can get around the country fairly easily by train, though it's best to use the fast (and slightly more expensive) **TALGO** trains for intercity travel—unless an even faster high-speed **AVE** line is available. They are truly high speed: You can hurtle between Madrid and Barcelona, for example, in less than 3 hours with 20 trains a day in each direction. The Spanish national rail network, **RENFE** (www.renfe.es), has complete schedules online. You can purchase tickets and reserve seats on the high-speed trains from the comfort of your own computer.

If your itinerary calls for a number of long-distance rail trips and you're willing to forego the high-speed trains, you may find that a **Eurail Spain Pass** is the most economical and convenient option. It's valid for unlimited travel for 3 days within a 2-month period, and you can buy extra travel days up to a maximum of 10 days. Prices start at $272 for first class, plus $40 for each additional day. Second class (a better value and hardly a hardship) starts at $218 with additional days costing $33. (Kids 4–11 pay about half fare on any of these discount passes.) The pass is not good on hotel trains or high-speed trains, although it does provide a discount when purchasing tickets for these trains. You must buy a Eurail Spain Pass from

outside Europe; contact **Rail Europe** (☎ 877-272-RAIL (272-7245); www.raileurope.com).

By Car

The Spanish highway network is surprisingly good and getting better all the time, as long-distance superhighways near completion. Be wary of maps and online mapping services, as some roads shown as completed have long hiatuses that shunt traffic onto rural highways, where you may find yourself stopping to let a herd of sheep cross the road.

Several major highways radiate out from Madrid, at the very center of Spain. Highway **A-2** leads to Zaragoza and Barcelona in the northeast, and the **A-3** heads directly east to Valencia. The **A-6** runs northwest toward Galicia (take this for Segovia and Ávila), and the **A-5** heads southwest toward Extremadura and Sevilla. The **A-42** is a direct highway to Toledo. Madrid is encircled by three major ring roads: the **M-30,** the **M-40,** and the **M-50.** Traffic can be sluggish, especially at rush hour when it slows to a standstill.

Weigh your travel needs carefully when selecting a rental car. Smaller cars are more economical to drive and easier to handle on narrow streets and in claustrophobic parking garages, but it's wise to select a vehicle with a closed trunk to keep luggage out of sight. If available, choose a diesel vehicle to save 20% to 30% on fuel costs. Air-conditioning is usually standard—and not a luxury during hot summer months. Check with your credit card company ahead of time to see if your card covers damages to the vehicle; if not, pay extra for the collision damage coverage. It is only too easy to crumple a fender and end up paying a 500€ fee to have it repaired. For details on renting a car, see "Car Rentals" in the "Fast Facts" section below.

By Bus

Spanish bus service is better than bus service in most of North America. But rarely do the buses offer significant savings over trains, and they are always less comfortable and usually slower. Buses are fine for local sightseeing from urban centers, or to connect between rural villages, where the "station" is likely to be the bar at the nearest crossroad. Regional bus lines tend to dominate bus service. You'll find information on using the local and regional buses in each of the chapters in this guide.

Tips on Accommodations

Booking in Advance

During busy seasons, it's usually wise to book accommodations in advance, especially in popular areas like beach resorts or areas with limited accommodations, such as mountain retreats. It gives you peace of mind and can save a lot of time if you don't have to search for lodging on arrival. Use the lodgings listed in this book as your first recourse. If you need to dig deeper, the best of the online sites in Spain is **Venere** (www.venere.com), which includes many smaller lodgings that may be overlooked by larger international online booking sites. Sometimes it is worth checking a rate you find on Venere against the hotel's own website for last-minute specials. If you're traveling with a laptop, you can reasonably book for the next 2 to 3 days ahead while on the road, giving you maximum flexibility. In fact, if you are traveling off season or in less-visited regions (or simply have a high tolerance for uncertainty), you may be able to secure substantial discounts on last-minute or even walk-in bookings.

Types of Accommodations

Most lodgings in this book are either **hotels** or **hostales,** which can be hard to tell apart. Hotels generally occupy their entire building and may have more services, while *hostales* often share a building with residential apartments or other *hostales*. They are often small, family-run operations. Both hotels and *hostales* are rated on a star system by the national government, but ratings more closely reflect services and amenities rather than overall quality. As a general rule, don't step below two stars unless your budget is *very* tight. Outside resorts and urban areas, four-star hotels are often very reasonable and even five-stars can be a bargain on weekdays.

King Alfonso XIII started the **parador** system in the 1920s. These state-run hotels are usually four-star and five-star properties, and some have the highest possible designation of five-star Gran Lujo. The majority of *paradores* are located in historic buildings with especially prized locations, and their restaurants emphasize traditional cuisine of the area. While often expensive, the *paradores* offer extraordinary discounts when one of the travelers in a room is under 30 or over 65, or if you purchase 5 nights (which can all be in different *paradores*) in advance. For details, see **www.parador.es**.

Spain also has its share of **hostels** (not to be confused with *hostales*), usually offering shared bathrooms and often dormitory-style rooms. Most are affiliated with IYH (International Youth Hostels) and cater primarily to young backpackers.

Spain also rates **apartmentos turisticos**—apartments designed for short-term stay—on a scale of one to three keys. For information on apartment rentals, see "Apartment, Villa, or Condo Rentals" in the "Fast Facts" section below.

Rural hotels, inns, and country houses are also rated by the government on a one- to three-star system, but typically vary little from their urban equivalents. The province of Cádiz in Andalucía operates a superb system of family-oriented rural accommodations, mostly in natural areas. See **www.tugasa.com** for details.

Fast Facts

Apartment, Villa, or Condo Rentals

Renting an apartment is most practical in cities where you plan to spend a fair bit of time. **Homes for Travellers** (www.homesfortravellers.com) concentrates exclusively on Madrid and has a high standard in representing apartments in desirable neighborhoods. In Granada, **Apartamentos Santa Ana** (www.apartamentos-santaana.com) books apartments in three old buildings with historic character, while **Accommodation Valencia** (www.accommodation-valencia.com) usually has a choice of about 45 apartments. **Friendly Rentals** (www.friendlyrentals.com) represents apartments in Sevilla, Barcelona, Madrid, Granada, San Sebastián, Valencia, Sitges, Santander, and Mallorca. Although it's a fairly large operation, there is a strong commitment to personal service. **Spain Select** (www.spain-select.com) has an array of upscale seaside villas and rural homes. When booking any type of lodging, inquire carefully about deposits and payment requirements, as well as hidden costs such as cleaning fees and surcharges for additional guests.

ATMs/Cashpoints

The easiest way to get euros in Spain is at an ATM (or cashpoint), using your bank or credit card. Keep in mind that credit card companies charge interest from the day of your withdrawal, even if you pay your monthly bill on time. You'll find 24-hour ATMs/cashpoints throughout Spain, even in small towns. Most accept Maestro/MasterCard, Cirrus, and Visa. Go to your bank card's website to find ATM locations at your destination.

Banking Hours

Do your banking before lunch. Most banks are open weekdays from 8:30am to 2pm, though some larger banks, especially in big cities, may reopen in the afternoon. Some banks are also open until 1pm on Saturday.

Bike Rentals

Bike sharing is catching on in Spain, with Barcelona, Valencia, Sevilla, and Córdoba leading the way in offering free or inexpensive bicycles to pick up and drop off at convenient locations throughout each city. See destination chapters for more information on biking.

Business Hours

Shops and offices are generally open Monday to Saturday from 9:30 or 10am to 1:30 or 2pm and again from 4:30 or 5pm to 8pm. Some shops stay open later in the evening, and larger department stores and shopping malls often stay open all day without interruption—usually from 10am to 9 or 10pm. Museums usually open at 10am, and many close roughly between 2 and 4pm, reopening until at least 7pm and sometimes as late as 9pm. Many museums are open mornings only on Sunday, and many are closed on 1 weekday, often Monday or Tuesday.

Car Rentals

Although the minimum driving age in Spain is 18, drivers must be at least 21 to rent a car. All drivers must have a valid driver's license, passport, and credit card. Drivers from North America are required to have an International Driving Permit (which is available from AAA; www.aaa.com). It's unlikely that you will be asked to show the IDP when picking up your rental car, but it is essential if you are stopped for a traffic violation. Start researching rental rates at U.S.-based **Auto Europe** (☎ 888-223-5555; www.autoeurope.com) and then compare their best deals with the major car-rental agencies in Spain: **Avis** (www.avis-europe.com), **Hertz** (www.hertz.es), **Europcar** (www.europcar.com), and **National Atesa** (www.atesa.es).

Customs

As a member of the European Union, Spain follows the same customs regulations as other E.U. countries, though it is rare for travelers to be stopped as they leave the airport arrivals area. Travelers may bring into Spain a kilogram (2.2 lb.) of any food except meat, meat products, milk, or dairy products. Infant formula or infant food still sealed in its original packaging will be allowed. Customs officials may also make exceptions for special diet foods, but be prepared with documents that demonstrate a clear medical need. Travelers may bring items for personal or family use and for gifts, provided they are not considered commercial merchandise by Customs officials. Anyone over age 18 may carry a maximum of 200 cigarettes, 100 small cigars, 50 cigars, or 250 grams (about 8 oz.) of rolling tobacco. Visitors can also bring in 1 liter (33.8 oz.) of spirits and 2 liters (67.6 oz.) of wine or beer, 50ml (1.7 oz.) of perfume, and 250ml (8.5 oz.) of *eau de toilette*.

Dining

Few things about Spain so flummox visitors as Spanish dining habits. The midday meal, often the largest of the day, occurs between 2 and 4pm, while few restaurants open for the evening meal much before 9pm and many as late as 10pm. After a day or two you'll understand the logic of the Spanish schedule. A late lunch is a good break from the midday heat, and you often get great deals on a *menú del día,* a three-course meal with wine and coffee at a low fixed price. If you have trouble waiting until 10pm for supper, let tapas fill the gap. Bars roll out the snacks from 7 to 9pm, and walking from bar to bar to nibble and nosh is both sustenance and entertainment.

Electricity

Like most of continental Europe, Spain uses the 220–240-volt system with two round prongs on the plug. North American (110–120-volt) electronics such as laptops with dual voltage transformers and shavers with dual-voltage switches can be used with a simple adapter. (Some hotels include a 110-volt outlet for shavers in the bathroom.) Other appliances, such as hair dryers, require a clunky voltage converter; using such appliances with simple plug adapters instead of converters will most likely destroy the appliance and blow fuses. U.K. 240-volt appliances need a continental adapter, which is widely available in the U.K. but usually impossible to find in Spain.

Embassies & Consulates

In case of emergency, most embassies have 24-hour referral service.

The **United States Embassy** is in Madrid at C/ Serrano, 75 (☎ 915-872-303). U.S. consulates are in A Coruña, at C/ Juan Vieja, 10 (☎ 981-213-233); Barcelona, at Paseo Reina Elisende de Moncatde, 23 (☎ 932-802-227); and Fuengirola, at C/ Las Rampas, Fase II (☎ 952-474-891). The Sevilla consulate is at Paseo de las Delicias, 7 (☎ 954-231-885); the Valencia consulate is at C/ Paz, 6 (☎ 963-516-973); and the Palma de Mallorca consulate is at C/ Porto Pi, 8–9 (☎ 971-303-707).

The **Canadian Embassy** is in Madrid, at C/ Núñez de Balboa, 35 (☎ 914-233-250). The Barcelona consulate is at C/ Elisenda de Pinós, 10 (☎ 932-042-700); and the Málaga consulate is at Plaza de la Malagueta, 3 (☎ 952-223-346).

The **United Kingdom Embassy** is in Madrid, at C/ Fernando El Santo, 16 (☎ 917-008-200). The Alicante consulate is at Plaza Calvo Sotelo, 1 (☎ 965-216-190); the Barcelona consulate is at Avenida Diagonal, 477 (☎ 933-666-200); and the Bilbao consulate is at Alameda Urquijo, 2 (☎ 944-157-600). The consulate in Ibiza is at Avenida Isidoro Macabich, 45 (☎ 971-301-818); and the consulate in Málaga is at C/ Mauricio Moro Pareto, 2 (☎ 952-352-300).

The **Irish Embassy** is in Madrid, at Paseo de La Castellana, 46 (☎ 934-915-021). The Barcelona consulate is at Gran Vía Carlos III, 94 (☎ 934-915-021); the Bilbao consulate is at C/ Elcano, 5 (☎ 944-230-414); and the Málaga consulate is at Avenida Las Boliches, 15 (☎ 952-475-108). The consulate in Palma de Mallorca is at C/ San Miguel, 68 (☎ 971-722-504); and the consulate in Sevilla is at Plaza de Santa Cruz, 6 (☎ 954-216-361).

The **Australian Embassy** is in Madrid, at Plaza del Descubridor Diego de Ordás, 3 (☎ 913-536-600). The Barcelona consulate is at C/ Gran Vía Carlos III, 98 (☎ 934-909-013); and the Sevilla consulate is at C/ Federico Rubio, 14 (☎ 954-220-971).

The **New Zealand Embassy** is in Madrid, at Plaza de la Lealtad, 2–3 (☎ 915-230-226). The Barcelona consulate is at C/ Travesera de Gracia, 64 (☎ 932-090-399).

Emergencies

For all emergencies, including medical, dial the pan-European emergency telephone number ☎ 112.

Entry Requirements

Citizens of the United States, Canada, Australia, and New Zealand need a valid passport for at least 6 months to enter Spain for up to 90 days. You could be asked to show a return ticket to confirm your departure date. Citizens of European Union countries (including Ireland and the United Kingdom) and Switzerland, Norway, Iceland, or Liechtenstein may present a passport or national identification card. If you do not have a passport, allow plenty of time before your trip to apply. Processing normally takes 3 weeks but can take much longer during busy periods, especially spring. If you need a passport in a hurry, you'll pay a higher processing fee.

Event Listings

Local tourist offices (and their websites) are often good sources of information on upcoming events and may have schedules for performing arts companies. In Madrid and Barcelona, look for the **Guía del Ocio** leisure guide at newsstands; in Sevilla, it's **El Giraldillo.**

Family Travel

Spaniards are very family-friendly, and it's not hard to find accommodations for families at all price levels. Children 11 and under may be able to stay for free in their parent's room; be sure to ask. Restaurants welcome children, and it is not unusual to see youngsters dining with their parents at 10pm. You'll rarely find a children's menu, but you can ask for half portions, or have the kids dine on simple tapas such as *tortilla española* (egg and potato omelet), *albondigas* (meatballs), or grilled ham and cheese sandwiches, called *mixtos.* Reduced and free admissions for children are usually available at museums and other attractions. The **Spanish National Tourist Office** website (www.okspain.org) has a good listing of child-oriented attractions and activities. Check **www.travelwithyourkids.com** for general information about planning, packing, and preparing kids for a foreign culture. **Family Travel Forum** (www.familytravelforum.com) offers destination-specific advice.

Gay & Lesbian Travelers

The website **www.gayinspain.com** is a good

resource of gay-friendly lodgings, shops, restaurants, and attractions in Spain. The country's laws are a model of open-mindedness, having legalized homosexuality between consenting adults in 1978, banned discrimination based on sexual orientation in 1995, and legalized marriage between same-sex couples in 2005. In practice, Spain is among Europe's most open societies. Some of the more vibrant gay scenes are in Madrid's Chueca district, Barcelona, Granada, and Cádiz, as well as the resort areas of Sitges on the Costa Daurada and Torremolinos on the Costa del Sol. For guided tours, often with an educational focus, check U.S.-based tour operators **Atlantis Events** (www.atlantis events.com) or **Coda International Tours** (www.coda-tours.com).

Health

No vaccinations are required for travel to Spain, and the tap water is perfectly safe to drink. Your general concerns should be the same as they are at home: Be careful how much you eat and drink, and limit your sun exposure. (Indeed, the sun in southern Spain may be much more intense than it is back home.)

Pack an adequate supply of any prescription medicines in their original containers with pharmacy labels in your carry-on luggage, and bring an extra copy of your prescription. Spanish pharmacies can fill prescriptions, although it is a good idea to know the generic name of any medications, since the pharmacist might not recognize an American brand name.

Ask your hotel to recommend an English-speaking doctor, or consult your country's consulate. For emergency medical or dental attention, go to the *centro de urgencia* (emergency room) at the nearest hospital. Non-E.U. residents can consult national health service doctors for a relatively small fee; ask at your hotel for a list of doctors.

The following government websites offer up-to-date health-related travel advice. In Australia, go to **www.dfat.gov.au/travel**; in Canada, go to **www.hc-sc.gc.ca/index_e.html**; in the U.K., go to **www.nhs.uk/nhsengland/Healthcare abroad**; in the U.S., go to **www.cdc.gov/travel**.

Contact the **International Association for Medical Assistance to Travelers** (**IAMAT**; ☎ 716-754-4883, or 416-652-0137 in Canada; www.iamat.org) for tips on travel and health concerns in Spain, and for lists of local, English-speaking doctors. The **United States Centers for Disease Control and Prevention** (☎ 800-311-3435; www.cdc.gov) provides up-to-date information on health hazards by region or country and offers tips on food safety. **Travel Health Online** (www.tripprep.com), sponsored by a consortium of travel medicine practitioners, may also offer helpful advice on traveling abroad. You can find listings of reliable medical clinics overseas at the **International Society of Travel Medicine** (www.istm.org).

Holidays

In addition to shops and offices, you may even find some museums and restaurants closed on the holidays listed below. But the opportunity to observe and even participate in activities usually more than compensates for any inconvenience.

National holidays are as follows: January 1 (New Year's Day), January 6 (Epiphany), Maundy Thursday (date varies), Good Friday (date varies), Easter (date varies), May 1 (Labor Day), August 15 (Assumption), October 12 (National Day), November 1 (All Saints' Day), December 6 (Constitution Day), December 8 (Immaculate Conception), December 25 (Christmas).

Insurance

Having adequate insurance coverage will give you peace of mind at the very least. But check your own health and homeowner coverage before purchasing additional insurance for lost luggage, medical expenses, or evacuation. Also check with your credit card companies, as some may protect you if you have charged a trip on their card and the tour operator goes out of business. If you feel you need additional coverage, visit **www.InsureMyTrip.com** to compare coverage and prices from 18 different insurance providers. Package plans are usually sold for a single trip and generally cover trip cancellation, lost luggage, medical and evacuation expenses, and other circumstances.

TRIP-CANCELLATION INSURANCE

Trip-cancellation insurance helps you retrieve your money if you have to back out of the trip due to illness or accident or if there is a natural disaster or political turmoil at your destination. Some newer policies will cover you if you cancel for *any* reason. Since the coverage can also protect you if the tour operator goes bankrupt, always purchase trip-cancellation insurance from a third party—never from the tour provider. **Travel Safe Insurance** (www.travelsafe. com) is a good place to start to explore options and costs. It's especially worth considering if you are purchasing an expensive trip and have health concerns.

LOST-LUGGAGE INSURANCE

Many American homeowner's policies will cover lost or stolen cameras and other equipment, but, again, be sure to check with your agent to see if you need a special rider for an expensive item. In reality, more luggage checked aboard an airplane is simply—and usually inexplicably—delayed, rather than permanently lost. If your bag never shows up, you will almost certainly be disappointed with the amount of the airline liability, so lost-luggage insurance could be a good investment. Be sure to file a lost-luggage claim, detailing all the contents of your bags, before you leave the airport.

MEDICAL INSURANCE

Be sure to determine whether your health plan covers you while overseas. Most U.S. insurers, including Medicare and Medicaid, cover overseas emergency treatment only and will require you to pay the Spanish healthcare provider up front and then seek reimbursement when you return home. You can explore international medical insurance rates and coverage from **Medex** (www.medexassist.com), which also provides coverage for emergency medical evacuation. Emergency evacuation coverage is rarely provided in standard American healthcare policies, especially not for high-risk activities such as skiing, bungee jumping or hang gliding.

Internet Access

Wi-Fi has become common in most hotels and is increasingly offered as a free amenity, except in some business hotels, which charge up to 20€ a day for the "privilege." Hotels without in-room Internet connections may provide access through a public computer. Internet cafes are common. Free Wi-Fi hot spots are often found at public libraries, some museums, and a few cafes and fast-food operations.

Language

Castilian Spanish (called Castellano in Spain) is the official national language, and you can use it to do business anywhere in the country. Regional languages, however, enjoy equal status with Castellano in their respective areas: Euskera in the Basque Country, Gallego in Galicia, and Català in Catalunya. In fact, street and directional signage is likely to be in the local language first and Castellano second. Most people, however, will be happy to speak Castellano with you. English is almost always the non-Iberian language of choice for travelers who do not speak Castellano or a regional tongue. Consult "Useful Phrases & Menu Terms" (see p. 701) for some basic Castellano words.

Legal Aid

Consult your country's consulate (see p. 695) for assistance with legal matters. They can make sure you are aware of your rights and provide you with a list of attorneys. You will have to pay attorney's fees yourself. The consulate may also contact your family if you find yourself in serious legal trouble.

Lost Property

Be sure to fill out a claim form before leaving the airport if your luggage does not arrive with your flight. Report any stolen goods to the police. While it is unlikely that your goods will be recovered, you will need a report to support your insurance claim. If your credit cards are lost or stolen, notify the companies immediately so that the cards can be cancelled. Report the loss to the police as well, as your credit card company may require a police report number or record. Credit card emergency numbers in Spain are as follows: **Visa** (☎ 900-991-124), **MasterCard** (☎ 900-971-231), and **American Express** (☎ 902-375-637). Use the same number to report stolen or lost American Express traveler's checks. Credit card companies might wire you an immediate cash advance or make sure you receive a new credit card in a couple of days.

If you lose your passport, immediately report the loss to your consulate or embassy (see p. 695, "Embassies & Consulates.").

Mail & Postage

Postcards and letters weighing up to 20 grams sent to the United Kingdom and Ireland cost .62€; to the United States, Canada, Australia, and New Zealand, .78€. You can buy stamps at all post offices and at tobacco stores.

Money

Spain's currency is the euro. Euro banknotes come in denominations of 5€, 10€, 20€, 100€, 200€, and 500€, and coins of .02€, .05€, .10€, .20€, .50€, 1€, and 2€. For the most up-to-date currency conversion information, go to **www.xe.com**.

The best way to get cash in Spain is at ATMs/cashpoints (see p. 693). Very few shops, restaurants, and hotels do not accept credit cards but some may add a small transaction fee. Always have some cash for incidentals and sightseeing admissions. Avoid exchanging money at commercial exchange bureaus and hotels, which typically charge the highest transaction fees. For more detailed advice on using cash versus plastic and saving money on charges, see chapter 2, "Strategies for Seeing Spain."

Passports

If you do not have a passport, allow plenty of time before your trip to apply. Processing normally takes 3 weeks but can take much longer during busy periods, especially spring. If you need a passport in a hurry, you'll pay a higher processing fee.

FOR RESIDENTS OF AUSTRALIA

Contact the **Australian Passport Information Service** at ☎ 13-12-32, or visit the government website at www.passports.gov.au.

FOR RESIDENTS OF CANADA

Contact the central **Passport Office,** Department of Foreign Affairs and International Trade, Ottawa, ON K1A 0G3 (☎ 800-567-6868; www.ppt.gc.ca).

FOR RESIDENTS OF IRELAND

Contact the **Passport Office,** Setanta Centre, Molesworth Street, Dublin 2 (☎ 01-671-1633; www.irlgov.ie/iveagh).

FOR RESIDENTS OF NEW ZEALAND

Contact the **Passports Office** at ☎ 0800-225-050 in New Zealand or 04-474-8100, or log on to www.passports.govt.nz.

FOR RESIDENTS OF THE UNITED KINGDOM

Visit your nearest passport office, major post office, or travel agency or contact the **United Kingdom Passport Service** at ☎ 0870-521-0410 or search its website at www.ukpa.gov.uk.

FOR RESIDENTS OF THE UNITED STATES

To find your regional passport office, either check the U.S. State Department website or call the **National Passport Information Center** toll-free number (☎ 877-487-2778) for automated information. Note that to obtain a passport for a child in the U.S., the child must be present, with both parents at the place of issuance; *or* a notarized statement from the parents is required.

Pharmacies

To find an open pharmacy outside normal business hours, check the list of stores posted on the door of any drugstore or call ☎ 012. By law, there's always a drugstore open around the clock in every neighborhood. Drugstores are called *farmacías.* When open, they display a neon green cross.

Safety

Most crime in Spain, as in most countries, occurs in the big cities, but you should be watchful and careful wherever you go. Plan your route before leaving the hotel so that you minimize your need to consult a map. Stick to major, well-traveled streets and don't make it easy for purse snatchers. Carry bags and cameras on the side away from the street and never put wallets in your back pocket. When sitting in a public place, keep purses on your lap or at least strapped to an arm or leg. Never leave valuables unattended in a car. If you want to give money to street performers, have it ready in your palm before you approach them, to avoid being targeted by pickpockets in the crowd.

Senior Travelers

Seniors can expect to receive reduced or even free admission to most museums and other attractions, and sometimes to performing arts events. The discounts might kick in at age 60 or 62, but certainly by age 65. In addition, the Spanish *parador* system (www.parador.es) often offers special discounted rate packages for travelers over age 55. See chapter 19, "The Best Special Interest Trips," for more senior travel options.

Smoking

A law banning smoking in public places, including on public transportation and in offices and hospitals, was enacted in early 2006. However, only larger bars and restaurants are forced to provide a nonsmoking section, while smaller establishments are simply allowed to choose whether to become smoking or nonsmoking. The few nonsmoking bars (about 5%) have prominent signs. If you feel strongly about avoiding secondhand smoke, ask establishments if they have a *no fumadores* (nonsmoking) section, or choose a restaurant with an outdoor terrace.

Spectator Sports

What Americans call soccer is called football in Spain, and it's a national passion. Fans pack bars to watch the matches on big-screen televisions, and even some of the swankier restaurants tune to the bigger matches. You'll have to plan far in advance to score tickets to a match. Among the teams to watch are Real Madrid and Atlético de Madrid, FC Barcelona and RCD Espanyol (also in Barcelona), and Valencia CF. Check for seat availability at the all-around ticket vendor **ServiCaixa** (www.servicaixa.com).

Taxes

The value-added (VAT) tax (known in Spain as IVA) ranges from 7% to 33%, depending on the commodity. Food, wine, basic necessities, and hotels are taxed at 7%; most goods and services (including car rentals) at 13%; and luxury items (jewelry, tobacco, and imported liquors) at 33%. Non-E.U. residents are entitled to a reimbursement of the 16% IVA tax on most purchases worth more than 90€ made at shops offering "Tax Free" or "Global Refund" shopping. Forms, obtained from the store where you made your purchase, must be stamped at Customs upon departure. For more information see **www.globalrefund.com**.

Telephones

For national telephone information, dial ☎ **11888.** For international telephone information, call ☎ **11886.** You can make international calls from booths identified with the word *Internacional.* To make an international call, dial ☎ 00, wait for the tone, and dial the country code, area code, and number. To call locally or around the country, dial the full 9-digit number. Note that the conventions for where to break the 9-digit number vary by region, but the entire country is now on 9-digit dialing.

To dial direct internationally, dial 00 and then the country code, the area code, and the number. Country codes are as follows: the United States and Canada, 1; the United Kingdom, 44; Ireland, 353; Australia, 61; New Zealand, 64.

Make international calls from a public phone, if possible, because hotels charge inflated rates for direct dial—but bring plenty of *schede* (change). A reduced rate is applied from 11pm to 8am on Monday through Saturday and all day Sunday. Direct-dial calls from the United States to Spain are much cheaper, so arrange for whomever to call you at your hotel.

International phone cards (*scheda telefonica internazionale)* for calling overseas come in increments of 50, 100, 200, and 400 *unita* (units), and they're available at *tabacchi* (tobacco shops) and bars. Each *unita* is worth .15€ of phone time; it costs 5 *unita* (.65€) per minute to call within Europe or to the United States or Canada, and 12 *unita* (1.55€) per minute to call Australia or New Zealand. You don't insert this card into the phone; merely dial ☎ 1740 and then *2 (star 2) for instructions in English, when prompted.

To call the free national telephone information (in Italian) in Spain, dial ☎ 12. International information is available at ☎ 176 but costs .60€ a shot.

To make collect or calling-card calls to the U.S., drop in .10€ or insert your card and dial one of the numbers here; an American operator will come on to assist you (because Spain has yet to discover the joys of the touch-tone phone). The following calling-card numbers work all over Spain: **AT&T** (☎ 172-1011), **MCI** (☎ 172-1022), and **Sprint** (☎ 172-1877). To make collect calls to a country besides the United States, dial ☎ 170 (.50€), and practice your Italian counting in order to relay the number to the Italian operator. Tell him or her that you want it *a carico del destinatario* (charged to the destination, or collect).

Time Zone

The Spanish mainland and the Balearic Islands are on Greenwich Mean Time plus 1 hour in the winter and 2 hours in the summer. Daylight saving time is in effect from the last weekend in March (when the clocks are turned forward 1 hr.) to the last weekend in October (when the clocks are set back 1 hr.). In practice, this means that Spain is 6 hours ahead of Eastern Standard Time (EST) in the United States, 1 hour ahead of London, and 9 hours behind Sydney.

Tipping

More expensive restaurants may add a 7% tip

> *Public telephone booths in Madrid.*

to the bill, and cheaper ones incorporate it into their prices. This is *not* a service charge, and a tip of 5% to 10% is expected from tourists in these establishments, although locals rarely leave more than a few euros. For coffees and snacks, most people just leave a few coins or round up to the nearest euro. Taxis do not expect tips, although they might hope for something from tourists. Tip hotel porters and doormen 1€ and maids about the same amount per day.

Toilets

Use the terms *aseos, servicios,* or *lavabos* to ask for directions to restrooms. Once you find them, they will be marked *SEÑORES, HOMBRES,* or *CABALLEROS* for men and *DAMAS* or *SEÑORAS* for women. Bars and restaurants have facilities for their patrons, as do some tourist offices. Museums are always a reliable source of clean restrooms—even those that do not charge admission. Stop in for a restroom break and you may discover a fascinating exhibition.

Travelers with Disabilities

With its hilly terrain and old quarters of narrow, cobbled streets, Spain can present challenges for travelers with disabilities. But the country is beginning to address disability issues, and newer hotels and upscale restaurants tend to be wheelchair accessible. It's always wise to confirm when booking a room or making a reservation. Historic buildings, especially, may have narrow doors and steep stairs and lack elevators. Lodging booklets available for order from the Spanish National Tourist Office website (www.okspain.org) identify establishments that are handicapped accessible.

For travelers who prefer to leave the planning to someone else, **Flying Wheels Travel** (www.flyingwheelstravel.com) offers escorted tours and custom itineraries for travelers with disabilities; check for Spanish destinations. U.K.-based **Tourism for All** (www.tourismforall.org.uk) has lists of tour operators and is a good source of general information, as is the **Society for Accessible Travel and Hospitality** (www.sath.org) in the U.S.

Water

Not only is tap water safe all over Spain, but it generally tastes pretty good. It's wise to carry bottled water with you during warm weather, but do your pocketbook and the environment a favor by refilling a screw-top bottle from the tap.

Useful Phrases & Menu Terms

Phrases

ENGLISH	SPANISH (CASTELLANO)	PRONUNCIATION
good day	buenos días	*bweh*-nohs *dee*-ahs
how are you?	¿cómo está?	*koh*-moh es-*tah*
very well	muy bien	mwee byehn
thank you	gracias	*grah*-thee-ahs
you're welcome	de nada	deh *nah*-dah
goodbye	adiós	ah-*dyos*
please	por favor	por fah-*vohr*
yes	sí	see
no	no	noh
excuse me	perdóneme	pehr-*doh*-neh-meh
where is . . . ?	¿dónde está . . . ?	*dohn*-deh es-*tah*
the station	la estación	lah es-tah-*syohn*
a hotel	un hotel	oon oh-*tehl*
the market	el mercado	ehl mehr-*kah*-doh
a restaurant	un restaurante	oon rehs-tow-*rahn*-teh
the toilet	el baño	ehl *bah*-nyoh
the road to . . .	el camino a . . .	ehl kah-*mee*-noh ah
to the right	a la derecha	ah lah deh-*reh*-chah
to the left	a la izquierda	ah lah ees-*kyehr*-dah
I would like . . .	quisiera . . .	kee-*syeh*-rah
I want . . .	quiero . . .	*kyeh*-roh
to eat	comer	ko-*mehr*
a room	una habitación	oo-nah ah-bee-tah-*syohn*
do you have . . . ?	¿tiene usted . . . ?	tyeh-neh oo-sted
a book	un libro	oon *lee*-broh
a dictionary	un diccionario	oon deek-syoh-*nah*-ryoh
how much is it?	¿cuánto cuesta?	*kwahn*-toh *kwehs*-tah
when?	¿cuándo?	*kwahn*-doh
what?	¿qué?	Keh
there is (is there. . . ?)	(¿)hay (. . . ?)	aye
what is there?	¿qué hay?	keh aye
yesterday	ayer	ah-*yehr*
today	hoy	oy
tomorrow	mañana	mah-*nyah*-nah
good	bueno	*bweh*-noh
bad	malo	*mah*-loh
better (best)	(lo) mejor	(loh) meh-*hohr*
more	más	mahs

Phrases

ENGLISH	SPANISH (CASTELLANO)	PRONUNCIATION
less	menos	*meh*-nohs
do you speak English?	¿habla inglés?	*ah*-blah een-*glehs*
I don't understand	no entiendo	noh ehn-*tyehn*-doh
what time is it?	¿qué hora es?	keh *oh*-rah ehss
the check, please	la cuenta, por favor	lah *kwehn*-tah por fah-*vohr*

Emergencies

ENGLISH	SPANISH (CASTELLANO)	PRONUNCIATION
a doctor	un médico	oon *meh*-dee-koh
an ambulance	un ambulancia	oon am-boo-*lahn*-tsah
call the police!	¡llame a la policía!	*ya*-may ah lah po-lee-*see*-ah
help!	¡ayuda!	eye-*yooh*-dah

Numbers

ENGLISH	SPANISH (CASTELLANO)	PRONUNCIATION
1	uno	*oo*-noh
2	dos	dohs
3	tres	trehs
4	cuatro	*kwah*-troh
5	cinco	*theen*-koh
6	seis	says
7	siete	*syeh*-teh
8	ocho	*oh*-choh
9	nueve	*nweh*-beh
10	diez	dyehth
11	once	*ohn*-theh
12	doce	*doh*-theh
13	trece	*treh*-theh
14	catorce	kah-*tohr*-theh
15	quince	*keen*-seh
16	dieciséis	dyeh-thee-*says*
17	diecisiete	dyeh-thee-*syeh*-teh
18	dieciocho	dyeh-thee-*oh*-choh
19	diecinueve	dyeh-thee-*nweh*-beh
20	veinte	*bayn*-teh
30	treinta	*trayn*-tah
40	cuarenta	kwah-*rehn*-tah
50	cincuenta	theen-*kwehn*-tah
60	sesenta	seh-*sehn*-tah
70	setenta	seh-*tehn*-tah
80	ochenta	oh-*chehn*-tah
90	noventa	noh-*behn*-tah
100	cien	*thyehn*

Meals & Courses

ENGLISH	SPANISH (CASTELLANO)	PRONUNCIATION
appetizers	entremeses	en-treh-*meh*-sehs
breakfast	desayuno	deh-sah-*yoo*-noh
dessert	postre	*pohs*-treh
dinner	cena	*theh*-nah
lunch	almuerzo	al-*mwehr*-thoh
main course	primer plato	*pree*-mehr *plah*-toh
meal (used for lunch)	comida	ko-*mee*-thah

Table Settings

ENGLISH	SPANISH (CASTELLANO)	PRONUNCIATION
bottle	botella	boh-*teh*-lyah
cup	taza	*tah*-thah
fork	tenedor	teh-neh-*dor*
glass	vaso	*bah*-soh
knife	cuchillo	koo-*chee*-lyoh
napkin	servilleta	sehr-vi-*lye*-tah
spoon	cuchara	koo-*chah*-rah

Decoding the Menu

ENGLISH	SPANISH (CASTELLANO)	PRONUNCIATION
baked	al horno	ahl *ohr*-noh
boiled	hervido	ehr-*vee*-thoh
fried	frito	*free*-toh
grilled	a la plancha	ah lah *plan*-chah
medium	medio hecho	*meh*-dyo *eh*-choh
rare	poco hecho	*poh*-koh *eh*-choh
roasted	asado	ah-*sah*-thoh
spicy	picante	pee-*kahn*-the
well done	muy hecho	mwee *eh*-choh

Beverages

ENGLISH	SPANISH (CASTELLANO)	PRONUNCIATION
beer	cerveza	thehr-*veh*-thah
coffee	café	kah-*feh*
milk	leche	*leh*-cheh
red (wine)	tinto	*teen*-toh
rosé	rosado	roh-*sah*-thoh
tea	té	teh
water	agua	*ah*-gwah
white (wine)	blanco	blahn-*koh*
wine	vino	*bee*-noh

Meat

ENGLISH	SPANISH (CASTELLANO)	PRONUNCIATION
beef	buey	*bway*
chicken	pollo	po-*lyoh*
cooked ham	jamón York	hah-*mohn* york
cured ham	jamón serrano	hah-*mohn* seh-*rah*-noh
duck	pato	*pah*-toh
ham	jamón	hah-*mohn*
lamb	cordero	kohr-*deh*-roh
meat	carne	*kahr*-neh
pheasant	faisán	fahy-*thahn*
pork	cerdo	*thehr*-doh
rabbit	conejo	koh-*neh*-hoh
ribs	costilla	kos-*tee*-lyah
sausage	salchicha	sahl-*chee*-chah
sirloin	solomillo	so-loh-*mee*-lyoh
spicy sausage	chorizo	choh-*ree*-thoh
steak	bistec	*bee*-stehk
turkey	pavo	*pah*-voh
veal	ternera	tehr-*neh*-rah

Seafood & Shellfish

ENGLISH	SPANISH (CASTELLANO)	PRONUNCIATION
bass	lubina	loo-*bee*-nah
cod	bacalao	bah-kah-*lah*-oh
crab	cangrejo	kan-*greh*-hoh
crayfish	cigala	see-*gah*-lah
fish	pescado	pess-*kah*-thoh
flounder	platija	plah-*tee*-hah
fresh (water)	boquerón	boh-*keh*-rohn
lobster	langosta	lahn-*goss*-tah
mackerel	caballa	cah-*ba*-lyah
mussel	mejillón	meh-hee-*lyohn*
octopus	pulpo	*pool*-poh
oyster	ostra	*ohs*-trah
prawn	gamba	*gahm*-bah
salmon	salmón	sal-*mohn*
salt (water)	anchoa	ahn-*choh*-ah
sardine	sardina	sahr-*dee*-nah
scallop	peregrina	peh-reh-*gree*-nah
shellfish	mariscos	mah-*reess*-kohs
shrimp	camarón	ka-mah-*rohn*
sole	lenguado	len-*gwah*-tho

squid	calamar	kah-lah-*mahr*
swordfish	pez espada	*peth* ess-*pah*-thah
trout	trucha	*troo*-chah
tuna	atún	ah-*toon*

Vegetables & Legumes

ENGLISH	SPANISH (CASTELLANO)	PRONUNCIATION
carrot	zanahoria	thah-nah-*oh*-ryah
cabbage	col	kohl
celery	apio	*ah*-pyoh
chickpea	garbanzo	gahr-*bahn*-thoh
corn	maíz	mah-*eeth*
eggplant	berengena	beh-rehn-*jeh*-nah
fava (broad) beans	habas	*ah*-bahs
green beans	judías	hoo-*dee*-yahs
lentil	lenteja	lehn-*teh*-hah
lettuce	lechuga	leh-*choo*-gah
mushroom	seta	*seh*-tah
onion	cebolla	theh-*bo*-lyah
potato	patata	pah-*tah*-tah
salad	ensalada	enn-sah-*lah*-dah
spinach	espinaca	ess-pee-*nah*-kah
tomato	tomate	toh-*mah*-teh
vegetables	verduras	vehr-*doo*-rahs

Miscellaneous

ENGLISH	SPANISH (CASTELLANO)	PRONUNCIATION
banana	plátano	*plah*-tah-noh
bread	pan	pahn
butter	mantequilla	mahn-teh-*kee*-lyah
caramel custard	flan	flahn
cheese	queso	*keh*-soh
egg	huevo	*weh*-boh
fruit	fruta	*froo*-tah
ice cream	helado	eh-*lah*-doh
omelet	tortilla	tohr-*tee*-lya
pepper	pimienta	pee-*myen*-tah
rice	arroz	*ah*-rohth
salt	sal	sahl
sugar	azúcar	ah-*thoo*-kahr

Index

Photo Credits

Note: l= left; r= right; t= top; b= bottom; c= center

Cover Photo Credits: Front cover (l to r): © Markel Redondo; © Javier Larrea/age fotostock; © Steve Vidler/Super-Stock. Back cover (t and b): © Denis Doyle. Cover flap (t to b): © White Star Agency/age fotostock; Detail of the Portico de Gloria depicting the apostles, by Mateo/Cathedral of St. James, Santiago de Compostela, Spain/The Bridgeman Art Library; © Robert Harding Picture Library Ltd/Alamy; © Science and Society/Superstock. Inside front cover (clockwise from tr): © Markel Redondo; © Diego Vivanco; © Sergi Camara; © Niccolò Guasti; © Jorge Guerrero; © Jorge Guerrero; © Denis Doyle; © Paul Harris; © Markel Redondo; © Markel Redondo. **Interior Photo Credits:** AGE: © Aguililla & Marín/age fotostock: p368; © Felix Alain/age fotostock: p392; © ARCO/Dona, S/age fotostock: p480; © Gonzalo Azumendi/age fotostock: p340; © Markus Bassler/age fotostock: p188, p339; © Alberto Berti/age fotostock: p498(bl); © bw media photoagentur/age fotostock: p700; © Peter Cassidy/age fotostock: p127(tr); © Marco Cristofori/age fotostock: p25, pp68-69; © Mitch Diamond/age fotostock: ppxii-1; © Nevio Doz/age fotostock: p675(r); © Elan Fleisher/age fotostock: p377; © Foodanddrink Photos/age fotostock: p127(cl); © Foodfolio/age fotostock: p127(tc); © Guiziou Franck/age fotostock: p302; © Isidoro Ruiz Haro/age fotostock: p367(t); © José Antonio Hernaiz/age fotostock: pp510-11; © Hughes Hervé/age fotostock: pv(t), p258; © Rafael Jáuregui/age fotostock: p498(cl); © Reinhard Kliem/age fotostock: p148; © Javier Larrea/age fotostock: p127(tl); © Javier Lobato/age fotostock: p503; © Joan Mercadal/age fotostock: p280; © Nacho Moro/age fotostock: p354; © Nils-Johan Norenlind/age fotostock: pp32-33; © Passport Stock/age fotostock: p141(r); © Stuart Pearce/age fotostock: p507; © Sergio Pitamitz/age fotostock: p81; © Paul Raftery/VIEW/age fotostock: p329; © Quim Roser/age fotostock: p409(t); © Neil Setchfield/age fotostock: p475(r); © Siepmann/age fotostock: p556(b); © Marco Simoni/age fotostock: p573; © Felix Stenson/age fotostock: p255(bl); © Xavier Subias/age fotostock: p369(tl); © Michael Thornton/age fotostock: pp262-63; © Tramonto/age fotostock: p105(2nd from tr); © Lucas Vallecillos/age fotostock: p255(tr); © Value Stock Images/age fotostock: p538; © Vidler/age fotostock: p373; © Zorka Vuckovic/age fotostock: p526(r); © White Star Agency/age fotostock: p105(tl); © Adam Woolfitt/age fotostock: p630(b), p633; Alamy: © AA World Travel Library/Alamy: p212; © Daniel Acevedo/Alamy: p325; © The Art Archive/Alamy: p211(tr); © Author's Image Ltd/Alamy: p76(r), p78(b); © Bildarchiv Monheim GmbH/Alamy: p156, p166, pp194-95; © Tibor Bognar/Alamy: p243(r); © Mark Boulton/Alamy: p246, p248; © Cephas Picture Library/Alamy: p64, p215; © Michelle Chaplow/Alamy: p127(bc); © Classic Image/Alamy: p211(tl); © CuboImages srl/Alamy: pp254-55(t), p256; © Mike Cumberbatch/Alamy: p561; © Mary Evans Picture Library/Alamy: p674(r); © Mark Eveleigh/Alamy: p134(l); © Alexei Fateev/Alamy: p389; © Josep Ferrer/Alamy: p370; © Kevin Foy/Alamy: p127(bl); © Geoffrey Grace/Alamy: p90; © graficart.net/Alamy: p369(3rd from tl); © Jeremy Green/Alamy: p143; © Robert Harding Picture Library Ltd/Alamy: p73, p355(br), p398; © Hemis/Alamy: pvii(b), p165, pp482-83, p429(tc), p671; © Peter Horree/Alamy: p7; © imagebroker/Alamy: p142; © Images & Stories/Alamy: p416; © Interfoto/Alamy: p498(2nd from bl); © Isifa Image Service s.r.o./Alamy: p176; © Ivy Close Images/Alamy: p210; © Jam World Images/Alamy: piii(t), p10, p180, p200; © Kazimierz Jurewicz/Alamy: p599(c); © Per Karlsson, BKWine 2/Alamy: p369(2nd from tl); © Graham Lawrence/Alamy: p344; © LOOK Die Bildagentur der Fotografen GmbH/Alamy: pvii(c), p82, p475(l); © MARKA/Alamy: p632; © Bob Masters/Alamy: p429(tr); © Tim Moore/Alamy: p234; © Moreleaze Travel Spain/Alamy: p355(tr); © North Wind Picture Archives/Alamy: p666(b); © Bernard O'Kane/Alamy: p355(bc); © parasola.net/Alamy: p504; © Alberto Paredes/Alamy: p216, p291; © David Pearson/Alamy: p626; © Photos 12/Alamy: p667(t); © Pictorial Press Ltd/Alamy: p214; © Picture Contact/Alamy: piv(b), p214; © Ingolf Pompe 52/Alamy: p62, p473; © Nigel Reed QEDimages/Alamy: p355(l); © Howard Sayer/Alamy: p360; © Carmen Sedano/Alamy: p44; © Alex Segre/Alamy: p242; © Rhys Stacker/Alamy: p304; © TNT Magazine/Alamy: pp318-19; © Travel Division Images/Alamy: p105(tr); © Ken Welsh/Alamy: p546, p565; Art Archive: The Art Archive/Royal Chapel Granada Spain/Gianni Dagli Orti: p663; Art Resource: Giraudon/Art Resource, NY: p321; Bridgeman: *The Coronation of the Virgin* by El Greco/Prado, Madrid, Spain/The Bridgeman Art Library: p99(t); *Dance on the Banks of the River Manzanares* by Goya/Prado, Madrid, Spain/The Bridgeman Art Library: p106; *Equestrian Portrait of Henri IV before the walls of Paris*/Musée de la Ville de Paris, Musée Carnavalet, Paris, France/The Bridgeman Art Library: p211(br); *The Garden of Earthly Delights* by Bosch/Prado, Madrid, Spain/The Bridgeman Art Library: p98; *The Holy Family of the Oak Tree* by Raphael/Prado, Madrid, Spain/The Bridgeman Art Library: p99(b); *Las Meninas or The Family of Philip IV* by Velazquez/Prado, Madrid, Spain /The Bridgeman Art Library: p20-21(t), p21(t, b and c); Detail of the Portico de la Gloria depicting the apostles, by Mateo/Cathedral of St. James, Santiago de Compostela, Spain/The Bridgeman Art Library: p254(b); Detail of the Portico de la Gloria depicting St. James, 12 century (stone), Mateo, Master (fl.1168-88)/Cathedral of St. James, Santiago de